Capitol
Courthouse
AND
City Hall

7th edition

Readings in American State and Local Politics and Government

DAVID L. MARTIN

Editor

Longman
New York & London

CAPITOL, COURTHOUSE, AND CITY HALL, Seventh Edition

Longman, Inc., 95 Church Street, White Plains, N. Y. 10601

Associated companies:
Longman Group Ltd., London
Longman Cheshire Pty., Melbourne
Longman Paul Pty., Auckland
Copp Clark Pitman, Toronto
Pitman Publishing Inc., New York

Senior editor: David J. Estrin
Production editor: Elsa van Bergen
Text design: Joseph Maslan
Cover design: Joseph DePinho
Production supervisor: Judith Stern

Library of Congress Cataloging-in-Publication Data

Capitol, courthouse, and city hall.

    1. Local government–United States. 2. State
governments. I. Martin, David L.
JS.C36 1988   320.973   87-3744
ISBN 0-582-28686-7 (pbk.)

Compositor: TC Systems
Printer and binder: RR Donnelley & Sons Co.

87 88 89 90 9 8 7 6 5 4 3 2 1

Contents

Preface

This seventh edition of *Capitol, Courthouse, and City Hall* is offered because we believe that American state and local government is a dynamic subject, best viewed from multiple perspectives. The decisions made at state capitols, county courthouses, and city halls daily affect the quality of our lives. The voices from those political arenas were what Bob Morlan tried to capture in his career as a political scientist: To bring varying viewpoints alive and kicking into the classroom for discussion remains the purpose of this book.

Recognition is due to two women who helped deliver this book: Mrs. Anne Morlan, who supported her husband on the earlier editions, and my wife Catherine, who continued the effort.

D. L. M.

In Memoriam
Robert L. Morlan
(1920–1985)
Scholar and Citizen

CHAPTER 1

Values and Criticisms of State and Local Governments

Why have 50 states and more than 80,000 separate local governments? We begin by looking at the contemporary role of the states, followed by Aaron Wildavsky's critique that federalism means inequality. Politically, states and local governments offer their citizens the opportunity to make significant policy choices. The goods and services produced by California or New York place them among the world's economic powers, and financially even the smallest, Vermont, would rank in the FORTUNE 500 largest business enterprises. In a federal system, decentralizing power to subnational governments in order to allow local preferences results in variation, and, as Wildavsky points out, inequalities. These first two selections discuss how well political mechanisms (can you identify them?) are working to accommodate diversity and change in the United States.

Can the states be revitalized? David Nice looks at the record, and Harry Hatry asks, "Would we know a well-governed city if we saw one?" They suggest criteria to judge how well state and local governments have handled increasingly complex responsibilities. The contrasting views in this opening chapter express the political tension that (as in the first selection's arch-support analogy) has added strength to the structure of American democracy.

1

The Contemporary Role of the States

ADVISORY COMMISSION ON INTERGOVERNMENTAL RELATIONS

Although states currently exercise important functions as intergovernmental middlemen, being heavily involved in intergovernmental financing, regulating and managing, their performance of their more traditional role remains strong. They continue as major polities.[1] Politically, the states still are the balance wheels of the federal system, helping to maintain the equilibrium between national and subnational interests. They constitute the prime impediments to centralization at the national level. Even in an era when federal largesse is welcomed, resistance is still marked. State reactions to the U.S. Department of Education's directives regarding institutions of higher learning are cases in point, as is Connecticut's resistance to allowing double-rigged trucks to use her highways.

Although managerial, administrative, and other factors contribute, the ability of states to act as balance wheels is based largely on their political power in a system characterized by plural power bases. This pluralism is tied to the uncentralized political party system in the United States, state responsibilities in regard to enfranchisement of voters and the conduct of elections, the power states wield in the presidential nominating conventions and in the electoral college, the attention given to their governors (individually or singly) and legislatures when they speak out on public issues, state potential for amending the Constitution by petitioning the Congress to call a convention for that purpose, and for ratifying proposed amendments.

Several recent developments have compromised state political strength to some extent. The Supreme Court's decision on *Cousins* v. *Wygoda* (1975)[2] gave precedence to the rules of the Democratic National Convention over Illinois statutes regarding the selection of that state's delegates to the convention, thus reducing state control of party matters and moving toward centralization of party power at the national level. State control of elections was weakened further by a 1981 Supreme Court decision that upheld the national Democratic Party's right to restrict participation in Democratic presidential preference primaries to party members.[3] Wisconsin's open primary, in which voters could participate regardless of party affiliation, was at issue. National political party reforms relating to selection of delegates undercut state party power as well. The *Voting Rights Act of 1965* and the 18-Year-Old Vote Amendment also infringed on state powers to control the franchise and conduct elections.

Moreover, in case after case, the Supreme Court's decisions to place individual rights ahead of states' rights have undercut state authority. One constitutional law casebook reported that of the 56,922 private cases (not involving the federal government or its officers) raising a federal question that were filed in the United States District Courts in 1976, a total of 17,543 were against state and local officials for civil rights violations.[4] In cases involving racial justice, equity, civil liberties, criminal justice and official immunity from

Advisory Commission on Intergovernmental Relations. *The Question of State Government Capability*, Report A–98, (Washington, D.C.: 1985), pp. 20–25. Footnotes have been renumbered.

suit, the Court has invoked the due process and equal rights clauses of the 14th Amendment in a manner that has diminished state authority. The *Brown* v. *Board of Education*[5] case in 1954 stimulated a wave of cases aimed at racial justice. *Reynolds* v. *Sims* (1964)[6] and subsequent reapportionment cases limited state options in drawing district lines for representation in legislative bodies. *Roe* v. *Wade* (1973),[7] recently strengthened by a 1983 decision, restricted state authority to ban abortions. *Gideon* v. *Wainwright* (1963)[8] established the right of the accused in criminal cases to counsel, thus, in effect, requiring states to provide it. Employment of personnel on a patronage basis came under attack in *Elrod* v. *Burns* (1976),[9] when the Court held that employees' First and 14th Amendment rights were violated when they were discharged for partisan reasons. *Branti* v. *Finkel* (1980)[10] followed this reasoning. . . .

Nevertheless, the states remain the repositories of much of the political power in the nation. A factor in maintaining this posture is the revitalization of their political processes, thanks in an ironic way to the reapportionment decision of the Supreme Court and the voting rights legislation of Congress. These processes now are more open, more competitive and characterized by broader participation than ever before. And from them are formed 50 different governing and representational systems, whose varying values, policy and program preferences, fiscal arrangements, and approaches to local governments suggest other than a managerial intergovernmental program role.

States, for example, still provide their citizens ample opportunity for choice among key public policies. Witness the diversity of public assistance support, legislation on punishment for capital offenses, funding for abortions, and ratification of the Equal Rights Amendment, as well as public sector collective bargaining and right to work laws. Opportunity for choice among values diffuses opposition to government and builds support for the regime.

The states' differing roles as direct service providers continue substantially intact, although sharing of functions is greater and governmental services in general are more intergovernmentalized. States are the dominant service providers—providing more than 55% of the expenditures in most of the states—in six functional areas: highways, state-local public welfare, hospitals, health, natural resources and corrections. In addition, they now pay most of the court and school costs. In other areas, such as water transportation, they often provide most of the financing and they have become increasingly important in mass transit services. Even when their traditional functions such as highways and health are heavily assisted by federal grants, states continue to support them with large outlays.

If one looks only at broad functional areas and not at their components, the picture is clouded and there appears to be a resultant diminution of the importance of state participation in service delivery. One must remember, however, that states provide some components of activities financed primarily by other governments. In the functional area of education, for example, where major responsibility for financing until recently rested with local governments, states have been major deliverers in public higher education, educating three-quarters of the nation's college students. Similarly, within the general area of police protection, states frequently provide crime laboratories.

Often overlooked are the major state responsibilities in the provision of criminal justice and the regulation of business. States are the prime designers of the criminal justice system and determine state and local responsibilities within it. Their courts handle more than 90% of the cases tried in the United States. They also provide other related services such as prisons and correctional institutions, state police, and financial and technical assistance for local activities in this area.

State responsibilities for the regulation of business encompass almost every phase of business activity, and include the enactment of commercial codes governing business relations; entrance into business; laws on contracts; legal provisions for property ownership, use and disposal; taxation; sale of securities; and unfair business practices, among other things. They regulate closely certain businesses such as utilities, banks, common carriers and insurance companies; license professions and occupations; and institute certain provisions relating to labor and employment. Moreover, to a limited degree, states engage in business themselves. They may sell alcoholic beverages; operate toll roads, bridges and wharfs; run lotteries; or maintain funds for malpractice insurance, for example. North Dakota goes furthest in this connection, operating a bank as well as grain elevators and a mill, and maintaining a casualty and bonding insurance business.[11] Moreover, states do all kinds of other things that affect the quality of life of their citizens, particularly in the exercise of the police power to protect the public, and theirs is likely to be the first response to major emergencies and disasters.

Although federal preemption has siphoned off some of the regulatory powers of the states, their overall regulatory capacity remains strong. While they were losing some authority to the federal government, they took on other areas of activity. Among the new areas are surface mining regulation, consumer protection, hazardous waste disposal, radiation risk prevention, and land use regulation (especially wetlands), to name only a few. In other areas, they increased both the scope and intensity of their regulations. Their traditional role in licensing professions has expanded to include new occupations and activities. Arizona, for example, now issues guidelines for the education of radiologic technologists and certifies them. States now do more in environmental protection, both on their own and at the instigation of the federal government. They also have moved to prescribe standards for both mobile and modular home construction, nuclear waste disposal, and nursing homes, for example, and prohib-

ited such actions as the use of children for pornographic pictures and job discrimination between sexes.

All of these activities, and many more, follow different patterns, for the most part, in each of the 50 systems. These diverse models reflect the various compromises reached within each state as a result of differing political and societal values and economic resources.

States remain the architects and empowerers of local governments within their boundaries, with substantially undiminished control. Only insofar as General Revenue Sharing and direct federal grants to local governments have shored up local political power has their position changed in this respect.

Long called the "laboratories of democracy," states today are making a reality of this textbook description, which applied only in a limited sense in the period from the late 1920s to the early 1960s. Actually, states ordinarily do not engage in calculated experiments in the scientific sense. They undertake innovations in order to solve the different problems they face. Such initiatives broaden the scope of choices for policymakers at all levels and enable small-scale testing of untried programs and procedures. Such innovations as sunset legislation, zero based budgeting, equal housing, no fault insurance, and the senior executive service had their beginnings in the states. Pioneering actions in gun control, pregnancy benefits for working women, limited-access highways, education for handicapped children, auto pollution standards and energy assistance for the poor are only a few instances of other innovative state actions. There is no reason to believe that such resourcefulness will not continue, but again within 50 different political cultures.

These numerous "independent" actions suggest that the states have not scrapped the traditional role that stems from their being differentiated political and representational systems. If anything, some would argue this role has been revitalized in the past decade and a half, even as the role of planner, partial banker and coordinator of big, largely intergovernmentally financed, programs emerged.

There are at least two basic roles, then, the states now have assumed, and neither eclipses the other. Sometimes they complement one another (as when the national government is looking for new policies that have been "tested" or when federal grant programs require cost-sharing or a differentiated approach to implementation). But in other instances, they conflict, as have the federal mandates, intrusive conditions attached to grant programs, and other federal actions that undermine the very political processes that federal actions in the mid-1960s did so much to reform.

To sum up, the states have assumed a major coordinative, planning and funding role in big domestic programs, and they have reasserted themselves as vital governing entities and representatives of 50 varying political, social and fiscal value systems. The two combined, whether complementary or in conflict, suggest a major revitalization of the states' overall functional role in the federal system. They have become its arch supports.

NOTES

1. See Daniel J. Elazar, "The States as Polities in the Federal System," *National Civic Review*, New York, NY, Citizens Forum on Self-Government, February 1981, pp. 77–82.
2. 419 U.S. 477.
3. *Democratic Party of the U.S.* v. *La Follette*, Docket No. 79-1631, decided February 24, 1981.
4. P. Bator, P. Mishkin, D. Shapiro and H. Weschler, *The Federal Courts and the Federal System*, 2nd ed., Supp. 1977, as cited in A.E. Dick Howard, "States and the Supreme Court," *Symposium: State and Local Government Issues before the Supreme Court*, reprinted from *Catholic University Law Review*, Vol. 31, Spring 1982, p. 279.
5. 347 U.S. 483.
6. 377 U.S. 533.
7. 410 U.S. 113.
8. 372 U.S. 335.
9. 965 U.S. 2673.
10. Docket No. 78-1654, preliminary publication (March 31, 1980).
11. Russell W. Maddox and Robert F. Fuquay, *State and Local Government*, 3rd ed., New York, D. Van Nostrand Company, 1975, p. 585.

2

Federalism Means Inequality

AARON WILDAVSKY

Federalism is in decline because it cannot be sustained without the underlying support of political culture. From its beginning until this very day, there have been two classic criticisms of the structure of American federalism: it is too strong or too weak. Either the structure is a sham (federalism as a front for a unitary state) or the structure is stultifying (federalism as an obstacle to effective government).

These criticisms have been countered by two styles of argument: political geometry and political sociology. The geometricians

Published by permission of Transaction, Inc. from SOCIETY, Volume 22, No. 22, copyright (1985) by Transaction, Inc.

take the structural thesis head on. They argue, for example, that federal structure is built into national policymaking so the central government is effectively prevented from subsuming state governments. Or they contend that the diversity of state governments aids implementation of policy by providing a proper variety of responses to local conditions. Or they say that federal structure tames conflict by diverting it into many small ones, occurring at different times and in various places. The argument from political sociology, by contrast, simply states that structure need not and does not equal function. Between structure and function, they say, lies society, which both bolsters federalism, by representing social differences within geographic locations, and mitigates its excesses by connecting the constitutional parts. The institutional form of political sociology was political parties. The tendencies to formal dispersion of power would be met by informal concentration in parties.

I consider two explanations for the loss of vigor (the structure remains but its social support weakens) in the federal system: the decline of political parties and the rise of a sectarian political culture dedicated to equality of results. All the perspectives, whether structural or social, supportive or critical, centralizing or decentralizing, share a set of assumptions that have increasingly come under question. As usual, the main assumption was that life would remain unchanged. Government would remain small. For most of American history, the question of federal finance was what to do with surpluses, not deficits. Until sometime in the 1960s, fiscal drag, raising too much revenue, was considered the big problem. Government that used up a third or more of citizen income or employed a fifth or more of the people or operated hundreds of programs and bureaus was unthinkable. So was the welfare state. So were modern technology, communications, and mass mobility.

Most unimaginable of all, these technical and demographic changes resulted in a fundamental change in the direction of political causality. Until recently, everyone's model was that citizens (alone or in groups) put pressure on government, which then responded well or badly. It was not government that pressured the people but the other way around. A great leader might manage to rouse people to a pitch of patriotism, but this was a sometime thing, saved for special occasions, like the good family china, lest through overuse its essential fragility lead to breakage. No one, it is safe to say, contemplated government setting up institutions to put pressure on it.

Before our eyes, the time that waits for no one destroyed the traditional arguments pro and con about American federalism. So swiftly that we barely caught a glimpse of what was happening as it passed us by, the premises of the debate shifted. In a phrase, plane political geometry became solid. The theory of dual federalism, in which the parts never penetrated except by benefit of constitutional clergy, was in disarray. So long as the image of the layer cake prevailed, a platonic arrangement if there ever was one, constitutional lawyers knew they should ask not only what was to be done but who was to do it. Parallel play, a space for states, a space for national government, a space for them together, was the neat theory. When Morton Grodzins observed in *The American System* that these parallel lines really met in real life, there was complexity but not consternation. The states and the federal government interpenetrated in numerous ways in almost every program. Daniel Elazar demonstrated in *The American Partnership* that cooperative federalism was the norm virtually from the outset. There remained the good feeling that American pragmatism had apparently triumphed over arid theory. The question of what exactly to call it was, for a time, superseded by calling it good. So long as a few bands of dark were still visible against the white, there was sufficient resolution to say it was something. We could have our federal cake (color me marble!)

and eat it too. As government grew, and as research became more sophisticated, swirls of marble gave way to veins going every which way, so crisscrossed that no one could say what was up or down or who was (simultaneously?) on top or bottom. How could we enjoy federal structure if we did not know what it was? The seemingly arcane disputes about a formula for designating the degree of federalism hid a deeper dilemma, for the political sociology of federalism fared no better, indeed worse, than the political geometry. After all, there was still the structure—states existed; senators would only come from states; and representatives ran in districts within states or the District of Columbia. Where was the social glue?

The social study of federalism talked about state and regional interests but rarely about values and practices. It was assumed that American political cultures were compatible with (and were an expression of) the variety and diversity necessary to maintain a federal system. A belief in uniformity, for instance, could be manifested by strong central rule, modified by delegating authority to geographic units. This delegation, though it belongs to a unitary conception of government, is often called decentralization. Noncentralization refers to independent centers of power in geographic areas that do (and are expected to) differentiate themselves. Though there may be some centralization in a federal system, and there might be decentralization (i.e., delegation), there must be noncentralization. A belief in equality, not only of opportunity but of outcome, would be hostile to noncentralization, for then there could be no substantial differences among states.

Uniformity is antithetical to federalism. The existence of states free to disagree with one another and with the central government inevitably leads to differentiation. Yet states must differ if they are to do more than obey central directives. Were there to be a change in values toward equality of condition, the political culture that undergirds federalism

would fall apart. You can have a belief in equality of opportunity to be different, but you cannot have a belief in equality of results to be the same and still have a federal system.

The special subject of political sociologists has been political parties. Though national parties were weak by European standards, parties in America were the only nationwide social support for the institutional structure of federalism. The decline of parties has not so much left sociologists unemployed as bereft of a rationale for why the unadorned federal structure should work as well as some of them supposed.

WEAK PARTIES

The confusion and concern over what to call federalism is a reflection of a deeper anxiety over what it is becoming. In ancient times, the ability to name an object or a person was equivalent to controlling it or the person. The Bible contains numerous episodes of Jacob or Moses or Manoa trying to discover the name of God and being told, one way or another, that this was improper. Brilliant studies of the definitions and metaphors used to characterize federalism in the past as well as the present suggest that the difficulty may be inseparable from the enterprise. One recent author finds 267 separable designations. If federalism is so far out of control that we do not know what to call it, so is our government, and so are we.

The most visible measure of the vitality of federalism is the party system. If parties (almost always modified by the word "decentralized") were in good shape, so was the federal system. As long as they existed together, the question of causality need never be asked, or, at least, answered. Did strong parties emerge from a strong federal structure or did strong parties create or maintain a strong federal structure?

In the mid-1960s, I collected a number of the best pieces on federalism in order to give students the advantage of a convergence of thought that had emerged in the literature. One basic agreement leaps from that literature: the significance of political parties. William Riker, in "Federalism: Origin, Operation, Significance," put the case squarely:

The federal relationship is centralized according to the degree to which the parties organized to operate the central government control the parties organized to operate the constituent governments. This amounts to the assertion that the proximate cause of variations in the degree of centralization (or peripheralization) in the constitutional structure of a federalism is the variation in degree of party centralization.

Like other writers on federalism, Riker inserts a kicker: "It is theoretically possible but practically difficult to measure the structure of the party system." If we cannot measure the structure of the party system, then how do we calibrate it with the structure of the federal system?

Morton Grodzins begins with the same confident assertion: "The nature of American political parties accounts in largest part for the nature of the American governmental system. The specific point is that the parties are responsible for both the existence and form of the considerable measure of decentralization that exists in the United States." Almost as soon as that sentence has expired, Grodzins begins to equivocate. Life is complicated. Demands for action by the national government may be attributed on occasion to failure by parties within states to offer appropriate policies. "Thus, even with respect to decentralization, the consequences of parties for government are not simple and do not always move in one direction." Causality is complex. "In the first place," Grodzins continues, "it can easily be shown that the causal relationship between party and government is a reciprocal one." Just as parties may shore up state structure, so may local control over nominations or the electoral college system, which are part of the structure of government, " 'cause' decen-

tralized government." Though parties aid in achieving a decentralized government, "governmental [here formal constitutional] factors are partially responsible for the manner in which parties are structured. So government 'causes' the form of party; party 'causes' the form of government." With so many factors potentially contributing to decentralized government, such as local attachments, geographic scope, and the wealth of the nation, which makes redundancy affordable, party can be only one of a number of causes.

By now we are not surprised to find a strong initial statement on the subject endlessly modified. No one does this with greater sophistication than David Truman in "Federalism and the Party System." He says:

In a federal system, decentralization and lack of cohesion in the party system are based on the structural fact of federalism. . . . Three factors derived from the existence of the states as separate and largely self-sustaining power centers— channeling of the claims of local socioeconomic interest groups, inviting their use as leverage against federal action by interests which are only tactically local, and providing for competing and frequently incompatible nuclei of decentralized intra-party conflict—. . . go a long way toward indicating that there is something in federalism which induces decentralization and lack of coherence in a party system.

We discover that "the interdependence of constitutional forms and types of political party is a fact, obvious enough in its simple statement but complex and baffling when the observer undertakes to explain these interrelations as they bear upon past changes in the political life of a people or to anticipate the form and direction of developments in the future." In contexts characterized by multiple and reciprocal causation, where "the cast has altered the mold," we learn that a "search for origins and for trends is thus bedeviled by the tendency to treat in linear, cause-and-effect terms a relationship which is circular and elusive."

So concerned is he with complexity, that Truman refuses to speak of the "party system," saying that would prejudge the question of whether there is one or not. A dive into the watery depth of federalism leaves everyone gasping for air. Yet, there are one or two things on which we can grab hold. Up through the 1950s, at least, parties still performed the distinctive function of nominating candidates. Even as presidential campaigns become more centralized, "the power over nominations remains decentralized." In understanding federalism, however, answers only lead to further questions. "The American party system," Truman continues, "thus tends to be characterized by decentralization of power with respect to its most crucial function, by structural confederation, and by a lack of coherence in matters of major policy. What have the facts of federalism to do with this? To what extent is this an inescapable consequence of the federal system itself?" To this question, Truman has an answer, which soon enough turns into its own question:

> The basic political fact of federalism is that it creates separate, self-sustaining centers of power, privilege, and profit which may be sought and defended as desirable in themselves, as means of leverage upon elements in the political structure above and below, and as bases from which individuals may move to places of greater influence and prestige in and out of government. . . .
>
> But, it has been argued here, the degree to which these become the dominant characteristics of the distribution of power within the political parties is a function of a variety of other governmental and social factors which are independent of the federal structure or are merely supportive of its tendencies.

Though federal structure alone encourages "an irreducible minimum of decentralization and disruption in the party system," Truman tells us other factors in society must also be taken into account. While it is easy to show that federalism has some sort of an in-fluence on the party system, Truman concludes, "the important question of how much effect it has remains unanswered and to a precise degree unanswerable."

I have gone through this maze of quotations to show that in the study of federalism every author takes two steps backward for every step forward. They all agree that party is the most important institutional force sustaining federalism, but how strong it is or why it is strong or how to appraise the various factors contributing to or detracting from its strength, no one knows.

Party stands for the social support, the political sociology undergirding federal structure. When we ask how parties contribute to federalism or how federal structure supports parties, we are actually asking: (1) Is there social support for federalism? and/or (2) Is there anything more to federalism than the bare bones of its structure? If the answer to the first question is no, so is the answer to the second. No wonder students of the subject have become worrywarts. What, then, will become of federalism if it has lost social support but retained its formal structure?

Putting the question this way, as if federalism were at the mercy of unknown but unfriendly forces, entirely apart from human volition, is like going to the Delphic Oracle for a clear answer. In an ultimate sense, there must be more forces at work in the world than anyone can comprehend. Assuming that we citizens had something to do with it, we can ask what the people have done to their parties and whether these actions, of which there are many, may not have something to do with their dissatisfaction.

What has happened to our political parties that they have ceased cementing the American political system? Better still, we might ask not what our parties have done to us, since we now allow them to do so little, but what we have done to them. In words of few syllables, we have deliberately and by design separated parties from society. In every way we could think of, we have cut parties off from social support. First and foremost, direct democracy through primaries has taken the nominating function, everywhere regarded as the primary purpose of parties, away from party leaders. Why work in a party year in and year out if one has little or no say in who will be nominated? Expression by independent political entrepreneurs, attracting a temporary array of supporters, replaces deliberation by party leaders. Discussion in party caucuses and conventions among people who know the candidates is replaced by staged media events or citizens voting in primaries who do not know one another, who do not know citizens in other states, and who certainly do not know the candidates. Caucuses are replaced by "cash-register" primaries, mechanically ringing up the results. A sense of place among people rooted in local party affairs and connected through them to national candidates gives way to a sense of frustration from not knowing enough about the candidates and, because of the proliferation of primaries, not being able to keep track of them.

The other side of the coin of downgrading financial "fat cats" is that there is no one who contributes enough to have a say. Instead of a constituency of contributors to add to other constituencies of accountability, there is another kind of specialist, the expert in campaign law and accounting, whose advice must be heeded for fear of not getting on the ballot, or even going to jail. Or there are sophisticated Political Action Committees (PACs) which organize to press narrow demands but have little or no concern for the integrative, across-the-board concerns of parties. Something in society has been traded for nothing.

All of us have noticed that campaign buttons and stickers are disappearing along with neighborhood headquarters run by neighborhood people. For this the financial restrictions are partly responsible, for the only way to reach people is to use the limited funds for television, radio, and other public media.

It may well be true that Jimmy Carter the candidate, as he claimed in 1976, owed no obligations to anyone. By the same token, it was also true that no one owed anything to him. When he got into trouble, there were few defenders. When he needed advice outside his own circle, there were few party leaders on whom he could rely, just as there were few on whom he was dependent. Like other presidents, to be sure, Carter could set up a White House office for governors and mayors. But, under the guise of protecting pure local government from corrupting contact with national party politics, their elections have almost entirely been switched to nonpresidential election years. So they all have less reason to guide and constrain each other.

There is no need to ask why parties have lost their social roots, since it is the purpose of public policy and national party rules to accomplish just that. Were there states determined to do otherwise, they would be prohibited from doing so, at least in the Democratic party, by the enforcement of national rules. The federal principle, insofar as it relies on national parties based on independent territorial units, no longer exists. Why not?

FOUR CULTURES

What matters most to people is how they live with other people. The critical questions are how individuals should behave toward others and how they would like others to act toward them. No one answers these questions alone; they are embedded in culture—the different forms of social relations and the shared values that justify them. Political cultures answer questions about life with other people: How is order to be achieved and maintained? How are the goods of this world to be secured and divided up? How is envy to be controlled, inequality to be justified or condemned, power to be exercised and legitimated?

The answers of the culture called hierarchical collectivism are to impose order through a division of labor in which larger and smaller decisions are parceled out to different people and reconciled by commands from the center. Inequality is legitimated by arguing it is essential to safeguard the collective, each element being taught to sacrifice for the whole. Envy is controlled by teaching people their place, by reserving ostentation to collective bodies, such as the state or church, and by examples of sacrificial behavior as the elite lead and die in battle. Wealth is created by saving to sponsor collective investment, thereby guaranteeing the collective obligation to the future, on which basis past sacrifices are justified. Authority goes with position from the top down, the exercise of power rationalized both as an antidote to disorder and on grounds of expertise, i.e., "papa knows best."

The culture of competitive individualism imposes order by maintaining agreement on freedom of contract. Leaders are chosen like every other commodity by bidding and bargaining. There is no permanent leadership (Will leaders not restrict equal opportunity to maintain themselves in power?), only different leaders for different purposes. Envy is mitigated by showing everyone they can have their chance too, or by blaming failure on personal incapacity or bad luck. For individualists, risk is opportunity, providing that winners can personally reap the rewards. By the same token, inequality of result is justified on grounds of fair competition. Where hierarchies can take long-term risks for future growth by characteristic techniques of shedding blame (secrecy, complexity, deception), individualists depend on markets to reward the most promising solutions while discarding the worst. Reliance on markets is legitimated by the claim that pursuit of private interests ultimately leaves everyone better off.

Taken together, the alliance of hierarchic and market cultures constitutes the modern establishment. From hierarchy comes order, including the rules for competition, and from individualism economic growth. There are tensions between them. Hierarchies care more about the division of labor defining who can do what, while individualists care about results, any combination of resources or people being all right so long as it maintains freedom of contract for the future.

The critical culture, the opposition to the establishment, is egalitarian sectarianism. Where competitive individualism believes in equality of opportunity, egalitarian sectarianism believes in equality of result. Sectarianism is an egalitarian community, rejecting all bargains that confer more gain on some than on others. Whether they be religious or secular, sectarians choose to live a life of purely voluntary association. From rejection of authority come their other fateful choices. They choose equality because that is the only way people will agree to live together without authority. They choose criticism because painting the society outside in lurid colors helps keep their people together against the splits that must threaten those who live without authority. The reasons are always at hand: collectivism stands for coercion; individualism breeds inequality. Leadership either should not exist (hence the endless discussions inside sects seeking consensus) or it should be perfect (hence the appearance of the charismatic leader of unusual personal qualities in whom the spirit of the Lord or of perfect justice shines). Envy may be mitigated by surface signs of equality—plain food, simple clothes, sharing wealth. Since perfect equality is rare, envy is handled by expulsions and schisms as would-be leaders are driven out for usurping authority, or they split and set up shop on their own. Wealth creation is not the concern of sects partly because they find it difficult, without authority, to tax their members, and partly because they can take that for granted, criticizing individualism for failure to redistribute the wealth that already exists.

By now it should be apparent that concepts of fairness differ according to the way of life each is supposed to support. For individualists, fairness is equal opportunity in competition. It is not success but failure (in theories, elections, or business) that is crucial, because markets for ideas or goods are regulated by dropping out the worst. That is why political democracy is mostly about getting people and parties out of office and has very little to say about what they should do when they get there, other than to leave gracefully when they lose. Fairness in a hierarchy is about following the forms specifying the relationships among the parts and the whole. Being treated fairly means being allowed to fulfill the responsibilities of one's station and supporting superiors to do the same. Fairness follows function in observing the division of labor and the boundaries between each specialty. The soldier must obey the superior officer, but the general may not invade the subordinate's home. To sectarians, fairness follows outcomes; equal is fair.

Just as the various political regimes all believe in equality but define it differently, so they all believe in "decentralization." For collectivists, decentralization means delegation; for sectarians, decentralization means central redistribution of resources among localities; only for individualism does decentralization mean competition among independent entities without central control other than by mutual agreement.

"Stolen rhetoric," as Mary Douglas calls values that can be shared among cultures because they do not point to particular acts—goodness, harmony, equality—also applies to "decentralization." Everyone appears to agree because the various cultures mean different things by these terms. Noncentralization, the independence of local entities from outside control, cannot be stolen by collectivists, any more than their talk about specialization and the division of labor can be appropriated by sectarians who, in turn, can hardly use rhetoric about the social survival of the fittest. This rhetoric cannot be shared because it prescribes and legitimates specific behavior in the present, behavior so contradictory to some political cultures that they would self-destruct.

In discussing America, it is especially important to observe the crucial distinction between individualism and sectarianism. Both share a desire to live with as few rules prescribing their behavior as possible. Where individualists choose to maintain equality of opportunity to achieve distinction, sectarians choose to escape authority by diminishing differences through equality of result. Thus the challenge the two cultures offer to authority is fundamentally different. Because sectarians form part of a collective, they reject all outside authority. Because individualists have no collective ideal, they will join with anyone, including hierarchical authority, provided their ability to bid and bargain is respected. Individualists prefer minimal authority; sectarians, none at all.

Though the United States is a single nation, Americans do not constitute a single culture. The attempt to explain the vast diversity of behavior observed in everyday life on the grounds of uniformity in shared national values is a major mistake of social science. Once we stop thinking that there are American (or German or Japanese) values uniformly distributed across the population, and liberate ourselves to think that varied ways of life may compete for allegiance within a national identity, we will be in a better position to gain self-understanding. When we ask about the mix of cultures within countries, we can ask what a change in the proportion of people who adhere to individualism, collectivism, or sectarianism can mean for the country concerned.

A brief analysis of the compatibility of the federal principle with the major cultures—the primary colors, so to speak—will prepare the way for mixing subtler political hues. At the outset we will eliminate authoritarian cultures, ruled by a single hierarchy, and state capitalism, where competition has been driven out by state control of markets, as incompatible with democracy.

Within a democratic government, rival hierarchies might compete for office but they do not so much share as delegate authority. An areal delegation of administrative authority, as in prefectures, is not the same as the independent centers of power, at least in regard to some important matters, required in a federal system. At its extreme, competitive individualism is no more compatible with a division of authority between the center and the states than is hierarchical collectivism; for competitive markets, except for maintenance of freedom of contract, do not recognize a center. They are inherently noncentralized. Sectarians could accept either central rule, where all individuals were equal, or a confederacy, where all states were equal, but not both, because one level of government would have to have more power over certain objects and, therefore, subjects than others. Their overriding desire to secure equality of results rules out any arrangement, like federalism, that prizes diversity. My hypothesis is that only hybrid regimes, combining at least two cultures (and, of necessity, their differing values and practices) can support federalism.

HYBRID REGIMES

Markets and hierarchies are the prototypical combination of centralization and noncentralization. Markets bring not only economic growth but also a belief in competition for its own sake. Hierarchy contributes authority and the stability to help make markets work. Both regimes, it should be stressed, institutionalize inequality, the hierarchy building it in beforehand as the price of order, markets encouraging it afterward as the main incentive for economic activity. This very tolerance (even encouragement) of inequality facilitates the diversity that lies at the heart of federalism. It is no deviation from principle for states to differ from one another and from the central government. It is inequality of result, not merely in income (some states choosing high tax, high services, others the opposite) but also in lifestyle, that distinguishes federalism as a living system from federalism as a front for a unitary power.

Sectarians could compromise. They could combine with collectivism, accepting the coercion inherent in authority in order to use the power of government to redistribute resources and otherwise enhance equality among citizens. Alternatively, sectarians might move toward market individualism, accepting inequality of reward in order to escape from the involuntary authority of hierarchy. Actually, we do observe egalitarians in conflict between social democracy (collectivism and sectarianism) and "small is beautiful" (individualism and sectarianism). In the United States, hierarchy has been weak but sectarianism has been strong.

The historic sectarian stance (beginning long before the antifederalists and continuing until the 1930s), that central government—the hierarchical principle—imposed artificial inequity on society, predisposed its adherents to an alliance with market forces in favor of state government and in opposition to the national executive power. Where individualism is the dominant regime, as in the United States, sectarians can reduce cultural dissonance (that is, maintain coherence in shared values and practices) by arguing that pure and unfettered competition, if actually practiced, would diminish differences among people. Equality of opportunity would then fulfill its promise by achieving equality of result.

Where collectivism is the dominant political culture, as in most European countries, sectarianism can overcome its internal dissonance by arguing that acceptance of authority would enable government to enforce sacrifices on the better off by redistribution of income to the worse off. Sectarian rage at inequality is transmuted into the positive use of authority to achieve not merely equality before the law, which is the norm of collectivism, but substantive equality of result.

The sectarian impulse is noncentralist. Based on purely voluntary organization, distrusting authority, suspicious of expertise, preferring face-to-face relations in small groups without social differentiation, sectarians could support not delegation of authority, which only makes it more remote, but non-centralization—small communities independent of the center. But—and there's the rub!—local discretion means local differences, and differences imply that everyone is not being treated the same.

So long as collectivism (of the Right or Left) remains the dominant political culture in Europe, the chances for noncentralization, for a genuine expansion of local autonomy, will remain slim. When conservative governments are in power, the social democratic opposition calls for transfer of functions to regions (non-centralization) where their power is greater. When social democrats are in office, they speak of decentralization, that is, delegation of powers in order to spread egalitarian policies around from the center. So long as hierarchy dominates markets, decentralization will remain a euphemism for delegation, that is, if I may abuse the expression, centralization "with a human face." The status quo will remain—talk of decentralization and practice of recentralization.

What about the United States? If federalism has not been entirely synonymous with American society, a symbol of its diversity and decentralization, it has long been equivalent to American government. In popular parlance, whenever the glories or defects of the peculiar American form of government are discussed, the name is federalism. When American government appears to be doing well, the cause is found in its federal arrangements. If those arrangements include the separation of powers and checks and balances, are not these also modes of dividing and containing power? If there are two of everything—legislatures, executives, courts, levels of government—is it not wonderful that the competition this creates produces order out of chaos? When we like it, this Noah's ark of ours is a marvelous compendium of unity and diversity. When things are going badly, and the parliamentary is preferred to the presidential model, a unitary to a federal form, the blame is placed on federalism. Then there are too many rather than too few governments, confusion instead of cohesion, redundancy instead of rationality, so federalism is found wanting. When, for instance, a president finds a malaise in the country, we know he is finding it hard to govern. He has too little, not too much power, too many, not too few competitors: federalism is failing. Why?

What is that we hear rattling around in the closet of American government? The bare bones of federal structure. The critics' conception of federalism as a structure without a sinew, bones without connective tissue, has come back to confront us. At long last, the often repeated fears that federalism would regress to its constitutional origins, dust to dust, structure to structure, working out the consequences of formal arrangements unmediated by social ties, are being realized. It is not just that the demography of the states is becoming somewhat more similar; it is, rather, that the values and practices that would legitimate and rationalize noncentralization have grown weaker.

A mixed regime is compatible with federalism. Should sects, markets, or hierarchies grow all-powerful, there would be no room for federalism. Should these political cultures coexist, the centralization of hierarchies and the noncentralization of markets, accompanied by criticism from sects, has proved to be viable. So long as sects are weak, they add to the variety of organizational forces. Sects tend to be small (large size is difficult without a division of labor), numerous (because they split often), and mobile (moving to get away from established authority). Unable to control central government, they resist its authority so as to maintain their local diversity. If sectarianism becomes stronger, so that it can hope to impose its preferences for equality of result on the central government, it will urge policies of uniformity. Some uniformity is one thing; a lot of uniformity is another. There is no escape from a compelling truth: federalism and equality of result cannot coexist.

READINGS SUGGESTED BY THE AUTHOR

Elazar, Daniel. *The American Partnership.* Chicago: University of Chicago Press, 1962.

Grodzins, Morton, ed. *The American System.* Chicago: Rand McNally, 1966.

Riker, William H. "Federalism: Origin, Operation, Significance." In Aaron Wildavsky, ed. *American Federalism in Perspective.* Boston: Little, Brown, 1979.

Truman, David. "Federalism and the Party System." In Aaron Wildavsky, ed. *American Federalism in Perspective.* Boston: Little, Brown, 1979.

3

Revitalizing the States: A Look at the Record

DAVID NICE

The American states have been the objects of substantial criticism for many years. While they have been assigned a major role in the operation of the federal system, many observers have expressed doubts regarding states' abilities to fulfill that role. Fifty years ago, Luther Gulick said in unmistakable terms:

> Is the state the appropriate instrumentality for the exercise of these sovereign functions? The answer is not a matter of conjecture or delicate appraisal. It is a matter of brutal record. The American state is finished. I do not predict that the states will go, but affirm that they have gone.

Nearly four decades later the question was still being asked of whether the states are the "fallen arch" of the federal system, occupying a prominent position but possibly unable to bear the burden of its responsibilities.

The states have indeed been plagued by a number of structural problems, mostly of their own making. Those problems have been widely discussed and debated, but considerably less attention has been paid to the substantial progress that the states have made in overcoming them. The pace has varied from state to state and from one issue to another, but the overall pattern is clear.

STATE PARTIES

A fundamental criticism has been leveled at the state political party systems for failing to provide adequate interparty competition and for being organizationally weak and ineffective. At minimum, the absence of interparty competition forces complete reliance on intraparty controls for responsiveness. A competitive system provides both kinds of controls.

The increased reliance on intraparty influence is reflected in the frequency and intensity of primary contests where interparty competition is absent. Where one party's nomination is tantamount to victory, interest in and conflict over that nomination naturally increase. However, the voters' role is still confined to a single phase of the process, the intraparty choice, rather than the two phases available in a two-party state.

Without the competition of a strong opposition, the dominant party tends to grow

National Civic Review, Vol. 72, No.7 (July–August 1983), pp. 371–376.

weak organizationally. As a result, the less competitive state typically experiences party division in primaries, less party voting in the legislature, and more uncontested general elections, all of which indicate party weakness. This weakness often produces a chaotic political recruitment system, a propensity for favoritism, an inability to put sustained support behind programs, and a confused electorate which has difficulty keeping track of rapidly changing coalitions.

In recent years, however, the state party systems have grown somewhat more competitive. Between 1965 and 1976, 36 states showed increasing competition, based on legislative and gubernatorial elections. The number of least competitive states has fallen significantly, and the number of highly competitive states has nearly doubled. We remain some distance, however, from high levels of interparty competition in all states. Larry Sabato's analysis of gubernatorial elections reached similar conclusions. The number of one-party states fell by half, and the number of competitive states more than doubled (*Goodbye to Goodtime Charlie*, Lexington Books, 1978). While party competition does not guarantee satisfactory voter choice, it is more likely to do so than is an election with no choice at all.

STATE LEGISLATURES

The legislatures have received a large share of the criticism directed at state governments. For decades, they were handicapped by limitations on the time members were willing or able to devote to legislative duties. Those limitations took the form of biennial sessions, limits on the length of sessions, and low salaries. The high rate of turnover compounded the time problem.

Legislative effectiveness was also limited by inadequate staffing and facilities which would ease the burden on legislators and provide more sources of information, as well as

handling routine matters. Finally, the legislatures were criticized for failing to give urban and suburban areas their fair share of representation, leaving rural areas in control.

The "reapportionment revolution" of the 1960s changed the composition of the state legislatures, largely by mandate of the federal courts, thereby eliminating one of the major shortcomings.

The legislatures have moved to give themselves more time in which to work. The number of states with annual sessions increased from only five in 1946 to 20 in 1966 to 36 in 1978.

Higher salaries and other reforms have increased the appeal of legislative service, with the result that turnover has declined. Between 1931 and 1976, the rate of turnover in state senates fell from 51 percent to 32 percent, house turnover from 59 percent to 37 percent. Consequently, the legislatures have a larger pool of experienced members to supply substantive and procedural expertise.

Legislative staffing has been expanded greatly in recent years, although the pace of progress has varied considerably from state to state. Between 1968 and 1974, there was an overall increase of 130 percent to a total of 16,000 in full-time, year-round professional, administrative, and clerical staff.

Overall, the typical state legislature in the 1980s is better suited to the demands of modern government than its counterpart in recent decades, and while the pace of reform has varied considerably the pattern is clear.

GOVERNORS

The governor's office in many states has been roundly criticized, because of both limits on tenure with their obvious constraints on gubernatorial effectiveness and the practice of electing a variety of other state executive officers. Even where formal limits were not a major problem, salaries in many states posed a practical time limit for many occupants of the statehouses. While a high salary does not assure excellence, low salaries often discourage capable chief executives from staying in the office and may lead some good candidates to avoid seeking the office.

Many governors' efforts have been frustrated by the presence of other elected state executive officers who are not part of the "team," as in the recent case of an elected attorney general who publicly expressed the view that a gubernatorial program was unconstitutional and was then called to defend it in court when opponents filed suit to block its implementation. The limited visibility of many of these officials may also reduce their public accountability and make them more susceptible to interest group influence. As the number of elective executives increases, the information costs associated with voting rise considerably, as do the problems of determining which officials are responsible for the condition of the state.

While governors in many states are still plagued by many weaknesses in the design of their offices, substantial progress has been made in attacking some of the fundamental problems. The four-year term, which was found in only 25 states in 1946, was practically universal—46 states—by the mid-1970s. Gubernatorial salaries have risen from an average of $11,512 in 1950 to an average of $40,963 in 1975. Nevertheless the pace of progress has been uneven, and gubernatorial salaries remain low in some states.

With longer terms of office and higher salaries, governors have in fact been staying in office longer in recent years. While less than 30 percent of governors remained in office more than four years during the 1950s, the proportion rose to more than 35 percent a decade later, with the biggest jump among those serving 10 years or more, from 4.6 percent to 10 percent.

Some progress has also been made in reducing the number of independently elected state officials, although the results have been more modest. In 1950 the average state had 13 state constitutionally elective statewide officials; the number was down to 10 by 1975. There was a total of 242 major elected executives (excluding governors and lieutenant governors) in 16 states in 1950, which Sabato found to be reduced to 187 by 1975.

STATE BUREAUCRACIES

While the federal bureaucracy seems to have become the target of choice in recent years, state bureaucracies have also received considerable criticism. Among the culprits have been: limited merit system coverage in many states; lower salaries than for comparable private sector positions; inability to achieve and maintain high levels of knowledge and expertise in agencies; high turnover; and chaotic administrative structures which fail to coordinate related activities, frustrate initiative, and make determination of responsibility difficult.

While these problems have not been eliminated, their extent and severity have been reduced. According to Sabato's figures, merit system coverage expanded by 11 percent between 1963 and 1975, although they still may be criticized for undue rigidity, unresponsiveness, and failure to actually achieve merit at times.

The educational attainments of state agency heads have also risen in recent years. A survey of state administrators in 1964 found that less than 40 percent held graduate degrees. Deil Wright found that by 1974 that figure had risen to over 50 percent (*Understanding Intergovernmental Relations*, Duxbury Press, 1978).

State administrators' salaries have also been on the rise in recent years. While much of the increase is illusory, a real increase remains when inflation is taken into account. As a result, state government positions have gained some ability to attract and retain qualified personnel.

The image of state bureaucracies has improved as well. Wright found federal aid administrators noticeably less critical of state personnel systems in 1975 than they were in 1965. While some of that may reflect changes in the ideological and partisan leanings of the aid administrators, more direct evidence shows that the states have made genuine progress.

REVENUE SYSTEMS

State revenue systems and their reliance on relatively inelastic taxes have also come under fire as public demands often outpaced revenue growth. State officials must then either adopt new taxes, raise existing tax rates, refuse to respond to public demands, or turn to the federal government for aid. When the political environment is hostile to tax increases and federal aid is not forthcoming, the states have been considered unwilling or unable to respond.

Despite the political risks, from 1959 through 1971, the states enacted 40 new taxes and 468 tax rate increases, an average of roughly one tax increase per state legislature each time it convened. As a result, Wright noted, over half of the growth in state tax revenues from 1958 to 1972 came from the adoption of new state taxes and rate increases, and state tax revenues grew faster (302 percent) during that period than did federal tax revenues (103 percent) or local tax revenues (245 percent). The Tax Foundation reported that between January 1982 and January 1983 alone, there were 43 increases in the 233 non-property tax rates in 23 states.

The states have also increased their reliance on income taxes, which most observers regard as more elastic than other tax types—although that depends on rate structures and exemptions. The number of states with general individual and corporate income taxes rose dramatically, so that they are now the norm rather than the exception. The proportion of state tax revenues derived from income taxes also has increased—27.3 percent

in 1982, according to the Tax Foundation. The result of this change may well be an increasing ability of states to finance public demands from state tax revenues without the trauma of rate increases.

STATE CONSTITUTIONS

A fundamental structural problem is the nature of many state constitutions. The typical state constitution is much longer than the U.S. constitution, largely because of the inclusion of all sorts of detailed provisions. The result of that excessive detail is to make change considerably more difficult. Because many of the provisions are in the form of limitations, state officials who want to act on a policy problem may find themselves unable to do so. Reformers have, therefore, called for constitutions which contain fewer restrictions on legislative and executive actions and which leave much detail to be treated as statute law. Some states have made progress in streamlining their state constitutions in recent years but the overall pattern is one of limited progress.

CONCLUSIONS

In general, the American states have undergone a process of revitalization in recent decades. Considerable progress has been made in remedying some of their fundamental shortcomings, although some have lagged behind. Why has this process of reforms occurred?

First, reform has been encouraged by a variety of groups, including the Citizens Conference on State Legislatures, the Committee for Economic Development, the National Municipal League, civil service reformers, and many others.

The growth of state government has also stimulated reform efforts. For most of this century, state government tax revenues and direct domestic public expenditures grew faster than the federal level and the local level. Moreover, the state government share of state-local spending roughly tripled, from 21 percent in 1902 to 63 percent in 1971, and the increase has continued across the country, with some variation. The increasing role of state government may have enhanced the need for reforms and may also have enhanced support for them by increasing the visibility of state government.

A third stimulus for reforms has been the somewhat lackluster image of state government. A series of surveys which asked citizens which level of government gave them the most for their money found that state government consistently came in third, well behind the federal government and also behind local government. That lackluster image may help to spur reform efforts, both by providing a base of citizen support and by shaping officials' perceptions of the need for change.

Finally, the national influences have affected the states. The increasing levels of interparty competition are undoubtedly due to national political currents in most cases. The growth of the federal government has stimulated reforms by indicating to the states that when they cannot or will not act, the federal government will. State officials appear to be responding to the "federal challenge" by revitalizing the state governments.

The long-term significance of the revitalization of state governments may be profound. While state officials have often expressed alarm at the growth of federal involvement in domestic policy, the states have often been poorly equipped to compete with the federal government. Of course, many factors have encouraged the growth of federal power, including increasing interdependence, the Depression, and political interests seeking some degree of nationwide uniformity in various programs. Nevertheless, in many instances groups have sought federal intervention only after the states proved to be unwilling or unable to act. More recently, states have increased their responsive capabilities and their ability to play a sustained and probably growing role in the federal system.

4

Would We Know a Well-Governed City If We Saw One?

HARRY P. HATRY

Would we know a well-governed city if we saw one? How should a city be rated? Results are the key. First and foremost, there should be evidence that the city's services are "good," that is, that they produce good results. There should be evidence that the *quality of life* is high, at least relative to other cities with similar characteristics, and that residents by and large have been pleased with services for the last few years. Another con-

National Civic Review, Vol.75, No.3 (May–June 1986), pp. 142–146.

sideration is the condition of the community's streets, bridges, water and sewer mains, and buildings.

Further, how equitable are the services? How does the government treat its disadvantaged and minorities? Do those residents, often living in less attractive sections of the city, also feel that they are receiving adequate services in terms of the condition and cleanliness of their streets, recreational opportunities, human services, police and fire protection, etc., services that have resulted in decent living conditions?

Have taxes (property, sales, etc.) been reasonable, indicating an *efficient* city? Has that government avoided periodic budget emergencies, had a high bond rating, and, based on fiscal indicators, demonstrated *fiscal strength?*

In these three key results criteria—service quality, equitableness, and efficiency—to be fair the city should be compared to places similar in age, area of the country, and basic demographics.

Unfortunately, most communities throughout the United States collect little information on the first two major criteria, i.e., service quality and equitableness. Residents, the media, and even public officials themselves seldom see such information. Few communities are making regular efforts to measure service quality and equitableness, although in recent years there has been considerably more interest. A number of city and county governments are attempting to do a better job on this key element of accountability.

Given the absence of information on service quality and equitableness, substitute criteria are often used to assess whether a city is well-governed or not. The use of these criteria is less satisfying and can even be misleading since a city could meet most or all of them and still not be achieving good service results. These substitute criteria are the following:

1. *Tranquility and the absence of squabbles (at least in public) among public officials.* Ob-

servers probably look first for the absence of confrontation and negative headlines in the newspapers. Cities with active warfare between the mayor and council or between the mayor and various community groups would generally be dismissed as not being well-run. The absence of scandals, prosecutions or claims of corruption involving city officials would likely be a prerequisite to a positive appraisal.

2. *Stability/continuity in office of government officials.* Frequent turnover in the highest levels of management, such as the city manager and department heads, is a negative. (Caution: in some situations, the chief officials may be doing a fine job of selecting, training and developing personnel. In such instances, the city might have more turnover among middle- and upper-level managers who may be offered substantial promotions in other communities.)

3. *Innovativeness.* Ah, innovativeness! This seems to be a favorite of observers. The frequent introduction of new, unusual projects is often taken as a sign of top-notch communities. It suggests that the government is not just a follower but also a leader. Innovativeness is probably the key indicator for most awards to public officials and communities. Though innovativeness is a good sign, it seems important to determine that the innovations have endured and that they provide major benefits to the community—not just that a city implemented an innovation.

4. *Participative management.* Participative management goes back decades, but in recent years it has begun to take off, especially as our country has shifted to become much more of a service economy. Thus, city evaluators have begun to look for employee-oriented management, the presence of labor-management committees, or some version of these such as quality circles, and high morale among

government employees. Note, however, that the link between employee satisfaction and effective production has not yet been clearly established. We still find situations where autocratic management appears to work well, at least under certain conditions.

5. *Active public-private partnerships.* This is a big thing these days, a favorite topic for the current federal administration. Indeed, for many years many communities have attempted to leverage government funds with private sector resources in development activities to make their cities at least more physically attractive. These days we look for public-private partnerships relating not only to the physical infrastructure and economic development but also to human service activities, including school systems.

6. *Analytical budgeting and planning.* City evaluators, particularly those with technical backgrounds, look for some form of advanced budgeting and planning process such as program budgeting, zero-based budgeting, strategic (multi-year) planning, and the like, as distinct from the classic, line-item budget approach. The assumption is that such a process will help the government focus on what's important, on both its short- and long-term objectives and how these can best be achieved, playing down nit-picking and avoiding seeing the trees while neglecting the forest.

7. *Citizen input into government decisions.* Since at least the early '60s, citizen input has more and more become a criterion for good government. The belief is that well-governed communities should use citizen advisory groups, neighborhood advisory boards, or other means for regularly and systematically obtaining input from citizens that helps government officials select programs and policies. We in the United States have begun to believe that citizen input during elections is not sufficient. Between elections, citizens

(who after all are the clients for the services of government) should be given opportunities to provide inputs to our public officials. The danger here is that officials will become too responsive, especially to the demands of select groups in the community at the expense of others, and will abdicate some of their responsibilities.

Each of these characteristics is good in a community. A government can, however, provide considerable opportunity for citizen input and never use it, or get overly selective input. A government can have a fine budget process and not make good decisions with it. A government may be very innovative but never maintain its innovations for long or achieve real benefits. The government may be very tranquil and stable yet be doing the wrong things or doing the right things in the wrong way.

Unfortunately, in local, state and federal governments only a small proportion of agencies, perhaps 5 to 10 percent, regularly assess the extent to which they are getting value for their dollars. Cities, counties and states seldom systematically examine the cleanliness and ridability of their streets, assess whether their health and social services have led to significant improvements for clients, or ask their clients—the citizens—for feedback on the helpfulness, timeliness and quality of services they have received.

Even more surprising, few cities measure on a regular basis and in a systematic way the efficiency (i.e., the productivity) with which services are delivered. (Efficiency and productivity here mean the amount of dollars and hours of employee time spent to achieve the amount of output produced.) The Urban Institute recently examined management-by-objective systems in city, county and state agencies, seldom finding objectives relating to service quality or effectiveness, or to service efficiency, productivity or even cost reduction. (On occasion, a department manager had an objective to stay within the city manager's budget, but this is not much of an incentive to save money, at least not without lowering the level of service.)

Yes, cities do obtain complaint data, and most appear to respond to complaints and other calls from constituents. But many citizens don't know how to complain, don't like to complain, or don't feel it would do any good, and this applies especially to the disadvantaged in a community. Yes, many officials travel about their jurisdictions, speak with constituents, and obtain a perspective on service quality, but this can be highly unrepresentative of conditions that exist throughout the whole community. Only a small number of cities or counties currently conducts annual or biennial surveys in order to obtain citizens' ratings of services. In the private sector, businesses periodically do market surveys and seldom take customers for granted. Peters and Waterman in their popular work *In Search of Excellence* reported that being close to customers and having a corporate belief in delivering quality service seemed to be highly correlated with successful businesses. Should not this also be the case with governments?

Recently, the Boston *Globe* reprinted a series of articles it originally ran June 16–21, 1985, on "City Services: Does Boston Deliver?" A team of reporters using a series of measurement procedures (in part developed at The Urban Institute) interviewed citizens and rated such factors as street cleanliness and park condition to generate information on the quality of city services. The disappointing element is that a newspaper had to do the measurement. The government was not doing it. This is not to criticize Boston; most cities are in the same situation.

The well-governed city in the decade of the 1980s will necessarily concern itself with entrepreneurship and the greater use of the private sector by the public sector.

Public services, as economists remind us,

have for the most part been monopolies: meaning no competition and, thus, little incentive for the organization to improve its efficiency or the quality of its services. This perhaps explains the lack of regular measurement of efficiency or service quality by governments. Since California's Proposition 13 in 1978 and the new administration in Washington since 1980, however, there is clearly a drive toward the greater use of the private sector and business to help deliver government services. Without getting into the philosophical arguments pro and con, this new drive can be turned to almost everyone's advantage.

Public officials will need to become more entrepreneurial, to look at a broader range of options, and to try new approaches. This does not have to mean privatization. City personnel, both management and non-management, spurred by the new private competition, could become more motivated to cooperate and overcome bureaucratic inefficiencies that handicap them in delivering services. In Phoenix and Minneapolis, for example, city personnel are effectively improving procedures to make government more competitive with private sector options. Public sector agencies and their unions are naturally greatly concerned and opposed to anything that smacks of privatization. The answer may be for public agencies to become more competitive and be able to demonstrate their ability to deliver services as well as private organizations. A well-governed city may be able to accomplish this.

With the growing complexity of modern society, including environmental threats, continued high rates of crime, influx of immigrants and refugees, and higher expectations, the demands on our cities will continue to grow. Over the next decade our less well-governed cities will need to break through to become well-governed cities and our currently well-governed cities to become even more so.

CHAPTER 2

Intergovernmental Relations

Fundamental to the study of American state and local government is an understanding of the constitutional framework within which they exist. Conflicting interpretations of the "proper" relationship between the **national and state governments have been an enduring theme in American history. The present debate over the "intent of the Framers" of the Constitution is considered in Professor Anderson's classic article, below.**

How these relationships between governments work in practice forms the rest of this chapter. Uniform state laws and interstate compacts allow state initiative and national cooperation without relying solely upon the federal government. The responsibilities of the states for their local governments are detailed by the Advisory Commission on Intergovernmental Relations. Finally, the courts may be called upon to referee between governments, or to hold them accountable for the constitutional treatment of citizens.

5

The Nation and the States: Rivals or Partners?

WILLIAM ANDERSON

Concerning the nature of the federal system and of the Constitution there are in general terms two opposing philosophies. On the one hand there are the states' righters, the bring-the-government-back-home group. To the extent that they hold a theory on the origin of the federal system it is that sovereign states came together to form the union, that even in indissoluble and perpetual union these states retained their sovereignty, and that therefore the central government is the mere creature of the states. They believe that in order to preserve personal liberties and local government the national government must be kept at a minimum, and that the assumption of new activities by the federal government is "unconstitutional." They express fears of "centralization" and of "big government." They want the powers of the various governments "strictly defined and separated." Some of them oppose any suggestion of the "welfare state" at whatever level; others believe that the state governments can handle welfare functions more democratically and efficiently than the national government.

In opposition are those who believe that the people are sovereign; that the people created both state and national governments and that therefore both levels of government are merely the agencies of the people. They believe that the Constitution is a flexible document which cannot be read solely in terms of what the framers of 1787 intended but must be interpreted in the light of changing conditions and needs. They are not afraid of centralization or big government as such, as long as democratic processes are preserved to control government. They do not believe that recent increases in the national government's activities have taken any powers away from the states; on the contrary, they believe that the state governments are stronger and more active than ever before. Finally, they are convinced that it is in the best interests of the nation as a whole not to limit to any great extent the powers of the central government.

Admittedly these contrasts are oversimplified. Not all in either camp hold all the related views. In many cases individuals are not consciously aware of holding one philosophy or the other; they merely react to specific actions and proposals with approval or disapproval. I do not intend to suggest that the

differences of opinion are clear-cut and easy to define; rather I would have us use these generalized characterizations merely as convenient points of reference.

Neither do I mean to imply that the nation is once again a "house divided," this time on the issue of intergovernmental relations, and doomed to be rent asunder. Certainly there are significant and basic differences of opinion, as I have outlined; there are tensions and frictions and even animosities among government officials at the various levels; there is a good deal of "viewing with alarm" and shaking of skeletons by numerous nonofficial groups. But there are wide areas of agreement, on purpose if not always on procedure. Excellent cooperation and smooth functioning mark many of the programs in which national, state, and local governments join hands. . . .

THE INTENT OF THE FRAMERS

The Constitution of the United States, after it was adopted, soon became a symbol of national unity, strength, and achievement. It took on for prideful Americans some of the aspects of the "crown" of the United Kingdom—that great symbol of British national and even imperial strength and unity. The framers of the Constitution were accordingly praised then and later by many patriotic speakers and writers as an assembly of demigods, or at least of men who were very near that level of ability, high purpose, and integrity. The bickerings, disagreements, and compromises of the Federal Convention were passed over in silence, while the Constitution was exalted into an almost sacrosanct and untouchable symbol of national greatness.

Along with this fetishism arose the feeling that everything about the interpretation and operation of the Constitution must be tested by the touchstone of "the intentions of the framers." This began even before the publication in 1843 of Madison's notes on the debates in the convention, one of the best sources of evidence as to what was intended. And today, more than one hundred and sixty-five years after the drafting of the Constitution, there are still frequent references to the framers and their "intentions." . . .

The Constitution simply did not spring forth perfect, complete, and self-explanatory. Most likely it never will be complete and perfect. Men disagreed about it when it was being drafted, when it came up for adoption, and when it was being put into effect. Many of the framers were participants in the early national government and in some of the state governments of that day, and they did not all agree as to what the Constitution meant or what its framers intended. Indeed, it is merely vain imagining to assume that such a thing as "the intention" of "the framers" in the full sense ever existed or ever can be discovered. Fifty-five delegates took part in the Federal Convention, and thirty-nine signed the final document. Hundreds of persons participated in the thirteen-state ratifying conventions, while many other citizens engaged in written and oral discussions of the Constitution.

Many questions that came up later probably never were considered by the framers. Consequently they can hardly be said to have had any intentions on these issues. The record of what they did discuss is quite incomplete, obviously, but what is available provides voluminous evidence of differences of opinion as to what was intended and as to what might be expected from the Constitution on the points that men did discuss. There were differences of opinion not only between the proponents of the Constitution and the opponents, but also among the proponents themselves. Even *The Federalist*, the essays published in New York in 1787 and 1788 to help bring about the adoption of the Constitution by the people of New York, displays a noticeably "split personality." In fact each of the two principal authors of these essays revealed within his own writings some vague-

ness, confusion, and even contradiction—perhaps Madison more than Hamilton.

This is not to say that nothing at all can be determined about the intentions of the framers. There obviously were areas of agreement among the sponsors of the Constitution. That document is itself the best evidence of what they agreed upon. . . .

. . . [T]he Constitution contains no term to suggest a treaty or agreement among the ratifying states—neither confederation, nor confederacy, nor federation, nor federal. The complete omission of any and every such word from the Constitution can hardly have been a mere oversight or inadvertence. . . .

The framers of the new plan called it a constitution. The word was already in use among the states to designate the written document that sets forth the framework of the government of a single state. There is in this word no idea of a treaty or of a plighting of faith among various individuals or states, rather it suggests integration or unity.

On the other hand the Articles of Confederation were cast more clearly in the form of a treaty or compact among states. . . .

The Articles were drawn up by "Delegates of the States in Congress assembled," and were ratified by the legislatures of the several states on behalf of the states as units. On the other hand the famous words with which the Constitution begins are "We the People of the United States . . . do ordain and establish this Constitution of the United States of America." Furthermore, the Constitution was ratified by special conventions of the people in each state, not by the legislatures.

This is surely one of the most significant verbal and structural differences between the Constitution and the Articles.

The "Sovereignty" of the States

One of the most notable clauses in the Articles of Confederation reads: "Article II. Each state retains its sovereignty, freedom and independence, and every Power, Jurisdiction and right, which is not by this confederation expressly delegated to the United States, in Congress assembled."

This seems to imply that the states were separately sovereign and independent before the Articles were adopted, that by their act of confederating they delegated to Congress whatever powers it was to have, and that all powers not expressly so delegated, plus the essence of sovereignty and independence, were retained by the states. This clearly put or left the states in the driver's seat.

The framers of the Constitution left out the word "sovereignty" entirely. It does not appear at all, to describe either the nation or the states. Since other words from the Articles were included in the Constitution, the presumption must be that the framers purposely and deliberately omitted the idea that the states were sovereign. In short, sovereignty was assumed by the people of the United States and this means popular supremacy over both the national government and the states.

Supreme Law of the Land

The only words in the Constitution that imply sovereignty or supremacy, outside of the preamble wherein the people take over the reins of authority, are to be found in the second paragraph of Article I, "the supreme law of the land" clause, which reads: "This Constitution, and the laws of the United States which shall be made in pursuance thereof; and all treaties made, or which shall be made, under the authority of the United States, shall be the supreme law of the land; and the judges in every state shall be bound thereby, any thing in the constitution or laws of any state to the contrary notwithstanding."

This clause, taken along with other phrases of the Constitution, has the obvious effect of putting the Constitution, laws, and treaties of the United States above the constitutions and laws of the several states. It is reinforced by the requirement that an official

oath "to support this Constitution," must be taken by all members of Congress, all state legislators, "and all executive and judicial officers, both of the United States and of the several states . . ." (Article VI, paragraph 3).

Together these provisions illustrate the completeness of the overturn in authority that took place when the Constitution replaced the Articles of Confederation. The former residual "sovereignty" of the states was eliminated, and in place of it the people of the United States established the supremacy of the United States Constitution and of the proper laws and treaties of the United States government. . . .

. . . [The framers] planned to and did create a full-fledged national government, to be based on the people and to legislate for and serve the people, without requiring the consent of the state governments and without being dependent upon them in any way when legislating, taxing, making treaties, and enforcing laws for the nation as a whole. This national government was to be officered by men who held no state offices, and who were not to be delegates of the state governments as such, but whose attachments would be to the Union, to the United States as a whole, and to its national government. So organized, the central government would be able to act autonomously, upon its own initiative, in the national interest, without regard to what the state governments might be doing in their respective territories. . . .

Despite the broad range of powers granted to the national government, no one, except for Hamilton in the early days of the Federal Convention, seems to have advocated the abolition of the states. The states were to be left, though in a reduced role, and were actually to have some part in helping to conduct the new national government (the state legislatures were to elect United States senators; to regulate elections for the United States as well as for themselves; to provide for appointing presidential electors; and so on). The primary intention was to create a new, effective, autonomous national government for all the people and for the whole territory of the United States, and to set it down over the states to serve the people directly. In effect a dual system of government came into existence, the national government established for the whole country and the state governments left to carry on their local functions within their respective territories. . . .

Finally, the framers did not desire that the Constitution they proposed should be rigidly binding on all future generations. It has remained for later protagonists of various political and economic causes, when appealing from the present Constitution—which they think they don't like—to the original Constitution—which they think they do like—to urge that the intentions of the original framers must be respected and obeyed no matter what changes in thought or in circumstances have taken place since then.

This attempt to turn back, as it were, the clock of constitutional interpretation and practice in order to be guided by an earlier view finds little support in the writings and reasonings of the original framers. For one thing, the framers inserted in the Constitution an article that provided for future amendments. This certainly showed that they expected the Constitution might require amendments in the future. Indeed, Hamilton, Washington, and other leading supporters among the members expressed disappointment with various provisions of the Constitution as it went before the people. The existence of the amending article was one reason why Washington thought it best to adopt the Constitution as it was and then proceed to get amendments later. . . .

In short, the framers and proponents of the Constitution realized that the Constitution was a manmade and imperfect instrument; that its meaning was not entirely clear but would call for interpretations; that it probably would be found in practice to be deficient in a number of respects, and so would call for formal amendments. They did not claim superhuman wisdom or skill for themselves, or set themselves up as wiser than those who

would come after them. They were content to leave the interpretation and the necessary modification of the Constitution to future congresses, legislatures, and supreme courts, and to the people of the United States. They recognized that constitutions are made "for posterity as well as ourselves," and that they must be adaptable to the "exigencies of ages" yet unknown (*The Federalist*, No. 34). . . .

The changes that have taken place in the Constitution since its adoption have not all been in one direction, nor have all been fully consistent one with another. On every constitutional issue that arises there are likely to be two or more positions that can be taken. Which of these will be approved as the basis for action will depend upon a variety of circumstances, of which the political views of those who must make the decision are highly important. It is largely a matter of chance whether those in office when a particular constitutional decision is to be made hold one set of political views or another.

In point of fact, however, there has been from the beginning one dominant trend, at least in the constitutional relations between the national government and the states—the trend toward spelling out and solidifying the supremacy of the national government.

This does not mean that the states have suffered an exactly corresponding loss in authority, or that they are actually less important, less active, or less serviceable than they used to be . . . the activities of the states after the Revolution were largely limited to legislating. As the functions and services of government have increased all along the line, and at all levels of government, national, state, and local, . . . the states have actually increased in importance. . . .

RESERVED POWERS AND THE TENTH AMENDMENT

To many leaders in state government the Tenth Amendment has appeared to be the most important provision among the first ten amendments. Its words and its consequences deserve much attention. It reads: "The powers not delegated to the United States by the Constitution, nor prohibited by it to the States, are reserved to the States respectively, or to the people." . . .

. . . [S]ome of the proponents of the Constitution thought that an express reservation of powers to the states was unnecessary, since it was patent on the face of the Constitution that the states were to remain in existence and that they would, therefore, continue to exercise powers not delegated by the Constitution to the United States government and not denied by the Constitution to the states.

As I see the situation, if the original states had been content to let well enough alone they might have been able to argue that each original state retained for itself, and by its own authority, the powers not delegated or denied, as seemed to be the situation under the Articles of Confederation. As it was, they desired the greater security that might come from having the reservation made explicit in the United States Constitution by an amendment. But a constitutional amendment like any other provision of the Constitution is ordained by the people of the United States. In seeking a constitutional amendment the states in effect acknowledged the supremacy of the people of the United States and submitted to receiving their powers from the people through the medium of the Constitution. . . .

The amendment, it seems to me, should be read with the enacting clause of the preamble as follows: "We the people of the United States . . . do ordain . . . [that] The powers not delegated to the United States by the Constitution, nor prohibited by it to the States, are reserved to the States respectively, or to the people."

In other words, it is the people of the United States who, in ordaining the Constitution, delegate some powers to the United States government, reserve other powers to the states or to the people, and place restrictions on both the national government and the states in the interests of the people. This carries out logically the idea expressed by Madison in *The Federalist*, No. 46, that "The federal and State governments are in fact but different agents and trustees of the people."

This view, I believe, is consonant also with the fact that nearly three fourths of the states have been subsequently brought into the Union under the Constitution, and they could not have had any prior "inherent" or "sovereign" powers as states which they could have retained for themselves by their own authority upon admission to the Union. The people of the United States surely are the source of the powers of all the states subsequently brought into the Union, which states had to accept the Constitution as a condition of their admission, so that the Constitution is for them both the means of conveying power to them and the measure of the powers conferred on them by the "reservation" in Amendment 10. And since all the states in the Union are constitutionally equal, I hold that all the states receive their powers from the people of the United States speaking through the Constitution. . . .

In short, at present, the reserved powers of the state are not a limit on or a bar to the exercise by Congress of the powers delegated to it. Indeed, the Tenth Amendment itself has been held to state "but a truism that all is retained which has not been surrendered" (Darby case). "From the beginning and for many years the amendment has been construed as not depriving the national government of authority to resort to all means for the exercise of a granted power which are appropriate and plainly adapted to the permitted end."

But Tenth Amendment or no Tenth Amendment, the states exercise under the Constitution a wide range of important powers. If state laws lack supremacy over the acts of Congress, they are nevertheless, from the individual's point of view, enforceable laws and laws that must be obeyed, just as fully as any act of Congress, as long as they do not violate any provisions of the Constitution or any valid act of Congress. . . .

"STATES' RIGHTS"

The struggle for states' rights—as against the supremacy of the national government—has been like a fire that smolders for a time and then flares up anew, in new places and with new combustibles, but which never really dies out. . . .

It is interesting to notice . . . that outside of Virginia and Kentucky the 1798 "resolves" of these two states [nullification] fell on deaf ears in the other southern states, and were vigorously condemned in the states north of the Mason and Dixon line. The Federalists opposed the resolutions strongly, and they actually gained in political strength in 1799 at the expense of the Republicans. Both Madison and Jefferson dropped the idea of state nullification as the means of wiping out the Alien and Sedition Acts, and returned to their more congenial and constitutional political weapons, the attempt to get people to elect Anti-Federalists to Congress.

Although both Jefferson and Madison were successively elected to the presidency (1800 and 1808), this fact cannot be attributed to their utterances in the Virginia and Kentucky Resolutions. And by 1830 Madison was clearly once more in the anti-nullification camp.

Another claim to the right of nullification arose a generation after the Virginia and Kentucky Resolutions, when South Carolina claimed the right to nullify a tariff law passed by Congress. Actual nullification was prevented by President Jackson's stern position against it. Nevertheless the slavery controversy soon thereafter raised a similar issue, and the conflict over federal control of slavery in the territories led on to southern secession and civil war.

Southern historians have discovered in the publications and utterances of some of the secession leaders statements that were almost lyrical in praise of states' rights. John C. Calhoun and other theorists of the South accepted as a historical fact that each of the thirteen original states had at the beginning been completely independent and sovereign in the full international sense of sovereignty. Calhoun further claimed that this sovereignty was by nature inalienable and indivisible, and that the Constitution was therefore only a compact among states, each of which continued to be fully sovereign. . . .

This theory was made explicit in the constitution of the Confederate states. As a practical matter the framers of that document followed rather closely the Constitution of the United States, but they began the preamble differently: "We, the people of the Confederate States, each State acting in its sovereign and independent character, in order to form a permanent federal government. . . ."

Ironically, the recalcitrancy of some of the states, which even in wartime pursued their theories of states' rights, is considered by many historians to be a major cause of the Confederacy's defeat. . . .

Since the Civil War, the states' rights doctrine—based on what Hamilton called "the inordinate pride of state importance"—has not led to bloody violence. As we have seen, however, it has in one form or another remained a factor in the politics of this nation. Although the Union victory in the War of Secession pretty well laid to rest Calhoun's theory of *absolute* sovereignty of each state, the "state-sovereignty theory," as Owsley termed it, which insists on a rigid reservation of powers to the states, is resuscitated regularly by those who oppose some extension or other of national powers.

But I believe and have tried to show that there is no constitutional basis for this theory. The people cannot be assumed to have undone with the left hand what they did with the right, to have reserved to the separate states powers that would defeat the powers conferred on the national government to promote the national security and the national welfare. If in the original Constitution they were not sufficiently clear about national objectives and national supremacy, by their subsequent actions they have done much to remove the uncertainty and doubt. . . .

THE CONSTITUTIONAL ESSENTIALS

"The Constitution, in all its provisions, looks to an indestructible Union, composed of indestructible States."

This statement in a Supreme Court decision of 1869 sets forth succinctly the basic fact about national-state relations under the Constitution of the United States—the importance and permanence of both the national and the state governments.

It is true, of course, as we have seen, that the national government has been established as supreme. No state may constitutionally nullify or obstruct the acts of the national government. Every state stands under the compulsory jurisdiction and process of the nation's Supreme Court to decide on the state's rights and duties under the United States Constitution and laws. The constitutional acts of Congress are also binding on the states. National citizenship is the primary citizenship for all the people in the United States—above state citizenship—and the national government may reach with its laws any and every citizen (as well as all aliens and other persons) in any state. The national Constitution is the highest written law for all the people of the United States, for the nation as a whole and for each of its parts—for the national government and for the state and local governments as well. The Constitution is without qualification the "supreme law of the land." . . .

One aspect of this complex system of government that many foreign observers and perhaps many Americans also do not understand is defined approximately by the terms "autonomy" and "free initiative." Congress and the President, the national policy-making authorities, may go ahead and act for the general welfare upon their own interpretation of the national powers without consulting or getting the consent of either the United States Supreme Court or the state governments. Each state government may do the same in acting for the welfare of its state without consulting the President, Congress, or the Supreme Court. If not sovereign the states are at least autonomous.

This apparent looseness of governmental structure strengthens the importance of each part of the system: each part, though subordinate to the whole, has certain "checks" on the other parts and on the whole. At the same time, paradoxical though this seems, it also ties the nation and its parts permanently together. For the threads between the President and the Congress, Congress and the Supreme Court, the Supreme Court and the state legislatures, the state legislatures and the Congress, Congress and the state governors, state governors and national executive agencies, national executive agencies and state divisions, state executive divisions and state legislatures, and so on, are so intricately interwoven that a break at any point would only temporarily snarl the threads; it cannot unravel the whole.

The relationship between the states and the nation that emerges from the complex governmental structure of the United States is sometimes called a partnership. I have used the term "partners" in the title of this [article], and in a way I believe it is a very apt term. But I want to make perfectly clear the sense in which I am using "partners" and "partnership."

It seems to me that there is between the nation and the states nothing like an ordinary business-partnership arrangement in which the partners have equal status and voting powers. Each state, being but a part of the entire people, is not an equal partner of the nation; at the same time, all the states combined *are* the nation and cannot be called its partners.

On the other hand the national government and the state governments are the agents of the nation and for its several parts, the states. They share the responsibility to promote the general welfare of all the people. In this sense they form a partnership, though not a partnership of equals, and not a partnership in any transient sense.

For what I have in mind it would be hard to find a more eloquent expression than that of Edmund Burke when he was criticizing the contract theory of the state. Said he:

Society is, indeed, a contract. . . . [B]ut the state ought not to be considered as nothing better than a partnership agreement in a trade of pepper and coffee, calico or tobacco . . . to be dissolved by the fancy of the partners. It is to be looked upon with other reverence. . . . It is a partnership in all science, a partnership in all art, a partnership in every virtue and in all perfection. As the ends of such a partnership cannot be obtained in many generations, it becomes a partnership not only between those who are living, but between those who are living, those who are dead, and those who are to be born.

As the distinct and separate agents of the people of the United States, a great nation among nations and one that we hope will endure to promote human welfare through many generations, the national government and the state governments have joint responsibility to respect each other, to consult with each other, and to cooperate with and assist each other to promote the national security and the general welfare. It is in this broad meaning that I speak of a partnership in national-state relations. . . .

6

Uniform State Laws and Interstate Compacts

DAVID L. MARTIN

If you are in business and have a disagreement with a supplier in another state regarding the terms of a commercial transaction, do you have to sue to resolve the problem? Or suppose you want to "give the gift of sight" or to donate other vital organs to another person when you die. What are your legal responsibilities? Perhaps a local college student is arrested for selling a "controlled substance." Which drugs are considered "controlled substances"?

The answers to these three questions, and many others, can be found in uniform state laws. The Uniform Commercial Code defines "the rules of the game" in business law. Since 1968, all fifty states have passed the Anatomical Gift Act governing the organ transplants made possible by advances in

---

This article was written especially for *Capitol, Courthouse, and City Hall,* Sixth Edition.

medical technology. During the 1970s, when the hazards of drug abuse became apparent, more than forty states agreed on which substances should be controlled.

None of these laws, effective across the nation, was adopted by Congress. Instead they were passed, in substantially identical form, by the legislatures of the fifty states, the District of Columbia, Puerto Rico, and the Virgin Islands.

When a problem goes beyond the legal jurisdiction of individual states, it is often studied by the National Conference of Commissioners on Uniform State Laws, which then drafts a model code for consideration and adoption by state legislatures. Commissioners are appointed by the governor of each state and meet annually in conjunction with the American Bar Association. Consisting of some 250 lawyers, judges, and law professors who serve without pay, the Conference's legal research expenses are financed by the states, the federal government, and bar associations. The Conference, functioning since 1892, is currently recommending more than eighty uniform acts, which have been adopted in varying degree by the states. (A tabulation of code adoptions appears every two years in *The Book of the States.*)

Uniform state laws are an important ingredient in American federalism, allowing for nationwide legislative alternatives at the states' initiative or when Congress is inactive. Some uniform acts, such as the one on reciprocal state divorce recognition, were spurred by U.S. Supreme Court decisions. All uniform acts, like other state laws, are subject to judicial review for constitutionality.

Originally limited to commercial matters and cooperative measures—such as the uniform act adopted during the 1930s to secure attendance of out-of-state witnesses at trials—more controversial proposals are now being considered. Current issues are reflected by proposed uniform legislation on residential landlord-tenant relationships (adopted by six-

teen states so far), consumer sales practices (seven states), and a consumer credit code (eleven states). Some proposed uniform acts meet stiff resistance in state legislatures: no-fault automobile insurance was opposed by many attorneys, since accident suits are a lucrative business for trial lawyers.

A uniform law proposed by the Conference may be amended considerably in the legislative process. Although forty-four jurisdictions have agreed on controlled substances in criminal law, of the forty-eight states passing the Gift to Minors Act, most made tax-law amendments. Even when the statutory language is identical, state court interpretations may vary.

Since each state must decide whether to adopt a uniform act as part of its laws, non-ratification can affect citizens in other states across the country. For example, the Uniform Child Custody Jurisdiction Act, passed by thirty-nine states, intends to remove the legal incentive for parents to move children across state lines in attempts to evade child custody decrees. A parent, having lost a custody battle in the original court or having been granted limited visitation rights, may be tempted to take the child to another state, hoping to obtain a more favorable ruling in the other court. An attorney from a state that has not adopted the uniform jurisdiction act commented, "We're an attractive island in the Midwest to take a child to live while seeking a different custody decree." Thus a parent with original custody may be affected by the laws of a state hundreds of miles away. However, even in the eleven states where reciprocal child custody has not been legislated, some judges have followed the policies of the uniform act in their rulings.

Uniform state laws ease the legal complications as citizens move from state to state. Varying state inheritance statutes have been simplified by a number of uniform laws. Such acts ensure that the terms of a will are carried out, prevent survivors from being harassed by outdated state probate laws, and facilitate the collection of estate taxes due on assets located in several states.

Uniform acts help eliminate, in the words of Chief Justice Warren Burger, "the barnacles picked up over the years" in state laws. As American society becomes more complex, state legislatures may find such model codes more attractive.

INTERSTATE COMPACTS: VEHICLES FOR COOPERATION

From American independence, states have entered into agreements with their neighbors. This fact was recognized in the United States Constitution: "No State shall, without the Consent of Congress . . . enter into any Agreement or Compact with another State . . ." (Article I, Section 10).

The original concerns over boundary lines, navigation, and the building of canals, bridges, and tunnels between adjacent states have been expanded and now include multiparty agreements on many subjects. For example, the International Registration Plan, a compact simplifying commercial vehicle fees, is open for approval by American states, Canadian provinces, and Mexican states.

The purposes of compacts can be classified within four primary categories:

1. Compacts are often the legal basis for cooperative metropolitan facilities. The New York–New Jersey Port Authority in 1921 authorized the first interstate financing, construction, and operation of public works. Mass transit, airports, parks and recreation, and regional planning and development are among the metropolitan concerns agreed on by adjacent states.

2. Compacts concerning river basin administration—for water allocation, flood control, waterway development, and pollution abatement—were the first to deal with regional problems on a com-

prehensive basis. Examples of these agreements are the Colorado River Compact (adopted by seven western states) and the Tennessee-Tombigbee Waterway Authority (five southern states). The federal government was authorized by Congress to become a participating member of the 1961 Delaware River Basin Compact, initiating federal-interstate compacts.

3. A number of compacts are regulatory in intent. The Interstate Oil and Gas Compact (passed by thirty states), originally designed to prevent overproduction among the states, has become a mechanism to conserve energy resources. Under the Gulf States Marine Fisheries Compact, an Alabama sportsman might launch his craft from a Florida boat ramp, fish in Louisiana waters, and have his catch box inspected by a Mississippi patrol boat. Mutual enforcement by eight states in the Ohio River Valley Water Sanitation Compact has been copied elsewhere.

4. Compacts may concern joint provision of services and the solving of interstate problems through consistent jurisdiction. If you are seeking a book that cannot be found in your state, your interlibrary loan request is circulated through the forty members of the Interstate Library Compact. Reciprocal recognition of teaching credentials issued by thirty-two states stems from their Agreement on Qualification of Educational Personnel. In the field of criminal justice, the federal government and forty-seven states have a joint Agreement on Detainers. The 1977 Nonresident Violator Compact deals with out-of-state motorists who ignore traffic citations. All fifty states agreed on the Supervision of Parolees and Probationers, and to the Interstate Compact on Juveniles under court supervision. Consistent treatment is the goal of the Compact on Mental

Health (adopted by forty-five states) and the Compact on the Placement of Children (forty-four states).

Whereas the 1930s through the 1960s regularly recorded increases in new agreements between states, the 1970s turned toward creation of compacts open to participants nationwide. Thus, compacts can be bilateral, regional, or nationwide in scope. The usual process is to draft an agreement on a common concern, which becomes operative when a specified number of states and Congress approve it. Congress in recent years, however, has been more reluctant in granting its consent. For example, the Southern Regional Education Compact was created in 1948 to avoid duplication of expensive graduate research facilities. It was also used to send black students out of the then rigidly segregated Deep South to law and other professional schools at state universities that would accept them. Congress never approved it. However, U.S. Supreme Court decisions have held that only

compacts affecting "political balance" in the federal system require congressional consent. (The Council of State Governments' *Interstate Compacts*, revised periodically, gives the compilation of agreements proposed and in force.)

The utility of interstate compacts is shown by the fact that the state that has the fewest—Hawaii, separated from the mainland—has ratified a dozen. New York has entered into more than forty agreements. The recent Minnesota-Wisconsin Port Authority Compact includes the port cities of Duluth and Superior as members. Vermont and New Hampshire have authorized their local governments to jointly build sewage-treatment plants. Thus, interstate compacts have expanded from state cooperation to include participation by the federal and local governments as well.

Interstate compacts and uniform state laws strengthen American federalism by allowing national cooperation without relying solely on the federal government.

7

States and Their Local Governments

ADVISORY COMMISSION ON INTERGOVERNMENTAL RELATIONS

How have all of the state reform activities affected local government, traditionally strongly interdependent with the states? Have improvements at the state level trans-

lated to advances for substate jurisdictions? Do the states treat their local units much as they always did, sometimes placing them in an intergovernmental straitjacket? Or, have

---

Advisory Commission on Intergovernmental Relations. *The Question of State Government Capability*, Report A–98 (Washington, D.C.: 1985), pp. 186–291, 304. Footnotes have been renumbered.

more urban-oriented legislatures loosened a few strings and allowed them more freedom to deal with their problems and aided them in areas where local efforts are insufficient? In short, what effect has state government reform had on state relations with their local governments? In order to deal with these questions, it is necessary, first, to examine what the role of state government is in regard to local units.

STATE RESPONSIBILITIES FOR LOCAL JURISDICTIONS

For almost all local jurisdictions—the notable exceptions being Indian reservations and the District of Columbia—state governments hold the key to many matters determining their well-being and success. The states are, in fact, major decisionmakers in local government affairs. In addition, they coordinate and supervise local administration of state programs; assist substate governments in improving their capability to carry on their own activities as well as those mandated for the administration of state law on the local level; bear a significant portion of the costs of local operations; intervene in local emergencies; and, to some degree, insure "good government" at the local level.

Moreover, in recent years states increasingly have become intergovernmental managers of federal programs administered at the local level. While this role is not new, it has expanded dramatically with the growth of federal assistance programs and the vesting of administrative responsibility for the new block grants in the states. Often the decision as to which local units will receive federal funds is made by the states. In addition, it may be necessary for them to plan, supervise, monitor, provide technical assistance and perform other oversight activities in connection with the federal-aid programs.

STATES AS DECISIONMAKERS FOR LOCAL GOVERNMENTS

As decisionmakers for local governments, states determine, either through the state constitution, or by statute or charter, what local governments there will be; the proper allocation of powers to and among them; their functional assignments; their internal structure, organizations and procedures for local operations; their fiscal options in regard to revenue, expenditures and debt; the extent of the interlocal cooperation; how their boundaries can be expanded or contracted and to some degree their land use patterns. When one government exercises this kind of influence over others, its decisions affect those subordinate governments critically.

Because there is no federal Constitutional provision for local governments, they owe their existence to the states. In the absence of a state constitutional restriction, the state legislature may create or abolish local governments at will. While public opinion and countervailing local political forces may prevent any precipitant moves to disestablish a local unit, the legal authority to do so is there. In the words of Judge John F. Dillon, local governments are "mere tenants at the will of the legislature."[1]

Likewise, the state constitution or, more usually, the legislature determines which units of local government can exercise which powers and functions. Often these allocations are made on the basis of traditions, and, usually, once a unit has authority to perform a function it rarely loses it. Nevertheless, the state decides whether cities, counties, towns, townships, or special districts, or all or none can or must engage in land use planning and zoning, operate the public school system, construct an airport or engage in other functions. In most states, without a specific grant of authority from the state, local units are unable to act. They have only the powers granted to them; and the courts, following Dillon's Rule, are inclined to interpret authorizations strictly. The rule states:

> It is a general and undisputed proposition of a law that a municipal corporation (read: local government) possesses and can exercise the following powers and no others: First, those granted in express words; second, those necessarily or fairly implied in or incident to the powers expressly granted; third, those essential to the declared objects and purposes of the corporation—not simply convenient but indispensable. Any fair reasonable doubt concerning the existence of power is resolved by the courts against the corporation and the power is denied.[2]

Other states are more liberal with the powers of their local units.

While it might seem that the determination of local government structure, organization, and procedures should be the preserve of the citizens of the locality concerned, such is not entirely the case. Both state constitutions and state legislatures prescribe forms of governments, duties of officials, and operating procedures for local jurisdictions. For example, in 1975 New York had 11 statutes running to 19 volumes containing 6,000 pages dealing directly with powers and structures of its local governments.[3]

In another example, a recent amendment to the Tennessee Constitution providing for an elective executive form of government included the following statement concerning the county legislative body:

> The legislative body shall be composed of representatives from districts in the county as drawn by the county legislative body pursuant to statutes enacted by the general assembly. Districts shall be reapportioned at least every ten years based upon the most recent federal census. The legislative body shall not exceed 25 members, and no more than three representatives shall be elected from a district.[4]

The Tennessee legislature then provided in detail for the establishment of the county executive form of government.

States determine the fiscal options of their local governments in a number of ways. In the first place, they decide what revenue sources local governments can use, a decision predicated on protecting the state's own income. Property taxes and license and service fees have been the traditional sources, but in recent years revenues from income or payroll taxes, sales taxes and other sources have been authorized in some states. Limits on the rates of taxes imposed are frequently attached. States also stipulate the purposes for which local funds may be spent, impose spending limits, set salaries and fees, require certain budgetary procedures and sometimes approve local budgets. In addition, their requirements that local governments engage in specific activities often necessitate local outlays for these purposes. Such state mandated activities limit local expenditure options by absorbing local revenues.

Nowhere is local discretion more hindered than in the incurrence of debt. State constitutions and statutes impose limits on the amount of debt, the purposes for which it may be incurred, procedures for repayment and the investment of funds set aside for repayment. Although instituted to preserve the credit of both the state and other local governments by preventing default on debt obligations, such arrangements frequently stimulate local ingenuity in circumventing the state constraints. One example is the issuance of revenue bonds, repaid from the earnings of the enterprise for which money was borrowed, that are not considered "debt" since the general credit of the local government is not pledged to their repayment.

State decisionmaking also extends to determining the extent of and procedures for interlocal cooperation and external structural changes. State law will prescribe what agreements are allowable and sometimes the procedures for entering into them. Frequently, the creation of substate districts for handling local matters is specified by state statute. State legislatures also set out the terms of, and procedures for annexation, extraterritorial jurisdiction and consolidation. In one instance, Indianapolis and Marion County, Indiana, the state legislature merged the two governments without a referendum.[5] In another, the Kentucky State Board of Education consolidated the Louisville and Jefferson County school districts.

Land use control is an area in which state involvement has grown in recent years. From 1922 until recently, local governments largely exercised authority over the use of land except where states determined the location of state facilities and took land by eminent domain for such purposes as highways, parks, prisons, educational institutions, hospitals and other public uses. Following the publication of a model zoning enabling act by the Department of Commerce in 1922, most states adopted legislation authorizing municipal governments to classify land within their boundaries and to regulate its uses. When the department published model legislation for local planning control in 1928, the states adopted this code as well.[6]

Because local control of land use did not work well in many instances, frequently permitting urban sprawl, traffic congestion, air and water pollution, and loss of prime agricultural land, states undertook to regulate land use at the state level, revoking powers previously allowed local governments. A variety of techniques were used. States resorted to the requirement of permits for certain types of development, established mechanisms to coordinate state land use-related problems, and required local governments to establish mechanisms for land use planning and zoning. More recently, they moved to participate in the coastal zone management program of the federal government, took on the management of wetlands, determined the siting of power plants and related facilities, acted to regulate surface mining and established rules for identifying and designating areas of critical state concern (e.g., environmentally fragile or historic areas).[7] Moreover, they began to

settle land-use disputes among local jurisdictions, to forbid exclusionary zoning and to handle large developments. All of these activities enabled states to engage in decisionmaking concerning land use to a greater degree than once was the case. As a consequence, local governments find that although state decisions often relieve them of some of the pressures relating to development, they also limit their options in this as well as in other areas.

STATES AS ADMINISTRATIVE SUPERVISORS OF LOCAL IMPLEMENTATION

All states coordinate and supervise to some degree local administration of state functions. These activities encompass a wide range of state actions extending from informal conferences through advice and technical assistance, requirement of reports, inspection, imposition of grant-in-aid requirements, review of local actions, prior approval of local action, orders, rulemaking, investigations, removal of local officials, and appointment of local officials, to state takeover of local administration. The employment of these devices to influence local administration varies widely, not only from state to state but from function to function within a state. In general, the less coercive appear to be the most effective and most frequently employed. The most stringent— substitute administration—rarely occurs and, when it does, it is in crisis situations such as financial, health or disaster emergencies. . . .

STATES AS ENHANCERS OF LOCAL CAPABILITY

States frequently engage in efforts to improve the capability of local governments to carry on their own activities. They also try to upgrade local abilities to administer state law on the local level. Toward this end, they offer a wide range of technical assistance in such matters as purchasing, accounting procedures, drafting of charters, and design of personnel systems, not to mention a host of other subjects.

Local governments do not rely on such technical assistance extensively. A General Accounting Office survey, reported in 1978, indicates that approximately 50% of local officials responding never asked the state for technical assistance. Nonetheless, state officials are contacted more often than any other type of outside organization—including the federal government—to meet local technical assistance needs. Apparently local officials perceived fewer programs and less paperwork in dealing with state officials than with federal agencies.[8]

All states now have state agencies specifically designated to assist local governments.[9] Although Pennsylvania set up the Bureau of Municipal Affairs in 1919,[10] widespread adoption of special agencies for local affairs did not occur until the 1960s. Following a recommendation of the Council of State Governments, endorsed by public interest groups representing local governments, and a 1964 recommendation from ACIR, states began to create or designate such agencies. Currently, 35 of the agencies are separate cabinet departments, nine are within other departments, and six are located in the governor's offices.[11]

The agencies offer a wide range of programs and services to local governments and try to promote intergovernmental cooperation, upgrade local management and planning capabilities, and facilitate the administration of programs in such areas as economic development and housing.[12] Some provide assistance for small jurisdictions in such matters as applications for federal grants. Few exercise control functions, emphasizing their assistance capabilities.

Other state aid may take the form of efforts to improve local government structure in order to enhance decisionmaking capacity and administration. This could involve the requirement for county executive (or manager)

government as occurred recently in Arkansas, Kentucky and Tennessee. It could include the extension of home rule or discretionary powers to local units broadening their authority to cope with local problems. Local boundaries might be altered by the state, as in Indianapolis, to make political jurisdiction correspond more closely to the geographic area of the problems. State statutes might impose merit systems, stipulate auditing practices, or require training for local officials. All of these are done by one or more states, although they are only examples of the many types of state assistance.

STATES AS BANKERS OF LOCAL GOVERNMENTS

A major facet of state involvement in local affairs is the part they play in financing local government. They are the principal external providers of funds to local governments. They transfer large sums of state money to the local units and, in addition, they serve as conduits of much of the federal money that local governments spend. Most of this is in the form of grants-in-aid, although states also share taxes as well as receipts from state businesses, such as liquor stores, and some other funds. They also provide payments to local governments in lieu of taxes on state property, share facilities, and sometimes give state real or personal property to local jurisdictions. State aid currently comprises approximately one-third of the funds local governments spend.[13] In addition, states pass through to local units about 27% of the federal funds they receive.[14]

STATES AS ENSURERS OF EQUITY, EFFECTIVENESS, EFFICIENCY, AND ACCOUNTABILITY

To a substantial degree, states are the ensurers of "good" government at both the state and local levels. Through their constitutions, statutes, and court decisions, they can mandate equity in representation, distribution of resources, and governmental operations. While they operate within the limits of human constraints, their legal controls over local units allow them to improve responsiveness of local institutions and to ensure accountability and openness of and access to governmental processes. They exercise significant control over such matters as apportionment for representation. They can establish formulas for the distribution of resources and require fair governmental practices. State "sunshine" statutes, aimed at ensuring open decisionmaking in public matters, can apply to state and local levels alike.

The steps states can take to ensure effective government cover a wide range of possibilities. On one hand, they can grant charters that allow local officials the leeway to deal with their problems. On the other end of the scale, they can oversee locally administered state programs to ensure that they accomplish the intended results, authorize sufficient revenues to carry out government programs and remove barriers to effective management. Often they can play a positive role through standard setting, technical assistance and advice. The same thing applies to encouraging efficiency. Although those who actually deliver government service are the largest factor in the efficiency of the operations, states can exert influence by promoting cooperation among localities, sharing expertise and promoting local competency. They can refrain from imposing procedures and requirements that impair economical government operations. State restrictions on local debt, accounting, purchasing and auditing requirements, while often necessary to prevent financial crises, must be imposed with care. Otherwise, requirements intended to encourage efficiency in some instances may produce the opposite effect.

Each state performs differently in these matters, a fact that makes nationwide assessment of their actions difficult. They have, as well, unique political cultures, economic and social systems, and other characteristics that make for different patterns of response to problems.

CRITICISMS OF STATE ACTIONS AFFECTING LOCAL GOVERNMENTS

The heavy reliance of local governments on the state affords the latter substantial options in regard to improvement of local governmental operations. The choices made, nonetheless, have not always provided the maximum opportunity for local excellence. They have, in the past, often retarded local efforts at effective and efficient decisionmaking and administration. In the words of a 1969 ACIR report:

> The deadly combination of restricted annexation and unrestricted incorporation; the chaotic and uncontrolled mushrooming of special districts; and limitations upon municipal taxing and borrowing powers; the deliverance of all important police powers of zoning, land use and building regulations into the hands of thousands of separate and competing local governments—these are but a few of the byproducts of decades of state governments; nonfeasance and malfeasance concerning urban affairs.[15]

Many critics would agree that states often have been unmindful of local problems, particularly those of big cities. In discussing the "reluctant states" in this connection, Roscoe C. Martin blamed part of the problem on the "state mind." He wrote, in 1965:

> Rural orientation, provincial outlook, commitment to a strict moral code, a philosophy of individualism—these are the components of the state mind. If they evoke memories of the oil lamp and the covered bridge, why this very spirit of nostalgia is also characteristic of the state mind. One of the most unhappy features of the state (and its leaders and institutions) is its intermittent and imperfect contact with the realities of the modern world.[16]

In Martin's view, this state of mind gave birth to certain myths that have had important influences on state policies toward local problems. Chief among the myths is the conviction that little government, both in the sense of local governments and a minimum of state government, is "both virtuous and democratic." Conversely, big government, be it state or federal, tends to be corrupt and undemocratic. Moreover, urban problems "spring from unhealthy soil" and lack the legitimacy of established claimants to state attention. States claim a lack of resources to deal with all these matters. Finally, the federal government, large and distant, is an object of distrust.

The "state mind" has had the consequence of engendering a dedicated intransigence and "negativism" on the part of the states, according to Martin. Their addiction to the status quo produces an unfavorable reaction to almost anything new. In summing up the effects of the state of mind and mythologies that he attributes to the states, Martin wrote:

> In summary, three overriding deficiencies flow from the state of mind and the mythology which grip the states. The first is in orientation—most states are governed in accordance with the rural traditions of an earlier day. The second is timeliness—the governments of most states are anachronistic; they lack relevance to the urgencies of the modern world. The third is in leadership—state leaders are by confession cautious and tradition-bound, which ill-equips them for the tasks of modern government.[17]

If Martin's analysis is correct, such a negative outlook on the part of the state does not augur well for local governments. Are the criticisms set out above valid at the present time? Have the states been willing to change in this important aspect of their responsibilities? What recent actions have they taken to improve their relations with their local governments? How do these balance others that increasingly circumscribe local options and initiatives?

CHANGING STATE STRATEGIES TOWARD LOCAL GOVERNMENTS

If, as the Walkers pointed out, "the acid test of the States' real strength lies in their relationship with their own localities,"[18] that relationship needs to be examined to determine if it permits localities enough freedom to manage their own affairs effectively and efficiently at the same time that it preserves state authority to deal with statewide problems. The dichotomy presented by building both strong state and strong local governments need not force a choice between the two. Strong, viable governments at both levels do not preclude effective sharing of responsibility and, in fact, may enhance it. The growing interdependence of states and their local governments, as reflected in the growth of shared functions and fiscal aids, underscores the necessity of increased cooperation and coordination between them. . . .

In the past quarter century, states have broadened local powers through increased grants of home rule and optional charters, through devolution of powers, and through permission to make interlocal agreements. Counties have been the principal beneficiaries of the greater autonomy, although other types of local jurisdictions also have profited. States have coupled this strengthening of local legal authority, however, with a dramatic increase in mandates on local governments to undertake new functions and activities. These requirements have proved costly to the localities. Despite the attachment of cost estimates in the form of fiscal notes to state legislation mandating local action, the expense has fallen largely on the smaller jurisdictions, thus limiting their options because of fiscal constraints. The trade-offs between more discretionary authority on the one hand and increased state mandating on the other have varied from state to state. Consequently, it is difficult to assess the overall impact of these two opposite developments.

NOTES

1. *City of Clinton* v. *Cedar Rapids and Missouri Railroad Company*, 24 Iowa 455, 462, 463 (1868).
2. John F. Dillon, *Commentaries on the Law of Municipal Corporations*, 5th ed., Boston, MA, Little, Brown and Co., 1911, Vol. 1, Sec. 237. Emphases in the original except "read: local government."
3. Joan Aron and Charles Brecher, "Recent Developments in State-Local Relations: A Case Study of New York," a paper prepared for the Conference on the Partnership Within the States: Local Self Government in the Federal System, November 18–20, 1975, pp. 1–2.
4. Article VII, Sections 1 and 2, adopted March 7, 1978.
5. Daniel R. Grant, "Urban Needs and State Response: Local Government Reorganization," in The American Assembly, *The States and the Urban Crisis*, edited by Alan K. Campbell, Englewood Cliffs, NJ, Prentice-Hall, Inc., 1970. For recent activity on city-county consolidation, see: Parris N. Glendening and Patricia S. Atkins, "City-County Consolidation: New Views for the Eighties," *1980 Municipal Year Book*, Washington, DC, International City Management Association, 1980, pp. 68–72.
6. Land Use Planning Reports, *A Summary of State Land Use Controls*, Report 2, Washington, DC, Plus Publications, Inc., January 1975, p. 1. For a discussion of the spread of innovations in land use legislation among the states, see Nelson Rosenbaum, *Land use and the Legislatures*, Washington, DC, The Urban Institute, 1976.
7. Council of State Governments, *State Growth Management*, Lexington, KY, May 1976, pp. 24–25. The Council has published a series of studies on state land use programs and policies developed by the Task Force on Natural Resource and Land Use Information and Technology. The Council sponsored the Task Force in cooperation with the U.S. Department of the Interior. The studies are: *State Alternatives for Planning and Management* (Final Report of the Task Force); *Land Use Management: Proceedings of The National Symposium on Resource and Land Information; A Legislator's Guide to Land Management; Land Use Policy and Program Analysis Number 1: Intergovernmental Relations in State Land Use Planning; Land Use Policy and Program Analysis Number 2: Data Needs and Resources for State Land Use Planning; Land Use Policy and Program Analysis Number 3: Organization, Management and Financing of State Land Use Programs; Land Use Policy and Program Analysis Number 4: State of the Art for Designation of Areas of Critical Environmental Concern; Land Use Policy and Program Analysis Number 5: Issues and Recommendation—State Critical Areas Programs;* and *Land Use Policy and Program Analysis Number 6: Manpower Needs for State Land Use Planning and Public Involvement in State Land Use Planning.*
8. U.S. General Accounting Office, *State and Local Government's Views on Technical Assistance* (GGK–78–58). Washington, DC, July 12, 1978, pp. ii, 38, 45.
9. ACIR, *State-Local Relations Bodies: State ACIRs and Other Approaches*, M–124, Washington, DC, U.S. Government Printing Office, March 1981, p. 37.
10. Joseph F. Zimmerman, "State Agencies for Local Affairs: The Institutionalization of State Assistance to Local Governments," mimeographed, Albany, NY, State University of New York at Albany, Graduate School of Public Affairs, Local Government Center, 1968.
11. ACIR, M–124, *op. cit.*, pp. 38–39.
12. *Ibid.*
13. ACIR, *The States and Intergovernmental Aids* (A–59), Washington, DC, U.S. Government Printing Office, February 1977, p. 9.
14. See Table 5, ACIR, *Recent Trends in Federal and State Aid to Local Governments*, M–118, Washington, DC, U.S. Government Printing Office, 1980, p. 8.
15. Advisory Commission on Intergovernmental Relations, *Urban America and the Federal System*, M–47, Washington, DC, U.S. Government Printing Office, 1969, p. 2.
16. Roscoe C. Martin, *The Cities and the Federal System*, New York, Atherton Press, 1965, p. 77. See, also: The American Assembly, *The States and the Urban Crisis*, edited by Alan K. Campbell, Englewood Cliffs, NJ, Prentice-Hall, Inc., 1970; Lee S. Green, Malcolm E. Jewell, and Daniel R. Grant, *The States and the Metropolis*, University, AL, University of Alabama Press, 1968; A. James Reichley, "The States Hold the Keys to the Cities," *Fortune Magazine*, June 1969; and Paul N. Ylvisaker, "The Growing Role of State Government in Local Affairs," *State Government*, Summer 1968.
17. *Ibid.*, p. 79.

18. Jeanne and David Walker, "Rationalizing Local Governments' Powers, Functions and Structure," in *States' Responsibilities to Local Governments: An Action Agenda,* prepared by the Center for Policy Research of the National Governors' Association, Washington, DC, 1975, p. 39.

The judiciary is often called upon to resolve cases involving intergovernmental relations, or the relative powers of state and local governments involving citizens. Judges are expected to remain aloof from politics, yet their daily decisions affect the governmental process. What happens when a majority of judges decide that prior law has become unrealistic policy and previous precedents (*stare decisis*) should be reversed? Should "government of the people, by the people, and for the people" be sued without its consent by its citizens? Since a plaintiff would in effect be suing himself, common law has traditionally held that governments enjoyed "sovereign immunity," although they might be sued for damages (torts) in their proprietary capacity in providing services as a corporation. In recent years, a large number of American legislatures have by statute made state and/or local governments liable for all their actions, at the cost of rising insurance premiums and nuisance suits from the greedy. If the legislature refuses to act, what should the courts do, as in the following "police brutality" case?

8

When Should Governments Be Liable?
Jackson v. *City of Florence*

SUPREME COURT OF ALABAMA

Action was brought to recover from city and several of its police officers for injuries which the officers allegedly, negligently or willfully inflicted on plaintiff during and following arrest.

SHORES, Justice. [For the majority]

This is an appeal from . . . the trial court's sustaining the defendant city's demurrer and motion to dismiss the plaintiff's complaint. . . . :

. . . The court is of the opinion that the demurrer is due to be sustained under the doctrine of

294 Ala. Reports 592; 320 So.2d 68 (1975).

municipal immunity from liability for injuries inflicted by an agent of the municipality acting in a governmental capacity which is well established by the opinions of the Supreme Court of Alabama . . .

The complaint claimed damages against the City of Florence and a police officer for personal injuries sustained by the plaintiff as a proximate result of the negligence and wantonness of the police officer acting in the line of duty. It was alleged that the police officer . . . negligently assaulted (Count I) and willfully or wantonly assaulted (Count II) the plaintiff, an unarmed, seventy-five-year-old, 130-pound man by the use of excessive force, resulting in the plaintiff's loss of his right eye. In his claim, the plaintiff asserted:

On August 1, 1972, I was arrested at The Shanty Restaurant . . . by Florence City Police Officers, Grady Smith and Lee Short, at approximately 6:55, p.m. The . . . officers took me to the police station at the City Hall in Florence, Alabama, where I was escorted into a small room by the two . . . officers. Then and there City police officer, Grady Smith, struck me in the face on or near my right eye, rendering me momentarily unconscious, and inflicting serious injuries to my right eye and face. I was neither permitted to seek medical attention by said officers for . . . injuries nor was any attempt made by . . . officers to get medical attention for me. Immediately following the . . . assault on me, I was taken by these officers upstairs in the . . . City Hall and put in a jail cell and kept there until the following morning. . . .

While in the jail cell and during the night of August 1, 1972, and the morning of August 2, 1972, I repeatedly requested to be taken to a doctor to get medical attention for my eye. Notwithstanding my repeated requests, I was not taken to a doctor until around 7:30 on the morning of August 2, 1972, at which time I was driven by City police officers to the Eliza Coffee Memorial Hospital in Florence, Alabama, and carried to the emergency room. Dr. Shaler Roberts of the Florence Clinic was called in to examine my

eye and found that it was damaged to such an extent that the eye had to be immediately removed.

Appellant acknowledges . . . that this is a "head-on" request for a re-examination and reconsideration of the broad question of whether Alabama municipal corporations should continue to enjoy immunity from liability for the wrongful acts of their agents acting within the line and scope of their employment. . . .

It is generally agreed that the doctrine of sovereign immunity developed in this country from the English doctrine, which grew out of the concept that the "King can do no wrong." That this occurred in America, given the historical background which led to the Revolutionary War, is "one of the mysteries of legal evolution."

Alabama first considered the question of tort liability of municipalities in 1854. . . . There followed a long line of cases holding that municipalities were liable for torts committed in the exercise of their corporate or proprietary capacity, but were immune from suit for the commission of torts in their governmental capacity.

The doctrine of governmental immunity in this country has been universally condemned in an unending number of published statements by legal scholars and jurists. It is frequently stated that the doctrine cannot be defended on any logical basis. By the turn of the century, it was being criticized as unjust and irrational from many sources; but, there is no doubt that the doctrine was, by that time, firmly established in Alabama law by decisions of this court, as it was in a majority, if not all, of the other states of the Union . . .

From that point forward, this court has accepted the interpretation placed on the statute, and has continued to distinguish between governmental functions and corporate or proprietary functions, which has had the effect of making the legislative enactment ineffective in so far as changing the law as it had been judicially declared in this state since 1854. The only change effected by the statute was to eliminate the reference to municipal charters as the source of a city's duty to maintain the streets in safe repair. It is an anomaly that, since the act itself made no distinction between governmental and corporate functions but imposed liability in "street" cases, this court was put in the awkward position, after the enactment of the statute, of having to declare, to remain consistent with its prior holdings, that the duty to repair streets was "intrinsically ministerial," since they have peculiar and local uses. . . .

Since that time, the litigant suing a municipality in tort must attempt to show that the function being performed which resulted in his injury was a corporate or ministerial one. Needless to say, this has resulted in some curious categories. Garbage collecting has been held governmental . . . but sewer disposal is corporate. . . . Repair and maintenance of streets is proprietary or corporate. . . . but operating a street sweeper to keep the streets clean is governmental. . . .

In its present state, the only clue to whether a particular function is governmental or corporate must be found in cases expressly declaring that particular function to fall within one or the other category. The incongruities which have resulted from this effort has itself been the subject of frequent comment, both in Alabama and elsewhere. . . .

The defendant city, in the instant case, argues just that again, i.e., that relief, if any, must come from the legislature, and we do not blame it. There is abundant authority to support the argument. . . . Yet, as case after case has come to this court urging it to correct this judicially created barrier to the courthouses of this state, the answer always given in denying that relief is that the relief sought, if to be obtained, must come from the legislature.

No one believes in the validity of the rule of stare decisis and the necessity for stability in the law more than we do. We are equally, if not more so, adamant in our belief in the profound wisdom in the doctrine of separation of powers. Such is critical, in our opinion, to the survival of our system of government. Under that doctrine, no branch of the government may substitute its judgment for any other. Each branch has inherent powers denied the others. . . .

The rule of governmental immunity for cities, bottomed, as it is, on the English concept that the "King can do no wrong," is the antithesis of the very concepts upon which our government was founded. In fact, recent events have demonstrated dramatically that the "king can do wrong" in America; and when he does, he must pay the penalty for such wrongdoing.

As alluded to earlier, by the turn of the century this judicially created rule of immunity was under severe attack. In fact, England had, by that time, overruled the decision on which the American cases are founded, and municipal immunity for tort is not recognized by the law of England at this time. . . .

As strongly as we believe in the stability of the law, we also recognize that there is merit, if not honor, in admitting prior mistakes and correcting them. . . .

We earnestly believe that the responsibility for correcting what is universally condemned as a bad rule of law rests with this court. The rule of municipal immunity cannot be rationally defended. . . .

In abolishing the doctrine of municipal immunity, Alabama joins a growing number of states in abolishing governmental immunity as to various governmental units: *Stone* v. *Arizona Highway Com.*, 93 Ariz. 384, (1963); *Muskopf* v. *Corning Hospital Dist.*, 55 Cal.2d 211, Cal.Rptr. 89 (1961); *Hargrove* v. *Cocoa Beach*, Fla. (1957); *Molitor* v. *Kaneland Community Unit Dist.*, 18 Ill.2d 11, 163 (1959); *Carroll* v. *Kittle*, 203 Kan. 841 (1969); *Myers* v. *Genesee County Auditor*, 375 Mich. 1 (1965); *Williams* v. *Detroit*, 364 Mich. 231 (1961); *Brown* v. *Omaha*, 183 Neb. 430 (1968); *Rice* v. *Clark County*, 79 Nev. 253 (1963); *B. W. King, Inc.* v. *West New*

York, 49 N.J. 318 (1967); *Becker* v. *Beaudoin,* 106 R.I. 562 (1970) . . .

In departing from our earlier holdings in this area, a departure which we believe is required to let the legislative will operate, and also by justice, we recognize that the decision would work hardship on municipalities in this state which have relied on the earlier cases.

Many states have considered this problem and have applied the new rule in various ways. When Kentucky abolished the rule of governmental immunity, it dealt with the problem of the new rule's applicability and said:

> *Three courses are open to us under such a situation as is presented here: (1) We can merely announce the new rule without applying it and suggest that it should be applied to cases brought to us in the future. (2) We can give relief to the appellant in the instant case but deny it to any others whose injuries occurred before the date of the opinion; or (3) We can apply the rule in the instant case and permit all others who have been injured, not barred by the statute of limitations, to take advantage of the new rule. . . .*

However, it is noted in that opinion, *Hancy* v. *City of Lexington* . . . in a prior opinion ". . . this Court gave warning that it was dissatisfied with the rule of municipal immunity." No opinion by this court has issued such a warning. For that reason . . . we believe that the second alternative constitutes a reasonable compromise. Therefore, this holding is applicable to the appellant in the instant case, and to all others suffering injury after the date hereof. There is ample authority for this treatment. . . .

In deciding, as we do, that municipal immunity for tort is abolished in this state after the date of this opinion, we recognize the authority of the legislature to enter the entire field, and further recognize its superior position to provide with proper legislation any limitations or protections it deems necessary in addition to those already provided. . . .

The judgment appealed from is reversed.

Reversed and remanded.

FAULKNER, JONES, ALMON and EMBRY, JJ., concur.

BLOODWORTH, J., concurs in the result.

HEFLIN, C. J., and MERRILL and MADDOX, JJ., dissent.

MERRILL, Justice (dissenting).

I would affirm the judgment of the circuit court and, therefore, I dissent.

The statement the "King can do no wrong" appears three times in the majority opinion, and a casual reader of that opinion might get the idea that that concept is the basis of American and Alabama decisions upholding the doctrine of governmental immunity. That obviously is not the case.

Most of the words in our revered Declaration of Independence, 200 years old in 1976, catalogue *wrongs* of the King, and those wrongs were the reasons for the support of our long war for independence from England and the rule and wrongs of the King. Then our own government, first under the Articles of Confederation and later the Constitution of the United States made certain that this new country would have no king.

Our doctrine of governmental immunity, both state and national, grew out of the common sense approach that the people had created a democracy under a republican form of government; that the government was the people, and the people's government should not be weakened by allowing the people to sue themselves when the government committed a tortious act while engaged in a governmental function. . . .

In Alabama, the people have tried the doctrine both ways insofar as the State government is concerned. The Constitution of

1819, our first, provided: "The general assembly, shall direct, by law, in what manner, and in what courts, suits may be brought against the State." Statutes were passed in accordance with this provision. . . . In the Constitutions of 1865 and 1868, the people said, "That suits may be brought . . ." But in the Constitution of 1875 and our present Constitution of 1901 . . . the people had changed their minds and said, "That the State of Alabama shall never be made a defendant in any court of law or equity." No king or kingly concept had anything to do with those provisions of our Constitution. . . .

It is my opinion that the holding in this case will be a heavy blow to law enforcement in Alabama. In practically every arrest or even detention for investigation, there is a physical touching of the suspect by the officer, either in frisking the person or handcuffing him, or both. An allegation and evidence that the officer used more force than was reasonably necessary would make a jury question in every suit against the officer and the municipality that employed him. Not only would the courts soon become clogged with such cases, but many of them would be filed merely as a permissible form of blackmail to force the city to settle for a dismissal or a lighter sentence or to force the officer to change his testimony in many such cases. Many arrests are made in unfriendly surroundings and the officer could easily be outsworn as to what happened. It is not to be expected that too many deputy sheriffs or policemen would physically block entrance to private or public buildings when faced with a large group of demonstrators, rioters or hoodlums when he knew that any act on his part, other than talking, would result in a suit against him and his employer.

Then, there is a tremendous economic impact on the municipalities. This policy decision changes the rule drastically and it will come upon municipalities in Alabama without warning because for over 100 years the appellate courts of this state have applied the doctrine of governmental immunity

when the agent or employee was engaged in a governmental function. . . . There will be consideration of . . . reducing other public services and hunting funds to pay additional and higher insurance premiums. It seems to me that some warning could have been given by this court that such a drastic change in the law was imminent. . . .

This dissent is already too long. I close with some words of Justice Thomas E. Brennan of the Supreme Court of Michigan. These words express my sentiments. . . . :

. . . When judges get into the area of deciding policy they get into trouble. Those who sought unsuccessfully and later successfully to abolish governmental immunity have thought it the wiser policy. The legislature has since vindicated the minority who felt otherwise. If the common-law rule holding the various levels of government immune from civil liability by reason of the tortious acts of their agents when engaged in governmental functions was indeed an ancient wrong crying out for redress, we must marvel that it has been re-perpetrated by a modern legislature. The truth is that the rule is not a wrong, ancient or recent. It is simply a rule of reason ordained for the common good. In the last analysis, the preservation of civil government is thought to be a greater good, even for the unfortunate plaintiff than compensation of his injuries from the public coffers. In a government whose power to borrow money is constitutionally circumscribed, it is thought to be a prudent policy to deny to civil juries the unfettered power to increase the public indebtedness.

This is no outmoded theory that 'the King can do no wrong.' It is merely a recognition that in a government of the people, by the people, and for the people, the wrongs inflicted by government upon the people are wrongs they inflict upon themselves. . . .

When fire rages, when the dam breaks, when the enemy attacks, the people, through their government must act.

They must act vigorously and boldly or they perish. It is not for judges, serene in their robes and far removed by time and space from the common peril, to brand them negligent in their travail and suffer their fortunes and their labors to be further taxed to pay compensatory damages to those who chanced to be injured in the community's efforts to overcome the disaster rather than in the disaster itself.

I would affirm the judgment of the trial court because this being a matter of important state policy, I remain of the opinion that it is a legislative rather than a judicial matter.

MADDOX, J., concurs.

CHAPTER 3

Legal Status and Powers
of State and Local Governments

The United States Constitution and the international treaties made under it are the supreme law of the land. Providing they do not conflict with it, state constitutions and interstate compacts may be adopted. The powers of local governments are set by state constitutions and state legislatures, either by general statute or by allowing cities and counties "home rule" to draft their own charters. Thus a local ordinance is subordinate to state law if the state has decided to legislate on the subject (called *preemption*), and both are subject to the provisions of the state constitution. Most state constitutions are lengthy documents containing the details of past political compromises, tending to make them quite inflexible. Completely rewriting a state constitution by holding a constitutional convention (with elected delegates), or piecemeal, through a revision commission (with appointed members), has usually been politically difficult to accomplish. The adoption of individual amendments by the legislature and ratification by the people is far more common.

In the first article in this chapter, Maxine Kurtz analyzes the elements generally found in state constitutions, and considers the problems of writing to cover all contingencies. Some states give their counties or cities home rule powers to do anything within the state's constitution; the pros and cons relating to this are debated in the second selection. A most important authority of local governments is the "general police power" to regulate for the health, safety, and common welfare of their inhabitants. When a group of college students wanted to live together (the *Belle Terre* v. *Boraas* zoning case), opinion of the U.S. Supreme Court was divided. Does this local regulation for community well-being infringe on individual students' constitutional freedoms of association? Finally, to secure life, liberty, and the pursuit of happiness, a city manager reflects on what might happen in his town if a citizen wanted to build a boat in his own yard.

9

What Should a Written Constitution Do?

MAXINE KURTZ

What are written constitutions of governments in this country? Fortunately, most definitions are in substantial agreement on four characteristics. First, they are grants of power. Second, they set limits on how that power should be exercised. Third, they establish an organization for the exercise of power. Finally, rights are reserved that make the constitution what lawyers, judges and others call a fundamental law. Let's look at these four characteristics in some detail.

One of the unique American contributions to concepts of government is that ultimate power is vested in the people. The federal and state constitutions agree on that source of power. This principle commonly is recited in the introductory phrases of such documents.

The grants of power to government by the people differ considerably between the national and state constitutions. The federal constitution has a nice, orderly list of powers delegated to the national government; the same characteristic is not true of state constitutions. Alexis de Tocqueville, in *Democracy in America*, explained the difference this way: "The obligations and the claims of the Federal government were simple and easily definable, because the Union had been formed with the express purpose of meeting certain great general wants; but the claims and obligations of the individual States on the other hand, were complicated and various, because their gov-

ernment had penetrated into all the details of social life. The attributes of the Federal government were therefore carefully defined, and all that was not included among them was declared to remain to the governments of the several states." This passage was written in 1832; it is equally true today.

State constitutions include: (1) the power to regulate, commonly called the police power; (2) the power to take private property for public use, commonly called eminent domain; and (3) the power to tax. Under the United States constitution, states may not exercise certain other sovereign powers, such as declaring war, making treaties with foreign nations without the consent of Congress, printing money and so on. Other powers commonly granted to states are not uniquely governmental, such as the authority to issue bonds, to contract, to hire and fire employees, and to own property.

Now, let's turn to the issue of limitations on power. There is little argument about the concept of a Bill of Rights. Eight of the original 13 states had such declarations in their constitutions, and the first 10 amendments to the federal constitution protect certain fundamental rights.

As new states were created, Congress required that their constitutions also protect certain rights. There are variations among the states as to which rights are protected and to what degree. This is a matter of local prefer-

Maxine Kurtz, "What Should a Written Constitution Do?" *National Civic Review*, November 1978, pp. 457–460. Reprinted by permission of the publisher. Footnotes in original omitted.

ence, except that provisions may not be inconsistent with the United States constitution. Currently, new rights are being discussed, such as a healthy environment. In essence, these are value questions rather than legal issues.

Constitutions include other limits on the use of power. These reflect public mistrust of the democratic system; an unwillingness to delegate to our elected representatives the responsibility for decision making on specific issues. Nobel prize nominee Kenneth Boulding was discussing this issue when he said: "A constitution is a sign of mistrust, in [a] sense. There is an optimum amount of mistrust. It's probably less than a lot of people think. The cost of trust is that you have occasional betrayals of trust. But this may be a low price to pay for the good things that happen by trust. And the cost of mistrust may be very high in terms of rigidity, bureaucracy, and stagnation. It's hard to reach the right balance. My own inclination is that the simpler a constitution, the better."

Early constitution writers concurred with Dr. Boulding, but political machines and domination of legislatures by private interests led states to rewrite their constitutions—and to make them much longer.

Those who write long, detailed constitutions are trying to foresee every contingency, but foreseeing the future is a difficult if not impossible task. A decade ago, most people thought that riots in urban ghettos were the most important problem on our nation's agenda. Today, in the face of energy problems, general unemployment, inflation, pollution and troubled international affairs, how many would agree? That's only a 10-year period—what if you try to see ahead a century? Or, consider how this country has changed since the end of the Civil War, which is only a little more than a century ago. There is a degree of arrogance in the assumption that we can be perceptive enough to write all of the details of government into our state constitutions.

What has been the effect of trying to write in such detail? Our constitutions are amended again and again and again (by comparison, the United States constitution has been amended only 26 times in 200 years). There is no alternative to frequent amendments to detailed constitutions if our state governments are to be able to cope with the challenges of our rapidly changing society. If we can't amend, the states wither away into empty shells, unable to perform their vital role in our federal system.

If this sounds like constitution writers are caught between a rock and a hard place, between possibly corrupt or non-responsive public officials on the one hand and powerless government on the other, they are. As Dr. Boulding suggested, each constitution is a compromise between trust and mistrust; each participant in revising that document must determine personally where that line is to be drawn.

Probably the most political part of any constitution is the organization of the government which is to exercise the powers. This deals with who is going to have what powers, and vested interests having a stake in maintaining the status quo will fight to the bitter end to avoid losing authority and independence.

The United States constitution requires that the states have a republican form of government. The legal definition of that term is simple: a government conducted by representatives chosen by the people. It is thoroughly imbedded in our political culture.

The major issue that has to be faced is how to balance accountability by our elected officials with the system of checks and balances. We divide powers among three branches of government. We divide the legislature into two branches (except in Nebraska) to prevent hasty, ill-considered lawmaking. In theory, this gives better representation to various interests in the same way as Congress does, but, in fact, state senators and representatives represent the population under the one man, one vote rule. We give the governor the right of veto [except in North Carolina] as an additional safeguard against poor laws, but since we do not trust the governor either, the legislature is given the power to override the veto.

We require the governor to carry out the laws, but we elect many subordinate officials so they are not subject to executive control. We put employees of the state under merit systems to avoid political spoils, and in some jurisdictions tighten the requirement to a degree that almost no one is responsible to the governor or to any other policy maker.

We earmark income to prevent the legislature from axing our favorite activity, and then wonder why there is not enough money to run the state.

We have more trust in the judiciary, so we do not put too many restrictions on them, except to require periodic confirmation of judges by election in one way or another. We divide administration and some powers between state and local governments, and grant varying degrees of home rule to certain local governments to prevent state interference in local affairs.

Municipal governments using city managers or strong mayors are far ahead of most of our states in employing basic management principles such as having authority equal to responsibility. But, given post-Watergate attitudes, we may be asking too much of today's citizens to propose strengthening state management in major ways. The field is ripe for innovation and constructive change, if the constitution writers and their constituents want to improve their governmental structure.

A constitution is a fundamental law. That involves the relationship between constitutions and laws, the amendment process and the franchise issue.

When courts say that a constitution is a fundamental law, they mean simply that no law enacted by a legislature can be valid if it goes against the provisions of the constitu-

tion. Put differently, legislators are bound by the constitution. The subject needs no elaboration; you are all familiar with courts declaring laws unconstitutional. The problem about that relationship is that constitutions can be stifling in their rigidity if they are too detailed.

Changes in the constitution must come from the same source that adopted the constitution in the first place, namely, the people. There are practical problems here, too. Most legislatures can propose amendments to be placed on the ballot, provided that some extraordinary majority, such as two-thirds of the membership, approves of the idea. Do you also allow amendments to be placed on the ballot by petition? If so, how easy do you make it to submit proposals in this way? If you make it too easy, all sorts of pressure groups with bright ideas load the ballot with proposals. The California ballot is a good example. If it is made too difficult or not allowed at all, needed reforms cannot be enacted. For example, would you really expect a legislature voluntarily to relinquish its power over districting?

Another recurring problem is the constitution as a whole becoming obsolete and cluttered with details and inconsistencies. Many constitutions provide for constitutional conventions to deal with broad changes. How are such conventions to be convened? Can only the legislature provide for such a comprehensive review or can the people initiate one? Does the whole constitution have to be opened for possible change or can the convention be limited to specific subjects?

Who can amend or rewrite a constitution? In other words, who are the voters? Here our democratic system has achieved significant progress. In the days when our nation was founded, only white, free, taxpaying males who were at least 21 years old could vote. Some colonies also imposed religious tests. Later, many governments required that voters be able to read and write, and live in the community for at least one year. Politicians were free to draw election district boundaries where they desired, so when people moved from rural areas into cities, the number of people represented by a single legislator could vary by several hundred percent.

Between court decisions and amendments to federal and state constitutions, the number of persons able to vote has grown enormously. Qualifications of race, sex, religion and literacy have disappeared. Residency requirements have been reduced to short periods such as one month, and taxpayer status has been eliminated for most elections. The minimum age has been lowered to 18 years. The one man, one vote rule has given city dwellers about the same level of representation as farmers, and the influence of special interests has declined to some extent.

A few years ago, Judge Raymond Broderick, who chaired the successful Pennsylvania constitutional convention, said: "A document which contains inflexible and limiting language may work today, but it will not work for tomorrow. Your constitution should contain only the basic structure for state and local government and the basic rights of your citizens. Restrictions upon the powers of state government should be eliminated from the constitution. All such restrictions should be statutory." To the extent that revisions of a constitution meet these criteria, the resulting government can be vital, dynamic, responsive, and a full partner in the federal system.

10

Home Rule for Local Governments: Pro and Con

DAVID L. MARTIN

Some of the most heated battles fought at state capitals occur between supporters who see home rule powers as a panacea for governmental problems and opponents who view such independence as reckless license. Given the following arguments on each side, which home rule powers would you grant as a state legislator?

PRO

1. Home rule power is necessary to achieve reorganization of government. Local units can alter their structure to meet their individual needs, giving flexibility for man-

CON

1. Home rule may be defeated on the issue of structural reform. The electorate may lack information or be opposed to a new form of government rather than decide on the mer-

---

From David L. Martin, *Running City Hall*. (University, Alabama: University of Alabama Press, 1982), pp. 20–23. Reprinted by permission of the publisher.

PRO

agement. Offices can be combined or consolidated as necessary to reduce personnel costs. Duplication and unclear overlapping of functions mandated by state law at different times can be streamlined. Local citizens and their elected officials can decide the form of government best suited to their needs.

2. Home rule units may create urban service areas, thus containing the proliferation of special districts. By establishing high service areas at the request of inhabitants and increasing taxes or imposing user charges to pay for these services, creation of single-function governments (independent special districts) can be avoided. Home rule allows increased intergovernmental cooperation between local units: they may freely enter into interjurisdictional agreements, joint contracting, and financing of joint projects.

3. If the state constitution provides that home rule should be "construed liberally," court interference can be avoided. Such a clause avoids a shopping list of home rule powers, leaving municipalities free to act as necessary unless there is state legislative preemption. Home rule units have the powers needed to carry out daily governmental functions without being second-guessed by the judiciary after expensive litigation.

4. Home rule provisions can define method(s) for state preemption, concurrent exercise of powers, and identifying a local as opposed to a statewide concern. An alternative is to leave this definition to the legislature or the courts to be decided on case by case, taking individual circumstances into account. Preemption can occur as the need arises, concurrently exercised powers can be shared, and changing circumstances will dictate whether it is a matter for local or statewide concern.

CON

its of home rule itself. Officials who might lose their jobs under reorganization often oppose home rule politically or successfully demand that a new local charter protect their position. Self-determination in matters of governmental structure may not include a substantive grant of regulatory power, meaning reorganization in form but not in operation, where it counts.

2. Home rule necessarily results in lack of uniformity among units of government. If at local option some jurisdictions have home rule powers and others do not, conflicts of applicability will inevitably arise. Eminent domain powers of special districts still take precedence over local home rule zoning ordinances, and state enabling legislation may be necessary to establish special service areas (especially outside city limits).

3. While the courts have followed constitutional provisions to "construe liberally," fights do occur over the precedence of home rule actions. If the state legislature enacts preemptive limitations, home rule units may challenge such restrictions in court. Previous state laws may conflict with actions taken under home rule and could be declared invalid. State legislators may resent judicial interpretation declaring statutes inoperative.

4. The distinction between statewide and local concerns is a source of endless litigation. Home rule becomes what the judges say it is. Political compromises determine the assumption of specific functions by local governments. The legislature can intervene by declaring an area to be of state concern, **constantly shifting the balance of power.** Efforts to allocate functions according to primacy of state or local interests result in an arbitrary and incomplete division of responsibilities.

PRO

5. Home rule without revenue-raising power is a hollow shell. Home rule units should be allowed flexibility in spending, incurring debt, and the ability to tax themselves to the limit their citizens desire. Financial referendum requirements are ineffective controls for fiscal management because so few voters turn out—unless there is a taxpayers' revolt. Any fiscal irresponsibility is the fault of elected officials, not a consequence of home rule itself.

6. Reorganization allowable under home rule will lead to greater efficiency. Administrative authority can be concentrated in the mayor or city manager, rather than a host of officials separately elected for each function. Home rule flexibility in operational procedures will allow experimentation for greater economy. If the people desire more checks and balances in government, under home rule they can decide the limitations necessary and write them into the city charter.

7. Home rule allows greater discretion in making routine decisions. City officials do not need the state legislature's authorization of everything. Without home rule, large cities have to submit a large volume of complex local legislation each session, while small towns will find it expensive to lobby at the state capital for the acts they need. Locally elected officials should have freedom to act in behalf of local government.

8. Municipalities (and counties) vary widely in their governmental needs. Home rule gives flexibility to deal with different **population sizes, growth problems, urban-rural makeup,** and socioeconomic composition. Without it, most state legislation passed has a

CON

5. Home rule with taxing authority erodes the state's revenue base and can lead to irresponsible local spending without state financial oversight. Home rule appears as a blank check to taxpayers who are reluctant to let local government's hands dig deeper into their pockets and are skeptical about how the money will be spent at local discretion. Public opinion surveys taken after home rule referenda appear to indicate that a major reason for rejection is voters' fear that home rule would mean new or increased taxes.

6. Incumbent officeholders and groups who feel they have a favorable position under the existing system are likely to oppose home rule. To gain political support necessary for adoption, the charter may specifically protect their positions. It may be more difficult and expensive to amend a home rule charter subsequently if a popular referendum is required than it would be to obtain new local legislation from the state legislature: To make a change under home rule requires convincing the voting electorate, not just the local delegation to the state legislature.

7. Home rule charters may be complex and highly technical. Voters are likely to be apathetic or else confused by charter amendments—plus some local interest group can lobby successfully for a change favoring it. State controls ensure that locally organized groups (such as public employee unions) do not use home rule to win special favors in charter amendments. Finally, those unsatisfied with local decisions under home rule will try to persuade the state legislature to intervene.

8. Of the many units legally eligible for home rule, only some have exercised the option. The calls for home rule often come from a relatively few large jurisdictions which need additional powers to meet citizen demand for urban services (which could be authorized by

PRO	CON

classification basis, making a "general" statute of narrow local applicability.

individual local legislation). Many local governments do not want and cannot afford additional responsibilities. Home rule may result in withdrawal of state financial support for certain functions.

9. Home rule relieves local governments from partisan discrimination by a state legislature controlled by the opposite political party. Without home rule, jurisdictions may not obtain necessary statutory authority because local legislation is tangled by party quarrels, legislative apportionment disputes, and carving up the city between legislative districts which give one party or another electoral advantage. In such partisan fights, it is tempting to block legislation crucial to local government's operation in order to obtain political compromise on other issues.

9. Local governments with partisan elections may (or may not) obtain home rule because of their political complexion rather than upon the merits of their situation. Home rule may be granted or refused on the basis of political loyalty, not need. Even with nonpartisan local elections, certain special interests may seek or oppose home rule, depending on whether it favors or might regulate them.

10. Home rule is a device allowing local initiative. It requires a psychological attitude as much as the legal formality for success. Home rule units have exercised their powers responsibly: only a tiny number have lost this power subsequently because of incapacity. Most state legislators hate to be charged with interfering in local affairs; moreover they can become entangled in local political squabbles. Denying home rule is really saying that local citizens are not capable of self-government.

10. Local pride biases consideration of alternatives. A system of strict state control does have its uses: legislators reap political rewards from sponsoring local bills. But even if one is disenchanted with local legislation, home rule is not a complete cure. Home rule may give some relief from inappropriate legislation, but it cannot undo adverse judicial decisions against the city. Since home rule powers are interpreted by the courts in light of national and state constitutional provisions, it is politically more difficult to reverse a judicial decision than to replace a legislator whose local bills do not please his constituents.

—————————————— **11** ——————————————

What Right to Regulate?
Village of Belle Terre v. *Boraas*

SUPREME COURT OF THE UNITED STATES

MR. JUSTICE DOUGLAS delivered the opinion of the Court.

Belle Terre is a village on Long Island's north shore of about 220 homes inhabited by 700 people. Its total land area is less than one square mile. It has restricted land use to one-family dwellings excluding lodging houses, boarding houses, fraternity houses, or multiple-dwelling houses. The word "family" as used in the ordinance means, "[o]ne or more persons related by blood, adoption, or marriage, living and cooking together as a single housekeeping unit, exclusive of household servants. A number of persons but not exceeding two (2) living and cooking together as a single housekeeping unit though not related by blood, adoption, or marriage shall be deemed to constitute a family."

Appellees the Dickmans are owners of a house in the village and leased it in December 1971 for a term of 18 months to Michael Truman. Later Bruce Boraas became a colessee. Then Anne Parish moved into the house along with three others. These six are students at nearby State University at Stony Brook and none is related to the other by blood, adoption, or marriage. . . .

This case brings to this Court a different phase of local zoning regulations from those we have previously reviewed. *Euclid* v. *Ambler Realty Co.*, 272 U.S. 365, involved a zoning ordinance classifying land use in a given area into six categories. The Dickmans' tracts fell under three classifications: U–2, which included two-family dwellings; U–3, which included apartments, hotels, churches, schools, private clubs, hospitals, city hall and the like; and U–6, which included sewage disposal plants, incinerators, scrap storage, cemeteries, oil and gas storage and so on. Heights of buildings were prescribed for each zone; also, the size of land areas required for each kind of use was specified. The land in litigation was vacant and being held for industrial development; and evidence was introduced showing that under the restricted-use ordinance the land would be greatly reduced in value. The claim was that the landowner was being deprived of liberty and property without due process within the meaning of the Fourteenth Amendment.

The Court sustained the zoning ordinance under the police power of the State, saying that the line "which in this field separates the legitimate from the illegitimate assumption of power is not capable of precise delimitation. It varies with circumstances and conditions." *Id.*, at 387. And the Court added: "A nuisance may be merely a right thing in the wrong place,—like a pig in the parlor instead of the barnyard. If the validity of the legislative classification for zoning purposes be fairly debatable, the legislative judgment must be allowed to control." *Id.*, at 388. The Court listed as considerations bearing on the constitutionality of zoning ordinances the danger of fire or collapse of buildings, the

416 U.S. 1 (1974). Footnotes omitted.

evils of overcrowding people, and the possibility that "offensive trades, industries, and structures" might "create nuisance" to residential sections. *Ibid.* But even those historic police power problems need not loom large or actually be existent in a given case. For the exclusion of "all industrial establishments" does not mean that "only offensive or dangerous industries will be excluded." *Ibid.* That fact does not invalidate the ordinance; the Court held:

> The inclusion of a reasonable margin to insure effective enforcement, will not put upon a law, otherwise valid, the stamp of invalidity. Such laws may also find their justification in the fact that, in some fields, the bad fades into the good by such insensible degrees that the two are not capable of being readily distinguished and separated in terms of legislation. *Id.*, at 388–389.

The main thrust of the case in the mind of the Court was in the exclusion of industries and apartments, and as respects that it commented on the desire to keep residential areas free of "disturbing noises"; "increased traffic"; the hazard of "moving and parked automobiles"; the "depriving children of the privilege of quiet and open spaces for play, enjoyed by those in more favored localities." *Id.*, at 394. The ordinance was sanctioned because the validity of the legislative classification was "fairly debatable" and therefore could not be said to be wholly arbitrary. *Id.*, at 388.

Our decision in *Berman* v. *Parker*, 348 U.S. 26, sustained a land-use project in the District of Columbia against a landowner's claim that the taking violated the Due Process Clause and the Just Compensation Clause of the Fifth Amendment. The essence of the argument against the law was, while taking property for ridding an area of slums was permissible, taking it "merely to develop a better balanced, more attractive community" was not, *id.*, at 31. We refused to limit the concept of public welfare that may be enhanced by zoning regulations. We said:

> Miserable and disreputable housing conditions may do more than spread disease and crime and immorality. They may also suffocate the spirit by reducing the people who live there to the status of cattle. They may indeed make living an almost insufferable burden. They may also be an ugly sore, a blight on the community which robs it of charm, which makes it a place from which men turn. The misery of housing may despoil a community as an open sewer may ruin a river.
>
> We do not sit to determine whether a particular housing project is or is not desirable. The concept of the public welfare is broad and inclusive. . . . The values it represents are spiritual as well as physical, aesthetic as well as monetary. It is within the power of the legislature to determine that the community should be beautiful as well as healthy, spacious as well as clean, well-balanced as well as carefully patrolled. *Id.*, at 32–33.

If the ordinance segregated one area only for one race, it would immediately be suspect under the reasoning of *Buchanan* v. *Warley*, 245 U.S. 60, where the Court invalidated a city ordinance barring a black from acquiring real property in a white residential area by reason of an 1866 Act of Congress, 14 Stat. 27, now 42 U.S.C. § 1982, and an 1870 Act, § 17, 16 Stat. 144, now 42 U.S.C. § 1981, both enforcing the Fourteenth Amendment. 245 U.S., at 78–82. See *Jones* v. *Mayer Co.*, 392 U.S. 409.

In *Seattle Trust Co.* v. *Roberge*, 278 U.S. 116, Seattle had a zoning ordinance that permitted a " 'philanthropic home for children or for old people' " in a particular district " 'when the written consent shall have been obtained of the owners of two-thirds of the property within four hundred (400) feet of the proposed building.' " *Id.*, at 118. The Court held that provision of the ordinance unconstitutional, saying that the existing owners could "withhold consent for selfish reasons or arbitrarily and may subject the trustee [owner] to their will or caprice." *Id.*, at 122. Unlike the billboard cases (*e.g.*, *Cusack Co.* v. *City of Chicago*, 242 U.S. 526), the Court concluded that the Seattle ordinance was invalid since the proposed home for the aged poor was not shown by its maintenance and construction "to work any injury, inconvenience or annoyance to the community, the district or any person." 278 U.S., at 122.

The present ordinance is challenged on several grounds: that it interferes with a person's right to travel; that it interferes with the right to migrate to and settle within a State; that it bars people who are uncongenial to the present residents; that it expresses the social preferences of the residents for groups that will be congenial to them; that social homogeneity is not a legitimate interest of government; that the restriction of those whom the neighbors do not like trenches on the newcomers' rights of privacy; that it is of no rightful concern to villagers whether the residents are married or unmarried; that the ordinance is antithetical to the Nation's experience, ideology, and self-perception as an open, egalitarian, and integrated society.

We find none of these reasons in the record before us. It is not aimed at transients. Cf. *Shapiro* v. *Thompson,* 394 U.S. 618. It involves no procedural disparity inflicted on some but not on others such as was presented by *Griffin* v. *Illinois,* 351 U.S. 12. It involves no "fundamental" right guaranteed by the Constitution, such as voting, *Harper* v. *Virginia Board,* 383 U.S. 663; the right of association, *NAACP* v. *Alabama,* 357 U.S. 449; the right of access to the courts, *NAACP* v. *Button,* 371 U.S. 415; or any rights of privacy, cf. *Griswold* v. *Connecticut,* 381 U.S. 479; *Eisenstadt* v. *Baird,* 405 U.S. 438, 453–454. We deal with economic and social legislation where legislatures have historically drawn lines which we respect against the charge of violation of the Equal Protection Clause if the law be " 'reasonable, not arbitrary' " (quoting *Royster Guano Co.* v. *Virginia,* 253 U.S. 412, 415) and bears "a rational relationship to a [permissible] state objective." *Reed* v. *Reed,* 404 U.S. 71, 76.

It is said, however, that if two unmarried people can constitute a "family," there is no

reason why three or four may not. But every line drawn by a legislature leaves some out that might well have been included. That exercise of discretion, however, is a legislative, not a judicial, function.

It is said that the Belle Terre ordinance reeks with an animosity to unmarried couples who live together. There is no evidence to support it; and the provision of the ordinance bringing within the definition of a "family" two unmarried people belies the charge.

The ordinance places no ban on other forms of association, for a "family" may, so far as the ordinance is concerned, entertain whomever it likes.

The regimes of boarding houses, fraternity houses, and the like present urban problems. More people occupy a given space; more cars rather continuously pass by; more cars are parked; noise travels with crowds.

A quiet place where yards are wide, people few, and motor vehicles restricted are legitimate guidelines in a land-use project addressed to family needs. This goal is a permissible one within *Berman* v. *Parker, supra.* The police power is not confined to elimination of filth, stench, and unhealthy places. It is ample to lay out zones where family values, youth values, and the blessings of quiet seclusion and clean air make the area a sanctuary for people.

The suggestion that the case may be moot need not detain us. A zoning ordinance usually has an impact on the value of the property which it regulates. But in spite of the fact that the precise impact of the ordinance sustained in *Euclid* on a given piece of property was not known, 272 U.S., at 397, the Court, considering the matter a controversy in the realm of city planning, sustained the ordinance. Here we are a step closer to the impact of the ordinance on the value of the lessor's property. He has not only lost six tenants and acquired only two in their place; it is obvious that the scale of rental values rides on what we decide today. When *Berman* reached us it was not certain whether an entire tract would be taken or only the buildings on it and a scenic easement. 348 U.S., at 36. But that did not make the case any the less a controversy in the constitutional sense. When Mr. Justice Holmes said for the Court in *Block* v. *Hirsh,* 256 U.S. 135, 155, "property rights may be cut down, and to that extent taken, without pay," he stated the issue here. As is true in most zoning cases, the precise impact on value may, at the threshold of litigation over validity, not yet be known. . . .

MR. JUSTICE MARSHALL, dissenting.

This case draws into question the constitutionality of a zoning ordinance of the incorporated village of Belle Terre, New York, which prohibits groups of more than two unrelated persons, as distinguished from groups consisting of any number of persons related by blood, adoption, or marriage, from occupying a residence within the confines of the township. Lessor-appellees, the two owners of a Belle Terre residence, and three unrelated student tenants challenged the ordinance on the ground that it establishes a classification between households of related and unrelated individuals, which deprives them of equal protection of the laws. In my view, the disputed classification burdens the students' fundamental rights of association and privacy guaranteed by the First and Fourteenth Amendments. Because the application of strict equal protection scrutiny is therefore required, I am at odds with my Brethren's conclusion that the ordinance may be sustained on a showing that it bears a rational relationship to the accomplishment of legitimate governmental objectives.

I am in full agreement with the majority that zoning is a complex and important function of the State. It may indeed be the most essential function performed by local government, for it is one of the primary means by which we protect that sometimes difficult to define concept of quality of life. I therefore continue to adhere to the principle of *Euclid* v. *Ambler Realty Co.,* 272 U.S. 365 (1926), that

deference should be given to governmental judgments concerning proper land-use allocation. That deference is a principle which has served this Court well and which is necessary for the continued development of effective zoning and land-use control mechanisms. Had the owners alone brought this suit alleging that the restrictive ordinance deprived them of their property or was an irrational legislative classification, I would agree that the ordinance would have to be sustained. Our role is not and should not be to sit as a zoning board of appeals.

I would also agree with the majority that local zoning authorities may properly act in furtherance of the objectives asserted to be served by the ordinance at issue here: restricting uncontrolled growth, solving traffic problems, keeping rental costs at a reasonable level, and making the community attractive to families. The police power which provides the justification for zoning is not narrowly confined. See *Berman* v. *Parker,* 348 U.S. 26 (1954). And, it is appropriate that we afford zoning authorities considerable latitude in choosing the means by which to implement such purposes. But deference does not mean abdication. This Court has an obligation to ensure that zoning ordinances, even when adopted in furtherance of such legitimate aims, do not infringe upon fundamental constitutional rights.

When separate but equal was still accepted constitutional dogma, this Court struck down a racially restrictive zoning ordinance. *Buchanan* v. *Warley,* 245 U.S. 60 (1917). I am sure the Court would not be hesitant to invalidate that ordinance today. The lower federal courts have considered procedural aspects of zoning, and acted to insure that land-use controls are not used as means of confining minorities and the poor to the ghettos of our central cities. These are limited but necessary intrusions on the discretion of zoning authorities. By the same token, I think it clear that the First Amendment provides some limitation on zoning laws. It is inconceivable to me that we would allow the exercise of the zoning power to burden First Amendment freedoms, as by ordinances that restrict occupancy to individuals adhering to particular religious, political, or scientific beliefs. Zoning officials properly concern themselves with the uses of land—with, for example, the number and kind of dwellings to be constructed in a certain neighborhood or the number of persons who can reside in those dwellings. But zoning authorities cannot validly consider who those persons are, what they believe, or how they choose to live, whether they are Negro or white, Catholic or Jew, Republican or Democrat, married or unmarried.

My disagreement with the Court today is based upon my view that the ordinance in this case unnecessarily burdens appellees' First Amendment freedom of association and their constitutionally guaranteed right to privacy. Our decisions establish that the First and Fourteenth Amendments protect the freedom to choose one's associates. *NAACP* v. *Button*, 371 U.S. 415, 430 (1963). Constitutional protection is extended, not only to modes of association that are political in the usual sense, but also to those that pertain to the social and economic benefit of the members. *Id.*, at 430–431; *Brotherhood of Railroad Trainmen* v. *Virginia Bar*, 377 U.S. 1 (1964). See *United Transportation Union* v. *State Bar of Michigan*, 401 U.S. 576 (1971); *Mine Workers* v. *Illinois State Bar Assn.*, 389 U.S. 217 (1967). The selection of one's living companions involves similar choices as to the emotional, social, or economic benefits to be derived from alternative living arrangements.

The freedom of association is often inextricably entwined with the constitutionally guaranteed right of privacy. The right to "establish a home" is an essential part of the liberty guaranteed by the Fourteenth Amendment. *Meyer* v. *Nebraska*, 262 U.S. 390, 399 (1923); *Griswold* v. *Connecticut*, 381 U.S. 479, 495 (1965) (Goldberg, J., concurring). And the Constitution secures to an individual a freedom "to satisfy his intellectual and emotional

needs in the privacy of his own home." *Stanley* v. *Georgia*, 394 U.S. 557, 565 (1969); see *Paris Adult Theatre I* v. *Slaton*, 413 U.S. 49, 66–67 (1973). Constitutionally protected privacy is, in Mr. Justice Brandeis' words, "as against the Government, the right to be let alone . . . the right most valued by civilized man." *Olmstead* v. *United States*, 277 U.S. 438, 478 (1928) (dissenting opinion). The choice of household companions—of whether a person's "intellectual and emotional needs" are best met by living with family, friends, professional associates, or others—involves deeply personal considerations as to the kind and quality of intimate relationships within the home. That decision surely falls within the ambit of the right to privacy protected by the Constitution. See *Roe* v. *Wade*, 410 U.S. 113, 153 (1973); *Eisenstadt* v. *Baird*, 405 U.S. 438, 453 (1972); *Stanley* v. *Georgia*, supra, at 564–565; *Griswold* v. *Connecticut*, supra, at 483, 486; *Olmstead* v. *United States*, supra, at 478 (Brandeis, J., dissenting); *Moreno* v. *Department of Agriculture*, 345 F. Supp. 310, 315 (DC 1972), aff'd, 413 U.S. 528 (1973).

The instant ordinance discriminates on the basis of just such a personal lifestyle choice as to household companions. It permits any number of persons related by blood or marriage, be it two or twenty, to live in a single household, but it limits to two the number of unrelated persons bound by profession, love, friendship, religious or political affiliation, or mere economics who can occupy a single home. Belle Terre imposes upon those who deviate from the community norm in their choice of living companions significantly greater restrictions than are applied to residential groups who are related by blood or marriage, and compose the established order within the community. The village has, in effect, acted to fence out those individuals whose choice of lifestyle differs from that of its current residents.

This is not a case where the Court is being asked to nullify a township's sincere efforts to maintain its residential character by preventing the operation of rooming houses, fraternity houses, or other commercial or **high-density residential uses.** Unquestionably, a town is free to restrict such uses. Moreover, as a general proposition, I see no constitutional infirmity in a town's limiting the density of use in residential areas by zoning regulations which do not discriminate on the basis of constitutionally suspect criteria. This ordinance, however, limits the density of occupancy of only those homes occupied by unrelated persons. It thus reaches beyond control of the use of land or the density of population, and undertakes to regulate the way people choose to associate with each other within the privacy of their own homes.

It is no answer to say, as does the majority, that associational interests are not infringed because Belle Terre residents may entertain whomever they choose. Only last Term MR. JUSTICE DOUGLAS indicated in concurrence that he saw the right of association protected by the First Amendment as involving far more than the right to entertain visitors. He found that right infringed by a restriction on food stamp assistance, penalizing households of "unrelated persons." As MR. JUSTICE DOUGLAS there said, freedom of association encompasses the "right to invite the stranger into one's home" not only for "entertainment" but to join the household as well. *Department of Agriculture* v. *Moreno*, 413 U.S. 528, 538–545 (1973) (concurring opinion). I am still persuaded that the choice of those who will form one's household implicates constitutionally protected rights.

Because I believe that this zoning ordinance creates a classification which impinges upon fundamental personal rights, it can withstand constitutional scrutiny only upon a clear showing that the burden imposed is necessary to protect a compelling and substantial governmental interest, *Shapiro* v. *Thompson*, 394 U.S. 618, 634 (1969). And, once it be determined that a burden has been placed upon a constitutional right, the onus of demonstrating that no less intrusive means will adequately protect the compelling state interest and that the challenged statute is sufficiently narrowly drawn, is upon the party seeking to justify the burden. See *Memorial Hospital* v. *Maricopa County*, 415 U.S. 250 (1974); *Speiser* v. *Randall*, 357 U.S. 513, 525–526 (1958).

A variety of justifications have been proffered in support of the village's ordinance. It is claimed that the ordinance controls population density, prevents noise, traffic and parking problems, and preserves the rent structure of the community and its attractiveness to families. As I noted earlier, these are all legitimate and substantial interests of government. But I think it clear that the means chosen to accomplish these purposes are both overinclusive and underinclusive, and that the asserted goals could be as effectively achieved by means of an ordinance that did not discriminate on the basis of constitutionally protected choices of lifestyle. The ordinance imposes no restriction whatsoever on the number of persons who may live in a house, as long as they are related by marital or sanguinary bonds—presumably no matter how distant their relationship. Nor does the ordinance restrict the number of income earners who may contribute to rent in such a household, or the number of automobiles that may be maintained by its occupants. In that sense the ordinance is underinclusive. On the other hand, the statute restricts the number of unrelated persons who may live in a home to no more than two. It would therefore prevent three unrelated people from occupying a dwelling even if among them they had but one income and no vehicles. While an extended family of a dozen or more might live in a small bungalow, three elderly and retired persons could not occupy the large manor house next door. Thus the statute is also grossly overinclusive to accomplish its intended purposes.

There are some 220 residences in Belle Terre occupied by about 700 persons. The density is therefore just above three per household. The village is justifiably concerned with density of population and the related problems of noise, traffic, and the like. It could deal with those problems by limiting each household to a specified number of adults, two or three perhaps, without limitation on the number of dependent children. The burden of such an ordinance would fall equally upon all segments of the community. It would surely be better tailored to the goals asserted by the village than the ordinance before us today, for it would more realistically restrict population density and growth and their attendant environmental costs. Various other statutory mechanisms also suggest themselves as solutions to Belle Terre's problems—rent control, limits on the number of vehicles per household, and so forth, but, of course, such schemes are matters of legislative judgment and not for this Court. Appellants also refer to the necessity of maintaining the family character of the village. There is not a shred of evidence in the record indicating that if Belle Terre permitted a limited number of unrelated persons to live together, the residential, familial character of the community would be fundamentally affected.

By limiting unrelated households to two persons while placing no limitation on households of related individuals, the village has embarked upon its commendable course in a constitutionally faulty vessel. Cf. *Marshall* v. *United States*, 414 U.S. 417, 430 (1974) (dissenting opinion). I would find the challenged ordinance unconstitutional. But I would not ask the village to abandon its goal of providing quiet streets, little traffic, and a pleasant and reasonably priced environment in which families might raise their children. Rather, I would commend the village to continue to pursue those purposes but by means of more carefully drawn and even-handed legislation.

I respectfully dissent.

12

Noah Builds an Ark in Decatur

G. CURTIS BRANSCOME

The building inspectors had taken to the field, and Jennifer Smith had settled down for another routine day of running the front desk at the licenses and inspections department at city hall. Ms. Smith had been at her job for 10 years. She could handle the permits and the inspection reports without thinking, neatly compiling, cataloging, and filing them. Her knowledge of the codes was extensive, and she was allowed to issue many permits without even consulting with the assistant chief inspector.

The first man through the door this morning had a sense of urgency about him.

"They tell me I need a building permit," he said.

Ms. Smith prided herself on her friendly and helpful service.

Public Management, Vol.67, No.1 (January 1985), pp. 21–23. Copyright © 1984 by G. Curtis Branscome. All rights reserved.

"You've come to the right place. What do you want to build?"

"An ark."

"An arch? You mean like at McDonald's? "I'm sorry, our code defines those as advertising signs, and we don't permit them."

"No, No. I mean an *ark*. A big boat."

"Oh, I see. And where do you want to build this boat?"

"At my house. 269 West Hill Street."

Ms. Smith really liked it when she could help someone. She had never heard of requiring a building permit for a boat. She thought she'd engage in a little friendly chit-chat before she gave him the good news.

"Where do you fish?" she asked. "Up on Lake Lanier?"

"I'm not much of a fisherman," he replied.

"Must be a sailboat," she thought. A picture she had once seen in the newspaper flashed through her mind. A man had built a sailboat in his basement and had no way of getting it out.

"Going to build it in your garage?" she asked.

"Well, it's kind of large. I was thinking about building it in my front yard."

"Can't do that. City code prohibits parking a boat anywhere other than in a garage or behind the front building line. While it was being built, we would consider it parked."

"I guess I could fit it into my backyard."

He "guesses" he could fit it in? Ms. Smith began to get interested in this project. "Just how big is this boat going to be?"

"It'll be 300 cubits long, 50 cubits wide, and 30 cubits high."

Ms. Smith didn't know how long a cubit was, but then she wasn't into boats and had no idea how you measured one. "300" sounded like a large number.

"I believe you'll need to speak to Assistant Chief Inspector Ricketts," she said. "Just have a seat, and he'll be with you in a minute. What's your name, please?"

"Noah."

"Well, Mr. Noah, I'll let Mr. Ricketts know you're here."

Mr. Ricketts' cubicle was a jumble of plans, specifications, and code books. He was a pleasant, church-going man, but he maintained a gruff facade. He had to, because it was his job to tell builders and developers "no" so that he could get the code exceptions down to as few as possible. Then the chief inspector could be "Mr. Nice Guy" and approve those exceptions. If it got to Mr. Ricketts' desk, it meant that it was time to say "no."

"Mr. Ricketts, there is a Mr. Noah here who needs to talk to you about building a boat," announced Ms. Smith.

"A boat? Why in hell does anyone need to talk to me about building a boat?"

Ms. Smith explained. He trusted her instincts. He could see the stream of complaining neighbors going to the city council. "Send him in."

"Mr. Noah, how big is this boat going to be? In feet?"

"It's going to be 450 feet long, 75 feet wide, and 45 feet high."

"There's no way you could begin to meet the sideyard and rearyard setback requirements," thundered Mr. Ricketts. "Why, no accessory structure can be closer than 10 feet to the property line on the side or the rear. This doesn't sound like an accessory structure to me, anyway. Let me see your plans."

"I don't have any plans," replied Noah.

"Any structure this large requires plans with the seal of a registered architect or engineer. You can't get a permit without that. How in the world were you going to build without plans?"

"I was going to build it the way God told me to," said Noah.

Bingo! Mr. Ricketts understood the situation now. This weirdo was trying to sneak in a church for some strange cult. "You're in an area zoned single family residential. What you are talking about is not a permitted use. We can't give you a building permit."

A confused and anxious Noah left the office. He had to get started on his ark. Whom could he turn to? As he made his way through city hall, he saw the sign: City Manager's Office. It was a large office, with nice carpet and heavy substantial furniture. "Maybe this guy can help me," thought Noah.

Noah had come to the right place. Phil Hawkins, the city manager, had recently been to a seminar on "The City Manager as a Facilitator." He was fired up. He could be an ombudsman and help people find their way through the maze of rules and regulations! He had an open door and a sympathetic ear.

After listening to Noah's problem, Mr. Hawkins laid out the options. "Mr. Noah, there are a couple of ways we can solve this land use problem. One way would be to go to the zoning board of appeals and get a variance. It seems to me that the key point is that we would have to convince the board that this is not a permanent structure. How are you going to get this big boat out of your backyard?"

"It's going to float out when the flood comes."

"Listen, Mr. Noah, you've got to be serious about this. Those board members aren't dummies. They know that property is on a hillside and that we're 1,000 feet above sea level." "Float out on the flood," he chuckled to himself. "I'd better write that down so I can tell the guys at the next seminar."

Rocking back in his chair and puffing on his pipe, the city manager presented his other option. "What you could do is rent a vacant lot in the commercial district. Boat building would be a permitted use there. Here's a list of three vacant lots that I know are available. Bring us back a lease on one of those and I think we will be in business."

Noah hadn't budgeted for the cost of leasing land and he was on a tight budget, but time was running out. He breathed a sigh of relief: at least he was making progress. He left to lease some property.

After two weeks of negotiating, he finally signed a lease. He knew he had made a bad deal on it. Probably there was no way he could contain his desperation. The owner of

the property certainly had taken advantage of him.

Ms. Smith recognized Noah when he returned, but she knew that the city manager had taken a personal interest in Mr. Noah. "Well," she thought, "I'm going to let someone else give him the bad news."

"Hello, Mr. Noah. What can I do for you?" She noted that he did have a roll of plans under his arm.

"I have my lease, and I came to see about a building permit," he replied.

"The rules say we can't issue a permit until we have a sign-off from the city engineer. He'll have to approve your storm water retention plan and your sedimentation and soil erosion control plan. And, by the way, how tall is this boat going to be?"

"30 cubits," Noah said.

"In feet?"

"Oh, that's about 45 feet."

"O.K. Any construction over 30 feet in height requires the approval of the fire marshal. You'll also need his sign-off before I can issue a permit."

A dejected Noah trudged off to see the city engineer. Harvey Holton, the city engineer, was a no-nonsense guy. He believed in the book and in those numbers that he could verify by recalculating them in his desktop computer.

"That's right," he told Noah. "You must have a storm water retention study done. The rate of runoff cannot be any faster after development than it was before development."

"But," protested Noah, "it is already being used as a parking lot and is totally paved."

"Look, Mr. Noah. The code says you gotta have the study, and it must be done by a registered engineer. I mean, there is grass growing in cracks in that asphalt, and your development is going to shade out that grass and kill it. All these factors must be considered."

"What is this about a sedimentation and soil erosion control plan?" Noah asked with trepidation.

"That's something the state makes us do. You'll probably have to put straw bales or some other silt barrier around the construction site. However, a registered engineer will have to study it and come up with the plan."

"But it is a paved lot . . . ," began Noah, but his voice trailed off as he looked at the impassive face of the city engineer.

"How long will it take to get these plans reviewed and approved?" asked a plaintive Noah.

"If, and I emphasize *if*, all the calculations are correct, it shouldn't take over a month to review storm drainage. After I approve the soil erosion plan, I am required to send it to the agricultural conservation and stabilization service for approval. There's no telling how long it will take those guys."

"Agricultural conservation and stabilization service?" stammered Noah. "There's no farmland for miles around here."

"Hey. I don't make the rules," said the city engineer as he turned back to his computer.

Noah wanted all the bad news in one day, so he went on to see the fire marshal. Willie Johnson was a dedicated public servant. He hated fires and the damage and suffering they caused. His wife had cross-stitched his favorite saying for him to hang on his office wall: "An ounce of prevention is worth a pound of cure."

"You want to build a wooden boat in the fire district?" an incredulous Mr. Johnson asked. "Look here, Mr. Noah, all construction in the fire district must be of noncombustible material. You can't build a wooden boat in the fire district!"

"I've got to build a wooden boat," said a desperate Noah. "I've been told to build a wooden boat. Isn't there anything I can do?"

Reluctantly, Willie Johnson said, "Yes. Some fire-retardant treated lumber has been rated noncombustible. I don't like it, but it's in the code. However, we require a certificate from the factory, and each and every piece must be stamped with the Underwriter's Lab-oratory rating at a maximum of four-feet intervals."

"What type of occupancy do you plan for this boat?" asked Mr. Johnson.

"I am going to collect two animals of every species that live on the earth."

"Boy, that's going to be some job! Let's see . . . a zoo in a structure over 35 feet tall. I would have to classify that as a high life-threatening situation. This boat is going to have to be fully sprinkled. Also, you will have to install a fire alarm system with both heat and smoke detectors tied directly into our central alarm system."

As he rose to go, Noah's eyes had a glazed look. "By the way," said Mr. Johnson, "I think I should warn you. Each and every exotic animal brought into the city requires a permit from the chief of police."

Months later, Noah sat on his patio drinking a glass of wine. His plans had still not been approved. His construction financing commitment had expired. A spatter of rain chased him into the house.

It rained for 40 days and 40 nights. Life as we know it vanished from the earth.

POSTSCRIPT

July recorded the second heaviest rainfall since records have been kept. The first two days of August opened with continued torrential downpour. Everyone had a touch of cabin fever, including me. I was just a little "stir crazy." Another developer had just complained about some code requirement. The two things came together in my mind. "What would happen," I said to myself, "if Noah tried to build his ark in Decatur today?"

Codes are important. The people who must enforce them have a difficult job. While the characters in this piece are entirely fictional, the code requirements are not. This piece is not a reflection on the fine and dedicated people I work with. It is just that I had an image of poor old Noah trying to build an ark in a city today and could not get it out of my mind until I committed it to paper.

CHAPTER 4

The Problem of Representation

Since the early 1960s, when the courts decided to enter the political thicket of representation, the cases presented have gone beyond ensuring "one person, one vote" from equal-sized districts. The opening selection reviews electoral systems commonly used, and asks if there is a best way. Research by political scientists has revealed that single-member districts tend to promote election of minorities (ethnic or partisan, if geographically dominant within the district) as well as representatives more interested in neighborhood or constituency service; and at-large elections show more successful women candidates. Such studies are often quantitative, and the evidence is subject to different interpretations, as illustrated by two contrasting views on how second or runoff primaries affect minorities and women.

Elbridge Gerry was a signer of the Declaration of Independence and the fifth vice president of the United States. He was also a governor of Massachusetts, and drew electoral districts for political advancement; one was in the shape of a salamander, which the painter Gilbert Stuart called a "gerrymander." The 1986 decision of the U.S. Supreme Court to examine gerrymandering, in *Davis* v. *Bandemer*, has prompted suggestions of criteria to be followed when drawing electoral districts for fair representation after the 1990 Census.

After reading these selections, consider the representational systems in your own community. What types of people are elected? Which electoral rules of the game favor them?

13

Local Electoral Systems: Is There a Best Way?

WILLIAM J. D. BOYD

Various electoral systems have evolved for local governments in the United States. It is impossible to state categorically that one is better than the rest, although a proportional representation system would be much fairer than a weighted voting system. Depending on a city's or county's political tradition—and pressures to preserve or change that tradition—a voting mechanism can be found that will help, but only help, to achieve a specific representative structure. There are many factors to be considered and the method of voting itself can never assure desired results.

SINGLE-MEMBER DISTRICTS

A major benefit of single-member districts is that they provide geographic representation within a community. If the district lines are fairly drawn they assure minority groups of getting at least one representative. Campaign costs are usually considered to be lower in a single-member district system but this is very difficult to prove.

In these days of public awareness of many governmental crises, council members have to think in terms of what is good for the entire community, so the danger of provincialism may be reduced. The same is increasingly true of county legislators. At the same time, single-member districts do provide someone who will be interested and concerned over the lack of a stoplight at a particular corner or chuck holes on a certain street, or any of the myriad small problems that are still big concerns to people in the immediate neighborhood. It also allows for representation from rural portions of counties.

In local governments utilizing partisan elections, or even nonpartisan elections where local party labels are used, single-member districts allow for the formation of political organizations along more rational lines. Political clubs or other such organizations are closer to the people and give them the sense of belonging to the community and having a place where their opinions will be heard and respected.

One of the greatest assets of a single-member district is its contribution to the short ballot. Americans must vote to fill more public offices than any other people. In a typical eastern state, it runs to 70 or more different posts every four years. In western states, with numerous initiative and referenda items, the situation is more confused. Filling a single legislative position at any level of government simplifies the ballot and increases the chances of the voter making an intelligent choice.

Conversely, under this system poorly educated members of lower socio-economic groups may well fall victim to a return of machine politics, at least within their ward. In big cities the political machines gradually col-

William J. D. Boyd, "Local Electoral Systems: Is There a Best Way?" *National Civic Review*, Vol.65, No.3 (March 1976), pp. 136–140, 157. Reprinted by permission of the publisher.

lapsed over the years with the rise in literacy and general education of the populace, but they recently have enjoyed a renaissance in certain areas.

In cities with partisan elections, single-member districts tend to be one-party enclaves. Therefore, victory in the primary is tantamount to election. As voter turnout for primaries is generally much lower than for general elections, the ward system encourages the development of political machines.

Single-member district representatives frequently take a narrow view of major public issues. There is a practice of trading votes with members from other areas. They may thwart the will of a majority of people of the city or county in return for special favors in their district.

In virtually every instance the council draws the district lines. Therefore, although the federal courts have made it clear that even local government legislative districts must have essentially equal populations, there is no protection as yet against political gerrymandering. Racial gerrymandering is also possible, although it has been declared unconstitutional by the United States Supreme Court. It is difficult to prove why legislators draw districts one way or another so long as they are of equal population. It is possible to draw the lines so that no member of a minority group is able to gain election to the council even though the group may represent as much as one-fourth of the city's population.

The single-member district can become provincial. It lends itself to the emergence of demagogues who would never be elected citywide or countywide but who can base their appeal on narrow, emotional issues to win within their district. Many argue that single-member districts heighten rather than relieve racial tensions. This has been the highly disputed claim made in some communities which have gone from an at-large to a district system. Some claim that under the new system there are now more members with strong racial biases sitting on the council than ever before.

AT-LARGE ELECTIONS

The movement toward at-large elections was largely a product of the Progressive era and subsequent periods in which civic reform efforts sought to eliminate political machines. Immediately prior to the Second World War most big cities in the United States (and many smaller communities throughout the northeast and midwest) were controlled by powerful local political organizations. The general rise in the educational level, increased prosperity, the Americanization of the pre-war European immigrant groups and a general revulsion against politics as usual led hundreds of communities to switch to at-large elections.

Frequently this movement was coupled with the abandonment of partisan elections, at least to the extent that the national political parties were forbidden to run local candidates under their label. Often, local political parties evolved, for example, the Charter party in Cincinnati. These were coalitions of civic-minded individuals who would work together for the election of a slate for the city council in opposition to the two national parties.

The at-large election system is credited with the defeat of the political machine, with bringing to the council people who perforce must view the problems of the community as a whole and thus be more apt to take a long-range view, and, in conjunction with nonpartisan elections, with encouraging people who would otherwise be unwilling to run (for fear of being tainted by the label "politician") to seek public office as a civic responsibility.

Under an at-large system it is not unusual for all or a majority of members of the council to come from a small section of the city or county. Councils elected at large, particularly in small-to-medium size cities, tend to be composed of upper middle-class Caucasians, generally Protestant. Although there are exceptions, the "establishment" invariably dominates the council.

Many claim the resulting councils fail to represent or understand large numbers of minority group members and the lower middle-class, blue-collar worker. Such councils are accused of being the country-club set, willing to undertake grandiose capital investments for the beautification of the downtown business district, the development of a shopping mall, and other such modernization projects, but unaware of the potentially devastating social and economic impact on the lives of the economically deprived residents of the community.

At-large elections can also lend themselves to rather violent shifts in public sentiment within the community. Even though most communities stagger the terms of the councilmembers, majority control is usually determined in each election. It is not unusual, therefore, for a moderately progressive council to be suddenly swept out and replaced by a sternly reactionary one; conversely, the extended student franchise can and has resulted in sudden radical victory. A steady reform movement can be overturned with one spectacular election (sometimes associated with national, not local, political trends). Such fits and starts are highly detrimental to community unity.

The increasing alienation of the public is frequently attributed to the at-large election system by its opponents. People are less aware of who their councilmembers are and know the names of only one or two prominent individuals.

Running at large tends to favor candidates who have more campaign money or those who have already built up a substantial reputation through the newspapers and other media. Their prominence in business affairs may be unrelated to their abilities to govern a city but their greater notoriety gives them disproportionate advantage in an election.

Ironically, on the county level, at-large elections may foster or perpetuate a political machine—exactly the reverse of earlier municipal experience. Most of the rural "courthouse gangs" are located in counties with at-large systems.

VARIATIONS OF THE AT-LARGE SYSTEM

In order to eliminate some of the weaknesses of the system, many variations have been developed.

Councilmembers are nominated by district and elected at large. The advantage is that this gives geographic representation to the council. The public knows who the district councilmember is and who to hold responsible for attention to neighborhood problems. At the same time, since the representatives are elected citywide or countywide they cannot afford to be provincial in attitude and stand as a stumbling block to community progress.

The disadvantage is that frequently the majority segment of the community will have the dominant voice in the election of representatives from minority districts. Many blacks feel this is worse than no representation at all, as it tends to confuse members of the black community, dividing them and placing them in an untenable position.

Some communities try to rectify these problems by having single-member districts and at-large elections. Single-member districts have residency requirements, the at-large seats do not. Geographic representation is preserved yet there are enough at-large representatives to ensure consideration of city/county problems. One criticism of this system is that those who are elected at large frequently consider themselves more important than the district representatives. Also, the at-large councilmen may view themselves as potential rivals of the mayor or county executive.

The place system. With this device candidates run for a specifically numbered council seat. They are, therefore, running against only those people who file for that seat, not against the whole field. Many believe this system, which first began in the south, was racially inspired. It prevented the so-called bullet vote by the black community.

Bullet voting is a process by which any substantial minority, be it political, racial or ethnic, may bring to bear its full power by concentrating its vote on a single seat. For example, in an at-large election with five offices to be filled, there might be nine major candidates running, and two or three others without much chance. A majority of the total vote is not required, the five with the highest vote are elected. Each person can vote for five candidates.

By concentrating their strength and casting a single vote for only one person, none of the minority group's four other votes goes to add to the totals of other candidates. The odds are very good that the candidate of the group that bullet votes will finish as one of the top five. Many criticize this practice. While their "own" person might not win if the minority exercised the full franchise, they might easily help elect two or three "friendly" candidates. Many times a group will feel it is worth the cost. It requires a thorough "get out the vote" campaign and disciplined leadership for a group to use bullet voting but it has had many notable successes.

The place system has advantages and disadvantages. A popular member of the council may well have no opponent file for the seat, thus assuring automatic reelection. It is also possible for one contest to be rather uninspired, drawing relatively few voters, while another seat may be hotly contested. Last-minute filing for a position also can lead to a variety of surprising developments.

Proportional representation, which is now used in only one city (Cambridge, Massachusetts) used to be much more popular. (It is also used for New York City's community school boards elections, and by some universities, labor and professional associations.)

The system became suspect when communist members were elected to the New York City council, and in 1946 the communists and proportional representation were defeated. The "un-American" argument was used elsewhere, and Cincinnati, Cleveland and several other cities abandoned proportional representation in the following few years.

This is a complex system whereby voters mark their first, second, third, etc., choices for various candidates. Seats are thus filled by an at-large election with a system of preferential voting. Proportional representation most accurately reflects all the elements within a community, and, since the election is at large, candidates are rarely tied to a single geographic area. It makes it possible for nonparty people to win and for all segments of the population to gain representation.

This virtue can be a vice. If there is substantial extremist sentiment within the community, candidates can make narrow appeals to these groups and will be assured of election, one of the disadvantages of the district system. It is, however, far more accurate in representing the people, and no sizable minority is totally deprived of a voice, as can happen in either the district or other at-large systems.

Cumulative voting. Illinois uses cumulative voting for its House of Representatives. Each voter may cast three ballots, which is equal to the total number of representatives to be elected to each district. The voter may then cast all three votes for one candidate, two for one and one for another, one for each of three candidates or one and one-half for each of two candidates. Unfortunately, the parties might nominate only the number of candidates they expect to win in that district. The primary then becomes the more important election, frequently dominated by machine politics.

Weighted voting, still constitutionally suspect, is used in a few county governments in New York and Illinois. There is no ready example of its use on the municipal level. Under this system a legislator casts a number of votes on the council weighted according to the number of people in the district. This is utilized in county government, as it allows preservation of town or township boundaries. Critics claim this distorts the true representative system, granting undue power to the opinion of a single legislator casting multiple votes.

Limited voting is widely used throughout Connecticut, in Philadelphia, and on a modified scale in New York City. In a community like Hartford the system works in this way: There are nine members of the city council to be elected, and each citizen may vote for six. Thus the major party is pretty well assured of gaining a two-thirds majority of the council while the minority is still certain of getting at least one-third. If people are voting along ethnic lines, it also assists in representation of the minority group.

Variations can appear and in some instances the majority party may deliberately nominate only the number of candidates it expects to win, and the minority party will take similar action. In this way the outcome of the final elections has already been decided.

The system is also constitutionally suspect, although it has generally been upheld in the lower courts. A minority within a community may represent 45 percent of the population, not one-third. Yet the very nature of limited voting establishes from the beginning a set percentage of the seats that will go to the minority irrespective of numbers. It can result in either their over- or under-representation and is suspect on the basis of one man, one vote.

There is also the problem of whether or not the city has primaries or runoff elections. There is a great deal of variety here. Some communities have nominations by party caucus, others by an open primary, and still others by a closed primary (in partisan elections where only the enrolled members of the party may take part). The primaries can be settled on a straight plurality basis or, if there is no clear-cut winner, there can be a runoff. This can be further refined by using preferential voting in the primary, making a runoff unnecessary. Under that system a person would vote for first, second and third choice of candidates for a single office. Its virtue is that, if there are large factions within the community or political party, a person who represents the plurality faction but is very unpopular with all others could not win the party's nomination.

To determine the right system each community must study and work within the framework of its own political tradition.

14

Runoff Primaries

LORN FOSTER

I would like to thank the members of the sub-committee for the opportunity to present my views on the issue of runoff primaries which are held in nine Southern States and Oklahoma. This issue, which Rev. Jesse Jackson brought to national attention during his campaign for the Democratic Party's presidential nomination, is a matter of great importance; the members of the subcommittee should be commended for investigating this issue.

Reverend Jackson, among others, contends that runoff primaries, also known as second primaries, discriminate against minorities by reducing minority candidates' chances of winning their party's nomination for office. If three or more candidates run for nomination in a partisan primary and none receives a majority of the votes cast, several States require a runoff or second primary. In the runoff, only the two highest vote getters compete, and the winner is the party's nominee.

In a number of contests for elective office—Federal, State and local—black candidates have led in the first primary while two or more white candidates have divided white voters. In the second primary, however, white voters united behind the remaining white candidate and, since the black population is probably a minority, the black candidate was defeated. The runoff primary generally has a negative effect upon blacks in districts in which they are a minority and there is a racial block voting.

The most often cited example of this is the 1982 Democratic congressional primary in North Carolina's second district. There H. M. "Mickey" Michaux, a black candidate, led in the first primary with 44.5 percent of the vote, but lost in the runoff when white voters coalesced behind Tim Valentine, a white candidate who had received only 32.7 percent of the vote in the first round.

Jackson argues that the Michaux-Valentine race is indicative of the runoff's discriminatory effect on minority candidates. But before examining this proposition, a look at circumstances in which runoff primaries were adopted will help us put present problems in their historical context.

Southern States began to institute runoff primaries around the turn of the century during the same period in which statewide "white primaries" were begun. South Carolina began using runoff primaries in 1896, and Mississippi became the State to mandate runoffs by law in 1902. By 1939, nine Southern States had adopted the procedure.

Because runoff primaries were instituted at the same time States were disenfranchising blacks by other means, some analysts have concluded that runoffs were not intentionally discriminatory. These analysts linked the procedure to the existence of one party politics in the South. Runoff primaries, they argue, facilitated intraparty factional competition by allowing several candidates to vie for the nomi-

Hearings before the Subcommittee on Civil and Constitutional Rights of the Committee on the Judiciary, U.S. House of Representatives, 98th Congress, 2nd Session. *Voting Rights Act: Runoff Primaries and Registration Barriers.* Serial No. 119, June 28 and July 26, 1984, pp. 15–18. (Washington, D.C.: U.S. Government Printing Office, 1985).

nation without sacrificing majority decisions.

Other analysts, however, believe that the runoff primaries were intended to reinforce the exclusion of blacks from political power. According to this view, significant numbers of blacks continued to vote in the South even after "disenfranchisement" was well underway (9 percent of blacks in Mississippi in 1896 and 14–15 percent in South Carolina and Virginia in 1904 were registered to vote). Black political participation, no matter how slight a deviation from complete black subordination, horrified many white supremacists. They feared that opposing politicians might abandon their allegiance to white supremacy and form political alliances with the large pool of potential black voters.

Runoff primaries were probably intended both to facilitate intraparty competition and to exclude blacks. The runoff primary protected Southern Democratic Parties from external opposition—particularly opposition by blacks or by groups making appeals to blacks. Thus, the exclusion of black voters or dilution of their votes has shaped the character of southern politics for nearly a century.

Those who argue most strongly for the abolition of runoff primaries focus on the experience of black candidates. In jurisdictions where there is a large but less than majority black population and there is racial block voting, black candidates who win in the first primary are often defeated in the second. This was true for H. M. Michaux in North Carolina, James Clyburn of South Carolina, Charles Evers of Mississippi, and many others.

It is possible, however, for runoff primaries to benefit black candidates. In a district with a solid black majority, for example, it could give blacks the same advantage it now gives whites, allowing the black vote to split candidates in the first round but coalesce in the second in support of the black frontrunner. This would be possible in three southern congressional districts: Georgia's fifth, Louisiana's second, and Mississippi's second.

As the American political scene changes, runoff primaries may become more helpful to blacks. For example, some political scientists suggest that as blacks become more successful at winning primaries and elections, it will be increasingly difficult to maintain unity behind a single minority candidate. Similarly, problems may arise in States with two different but sizable minority populations. In Texas, for example, blacks and Hispanics have often agreed on a single candidate in an election. But if more minority candidates seek office—which seems likely, particularly if runoffs are eliminated—the runoff might work to the advantage of the minority candidate.

Runoff primaries, however, have rarely worked to the advantage of the minority candidates. There are very few districts in which blacks are a majority. As long as white majorities and racial block voting are the rule—and it appears that they will be for some time to come—runoff primaries are not likely to be helpful to minority/black candidates.

Some supporters of the runoff primary argue that the runoff encourages white candidates to seek coalitions across racial lines and thus increases the influence of black voters. According to this argument, runoffs may indirectly benefit the black community, even if it hurts black candidates. In a runoff between two whites, the candidates might compete for the black vote by showing responsiveness to black concerns.

Mississippi Gov. William Winter's victory in 1979 and Lester Maddox's loss in 1974 were cited frequently as examples of moderate or liberal whites who came in second in the first primaries but won in runoffs. These moderate or liberal whites presumably are more responsive in minority concerns than their conservative counterparts would be.

There are two problems with this argument. First, there are an equal number of cases in which the moderate or liberal candidate has lost in the second primary. In 1966, for example, Lester Maddox defeated a more moderate candidate in the runoff after losing in the first primary.

Second, blacks are often placed in the position of choosing the lesser of two evils. The issue becomes not who will best represent black interests, but who will be least antagonistic to black interests. In these cases, the interests of blacks essentially are left unrepresented. Moreover, there is no reason that blacks should have to rely completely on whites, however liberal they may be, to represent black interests.

Another argument is that runoff primaries enhance majority rule and ensure broad-based community support. The majority requirement is also supposed to increase the chances of eliminating extremist candidates.

American politics, however, relies overwhelmingly on plurality elections. Forty of the fifty States and the vast majority of municipalities do not require a majority vote to nominate or elect the candidate. Moreover, turnout usually decreases in runoff elections. In fact, the winning candidate in the second round sometimes occasionally receives fewer votes than the frontrunner did in the first round. In the 1972 Texas senatorial primary, for example, turnout decreased by 130,000 votes as Harold Barefoot Sanders defeated Ralph Yarborough—even though Yarborough received 25,000 more votes in the first primary than Sanders did in the second.

Ironically, the jurisdictions that have insisted on majority vote requirements are the very ones that have historically maintained major barriers to voting.

Another major argument in favor of runoff primaries is that their elimination will not necessarily increase the number of black office holders. Some analysts contend that eliminating the runoff may make it easier for blacks to win nominations, but not general elections.

Robert Clark of Mississippi, for example, ran for Congress in 1982 and won the first primary with a clear majority. Despite being the Democratic nominee and having some strong white support—most notably from Gov. William Winter—Clark lost the general election to a white Republican. Winning the nomination does not guarantee winning the election even in solidly Democratic States.

The problem, according to this argument, is racism, not the electoral process. Since objections to runoff primaries are based on the existence of racially based voting, it is reasonable to assume that many white Democrats would vote Republican rather than support a black Democratic nominee.

The elimination of runoff primaries would probably allow large minority groups to win more nominations. This could set off a chain reaction: If the chances for nomination are better, more minority candidates will be encouraged to run for office. This could lead to increased political participation by minorities, and to the election of more minority candidates to office.

15

Sex and the Second Primary[1]

CHARLES S. BULLOCK III AND LOCH K. JOHNSON

The 1984 presidential candidacy of the Reverend Jesse Jackson focused public attention on the controversy over the second, or runoff, primary.[2] "We demand an end to second primaries," he often declared on the campaign trail (see, for example, Mollison, 1984, and Jackson, 1984a). As the first serious black presidential contender, Jackson brought widespread attention to an argument that had previously been confined chiefly to litigation (see, for example, *White* v. *Register*, 1973, and *Zimmer* v. *McKeithen*, 1973). He argued that nomination rules requiring a candidate to win a majority (rather than a plurality) of the votes cast dilute the influence of minorities in the electoral process.

In Jackson's view, blacks are not the only group disadvantaged by the runoff procedure. Women and Hispanics—part of his "rainbow coalition"—are affected in a similar way: white males and their supporters rally in the second primary to thwart the ambitions of women and minority groups. Jackson has projected that eliminating runoff primaries would lead to "the addition of 10 to 15 blacks or women to the U.S. Congress" and this "could be dramatic inasmuch as progressive legislation such as the nuclear freeze or the ERA, which both lost by narrow margins, might be passed" (Jackson, 1984b: sec. D, p. 7). If Jackson is accurate, even larger numbers of women and racial minorities would be elected to state and local governing bodies but for the runoff requirement. Eleanor Smeal, past president of the National Organization for Women (NOW), agreed with the Jackson perspective. The runoff is "no help to women," she emphasized in June 1984 (Smeal, 1984).

This research examines the effect of runoff primaries on the candidacies of women. It will be insufficient to sustain the Jackson-Smeal proposition merely to show that some women who led in the primary lost the runoff. A similar fate has greeted many male primary leaders. To build a case that runoffs are unfair to women, it is necessary to show that the results of runoffs involving women differ from all-male second primaries. Specifically, if runoffs are biased against women, then females who were front-runners in primaries will win runoffs less often than male front-runners. The fate of female front-runners will be compared with that of males who led going into male-female runoffs and males who led **prior to male-male runoffs.** Our test of the Jackson-Smeal hypothesis incorporates a multi-state and multi-year data set. Several potential correlates of a runoff bias against women—should bias exist—will be considered. These include the office contested, time, subregion, and competitiveness in the first primary.

FACTORS THAT MIGHT AFFECT WOMEN IN RUNOFFS

Runoffs are criticized because they can alter the outcome produced by the first primary.

Reprinted from *Social Science Quarterly*, Vol.66, No.4 (December 1985), pp. 933–942, by permission of the authors and the University of Texas Press.

They give the runner-up a second opportunity to win the nomination by attracting the followers of the other candidates bested by the primary leader. Using a variety of appeals, the runner-up will seek to expand his/her base of support. Overtures may stress ideology, play up the notion of the "little guys" fighting against the front-runner, call for a rallying of friends and neighbors, offer future considerations for the followers of the eliminated candidates, bid for endorsements from the eliminated candidates by offering to help retire their campaign debts (Ewing, 1953/1980), and so forth.

While it is uncommon for a male facing a woman in a runoff to call openly upon men to unite and defeat her, runoffs could disadvantage women in two ways. A woman might win a plurality in a multi-candidate field. However when she faces a single male in the runoff, she might lose because some voters doubt that women have the temperament or training to excel as officeholders (Deckard, 1983:304; Chamberlin, 1973:258; Costantini and Craik, 1972; Tolchin and Tolchin, 1974; Lee, 1977; Boneparth, 1977), or because of opposition to policy stands associated with women or the women's movement (Hill, 1981; Mandel, 1981). Second primaries may also handicap women because of their added cost. Women may encounter more difficulties than men in raising campaign funds and therefore be dependent on volunteers who must be mobilized again (Deckard, 1983:367; Currey, 1977).[3]

To the extent that some voters oppose the election of women for sex-related reasons, they may be more numerous or hold their beliefs with greater intensity when prominent offices are at stake. There may be more voters who hesitate to vote for a woman for governor, senator, or other statewide positions than for the state legislature or a local office. The history of officeholding by women supports the possibility of a higher-office bias. Victorious campaigns for more prominent offices have come less often and more recently than the winning of lower offices (Deckard,

1983:362–67). Women have had greater success in winning city council than mayoral positions (Welch and Karnig, 1979; Karnig and Walter, 1976; Merritt, 1977) and in winning seats in the lower than the upper chamber of state legislatures (Diamond, 1977). In a survey of Milwaukee voters, Hedland et al. (1979) found less willingness to support a woman candidate for a judgeship than for a school board seat, thus indicating that the office at stake makes a difference. Whether a bias exists against women seeking higher offices will be explored by looking at election results for four sets of positions.

A second variable that might be associated with a sex bias in runoffs is time. The last 20 years have witnessed major changes in sex roles. Millions of women fill a variety of positions that in the past were predominantly, if not wholly, the preserve of males. More women actively campaign for political office than ever before; today, for the first time, there are two women in the U.S. Senate in their own right, without having "inherited" the seat of a deceased husband. Moreover, the number of women in Congress stands at an all-time high with most of them having achieved the position through their own political skills and not those of their former husbands as was common in the past (Gertzog, 1979). The number of women in state legislatures is at an all-time high, too: 1,076. The presence of growing numbers of women in public office suggests that the public has become more willing to vote for female candidates. Therefore we expect less evidence that women will be disadvantaged in runoffs now than earlier.

A third variable is the state in which the runoff occurs. Historically the Deep South has been considered to be less progressive than the Rim South (Havard, 1972). If traditional ideas about a woman's role are tied to a more general opposition to change, then women may encounter greater difficulties in Deep South states than in the remainder of the region. Deep south is here defined as Alabama, Georgia, Louisiana,[4] Mississippi, and South

Carolina; the Rim South consists of Arkansas, Florida, North Carolina, Oklahoma, and Texas. These are the only states that use a runoff system for offices above the local level.

A fourth variable is the number of candidates in the primary. In a multi-candidate primary field, the vote is more fractured and, with a larger share of it up for grabs, the runoff is less predictable. The larger the field in the primary, the more important the personalities of the candidates (or other variables difficult to quantify) may be in the runoff (cf. Key, 1949:97). At this point we have no reason to expect that the heightened unpredictability produced by a large initial field will either adversely or favorably affect female candidacies.

A fifth variable is the vote margin that the primary leader held over the runner-up. We expect that regardless of whether one of the runoff candidates is female, the likelihood that the primary front-runner will win the runoff is positively related to the size of the lead over the primary runner-up.

Incumbency is the sixth variable. Studies of elections for various offices have found that incumbents are advantaged (Bibby et al., 1982; Common Cause, 1977; Shin and Jackson, 1979). And while incumbents who are forced into runoffs are less likely to be re-elected than are incumbents generally, Georgia incumbents won 55.5 percent of their runoffs over two decades (Bullock and Johnson, 1985). This figure, however, is little better than what would occur by chance. Therefore we expect that the presence of an incumbent will have little effect on the success of women in runoffs.

To this point, the concern has been with whether the leader in the primary has the momentum to capture the nomination. A very different perspective is that of the candidate who acknowledges the greater initial strength of an opponent but hopes that the leader will be denied majority support in the first primary. The first objective of the weaker candidate is to get into a runoff with the leader. If

that is achieved, then the runner-up will try to unite the majority of the voters whose first choice was not the primary leader.

In this paper male-versus-male runoffs are used as a benchmark against which to compare runoffs that include a woman. The first topic analyzed is the extent to which runoffs alter the order of finish from the primary. Next we consider whether the order of finish is altered more often in runoffs when a woman, rather than a man, led the first primary.

DATA

This paper is based on 834 runoff elections in the 10 states that use this system to select nominees when no candidate wins a majority in the initial primary. The time period is 1970–83. Of special interest are the 109 runoffs that involved a woman. Results for contests in which a woman participated will be compared with the outcomes of all-male runoffs. The objective is to determine if the presence of a woman affects the results and if women are disadvantaged by the use of runoffs.

The bulk of the elections analyzed are for the lower chambers of state legislatures. In addition, runoffs for state senates, the U.S. House and Senate, and statewide nonjudicial offices are included. While there are runoffs from all 10 states, only congressional and gubernatorial elections were included from Alabama, North Carolina, and South Carolina since these states do not make available primary and runoff results. The returns for the congressional and gubernatorial elections were culled from appropriate issues of the *Congressional Quarterly Weekly Report*. Results from Texas are more complete than for the three states discussed above, but do not include figures on the state house since these are not readily available. Data on state legislative primaries and runoffs were obtained from state officials in the other states.[5]

RESULTS

The first objective of this research is to determine whether primary front-runners fare better or worse in runoffs with a woman. When a woman is in the runoff, the primary leader holds on to win 80.7 percent of the time. In all-male contests, the front-runner wins the runoff 66.8 percent of the time. When women led the primary, they won 76.6 percent of the runoffs. Men in runoffs with a woman who finished second won 85.5 percent of the time. The success rate for female front-runners falls between that of males who led other males and males who led women in the primary.

Runoffs obviously do not deny women the opportunity to hold office. Of 47 women who would have been elected in a plurality system, 36 won runoffs. Another 9 women who would have lost in a plurality system overcame a deficit in the primary and won the runoff. Consequently, the 109 runoffs involving women produced only 2 fewer female elected officials than a plurality rule would have. The number of women elected is almost the same, but the identities of the winners differ since 9 runners-up are substituted for 11 front-runners.

While women win runoffs more than three-fourths of the time after leading in the primary, some conditions may enhance the chances for success. Also to be explored is whether women who come from behind to win runoffs share common features.

As was hypothesized, women have less success when seeking higher offices. Although there are few cases, Table 1 shows that women front-runners in contests for Congress and statewide positions are less successful than those seeking state legislative positions. However female front-runners' success compares favorably with that of front-runners in all-male runoffs. Differentiation by office does not carry over to female-

TABLE 1. SUCCESS IN RUNOFFS, CONTROLLING FOR OFFICE

| | Women's Place in Primary | | Success of Primary Leaders in All-Male Runoffs |
	1st	2d	
Statewide			
Woman won	50.0%	0.0%	57.1%
Woman lost	50.0%	100.0%	
(N)	(2)	(5)	(42)
U.S. House			
Woman won	66.7%	50.0%	64.8%
Woman lost	33.3%	50.0%	
(N)	(6)	(2)	(74)
State Senate			
Woman won	85.7%	0.0%	67.4%
Woman lost	14.3%	100.0%	
(N)	(7)	(8)	(144)
State House			
Woman won	78.1%	17.0%	67.7%
Woman lost	21.9%	83.0%	
(N)	(32)	(47)	(465)

TABLE 2. SUCCESS IN RUNOFFS, CONTROLLING FOR SUBREGION

	Women's Place in Primary		Success of Primary Leaders in All-Male Runoffs
	1st	2d	
Deep South			
Woman won	81.3%	17.9%	67.2%
Woman lost	18.8%	82.1%	
(N)	(16)	(28)	(391)
Rim South			
Woman won	74.2%	11.8%	66.2%
Woman lost	25.8%	88.2%	
(N)	(31)	(34)	(334)

male runoffs in which the male led the primary. Women almost always lose after a second place finish in the primary and do worse than similarly situated males, regardless of the sex of the males' opponent.

Contrary to expectations, women in the Deep South do better than their sisters in the Rim South. Success rates for Deep South women are at least 6 percentage points higher than Rim South women, *regardless of whether they ran first or second in the primary.* (See Table 2.) Moreover, female primary leaders in the Deep South win 14 percent more of the runoffs than do males who led prior to all-male runoffs. Deep South results give no evidence of sexual bias, with female front-runners winning at the same rate as do male front-runners who had a female opponent in the runoff. In the Rim South, women primary leaders do 14 points less well than males who led against women but are 8 points more successful than primary leaders in male-male runoffs. This hints at the possibility that Rim South voters are less willing to vote for women.

Dichotomizing the time period reveals no change in the success rates of female front-runners. Table 3 does indicate, however, that women who place *second* are twice as likely to overtake male primary leaders during the more recent period. This is an encouraging omen for women who run second and

provides some support for the hypothesized relationship with time. Since 1977 the sexes have differed little in their success in female-male contests, with female primary leaders winning 76.9 percent of their runoffs while male primary leaders won 79.3 percent of the time. Success rates for leaders in male-male runoffs are similar for both periods and are much below the rates in female-male contests.

The number of candidates in the primary has no consistent relationship to the success of female primary front-runners or those who finish second in the primary.[6] While variations exist, success rates fail to increase or decrease in step with the number of primary candidates. Our initial null hypothesis is borne out.

Size of the vote margin in the primary is not linearly related to women's runoff success. While all women front-runners with the largest vote margins in the primary won runoffs (fourth quartile), the least successful were not those who had the smallest percentage point leads in the primary. Instead, as Table 4 shows, the least successful female front-runners were in the second quartile. Among women who ran second in the primary, those who trailed by the narrowest margins overcame the initial deficit in 38.9 percent of the cases. Women runners-up not in the first quartile were less successful, winning only 3

TABLE 3. SUCCESS IN RUNOFFS, CONTROLLING FOR YEAR

	Women's Place in Primary		Success of Primary Leaders in All-Male Runoffs
	1st	2d	
1970–76			
Woman won	76.2%	9.1%	67.6%
Woman lost	23.8%	90.9%	
(N)	(21)	(33)	(408)
1977–82			
Woman won	76.9%	20.7%	65.6%
Woman lost	23.1%	79.3%	
(N)	(26)	(29)	(317)

of 44 runoffs. Female runners-up are less likely to win nominations than are male runners-up in female-male runoffs in the intermediate categories. Women who enter runoffs with a small deficit are more successful (38.9 percent) than are comparably situated male runners-up who faced women (20.0 percent victorious), but less successful than are males who were narrowly behind prior to male-male runoffs (46.0 percent). Only all-

TABLE 4. SUCCESS IN RUNOFFS, CONTROLLING FOR SIZE OF PRIMARY MARGIN

	Women's Place in Primary		Success of Primary Leaders in All-Male Runoffs
	1st	2d	
First Quartile (Smallest Primary Margin)			
Woman won	80.0%	38.9%	54.0%
Woman lost	20.0%	61.1%	
(N)	(10)	(18)	(213)
Second Quartile			
Woman won	60.0%	9.1%	61.7%
Woman lost	40.0%	90.9%	
(N)	(15)	(11)	(206)
Third Quartile			
Woman won	72.7%	6.3%	73.1%
Woman lost	27.3%	93.7%	
(N)	(11)	(16)	(141)
Fourth Quartile (Largest Primary Margin)			
Woman won	100.0%	5.9%	84.9%
Woman lost	0.0%	94.1%	
(N)	(11)	(17)	(165)

NOTE. First quartile has the most closely contested primaries, i.e., those in which the front-runner has the smallest margin measured in percentage points over the candidate who finished second. Quartiles are based on the distribution for runoffs involving women.

male runoffs conformed to the anticipated pattern, that is, runoff success increased with the size of the primary margin.

Women front-runners do worse when there is an incumbent running than when competing for an open seat.[7] The small number of instances in which there was an incumbent in female-male runoffs keeps us from making much of this finding.

Results thus far have been bivariate. To determine if differences observed in the bivariate analysis hold up, multivariate logic was used. The dependent variable is whether the candidate who led the primary field also won the runoff. Independent variables considered were whether a woman was in the runoff, the number of candidates in the first primary, whether one runoff candidate was an incumbent, a dichotomous measure for subregion, four dummy variables for the office contested, and a set of dummies for the year of the election.

Several models were estimated; incumbency and whether there was a woman were the only statistically significant variables. In confirmation of the bivariate results, the primary front-runner is more successful when one of the runoff candidates is female. The presence of an incumbent reduced the likelihood that the recipient of the primary plurality would win the runoff. Although not statistically significant, there is some indication that primary winners are more successful in state legislative contests than when other positions are at stake, as was reported in Table 1. Subregion is less strongly related to runoff success and therefore was not included in Table 5. Inclusion of subregion results in incumbency no longer achieving statistical significance. When separate models were estimated for each election year, it was rare for any variable to be significant.

SUMMARY AND CONCLUSIONS

Contrary to the Jackson-Smeal proposition, uniform discrimination against women front-runners was not found here. Women who won pluralities in primaries were more likely to win runoffs than were male primary leaders in all-male runoffs. Three-fourths of the female front-runners won, compared with 67 percent of the men who led going into all-male second primaries. A hint of voter bias against women comes from the high success rate of males who led women in the primary. These males won 85.5 percent of the time.

Closer inspection raises an alternative explanation to bias to account for the difference in the success rate of female and male primary

TABLE 5. MULTIVARIATE MODEL OF RUNOFF SUCCESS

WIN = 0.452 − 0.366* INC + 0.801** SEX + 0.434 STHOUSE + 0.341 **STSEN**
         (.184)   (.285)   (.278)   (.213)

   Chi-square = 16.39**
   Correct predictions = 67.2%

WIN: Primary leader wins runoff
INC: Incumbent involved in the runoff
SEX: Woman involved in the runoff
STHOUSE: State house election
STSEN: State senate election

NOTE. Standard errors are given in parentheses.
  * $p < .05$.
  ** $p < .01$.

leaders. The greater success of males results from the poor showing of women who trailed in the primary by moderate amounts. As reported in Table 4, in the second quartile women runners-up won only 9 percent of the runoffs—far below the 40 percent success rate of males who trailed females or the 38.3 percent success rate of males who trailed other males by comparable amounts. A similar pattern exists in the third quartile. Perhaps these patterns stem from the difficulties women have often had in soliciting campaign funds (Deckard, 1983:367). Candidates who seem less likely to overtake the front-runner may find funds especially scarce (cf., Jacobson and Kernell, 1981:35–36). Women not close on the heels of a male front-runner may have more difficulty raising money than comparably situated males, especially when competing in more expensive statewide or congressional contests.

The frequency with which women who got pluralities—even narrow pluralities—go on to win nominations demonstrates that the second primary is not an insurmountable obstacle for strong women candidates. There was no change in the incidence of success for female front-runners across time. The only longitudinal change has been a stronger showing in recent years by women who finished second in the primary. This may reflect changing voter attitudes or better-run campaigns as women gain more political experience.

Some female candidates may hope that if only they can squeak through to qualify for a runoff, then they might augment their coalition with support from candidates who were eliminated. The finding here indicates the limited conditions under which such hopes may be realized. If a woman does not run a close second, she has little chance of ultimately winning the nomination.

While female primary leaders are less likely to win nominations when seeking the more prestigious positions, their rate of success (57.1 percent for statewide and congres-

sional elections) approaches that for males who lead going into all-male runoffs (62.1 percent). Even where women front-runners are least successful, they fare little worse than comparable males.[8]

Since their sex does not preclude women from winning runoffs, other variables must account for instances in which female front-runners lose. Factors that may play a role include campaign funding and other resources, charisma, name recognition, political organizational ties, and the issue or ideological stands of the candidates, with a bias against liberals in some areas (see Currey, 1977). SSQ

NOTES

1. We appreciate the work of our research assistants Randy Austin and Bobby Reid
2. On the runoff primary, see Key (1949, 1964) and Bullock and Johnson (1985).
3. For an overview of barriers faced by women in politics, see Carden (1974), Chafe (1972), Flexner (1959), Freeman (1975), Jaquette (1974), Lewis and Baidema (1972), and Ware (1970).
4. Louisiana is included as a runoff state although its electoral system is unique. Candidates who win majorities in its nonpartisan first election are elected. When no one wins a majority, a runoff is held between the top two finishers to determine the officeholder.
5. Efforts to obtain primary and runoff election results met with varying degrees of success. In addition to the gaps noted in the text, results for some years were unavailable from some states. Oklahoma state legislative results begin with 1972 and those from Louisiana and Mississippi begin with 1975.
6. This and other tables that show no difference across categories have not been presented in order to conserve space but can be obtained from the authors.
7. We did not have materials available from which to determine the incumbency status of all elections. We were particularly likely to lack this information for the earlier years.
8. There is some difficulty in determining the presence of female candidates from official returns. It is impossible to identify blacks on official re-

turns. We have made a limited effort to discover black-versus-white runoffs, primarily in urban areas of Georgia, by reviewing newspaper accounts. Our conclusion based on a small, urban Georgia sample is that black primary leaders lose runoffs at about the same rate as white primary leaders (Bullock & Johnson, 1985). Whether this finding holds up in other contexts remains to be seen.

REFERENCES

Bibby, John F., Michael J. Malbin, Thomas E. Mann, and Norman J. Ornstein. 1982. *Vital Statistics on Congress, 1982* (Washington, D.C.: American Enterprise Institute).

Boneparth, Ellen. 1977. "Women in Campaigns—From Lickin' and Stickin' to Strategy," *American Politics Quarterly*, 5 (July):289–300.

Bullock, Charles S., III, and Loch K. Johnson. 1985. "Runoff Elections in Georgia," *Journal of Politics*, 47 (August):936–46.

Carden, Maren Lockwood. 1974. *The New Feminist Movement* (New York: Russell Sage Foundation).

Chafe, William Henry. 1972. *The American Woman: Her Changing Social, Economic and Political Roles, 1920–1970* (New York: Oxford University Press).

Chamberlin, Hope. 1973. *A Minority of Members, Women in the U.S. Congress* (New York: Praeger).

Common Cause. 1977. *In Common*, 8 (Fall):28.

Costantini, E., and K. H. Craik. 1972. "Women as Politicians: The Social Background, Personality, and Political Careers of Female Party Leaders," *Journal of Social Issues*, 28 (2):217–36.

Currey, Virginia. 1977. "Campaign Theory and Practice—The Sender Variable," in Marianne Githens and Jewel Prestage, eds., *A Portrait of Marginality* (New York: David McKay): pp. 150–71.

Deckard, Barbara Sinclair. 1983. *The Women's Movement*, 3d ed. (New York: Harper & Row).

Diamond, Irene. 1977. *Sex Roles in the Statehouse* (New Haven: Yale University Press).

Ewing, Cortez A. M. 1953. *Primary Elections in the South: A Study in Uniparty Politics*. Reprint ed. (Westport, Conn.: Greenwood, 1980).

Flexner, Eleanor. 1959. *Century of Struggle* (Cambridge: Harvard University Press).

Freeman, Jo. 1975. *The Politics of Women's Liberation* (New York: Longman).

Gertzog, Irwin N. 1979. "Changing Patterns of Female Recruitment to the U.S. House of Representatives," *Legislative Studies Quarterly*, 4 (August):429–45.

Havard, William C., ed. 1972. *The Changing Politics of the South* (Baton Rouge: Louisiana State University Press).

Hedland, Ronald D., Patricia K. Freeman, Keith E. Hamm, and Robert M. Stein. 1979. "The Electability of Women Candidates: The Effects of Sex Role Stereotypes," *Journal of Politics*, 41 (May):513–24.

Hill, David B. 1981. "Political Culture and Female Political Representation," *Journal of Politics*, 43 (February):159–68.

Jackson, Jesse. 1984a. "Moving to the Common Ground," *Washington Post* (National Edition), 9 April 1984.

———. 1984b. "Rainbow Coalition is a Success," *Atlanta Journal and Constitution*, 22 April 1984, sec. D, p. 7.

Jacobson, Gary C., and Samuel Kernell, 1981. *Strategy and Choice in Congressional Elections* (New Haven: Yale University Press).

Jaquette, Jane. 1974. *Women in Politics* (New York: Wiley).

Karnig, Albert K., and Oliver B. Walter. 1976. "Election of Women to City Councils," *Social Science Quarterly*, 56 (December):605–14.

Key, V. O., Jr. 1949. *Southern Politics in State and Nation* (New York: Knopf).

———. 1964. *Politics, Parties, and Pressure Groups*. 5th ed. (New York: Crowell).

Lee, Marcia M. 1977. "Toward Understanding Why Few Women Hold Public Office," in Marianne Githens and Jewel Prestage, eds., *A Portrait of Marginality* (New York: David McKay): pp. 118–38.

Lewis, Linda, and Sally Baidema. 1972. "The Women's Liberation Movement," in Lyman T. Sargent, ed., *New Left Thought: An Introduction* (Homewood, Ill.: Dorsey): pp. 83–93.

Mandel, Ruth. 1981. *In the Running: The New Woman Candidate* (New Haven: Ticknor and Fields).

Merritt, Sharyne. 1977. "Winners and Losers: Sex Differences in Municipal Elections," *American Journal of Political Science*, 21 (November):731–45.

Mollison, Andrew. 1984. "Jackson Calls for a New Coalition," *Atlanta Journal and Constitution*, 4 November 1984.

Shin, Kwang S., and John S. Jackson III. 1979.

"Membership Turnover in U.S. State Legislatures: 1931–1976," *Legislative Studies Quarterly*, 4 (February):95–104.

Smeal, Eleanor. 1984. "Eleanor Smeal Report," *Eleanor Smeal Newsletter*, 2 (28 June):1.

Tolchin, Susan, and Martin Tolchin. 1974. *Clout: Womanpower and Politics* (New York: Coward, McCann and Geoghegan).

Ware, Cellestine. 1970. *Woman Power: The Movement for Women's Liberation* (New York: Tower).

Welch, Susan, and Albert K. Karnig. 1979. "Correlates of Female Office Holding in City Politics," *Journal of Politics*, 41 (May):478–91.

White v. *Register*. 1973. 412 U.S. 755.

Zimmer v. *McKeithen*. 1973. 485 F.2d 1297.

16

Gerrymandering in the Courts: Threshold of a Second Reapportionment Revolution?

TONY STEWART AND SYDNEY DUNCOMBE

The legislative apportionment debate of the early 1960s focused largely on the political wrongs and unconstitutionality of the malapportionment and racial gerrymandering that were common throughout the states. In Vermont, for example, each town was entitled to a representative regardless of its population. As a result, the smallest town in the state, with a population of 38, had one state representative, as did the largest city, Burlington, with a population of 35,531. In Florida 15 percent of the population elected a majority of the state House membership.

Racial gerrymandering was made possible through "splintering" and "concentrating" minorities within certain legislative districts. In Georgia, a large black population was without any representation in the state legislature from 1907 to 1965. The roadblocks to black voter registration during this period also were a contributing factor.

In the 1960s and 1970s the United States Supreme Court identified malapportionment

as the key issue and fundamentally eliminated the practice by developing and applying the "one person, one vote" principle. Racial gerrymandering was also declared unconstitutional in 1960, in *Gomillion* v. *Lightfoot*, in which the court declared that "when a legislature . . . singles out a readily isolated segment of a racial minority for special discriminatory treatment, it violates the Fifteenth Amendment" (see the Review January 1978, page 10). Although this case dealt with the Alabama legislature altering the Tuskegee city boundaries to deny black voter influence in city elections, this same case law and the Fourteenth Amendment's equal protection clause were later applied to legislative districts.

Subsequent court rulings resulted in the same fate for malapportionment of representation at the congressional and state levels: *Baker* v. *Carr*, 369 U.S. 186 (1962); *Gray* v. *Sanders*, 372 U.S. 368 (1963); *Wesberry* v. *Sanders*, 376 U.S. 1 (1964); and *Reynolds* v.

National Civic Review, Vol.75, No.2 (March–April 1986), pp. 88–98.

Sims, 377 U.S. 533 (1964). The court majority pronounced in *Gray* v. *Sanders* (Georgia) an end to malapportionment practices by writing: "The concept of political equality from the Declaration of Independence, to Lincoln's Gettysburg Address, to the Fifteenth, Seventeenth, and Nineteenth Amendments can mean only one thing—'one person, one vote.' " Further, in *Reynolds* v. *Sims*, the court declared that "to the extent that a citizen's right to vote is debased, he is that much less a citizen. . . ."

The states thus reached the mid-1980s with a set of constitutional guidelines to prevent malapportionment and racial gerrymandering. First, any state legislative district plan with a total population variance of less than 10 percent would automatically satisfy the "one person, one vote" principle. Plans exhibiting a total variation betwen 10–16 percent would be acceptable on the basis of a "rational state policy" such as protecting local political subdivision boundaries (compact and contiguous territory) when drawing state legislative districts. Second, an intent to discriminate racially with the purpose of denying minority representation in a state legislative reapportionment plan would be unconstitutional.

Many scholars and judges assumed that these basic guidelines were sufficient to guarantee equal representation, which in turn would result in fair and effective representation in the state legislatures. Numbers of court cases, however, are challenging that assumption, producing mounting evidence to indicate that population equality among districts and the abolition of racial gerrymandering are inadequate to produce fair and equal representation.

Other types of political gerrymandering, specifically partisan, can result in discrimination as harmful and invidious as malapportionment or racial gerrymandering. In *Zobel* v. *Williams*, 457 U.S. 55 (1982), Justice William J. Brennan reasoned that the equal protection clause does not make some groups of citizens

more equal than others, and Justice John Paul Stevens, III, proscribed gerrymandering against other cognizable groups as equally violative of constitutional protections.

Gerrymandering is the drawing of legislative district boundary lines to give advantage to one party or one group of legislators or citizens, i.e., partisan, incumbent and racial.

Partisan gerrymandering is the process of redrawing district boundaries to benefit one political party. The two major techniques are "concentrating" the votes of the out party in a minimum number of districts and "splintering" the minority party's voting strength among several districts.

Malcolm Jewell and David Olson explain "concentrating" this way:

> The electoral and districting systems may distort the effects of voting so that a party whose legislative candidates win a majority of votes may fail to win a majority of legislative seats. . . . A simple example will show how that system can turn a voting majority into a legislative minority. Assume that a state has 10 single-member districts with 10,000 votes cast in each. The Democrats win 4 districts, each by a margin of 8,000 to 2,000. The Republicans win 6 districts, each by a margin of 6,000 to 4,000. The Democrats, with 56 percent of the total vote, will have won only 4 of the 10 seats because their supporters were so heavily concentrated in 4 districts that they won those by lopsided margins, and wasted votes.[1]

"Splintering" makes it difficult for the minority party to win the number of seats to which it would be entitled according to popular vote support. In drawing suburban districts in Illinois in 1973, for example, the legislature crossed the Chicago city line nine times to splinter the Republican suburban vote and so elect more Democrats (see the Review, January 1978, page 19).

Both practices produce a significant disadvantage for the out political party. According to Hardy, Heslop and Anderson, "The telltale sign of a partisan gerrymander is that the percentage of the seats held by the majority party in the legislature is significantly higher than its percentage of the two-party vote in the preceding election."[2]

Incumbent gerrymandering is the redrawing of legislative district boundary lines to safeguard the seats of incumbents. For example, a Republican representative who won with only a 51 percent majority may succeed in getting the boundaries of the legislative district redrawn to include several strongly Republican precincts from a neighboring district and exclude several strongly Democratic precincts of nearly equal population. The Democratic representative of the nearby district may cooperate, gaining some strongly Democratic precincts and losing some Republican precincts. At the next election, the Republican representative's margin of victory may increase from 51 percent to a safer 57 percent, while the margin of the Democrat may increase from 52 percent to 58 percent. Both representatives have gained "safer" seats from this incumbent gerrymandering.

Racial gerrymandering is the drawing of legislative district lines to benefit one racial group to the detriment of one or more others. This may involve dispersing the votes of a minority group evenly throughout several districts so that white voters gain a majority in all districts. This process has been described as negative racial gerrymandering in some litigations. Racial or ethnic gerrymandering may also work in reverse—lines can be drawn to concentrate voters in one area or district to assure the group of at least one state legislator, whereas it may not have had a single representative if the members of the group were more widely dispersed. Some courts have defined this process as positive racial gerrymandering.

The implementation of political gerrymandering is set into motion through the organizational structure of each legislature. Some states' reapportionment bills are introduced through a joint Senate-House committee. Other states form separate reapportionment committees in each house, thus often producing conflicting bills. Yet other states, with Idaho as an example, have used a more unique method of creating five or six regional apportionment committees. The legislators of each region are given a quota of seats and then are free to divide the districts within that region. Trade-offs among legislators become intense with this system. Still other states, such as Indiana, pass two divergent House and Senate reapportionment bills in order to turn over the issue to the legislative leadership and a conference committee. A few states avoid all these gerrymandering procedures by using a bipartisan or nonpartisan reapportionment commission.

The one addition to the process in recent years has been the use of computer technology. Previously, legislators relied on their own and party officials' political knowledge to divide precincts. Today there are computer devices that can draw precise maps from a computer program with the built-in past voting behavior and party registration of every precinct in the state. Little is now left to political chance.

The use of few judicial standards other than substantial population equality and the unconstitutionality of negative racial gerrymandering have left state legislatures free to engage in other types of political gerrymandering. The results have been some bizarre legislative boundaries, creating "safe" districts for either the incumbents or the political party in power at the time of reapportionment. Today's political science literature and court records are filled with examples of these roadblocks to fair and competitive democratic contests in both congressional and state legislative district races.

The problem of partisan apportionment of state legislative districts remains no less severe than that of congressional districts. Jewell and Olson discovered that Democratic gerrymandering in Michigan in the 1960s resulted in the Republicans electing only two of the 37 state representatives from Wayne

County (Detroit) despite the fact that Republicans received 28 percent of the popular vote. In Indiana in 1982, the Republican State Committee paid $250,000 to a prominent computer firm to draft a partisan plan. According to David Wells, "the plan worked as intended: the Democrats won a clear majority . . . of the votes cast for the . . . lower house, yet ended up with only 43 percent of the seats."[3]

The federal courts are continuing to safeguard against the abuses of malapportionment and negative racial gerrymandering. In Illinois in 1981, a federal court ruled in favor of the plaintiffs on grounds of dilution of minority voting strength in the Chicago area. The San Carlos Apache Tribe won a 1982 suit against Arizona for the racial gerrymandering of both state legislative and congressional districts. Another example of continued progress in protecting racial minorities from negative gerrymandering was in the 1982 case *Busbee* v. *Smith*, in which a three-judge panel found against a blatant case of racial discrimination by the Georgia legislature.

The problem of malapportionment has basically been resolved. In fact, today most states' overall range relative deviation is below 10 percent for state legislative districts and under one percent for congressional districts. The one major exception to this rule is the United States Supreme Court's acceptance of an 89 percent deviation in the Wyoming 1982 state legislative reapportionment plan (see the REVIEW, April 1984, page 181, and September 1983, page 435).

The growing issue for the courts is whether partisan and incumbent gerrymandering will suffer the same fate as malapportionment and racial gerrymandering. Many studies testify to the ill effects resulting from such "safe" districts: First, political participation is greatly diluted. Potential candidates and voters realize that the election results are predetermined, thus reducing candidate recruitment, voter turnout, party volunteers, and discussion of issues in the campaign. This causes a weakening of the two-party system.

Second, "safe" districts remove the incentive for legislators to be responsive to their constituents. Third, political gerrymandering weakens political parties by encouraging them to field weak candidates. The political system provides less opportunity for diverse points of view.

The courts are faced with the additional argument that each citizen has a constitutional right to cast a ballot and not to have that vote impinged on or diluted by some form of politically invidious discrimination through a technique known as gerrymandering.

The most conclusive evidence to date of the negative impact of partisan and incumbent gerrymandering on the electoral process appears in cases in Indiana and Idaho. The Republican-controlled Indiana legislature passed a reapportionment law in 1981; the Idaho legislature, also controlled by a large Republican majority, adopted a reapportionment plan in 1982 after three attempts that were vetoed by the Democratic governor.

Indiana. Apportionment bills were introduced in the House on February 13, 1981, and in the Senate on February 24. Both actions served as "vehicle bills" devoid of significant content; each passed its respective house and was referred to a special reapportionment conference committee. All of the appointed conferees were Republican legislators; four Democrats were selected as "advisors" with no vote and no access to the mapmaking process.

To aid in the reapportionment process, the Republican State Committee contracted with Market Opinion Research, Inc., to produce a plan based on past voting patterns in the state's precincts. This apportionment plan was approved by the all-Republican conference committee and the legislature on a party-line vote, signed by Republican Governor Robert Orr, and implemented for the 1982 state legislative races.

The Democrats complained of the partisanship of the new law by pointing to the statistics for the 1982 state House races in which Democratic candidates received 872,430 votes statewide, or 51.9 percent of the vote, but won only 43 percent of the House seats. Republican candidates received 808,681 votes statewide, or about 48.1 percent of the vote, but won 57 percent of the House seats. Members of the Democratic party, along with a number of other plaintiffs, brought suit in the United States District Court for the Southern District of Indiana based upon partisan gerrymandering in violation of the equal protection clause of the United States constitution (*Susan J. Davis, et al.* v. *Irwin C. Bandemer, et al.*, Cause No. IP 82-56-C and Cause No. IP 82-164-C, 1983; see also page 99).

Idaho. On March 24, 1982, the legislature passed a reapportionment bill which was signed by the governor. Immediately, a number of private citizens and local government entities brought suit in the state district court challenging the act as violating the state constitutional prohibition against breaking county boundaries. The plaintiffs also presented detailed voting data and expert testimony charging incumbent and partisan gerrymandering. The plaintiffs prevailed in a series of decisions based on the county division prohibition, but the district court and Idaho Supreme Court acknowledged and criticized the use of political gerrymandering by the legislature (*Hellar* v. *Cenarrusa*, III, Idaho Supreme Court Opinion No. 27, 1984; and U.S. District Court for the District of Idaho Civil No. 84-1091, 1984).

As a consultant and expert witness for the plaintiffs, Tony Stewart researched the legislative election results for every precinct in the state for all elections between 1960 and 1982. Among the findings presented to the state and federal courts were that after significant political (partisan and incumbent) gerrymandering by the Republican-controlled legislatures of 1972 and 1982: (a) there was a dramatic increase in the spread between the Republican party's legislative popular vote and the number of seats held in the legisla-

ture; (b) the number of uncontested legislative races grew rapidly after each reapportionment; and (c) voter participation went down in state legislative races within districts that had been gerrymandered.

A closer review of the Idaho data gives strong weight to the argument that political gerrymandering discourages voter participation and distorts the electoral decisions of those who do vote. First, the Idaho Republican statewide legislative popular vote in 1960 was 50.46 percent and the party held 51.46 percent of the legislative seats, but by 1982, with a popular vote of only 51.09 percent, the Republicans controlled 68.57 percent of the legislative seats. Second, during the 1960–1964 election period, only 11.38 percent of the legislative races were uncontested; the 1972–1980 period saw 21.33 percent of the races uncontested; and after the 1982 reapportionment, 33.3 percent of all races were uncontested. Third, after carefully identifying 14 gerrymandered districts in the 1982 reapportionment law from such sources as state legislators' court testimony and bizarre configurations (split counties), Stewart compared these with the remaining 21 legislative districts as to voter participation. The results showed a dramatic difference: In 12 of the 14 politically gerrymandered districts, voter participation fell well below that year's statewide average turnout of 58.5 percent of the registered voters, but 17 of the 21 remaining legislative districts had a significantly higher turnout.

Such findings give great weight to the argument that the representative democratic process is significantly harmed by gerrymandering tactics. Idaho District Court Judge Dar Cogswell pronounced such a judgment in his *Hellar* v. *Cenarrusa*, memorandum decision: ". . . when a plan is initially conceived with the objective of protecting or preserving the office of elected senators or representatives, bypassing our constitutional mandate, only disaster can result, with an open invitation to partisan gerrymandering."

The Indiana and Idaho cases illustrate the invidious discrimination that results from political gerrymandering. It is these developments that focus attention back to the courts.

Most political science literature has been cautious about predicting an end to political (specifically partisan) gerrymandering. The 1973 Supreme Court ruling in *Gaffney* v. *Cummings*, 412 U.S. 735 (1973), is often referred to as a precedent for continued partisan gerrymandering, and the rulings in *White* v. *Weiser*, 412 U.S. 783 (1973) and *Burns* v. *Richardson*, 384 U.S. 73 (1966) as precedents for incumbent gerrymandering.

In *Gaffney* v. *Cummings*, however, it is important to note that the court commended the Connecticut legislature for *bipartisan* gerrymandering in which both political parties would be provided with roughly proportional representation in the legislature according to their respective past voting strength among the electorate. At no time did the court suggest that it would have reached the same conclusion if one of the political parties had devised a reapportionment plan that minimized or eliminated the strength of the other party.

A major development with regard to political gerrymandering occurred on December 13, 1984, in *Davis* v. *Bandemer*, when the three-judge federal district court, by two-one, declared Indiana's state legislative apportionment law in violation of the equal protection clause through partisan gerrymandering by the Republican-controlled legislature against the Democratic party. The court declared:

> . . . The plaintiffs' right to vote, as secured by the Equal Protection Clause, is impinged upon by partisan gerrymandering . . .
> . . . In fact, several Justices have espoused their belief that undue emphasis on numerical equality may permit obvious partisan gerrymandering. Karcher, at 2670, 2683, 2688 (Stevens, J. concurring; White, J. dissenting; Powell, J. dissenting, respectively).
> . . . Thus political gerrymandering is a violation of the Equal Protection Clause because it

> *invidiously discriminates against a cognizable, identifiable group of voters.*

The *Davis* case was appealed by the defendants to the United States Supreme Court, which agreed to accept the case in March 1985. Thus the stage is set for what could become the removal of the third major obstacle to a truly fair, effective and representative reapportionment system for this country. Since present reapportionment guidelines remain constitutionally inadequate, this case becomes of major constitutional importance. In his *New Leader* article, Wells concludes that:

> *A supreme court decision declaring gerrymandering unconstitutional would shake the foundations of American politics almost as much as the one man, one vote rulings did. . . .*
> *The Indiana case is perhaps the perfect vehicle for supreme court action in this area. The defendants openly admit that they gerrymandered, and Democrats and Republicans are neatly offsetting one another on both sides of the question. No one will be able to accuse the court of making a partisan decision. Whatever it is, members of each party will be loudly cheering and booing— at the same time.*

Some attention has already been given to the issue of partisan gerrymandering by some members of the court. Justice Stevens, in his concurrence in *Karcher* v. *Daggett*, 103 S.Ct. 2653 (1983), presented an eloquent argument for the unconstitutionality of partisan gerrymandering under the equal protection clause of the Fourteenth Amendment. He also developed four meaningful standards that could be used by the court to judge partisan gerrymandering:

1. Population inequalities could be sufficient evidence of political gerrymandering.
2. Bizarre or unusually shaped districts could require a state to explain its purpose.
3. Splitting of long-established political subdivision boundaries could serve as

prima facie evidence of unconstitutional gerrymandering.

4. The use of partisan guidelines, rejection of diverse input, or no justification for selecting one plan over another that adversely affects the plaintiffs could be grounds for the majority to be required to explain its reasoning for the reapportionment plan adopted. In this process the plaintiffs must prove that they are of an identifiable and salient political group who have been adversely affected.

Other justices have taken note of the partisan gerrymander issue in both concurring and dissenting reapportionment opinions. In fact, several justices have recognized that numerical equality of districts has not effectively prevented partisan gerrymandering.

The possibility of obtaining a constitutional prohibition to either congressional or state legislative incumbent political gerrymandering must be viewed with far less optimism. In *White* v. *Weiser,* The Supreme Court, while affirming a lower court's invalidation of the Texas plan for the state's 24 congressional districts, did not, however, disparage the state's effort to maintain the existing relationships between incumbent congressmen and their constituents. Or, in the context of state legislative reapportionment, the Supreme Court in *Burns* v. *Richardson* said, " The fact that district boundaries may have been drawn in a way that minimizes the number of contests between present incumbents does not in and of itself establish invidiousness."

Again we suggest that the advocates of incumbent political gerrymandering could possibly read these decisions too broadly. Justice Marshall, in concurring in part in *White* v. *Weiser,* said:

Whatever the merits of the view that a legislature's reapportionment plan will not be struck down merely because "district boundaries may have been drawn in a way that minimizes the number of contests between present incumbents" (Burns v. Richardson), . . . it is entirely an-other matter to suggest that a federal district court which has determined that a particular reapportionment plan fails to comport with the constitutional requirement of "one man, one vote" must, in drafting and adopting its own remedial plan, give consideration to the apparent desires of the controlling state political powers (emphasis added).

Reapportionment plans which result in blatant incumbent gerrymandering often produce other problems such as bizarre districts, partisan gerrymandering, or larger population deviations than optional plaintiffs' plans, and can conflict with state constitutional guidelines. Thus the problem of incumbency gerrymandering can lead to unfairness and conflict with other constitutional requirements of apportionment.

We suggest that the court has ample evidence to persuade a conclusion that political (partisan) gerrymandering denies a significant segment of the citizenry equal protection of the laws under the Fourteenth Amendment. A persuasive argument also exists to suggest that partisan gerrymandering impedes the guarantee of a Republican form of government under Article IV, Section 4, of the United States constitution.

The reapportionment revolution of the 1960s focused on malapportionment and racial gerrymandering. Emerging from the many reapportionment cases of the 1960s and 1970s were the one-person, one-vote doctrine, implementing guidelines, and precedents against the use of racial gerrymandering. This was a major step forward in legislative apportionment.

We are now on the threshold of a second reapportionment revolution in which the courts will focus on partisan and incumbent gerrymandering as well as on malapportionment and racial gerrymandering. The use of perfect population equality among legislative districts and the absence of racial gerrymandering will no longer be sufficient to guarantee the constitutionality of an apportionment plan. Partisan gerrymandering was raised by some members of the court in *Karcher* v. *Daggett*, and Justice Stevens presented an eloquent argument against this type of gerrymandering and developed review standards. Partisan and incumbent gerrymandering were also raised as issues in the Idaho Supreme Court case *Hellar* v. *Cenarrusa*, in which a system of legislative districts relatively equal in population was struck down. In *Davis* v. *Bandemer*, a three-judge federal district court struck down Indiana's legislative apportionment law as a violation of the equal protection clause because of partisan gerrymandering. The *Davis* case was appealed to the U.S. Supreme Court in March 1985, which may be ready to broaden its rulings on reapportionment to include a test of partisan gerrymandering.

A series of legislative reapportionments in Indiana and Idaho has resulted in partisan gerrymandering which has increasingly favored the legislative majority. Moreover, there is clear evidence that gerrymandering has been used to keep incumbent legislators from having to run against each other. One result in Idaho was that voter turnout was lower in most 1982 Idaho legislative races in gerrymandered districts than in non-gerrymandered districts. Reapportionment literature has also shown many instances in which

blatant incumbent gerrymandering and partisan gerrymandering in California, Colorado and other states have produced bizarre shaped districts and gross unfairness in representation.

The courts and legislatures will increasingly face these two issues in the late 1980s and during the decade of the 1990s. Will they reject these types of gerrymandering which have historically produced voter confusion, lower voter participation and a reduction in the number of contested and competitive legislative races, and often predetermined the election outcome in favor of the majority party or incumbents? A negative response to this question strikes at the very core of representative democracy. We do not think the courts will take the negative response.

NOTES

1. Malcolm E. Jewell and David M. Olson. *American State Political Parties and Elections*. The Dorsey Press, Homewood, Illinois, 1982, p. 236.
2. Leroy Hardy, Alan Heslop and Stuart Anderson, ed., *Reapportionment Politics*. Sage Publications, Beverly Hills, 1981, p. 22.
3. "Indiana's Test Case: The Politics of Gerrymandering," *The New Leader*, October 7, 1985, p. 9.

—————————————————————— **17** ——————————————————————

Davis v. *Bandemer*: A Summary

SUPREME COURT OF THE UNITED STATES

The Indiana Legislature consists of a 100-member House of Representatives and a 50-member Senate. Representatives serve 2-year terms, with elections for all seats every two years. Senators serve 4-year terms, with half of the seats up for election every two years. Senators are elected from single-member districts, while representatives are elected from a mixture of single-member and multi-member districts. In 1981, the legislature reapportioned the districts pursuant to the 1980 census. At that time, there were Republican majorities in both the House and the Senate. The reapportionment plan provided 50 single-member districts for the Senate and 7 triple-member, 9 double-member, and 61 single-member districts for the House. The multi-member districts generally included the State's metropolitan areas. In 1982, appellee Indiana Democrats filed suit in Federal District Court against appellant state officials, alleging that the 1981 reapportionment plan constituted a political gerrymander intended to disadvantage Democrats, and that the particular district lines that were drawn and the mix of single- and multi-member districts were intended to and did violate their right, as Democrats, to equal protection under the Fourteenth Amendment. In November 1982, before the case went to trial, elections were held under the new plan. Democratic candidates for the House received 51.9% of votes cast statewide but only 43 out of the 100 seats to be filled. Democratic candidates for the Senate received 53.1% of the votes cast state-

wide, and 13 out of the 25 Democratic candidates were elected. In Marion and Allen Counties, both divided into multi-member House districts, Democratic candidates drew 46.6% of the vote, but only 3 of the 21 Democratic candidates were elected. Subsequently, relying primarily on the 1982 election results as proof of unconstitutionally discriminatory vote dilution, the District Court invalidated the 1981 reapportionment plan, enjoined appellants from holding elections pursuant thereto, and ordered the legislature to prepare a new plan.

Held: The judgment is reversed.

JUSTICE WHITE delivered the opinion of the Court with respect to Part II, concluding that political gerrymandering, such as occurred in this case, is properly justiciable under the Equal Protection Clause. Here, none of the identifying characteristics of a nonjusticiable political question are present. Disposition of the case does not involve this Court in a matter more properly decided by a coequal branch of the government. There is no risk of foreign or domestic disturbance. Nor is this Court persuaded that there are no judicially discernible and manageable standards by which political gerrymandering cases are to be decided. The mere fact that there is no likely arithmetic presumption, such as the "one person, one vote" rule, in the present context does not compel a conclusion that the claims presented here are nonjusticiable. The

No. 84–1244. Argued October 7, 1985—Decided June 30, 1986

claim is whether each political group in the State should have the same chance to elect representatives of its choice as any other political group, and this Court declines to hold that such claim is never justiciable. That the claim is submitted by a political group, rather than a racial group, does not distinguish it in terms of justiciability.

JUSTICE WHITE, joined by JUSTICE BRENNAN, JUSTICE MARSHALL, and JUSTICE BLACKMUN, concluded in Parts III and IV that the District Court erred in holding that appellees had alleged and proved a violation of the Equal Protection Clause.

(a) A threshold showing of discriminatory vote dilution is required for a prima facie case of an equal protection violation. The District Court's findings of an adverse effect on appellees do not surmount this threshold requirement. The mere fact that an apportionment scheme makes it more difficult for a particular group in a particular district to elect representatives of its choice does not render that scheme unconstitutional. A group's electoral power is not unconstitutionally diminished by the fact that an apportionment scheme makes winning elections more difficult, and a failure of proportional representation alone does not constitute impermissible discrimination under the Equal Protection Clause. As with individual districts, where unconstitutional vote dilution is alleged in the form of statewide political gerrymandering, as here, the mere lack of proportional representation will not be sufficient to prove unconstitutional discrimination. Without specific supporting evidence, a court cannot presume in such a case that those who are elected will disregard the disproportionally underrepresented group. Rather, unconstitutional discrimination occurs only when the elec-

toral system is arranged in a manner that will consistently degrade a voter's or a group of voters' influence on the political process as a whole. The District Court's apparent holding that *any* interference with an opportunity to elect a representative of one's choice would be sufficient to allege or prove an equal protection violation, unless justified by some acceptable state interest, in addition to being contrary to the above-described conception of an unconstitutional political gerrymander, would invite attack on all or almost all reapportionment statutes.

(b) Relying on a single election to prove unconstitutional discrimination, as the District Court did, is unsatisfactory. Without finding that because of the 1981 reapportionment the Democrats could not in one of the next few elections secure a sufficient vote to take control of the legislature, that the reapportionment would consign the Democrats to a minority status in the legislature throughout the 1980s, or that they would have no hope of doing any better in the reapportionment based on the 1990 census, the District Court erred in concluding that the 1981 reapportionment violated the Equal Protection Clause. Simply showing that there are multi-member districts and that those districts are constructed so as to be safely Republican or Democratic in no way bolsters the contention that there has been a *statewide* discrimination against Democratic voters.

(c) The view that intentional drawing of district boundaries for partisan ends and for no other reason violates the Equal Protection Clause would allow a constitutional violation to be found where the only proven effect on a political party's electoral power was disproportionate results in one election (possibly two elections), and would invite judicial interference in legislative districting whenever a political party suffers at the polls. Even if a state legislature redistricts with the specific intention of disadvantaging one political party's election prospects, there has been no unconstitutional violation against members of that party unless the redistricting does in fact disadvantage it at the polls. As noted, a mere lack of proportionate results in one election cannot suffice in this regard.

Justice O'Connor, joined by The Chief Justice and Justice Rehnquist, concluding that the partisan gerrymandering claims of major political parties raise a nonjusticiable political question, would reverse the District Court's judgment on the grounds that appellees' claim is nonjusticiable. The Equal Protection Clause does not supply judicially manageable standards for resolving purely political gerrymandering claims, and does not confer group rights to an equal share of political power. Racial gerrymandering claims are justiciable because of the greater warrant the Equal Protection Clause gives the federal courts to intervene for protection against racial discrimination, and because of the stronger nexus between individual rights and group interests that is present in the case of a discrete and insular racial group. But members of the major political parties cannot claim that they are vulnerable to exclusion from the political process, and it has not been established that there is a need or a constitutional basis for judicial intervention to resolve political gerrymandering claims. The costs of judicial intervention will be severe, and such intervention requires courts to make policy choices that are not of a kind suited for judicial discretion. Nor is there any clear stopping point to prevent the gradual evolution of a requirement of roughly proportional representation for every cohesive political group. Accordingly, political gerrymandering claims present a nonjusticiable political question.

White, J., announced the judgment of the Court and delivered the opinion of the Court with respect to Part II, in which Brennan, Marshall, Blackmun, Powell, and Stevens, JJ., joined, and an opinion with respect to Parts I, III, and IV, in which Brennan, Marshall, and Blackmun, JJ., joined. Burger, C.J., filed an opinion concurring in the judgment. O'Connor, J., filed an opinion concurring in the judgment, in which Burger, C.J., and Rehnquist, J., joined. Powell, J., filed an opinion concurring in part and dissenting in part, in which Stevens, J., joined.

—— **18** ——

How to Inhibit Gerrymandering: The Purpose of Districting Criteria

DAVID I. WELLS

The basic purpose underlying the establishment of criteria—or, as they are sometimes called, guidelines or ground rules—in the process of delineating legislative districting boundaries should be to inhibit gerrymandering to the greatest extent possible. In this context, gerrymandering may be defined as the drawing of district boundary lines in such a way as to secure special, unmerited advantage for one party, faction or group over another, or for some prospective candidates over others.

Districting criteria can serve this purpose because, if they are properly administered and strictly enforced, they diminish, to a greater or lesser degree, the discretionary powers of those who draw the lines, and it is precisely that power—the ability to determine the placement of district lines—which is the very essence of gerrymandering. Clear, precisely worded criteria can transform the districting process into a rational and logical procedure in which, unlike gerrymandering, the cards are not stacked in advance for or against any party, faction, group or potential candidate.

Whatever the specific guidelines are, if they are to serve their purpose, it is vital that they be applied in a very specific order of priority. Merely to set forth districting rules without specifying an order of priority would serve little purpose, for it would enable those who apply the provisions to pick and choose from among the various rules. Rules which are more favorable to one party or group could be given preference over others which are less favorable. A specified, logical order is essential if the guidelines are to reduce or eliminate gerrymandering.

There need be only four basic criteria: two of them rather simple, the other two somewhat more complex and requiring some amount of elaboration. The simple ones are *contiguity* and *compactness*; the ones requiring some spelling out are *reasonable equality of population* and the *avoidance of excessive division of governmental jurisdictions*. And I would apply these in the following order: first, contiguity (as I will proceed to define it); second, reasonable equality of population; third, minimal division of governmental units; and fourth, compactness.

Contiguity. Contiguity is inherent in the concept of the word "district." Yet over the years, in many states, parcels of land not effectively connected to one another have been politically attached to form districts. It should, therefore, be required that, to the extent possible, districts must consist of contiguous territory: that is, pieces of land physically adjacent to one another.

In most parts of most states, this requirement can be met quite easily. In some situations, however, depending on the geography of particular areas, the construction of districts made up of pieces of land separated by

National Civic Review, Vol.71, No.4 (April 1982), pp. 183–187.

bodies of water is sometimes unavoidable. In such cases, a requirement should be included that the separate parts of such districts must, wherever possible, be connected to one another by some man-made means: by bridges or tunnels where they exist or by regularly scheduled ferry service where they do not. In other words, the general rule of thumb should be that districts be established in such a way that it is not necessary to go outside of the district in order to travel from any one part to any other part. The only exception should be for islands which are not connected to the mainland or other islands by bridges, tunnels or ferries. In such cases, the island should be included in the same district as the nearest area within the same governmental jurisdiction.

Reasonable Equality of Population. The one-man, one-vote rulings of the 1960s require the establishment of districts with reasonably equal populations. Prior to those rulings, there were very wide variations among district populations and a resulting wide disparity in the political power of the residents of different areas. (To require that districts be exactly equal in population, however, without allowing for small deviations to accommodate other logical districting rules, actually facilitates gerrymandering, for it permits those who draw the lines to justify virtually any districting arrangement they choose to establish as long as the the resulting districts have equal populations.)

After some experimentation in the late '60s with very tight equal-population requirements, the U.S. Supreme Court expressly reaffirmed an earlier holding in which it had ruled that, except at the congressional level, "deviations from the equal population principle are constitutionally permissible . . . so long as the divergences are based on *legitimate considerations incident to the effectuation of a rational state policy* (emphasis added)."

In light of this, it seems to me that a state is well within its rights in establishing a set, specified and reasonable maximum popula-

tion deviation for state legislative districts (and presumably for local legislative districts, as well). For example, a 5 percent maximum deviation from the state average would seem to be well within what is both reasonable and legally acceptable. But such a deviation should be permissible only if it results from the application of the other criteria, not if it is arbitrarily applied in some areas and not in others. (For example, a deviation of up to 5 percent should be acceptable if it can be shown to be the result of a desire to avoid splitting up a county or town or city.) In effect, therefore, with regard to the population equality requirement at levels other than the congressional, reasonable allowable deviation would mean that:

a) Where there is no justification for a deviation, all districts must be equal.

b) Where there is justification—based on the other criteria—such deviations may go up to the specified maximum deviation.

c) No deviation may exceed the specified maximum *regardless* of whether or not it can be justified on the basis of the other criteria.

At the congressional level, by contrast, any statutory or self-imposed maximum deviation must be far smaller than at the state or local level, and must be applied with great caution, for the Supreme Court has not made it clear whether or not even a very small deviation would be acceptable. Certainly, at this level, no deviation of more than, say, 1 percent at most from the state average should even be contemplated. (The Court probably would be unlikely to strike down a congressional districting plan solely on the basis of population variations of less than such a small figure, but this is speculation.)

Avoidance of Excessive Division of Governmental Jurisdictions. Any set of guidelines should include one or more provisions designed to minimize the division of counties, towns and cities among legislative districts, not primarily because there is anything sacrosanct about the existing boundaries of such units or because the boundaries are geographically "logical," but for two other reasons: first, because the political machinery of most states is based on counties, towns, cities and other units of government, and therefore the smooth functioning of the political system would be facilitated by avoiding the needless fragmentation of such units; second, and, to my mind, more importantly, because keeping such fragmentation to a minimum serves as an important deterrent to gerrymandering. This is because the borders of counties, cities and towns are reasonably permanent; they are not frequently or easily changed and they are unlikely to be altered in order to win political advantage in the process of delineating district lines. If the boundaries of governmental units were ignored, it would be quite difficult to prevent those who draw the lines from splicing or severing territory at will, but the existing borders of such political subdivisions provide convenient, logical starting and stopping places for legislative districts, and these units make convenient building blocks for the establishment of districts. This is particularly true in rural and suburban areas. (In cities, where there are generally no similar internal lines to inhibit potential gerrymandering, only a compactness requirement can serve this function.)

In addition to a provision designed to prevent excessive fragmentation of governmental units—beyond the degree required by the population-equality requirement—it is also desirable to include, as a kind of corollary to this criterion, a provision or set of provisions spelling out precisely how governmental units are to be divided up on those occasions when their division is unavoidable. Such a guideline might read, for example, as follows: "If, in order to comply with the population-equality rule, it shall be necessary to divide the territory of any county or counties among more than one district, there shall be

as few such divisions as possible; geographic location permitting, more populous counties shall be divided in preference to less populous ones; and such counties shall be divided among as few districts as possible."

This kind of guideline is necessary for the same reason that a specific priority-order is required among the various guidelines themselves: to prevent those who draw the lines from being able to pick and choose among a large number of alternatives. To allow a choice among many alternatives would defeat the basic purpose of guidelines: the limitation of discretion.

Compactness. Although it has the lowest priority among the guidelines suggested here, an enforceable compactness provision is, nevertheless, essential as an anti-gerrymandering tool. This is because probably the most common form of gerrymandering is that which seeks to create political advantage by stringing together isolated pockets of territory—often widely separated and scattered geographically—where the party or faction in control of the process has significant voting strength. It is this type of gerrymandering which produces the classic bizarre shapes which most of us associate with gerrymandering—and which, indeed, gave that practice its name almost two centuries ago. This form of gerrymandering tends to be particularly prevalent in large cities where, as previously indicated, there are frequently no internal jurisdictional lines to inhibit gerrymandering and to prevent district lines from wandering in and out of streets at will, creating odd-looking indentations, protuberances and squiggly lines. And in large cities, as is well known, the inclusion or exclusion of just a few blocks can often mean the difference between victory and defeat for a candidate on election day.

Because of the irregular shapes of the many counties, towns and cities, as well as the uneven distribution of population, no districting plan can be expected to produce districts all of which have neat, compact shapes.

Some departures from absolute geometric compactness are unavoidable. It is possible, however, to keep such departures to a minimum. To do so, it is necessary to deal not with single districts, but with the totality of a districting arrangement. No compactness rule will work properly if it merely sets up an arbitrary rule relating to how each district must be delineated, for a standard which would be logical for one district or for one area of a state might be totally inapplicable to another. Instead, the most effective way to achieve the maximum degree of compactness possible, given the irregular shapes of counties, towns and cities, the absence of any semblance of uniformity among them, and the need to equalize district populations, is to require that after all the other districting guidelines have been followed, the total length of the boundaries of all the districts created must be as short as possible. Such a rule would prevent the arbitrary pushing of a particular boundary line a few blocks in one direction or another to achieve political advantage, but will permit minor departures from compactness to achieve a greater degree of population equality among districts.

It will be noted that the criteria suggested here take no account of demographics. Only geographic factors are used. This is because I believe that the use of demographic factors is justifiable only by those who, unlike myself, believe that there is something inherently desirable about politically or ethnically or ideologically homogeneous districts as contrasted to heterogeneous ones. While under almost any districting arrangement most districts will turn out to be homogeneous (and therefore "safe" in the political sense), there is nothing inherently wrong or undesirable about districts which include in them a mix of ethnic groups or of Republicans and Democrats or of liberals and conservatives. But that, of course, is the subject of another discussion altogether.

There are some who contend that those of us who advocate very precisely framed guidelines are attempting to take the politics out of the districting process. I do not accept that characterization. Rather, those of us who wish to thwart gerrymandering in reality have greater faith in the political system than those who would like to see everything "fixed" and prearranged in advance. We, in contrast, would merely like to see the so-called "great game of politics" played with ground rules which do not, in and of themselves, favor any of the participants in the game.

CHAPTER 5

Conducting Campaigns

State and local campaigns have come a long way from candidates shaking hands on Main Street. This chapter discusses four techniques that are changing the nature of campaigning, beginning with computer targeting of direct mail. Are the vast amounts given by political action committees (PACs) unduly influencing candidates, or are they a useful way of aggregating small contributions, allowing group access? Different states have experimented with different responses to regulating campaigns. In "Political Parties and the Dollar," Herbert Alexander examines the future of PACs in an era of single-interest fund-raising. After forty years of experience, pollster Burns Roper raises questions about political surveys. In politics as in sports, it's not over until the final count!

19

Mailing for Dollars

LARRY J. SABATO

I know that if the Democrats take complete control of our nation's government again in 1984, they'll immediately reinstitute their high-tax, big-government policies, slash our nation's defenses and utterly destroy the progress we've made.

Ronald Reagan, in a June 1984 letter for the National Republican Congressional Committee

Psychology Today, Vol.18, No.10 (October 1984), pp. 38–43. REPRINTED WITH PERMISSION FROM PSYCHOLOGY TODAY MAGAZINE. Copyright © 1984 American Psychological Association.

> Today, under the Republicans, individual liberties are being eroded, women and minorities are being pushed back to their traditional second-class roles, protection of the environment is being destroyed and essential services in education, health, child care and income security for the elderly are being dismantled.
>
> *Charles T. Manatt, chairman, Democratic National Committee, in a February 1984 letter*

If we are to believe the hyper-inflated claims in both political parties' direct-mail letters, then the United States is headed for disaster, whether Ronald Reagan or Walter Mondale wins the Presidency next month. Literally millions of these political solicitations have been mailed by both sides during the 1984 campaign, and while these letters may not directly capture many votes, they produce the money that can ultimately sway voters through advertisements and television commercials.

Even though widespread mailings produce a trickle of results initially, they provide something quite valuable in the long haul: the names of people apt to contribute and likely to do it again in the future. With such lists of people, direct mail can be targeted, allowing candidates and groups to sell their message, or appeal for funds to groups they most want to reach at relatively low cost.

A 1978 survey showed that more people (63 percent) look forward to the mail than to such daily activities as watching television, hobbies, eating dinner and sleeping. And contrary to the popular image of the wastebasket crammed with unopened "junk mail," another study found that 75 percent of people who receive political mailings actually read them.

"If it were not for direct mail, it is likely that a significant number of Americans would get no mail at all," says Carl D. Bauer, a clinical psychologist in Colorado Springs, Colorado. "We are not living in an age of copious letter-writing, a factor which may indeed have a bearing on the popularity of unsolicited mail. For some people, almost any kind of communication is better than none at all."

Direct mail has become an art form that persuades us to believe in an issue and then send in money as proof of our convictions. If you have previously "given," been politically active, been introduced to the cause or candidate and agree on an issue or if you have a strong dislike for the opponent or have contributed or purchased goods by mail, then you are a perfect target for more direct mail.

You've probably received more than your share of political solicitations during the last few months, and you may even have made a few contributions. If so, you may have been manipulated by one or more of the following techniques used in most mailings.

THE ENVELOPE

The more personalized the envelope looks, the more likely you are to open it. If the envelope cannot be individually typed or handwritten, window envelopes that allow the typed address on the letter itself to show through are the next best choice. Since they resemble bills, you are more likely to open them. Direct-mailers prefer "live stamps," especially colorful commemoratives, to meter or bulk mail, because they are attention grabbers. When researchers at the Alcohol Research Group of the University of California School of Public Health at Berkeley took a mail survey of more than 2,300 San Francisco residents, they found that those who received a return envelope with a commemorative stamp were more likely to reply than those whose return postage was a regular stamp or metered postage.

"Teaser copy," such as "Immediate Reply Required," is printed on the mailing envelope as an enticement. Richard Viguerie, direct-mail guru of the New Right, designed a packet for the National Tax Limitation Committee announcing, "Federal Tax Reduction Information Enclosed" on the envelope. Another of his envelopes threatened, "Notice: this letter is not to be opened by anyone other than the addressee."

The return envelope is even more carefully and attractively designed, usually in contrasting colors from the rest of the package and often marked "Personal" in red ink. Ideally, your name is typed in the return-address space. On some envelopes, there is a small calendar with a date circled to remind you of the deadline to contribute. The envelope is addressed directly to the politician or spokesperson for the group, again with live stamps.

STATIONERY

Instead of an impersonal campaign letterhead, many politicians use a facsimile of personal or business stationery. The letter is printed on heavy brown or ivory bond paper (not starchy, official white), with a dark blue or brown letterhead for maximum contrast. To make them appear to be individually typed, most letters are printed in a standard typewriter face in black ink. For easier reading, paragraphs are usually indented and kept short, rarely do they go more than five or six lines long. Sometimes they consist of a single sentence.

LANGUAGE

The language of direct mail is emotional, often filled with invective. There are no rules. "To raise money by mail, you don't have an hour of explaining things across the table to someone," says Robert Smith of Craver, Mathews, Smith and Company, an Arlington, Virginia, direct-mail firm. "You have to do it in a couple of pages of print. The message has to be extreme, has to be overblown; it really has to be kind of rough." In a 1976 letter for the National Conservative Political Action Committee, for example, Senator Jesse Helms wrote, "Your tax dollars are being used to pay for grade school courses that teach our children that cannibalism, wife swapping and the murder of infants and the elderly are acceptable behavior."

William Lacy of the direct-mail consulting firm of Bruce W. Eberle and Associates Inc. of Vienna, Virginia, says letters are usually written at the sixth- or eighth-grade level to make the point quickly and directly. The opening paragraph, the most crucial part of the letter, is designed to capture attention immediately. It explains in an intimate way the purpose of the letter, what you and the candidate have in common and how vital the candidate's election is to your own future. Phrases like "I need your advice," "This is the most urgent letter I have ever written in my life" and "I believe you've been waiting years to receive this letter" are common.

The tone of the writing is conversational, personalized with "you's" and "I's" and littered with connective phrases like "But that's not all," "It would mean a lot to me personally" and "You have done so much already that any additional help at all would be terrific!"

Other phrases try to get you involved: "You and I can save America" or "Will you go to the White House with me on Oct. 1st?" Eight million letters from the Republican Presidential Task Force were sent in 1982 to "only proud, flag-waving Americans like you who we know are willing to sacrifice to keep our nation strong."

Scratchy "blue-pen" underlinings, dashes and check marks, ostensibly added by the candidate to emphasize parts of the letter, are also used to make the letter seem more personal. Other personalizing techniques include interspersing your name throughout the text ("And now, Mr. Small . . .") and inserting your name at the top of pages after the first ("Page 2 of letter to Irving Small").

The letters convey urgency by giving a deadline for contributions. This is often the last day of a given month, because direct-mailers believe that they will capitalize on your propensity to pay bills at the same time. Mondale's February 1984 plea outlined a payment plan: "If you can possibly afford to send four contributions, one for each wave of primaries, you can postdate those checks and I will deposit only one check every two weeks. For example, you could date one today, another March 10, a third March 24 and one more April 7."

The request for contributions is usually made several times; as much as one-fourth of the letter may be devoted to such appeals. You're more likely to give, direct-mail experts say, if the request is for a specific project or if you're told exactly what your money can buy.

The final paragraph typically concludes on a dramatic and personal note. "I need help from my friends. Can I count on you, Harry?" "The survival of America is on the line. Let me hear from you today!" Mondale wrote in a February letter: "Your generosity and commitment to America has touched me and Joan deeply. We have both drawn strength from you."

The signature and postscripts are important, direct-mailers say, because people generally flip the letter to the end after reading the initial paragraph. The signature is usually a facsimile of the candidate's. The postscript may also be in the signer's handwriting and usually gives the most important reason for contributing in phrases meant to evoke guilt, urgency, patriotism or anger toward the enemy. "The Democrats hope you'll ignore my letter." "I will be given a list of contributors

soon, and I certainly hope your name is on that list."

LENGTH

Surprisingly, direct-mailers believe that long letters have more influence and produce more results than short ones. One particularly effective letter, for George McGovern in 1972, ran seven full pages. Craver, Mathews, Smith and Company, which generally handles left-of-center candidates, prefers letters running a minimum of four pages, two front and back, single-spaced. Long letters worked well for George Bush in 1980. Direct-mailer Robert Odell, of Bethesda, Maryland, who was working then for Bush says, "When you try to skirt the issue and do a short letter, you end up with short results."

THE DONOR CARD

Direct-mail experts report that people tend to donate more money when the suggested amounts on the donor card are presented in descending order ($500, $250, $100 and $50) and when there is a blank left at the high end of the scale for larger contributions. Some cards remind you of potential tax credits. Others ask you to sign a statement, "Yes, Mr. Candidate, I want to help you rid Washington of super-liberals. . . ." Even if you don't contribute, you are often asked to sign your name and return the card, "Sorry, Mr. Candidate, I'm afraid I cannot contribute to your cause even though I know you want to make our country safe for democracy." In a mailing for the Conservative Caucus, Viguerie had respondents signify whether or not they would contribute by affixing one of two flags to the reply card in an anti-SALT package—either the "Stars and Stripes" or the "White flag of Surrender"—against a blood-red background.

GIMMICKS

In a February 1984 letter from the Democratic National Committee, chairman Manatt enclosed "your official 1984 Presidential Strategy Ballot . . . your opportunity to speak out and . . . help save our nation from the disastrous policies of Ronald Reagan and the Republican Party." Recipients were asked to select their choice from the declared Democratic candidates for President and rank the importance of a dozen or so "critical national concerns," including the environment, government spending and women's rights. The results of the survey, Manatt wrote, "will be considered carefully by the leadership of our Party . . . I urge you to return your ballot to me as quick as possible. . . . And please include a contribution if you possibly can."

Such "mock election" ballots, "critical issues" surveys and the like are what direct-mailers call "participation devices." If you are motivated enough to complete the form, odds are you will also "check off" a contribution in the space that usually appears at the end of such surveys. No one knows for sure what use politicians and groups make of these surveys, but it is a safe bet that since the sample of responses is not scientific, the answers carry little weight.

The status gift is another gimmick. In 1980, Ronald Reagan sent each "first supporter" a "commemorative edition" wallet-sized photograph of himself complete with a facsimile of his signature. In a successful 1976 mailing, Gerald Ford posed with his family and dog Liberty to promote contributions to the Republican National Committee. The mailing was made just as he was leaving office. Other gift gimmicks have included American flags, lapel pins and "membership" cards. In 1982 the Republican Presidential Task Force sent contributors "The New Force," "a special insider's briefing on the real stories behind what's happening at the White House, on Capitol Hill and around

the world." And in the same year President Reagan offered "personally commissioned medals of merit" to certain contributors.

ENCLOSURES

Direct mailings will often include other materials designed to make you a believer. Odell used reprinted news articles with "personal notes" printed in the top margins in mailings for George Bush: "To Irving Small—I thought you might be interested in these recent clippings—G.B." Some of the Irving Smalls returned the annotated clippings with notes: "Thanks for lending this—I'm returning it because I'm sure you'll want to keep your copy."

Mondale's February solicitation included a copy of a "touching and eloquent" handwritten letter he received from Betty E. Miller of Ft. Myers, Florida: "Both my husband and I are disabled from work-related accidents," Miller wrote, "and I am in a wheelchair most of the time. We are still waiting for Social Security to approve us, so our finances are terribly limited. All of us agreed that we would donate $250.00 to you and that was to be our Christmas present to all of us. . . . We are all very proud to be working to change our country's image, priorities and love, to what it was before 1980."

Another popular device is the "wife letter," one of the best examples of the soft sell. In 1978, Republican Dan Crane won a House of Representatives seat in part, it appears, because of a letter from Judy Crane. Written in longhand on personal, pastel stationery and mailed in an envelope with live stamps, the letter was shipped back to the candidate's hometown for a local postmark. In the four-page letter, Crane told of her family history, marriage and children, connecting them all to her husband's concerns on crime, inflation, taxes, energy and foreign affairs. A photo of the happy family with pet dog was enclosed with a facsimile hand-scrawled inscription. Some voters thanked Crane for the snapshot and reporters found it displayed in many homes throughout the district.

In March, Jesse Helms's wife sent a personal letter with a somewhat different tone: "You have been such a loyal supporter and good friend of Jesse's over the years, that I felt that I could call on you for help. Frankly, I don't know where to begin. I can't tell you how hurt I am by the vicious misrepresentations constantly being spread about Jesse. When they attack his character and call him things like Prince of Darkness I have to draw the line. . . ."

In many respects, direct mail is a subtle art, disturbingly so when we realize how eas-

ily many of us are manipulated. Conversational writing, sprinkled with personalizing "you's" and "I's," dubious "prizes" and other gimmickry do influence some people to make contributions.

Yet, in essence, direct mail is probably the least subtle technique of modern election campaigns; all too often the result is little more than mass-produced, roughly refined hate mail. It is standard practice to exaggerate broadly, just on or over the edge of lying: "I wouldn't quote somebody *completely* out of context," says one direct-mailer. "I wouldn't write something that was *blatantly* untrue."

At its worst, then, direct mail is the conveyor of misinformation. At best it is the purveyor of oversimplification and emotionalism.

20

Placing Limits on PACs

CANDACE ROMIG

As Pac-Man fades from the videogame screen, PACs of another kind are having an increasing impact on state politics.

PACs are political action committees, groups of two or more individuals who have banded together to collect and distribute funds to influence political campaigns. While most public attention and concern about PACs has been focused on campaigns for federal office—Congress and the presidency—their influence on state elections is growing.

State legislators view PACs with mixed feelings.

The leader of the Democratic majority in the Washington state House of Representatives, for example, sees them as a fact of life.

"We have PACs because people have the right to organize with others of like viewpoint," says Representative Dennis Heck.

On the other hand, PACs are opposed by Republican state Representative Mae Schmidle of Connecticut who believes that by making a contribution to a committee rather than a candidate, donors suffer the loss of individual determination.

Basic to the debate is the issue of whether PACs are good or bad for the political process.

State Legislatures, Vol.10, No.1 (January 1984), pp. 19–22. Copyright 1984 National Conference of State Legislatures.

TABLE 1. FEDERAL LAW ON PACs

In 1976, the U.S. Supreme Court decided in *Buckley* v. *Valeo* that the 1974 Federal Election Campaign Act (FECA) in limiting political campaign spending and a candidate's use of personal funds was unconstitutional because it violated First Amendment guarantees of freedom of speech and open political debate. Under a system of public financing of federal elections, however, an exception was made that allowed limits on campaign spending and the use of personal funds. Disclosure requirements and contribution limits have been upheld by the Court.

In reaction to the *Buckley* decision, PACs have proliferated. The FECA prohibits PACs from contributing more than $1,000 per election directly to any candidate for federal office. Under the law, they are allowed to contribute as much as $20,000 annually to political committees of a national party or no more than $5,000 to any other PAC per year. Under specified criteria, a PAC calling itself a "multi-candidate committee" is restricted to contributions of $5,000 per election to any candidate for federal office, $15,000 per year to national party political committees, and $5,000 to other PACs. Corporations and labor unions are prohibited from making direct campaign contributions to candidates or political committees.

Although federal law pre-empts state law in regulating the role of PACs in federal elections, states often refer to the federal guidelines to determine how to regulate PACs at the state level. Such state regulations, of course, vary widely.

A question commonly asked, for example, is to what extent are PACs responsible for the decline of political parties?

Representative Heck believes the proliferation of PACs is parallel to social pluralism, with self-interest as the primary concern of each group vying for a "slice of the American pie."

Common Cause, however, cites a common complaint about PACs: Too many constituencies—the poor, elderly, infirm, children and youth, for example—do not have PACs and have little or no prospects of forming them.

Ironically, Common Cause was a prime mover of the post-Watergate election reforms that helped spur the development of PACs.

According to a recent Harris survey, 62 percent of the public thinks that excessive campaign spending is a very serious problem. People distrust the influence of the wealthy, big business, and big labor in campaigns more

TABLE 2. 'INDEPENDENT EXPENDITURES'

Both supporters and opponents of PACs decry the use of "independent expenditures" in state and federal political campaigns. This is an expense for or against a candidate without the knowledge or sanction of the candidate or the candidate's political committee. A fundamental principle in politics is that a candidate should be in charge of the campaign. Since timing and strategy are crucial, an independent expenditure can confuse and upset the process.

Corporations and labor unions rarely use independent expenditures, but when they do the efforts are often in the form of "in-kind" contributions. Still if restrictions on PACs are perceived to be unrealistic, then those with large memberships will seek other ways to participate in campaigns—perhaps through greater use of independent expenditures.

Lack of accountability is the biggest problem with independent expenditures. A bill has been introduced in Congress to allow free response time to candidates who are the subject of campaign advertisements funded by independent expenditures on radio or television. Meanwhile, Common Cause has brought court action against the use of independent expenditures.

than they do the influence of ideological PACs or candidates who contribute to their own causes.

Only three states—Alabama, South Carolina, and Wyoming—do not require candidates or PACs to file disclosure reports before elections. On the other hand, 22 states require disclosure reports at least *twice* before a general election. Meanwhile, independent commissions have been established in 25 states to enforce campaign financing laws.

Statutory limitations on contributions vary widely among the states. Only 20 limit PAC contributions. New York, though, does not recognize PACs as legal entities.

Meanwhile, seven states—Massachusetts, Montana, New Hampshire, Ohio, Oklahoma, Tennessee, and West Virginia—prohibit the use of corporate funds to establish or administer a PAC. Maryland, Ohio, and Oregon specifically set different contribution limits for out-of-state PACs to distinguish between the influence of national and state-based groups.

Montana recently became the first state to limit the amount state legislative candidates can receive from *all* PACs in each election.

The flavor of state campaign finance reform across the nation can be sampled by examining developments in several states.

California. The Legislature recently established a Joint Legislative Committee on Election Law Reform chaired by Senator Bill Lockyer and Assemblyman John Vasconcellos. Its mission is to review state election laws and suggest improvements to ensure governmental integrity, to remove legislative candidates whenever possible from the "demeaning and distracting task of raising enormous campaign funds," and assure the public that the Legislature is acting in its interest to restore confidence in state politics.

The committee is studying a proposal to establish expenditure limits under a public financing system. Under discussion is a threshold of $20,000 for Assembly races and $40,000 for Senate races to qualify for public funding. Expenditure limits would also be suspended

if an opponent's campaign spending exceeded the statutorily set limit.

In addition, an innovative matching fund for public financing of campaigns is being discussed that would, if as hoped, provide an incentive to small donors to contribute to campaigns.

The total amount a candidate can receive from PACs may also be limited, with only one-third of a candidate's money coming from these sources. Caucus and political party contributions may also be limited in proposed legislation.

Connecticut. The State Election Commission tightened contribution limts for corporate and labor PACs. Labor PAC contributions have been cut by one-half to between $250 and $2,500 per candidate, depending on the office, with an aggregate limit of $50,000 per election. Corporate PAC limitations are twice those established for labor PACs. This year, legislation will be introduced to cut this limit by one-half again, and to impose limits on ideological PACs at the same level as corporate PACs.

Representative Mae Schmidle, ranking minority member of the Joint Government Administration and Election Committee, is supporting "truth-in-spending" legislation that would require PACs to notify their membership of how their money is spent. Because of heavy lobbying by labor groups, this proposal previously failed to pass.

Connecticut's law is fairly restrictive on contributions by out-of-state PACs. According to Jeff Garfield, election commission director, a PAC wanting to participate in a Connecticut race must register in the state and collect "fresh" money for the election.

A bill has been introduced to institute a system of partial public financing in this year's election, but reportedly it has a chance of being adopted only if both the majority Democratic and minority Republican leadership can be persuaded to back it.

Maine. The Legislature last year enacted a bill that requires stricter reporting procedures and a maximum limit on contributions of

TABLE 3. PAC CONTRIBUTION LIMITS FOR STATE ELECTIONS

Alabama	None
Alaska	$1,000 per year per candidate
Arizona	None
Arkansas	$1,500 per year per candidate
California	None
Colorado	None
Connecticut	If established by individuals— no limit. If established by labor organization, same as individual limit—$50,000 aggregate limit per election. If established by corporation, twice individual limit— $100,000 aggregate limit per election.
Delaware	$1,000 per statewide candidate, per election. $500 per non-statewide candidate.
Florida	$3,000 per statewide candidate, per election. $1,000 to others.
Georgia	None
Hawaii	$2,000 aggregate per candidate, per election.
Idaho	None
Illinois	None
Indiana	None
Iowa	None
Kansas	$3,000 to statewide candidates per election, $750 to others per election.
Kentucky	None
Louisiana	None
Maine	$5,000 per candidate per election.
Maryland	None, except for limits on out-of-state PACs to $1,000 per candidate, $2,500 per election.
Massachusetts	None
Michigan	$1,700 to statewide office, $450 to state senator, $250 to state representative.
Minnesota	Between $150 and $12,000 in non-election years depending on office. Limits are increased five times for contributions in election year.
Mississippi	None, except for $250 per primary for judicial candidates.
Missouri	None
Montana	$8,000 to governor and lieutenant governor. $2,000 to others statewide. $600–$3,000 non-statewide. House candidates cannot accept more than $600 and Senate candidates cannot accept more than $1,000 from all PACs.
Nebraska	None
Nevada	None
New Hampshire	None
New Jersey	$800 per gubernatorial candidate.
New Mexico	None
New York	Formula based on voter population.
North Carolina	$4,000 per candidate per election.
North Dakota	None
Ohio	None
Oklahoma	$5,000 to state candidates. $1,000 to local candidates.
Oregon	None
Pennsylvania	None
Rhode Island	None
South Carolina	None
South Dakota	None
Tennessee	None
Texas	None
Utah	None
Vermont	$5,000 per candidate per election.
Virginia	None
Washington	None
West Virginia	$1,000 per candidate.
Wisconsin	$1,000 to statewide. $500 to state assembly. Others: percentage of prior disbursements.
Wyoming	No limit

SOURCE. Common Cause

$5,000 per candidate per election. Critics are afraid of the effect the stricter requirements will have on small PACs.

Before the bill was passed, there were no requirements for PACs to disclose receipts or spending. According to the bill's sponsor, Democratic Representative James Handy, "PACs can exist on a year-round basis and should be responsible to report on a more regular basis than they have." He believes PACs should be regulated because they are not responsible to the public as candidates are. One unsuccessful proposal last year would have outlawed PACs altogether.

Maryland. The House Constitutional and Administrative Law Committee is working to correct loopholes in the state law that leave the definition of out-of-state PACs vague and that allow unlimited funds to be transferred between PACs. Legislation will be introduced this year to define PACs more precisely and to put them under a standard contribution limit of $1,000 per candidate, with a total limit of $2,500 per election.

Minnesota. A bill to establish public financing of congressional campaigns is pending in conference committee in the Legislature. Democratic Senator Jerome M. Hughes, chairman of the Elections and Ethics Committee, believes that Minnesota's first-in-the-nation public financing of state elections has been very successful.

Montana. Last year, the state gained national attention as the first to limit the contributions that a legislative candidate can receive from all PACs. The limit is $600 for House candidates and $1,000 for Senate candidates; the law exempts in-kind contributions and contributions from political parties.

This measure, however, was the only successful element of a six-part package submitted to the Legislature. The other proposals, which may be introduced again this year, included:

Identifying PACs to reflect the interests that they represent, a "truth-in-labeling" measure;

Ensuring that all contributions be made at least six days before an election to give the news media a chance to report on campaign funding;

Regulating "in-kind" contributions such as volunteer services by persons paid by an outside interest for their work on a compaign;

Regulating independent expenditures; and

Establishing public financing.

Washington. Legislation passed last year sought to target last-minute, large campaign contributions by requiring that a telephone report or a mailed report be received by the state public disclosure commission within 24 hours if more than $500 was contributed. The law, however, has not been tested yet.

Meanwhile, the commission is examining how campaign money is actually spent. For example, it appears that spending for political consultants and media advertising increased tenfold since 1974. According to the commission's Graham Johnson, limits on contributions force a broader base of support, and he adds that campaigns with the largest number of donors win more often than those with a small number of large donors.

Washington's law to prohibit out-of-state PACs from participating in state campaigns was repealed in the 1970s.

Prospects are good this year to establish contribution limits, says House Majority Leader Dennis Heck. Although he dislikes restricting political participation in any manner, Heck thinks there is a problem in the ability of large contributors to influence legislation.

If Washington had an income tax, and if a state public campaign finance fund could be established through an income tax checkoff, then Heck might suggest modeling Washington's law to conform with federal regulations. In any event, he supports the "brightest sunshine laws possible" for campaign contributions from any source.

While a number of states have moved to

control PACs, and others can be expected to do so, a basic question remains: Is it really possible to loosen the links that have developed between today's political campaigns and PACs.

California state Senator Bill Lockyer, co-chairman of the Joint Committee on Election Law Reform, remains skeptical: "Separating money from politics is a giant desalinization project," he says. "It's like separating the salt from the sea."

What concerns Lockyer and others is that legislating reforms of the current political campaign system may result in worse consequences than the problems that are now perceived to exist.

21

Political Parties and the Dollar

HERBERT E. ALEXANDER

American politics is shifting from neighborhood precincts to socioeconomic bases representing a common occupation or ideology. Political Action Committees (PACs) are better able to adapt to these changing bases than are political parties, because PACs can focus on single issues or give priority to emerging issues and still survive with limited constituencies. Parties must be more broadly based in order to thrive.

The United States is best characterized as a pluralistic society, lacking both a centralized and a unified politics, and the American political system has been diffused in at least two ways. Horizontally, candidates, party and nonparty committees, and assorted PACs all campaign side by side—sometimes cooperating in coordinated campaigns, sometimes running parallel campaigns, sometimes running legally independent campaigns, sometimes only contributing one to the other. At least at the national level, the parties fragment into the national committee, traditionally rep-resenting the presidential wing of the party; the Senate campaign committee, representing the interests of senatorial candidates; and the congressional campaign committee, representing House campaigns. Vertically, political parties—the institutions whose primary purpose is to provide some semblance of cohesion in the political arena—are composed of layer upon layer of precinct, city, county, congressional, state, and national organizations, each having some autonomy and each deriving at least part of its resources from particular and often provincial economic and ideological interests. Thus, the structure of the parties can be seen as reflecting both the division of powers and the separation of powers.

DOLLARS AND DECLINE

All political actors—singly as candidates or jointly as committees or parties—are in competition for political dollars. Money is a scarce

---

resource; and growing numbers of political actors are in need of funds. Party committees compete for money not only against party committees and nonparty committees at each level but also against the party's own candidates at various levels.

The problems of campaign finance posed by diversity and the lack of centralization become apparent in an exposition of party finance structures. I contend that the once-dominant role of parties in American politics has been replaced largely by candidate and nonparty committees. The functions that parties historically performed have been taken over in part by other political actors. This fragmentation of American politics has worsened as party committees within the same party often come to view each other almost as rivals. The decline of party functions as well as the lack of centralized organization have taken their toll on resources available to party committees and hence on their strength. Parties increasingly are less able to mobilize support, receive a declining relative share of the political dollars, and have few means of discipline over the public officials they help elect.

Although the outlook for political parties appears bleak, there is hope for their revival. The national Republican party has taken new initiatives in financing its state and local organizations, which permitted Republican committees to play an increasingly prominent role in the 1980 and 1982 elections. If these initiatives can be developed further, and the Democratic party can adopt some similar techniques, the efforts of the parties may foreshadow a rise in their utility.

Although the Founding Fathers feared political parties would be divisive and made no provision for them in the Constitution, parties quickly and stubbornly emerged. Contrary to the[ir] fears, parties demonstrated themselves, at least sporadically, to be effective mechanisms for aggregating individual interests and resources into coherent programs—especially in the larger arenas of state and national politics.

At its most basic function, a party strives to attract large segments of the electorate to support its candidates on a ticket. The candidates usually are recruited from among a number of contesting persons through one form or another of intraparty competition. Prior to the Progressive reforms, intraparty competition had been managed primarily by the caucus system; since, the primary system has gained prominence.

Apart from the selection of candidates, which may or may not involve the party apparatus under the primary system, a party has an opportunity to realize its fullest potential: to mediate cross-pressures and conflicting interests into a workable program, with a reasonable degree of consensus, that the party candidates may advocate in their campaigns. When the citizenry is divided over public policy, a political party stands the best chance of formulating a common ground because it offers an ideological paradigm that is more encompassing than the interests of an individual candidate, who may be motivated by ambition or narrow issues rather than seeking broad policy goals. The party ideology has to be considered distinct from other "less acceptable" paradigms to serve its interest-aggregation function. For example, if one party generally advocates a laissez-faire approach to economics and the other party defends the more activist approach of Keynesian economics, individuals often will side with one party's program more than the other and will become aggregated into the larger political arena. A reasonable consensus of the body politic will have been formed, a program offering guidance for elected representatives will have been articulated, and the body politic should function smoothly.

The interest-aggregation function is complex. Democracy requires both consensus and competition. Some degree of consensus is necessary to achieve the enactment of public policies, but too much consensus may result in intolerance toward minority views, thus endangering the free and competitive discussions of the democratic process. The compromise or consensus and competition among the citizenry lies in the number of competitive parties; that is, the degree of compromise or consensus determines whether the system will be a two-party or a multiparty one. A caveat here is that in the American system, there are wide variations of views within each party. The compromise between consensus and competition among policymakers lies in the strength of the party organization; that is, the compromise lies in the degree of party discipline among elected public officials. The interest-aggregation function of parties is further complicated by the fact that individuals are not sorely moved by laissez-faire or Keynesian economic issues or their variations but embody views about other, often conflicting, social and political issues that may cut across both economic issues and party identifications.

Candidate recruitment, interest aggregation, and mediation between the citizenry and elected officials are the highest purposes of parties. These are ambitious goals, which American parties seem less and less able to achieve.

Parties always have had challenges in fulfilling their roles in the political arena, but today the problems almost seem insurmountable as nonparty committees assume a larger part in candidate funding. Many candidates seek independence from party mechanisms. The resources necessary to win elections cannot be obtained only through party committees. Most individuals and PACs seem to prefer to contribute directly to specific candidates rather than to parties; and the deciding electoral factors tend to be candidate personalities and stands on issues rather than party identification and party platform.

The latter decades of the nineteenth century marked the height of party strength. The shift away from party-oriented politics began as an effort to reduce political corruption. Party organizational strength was due less to ideology or program than to patronage; support for the winning party often translated into employment benefits or other rewards. The patronage-based parties were strongest in the ward, city, and county organizations, particularly in urban areas; the state and national parties, with fewer reward opportunities, sought similar loyalties with less success. Nevertheless, patronage was practiced at all levels. Public attitudes toward patronage changed in the Progressive era, and many reforms that struck at the heart of party organizations were enacted. A civil service system replaced the patronage system; favoritism in government contracts came under close public and legal scrutiny; and, threatening a purpose of parties, direct primary systems undermined the recruitment and nominating functions of party-controlled caucuses and conventions.

Party strength gradually but steadily declined as the New Deal reforms caused government to assume many of the social welfare functions previously performed by parties. The direct primary spread in popularity, most often not permitting even preprimary party endorsements. The electorate began to change as well. With more and more voters attaining a college education, fewer were willing to accept the cues from party organizations, preferring independent voting or split balloting instead. And the revolution in communication technology made parties less vital as a medium between public offices candidates, and voters; television quickly became more efficient means for candidates to reach mass constituencies than the personal contact offered by parties.

Within the past twenty years party strength has continued to wane because of a number of social shocks—the civil rights movement, the Vietnam War, and Watergate, in particular—that systematically undermined public respect for a number of mainstream institutions, including political parties. Party identification is also weakened when voters are upwardly mobile, move to a different area of the country, or marry outside their religious or ethnic group. In addition, issues increasingly cut across liberal and conservative lines. The middle-aged union member who has long supported liberal Democratic economic policies may be vehemently opposed to liberal Democratic social policies. Lifelong Republicans who agree with the party's probusiness orientation may be alienated by the anticorporate populism of the party's New Right wing.

As political parties became less important to public officials and voters alike, party programs decreasingly were of concern to policymakers. As campaign costs rose, campaign resources had to come from a variety of political actors. Instead of candidates bending to fit the party program, parties had to learn to do the accommodating. Unlike the strong party discipline among policymakers in Great Britain, American parties have had limited influence over members of Congress. From 1965 to 1980, the average Democratic legislator voted with the party majority on party-line issues only 64 percent of the time; the average Republican legislator fared slightly better with a 67 percent party unity score. Such low party unity scores in Congress should not be surprising, considering that during campaign periods it has not been uncommon for party-endorsed candidates to denounce publicly provisions of the party platform. Candidates have felt allegiances to specific constituencies representing specific interests, and parties have suffered from the single-mindedness of single-issue politics.

With the parties' nomination function taken over by primaries and their communication function carried largely through the electronic media, party structures have become weakened in their third function, that of interest aggregation among both the citizenry and policymakers. The era of multi-issue party organizations dominating the political scene has given way to the present era of candidate-oriented campaigns, accentuated by a fragmented interest group system and an electorate increasingly concerned with single,

diverse, often divisive issues. Candidates who receive funds from PACs relate to the PACs on a one-to-one basis, not leaving policy mediation to the parties. Once elected, incumbents continue their personal relationships with interest groups.

Inflation, the ascendancy of high-priced campaign professionals, increased reliance on broadcast and direct mail advertising, and other factors have driven up the cost of political campaigns. By 1980, the cost of politics at all levels—candidate campaigns, party activities, and ballot issues—exceeded $1.2 billion. As always, increased campaign demands have called for greater amounts of money, which in turn have prompted various reforms. The Tillman Act of 1907, the Federal Corrupt Practices Act of 1925, the Hatch Act (1939), and the Federal Election Campaign Act of 1971 (FECA) and its subsequent amendments were designed to regulate the sources and/or expenditures of campaign funds. The FECA was strengthened in 1974 by the creation of an independent regulatory agency, the Federal Election Commission (FEC), to enforce the civil provisions of the FECA, compile financial statements from candidates for public disclosure, and administer the presidential public financing program.

The FECA generally treats the parties favorably. Whereas contributions to candidates are limited to $1,000 from individuals and $5,000 from nonparty multicandidate committees per election, some party committees are permitted to make significantly larger contributions. Party assistance to federal candidates can be broken down into two categories: direct contributions and coordinated expenditures. No more than $5,000 in direct contributions—in either funds or valued goods or services—may be made per election by the **state and affiliated local party committees combined, or the national party committees combined. (Local party committees may contribute $5,000 to House and Senate candidates separately if they can prove they are independent from their state committees.)**

Major party senatorial campaign committees and their respective national party committees share a $17,500 contribution limit per calendar year to a Senate candidate.

Party committees are able to give larger amounts of assistance to federal candidates through coordinated expenditures; these are payments by a party committee in connection with a candidate committee for services and materials benefiting the candidate. Candidates need not count such assistance as expenditures nor report them to the FEC. Based on a formula that takes into account cost-of-living increases, a state's voting-age population, and whether it has one or more congressional districts, the limit for coordinated expenditures was as low as $18,440 for some 1982 House races and $20,000 for some Senate contests, or as high as $655,874 for a U.S. Senate race in California.

Through an "agency agreement," one party committee can transfer its spending authority to another. In a recent decision, the Supreme Court ruled that a state party committee could transfer its spending authority to the national committee of the same party. In the California contest, such an agreement enabled the National Republican Senatorial Committee to spend $1,311,272 on behalf of Pete Wilson's senatorial campaign—more than in any other Senate campaign.

The FECA says that individuals may contribute $5,000 to the federal election account of any of the nation's fifty state and affiliated local party organizations, plus the District of Columbia; individual contributions to a national party committee are limited to $20,000 per calendar year. An individual may contribute no more than $25,000 per calendar year to all candidates and committees relating to federal elections. Multicandidate committees also fall under the $5,000 contribution ceiling to state and affiliated local party organizations, but are limited to $15,000 in contributions to a national party committee. There is no overall limit on aggregate contributions made by multicandidate committees.

The public financing reforms of presidential campaigns, first implemented in 1976, create rules different from other federal campaigns for the participation of individuals, committees, and parties. Candidates can accept or reject the public funding. Candidates seeking a party's nomination for president face the same contribution restrictions applicable to all candidates for federal office. Once a presidential candidate accepts public funds, expenditure ceilings also are placed upon the candidate as part of a contractual arrangement in exchange for public monies. An eligible prenomination candidate can submit to the FEC contributions from individuals that can be matched up to $250 per contributor by an equal amount of federal funds. Public funds cannot exceed a total of 50 percent of the overall $10 million (plus cost-of-living adjustment) allowed to conduct the parties' nominating conventions. The actual federal subsidy to each party to finance its convention in 1980 amounted to $4,416 million.

In the general election, the public funding program prohibits all private contributions to presidential nominees who accept public funds. Instead, presidential campaigns are funded by public monies—$29.4 million for each major party candidate in 1980—that are given directly to the candidate committees, bypassing the party apparatus. Federal election laws clearly delineate party roles in the presidential campaigns. A national party committee exclusively can make coordinated party expenditures on behalf of the party's nominee. These expenditures are limited by the voting-age population formula as applied to the nation as a whole—allotting a maximum of $4.6 million in coordinated party expenditures on behalf of a presidential candidate in 1980.

In the 1976 elections, state and local party committees had been squeezed out of the presidential campaign. Federal election laws applied a $1,000 expenditure limit to state and local parties, an insufficient amount to make local organizing worthwhile. This was changed in the 1979 amendments to the act. Currently, state and local party committees may make unlimited expenditures on behalf of the presidential ticket for certain volunteer campaign activities. A state or local party committee may pay for campaign materials, such as bumper stickers, brochures, and yard signs, that are distributed by volunteers on behalf of party nominees in a general election. Expenses for phone banks also may be covered by state and local committees, provided the phones are operated by volunteers. A state and local committee may spend unlimited funds on voter-registration and get-out-the-vote drives on behalf of the party's presidential nominee. These grass-roots activities are exempted from federal regulations as long as they are paid for from funds permissible under the act, and these funds are not transferred from accounts held by the national party committee.

The restrictions on the flow of money into presidential campaigns may seem like an effective way to minimize campaign costs, but appearances can be deceiving. Total funds spent to further Ronald Reagan's election in 1980 amounted to $64 million; about $54 million was spent on Carter's behalf. These general election sums stand in stark contrast to the $34 million in public and national party funds provided. The additional funds come from a variety of legal sources. Independent expenditures, soft money, and corporate and labor communication costs and coordinated expenditures are some of the more significant sources. These different mechanisms for channeling political money into presidential general election campaigns are distinct enough to warrant the notion that multiple campaigns are conducted within each federal election. One such campaign, which involves only the presidential election, is waged mainly with public funds, is limited by law, and is controlled by the candidates. A second campaign is funded by various private sources that are unlimited but can be coordi-

nated with the candidate's campaign; individuals, state and local parties, and PACs fall into this category. A third campaign involves those expenditures that remain outside federal restraints—namely, independent expenditures.

This overview of the presidential campaigns illustrates the many openings for disbursement in a pluralistic society such as ours. It also suggests the problems of strict regulation of money in the political arena, because money seems to carve new channels when it is restricted at any given point.

With the steadily rising funds spent in federal elections, it appears that campaign finance reforms have not limited access to financial resources as much as they have changed the means through which those resources are channeled. The era of the large contributor clearly has come to an end with the FECA's $1,000 contribution limit; however, there are other avenues for a wealthy individual to put large sums of money into politics. One of the more significant avenues is independent expenditures. Protected by the constitutional right of freedom of speech, an individual or nonparty committee can spend unlimited funds to influence a candidate's election if all expenditures are made by the individual or committee without consultation with the candidate or the candidate's staff. Cecil R. Haden, for instance, a Houston businessman, spent $599,333 on national advertisements to further the campaigns of John Connally and Ronald Reagan in 1980. Stewart Mott, heir to a fortune made in General Motors, spent $110,179 to complement the campaigns of Senator Ted Kennedy and John Anderson; an additional $108,301 in independent expenditures was made by television's Norman Lear. Conducting an independent expenditure campaign requires political sophistication, which tends to limit the number of individuals who make such expenditures. In the 1979–80 election cycle, thirty-three persons made independent expenditures amounting to $1.2 million.

Nonparty committees utilized independent expenditures to a much greater degree. In the same election cycle, 105 nonparty committees spent $14.1 million independently, while 80 other groups spent an additional $.7 million. In some Senate and House races, independent expenditures were credited as having been a decisive element in the election outcome. The greatest share of independent expenditures, $13.7 million, was spent on presidential campaigns, primarily for the benefit of Reagan.

While both corporations and labor unions are prohibited from making direct contributions or expenditures to influence the outcome of federal elections, they can fund Political Action Committees through a separate segregated account, pay for internal communication costs, and finance voter-registration and get-out-the-vote drives. By the end of 1980, there were 2,551 PACs registered with the Federal Election Commission. Of these, corporate PACs accounted for nearly half the total, while labor PACs accounted for fewer than an eighth. The remaining PACs were not connected to an organization, or were associated with trade, membership, or health organizations; cooperatives; or corporations without stock. The disparity between the numbers of corporate and labor PACs was beginning to be reflected in their respective expenditures: Corporate PACs in the 1979–80 election cycle spent an aggregate amount of about $31.4 million in federal elections; labor PACs, about $25.1 million.

PACs with no connected organizations, often referred to as ideological PACs, held the lead in disbursements with a total of $38.6 million, closely followed by trade association PACs at $32.8 million. Altogether, PACs in the 1980 elections spent $131 million. PAC contributions slightly favored Democratic candidates over their Republican counterparts, demonstrating a stronger bias in favor of incumbents rather than for party affiliation. The bulk of ideological PAC disbursements were made as independent expenditures,

$13.1 million, which clearly favored Republican candidates regardless of incumbency.

PAC expenditure totals should not be taken as an index of contributions to candidates or of candidate support. For example, while corporate PACs' contributions to federal candidates in 1980 accounted for 69 percent of the PACs' total adjusted expenditures, labor PACs' contributions accounted for just 57 percent of their expenditures, and nonconnected PACs, just 14 percent. This last figure, by far the lowest of any PAC category, is largely due to the high fund-raising costs of nonconnected groups (which often solicit contributions by direct mail) and their tendency to use independent expenditures, which are not counted as contributions. Corporations and labor organizations, on the other hand, are allowed to spend treasury money to defray costs pertaining to the establishment, administration, and fund-raising costs of their PACs.

Labor unions made up for some of their declining PAC power in the form of internal communications. Election law allows labor unions, corporations, and membership groups to pay for partisan communications to their stockholders, to executive and administrative personnel and their families, or to members and their families. These expenditures need to be reported only if they exceed $2,000 per election. Approximately $3.9 million spent on partisan, internal communications during the 1979–80 election cycle was reported to the FEC. Of this amount, labor organizations spent close to $3 million, membership groups spent about $1 million, and a sole corporation spent less than $4,000. Total unreported communications costs of less than $2,000 probably aggregated significantly greater amounts. A breakdown of the reported communications expenditures in 1980 showed a bias favoring Democratic candidates over Republicans by about seven to one.

Individuals, labor unions, and corporations may funnel unlimited amounts of money into politics through "soft money" contributions. Political contributions to federal candidates that otherwise might be illegal, such as individual contributions in excess of $25,000 or direct corporate and union contributions, can be used to fund voter-registration and get-out-the-vote drives managed by state and local party committees. The 1979 amendments to the FECA provide state and local party committees with a special exemption from federal expenditure restrictions in the conduct of selected volunteer activities, including get-out-the-vote activities. The latter activity, because it is not expressly advocating the election of a particular federal candidate, falls outside the purview of federal contribution restrictions as well. A corporation or labor union, for instance, could contribute $100,000 from internal funds to a state party committee for voter registration activities if state law permits such contributions. The funds, of course, would benefit the party's presidential nominee in two ways: the registration of voters would be targeted by the party committee in areas providing the most likely partisan advantage; and party funds would be freed by the contribution to be spent in other partisan activities.

Soft money can assume particular importance in party campaigns when carefully orchestrated by the party's national committee. State election laws, which are applicable to state and local party voter-registration drives, vary from state to state. Thirty-two states, including some of the most populous states, such as California, permit direct corporate contributions, and forty-one states permit direct labor contributions. The limits on individual contributions also vary, with no limit in twenty-five states. Money can be directed by the party's national committee from, say, a corporation in a state that prohibits corporate contributions and sent to a party committee in a state that allows corporate contributions. For example, in the 1980 elections Missouri allowed corporate money but Texas did not. The Republican party facilitated the exchange of corporate money in Texas for individual

contributions raised in Missouri for the states' respective get-out-the-vote activities. The contributions were neither limited nor reported at the federal level. Altogether, under national committee guidance, the Republicans spent some $15 million in hard and soft money through strategic use of state and local committees.

PARTY FINANCES

Competing against candidates, nonparty committees, corporations, and organized labor for political money, party committees stand as one source among several for campaign resources. Aggregating all party committee disbursements in the 1980 federal elections—national, state, and local party operations, and contributions to and expenditures on behalf of federal candidates—party committees account for approximately $198 million of the total federal campaign spending dollars, while nonparty sources account for about $500 million. Although parties provide an important share of campaign money, they rank second to individual contributions made directly to candidate committees (more than $250 million), and are followed closely by PAC money and federal funds ($131 million and $100 million, respectively).

The party's runner-up status as a source of political money falls even further behind when operating expenses and other costs not associated with candidate promotion are subtracted from the total. In 1980, party committees as a source of contributions to and expenditures on behalf of all federal candidates amounted to $23.6 million; aggregate PAC contributions to and expenditures on behalf of all federal candidates exceeded $72 million. Thus, for every dollar parties contributed directly to candidates' campaigns, PACs gave three dollars (not counting independent expenditures). If candidates paid attention to where their money came from, parties in 1980 were not in a favorable position to gain loyalty relative to interest groups and individuals.

Besides the disadvantageous competition against nonparty resources, party committees also suffer from an imbalance. The Republican party has developed fund-raising skills far superior to those of the Democratic party. This difference is demonstrated amply in figures of party spending in the 1980 elections. Republican national, state, and local committees operated on budgets of about $170 million, while the Democrats operated on slightly more than $37 million—well over a four-to-one ratio. Accordingly, the Republican party was able to support its candidates to a much greater extent than the Democratic party could. Although each party contributed to or spent on behalf of its candidates about 10 percent of its total budget, the difference in absolute figures was substantial. Republican committees made $4.5 million in contributions to federal candidates, whereas Democratic committees afforded less than $1.7 million. Republican committees spent $12.4 million on behalf of their candidates in coordinated expenditures; Democratic committees, $4.9 million.

This disparity between Republican and Democratic finances originated in part from fund-raising strategies. Although Democrats traditionally have not been able to match the levels of Republican fund raising, the gap has widened in recent years. Until the contribution limits of the 1974 amendments to the FECA, big contributions dominated the financing of both parties. In 1956, donations to the Republican party of $500 or more constituted 74 percent of its total receipts. In 1964, 69 percent of the Democrats' money came from big contributors. In preparation for the 1964 elections, the Republicans began to experiment with a new fund-raising technique: direct mail solicitation. Barry Goldwater's ultraconservative ideology alienated many of the Republicans' traditional large contributors, forcing him to expand his prenomination solicitation of small contributions through the mail into a larger program for the general election once he was nominated. The experiment proved successful, raising $5.8 million from 651,000 contributors. Following a similar pattern, George McGovern in 1972 also successfully employed direct mail fund raising. Following the McGovern campaign, the Democratic party failed to exploit the list of 600,000 contributors, turning instead to money raised through telethons, special events, and wealthy individuals.

The Republican party pursued a different track. For the first time, the Republican National Committee—rather than candidate committees—utilized a direct mail drive to partially finance Nixon's 1972 campaign. The Republican National Committee (RNC) expanded its contributor lists so that by 1976 it was funded primarily by small contributors. Republican committees received 58 percent of their total receipts in contributions of less than $100; Democratic committees received 37 percent of their total in comparable gifts. Since then, the Republicans have successfully pressed ahead. Sometimes in competition with Richard Viguerie, mail fund-raising consultant for Goldwater, George Wallace, and later New Right groups, the RNC boosted its contributor list to 1.2 million names by 1980. In that year, 73 percent of RNC receipts were small contributions, generally in response to mail and telephone solicitations. The average contribution to the RNC in 1980 was $38; direct mail contributions totaled $40,226,300.

In contrast, the Democratic National Committee (DNC) in the 1979–80 election cycle received $4,150,522 in direct mail responses from 133,000 small contributors—roughly 20 percent of all DNC receipts. The Democrats relied very heavily on major contributors and fund-raising events, accumulating from these sources totals similar to the RNC's, $9.5 million and $10 million, respectively. Thus, the average contribution to the DNC in 1980 was $500. The major party differences are starkly illustrated by these comparisons.

The 1979 FECA amendments permitted grass-roots activities by state and local party committees that had been restricted in the 1976 presidential campaigns. Grasping at the opportunity, Republican state and local committees raised sufficient funds from all sources to spend nearly $33 million on federal elections in the 1979–80 election cycle. Democratic state and local committees spent almost $9 million. These figures would be significantly greater if state and local committee spending on nonfederal campaigns but on behalf of the entire ticket were included.

In comparison to the national party committees, all state and local party committees combined spent 21 percent of the party dollar on the 1980 federal elections. This was a much larger proportion than the percentages state and local committees spent in 1976. Despite the rise in grass-roots activities, party structures have undergone a trend toward "nationalization" beginning in the Progressive era and catalyzed by the reforms of the 1970s. The declining utility of parties in terms of patronage struck hardest at the heart of state and local organizations, where most of the reward opportunities were available. Allegiances to the local party machines faded, and so did their resources. To the degree that public policy increasingly has been formulated in Washington rather than state and local communities, at least since the New Deal, this trend toward nationalization of fund-raising became inevitable. Public attention increasingly has shifted to the national level, facilitated by expensive electronic media and professional electioneering.

The trend toward nationalization of parties also has been upheld by several U.S. Supreme Court decisions. The first court test was the 1975 *Cousins* v. *Wigoda* decision, stemming from national party rules established during the 1968 Democratic national convention. The 1968 convention reformulated procedures for the selection of delegates to the pending 1972 Democratic national convention, including an affirmative action program,

which state and local party organizations were required to follow. One of the few remaining party bosses at the time, Chicago Mayor Richard Daley, formed a slate of Illinois delegates in accordance with the Illinois Election Code, which ran counter to national party rules. An opposition delegate slate contested seating the Daley delegation before the convention's credentials committee on the grounds that the Illinois Democratic party had violated national party rules. The opposition delegation was seated by the convention, and the Supreme Court confirmed a qualified right of the national party to determine the selection of delegates to its conventions over the state laws and state party procedures. A similar favorable decision was issued in February 1981 in *Democratic Party of the United States* v. *Lafollette*, which upheld the primacy of national party rules calling for a closed primary over Wisconsin state laws calling for an open primary. These court cases were the result of efforts by the Democratic national party to gain control over the procedures used by state and local committees to select delegates to the nominating conventions.

The Republican party also has undergone a nationalization trend, but of a different character. The Republican national party has used its ample resources to enter into numerous "agency agreements," a process by which the national party may assume the state party's right to make coordinated expenditures in favor of federal candidates. Some $15 million of Republican state and local committee funds went into the 1980 general elections in support of the presidential ticket. Transfers of funds have been common. Joint fund-raisers with the national and state party organizations, often made possible through the national party's resources, have netted considerable sums for state and local activities. One such 1980 fund-raising event garnered $2.8 million for the Texas Republican party, an amount that became part of the $15 million noted above. Besides financial support, party coordinators established a local elections division that provided staff, technical, and financial assistance to state legislative campaigns; offered sophisticated computer services to state parties for electioneering; and conducted various campaign seminars for local party leaders and candidates. The extent of this assistance to state and local parties was well beyond the capability of the Democratic National Committee.

A substantial portion of state and local committee receipts has been raised from the committees' own sources. Of the 3.8 percent of the nation's adult population who say they contributed to political parties in 1980, 48.1 percent gave to national committees, 22.1 percent gave to state parties, and 29.8 percent gave to local parties.

State and local parties remain an important element of the nation's political system. Although they are becoming increasingly dependent on the resources and skills of the national parties, the state and local committees are responsible for the implementation of their own activities. And with the acquisition of greater resources, these grass-roots organizations have played a larger role in activities relevant to the presidential campaigns. In statewide elections these committees often are considered crucial factors. If they can be developed by their national organizations, as the Republican party is attempting to do, and remove the restrictions on their activities in congressional campaigns, state and local parties will perform a more important role in campaigns but largely will owe allegiance to national directives. Although state and local committees probably will play an enhanced role in the campaign process, there appears to be no returning to the powerful local organizations of the prereform era.

NATURAL LIMITS

Considered in the aggregate, American politics is not overpriced but underfinanced. Campaigns are expensive, but our system of elections creates a highly competitive political arena within a universe full of nonpolitical sights and sounds also seeking attention. Candidates, parties, and special interest groups are not just in competition with one another but also in competition with commercial advertisers possessed of larger budgets and advertising on a regular basis, often through popular entertainment programs on television and radio. The $1.2 billion spent on politics at all levels in 1980 needs to be viewed in perspective of the fact that the nation's leading commercial advertiser, Procter and Gamble Company, spent $649 million promoting its products in 1980.

One wonders how much more money is available for politics. Undoubtedly, there are large reserves of political dollars yet untapped. Richard Viguerie believes he can continue to expand his contributor list for the next three to five years through the electronic media. Republican fund-raisers also are striving to expand their lists, and the Democrats finally have decided to build their own direct mail drive. The consequence is a deluge of mail solicitations. Barbara Newington, a large contributor to campaigns, reported needing a suitcase to carry all the mail solicitations that accumulated after she left home for three days. Mail lists are often shared or sold to various groups, and a single fund-raising firm will service several clients. Once a person responds to a mail solicitation, he or she is solicited repeatedly by the same candidate or committee, or by anyone else who obtains the "proven contributors" list. If the saturation point has not been reached yet, the proliferation of direct mail drives probably will bring it about soon.

The Democratic party faces an even more formidable obstacle to its quest for an effective mail drive. The DNC's ambition to achieve a list of 600,000 proven contributors by 1984 was reached. It is always difficult to find contributors, and the amounts it receives through the mail are smaller than the Republicans' average response to mail solicitations. A direct mail fund-raising program will be helpful to the Democrats, but it may never be able to match the strength of the Republicans' program.

To the extent that natural limits do not rein in the growth of campaign spending, balances of power are altered. The higher the costs, the more need for a candidate or party to raise money, the more concern about where the money is to come from, hence the more concern about the public policy interests of groups that have the money and are willing to give it.

While candidates, parties, and PACs all are competing for scarce political dollars from individuals, they often turn to each other for financial support. Candidates and parties will sometimes expend their own resources to champion the causes of a special interest group, as has been seen in some Democratic candidates' support for the nuclear freeze movement; and PACs are one of the major sources of campaign funds to meet the political advertising and other expenditure needs of candidates and parties. PACs are better able to adapt to the emergence of single-issue politics, and thus are able to appeal to many potential contributors. People give because they share ideas and concerns that PACs advance, and they seek to elect candidates with congenial views. Out-of-state funding helps to nationalize politics, directing candidates to national issues and away from the provincial interests of a state or district.

To the degree that public policy is formulated in Washington rather than in state and local communities, a trend toward nationalization of campaign fund-raising is inevitable. As government has expanded and increased its role in the economy and in social issues, affected interests have become more active in politics. In general, the greater the impact of federal government decisions, the more people are likely to be interested in politics and in organizing PACs to raise funds for sympathetic candidates at the national level.

A systemic condition exists. Candidates want to win. Campaign costs are high. There are only a limited number of local people who can or will give. So candidates start early to gear up their fund-raising, based on where they think the money is. When candidates are unable to adequately finance a campaign from constituents within a state or district, they seek funds from PACs, from political parties, lobbyists, out-of-staters, or if possible they spend their personal funds. Another layer of sources is added on when presidential candidates or party leaders, through their personal PACs, contribute to favored party candidates. These personal leadership PACs compete with party PACs in soliciting funds, yet they undoubtedly raise some money that the parties themselves could not raise; to the extent such funds are contributed to other party candidates, the party effort to win election is advanced.

Often the money candidates seek is available from PACs. Not often enough is enough money available from the parties. As the availability of political money expands with the number of PACs, both the Democratic and Republican parties have initiated new efforts to appeal especially to business interests whose PACs are more numerous than those of any other segment of the population. House Democrats, for instance, have established a task force specifically for the purpose of seeking a larger share of campaign contributions from business-related PACs.

The 1950s saw the rise of a political reform movement—in New York, California, and elsewhere—that sought to disgorge the patronage-hungry, nonideological political party machines. The effort was to replace them with an issue-oriented politics that would appeal to the increasing number of college-educated and suburban-dwelling voters who value ideas and dialogue and who are dedicated to such overarching causes as peace, the environment, civil rights, and equality of opportunity. The reform movement succeeded in large measure, but through the years the issues changed. Broadly ideological groups were joined by single-issue groups that favor or oppose such specific issues as abortion, ERA, gun control, or nuclear disarmament. These organizations are made up of members who care about one issue more than about others, to the point that they oppose incumbents who vote "wrong" on that issue despite perhaps many "right" votes on other matters.

Ironically, though these latter groups have taken a singular form not anticipated by their precursors, they are supremely issue oriented, as political goal reformers long sought. They represent a shift away from the party dominated precinct politics of the past to a new politics in which the socioeconomic unit has replaced the neighborhood as a meaningful political division. As political parties diminish in significance, people join groups that can demonstrate their effectiveness on issues their members care about. These organizations become "reference groups," utilizing ideological beliefs and occupational interests as touchstones of self-identification, affecting their political behavior as exemplified in their patterns of contributing, voting, and volunteering.

Politics simply is not played by the old rules anymore. Instead of a reasonably cohesive body politic broken down primarily by party lines, today parties have lost a great deal of their utility, many of their functions have been absorbed by other institutions or left unfilled. The reforms of the political process, including campaign finance laws, have helped give rise to a plurality of institutions providing candidate support and dialogue with the community. American politics now lends itself to influence by single-issue interests oriented toward individual candidates, as well as by the multi-issue programs of parties.

This pluralistic nature also is reflected in the financing of politics. Campaigns are expensive, and political dollars are scarce. What can properly be called the nation's tuition for political education, the costs of free and com-

petitive elections, has to be shouldered by someone. Candidates, parties, interest groups, individuals, and government all have been paying the bills. In and around a maze of federal, state, and local regulations, political dollars have been channeled into campaigns through a multiplicity of mechanisms. Although PACs have demonstrated considerable promise, fortunately no one source of campaign funds is sufficient in any given election. That reality, along with the continued financial recovery of the parties (especially the Republican) means that whatever hopes the large New Right independent expenditure groups might have had for unilaterally bringing about a "conservative agenda" are probably unrealistic and that such groups are not destined to become a dominant force in American politics. The new single-issue, ideological, and PAC constituencies are as much in need of a mediating political institution as the old ethnic constituencies. The power of such potentially disruptive groups can be minimized by the continued financial growth of political parties. Political scientist Michael J. Malbin has made this point in regard to independent expenditure groups. Among other things, Malbin suggests, in the January/February 1982 issue of *Regulation,* that Congress extend the state and local party exemptions for unlimited spending on volunteer activities that is permitted in presidential elections, to **campaigns** for the Senate and House as well.

However well the parties have been treated, federal election laws have facilitated the proliferation of competing interest groups, eclipsing to some extent the importance of parties. The major parties, especially the Republican, are making strides in regaining a place in the game. Through fund-raising techniques that so far have proven effective, the Republican party played a significant role in recent elections, and probably will continue to do so in future elections. The Democrats have begun imitating Republican tactics; and though they probably will not achieve the same degree of success, expanded fund-raising will give the Democrats a needed boost. Organizational discipline within the parties also may rise as state and local party committees increasingly look to the national organizations for the training and resources to become professional campaigners. It remains to be seen whether the enhanced fund-raising and organizational skills of the parties will translate into party discipline over elected policymakers. Thus far, there have been no visible efforts by the Republican party to allocate party funds in a disciplinary fashion to candidates, nor have any serious efforts been made by the party to gain influence over the selection of party whips in Congress. Candidates may be becoming more indebted to the assistance of professional party organizations, but the existence of a variety of sources of campaign funds and expertise will keep American politics far from reviving an "era of the parties."

22

Political Polls

BURNS W. ROPER

Political polling fascinates me. I find it exciting, exacting, challenging, and extremely useful—useful not alone as campaign intelligence, but as analysis of the dynamics of an election, the forces at work in it, and the nature of a winning candidate's mandate. At the same time, there are many things that concern me about political polls.

I do not think that polling prior to the start of an election year does either the candidates for office or the public at large a service. Early polling does not reflect real preferences. It tends to reflect two things only: candidate name recognition and the public's whim of the moment. The question that is normally asked begins with the phrase "If the election were being held today." In fact the election is not being held today and people do not answer such a question from the same thoughtful perspective that they use to decide their vote on election day. This was dramatically illustrated when Gary Hart's support went from about 7 percent in a national poll to 37 percent two weeks later in the same poll. No positive program was put forth by Hart during that two week period. Walter Mondale committed no gaffe that would justify such a change during that time. The 7 percent figure for Hart could not really be described as public opinion; neither could the 37 percent figure.

In addition to advantaging the better known candidates, early polls have the long-range effect of turning the electorate off, of boring them to tears by midsummer, so that the public is totally tuned out—until about two or three weeks before the election itself. Publishing polls prior to a state primary indicating the likely outcome of that primary is foolish indeed, particularly in the early part of the campaign. I do not think the candidates are foolish to commission private polls at that time, for it is a time when opinion is so volatile and fluid that a well conceived poll can easily indicate how the present situation can be exploited. The fortunes of a particular candidate can be mightily, even if ephemerally, enhanced. The successful private poll indicating a strategy for changing the standings over the next week or ten days serves to insure that the published poll will be wrong. At the time of the early primaries, most voters are not selecting the next president of the United States and leader of the free world. They are engaging in an early spring rite, and their preferences are about as solid and meaningful as the way amateurs at a horse race bet on horses based on the colors the jockeys are wearing: "I think I like the candidate in the green stripes better than the one in the pink polka dots—today at least."

I am also bothered about the abuse or excuse of sampling error in many election polls. A poll with a plus-or-minus-four-percentage-points sampling error that shows a six-point lead for candidate X will frequently be termed a statistical toss-up because candidate X could be four points lower than indicated and his opponent four points higher. Hence, candidate X could be behind by two points rather than ahead by six. While this is true, it is equally likely—or unlikely—that candidate X could be four points higher than indicated and his opponent four points lower. Candidate X would then have a fourteen-point lead. This could hardly be termed a toss-up. Actually both of these extremes are highly unlikely. If there is a six-point lead for candidate X and a plus-or-minus four-percentage-points margin of error, it is extremely unlikely that candidate X is behind. It is also extremely unlikely that he is a dozen or more points ahead. The most likely result is that candidate X is six points ahead, or five, or seven, or four, or eight. To describe a race such as this as statistically even is either not to understand statistics, or it is a purposeful cop-out.

One of the media carried this sampling error nonsense to an extreme. They conducted tracking studies prior to major primaries last year, conducting 200 telephone interviews a night and combining the three most recent nights to arrive at the latest reading. These 600 interviews produced fewer than 500 likely voters. Thus, the survey is subject to about a plus-or-minus-six-percentage-point error. Therefore, if candidate X does not have more than a twelve-point lead over his nearest opponent, the survey is deemed a statistical toss-up and too close to call. In theory, the reason for daily tracking polls is to catch last-minute changes—to heighten the sensitivity of the measurements. Only 200 calls are done a night, presumably to hold down the cost of daily polling. What is the value of the daily tracking poll if a twelve-point lead, which could be as large as twenty-four points but could also be as small as zero, is considered too close to call? Almost no election that anyone is interested in is won by more than twenty-four percentage points. If one is, we hardly need polling in advance to determine who the likely winner will be.

In an election year, we are treated to the between-conventions poll—the poll after the Democratic nominee is finally decided and before the Republican convention takes place. This is a staple commodity that always creates news and misleads the public, as well as the press itself. Possibly the most dramatic case of the between-conventions poll and its distortion of public opinion was in 1976. Jimmy Carter had won what proved to be a surprisingly easy, unifying nomination. The Republican convention, scheduled second on the assumption that there would be little contest over a Republican incumbent, actually turned out to be the more exciting of the two conventions, a bitter race having developed between Gerald Ford and Ronald Reagan. As a result of unity in the Democratic party and dissension in the Republican party, the major national polls in the between-conventions measurements showed leads of well over thirty percentage points for Jimmy Carter over Gerald Ford. That this was strictly the result of unity around the Democratic candidate and dissension over the Republican candidate was shown when, less than two weeks later, Carter's so-called lead of thirty-six points, according to one between-conventions poll, had plummeted to only fourteen points. I contend that Carter never had a lead of thirty-six points. I do not mean that the pollsters fabricated that results. I mean that the measurement was taken at such a misleading point in time that the thirty-six-point margin it produced was unreal.

In an election year such as 1984, if between convention polls are done, a reverse distortion is likely to take place. If the Democratic fight is bitter, and there is no Republican fight at all, a between-conventions poll could reflect continuing Democratic bitterness versus continuing Republican unity. The first real measurement of the standing of the presidential candidates does not occur until at least a week after the second party's nominee is chosen. The worst possible reflection of candidates' strengths is obtained in between-conventions measures.

In addition to the way polls are presented and interpreted, I have some criticisms of them from a technical point of view. One of the trickiest parts of an election poll is to determine who is likely to vote and who is not. I can assure those concerned that this determination is largely a matter of art. A frequently used criterion to separate voters from nonvoters, or more likely voters from less likely voters, is past voting behavior. While I recognize that those who have a history of voting will vote in higher proportions this year than those who have not voted, it has always bothered me to use past voting behavior as a measure of a coming year's electorate. Past voting behavior cannot be used in the case of a survey respondent aged eighteen, nineteen, twenty, or twenty-one. I think it also has the potential for being misleading in terms of new candidates and new issues. A good example

is 1984. Jesse Jackson is credited with substantially increasing black registration and black turnout. His role, coupled with the successful candidacies of Wilson Goode and Harold Washington, on top of the past successes of Tom Bradley and other blacks, may well have caused many blacks who never voted before to vote for the first time. A measure based on past voting behavior would have eliminated them as likely voters.

Another technical problem is deciding in advance what the turnout is likely to be and then either eliminating or weighting down those who seem less likely to vote. This is done in order to get the survey sample down to a predetermined percentage. I would much rather say logic and good sense indicates that a person who says this and does that will be a voter. How many people qualified on that basis last year, and how does that compare with similar measures in past election years? I prefer to apply a uniform set of criteria and see whether that indicates a larger or smaller turnout than to decide on the basis of some kind of external criteria—or hunch—what the turnout is likely to be. Then we can seek out the most likely group of people to fit that number.

I am concerned about whether election polls are predictions or not. The worst example in this area is the pollster who, prior to the election, claims that a poll is merely "a snapshot in time." It merely measures how the election would be if it took place at that particular time, which it will not. When this same pollster, the Wednesday after the election, claims to have been within one point of the winner's margin, he is trying to have it both ways. Before the election, it was a snapshot in time which he could point to protectively if the election came out differently. If the result is very close, he can claim an accurate prediction without ever using the word prediction.

I am sure there are pollsters who honestly believe that a crash, last minute poll conducted at great effort and expense in the final hours of the campaign is a snapshot in time, not a prediction. I find this an incredible view. Why would a pollster wait until the very last minute, employ extraordinary methods to conduct interviewing as close to the election as possible, and speed up the processing so that reporting of the poll can be done Monday night or Tuesday morning of election day— unless its purpose is to predict? If a pollster does not want his poll interpreted as a prediction, he should not make a late-in-the-campaign measure. The later the poll is conducted and reported, the more difficult it will be for the pollster to contend that it is only a snapshot in time, not a prediction.

An aspect of polling that received a good deal of criticism in 1984 was the use of exit polls to make early projections—or as the networks euphemistically term it, to "characterize" the election. I think the media have every right under the First Amendment to make such projections or characterizations prior to the closing of the polling places. Also, I have seen no evidence to support the contention, nor do I see any logic supporting it, that early projections of the results affect the ultimate outcome of the race being projected, or of companion races for lesser offices. If you are for Reagan and I am for Mondale and NBC says "Forget it fellows—the whole thing's over–we project Reagan the winner," there is an equal disincentive for us both to vote. Reagan does not need your vote; he has already won. My vote cannot help Mondale; he has already lost. But what about the lesser races? Assuming that there is a correlation between Reagan supporters and supporters of senatorial candidate X on the one hand and between Mondale supporters and supporters of senatorial candidate Y on the other, then the disincentive I have just described not only loses one vote for Reagan and one vote for Mondale, but also one vote for Senate candidate X and one vote for Senate candidate Y. I can understand that early projections might reduce the size of the overall vote. I cannot agree that they would turn an otherwise winner into a loser.

I think the networks have a badly warped sense of values in persisting in projecting or characterizing the election outcome before the polls close. Many people think they are tampering with the election process, whether they are or not. I fail to see what great gain, either in terms of the public's right to know or in competitive network advantage, the networks realize by early projections. If I remember correctly, NBC was first with an early projection in 1980 and loudly trumpeted the fact that it was first. The NBC "Nightly News" thereafter dropped to third place in its share of the audience. The networks are risking unnecessary encroachments and restrictions on their First Amendment rights and should cease and desist in their own best interests, as well as in the nation's best interests. It would be unfortunate, for example, if exit polls were banned and their value were lost simply because they are reported prematurely.

Most of the concerns I have voiced about political polls thus far are comparatively easy to deal with. Another concern, I fear, is not so easy. I was very disturbed by the failure of the polls to indicate the magnitude of the Reagan victory in 1980 and by the persistent tendency of the polls to overmeasure the front-runner in 1982. In 1980 the consensus of the polls was that Reagan had a narrow edge, but it was close. While I reject the idea that he won in a landslide, he certainly won a comfortable victory, not a squeaker. In 1982, the polls indicated that Cuomo was an easy winner; instead, he had a narrow victory. The polls indicated Senator Weicker by a dozen points; he won by closer to five. The polls indicated a narrow victory for Millicent Fenwick; she lost. The polls indicated that Clements would beat White in Texas; White beat Clements. The polls indicated Bradley would beat Deukmejian; Deukmejian won. And on and on.

Presumably our polling techniques have become more and more sophisticated, yet we seem to be missing more and more elections. Why? Many pollsters think it is simply a matter of timing. The polls are not done quite late enough to catch last minute trends. I seriously question whether there was any last minute trend to Reagan's victory in 1980. I know some pollsters point to evidence that there was, but I think there is at least equally strong evidence that there was not. There is strongly suggestive evidence of closet voting in the 1980 election—of lifelong Democrats who knew they could not vote for Carter again but were not about to admit they would actually vote for Reagan. They said they would probably end up voting for Carter, when they knew they were going to vote the other way.

I am not sure why the polls so over-measured the success of front-runners in 1982. For the most part, the front-runners were incumbents. Whether there was an anti-incumbent sentiment that set in, I do not know. If so, I am concerned that the polls failed to pick up that antiincumbent sentiment. One scenario that would fit the front-runner character of the polls' failure, is that the public is unhappy enough with and cynical about most politicians; it does not want to give anyone an unqualified mandate. My suggestion about this is not consistent with the voter apathy we keep hearing about, but it has the virtue of fitting the data. A poll says X is going to clobber Y. People who have a preference for X over Y, but less than unbridled enthusiasm for X, end up either not voting or actually voting for Y to cut down X's win and to keep X from deciding he has a mandate to do what he damn well pleases.

I am not sure this is happening. I am not sure what is happening, and that concerns me most of all. I do not think it is a simple matter of polling two days later. Part of it may be increasingly conflicting pressures within any given voter. Fewer and fewer people today vote Democratic because they have always voted Democratic. Fewer and fewer people today vote Republican because they were born Republicans, their fathers were Republicans, and their grandfathers were Republicans. "This part of me argues for this candidate, that part of me argues for his opponent. I am no longer bound by tradition or orthodoxy and so I'm not really sure what I'm gonna do next Tuesday."

As I look back on our data for the 1980 election, I still see what I saw then. But I now realize how much more power it had then than I thought at the time. Our data clearly showed the public disaffection with Jimmy Carter, largely because he was seen as being ineffectual, indecisive, lacking in leadership ability, and not forceful. At the time, I thought his clear wins over Reagan on being compassionate, for the working people, and for the little guy, would at least offset the negative appraisals concerning leadership. In retrospect, it is now clear that leadership overshadowed compassion. I cannot say why the polls are missing the mark, but I would say to my colleagues: do not assume that merely polling forty-eight hours later will solve all of the problems.

CHAPTER 6

State Legislative Processes

Firsthand accounts of legislative life open this chapter. Political scientist
Frank Smallwood reflects on his experience as a Vermont state senator,
and Larry Sonis recounts one day's demands as a West Virginia
representative. Observe how their individual actions are affected by
being in a multimember legislative body. Why is compromise a
legislator's stock in trade?

A significant change in state legislatures over the past twenty years
is their emerging full-time operation, with most now meeting every
year. Four selections examine factors that affect the legislative process:
political parties, legislative staff, lobbyists, and the news media.
Although more voters consider themselves independents, Alan
Rosenthal points out why the demise of political parties has been
exaggerated, since in a majority of states control of one of the legislative
houses or the governorship is likely to be split between the Republicans
and the Democrats. Expertise needed by legislators in order to make
informed decisions has led to a full-time, professional staff, even if the
legislature has time-limited sessions; this leads to questions about who is
running the show. Lobbyists are a key information source, but is their
credibility self-policing? The natural skepticism of reporters, and how
the processes of legislating and journalism are different are explained by
a journalist who also served as a state legislator.

Opinion polls reveal public distrust of many states' legislatures.
Checks and balances adopted in the past decade include legislative
vetoes over administrative actions, and sunset laws for the automatic
ending of state programs and agencies unless they are specifically
reauthorized by the legislature. In some states, citizens can directly
legislate through the devices of initiative or referendum, and can recall
public officials from office prior to the expiration of their terms, as
Joseph Zimmerman explains in "Populism Revived."

23

Reflections on the Legislature

FRANK SMALLWOOD

Anybody who has been involved in the legislative process for any reasonable period of time is eventually forced to recognize the fact that a legislature is basically a "reactive" body which tends to respond to most key problems on an after-the-fact basis. As Jimmy Breslin notes in *How the Good Guys Finally Won,* a legislature "is not a place of positive action. It is an institution designed only to react, not plan or lead."

One of the basic reasons for this is that a legislature consists of a variety of voices which are, more often than not, attempting to sound off on a hundred different themes at once. Under the circumstances it is difficult for such a divergent body to get out ahead on very many major policy issues. A striking case in point involved the energy shortages that hit Vermont during the winter of 1974. Not one major bill dealing with the energy crisis was seriously debated during the 1973 legislative session, but we were deluged with such bills during the 1974 session. In essence, we were reacting to the crisis after it had hit us so hard that it could no longer be ignored.

This type of reactive approach creates a lot of problems and undoubtedly helps to account for the fact that legislative bodies in general, and state legislatures in particular, suffer from a generally poor public image. It's questionable, however, whether this is a fair appraisal. As political scientist Alan Rosenthal has observed, state legislatures are likely to be characterized "as weak sisters to admin-

istrators and governors. Yet probably more than any other American institution, state legislatures have recently undergone significant change."

Another political scientist, Ira Sharkansky, makes a similar point in *The Maligned States* when he observes that "one of the ironies of American politics is that the states receive so much negative publicity. They do not deserve to be whipping boys. The states are sources of strength." I agree with this observation. Despite all our problems, Vermont was ahead of the United States Congress in many areas of political innovation and creativity. Although we engaged in our share of frustrations, we were also making some very real strides in getting on top of many key issues, such as environmental planning, campaign-finance reform, open government and "right-to-know" legislation, and the like.

Part of the difficulty in evaluating the effectiveness of the state legislatures results from the fact that we fail to make such evaluations on the basis of what a legislative body is designed to accomplish. When the average citizen thinks about the legislature, he is likely to conclude, "Oh yes, that's where they make the laws." So far so good. But making laws is only one part of the legislative process. Actually, a legislature is designed to perform a multiplicity of roles, which is a point made by Professor Duane Lockard, who once served in the Connecticut Senate, when he observes

Excerpted from Frank Smallwood, *Free and Independent.* (Brattleboro, Vermont: Stephen Greene Press, 1976), pp. 216–218, 222–224.

that a legislature is "vitally important as an agency that reflects the views of different elements of the state, that allocates resources between the public and private sector and also within the government, that provides some kind of overview of the bureaucracy, and that mediates conflicts between competing forces."

When viewed in this light, the legislature performs a wide variety of different functions in our political-governmental system. First, it carries out a legitimizing role (creating and ratifying legislation by enacting statutory law). Second, it performs a distributive role (allocating revenues and tax burdens). Third, it performs a political role (mediating conflict and reconciling different pressures from divergent special interest groups). Fourth, it performs a representative role (reflecting constituency views and dramatizing issues so that they become the subject of open public debate). And finally, it carries out the role of watchdog (overseeing the executive branch).

Because of this multitude of roles, the legislature is a political body, and, in the words of political scientist Malcolm Jewell, "politics is the key to understanding the American state legislature." In effect, it serves as a lightning rod to which all the conflicting pressures of American society are drawn, and its primary job is to de-fuse these pressures so that the political system can function intact without blowing wide apart. . . .

There had also been disappointments, but they are an integral part of the political process. The essence of politics, especially legislative politics, is compromise, which means that no participants can gain (or lose) everything they may be after.

Most important of all, I learned a great deal about the dynamics of practical politics; and also a great deal about myself in relationship to the demands that grow out of the political life.

From the outset it was obvious to me that there are certain basic human traits that ap-

pear to be desirable in any political personality: a basic sense of fairness and integrity, a reasonable degree of intelligence, an ability to laugh and maintain a sense of balance in the face of conflicting pressures. These factors certainly are important, yet there is another equally important set of requirements that I completely underestimated: the personal time and energy demands that we place on our public servants in a democratic system of government.

To state it as bluntly as possible, anyone who is interested in making a major commitment to politics had best be prepared literally to give up all else if this commitment is to be fulfilled. As Stimson Bullitt observed in *To Be a Politician*, "politics is an all-or-nothing venture." There's no way—at least I found no way—to pursue the political life on a casual, leisurely, half-time basis. Unexpected demands pop up all over the place, often at the most inconvenient time. Drop everything, Frank, there's some new crisis out there somewhere that will take the rest of your afternoon (and probably your evening as well). The pressures of political life are so chaotic and so unpredictable that plain, hard physical stamina becomes of overriding importance to anyone who hopes to pursue a political career. What I'm talking about here is simple raw energy. You can be bone-tired, but if constituents want to see you on something that they think is important, you'd better be ready to draw on some hidden inner reserves in an effort to respond to their needs. The political life is a tiring, grueling, continuous depletion of personal energy reserves. This is the first, and most significant, insight I gained about the political process.

A second basic fact that emerged very early is that a great deal of your physical and mental energy is expended on routine business that may not appear to be of any particular earth-shaking importance. The point here is that you are a public servant. Certain issues may not be terribly important to you, but if they are important to your constituents, you'd better listen and pay attention. Although some of the bills we considered in committee bored me nearly to death, they represented legitimate concerns on the part of selected segments of the public, and there was no way I could conscientiously ignore these concerns. In short, a great deal in the political process does not—repeat does not—involve the big glamorous policy issues. Most of the work is sheer routine and hardly awe-inspiring. If you are not prepared to face this fact, stay away from the political arena.

Third is the matter of privacy, or, more accurately, lack of privacy. Once you have entered the public arena, a great deal of your business becomes public business. If you're on some kind of an ego trip and like to read your name in the newspapers, it's great; but if you really want to pack off and get away from it all, that's a different matter. There's very little room for personal privacy in the world of politics. This is another of the basic facts of political life.

Finally, you've got to have a pretty thick skin, and a sense of inner direction that is strong enough to guide you through some turbulent waters. It's not so much that everybody is trying to cut up everybody else all the time; the knives weren't that sharp, at least in Vermont. Rather it's the ability to reach specific conclusions in areas of considerable uncertainty; the ability to reconcile yourself to the reality that much of what you do will inevitably be misinterpreted and/or misunderstood; the ability to recognize that you have to provide leadership in helping people to understand and face complex issues that they would like to oversimplify. Dartmouth's former president John Dickey used to tell me that one of the key tests of leadership was "the capacity to be undismayed in the face of adversity and uncertainty." I was a little fuzzy on the concept when he first explained it to me, but I understood it much, much better after I finished a stint in the political arena.

24

"O.K., Everybody. Vote Yes": A Day in the Life of a State Legislator

LARRY SONIS

The phone beat my alarm clock in their daily contest to see which could wake me up first. I muttered a profanity, rubbed my eyes, and stumbled out of bed.

The West Virginia legislature was in session. And I was a member.

I shuffled across the floor and picked up the receiver. My elbow knocked a stack

---

of printed House bills off the table.

"Larry?" the caller began excitedly. "I have to tell this to somebody. I shouldn't be talking to you. Something has to be done. Can we talk confidentially?"

"Sure," I told her automatically, not realizing in my half-sleep that I'd just given my word of honor to keep my mouth shut even if she were about to tell me that the Speaker, before his plastic surgery, was a Nazi war criminal.

She went on to explain how a statehouse telephone bank for "hot-line" citizen complaints had been used regularly for long-distance calls in a political campaign. I caught a guilty glimpse of myself, using a state WATS line to call a personal friend in Atlanta.

When the woman finished her story, I advised her to notify the County Prosecutor's Office.

Now fully awake, I lapsed into my morning ritual. Coffee, orange juice, yogurt, and a perusal of *The Charleston Gazette*. I turned on the radio for background music and sat down on the couch.

An announcer on the radio was reading wire copy: "The House Finance Committee . . . public hearings today . . . take the sales tax off food. . . ."

I chuckled. Hell, the food tax removal was dead this year. But the leaders who had already decided to engineer the bill's funeral would make a big deal out of the public hearings on it anyway. Sincere witnesses would testify. A forum would be provided. And the bill would die.

Why bother? Well, I thought, the Legislature is part theater. Hold a hearing and people think you're doing something. A well-run hearing enables a politician to take a stand on principle while avoiding the necessity of a floor vote, which is perilously closer to meaningful action. The Legislature, I had learned, is chock full of neat tricks for avoiding commitment.

I finished scanning the *Gazette*, took a hurried shower, and opened the front door.

There, on the doormat, was a bag of fruit, left by a neighbor with a complimentary note.

This was a phenomenon I'd noticed right after my election. It seems nearly everybody wants to play Santa Claus in the presence of a legislator. People buy you drinks at the bar. They give you garden vegetables and Christmas cookies. Their associations and businesses send you watch calendars, pens, paperweights, neckties, and cuff links.

I placed the fruit inside the door and went down the street to the bus stop. As I waited, a car drove by and slowed to a halt. I could see an arm inside the car waving me over. On the assumption that dangerous psychopaths don't lure their victims so brazenly, I bounded into the waiting auto.

Once inside, I realized I'd been picked up by a lobbyist for the auto dealers, who proceeded to tell me good-naturedly how he had been thoroughly destroying a bill of mine aimed at protecting consumers against auto repair ripoffs. An affable and savvy professional, he was able to tell me in so many words that he thought I was a jerk for sponsoring the bill, without angering me. He dropped me in front of the Capitol.

"THAT'S RIGHT"

I walked up the front stairs and into the large hallway next to the House of Delegates chamber. Outside the chamber, textbook protesters and teachers confronted each other. Kanawha County's schoolbook controversy had come to the Legislature.

A delegate approaching the chamber was stopped by a protester and shown a junior high school library book. "That's right," the delegate said. "We've got to get the filth out of the schools."

Moments later, the same delegate was stopped by a teacher who urged that the Legislature not bow down to the demands of the protesters. "That's right," the delegate said.

"We've got to keep censorship out of the schools."

I walked into the chamber and strode down the aisle toward the Sergeant-at-Arms' quarters, a long room just behind the Speaker's podium. The chamber itself, ornate with its marble walls and plush, red carpeting, exudes grandeur, muddied here and there by one of the few remaining spittoons.

Waiting for me at my mailbox were four "approval slips," indicating that bills drafted by the Legislative Services Office were ready for me to sign and be introduced in my name.

I had put in my share of so-called "grandstand" bills, noble ideas with great purpose but a snowball's chance in hell of passing. As a freshman, I introduced a "program" including the abolition of five constitutional offices, tax reforms, and the creation of bipartisan, independent commissions on ethics and elections.

I hoped they'd pass. I believed in them. But, in my heart and while staring into a mirror, I knew they weren't going to go anywhere at this session. I rationalized my introducing them on the grounds that they might at least generate some consideration and public awareness for the ideas they embodied. What they were sure to generate, however, was stacks of paper and hours of work for the well-paid attorneys who translated my "program" into statutory language.

Other grandstand bills were less pretentious than mine. One delegate, for example, submitted legislation to command expansion of the highway between Lens Creek, Drawdy, and Madison Mountains. He didn't tell his constituents that the House would never vote such a specific command—that the real way to get the highway fixed was through negotiation with the state highways department and adequate provision of money in its budget.

Duplicate bills, too, ate up dozens of hours in staff time. Perennials were tax relief and "sock it to the utilities" measures, which ended up being introduced separately by half a dozen delegates who distinguished their versions from each others' by changing a non-

substantive word or two among their proposals.

After signing the approval slips, I left them on a desk where a per diem employee would show up later to carry them downstairs to Legislative Services.

I then walked to my desk in the chamber. Waiting for me there was a "meals and miscellaneous" expense form to sign. The expense money (around $15 a day—this was before the recent increase) was supposed to pay for a legislator's meals and job-related sundry expenses during the session. However, special-interest groups picked up the tab for many dinners, and some lawmakers went ahead and claimed full expenses anyway. Furthermore, since we were given free stationery, free office supplies, and free secretarial help, it was difficult to fathom what "miscellaneous expenses" we might incur doing our jobs. But I signed the form.

A stenographer then appeared beside my desk and asked me if I'd like to get some mail "out of the way."

"Yeah," I said, "if you've got the time, now is fine."

We started knocking off the dictation in near record time. Most of the letters I was answering were mechanical queries, complaints, or exhortations, with contents that could have been expressed by checking a little box. I answered each one.

The stenographer then confided to me a story about a delegate who irritated a colleague of hers. The ambitious solon had taken it upon himself to personally respond to each and every person who had signed a petition of which he had received a xeroxed copy. He sent the secretary scurrying to the phone books to look up their addresses and prepare thank-you letters for each one. Since paper, postage, and printing expenses are paid by the taxpayers and charged to the Legislature as a whole—without a delegate-by-delegate breakdown—staff irritation was about the only disincentive to such extravagance.

As we neared the bottom of the stack of mail, I found the annual letter from the horse racing industry, offering me a share of the more than $100,000 worth of free track privileges it offers to lawmakers.

Finished with the mail, I walked across the hallway between the House and Senate and stopped briefly at the office of a friend. We started talking about the hot potatoes of the session, one of the hottest of which was abortion. I remembered a campaign rally at which the local chapter of the National Organization for Women asked legislative candidates to raise their hands if they would be willing to sponsor an abortion compliance bill. After the election, when they were recruiting a co-sponsor for the bill, NOW's lobbyists were told "no" by one of the hand-raisers.

My friend and I traded political gossip like two high school sophomores for a few more minutes, and then I headed back toward the House chamber for the 10 A.M. session.

On the way, I stopped by a House staff office and noticed that one staff member seemed irritated.

When she told me which legislator she was angry with, I guessed her complaint. He was a congenial soul, I was told, honest and considerate in almost every respect, except for one peculiar hangup. He was a kleptomaniac. This legislator had stopped by the staff member's desk a few minutes before me and, while standing there smiling and talking to her, had removed her scotch tape dispenser and put it in his coat.

By now, the bell had rung, signaling the start of the session. I quickly commiserated with the theft victim, and then hurried toward the chamber. The doors had closed, which meant the prayer was already under way.

"TAKE A WALK"

With a moment to spare, I paused and overheard several major lobbyists discussing a bill. One of them, a former legislator who knew most members and key staff personally, was frequently sought out because of his access and firsthand knowledge. Numerous ex-legislators in West Virginia have become valuable advocates for coal, banking, and other special interests following their terms of office. Why let a little thing like being soundly beaten at the polls keep you from helping to shape legislation for your fellow citizens?

Shortly before entering the chamber, I was pulled aside by a lobbyist interested in defeating a consumer protection bill. He told me he realized what my position was (opposite his), but he would appreciate it if I could "take a walk" so as not to be present to cast my disagreeable vote. He told me another delegate had promised him to do so, and he just needed a couple of other absentees to swing the margin his way.

I smiled and went inside. Just as predicted, when the vote on the bill was taken, I noticed the delegate who had promised to walk had indeed taken a walk. He conveniently reappeared after the vote.

Next came a crucial vote on a tax reform amendment. A normally liberal delegate came up to me and, apologetically, told me he wished he could vote with me but he had promised the "leadership" he would oppose the measure. For reasons of his own, he proceeded to vote against his own conscience. Subsequently, he was appointed to a major conference committee.

The food tax was still a hot item despite its inevitable defeat. At one point, a senior member ambled over to my desk to explain his opposition to the proposal. In true veteran-to-neophyte fashion, he lied about the state budget and its revenue estimates while maintaining a straight face.

Interestingly, as the "young turks" worked toward trying to get the tax relief measure approved on the floor, a colleague told me "they're booing" at Rockefeller for Governor Headquarters. John D. Rockefeller IV, who was then the Democratic gubernatorial candidate, favored the proposal. However, some of his coterie, wanting their man to get credit for the measure while in office, took a dim view of "prematurely" acting on it.

The oddest debate on the food tax occurred on a motion to remove the bill from the reluctant Finance Committee and bring it to the floor for a vote. Several delegates who favored the food exemption nevertheless rose to their feet to denounce this "attack on the committee system."

In trying to understand how they could favor the tax relief bill but oppose the only motion which realistically might bring it to a vote, I conjured up a picture of a couple sitting on a front porch. "Ethel," the husband might say, "I'd sure like to see the tax off food." "Yes, Homer," the wife replied, "but, you know, we've got to uphold that committee system up there."

"OK, EVERYBODY. VOTE YES."

Among the other bills that were before us, pork barrels abounded. Literally millions of dollars were earmarked for a slew of goodies ranging from state funding for a national track and field hall of fame in Kanawha County to subsidizing a chronically flooded historical site. The projects were tied together politically into a coalition vote since none could easily survive on its own merits as a "priority" use of state tax dollars. Thus, as we prepared to vote on a pork barrel for Wood County, a Kanawha County delegate blurted out, "OK, everybody. Vote yes. Wood County is going for the Hall of Fame."

Less popular were the measures that threatened the time-honored customs of legislative patronage. For example, we were considering a motion to insist that the House adhere to its rules, which imposed a numerical ceiling on the number of staff jobs per session. Even the leadership had been embarrassed when it was discovered that more assistant doorkeepers were to be hired for the session than the House had doors.

After taking part in the anti-patronage revolt by pushing the motion, I was summoned into the office of a prominent leadership figure. "Won't you guys at least telegraph your shots in advance?" he asked me. "We could have worked something out if you'd come by first."

I left his office, and, outside in the hallway, I thought about how the Speaker and other legislative leaders get chosen by the Democratic caucus. A lot of it depends on who promises what to whom. The supporters of one candidate for speaker had offered me a committee chairmanship and a Finance Committee slot if only I would vote for their guy.

I continued walking and soon arrived at my first committee meeting.

The chairman began the meeting by stating that we would take up a bill the Speaker wanted considered.

"What is it?" a delegate asked.

"Uh," the chairman replied, "well, it's . . . uh . . . what it would do . . . well, the Speaker wants it."

Another committee member then bailed the chairman out and explained the bill, which was harmless enough. It passed despite the chairman's ignorance of its content.

Shortly thereafter, another delegate entered the room to tell us he had introduced one bill just to placate a constituent—and would we please help him out by killing his bill. The committee obliged him, but not until a few members speculated on how funny it would be to send his bill to the floor and watch him squirm. The committee adjourned for lunch.

Lunch was short. I ate at my chamber desk in about ten minutes. During the meal, a senior member of the permanent House staff came up to my desk and lavished praise on the "fine work" I was doing and told me how much he admired my floor speeches and public statements. Moments later, I overheard him asking a nearby colleague of mine, "You think you can keep Sonis quiet this session?"

The Democratic caucus, closed to the public as usual, was held around 12:30 that afternoon. Inside, delegates loosened their ties and spoke candidly about a pending teacher pay raise. A show of hands indicated a pay raise would pass by a narrow margin.

Later, when the Legislature went public again, the teacher pay raise sailed through the House by an overwhelming majority. One delegate who had opposed the raise in the private caucus spoke to a group of teachers outside, taking partial credit for the victory.

HEART-TO-HEART TALK

On the way to my afternoon committee meeting, a normally aloof delegate approached me with an earnest look. "Uh-oh," I thought. He told me he had information that a colleague had pushed for an item in the state budget to upgrade a park facility that happened to be located near a motel in which the colleague had an interest. "Why don't you embarrass him on the floor?" the delegate asked, handing me a scrawled note and adding, "Think about it."

I walked upstairs to the committee meeting and joined a half dozen or so other delegates. When a quorum didn't materialize, we disbanded. A few of the more diligent members grumbled about the Legislature's prevailing work habits.

After the attempted meeting, the chairman of a major committee, who noticed I had been voting with his antagonist lately, called me into his office for a private, "heart-to-heart" talk.

With tears in his eyes, he accused his rival of having helped to publish an "obscene" and "communistic" student newspaper—of which he happened to have a copy in his desk drawer. He urged me to join with him and the "leadership" and "get something done," instead of trying to "make trouble," which could only hurt me, he added.

I returned downstairs with some time to kill before the afternoon floor session. A lobbyist approached me and asked me where I stood on a certain bill. I told him.

Another delegate, who had heard me explain my position, stopped me as I headed into the chamber. "Why did you tell him where you stood?" he asked. "You could have kept him guessing and gotten a steak dinner out of him."

Inside the chamber, we were about to vote on the track and field hall of fame appropriation. "Boy I hate to vote for this damned thing," complained one delegate who had made a personal assurance months before that he now regretted.

As the bills came up, many delegates looked around the room for indications on how to vote. Some looked to a floor leader or committee chairman for a thumbs up or thumbs down. Others bent their ears to a colleague who might know something about the bill. On any given topic, probably about a third of the membership is familiar with the bill, another third knows the issue generally, and another third is playing follow the leader.

As we proceeded through the legislative calendar, the debates, bill explanations, and button-pushing roll-call votes continued. One delegate improved on Pythagoras when, in expressing his outrage at how his county was being mistreated, he lashed out at the "Charleston-Huntington-Morgantown-Wheeling triangle."

THE RULES COMMITTEE RULES

The calendar was limited, however, because the session was nearing its end and the Rules Committee was in control. You see, during the last two weeks of a legislative session, when the volume of business is largest, the decision to defeat a bill is made, not by the 100 elected delegates in the House, but by the handful of delegates who make up the House Rules Committee. The Rules Committee may be the most effective device yet invented for wresting control of the Legislature from a majority of the elected representatives and putting it in the hands of a few key people. Here's how it works:

When a bill is reported to the floor from committee, it is put on the "calendar" so the House may vote on it. However, legislators tend to behave a bit like students with homework: they postpone major assignments. As a result, the "calendar" of bills gets unwieldy during the last two weeks of the session.

The Rules Committee was invented, in theory, as a "traffic cop" to go into action late in the session and "schedule" the consideration of bills, thus avoiding a logjam of last-minute legislation. The Committee is made up of the floor leaders, committee chairmen, and a few extras, usually people who worked their way into the inner circle by carrying water for the leadership or by voting right in the election for Speaker.

Under a resolution routinely approved early in the session by a coalition of leadership folks and naive freshmen, the Rules Committee is granted authority to put bills on a "special calendar" that takes precedence over the "regular calendar" of the House. In theory, the Committee only schedules bills to ensure an "orderly" flow of business. In practice, the Committee has assumed the power to judge bills on the basis of substance and policy.

In practice, also, if your bill is not chosen by the Committee for the "special calendar" chances are it will never make it to the floor for a vote. As soon as the special calendar has been completed each day, the House automatically adjourns. And just try getting the two-thirds vote necessary to suspend the rules and get your bill to the floor. (I tried once, and got six votes, plus a lot of scorn for my outlandish violation of "rules of the game.") So year after year, the session ends without the "regular calendar" ever being voted on, and the bills left there die a quiet, *de facto* death.

In effect, the Rules Committees have become mini-legislatures. It takes seven legislators to control the House Committee, and six to control the smaller Senate Committee. The intelligent lobbyist concentrates on them. After all, a cynic might ask, why buy a majority of the entire Legislature when you only need to pay for 13 members.

EVENING LESSONS

With all the scheduled special calendar items taken care of, the House adjourned for the day. I began gathering up a stack of homework and looked around the chamber as most of the delegates wandered out.

In front of me, a public relations aide had brought a draft of a weekly newspaper column to a delegate to be checked out before sending it to the hometown editor for publication. Another representative had a large stack of manila envelopes on her desk, and was dutifully signing the copies of bills she was mailing to grateful constituents. At the podium stood another lawmaker, beaming into the camera alongside schoolchildren from the district.

I left the scene and returned home briefly, driving back to the Capitol to leave a few bill requests with legislative services. Then I headed downtown, providing a lift to a colleague anxious to get to the Daniel Boone Hotel, the traditional grand central station for out-of-town delegates during the session.

This delegate, who had been strongly supported by the West Virginia Education Association, was offering his thoughts on politics. "I figured when I ran that it would be helpful to be expedient with at least one major interest group," he said. "So, hell, why not teachers?"

I dropped him near the Boone, where I also had to go to tape a radio show with a news reporter (a former legislator himself). The legislator-turned-broadcaster had a half-hour program, which he told me went to a string of radio stations in the rural, central part of West Virginia.

"I've got Delegate Sah-nus here with me," he told his audience as the tape recorder got rolling, "and I thought I'd ask him about two things I see here he's introduced. This abortion reform bill. And the bill to make Martin Luther King's birthday a holiday."

"Delegate Sah-nus," he said, "some people say abortion's murder. What do you say?"

I sensed I was in for an uncomfortable half hour, and I plunged into the subject expecting similar lines of questioning. I wasn't disappointed. When he got to the King bill, my interviewer prefaced his question by noting that he had seen a "report" that black people had been multiplying at a more rapid rate than white people.

After the radio show, I was leaving the hotel when an older member, who, it is fair to say, had had a few, approached me with a warm, kindly smile.

"I was like you boys once," he beamed. "Hell, I know you're right. You just go about it the wrong way. You'll learn when you get my age."

"If you agree with us, why don't you vote with us?" I asked him.

"How you vote don't matter, really, in the long run," he said, "You'll learn that, too, when you get my age."

I didn't stop to chat, but hurried across town to where the county teachers association was having its annual legislative dinner. We were scattered neatly around the tables . . . teacher, legislator, teacher, legislator, etc. After the dinner, each lawmaker was asked to rise and recite his or her views on the teachers' program. We did it in turn, over and over again, and some of us got it right.

As I left the dinner, I began to relax and mull over the day's events. I drove across the Kanawha City Bridge and headed home. Upon arriving, I walked upstairs and tossed my coat on the couch. The phone was ringing.

I spent the next half hour answering calls, highlighted by an irate father who insisted on having my views on whether sex education books were proper in displaying human genitals. Finally, I decided I needed to sleep and stopped picking up the receiver. I climbed into bed. The phone kept ringing until around midnight.

— 25 —

If the Party's Over,
Where's All That Noise Coming From?

ALAN ROSENTHAL

It's been over 10 years since columnist David Broder wrote his book about the failure of politics in America. In *The Party's Over*, he asserted that, "the governmental system is not working because the political parties are not working." The conventional wisdom is that if the parties were not working in the early 1970s, they are working no better in the mid-1980s.

The conventional wisdom needs to be qualified. There are three meanings of party—party in the electorate, party as organization and party in office. It helps to distinguish among them. Party in the electorate is undoubtedly weaker than it used to be. As far as American voters are concerned, party affiliation no longer matters terribly much. A third or so of the electorate identify, not as Democrats or Republicans, but rather as Independents. And, most of the others are weak or erratic in their loyalties. Party as organization is certainly different than it used to be. The old grass roots continue to wither away, and neither state nor local parties play the role they once did—not in Connecticut or Michigan, not in Chicago or New York City, and not in Allegheny County, Pennsylvania, or Hudson County, New Jersey. Still, there is renewed vitality of the national committees in Washington, D.C., the establishment of party offices and cadres in state capitals, and new forms of ideologically inclined caucuses in more than a few places. Although it is not all decline, parties in the electorate and as organizations are weaker than before.

Party in office, however, may be stronger than it used to be. Governmental parties have recently become more active. It is true that merit systems have generally replaced patronage as a means of making appointments, but partisan affiliation still counts heavily when it comes to filling top positions in the federal government and in the executive departments and agencies of many of the states. Moreover, something has been happening in Congress. Particularly in the House, the majority caucus has become a more vital institution, discipline is being exercised, and on some of the major issues the parties take cohesive positions in opposition to one another.

If parties are astir in Congress, what are they doing in state legislatures? In order to find out, we recently surveyed partisan behavior in the senates and houses of 44 of the nation's states (the exceptions being Alaska, Arkansas, Hawaii, Pennsylvania, Tennessee and West Virginia, which did not respond to our inquiry).[1] On the basis of this exploration, it can be reported that in a surprising number of legislatures the parties are alive and kicking, and partisanship is making a considerable amount of noise.

A GROWTH IN PARTISANSHIP

Where political parties exist, partisanship also exists—in one form or another. As defined in

State Government, Vol.57, No.2, (Summer 1984), pp. 50–54.

the dictionary, "partisanship" is basically adherence to or support for a party (or faction, person or cause). It is the act of *taking sides*.

In state legislatures today, there is a good deal of taking sides—by some members as Democrats and others as Republicans. Roughly one-quarter of the 44 legislatures surveyed could be considered "very" partisan and another half "somewhat" partisan. Partisanship matters in these states, but it is not the only factor (nor always the most important one) shaping the behavior of legislators. Kansas' regional rivalry between east and west may be more basic there; New Hampshire's ideological alignments may be stronger; and Maryland's conflict between legislators from the rural, western part of the state allied with those from the Eastern Shore and legislators from Baltimore City and the suburbs may be more pervasive.

Nevertheless, partisanship is on the rise. It is on the rise in states where it means relatively little, such as Oklahoma, South Carolina, Texas and Vermont. It is on the rise also in states where it means a lot, such as California, Michigan, New Jersey and Wisconsin. Overall, during the past decade partisanship seems to have increased in roughly 40 percent of the states and decreased in only 10 percent, remaining at about the same level in the rest.

What accounts for this trend? There are a number of reasons, and different ones in different places. We shall focus on two of the most important reasons here—one having to do with party organization and the other with electoral activity.

PARTY ORGANIZATION

The vitality of party organization bears some responsibility for the upsurge of legislative partisanship today. Party caucuses, the principal mechanisms of such organization, have made a difference in most places. In fact, among the states surveyed here, only Alabama, Louisiana, Mississippi and Texas in the South and nonpartisan Nebraska are entirely without caucuses.

One of the critical functions caucuses perform is organizational. With each newly elected legislature, they select their party's leaders—the majority and minority leaders, the assistant leaders, the whips, etc. They also nominate candidates for the top positions of president or president pro tempore in the senate and speaker in the house. Despite the appearance of a bipartisan coalition from time to time (even in partisan places like California, Minnesota and Washington) to elect top leadership, the majority party caucus usually prevails. It controls the basic organization of the chamber.

Another critical function is positioning. The extent to which a caucus engages in positioning depends partly on the frequency of stands taken. In states like Arizona, California, Delaware, Iowa, Maine and Michigan caucuses take rather frequent stands. Positioning depends partly also on the firmness of the stands taken. There is nothing firmer than the "binding" caucus, where a majority of members votes to commit the minority to the majority position. Attempts to bind are rare, however. Instead of exercising party discipline, caucuses generally work to build a consensus on the basis of what members want to achieve, then they take a position on an issue or bill, and finally they try to persuade undecided or wavering members to go along.

Caucuses also perform informational and procedural functions. Members exchange views and learn from one another; leaders get feedback from rank and file; and rank and file get cues from leaders. At the same time, strategies and tactics are planned, mainly to deal with issues on the floor so that the caucus position is advanced.

Party caucuses are in good health today in part because they are staffed by able professionals. With the growth of staffing in state legislatures over the past 20 years, there are now several types of staff operating. Among them are those of partisan hue, working for caucuses or legislative party leaders. They assist leaders, work for standing committees, do research, write speeches, conduct constituent service, and handle the media. A majority of the nation's legislatures now employ caucus staff of one size or another. The largest, amounting to 10 or more people for each of the four caucuses, are found in California, Connecticut, Illinois, Indiana, Michigan, Minnesota, Missouri, New Jersey, New York, Ohio, Rhode Island and Washington.

These staffs do make a difference. Some years ago the effects of partisan staffing were explored in a study of the Wisconsin Legislature. The study showed that caucus staffs engendered greater cohesion within the parties and conflict between them and more forceful attacks by the minority and defense by the majority.[2] In short, caucuses and their staffs contribute to partisanship—the process of taking sides.

ELECTORAL ACTIVITY

A potent stimulus to the recent rise of partisanship is the growing concern—even preoccupation—of legislators with elections. As a result, there is an increase in electorally related activity, not only in districts throughout the state but in the legislature as well. Electoral efforts and legislative partisanship, for example, have been linked in the state of Washington. The former speaker there explained: "You might think that Washington would be very nonpartisan. . . . In some ways, though, we are very party-conscious, if only because party—at least my own Republican Party—has become a formidable election machine."[3] It may sound peculiar, but the legislature has become politicized—that is, substantially more politicized than before. And biennial elections may have become the dominant feature of legislative life.

Electoral concerns are manifest in the ways in which issues are now being used. We tend to think of issues as results of the legislative process, representing the public policy objectives of the parties and members in the legislature. That is their principal role, but they also serve as vehicles in the partisan quest for power.

It is nothing new for political parties to calculate the potential effects that the position they take on a bill will have on their electoral prospects. Indeed, there is the story of the legislative staffer who, in the heat of the process, cautioned a party leader: "If you pass this bill, you're going to screw up the state for the next 30 years." "We can't worry about the next 30 years," the party leader countered, "we have to worry about the next election." What is new is the increase in positioning and posturing. The parties are going further than simply taking into account the electoral effects of their legislative positions. They are raising and exploiting issues in order to gain partisan advantage, and not necessarily to enact legislation to their partisan liking. This has become an almost regular practice in places like Arizona, California, Connecticut, Iowa, Michigan, New Jersey, New Mexico, New York, Washington and Wisconsin.

One way that a party attempts to secure an edge electorally is by "making a record" that will help it and hurt the opposition. Floor amendments requiring roll-call votes are the customary way to make a record. Typically, Democrats will try to get Republicans on record against teachers or against environmental interests, while Republicans will try to get Democrats on record against economic development. A variant of "making a record" is what can be called "the minority party game." Since the minority has little control over the legislative agenda or the legislative product, it may be more likely to act irresponsibly. It does so when it tries to embarrass the majority, to put the majority on the spot. This game often involves revenues or expenditures, with a typical minority stance being to reduce taxes and cut the budget.

When one party controls the legislature and the other the governor's office, partisan exploitation of issues tends to be greater. Divided government often gives rise to the "get the governor game" in the legislature. New Jersey provides an illustration of how this game can be played. Republican Thomas Kean took office as governor of New Jersey in 1982 and confronted a Democratic-controlled legislature, including an Assembly led by a partisan and aggressive speaker. For the first two years of the Kean administration, conflict was intense as both parties threw everything they had into the 1983 Senate and Assembly elections. In an attempt to win control of the legislature, the governor headed a vigorous Republican campaign, albeit one that did not succeed. The Democrats were furious at the governor for the role he played, but he defended himself: "I did what I did as head of the party to elect Republicans, and I am not sorry. I did what I had to do." Although there was talk after the election of conciliation, the Democrats had an incentive to weaken Kean who would probably be at the top of the Republicans' 1985 ticket. "If there are coattails and your candidate loses," went their rationale, "you lose, too."[4] And they had no desire to lose.

One issue that can ordinarily be counted on to provoke partisanship, if only on a decennial basis, is legislative redistricting or reapportionment. Since the most recent reapportionment plans were enacted only a few years ago, the results are still fresh in legislative memory. Among the states we surveyed, in one out of three cases partisan considerations had at least some bearing on the reapportionment process and in another one out of three its bearing was very significant.

In addition to taking continuing advantage of issues and perennial advantage of redistricting, the legislative parties also provide material support to their candidates—incumbents and challengers alike, and particularly those in close races. Recently, legislative leaders have come to play an important part in this business, thus bringing the electoral and the legislative arenas closer together.

It began in California almost 30 years ago, when Jesse Unruh had money left over from his own campaign and parceled it out to other Democrats. Since then, the role of leadership in raising and allocating funds has progressed further in California than anywhere else. California's legislators today rely on their personal organizations, individual contributions and PACs. But they also expect their leaders to raise funds for them. Thus, when Leo McCarthy announced his candidacy for governor and started seeking money for his own campaign instead of for those of his Assembly colleagues, a majority of Democrats tried to oust him from the speakership in the middle of his term.

California's new leaders learned their lesson. By way of illustration, in 1982 Speaker Willie Brown raised $1.7 million and allocated it to Democratic candidates for the Assembly, including six who received more than half their support from him and all of whom won. Brown, it is said, has admitted to spending half his time as a speaker raising money (and, according to one sardonic observer of California politics, spending the other half of his time paying it back). When asked if he thought this was a healthy trend, Brown replied: "For the Speaker's survival purposes, it is very healthy."[5] Leaders, like Willie Brown, can offer their members staff, office space, chairmanships and—probably as critical as anything else—large chunks of money. "When you receive that kind of money," one participant commented, "you get grateful."

Legislative leaders not only in California but in Arizona, Connecticut, Illinois, Michigan, Minnesota, New Jersey, New York, Ohio, Oklahoma, Oregon, Washington and Wisconsin also play a significant role in campaign finance. Sometimes the money distributed to party members comes out of the leader's own war chest, as in Arizona. There Burton Barr, the Republican minority leader in the house, can raise a large amount, but spends little of it on his own campaign. The excess is given to Republican incumbents, with most going to those in key races. Some-times leaders set aside special accounts or establish special caucus funds. In New Jersey the speaker, Alan Karcher, set up his own PAC, raised over $125,000, and distributed it to Democratic candidates in 1983. Karcher's PAC, in fact, was among the 10 highest spending PACs in the campaign.[6]

Whatever the banking and accounting system, the principal mechanism by which money is generated seems to be the big fundraiser. Michael Madigan, formerly minority leader and now speaker in Illinois, helped elect a Democratic house in 1982 and since then has raised over $250,000 with a single Chicago event. Massachusetts Senate President William Bulger has a reputation for sponsoring very successful affairs, such as those held at Anthony's Pier Four which are considered major occasions in Boston and "amazing sights to behold." Vernal Riffe, the speaker in Ohio, is as accomplished as any-one along these lines, and over a period of a few years, he has raised hundreds of thousands of dollars for Democratic candidates who, when elected, are expected to be members of the "team." New York's legislative leaders are similarly effective, and it has been written that: "Whatever the influence of local party bosses, however, Democratic lawmakers seeking political help today are more likely to turn to their own legislative leaderships."[7]

If leaders do not raise and allocate funds themselves, in most of the rest of the states they help their party's candidates in other ways: by singing their praises at dinners, receptions and barbecues, as in North Carolina; by attending fundraisers and writing letters, as in Maryland; and even by door-to-door campaigning in targeted districts, as in Iowa.

Still another form of electoral support, which leaders in a number of states can furnish, is staff. In some places legislators have personal staffs to call on for help during campaigns. In others, however, the only people they can turn to for help are those working either directly or indirectly for leaders and generally on the payroll of leadership or caucus staffs. Much of the work done by these so-called "political support staff"—newsletters, press releases, radio spots and so forth—naturally can be used for partisan purposes, and one of the most partisan purposes of all is that of winning elections. However, there are limits. As state employees, staffers generally are not permitted to work on campaigns during regular office hours. Therefore, some of them work in members' districts after hours, in the evenings or on weekends, and some manage to spend time in the districts, discretely to be sure, but during the workday nonetheless.

THE EFFECTS OF PARTISANSHIP

Partisanship undoubtedly affects the legislature as an institution. Generally speaking, it is a unifying force, in what has become a fragmented body with individualistic members. One result is that Democrats and Republicans tend to stick together in opposition to one another, especially on major issues of revenue and expenditure.

In many of the closely contested states, where majority and minority parties switch status suddenly and frequently, partisanship works well. It contributes positively to the process. Democrats and Republicans have respect for each other, and when they wage battle it is in civil fashion. But in some places partisanship may affect the process adversely—in Wisconsin, for example, where partisan divisions have widened and individual members have become less disciplined than before. In California the election in 1978 of the so-called "Proposition 13 Babies" and the Democrats' reapportionment behavior have led to intense partisan conflict. Things had gotten so partisan and so heated in the Golden State that many Republican Assemblymen came out in support of the Gann Initiative. Despite the draconian effect the proposition would have had on the legislature, minority members apparently felt that they had little to lose.[8]

However partisanship affects Democrats and Republicans in a particular state, it does reinforce the preoccupation with elections of legislators almost everywhere. Twenty years ago, according to a veteran lobbyist in California, the legislature "was made up of a group of people who seemed to place more emphasis on the issues, on the art of legislating." Now, he observed, it is made up of people who place more emphasis on "the art of politicking, getting elected and staying elected."[9] If that's where California is, can the other states be very far behind? Probably not, for in more and more states, and particularly the larger ones, winning power has become more important to legislators and legislatures than exercising it. Partisanship certainly has made its contribution.

NOTES

1. We rely heavily on information provided by key members of the legislative staffs, one or two in

each of the 44 states responding. Surveys were mailed out in September 1983 and nearly all had been returned by the end of October. Follow-up telephone interviews were conducted in December with respondents from 10 of the states.

2. Alan Rosenthal, "An Analysis of Institutional Effects: Staffing Legislative Parties in Wisconsin," *Journal of Politics* 32 (August 1970): 351–62.

3. Quoted in National Conference of State Legislatures, "Is the Party Over? Political Parties in State Legislatures," *State Legislatures* 7 (November/December 1981): 25.

4. Quoted in Dan Weissman, *Star-Ledger*, November 13, 1983.

5. Reported in *New York Times*, February 8, 1984.

6. Arthur K. Lenehan, "Political Fund-raising Systems Appear Ripe for Reform Effort," *Star-Ledger*, March 27, 1984.

7. "Special Report: The New Face of State Politics," *Congressional Quarterly Weekly Report*, September 3, 1983, 1835.

8. Charles M. Price, "The Gann Legislative Reform Initiative in California: Trick or Treat?" *Comparative State Politics Newsletter* 4 (December 1983): 15.

9. Jerry Gillam and Carl Ingram, "Capitol View— Need for Moose Milk," *Los Angeles Times*, January 29, 1984.

26

The Changing Role of Legislative Staff in the American State Legislature

JOHN N. LATTIMER

It is difficult to generalize about the changing roles played by legislative staff across the 50 states. Each state has its own patterns of development, political culture, and legislative mores. All legislatures, however, have been

affected by certain historical developments, such as changes in fiscal federalism and in the political culture. These changes have had a dramatic effect on the roles played by staff. This essay will examine these past changes

State and Local Government Review, Vol.17, No.3 (Fall 1985), pp. 244–250. Copyright 1985 Carl Vinson Institute of Government, University of Georgia.

and how they have shaped both state legislatures and staff roles. That discussion will be used as a means of predicting the future course of staffing in the American state legislature.

THE DEVELOPMENT OF STATE LEGISLATURES—A HISTORICAL PERSPECTIVE

Legislative staff develop as a function of the political environment in which the legislatures themselves develop. Although some legislatures have changed more slowly than others, all are subject to and have been affected by these same political forces. Moreover, while legislatures differ in size and not all have the large staff bureaucracies of New York and California, the functions performed by staff do exist in most states. The crucial relationships of staff to staff, staff to the institution, and staff to the individual legislator often follow the same patterns of historical development throughout the country. Understanding these staff relationships in the context of institutional change is important in assessing the role of staff in molding the legislature.

The development of state legislative staff in the United States can be divided into five stages. The first stage comprises the period from the hiring of the first staff in the Virginia House of Burgesses to the development of the first central, nonpartisan, multipurpose service agency in the mid-1930s. While nineteenth century legislative staff were hired on a partisan basis and had a close institutional relationship to the legislators they served, few of them were full-time and few developments during this period would shed much light on legislative relationships today.

THE AGE OF THE EXECUTIVE (1934–1964)

The second stage could be called the Age of the Executive and characterized by the old saying that "the Governor proposes and the legislature disposes." From the mid-1930s to the mid-1960s, interest focused on state executive organization and administration and followed the reform movements of the "progressives" and "muckrakers" during the early part of this century. During this period, state legislatures met once every other year and in short sessions. They made decisions on gubernatorial requests either "up" or "down." They rarely proposed substitute legislation or "marked up" legislation in committee. Committees were weak and staff, mostly clerks and secretaries, were essentially used to provide administrative support to the process of legislating, to maintain the statutes and draft legislation (e.g., New York Drafting Commission—1909), or to undertake spot research and interim committee staffing (e.g., Kansas Legislative Council—1933). During the early years, the majority of those states providing central, "professional," and nonpartisan research services did so through their state libraries (e.g., Massachusetts Legislative Reference Division—1908). In many states the governor provided the staff even to the point of using budget agency personnel to staff the appropriations committees. Although many central service agencies were established in the late 1940s and 1950s, they were essentially small spot-research organizations or legislative libraries. These "legislative council" type research agencies were developed by students of classical public administration which teaches that staff do not make political choices or decisions. Consequently, use of partisan staff was thought to be unethical, inefficient, and an improper use of public resources. This era can be characterized by a near total lack of committee, leadership, or partisan staff.

THE AGE OF THE INSTITUTION (1964–1974)

The next major development for state legislatures was the landmark "one person, one vote" decision in *Baker* vs. *Carr* in 1962. Essentially that decision took effect with the 1964 election, resulting in legislatures more closely representative of the electorate at large. Newly elected state legislators were younger and better educated, and they began to view both the legislature and politics as a profession rather than as an avocation.

At the same time, the "great society" of Lyndon Johnson and the "new federalism" of Richard Nixon promoted an era of unprecedented expansion in state government. By 1969, there were 581 federal assistance programs to state and local governments, with 109 authorized in 1965 alone. During this period, many state governments reorganized their administrative structures to cope with the huge proliferation of federal grant programs ($50 billion by 1974) and their complex administrative requirements. Across the country, state agencies expanded or added new bureaus or divisions to administer one federal program or another. In Illinois, four state agencies were over 90 percent federally funded in 1975 while five others were 50 percent federally funded. In 1964, state governments had total general expenditures amounting to $37 billion and 1.8 million employees. With federal funds approaching 20 percent of state general revenues by 1974, state expenditures had risen 224 percent to $120 billion and with matching rates averaging 33 percent of the grants (most of it "in-kind") the number of state employees had nearly doubled (3.2 million). More importantly, until the mid-1970s these funds were kept outside the purview of state legislatures. In 1978, the U.S. Supreme Court decided in a case pitting the Pennsylvania legislature against then Governor Shapp, that state legislatures had full authority to appropriate funds and design policy for the administration of federal programs.

To ensure they would retain an active role in shaping these sweeping changes in state government, legislatures had to change. In 1964, 19 legislatures held annual sessions, but this number had risen to 40 by 1974. In addition, they began to use computers for fis-

cal analysis, bill drafting, statutory retrieval, bill status, word processing, and voting. Individual legislators began to receive substantial increases in pay, allowances, and pensions as well as office space and secretarial support. The result was both a physical strengthening of the legislature and an increased role in state government.

These changes also affected staff. Legislatures, no longer content to rely on the executive branch, added staff in increasing numbers. They either developed or increased fiscal staff. For the first time, committees were assigned staff, and bills were routinely analyzed for both committee and floor action. These staff, however, were largely nonpartisan and did not participate directly in the development of partisan solutions to policy problems. Although nonpartisan research could be used for partisan purposes, legislators, alone or with help from lobbyists or party organizations, developed policy options. Therefore, the relationship of staff to legislators, while close in many instances, stopped at the caucus room door. Staff supported the activities of the legislature without participating in the major function of the institution—policy development and consensus building. Staff began to develop pride in the institution and to sense that they were no longer just lawyers or political scientists but that they worked in a distinct profession. Moreover, staff personnel systems were developed with job descriptions, regular personnel reviews, and chains of command: in essence the beginning of the legislative bureaucracy.

THE SUPER LEGISLATURE (1974–1984)

The second decade of the modern legislature was shaped by two forces, economics and Watergate, both of which had important implications for the continuing development of legislative staff. This 10-year period of unstable economics compelled state legislatures to deal with a 111 percent increase in inflation, two major recessions, and "Reaganomics." While inflation provided additional revenues, it also created political pressure for more public services. But the recessions and slowdown in federal aid made it nearly impossible to keep up with inflation, causing pressure for tighter controls over the budgetary process and better oversight of the executive branch. During this period, legislative budget and appropriations staff grew, matured, and were separated from general service agencies. They developed specialists in a variety of policy areas such as welfare and transportation. They also began to look at capital budgeting and estimating revenues using sophisticated econometric models. Continuing this trend of staff development and specialization, legislatures also established other institutional mechanisms to enhance legislative oversight, such as legislative auditors, agencies for program evaluation, and the review of administrative rules. In 1969, the *Book of the States*, published by the Council of State Governments, listed 179 "permanent" legislative agencies—29 of which were situated in state libraries or other executive departments. By 1980, the Council listed 282 "principal legislative staff offices," not including 27 joint regulation review committees, 17 "sunset" agencies, and numerous separate committee staffs.

The trends toward the election of professional legislators, begun in the previous period, continued. This new breed of legislator was no longer content to sit quietly on the back bench. Party discipline weakened, and members began to pressure leaders for more to do and for a greater voice in the operations of the institution. Consequently, leaders had to share some of their power and develop new skills in consensus building. The days of strong, autocratic legislative leaders had come to an end.

Other trends also continued: as legislators were in the state capital for a longer period and spent more time investigating state programs, they introduced ever-increasing amounts of legislation. Just to handle the increased volume of work, additional staff were needed to assist legislators, committees, and agencies. At the same time, the legacy of Watergate put a different kind of pressure on legislators. Reporters, trying to mimic Woodward and Bernstein, looked into every nook and cranny of their legislators' public and private lives. Single issue public interest groups followed every vote. The political implications of each vote in the legislature became of utmost importance to them. Consequently, a need developed for professional staff to assess the political implications of each public policy initiative. For the first time, the development of large numbers of partisan staff created intra-institutional tensions that would change the face of many state legislatures.

CONGRESSIONALIZATION OF STATE LEGISLATURES OR THE AGE OF DEMOCRACY? (1980–1990)

The final period overlaps the previous one. It begins in 1980 with the election of Ronald Reagan and at this writing is only half complete. The Reagan revolution has exacerbated the political problems of the previous decade by turning over a large number of federal programs to states through block grants and cuts in other domestic programs. Many of the programs cut or consolidated in block grants to states were programs of direct aid to local governments and local community groups. State government, and state legislatures in particular, became the focal point of the changing role of governments in the United States.

The new focus on the states has heightened the importance of state legislatures and further escalated the cost of elections. To maintain control of their membership and to retain their titles, legislative leaders have become super fund-raisers who dole out campaign monies to the faithful. Also they have increased the number of leadership positions, committee chairs, and staff as "chits" for votes during leadership battles. Money, previously made available to expanding central staffs, is now provided for committee, personal, and leadership staff.

To many it appears that the primary concern of leaders and rank-and-file legislators alike is the next election. Today's state legislature is characterized by the rise of the public information officer, of news releases, and of radio feeds. Legislators are constantly looking over their shoulders as single-interest groups have cropped up in staggering proportions and the new "wolfpack" journalism, now in full swing, makes their public and private lives an open book. The number of registered lobbyists has tripled and legislative behavior is scrutinized as it has never been before. The institution has become more politicized and the political culture surrounding the legislature has become mean spirited. Even the two chambers, always wary of each other, engage in open warfare. Is it any wonder that legislators will seek help from partisan staff hired to watch for the pitfalls and traps of modern American politics?

This is also an age of democracy. State legislatures are more representative than they have ever been and the individual legislator is closer to his or her constituents and more accountable. The tough politics of state legislatures have produced some of the best political leaders in the nation. Legislators have more resources at their fingertips to thoroughly debate the tough issues they face and to scrutinize executive branch operations. Their staffs have matured and have better educational backgrounds and experience to deal with the complex issues. Some of the real innovations in public programs are developed in state legislatures. For example, the Wisconsin legislature has changed the welfare system to guarantee a standard of living and promote private sector employment—an issue Congress has debated since the Nixon administra-

tion. In the vast majority of states, heightened political competition has forced state legislatures to reach consensus on some of the most divisive public policy issues of our time.

Although one could characterize this era as the deinstitutionalization of the legislative branch where leaders have lost control and we face institutional gridlock, this belies the evidence. Beginning with the recession of 1978-79, state legislatures have dealt equitably with the difficult issues of revenue shortfall, bank deregulation, tort liability, hazardous waste, school reform, safeguarding children (child abuse, child support enforcement, search programs for missing children), and the transition of many federal programs to state jurisdiction. When necessary, they have sought expert opinion and hired specialists to help sort out policy options. Legislative staff have used innovative techniques to find out what people believe about a variety of solutions to the knotty problems faced by their state legislatures. They have used survey research, focus groups, and statewide conferences to build consensus. More importantly, at a time when Congress appears to be incapable of making key decisions, state legislatures have made the tough choices—raising taxes and streamlining programs. State legislatures have taken the lead and are alive and well in America.

OUTLOOK FOR LEGISLATURES AND LEGISLATIVE STAFFING

Over the next five years, two factors will have a crucial influence on state legislatures. The first is the political battle to control reapportionment in 1991. David S. Broder, in *The Washington Post Weekly Edition* of October 28, 1985, points out in his article entitled "1991: Egad! They're Already Lining Up for Redistricting," that ". . . both parties are engaged in the political battle of 1991—the struggle for control of congressional redistricting in the 50 state legislatures." The Republican National

Committee started two years ago with its "1991 Plan" which is designed to dramatically increase the number of Republican legislative seats and governorships in preparation for the crucial 1991 reapportionment. The Democratic National Committee has responded by establishing "Project 500" to elect or retain 500 legislators in marginal districts and states in the next five years.

The political battle to control the state legislatures will have profound effects on state legislatures and their staffs. First, the three elections of 1986, 1988, and 1990 will turn over the entire legislature in most states. The legislature of the 1990s will have more women and minorities. The trends for younger and more professional legislators in each chamber will continue. Leaders will be under more pressure to provide personal staff to the rank-and-file members, and committee chairs will press for the power to hire their own committee staff. Personal staff can have a dramatic effect on intra-institutional relationships. They can redistribute power in the institution by making committee chairs and rank-and-file members more independent of leadership. They can also insulate central service staffs (both partisan and nonpartisan) from the members. As the cost of elections increases, partisan staff (personal, committee, and leadership) will become an ever more valuable political resource and may take funds away from central nonpartisan staffs.

The most dramatic change will take place as legislatures move into the electronic age and staff becomes more technically specialized. The use of high-speed information technology will speed up the legislative process by reducing the amount of paperwork and lengthy printing processes necessary to move legislation. Also, the portability of high-speed computers, telecommunications, and laser technology will make the never-ending campaign physically easier to handle. It will also give leadership an opportunity to control their members with more than just campaign funding. Press releases, issue briefs, research, and strategy will be designed and written in the capital and disseminated to individual members' district offices (in multiple copies if necessary) or at campaign stops. The escalating costs of campaigns and technical partisan staff may force recentralization of that staff under leadership control. It will be difficult for young untrained "campaign groupies" to survive in such a highly competitive, technologically advanced, and structured environment.

The coming years could be an exciting period for staff with the foresight and expertise to exist in the new state legislature's highly charged, rarefied atmosphere. It will provide opportunities to have a direct effect upon public policy. But with these new opportunities will come new professional responsibilities. As legislators become more concerned about the next election, the responsibility of minding the store will devolve almost solely upon staff. Staff will provide the institutional memory. They will have to guard against the forces that split the institution into small kingdoms; against petty battles over turf; and against forces that make consensus building difficult if not impossible. Escalating institutional costs and the consequent press criticism will force them to be good managers and to organize in the most efficient and effective manner. They will have to resist rigid staff bureaucracies that are incapable of changing as the institution changes. More importantly, they will have to participate in intra-institutional cooperation, both partisan and nonpartisan. For otherwise, staff can be responsible for the ultimate legislative disgrace—institutional gridlock.

It is not necessary to speculate about those forces that can bring the legislature to a halt. We merely need to look at the U.S. Congress. Personal staff of each member of Congress are used almost solely for constituent work, with little time spent on policy research. The multiplicity of caucuses, study groups, committees, subcommittees, and attendant chairs and vice chairs make it nearly impossible to fix responsibility for the legislative process and ultimately public policy.

Unlike Congress, however, state legislatures must meet constitutional deadlines to finish their business and constitutional mandates to balance budgets. Because the institution is not as complex as Congress and it is easier to fix responsibility for legislative actions, the staff bureaucracies of the 50 state legislatures will grow in a much slower and hopefully more rational manner than have those in Congress. Probably the most important difference between the operation of Congress and of state legislatures is the appropriations process. Most state legislatures, unlike Congress, do not allow substantive committees to make budget policy. This single difference means that state legislatures can and do make the toughest decisions in politics—the allocation of public resources.

The budget process aside, political competition and turnover in the state legislature may force state legislatures to develop as has Congress and produce two distinct groups of staff. One group will be older, longer-term central agencies staff with institutional memory. The second group will be a younger, inexperienced staff, lacking in institutional memory but bright, who will produce lots of good ideas that in turn will produce more and more legislation. Tensions will develop over issues of professionalism and turf. As in Congress, this intra-institutional tension can lead to the balkanization of staff resources where the allegiance of younger staff is to individual members or committee chairs, and battles over turf take the place of battles over public policy. It is difficult to reach consensus on the important issues of the day when self-advancement is predicated on how well the boss does in the institutional battles rather than on the design of operable public policy. Older central staff (partisan and nonpartisan) will tend to be more concerned about the institution, the development of public policy, and their own prerogatives within the institution.

As the use of partisan staff increases, the need for coordination of staff functions will force changes in the way various staff relate to legislators and to the institution. Partisan staff tend to form a barrier between nonpartisan staff and the legislators they serve. The tension that exists between partisan and nonpartisan staff can be overstated but is definitely a factor in certain developmental changes in state legislatures. Partisan staff to a certain extent can control events and access to leaders. Those nonpartisan staff who survive are the ones who accept the role of partisan staff and work closely with them to assist legislators.

As intra-institutional tensions develop, legislatures must find ways in which important legislative services are maintained in the most effective and efficient manner. Partisan staff must recognize that there are services not required of each caucus in each house. They must be sensitive to institutional concerns and the valid role of nonpartisan staff, as well as to personal and political needs. Political competition can lead to inefficiencies, taking scarce resources away from more important institutional needs.

Nonpartisan staff must recognize the need for partisan policy analysis which strengthens not only the legislative process but also the political system through the competition of well-developed ideas. More importantly, they must be aware that they are a part of the political system and be sensitive to the political environment in which they exist. If they are not, they face the real possibility of becoming irrelevant to the legislative process.

THE ROLE OF STAFF IN STRENGTHENING THE LEGISLATURE

There is little doubt that legislatures and their staffs develop in response to changes in the political environment. However, legislators tend to be poor institutional managers, so staff have the responsibility to recognize those changes and to respond with the highest quality, most professional, effective, and efficient services they can. The legislature is an organic institution, best served by staff who work with legislators to develop a system for continuously analyzing the institution's capability and effectiveness. Important changes in the legislature do not have to come along like earthquakes once every 20 or 30 years. They can take place incrementally. But in order for the institution to develop rationally, staff and legislators (particularly legislative leaders) must design a system for continuously assessing institutional needs.

Public policy needs and political competition are constantly forcing the institution to hire more highly trained and skilled personnel (both partisan and nonpartisan). The system must be designed so that they are placed in the proper institutional setting for efficiency and effectiveness. The existing system must be analyzed against a structure that fixes responsibility and accountability for staff services by establishing

clearly defined goals and tasks (partisan or nonpartisan, centralized or decentralized);

clear notions of professional and academic requirements for each task;

well-defined lines of authority for both legislators and staff;

a well-defined priority setting process;

clear operating rules; and

an institutional process for coordinating staff functions and resolving conflict.

A broad range of staff services may be provided to any legislature. They are provided through many different institutional devices across the country, but they are not always provided in the most effective or efficient manner (staff redundancies in New York are legendary).

The list [in Table 1] is organized by institutional constituency and function. While there are redundancies, it would be almost impossible to eliminate duplication in staff services. In a strict organizational sense, one can argue that almost none of these services need to be provided by partisan staff. Only caucus and leadership services are by definition partisan and then only because of the nature and not the substance of their work. On the other hand, only certain technical fiscal and oversight services cannot be effectively provided by partisan staff (e.g., computer, printing, revenue estimates, impact notes, audit, and rule and regulation review). Separate partisan computer and printing facilities would not be efficient, while four separate revenue estimates or fiscal notes would create chaos. The independence of the audit would be compromised by partisan involvement, while the technical nature and cumbersome machinery of rule and regulation review and statutory revision would not lend itself to effective partisan staffing.

Committee services, research, and policy development; certain fiscal, legal, and oversight services; and institutional public relations can be staffed effectively by either partisan or nonpartisan staff. How a legislature organizes these staff will probably depend on institutional history and the size and political diversity of the state. However, if efficiency and effectiveness are important, then these activities should be designed so that partisan staff are assigned tasks which are strictly partisan and important to the development of caucus positions. For example, good bill analyses can be effectively provided by nonpartisan staff. If done properly, there would be almost no difference between a partisan and a nonpartisan bill analysis. If central nonpartisan staff wrote all bill analyses, then the partisan staff would be free to concentrate on partisan policy development and strategy. However, if only partisan staff are used for bill analyses, especially of appropriations bills, that staff's tendency is to view changes in policy on marginal political terms. Nonpartisan staff tend to take a more pluralistic view of the overall long-term impact of legislation.

TABLE 1. STAFF SERVICES IN THE MODERN STATE LEGISLATURE

Committee Services
 administration, clerical
 bill analysis
 research and policy development
 press

Member and/or Caucus Services
 administration, clerical
 research
 bill drafting
 constituent services
 policy development
 press, public relations, and public education

Technical Services
 printing
 data processing
 facilities development and space utilization
 bill status and digest preparation
 purchasing and accounting
 enrolling and engrossing
 House and Senate journals

Research and Policy Development
 spot research
 interim policy development (single-issue, long-
  term research requiring member involvement
  and utilizing expert nonmembers)
 legislative library

 intergovernmental relations
 technology assessment
 library services
 internships

Fiscal Services
 revenue estimates
 debt and pension impact
 bond analysis
 fiscal notes
 budget review (overview, short- and long-term
  trends, possible trouble spots)
 appropriations

Legal Services
 bill drafting
 statutory revision and codification
 synopses of bills
 law library

Oversight Services
 audit, sunset review
 rule and regulations review
 program evaluation

Institutional Public Relations
 constituent or ombudsman services
 press
 public education

Policy development is clearly the most difficult staff function to place in an appropriate institutional setting. When undertaken by standing committees and partisan staff in the glare of the TV lights, it has a tendency to be adversarial and strictly partisan. Such a setting provides little opportunity for reflection and the development of bipartisan consensus. Policy development in the sense of consensus building is most effectively handled by central legislative agencies or joint committees with the involvement of outside experts and technical nonpartisan staff. Once the issues have been defined and well-crafted policy alternatives developed, then the partisan process can take over and ensure that those options stand

the test of the political arena. For it is the political process that ultimately decides which policy options are appropriate for a particular state. If, however, those options are developed only in a partisan arena, legislators run the risk of missing more appropriate or innovative alternatives that are almost impossible to see in a partisan context.

Finally, the responsibility for finding appropriate solutions to public problems is fixed first on legislative leaders and then on the rank-and-file members. For this reason, many legislative services may be more appropriately provided by partisan staff. This is particularly true in large states with diverse and highly competitive political cultures. Even in those states, efficiency and effectiveness would dictate that certain staff functions are inappropriate for partisan agencies. More importantly, all staff must recognize that they are part of a political process and will not last long if they live too far above the battle or if the battle becomes more important than the constituencies and institutions for which they fight.

27

The Lobbyist as an Information Source

ALAN FEEZOR

Those who live in Washington often think of it as the fountain of all knowledge, and certainly of all power. I tend toward a different view. Having observed the trends of recent years—fiscal conservatism, a distrust of grand social programs, heightened emphasis on intergovernmental relations, and the resurgence of state governments—I believe firmly that most major issues of the next five to eight years will be addressed primarily at the state legislative level, if they're addressed at all.

It is therefore increasingly important—in fact, it is vital—that state legislators and their staffs have the best possible information resources, and know how to use them. In my opinion, the best source of information for legislatures is now, and will continue to be, the lobbyist.

To develop this point, we need to reflect on the changing nature of the lobbyist's role.

As I see it, lobbying runs along a continuum. On one end, you have what I refer to as an "influence lobbyist" or an "influence lobby," and on the other end an "information lobby." The former would be more inclined to use political action committees, donations, old ties and old friendships in grass roots lobbying. The latter would define his or her job as a transfer of information.

Those are the two extremes, of course, and most of us fall somewhere between them. Still, the overall trend is clear. Although lobbyists have always been paid to exert influence, and still are, the growing sophistication of state legislatures and the rise of consumer groups are pushing them toward a greater emphasis on information. In fact, the two functions are inseparable: If you provide needed information in an appropriate way, you are able to influence policy.

We in the private sector rely on several information sources to build our arguments. We often try to use information generated by third parties or by state agencies, primarily because that information is less suspect and is considered by decision-makers to be more valid than anything we might generate. We try to use information from other states, either via our own network of communication or via such instruments as NCSL's legislative information service. When possible, of

---

State Legislatures, Vol.6, No.10 (November–December 1980), pp. 9–11. Copyright 1980 National Conference of State Legislatures.

course, we also use the technical information that we can generate within our own corporation. But this is useful only if it is accurate, if we have the credibility and reputation to make it believable and if we have the time to develop it. (The last of these—time—can be a real problem from a lobbying standpoint. Legislation tends to move so fast in state legislatures and our data bases may not be geared to produce the needed information immediately. Moreover, many lobbyists have limited resources, and the corporation may have other priorities. Only if a bill gets close to passage are we certain to make it a priority.)

As we move toward a greater emphasis on information, we adopt different approaches to presenting it. For example, we're moving away from the old emphasis on purely verbal testimony, and I think this is a good trend. We're beginning to look at everything from issue briefs to written position statements to technical impact statements, as supplements to the verbal testimony and the one-to-one lobbying we have traditionally employed.

Much of what we do depends on the *modus operandi* of either the committee or the legislature. It depends on the legislature, the staff and the legislator. Legislators, particularly committee chairmen, can set the tone and the demands for the kinds of information they need. If legislators are tired of simply hearing corporations say, "We're for this" and "We're against this," then challenge them to describe the negative impact of proposed legislations and to come up with solutions. Ask them: How will this affect the people of Kansas? What will be the cost of this particular bill in terms of regulatory costs or in terms of cost to the consumer? Put the onus on business.

We regularly confront the question of whether to deliver policy information through staffers or directly to legislators. The choice always depends upon the lobbyist's relationship with the legislator, and upon the visibility or sensitivity of an issue. In some cases,

the legislator may not want the lobbyist to be directly involved—or the lobbyist may not want to be. It's also a matter of timing. If information is delivered at an early stage, the lobbyist generally goes to staff; if it's delivered later, when we're trying to effect last-minute changes, we go straight to the legislator—because we must.

Our choice also depends upon the staffing of the legislature. In the larger states, we find a highly competent, full-time staff with a great deal of expertise and we can go to the staff with some degree of reliance. In some other states, you may have part-time legislatures and more modest staffing. Consequently, you tend to go to the legislators. It also depends upon the competence of the staff, their technical expertise and their attitude.

Legislative staff members today are stretched too thin; they also tend to be very young and idealistic—and may not be receptive to comments from the private sector.

A legislator, however, can set the tone for the staff. Legislators should know where the staff gets its information. Legislators should assure themselves that the staff is open-minded and solicitous of all points of view because this attitude will better serve lawmakers and their legislation. Legislators should be certain that their issue formulation is founded on broad-based information. The best input is always at the earliest stages before personalities get involved, before positions harden and before people are forced to react instead of act.

I think that state legislatures will continue to designate more resources for staffing. When they do, the people of the state will be better served and I will be more comfortable with the staff as a lobbyist.

How can the relationship between legislators and lobbyists be improved? First, the legislator needs to determine whether each lobbyist is an information or an influence lobbyist. You have to learn which ones you can trust and who will provide you with good information. Then work with them, consider and use them as technical assistants or as auxiliary staff members—again realizing that there are some limitations and they do have their bias.

Like anyone else, lobbyists respond to how they're treated. A legislator who views the lobbyist primarily as a source of entertainment, food or other indulgences will probably find his expectations fulfilled. The legislator who makes hard and fair demands for information—good technical assistance—will get that, and will benefit from it.

Legislators need to be up front in their dealings with lobbyists. Make use of the lobbyist at the earliest stage of the legislative process because it allows more flexibility, more creativity and more alternatives to come forward. It also allows the lobbyist to be affirmative. (I used to pray for opportunities to be *for* something instead of always against something.)

Legislators need to demand more than just testimony. They need to demand background information on general subject matter, historical perspectives, issue briefs, impact assessments and even legislative analysis. Legislators can even ask a lobbyist to take responsibility for forming an ad hoc study group to address an issue without the need for legislation, particularly on long-range problems.

Legislatures also need to adopt rules that provide opportunities for the orderly input of information. A bill that becomes law 36 hours after it's introduced is not good legislation. There will be a few exceptions, of course, but ordinarily legislators need to assure the proper time in terms of notice of hearings, notice of rules of procedure (both within the committees and within their chambers) that provide an orderly process for submitting and assessing information.

Finally, legislators need to make available to lobbyists the information sources they need to do their job. Most states have computerized bill status systems. Legislatures could consider—it might help defray the cost—allowing the bill status system to be contracted out on a subscription basis to firms which are willing to pay for it and which believe they need immediate access to the current status of the bill.

Although I advocate closer use of lobbyists, I recognize the dangers inherent in the heavy reliance on them. I do, however, feel that there are four checks which serve to restrain lobbyists.

First, legislators hear from other interest groups and can play their views against each other.

Second, the legislative staff can test the validity of information received from lobbyists.

Third, the legislator's own familiarity with the subject and the bill provides a check. If I know that a legislator has the reputation of doing his homework on a bill, I'm going to be damn careful about what I tell him.

The fourth and biggest check is personal credibility. Every single lobbyist I work with—and I work with more than 100—holds this sacred. It's probably more important than his lineage or his parenthood. It's a matter of personal integrity. Every good lobbyist knows that if he misleads a legislator and the legislator finds out about it, he'll never be able to go back to that legislator. If we're going to err, it will probably be on the side of honesty.

28

Legislatures and the Press:
The Problems of Image and Attitude

MARTIN LINSKY

Remember the story about the lady with the garbage problem? The constituent calls her legislator to complain that the garbage has not been picked up in front of her house for two weeks. The legislator asks, "Why didn't you call the garbage collector?" "Well," she responds, "I just didn't want to start that high."

Legislatures and legislators have never enjoyed a very good reputation, although individual legislators often have very fine reputations, especially in their own districts.

Part of the public attitude toward legislatures comes from American history and government texts. Such books too often present an unrealistic picture of the legislative process. They lay the foundation for the kind of disillusionment which is often seen when schoolchildren come to Washington and are dismayed to watch the U.S. Senate in "action," with only a handful of members on the floor and most of those who are there apparently not paying attention to the speaker.

Opinion about legislators and legislatures is also affected by constituents' views of their own representativ   Some people have had personal contact with their state legislator; others have a clear sense of him or her, developed indirectly from the views of those who know the legislator personally and by the impression conveyed in the local media.

Perhaps most important, however, much of the citizen's view of the institution and its members is developed from a more imper-

sonal vantage point. Only a handful of people have direct dealings with the legislature as an institution or with members other than their own. What most people think about the legislature, apart from what they think of their own legislator, is to a large extent a function of what they read in the newspapers or see on television. What is covered and how it is covered has an impact on the public sense of how, and how well, legislators do their work.

IMAGE AND ITS CONSEQUENCES

The media, both print and electronic, play a major role in determining the image of the legislature, and having a negative image has serious consequences for both legislatures and legislators.

A legislature which is held in low esteem cannot independently manage its own affairs. Members who support increases in legislative salaries or staff put themselves at risk at election time; inflation and increased workload are not compelling enough justifications if the real issue in the public mind is the worthiness of the institution itself.

Quality people are not attracted to serve in either elected or appointed capacities in a legislature in disrepute. And public attitude also makes a difference in the respect accorded legislative-made law. Increased law-

State Government, Vol.59, No.1 (Spring 1986), pp. 40–44.

making by the courts, and by the public directly through referenda, may be one manifestation of an institution that is not well-regarded. Governors are likely to run against the legislature or to go over the heads of the legislators to build support for programs among the people. The lower the esteem accorded the institution, the more often such circumvention occurs. Poorly-regarded legislatures find themselves having legislative priorities determined by others.

The public attitude toward the legislature as a whole also affects individual legislators. When legislative service is not well-regarded, legislators may not be able to use that experience as a credential for running for another office. The most ambitious members will have incentive to make names for themselves by demeaning the legislature and thus further undermining the credibility of the individual members.

Some of the negative attitude toward the average legislator and toward the institution itself is undoubtedly deserved. In the late nineteenth century, legislators were often on the payroll of railroads and other special interests, and corruption was a routine revelation. Legislatures still are touched by scandal with disturbing regularity. In recent years, legislators have been in deep trouble in Louisiana, Massachusetts, Oklahoma, Pennsylvania, and Texas, to name a few that come to mind. Yet with it all, there is no evidence that corruption is any more rampant in legislatures than it is in the executive or judicial branches of government, or in the private sector, for that matter.

Legislatures also create a lot of their own bad reputation independent of the corruption of a few of their members. The traditional end-of-session disarray characterized by late-night or even all-night sessions, parties, and members sleeping on couches in public places undermine public confidence. The success of former legislators, even legislative leaders, in turning their failed ambition for higher office into a lucrative business of lobbying their former colleagues on behalf of well-heeled powerful clients, diminishes faith of the average citizen that a broader sense of the public interest is being served.

Even so, the degree of bad conduct by legislatures does not seem commensurate with the bad press and the low esteem in which the institutions are generally held.

THE GAP IN UNDERSTANDING

Tension between legislators and reporters seems at times endemic. Frustrated legislators often accuse journalists of only being interested in selling newspapers or winning the ratings war, as if those commercial constraints were any less compromising for the press than the desire to win re-election is for them. Reporters are routinely accused of taking remarks out of context, overplaying the bad news, and giving coverage to the worst legislators, as if they were deliberately trying to undermine legislative credibility. The journalists, of course, see it quite differently, and that gap feeds misunderstanding between legislators and the press.

In fact, more of the problems between the press and legislatures are the result of inherent and legitimate conflict between the two institutions than are attributable to legislative failures or bad reporting. Consider for a moment these institutional dynamics:

First, legislatures are not designed to make good coverage easy. They are organized to give every point of view a chance to be heard, to consider every issue that anyone believes important, to take time before taking action, and to provide a forum for the full diversity of the population of the state. All of that makes them organizationally and inherently slow and inefficient. Getting a handle on legislatures is further complicated because they are multiheaded monsters: no one individual, not even the leaders, can speak for all the members. News, on the other hand, is oriented to action and change, and journalists need individuals to personify institutions and issues.

Second, there is a wide gulf between what kind of legislator, legislating, and legislative politics make good press, and what constitutes good performance in the eyes of legislators themselves. For instance, among legislators there is admiration for the workhorses, the legislators who do a lot of the behind-the-scenes work on legislation at the expense of personal publicity. There is contempt mixed with jealousy for the showhorses, the legislators who have a knack for being at the right place at the right time to get publicity or credit for a bill, even though they were not around when all the hard negotiating took place. Yet it is often the showhorses who make news. Inside the legislature, the individual who is willing to make the narrow case for his or her district's interests, even though it runs against the broader public interest, is respected for representing the people. To a reporter, and to the public, the legislator who is, for example, fighting against the expansion of the airport closer to the residential areas, is seen as parochially standing in the way of progress.

Third, good legislating does not always make good press. Good legislating takes place behind closed doors. Consensus is the goal. Compromises are made. But to a reporter, a legislator who resists compromise is "standing on principle." Good legislating is often done without publicity, or else it would not, and perhaps could not, be done. Much of the legislative process is invisible, and therefore unreported by the press and unappreciated by the public. When good work is done that way, the result is sometimes very unappealing from a news perspective: the legislation is centrist and moderate; and it is enacted overwhelmingly, without rancor or even any public debate at all.

Finally, the folkways of good politics also do not make for favorable coverage. In legislatures, unlike in sports, one day's teammates may be tomorrow's antagonists. Legislators sometimes reverse positions on a bill for reasons which seem very sound to them, but which are hard to explain to a reporter, since the mix between the politics and the substance of legislation may change overnight. Lawmakers see their actions as representing flexibility, not weakness, but again, the pattern is hard to explain. Inside the legislature, a member can justify a position on a bill by saying that any other would jeopardize re-election, but on the outside and with the press, such an explanation would be unacceptable.

A QUESTION OF VALUES

In addition to institutional differences, legislatures and the media operate with very different value systems.

From the point of view of the reporters, the journalistic values are clear. News organizations believe that some ways of packaging the news are more effective than others. That is not a commercial argument, although it can be made that way. It is the job of the press to tell the people what is going on in their government and to hold officials accountable, and it is a convention of the news business that certain kinds of stories do that well. Stories built around personalities, for example, are understood to be better read than stories about issues, institutions, or processes. Good stories have drama, especially conflict and confrontation. One type of drama which news organizations believe well conveys a tale is the profile-in-courage, the lone individual standing against the tide of the consensus or the conventional wisdom or the powerful. Stories with winners and losers, or good guys and bad guys, can be told in idioms which most people can grasp quickly. Scandals are big news. So are incidents which illustrate other human frailties such as hypocrisy, inconsistency or stupidity.

From the perspective of the legislature, those news values obviously create problems.

A good story for a reporter is very often a bad story for the legislator involved or for the legislature as a whole. The legislator who travels out of state to learn about alternative approaches to a problem, attend a professional seminar, or just share the joys and frustrations of public life with colleagues from around the country is on a "junket." The effort of a fifth-grade class to pass a law naming a state dinosaur dominates news coverage of the legislature in Colorado. A story about an overweight Illinois legislator and his candy supply displaces other legislative coverage and becomes a national story.

In short, the conflicts between legislators and reporters are more a function of the legitimate but different perspectives that they bring than of bad reporting or bad legislating. Journalists sometimes talk as if they represent the public at the state house; of course, that is precisely what legislators are elected to do. The press thinks it is supposed to make sure that the legislature addresses the key issues; the legislators think setting the legislative agenda is their job. The legislators want the journalists just to report what is said; the reporter believes that unless he puts what is said in context, the public will be misled. Coverage of the legislature is by its nature episodic, not continuous, but the legislator believes that the public episodes, such as hearings and debates, do not illustrate the heart of the legislative process.

SHAPING A LEGISLATIVE RESPONSE

Too often, legislators have reacted to negative press by criticizing the reporters and complaining about the coverage. It is usually a counterproductive strategy, although it may be right on target and even temporarily satisfying. Blaming the messenger, even when the messenger deserves some or all of the blame, is not likely to make the messenger feel better or be more responsive. Furthermore, doing so

can become an easy excuse for legislators and legislatures to avoid the hard but necessary work of understanding the press and cleaning up their own acts.

Legislatures and their members share the multifaceted responsibility of shaping a more effective media relationship and thus a more favorable public image.

First, legislators who understand the press on its own terms are in a better position to deal successfully with reporters who cover them. By knowing how journalists perceive the world and derive satisfaction and gratification, legislators can begin to develop a professional relationship with the press which will better suit their own personal and institutional needs. And, legislators can begin to do something about their public image.

For individual legislators, understanding the press means at least respecting the pressures reporters are under; deadlines, an angry editor, the competition, the need for terseness, or whatever. It means picturing each sentence on the front page of the daily paper or at the top of the six o'clock news before saying it, so there is no danger of being quoted out of context.

Second, the legislature and its leaders should be responsible for training for all legislators and all legislative employees so that the missteps and gaffes can be reduced to a minimum. Such programs exist in some states already. Pennsylvania and Georgia, for example, provide training and orientation sessions for both freshman and incumbent legislators. The goals are to make legislators aware of the significant role of the press in government and the constraints this imposes on them, and to teach them how to communicate effectively through the mass media. However, training is only one step in dealing with the broader institutional demands for improved press relations that most legislatures need.

Finally, the responsibility for educating the public about the legislative process rests with legislatures themselves. Each state legislature should have a broad public information program that goes beyond traditional coverage to reach directly into schools, service clubs, and businesses. Too often the picture delivered currently is one of the local legislators standing bravely against the institution and its leaders, with the message delivered, of course, by the legislator to the adoring audience that elected him or her. Legislative leaders must understand that they represent the institution as a whole, that they have a precious legacy entrusted to them, and that the job of presiding officer demands some relaxation of pure partisanship in favor of a broader view. Successful legislative leaders have not only represented the institution well, but they have taken on the responsibility for keeping the press informed about what is happening and going to happen. Ongoing background briefings will help build trust and confidence between press and legislators and will reduce mistakes made on both sides in the heat of a crisis.

Minnesota is widely recognized as a state which has worked hard in recent years to improve press-legislative relations, and to educate the public about the legislative process. The House and Senate information offices in St. Paul track legislation and provide the press and the public with accurate nonpartisan information about bills. In addition, the offices distribute educational materials to schools, town meetings, and other public forums. Every two years Minnesota holds a media day, an opportunity for legislators and reporters to discuss issues and conflicts in their relationship outside of the day-to-day press of business. Jean Steiner, the House public information officer in St. Paul, believes that maintaining the nonpartisan status of a public information office is essential to the credibility and success of a public relations effort for a legislature. Furthermore, the program must be active and on-going, not passive or sporadic. Jet Toney, director of the Georgia House Public Information Office stresses that the educational role of an information office cannot be simply that of a responder and conduit; the staff must seek forums for spreading the word about how the legislature really works.

THE TASK AHEAD

The process of changing public attitudes toward the legislative process is not easy, but it is crucial if legislatures are to perform their share of governing in the years ahead. That will be increasingly true as the federal government begins to devolve more and more responsibility to the states. How the press covers the legislature is a central element in determining what the public thinks of the legislature. To an extent, legislatures are their own worst enemies, designed to expose their own weaknesses and filled with people too quick to blame reporters for negative coverage.

Legislators and legislatures have it within their power to do something to restore their tarnished images, but they will have to begin by understanding the press, its drives and its constraints. The tensions that exist between reporters and legislators are real and predictable given the worlds in which they operate. Accepting those difficulties as facts of legislative life and working within them is the first step toward a professional, and more successful, relationship with the press, and ultimately a more respected environment for legislators to do the people's business.

29

Sunset Laws and Legislative Vetoes in the States

DAVID C. NICE

Recent dissatisfaction with government bureaucracies has spurred legislative efforts to gain more control over government agencies. State legislators, knowing that effective legislative oversight and control require sufficient legal authority, have moved in recent years to increase their legal powers over the bureaucracy.[1] Two significant aspects of that effort are legislative vetoes and sunset laws.

Observers disagree on the likely consequences of legislative control efforts. Some contend that stronger legislative controls will improve the performance of government programs. Other observers expect legislative controls to simply reduce government action in dealing with social and economic problems. The analysis which follows will seek to explain adoption of legislative vetoes and sunset laws. In addition, by examining which states have adopted legislative veto and sunset law provisions, we may be able to infer the likely consequences of each: improved performance or less government action.

The legislative veto appears to be a reversal of the traditional pattern of legislative enactment and executive veto in that an executive agency promulgates regulations which the legislature may veto. Proponents contend that the legislative veto provides a check on bureaucratic excesses and enables the legislature to make certain that agency regulations established under delegated authority are consistent with legislative desires. Critics charge, however, that the legislative veto violates the principle of separation of powers and serves as a tool for powerful interests seeking to block controversial programs.[2]

Sunset laws, which attach an expiration date to laws creating agencies and programs, are seen as a method for eliminating unnecessary spending.[3] More generally they alter the agenda-setting process by creating deadlines that periodically raise the issue of whether a program, grant of authority, or agency should be retained or eliminated. Advocates of sunset laws also contend that they stimulate program reviews which will make agencies more accountable and more responsive to legislative desires.[4]

Some observers contend, however, that sunset laws are ineffective for agencies with powerful clientele support; only agencies lacking such support face much risk.[5] Others fear that sunset laws play into the hands of well-organized interest groups seeking to eliminate programs they oppose and the hands of legislators seeking to extract favors from agencies.[6]

With their various limitations, legislative vetoes and sunset laws represent two vehicles for increasing legislative control over the bureaucracy. While they have shortcomings, as do all mechanisms of control, they provide significant additions to the legislature's arsenal of bureaucratic controls. The states have shown varying levels of enthusiasm for legislative vetoes and sunset laws. Some have provided for legislative vetoes while others have not. Some states have enacted comprehensive sunset legislation, while others have re-

State Government, Vol.58, No.1 (Spring 1985), pp. 27–32.

stricted it to certain agencies or regulations, and still other states have none at all.[7]

INFLUENCES ON LEGISLATIVE CONTROL EFFORTS

The structural characteristics of state governments may influence legislative efforts at controlling the executive branch. Legislative control of state bureaucracies has long been hampered by the structural weaknesses of the state legislatures themselves. Short sessions, a lack of staff support, high turnover, and other limitations on legislative effectiveness frustrate efforts at controlling the bureaucracy. A legislature with ample time, staff support, and a corps of experienced members is far better equipped to deal with agency oversight and control.[8] Edgar Crane found that more professionalized legislatures were in fact more likely to engage in comprehensive program review.[9] Keith Hamm and Roby Robertson found no relationship between legislative structure and adoption of legislative veto power but did find that sunset laws were more likely to be adopted where legislative salaries were *lower*.[10]

We would expect, therefore, more highly developed legislatures—those with longer sessions, more staff assistance, lower turnover, and reasonably organized leadership and committee structures—to enact comprehensive sunset legislation and legislative vetoes. In the former case, a more capable legislature is in a better position to carry out the evaluations which sunset laws require for maximum effectiveness. A more capable legislature is also in a better position to analyze proposed administrative regulations and judge them in an informed manner. By far the most comprehensive measure of legislative capability is the FAIIR rating, which includes the time available to the legislature, staff assistance, compensation, and measures of oversight capabilities.[11]

As Table 1 indicates, states with more capable legislatures, as measured by the FAIIR ranking, are more likely to have legislative vetoes, as expected, but less likely to adopt sunset laws. Nearly half (44 percent) of the states with low legislative capability (rankings 35–50) have comprehensive sunset laws, but only one of the states with high legislative capability has similar legislation. By contrast, nearly 60 percent of the states with high legislative capability have legislative veto powers, but less than one-third of the states with low legislative capability do.

In some states the executive branch is a fragmented, dispersed collection of agencies rather than an integrated structure under the control of a strong governor. Where the executive branch fails to provide its own mechanisms of coordination and integrated control, legislators may feel compelled to step into the breach. Moreover, a comparatively weak governor may be less equipped to fend off legislative incursions into what the governor considers executive territory. Joseph Harris, for example, noted that in the late 19th century, presidents had only limited control over the bureaucracy while congressional influence was substantial.[12] Hamm and Robertson reported that legislative vetoes are more common in states where gubernatorial veto powers are relatively weak, but their study did not include other aspects of gubernatorial power.[13]

Analysis reveals that states in which governors have more formal power, as measured by tenure potential, appointive powers, budget powers, and veto powers, are less likely to adopt sunset laws but are more likely to have legislative vetoes. Fully one-third of the states whose governors have limited formal powers have comprehensive sunset laws, but not one of the states which have a strong governor (in terms of formal powers) does. On the other hand, governors with high formal powers are twice as likely to face a legislature with legislative veto powers as are governors with low formal powers (see Table 2).

TABLE 1. STATES WITH SUNSET AND LEGISLATIVE VETO, CLASSIFIED BY FAIIR RATINGS(a)

	A. Sunset Laws		
	States with FAIIR Rating 1–17(b)	States with FAIIR Rating 18–34(c)	States with FAIIR Rating 35–50(d)
Comprehensive Sunset Law	1 (6%)	3 (18%)	7 (44%)
Limited Sunset Law	9 (53%)	8 (47%)	7 (44%)
No Sunset Law	7 (41%)	6 (35%)	2 (12%)
Total	17	17	16

	B. Legislative Veto FAIIR Rating		
	FAIIR Rating 1–17(b)	FAIIR Rating 18–34(c)	FAIIR Rating 35–50(d)
Legislative Veto	10 (59%)	7 (41%)	5 (31%)
No Legislative Veto	7 (41%)	10 (59%)	11 (69%)
Total	17	17	16

SOURCE. *Report on an Evaluation of the 50 State Legislatures* (Kansas City, MO.: Citizen Conference on State Legislatures, 1971).

NOTES. (a) Some caution in interpreting these findings is advisable in view of the age of the FAIIR ratings. Percentages rounded.

(b) Ratings 1–17 indicate legislatures with relatively high salaries, long sessions, substantial staff support, explicit rules and procedures, clear and complete records of legislative decisions and deliberations, well organized committee and leadership structure, and substantial public and media access to legislative actions.

(c) Ratings 18–34 indicate legislatures in an intermediate position between the two extremes, i.e., moderate salaries, medium-length sessions, and so forth.

(d) Ratings 35–50 indicate legislatures with relative low salaries, short sessions, limited staff support, ambiguous rules and procedures, unclear or incomplete records, poorly organized committee and leadership structures, and limited public and media access to legislative actions.

Because the legislative veto and sunset laws are comparatively recent innovations at the state level, the fact that some states have them while others do not may reflect general differences in the speed with which states adopt new ideas. Some states tend to be quick to enact new programs, while others tend to be slow.[14] Support for this possibility is provided by Crane, who found that extensive legislative review of programs was more likely to occur in innovative states than in laggard states.[15] Innovativeness may stimulate legislative adoption of new methods of program review in several ways. First, an innovative state, because of its greater attentiveness to and receptivity toward new ideas, may be more willing to try a new method of program review as an innovation itself. Second, the de-

TABLE 2. STATES WITH SUNSET AND LEGISLATIVE VETO, CLASSIFIED BY FORMAL GUBERNATORIAL POWERS

	A. Sunset Laws Governor's Formal Powers(a)		
	High	**Medium**	**Low**
Comprehensive Sunset Law	0 (0%)	4 (29%)	6 (33%)
Limited Sunset Law	9 (50%)	7 (50%)	8 (44%)
No Sunset Law	9 (50%)	3 (21%)	4 (22%)
Total	18	14	18

	B. Legislative Veto Governor's Formal Powers(a)		
	High	**Medium**	**Low**
Legislative Veto	10 (56%)	7 (50%)	5 (28%)
No Legislative Veto	8 (44%)	7 (50%)	13 (72%)
Total	18	14	18

SOURCE. Alan Rosenthal, *Legislative Life* (N.Y.: Harper & Row, 1981).
NOTE. (a) High includes high and somewhat high. Low includes low and somewhat low. Percentages rounded.

sire to innovate in substantive program areas may spur greater efforts at assessing those programs to determine where changes are needed. Finally, a state which is changing policies more frequently may have more need for program review than does a state which changes policies rarely. In the latter case, a proven program may require less attention than a new, untested one.[16]

In actual experience, however, these expectations are not met. States which have been historically quick to adopt new programs tend *not* to have sunset laws. Moreover, innovation appears unrelated to legislative veto provisions (see Table 3).

Partisan influences may also affect legislative efforts at controlling the bureaucracy. A variety of scholars have noted that legislative oversight is likely to be particularly vigilant when one party controls the legislature and the other party controls the governorship.[17] In that situation, the desire to embarrass the other party may provide the stimulus to oversight which is otherwise often lacking. Conversely, when the governor and legislature are controlled by the same party, bonds of party loyalty as well as self interest may cause legislators to avoid antagonisms with the executive branch. We would expect, therefore, states which experienced divided control on a regular basis to be more likely to enact sunset laws and legislative vetoes, each of which gives the legislature additional leverage on the state bureaucracy. Surprisingly, Hamm and Robertson found that divided control encouraged adoption of legislative vetoes but

TABLE 3. STATES WITH SUNSET AND LEGISLATIVE VETO, CLASSIFIED BY INNOVATIVENESS

	A. Sunset Innovation Score(a)		
	.520 or Higher	.410 to .510	Less than .410
Comprehensive Sunset Law	0 (0%)	5 (31%)	5 (26%)
Limited Sunset Law	5 (38%)	7 (44%)	10 (53%)
No Sunset Law	8 (62%)	4 (25%)	4 (21%)
Total	13	16	19

	B. Legislative Veto Innovation Score(a)		
	.520 or Higher	.410 to .510	Less than .410
Legislative Veto	7 (54%)	5 (31%)	10 (53%)
No Legislative Veto	6 (46%)	11 (69%)	9 (47%)
Total	13	16	19

SOURCE. Jack Walker, "Innovation in State Politics," in Herbert Jacobs and Kenneth Vines, eds., *Politics in the American States*, 2nd ed., (Boston: Little, Brown), 354–87.

NOTE. (a) High innovation scores indicate states which have historically been quick to adopt new programs. Percentages rounded.

discouraged adoption of sunset laws. We will return to that paradoxical finding shortly.[18]

The evidence reveals that states with more divided partisan control are more likely to adopt legislative veto provisions, as expected, but are *less* likely to adopt sunset laws (see Table 4). Three-fourths of the states with little divided control have adopted sunset laws, but less than half of the states with extensive divided control have. By contrast, less than one-third of the states with little divided control have legislative vetoes, but almost two-thirds of the states with extensive divided control do.

Partisan influences may also affect support for sunset laws and legislative vetoes in another way. Both represent attempts at trimming back the size of government or slowing its growth, with similar effects on govern-

ment spending.[19] Those results have traditionally been dear to the hearts of political conservatives. Conservative state party ideologies may encourage adoption of sunset laws and legislative vetoes as methods for controlling the size and cost of government.

Evidence, in fact, shows a modest but discernable tendency for states with more conservative Democratic parties to adopt comprehensive sunset legislation (see Table 5). Legislative veto provisions do not conform to expectations, however. Almost two-thirds of the states with liberal Democratic parties have legislative vetoes, but just under one-fourth of the states with conservative Democratic parties do.[20]

The size and cost of government may provide a direct stimulus to legislative efforts to control the bureaucracy as well. A larger

TABLE 4. STATES WITH SUNSET AND LEGISLATIVE VETO, CLASSIFIED BY DIVIDED PARTISAN CONTROL

	A. Sunset Extent of Divided Control(a)		
	60% or More	30% to 50%	20% or Less
Comprehensive Sunset Law	1 (9%)	1 (6%)	7 (35%)
Limited Sunset Law	4 (36%)	10 (62%)	8 (40%)
No Sunset Law	6 (55%)	5 (31%)	5 (25%)
Total	11	16	20

	B. Legislative Veto Extent of Divided Control(a)		
	60% or More	30% to 50%	20% or Less
Legislative Veto	7 (64%)	8 (50%)	6 (30%)
No Legislative Veto	4 (36%)	8 (50%)	14 (70%)
Total	11	16	20

NOTE. (a) Derived from various volumes of the *Statistical Abstract*. For each two years, unified partisan control of the governorship and both houses of the legislature is scored 0. If the governor's party controls one house of the legislature but not the other, score is 50%. If the governor's party controls neither house, score is 100%. Scores for 1971–1972, 1973–1974, 1975–1976, 1977–1978, and 1979–1980 were totaled and divided by 5 to produce an average score for the decade of 1971–1980.

bureaucracy, with more personnel, money, and programs is likely to affect more people and to therefore stimulate efforts at legislative control. More is at stake as government grows larger.[21] This possibility is supported by Crane's analysis, which found that legislative program reviews were more common in states with high public employment, taxes, and revenue, and by Hamm and Robertson with respect to legislative vetoes but not sunset laws.[22]

Analysis reveals that sunset laws, particularly comprehensive ones, tend to be found in states with relatively low levels of spending per person. Moreover, legislative veto provisions are essentially unrelated to state-local expenditures (Table 6). Neither finding is consistent with expectations.

CONCLUSIONS

The preceding analysis indicates that sunset laws have been most widely adopted in states with a relatively negative orientation to government. Institutionally weak legislatures, governors with limited formal powers, conservative Democratic parties, reluctance to innovate, and low levels of expenditure in the sunset law states all reflect that negative orientation. Legislative veto powers tend to be found in states with institutionally strong legislatures, governors with extensive formal powers, liberal Democratic parties, and divided control, a pattern which suggests a more positive orientation toward government but also disagreements over its control or direction.[23]

TABLE 5. STATES WITH SUNSET AND LEGISLATIVE VETO, CLASSIFIED BY DEMOCRATIC PARTY IDEOLOGY

	A. Sunset Democratic Party Ideology(a)		
	4–5	**3**	**1–2**
Comprehensive Sunset Law	6 (35%)	2 (12%)	2 (14%)
Limited Sunset Law	5 (29%)	10 (59%)	5 (36%)
No Sunset Law	6 (35%)	5 (29%)	7 (50%)
Total	17	17	14

	B. Legislative Veto Democratic Party Ideology(a)		
	4–5	**3**	**1–2**
Legislative Veto	4 (24%)	8 (27%)	9 (64%)
No Legislative Veto	13 (76%)	9 (53%)	5 (36%)
Total	17	17	14

SOURCE. Eugene McGregor, "Uncertainty and National Nominating Coalitions," *Journal of Politics* 40 (1978): 1011–42.

NOTE. (a) High scores indicate conservatism. Percentages rounded.

The inconsistent impact of legislative institutional capability on sunset laws and legislative vetoes also reflects differences in their modes of operation. With sunset laws, the legislature can schedule the decisions to coincide with a limited legislative session, even one which only lasts for two months. With legislative vetoes, however, the scheduling of decisions is in the hands of state agencies, which may promulgate new rules at any time of year. The legislature which only meets for two months each year is poorly equipped to monitor agency rule-making on a year-round basis. Legislative strategies for controlling the bureaucracy, therefore, appeared to reflect both political and institutional influences.

At a more general level, the differences between the states adopting legislative vetoes and sunset laws suggest two different orientations toward controlling the bureaucracy. The legislative veto, with its association with a positive orientation toward government, implies a recognition of the need for delegated authority. Rather than denying the need for bureaucratic or executive discretion and flexibility, the legislative veto seeks to provide safeguards for their use and can be used on a relatively continuous basis. By contrast, sunset laws reflect a generally negative orientation toward government. While some advocates contend that sunset laws can play a positive role in stimulating accountability and responsiveness,[24] the fundamental assumption in sunset legislation is that some programs and agencies are unnecessary and

TABLE 6. STATES WITH SUNSET AND LEGISLATIVE VETO, CLASSIFIED BY STATE-LOCAL EXPENDITURES PER CAPITA

A. Sunset State-Local Expenditures Per Capita, 1977		
$1310 or More	**$1120–$1309**	**$1119 or Less**

	$1310 or More	$1120–$1309	$1119 or Less
Comprehensive Sunset Law	1 (6%)	2 (12%)	7 (41%)
Limited Sunset Law	8 (47%)	10 (62%)	6 (35%)
No Sunset Law	8 (47%)	4 (25%)	4 (24%)
Total	17	16	17

B. Legislative Veto State-Local Expenditures Per Capita, 1977		
$1310 or More	**$1120–$1309**	**$1119 or Less**

	$1310 or More	$1120–$1309	$1119 or Less
Legislative Veto	7 (41%)	9 (56%)	6 (35%)
No Legislative Veto	10 (59%)	7 (44%)	11 (66%)
Total	17	16	17

SOURCE. Richard and Mary Nathan, *America's Governments* (N.Y.: Wiley, 1979).

should be terminated. It is, therefore, a basically negative approach to controlling the bureaucracy, both in principle and in terms of the states likely to have it.

NOTES

1. Morris Ogul, *Congress Oversees the Bureaucracy* (Pittsburgh: University of Pittsburgh Press, 1976), 11–13.
2. Felix and Lloyd Nigro, *Modern Public Administration*, 5th ed., (New York: Harper & Row, 1980), 461–62; Roger Davidson and Walter Oleszek, *Congress and Its Members* (Washington, D.C.: Congressional Quarterly, 1981), 337; Marcus Ethridge, "Legislative-Administrative Interaction as 'Intrusive Access': An Empirical Analysis," *Journal of Politics* 43 (1981):473–92; Louis Fisher, *Presidential Spending Power* (Princeton, N.J.: Princeton University Press, 1975), 74.
3. Nigro and Nigro, *Modern Public Administration*, 460.
4. Gerald Kopel, "Sunset in the West," *State Government* 49, 3 (Summer 1976): 138; Benjamin Shimberg, "The Sunset Approach: Key to Regulatory Reform," ibid., 145.
5. Louis Fesler, *Public Administration* (Englewood Cliffs, N.J.: Prentice-Hall, 1980), 329–30; Russell Maddox and Robert Fuquay, *State and Local Government*, 4th ed., (New York: Van Nostrand, 1981), 75.
6. Nigro and Nigro, *Modern Public Administration*, 461; Morris Fiorina, "Congressional Control of the Bureaucracy: A Mismatch of Incentives and Capabilities," in Lawrence Dodd and Bruce Oppenheimer, eds., *Congress Reconsidered*, 2nd ed., (Washington, D.C.: Congressional Quarterly, 1981), 337.
7. *The Book of the States*, 1980–81 (Lexington, Ky.: Council of State Governments, 1980), 120–24.
8. Malcolm Jewell, *The State Legislature*, 2nd ed., (New York: Random House, 1969), 128; William Keefe, "The Functions and Powers of the State

Legislatures," in Alexander Heard, ed., *State Legislatures in American Politics* (Englewood Cliffs, N.J.: Prentice-Hall, 1966), 47; Alan Rosenthal, *Legislative Life* (New York: Harper & Row, 1981), 315–16.

9. Edgar Crane, *Legislative Review of Government Programs* (New York: Praeger, 1977), 102.

10. **Keith Hamm and Roby Robertson, "Factors Influencing the Adoption of New Methods of Legislative Oversight in the U.S. States," *Legislative Studies Quarterly* 6 (1981): 144–46.**

11. *Report on an Evaluation of the 50 State Legislatures* (Kansas City, Mo.: 1971), 29.

12. Joseph Harris, *Congressional Control of Administration* (Washington, D.C.: Brookings Institute, 1964), 281–82.

13. Hamm and Robertson, "Factors," 144–45.

14. Jack Walker, "The Diffusion of Innovations Among the States," *American Political Science Review* 63 (1969): 880–99; "Innovation in State Politics" in Herbert Jacob and Kenneth Vines, eds., *Politics in the American States*, 2nd ed., (Boston: Little, Brown, 1971), 354–87.

15. Crane, *Legislative Review*, 117.

16. This is not to say that non-innovative states have an array of programs which have proven excellent but rather that more frequent changes in programs may call for more program review efforts, other things being equal.

17. Harris, *Congressional Control*, 280; Ogul, *Congress Oversees*, 18; Seymour Sher, "Conditions for Legislative Control," *Journal of Politics* 25 (1963): 526–51; Herbert Simon, Donald Smithberg and Victor Thompson, *Public Administration* (New York: Knopf, 1950), 525.

18. Hamm and Robertson, "Factors," 144–47.

19. Nigro and Nigro, *Modern Public Administration*, 460; Rosenthal, *Legislative Life*, 317.

20. Republican party ideology was examined but is essentially unrelated to sunset laws and legislative veto provisions.

21. William Keefe and Morris Ogul, *The American Legislative Process*, 5th ed., (Englewood Cliffs, N.J.: Prentice-Hall, 1981), 385–86; Sher, "Condition."

22. Crane, *Legislative Review*, 95; Hamm and Robertson, "Factors."

23. Care should be exercised in comparing the strengths of the relationships between various state characteristics examined here and adoption of measures to increase legislative control over the bureaucracy. Some of the state characteristics were measured more recently than others, and state government reforms in recent years may have introduced some measurement error into the older measures.

24. Kopel, "Sunset in the West"; Shimberg, "The Sunset Approach."

— **30** —

Populism Revived

JOSEPH F. ZIMMERMAN

The referendum, the initiative, and the recall were promoted by many governmental reformers in the 1890s and early 1900s as mechanisms for restoring popular control of state and local governments dominated by business corporations and/or bosses. The employment of direct legislation since 1978 to limit property taxes in California (Proposition 13)

State Government, Vol.58, No.4 (Fall 1986), pp. 172–178.

and Massachusetts (Proposition 2½) and the recall to change political party control of the Michigan Senate, highlight the need for an assessment of these popular control devices in terms of their impact upon representative government.

The origin of the first two devices is traceable to the colonial period. The referendum, based upon the concept of shared decision-making, is a natural extension of the New England town meeting and allows voters to determine whether referred matters are to become parts of the state constitution, state statutes, local charters, or local ordinances. Not surprisingly, the first referendum was held in the Massachusetts Bay Colony in 1640.[1]

The initiative, the process by which citizens by petitions place questions on the referendum ballot, dates to 1715 when the Massachusetts General Court (legislature) enacted a law requiring the selectmen to include in the warrant calling a town meeting any item accompanied by petition signed by 10 or more voters.[2]

The practice of submitting proposed state constitutions to the electorate became well established in the early decades of the 19th century and, commencing with the Rhode Island Constitution of 1842, provisions were incorporated in many constitutions forbidding the legislature to borrow funds or levy property taxes exceeding constitutional maxima without the sanction of the state's voters.

Citizen law-making entered a new era in 1898 when South Dakota voters amended the state constitution to provide for the statutory initiative and referendum by stipulating they "expressly reserve to themselves the right to propose measures, which measures the legislature shall enact and submit to a vote of the electors of the State" and "to require that any laws which the legislature may have enacted shall be submitted to a vote of the electors of the State before going into effect. . . ."[3] In the same year, San Francisco freeholders adopted a new city-county charter providing

for the initiative and the referendum.[4] South Dakota's and San Francisco's leads were followed by other states and local governments, and the use of the initiative and the referendum became relatively common during the subsequent two decades.

Whereas the referendum and the initiative allow voters to make the final decision on proposed laws, the recall is designed to remove public officers—legislators, executives, and judicial officers—from office prior to the expiration of their terms. In common with the other devices, the process of removing an officer is commenced by the circulation of petitions for voter signatures. The recall first was adopted by Los Angeles in 1903 when voters ratified a new city charter providing for the device.[5]

THE REFERENDUM

The Delaware constitution is the only constitution which does not provide for a referendum on constitutional amendments enacted by the state legislature. In the other states, the size of the legislative vote and referendum vote required for approval of a constitutional amendment varies from state to state.

Thirty-six state constitutions currently contain provisions for referenda on certain laws enacted by the state legislature such as ones pledging the "full faith and credit" of the state. In addition, voters in 25 states may petition for a referendum on a law enacted by the state legislature. The filing of the required number of signatures on petitions suspends the law, except appropriations and emergency ones in several states, until the electorate determines whether the law should be approved.

Mandatory Referenda. A relatively long list of state and local governmental actions—adoption of state constitutions and local charters or amendments, incorporation of municipalities, calling of a constitutional convention, annexation of land, mergers of local governments, and pledging the "full faith and credit" of the government—are subject to compulsory referenda in many states.

Serious objections are raised by many governmental observers to mandatory referenda on bond issues because such a requirement has led to more expensive ways of financing large governmental projects. The plebiscite requirement can be evaded by creating public authorities empowered to issue "moral obligation" bonds and by entering into lease-purchase agreements. Authorities are not subject to constitutional debt referenda requirements and a number of such authorities have been created in various states with the power to issue bonds backed by a "moral obligation" or "indirect" guarantee that a future state legislature will appropriate funds to meet interest and principal payments should the issuing authorities be unable to meet their financial obligations. These bonds carry a higher rate of interest than "full faith and obligation" bonds and, consequently, place a heavier burden upon taxpayers.

Lease-purchase agreements involve a state or a local government entering into an agreement to purchase large capital equipment or facilities on the installment plan. In other words, a government signs a long-term contract providing the government may use a facility constructed and financed by another government or a private firm with title to the project passing to the former government on a specified date. In common with "moral obligation" financing, lease-purchase financing is more expensive than "full faith and credit" financing.

The Citizens' Veto. The petition referenda, also known as the protest or direct referenda, provides for a citizens' veto by allowing voters by petitions to stop the implementation of a law until a referenda determine whether the law is to be repealed. This type of referenda is similar to the initiative in that action to place a law on the referenda ballot originates with the voters. Successful collection of the requisite

number of signatures results in a mandatory referenda.

The protest referenda may be employed in 24 states. However, in eight states— Alaska, Idaho, Massachusetts, Michigan, Missouri, Montana, South Dakota, and Wyoming—the petition referenda may be employed only against an entire law whereas in the other states the referenda may be used against part or all of a law. The constitutional provision authorizing this type of referenda typically excludes certain topics—religion, appropriations, special legislation, and the judiciary—from the referenda.

States lacking the petition referenda at the state level authorize its use at the local level. New Hampshire statutes, for example, authorize the owners of 20 percent either of the land area or lots to petition for a referenda on a change in land use regulations adopted by a town.[6]

The protest referenda can be employed by conservative or liberal groups, or by integrationists or segregationists. Whereas business groups typically do not employ the initiative to achieve their goals, such groups use the protest referenda to annul statutes. In 1982, the Massachusetts Soft Drink Association filed petitions for the first referenda in the nation on the subject of repealing a mandatory bottle deposit law enacted by the Massachusetts General Court. Although voters defeated a proposed bottle deposit law by a small margin in 1976, they rejected the repeal proposal in 1982.

There is no evidence that "conservative" groups make more use of the referenda than "liberal" groups, but there is evidence that voters take both a "conservative" and a "liberal" stance on different propositions on the same ballot. Massachusetts voters in 1982 approved a death penalty proposition, generally considered to be a "conservative" issue, and a bottle deposit proposition and a nuclear freeze proposition, which are considered to be part of the "liberal agenda."

THE INITIATIVE

The constitutions of 23 states contain provisions for one or more types of initiatives. In 17 states, the initiative may be employed in the process of amending the state constitution. And in 21 states, the initiative may be employed in the process of enacting ordinary statutes.

Initiatives may be classified as (1) state, (2) local, (3) constitutional, (4) statutory, (5) direct, (6) indirect, and (7) advisory. The first four categories are self-explanatory.

Direct Initiative. This type circumvents the entire legislative process as propositions are placed directly on the referendum ballot if the requisite number and distribution of valid signatures are collected and certified.

The state legislature in five states—Maine, Massachusetts, Michigan, Nevada, and Washington—is authorized to place a substitute proposition on the referendum ballot whenever an initiative proposition appears on the ballot. Although the constitution of Alaska provides only for the direct initiative and contains no provision for an indirect initiative, a section of the constitution allows the state legislature to enact a substitute which voids the initiative petition provided the substitute is "substantially the same."

On the substate level, the direct initiative commonly is employed to place local charters or charter amendments on the referendum ballot, as illustrated by voters in Summit County, Ohio, in 1980, successfully placing on the ballot a proposed home rule county charter which was ratified by the voters.

The major objection raised against the direct initiative is the fact initiated measures often are drafted imperfectly, violate the federal or state constitution, or produce unintended adverse effects. Opponents and proponents of a 1978 California proposition limiting smoking in public places agreed the proposal was defeated because of technical defects, including prohibition of smoking at jazz concerts but not at rock concerts.

Indirect Initiative. Employed in eight states, the indirect initiative involves a more cumbersome process as a proposition is referred to the legislative body for its consideration upon the filing of the required number of certified signatures. Failures of the legislative body to approve the proposition within a stipulated number of days, varying from 40 in Michigan to adjournment of the Maine legislature, leads to the proposition being placed automatically on the referendum ballot. In three states, additional signatures must be collected to place the proposition on the ballot as follows: one-half of 1 percent and 10 percent of the votes cast for governor in the last general election in Massachusetts and Utah, respectively, and 3 percent of the registered voters in Ohio. Only the Massachusetts constitution authorizes the indirect initiative for constitutional amendments and an amendment proposed by the initiative is not placed upon the referendum ballot unless the proposal is approved by at least 25 percent of the members of the General Court in two consecutive sessions.[7]

Relative to proposed statutes, Maine, Massachusetts, and Wyoming provide only for the indirect initiative. Michigan, Nevada, Ohio, South Dakota, Utah, and Washington authorize employment of both types.

The indirect initiative can have the salutary effect of prodding the legislature to take action to solve a major problem. Within a fortnight of the filing of 145,170 signatures on initiative petitions prohibiting the use of cats and dogs from pounds for medical research, the Massachusetts General Court in 1983 enacted the petition.

Advisory Initiative. This type of initiative allows voters to circulate petitions to place a nonbinding question on the ballot at an election and is a mechanism citizens and groups can employ to pressure legislative bodies to take a certain course of action.

Until the late 1970s, the advisory initiative was employed relatively infrequently and attracted generally only local notice. The growth of the environmental and nuclear freeze movements, along with movements opposing United States involvement in Central America, has resulted in national attention being focused upon such referenda as national and regional groups employ the initiative to place questions on election ballots. In 1983, for example, voters approved advisory initiative Proposition O directing the mayor and the board of supervisors of the city and county of San Francisco to notify President Ronald Reagan and Congress the voters favor the repeal of the provisions of the federal Voting Rights Act requiring the city and county to provide ballots, voter pamphlets, and other materials on voting in Chinese and Spanish as well as in English.

THE RECALL

The concept of the recall was incorporated into Article V of the Articles of Confederation and Perpetual Union which provided that states were authorized to replace their delegates to Congress. However, the voters only indirectly participated in this type of recall since the state legislature possessed the power of the recall.

The recall was a product of the populist and municipal reform movements which were in sympathy with the early 19th century Jacksonian distrust of government officials. Jacksonian democracy attempted to keep public officials continuously responsible to the electorate by providing that most public officers should be elected and their terms of office should be short; *i.e.,* six months to one year.

The constitutions of 14 states authorize the employment of the recall to remove state officers from office. These states also authorize, by statute, all or certain local governments to employ the recall against all or speci-

fied local government officers. In addition, 17 states authorize the recall of local officers by general law, special law, or a locally drafted and adopted charter.[8]

The reasons for the use of the recall in most states are not limited to a scandalum magnatum as the recall can be employed for any reason, including disagreement on a policy issue. The Michigan constitution stipulates "the sufficiency of any statement of reasons or grounds procedurally required shall be a political rather than a judicial question."[9] On the other hand, the Washington constitutional provision requires petitioners to recite "that such officer has committed some act or acts of malfeasance or misfeasance while in office, or who has violated his oath of office, stating the matters complained of, . . ."[10]

Restrictions on Use. Constitutional, statutory, and local charter provisions typically place restrictions on the exercise of the recall by the voters. The constitutions of Alaska, Idaho, Louisiana, Michigan, and Washington exclude judicial officers from the recall.

The Montana recall law is the only one that provides for the recall of appointed as well as elected state officers.[11] In addition, a number of local charters authorize the recall of appointed as well as elected officers. The city of Greeley, Colorado, has an unusual charter provision authorizing voters at an election held every six years to terminate the employment of the city manager.[12]

Constitutional and statutory provisions authorizing employment of the recall often prohibit its use during the first two months (Montana) or year of an elected officer's term of office and a second recall during the same officer's term of office unless the petitioners pay for the cost of the preceding recall election. Louisiana law prohibits a second recall attempt within 18 months of the previous unsuccessful recall election.[13]

There are no restrictions on the use of the recall, other than time period or frequency, in California, North Dakota, Ohio, South Dakota, and Wyoming. Kansas law enumerates

the grounds for recall—"conviction of a felony, misconduct in office, incompetence, or
failure to perform duties prescribed by law."[14]

Petition Requirements. The recall is similar
to the petition referendum and the initiative
in that action originates with the voters. The
first step in initiating voter removal of a state
officer in eight states—Alaska, Arizona, California, Georgia, Idaho, Kansas, Oregon, and
Washington—is the filing and publishing or
posting of a notice of intent to circulate a recall
petition.[15] A filing fee of one hundred dollars
is required in Alaska, but the fee is refunded if
verified signatures equal to 25 percent of the
votes cast for the office in question at the last
election are filed by the deadline for petitions.[16] Kansas also levies a one hundred dollar filing fee.[17]

Each recall petition must contain a declaration by the circulator that each signature is a
genuine one.[18] Petitions must be filed within a
stated number of days—ranging from 60 days
in Wisconsin to 270 days for state officers in
Washington—after the certifying officer noti-
fies proponents that the form and wording of
the filed proposed petition are correct.[19] Successful collection of the required number of
certified signatures results in a special election to determine whether the named offi-
cer(s) shall remain in office until the expiration of the regular term of office. The most
common petition requirement is signatures
equal to 25 percent of the votes cast for all
candidates in the last general election for governor in the involved unit or the officer whose
recall is sought.[20] In some states, there is a
geographical requirement relative to the minimum number of signatures for the recall of an
office elected on a statewide basis.

The Recall Election. The typical recall provision stipulates the process is terminated
should the public officer against whom the
petitions are directed resign the office. Should
the officer resign, the vacancy is filled in the
manner provided by law.

The reasons advanced in support of the
recall are printed on the recall ballot, but the
number of words is limited; 200 is the most
common limit.[21] The officer whose recall is
sought may submit a statement of justification
of conduct in office.

In nine states, voters in a recall election
simply vote on the question of whether the
officer should be recalled. A majority affirmative vote ipso facto removes the officer from
office in most jurisdictions. The vacancy resulting from an affirmative removal vote may
involve a second special election to select a
successor. If an officer is recalled, Montana
law directs that "the vacancy shall be filled as
provided by law, provided that the officer recalled may in no event be appointed to fill the
vacancy."[22]

A separate election on the question of re-
calling an officer has the advantage of allowing voters to concentrate on the question of
the removal without having their attention di-
verted by the claims of other candidates, but
suffers from the disadvantage of increasing
governmental costs if a special election is held
to fill the vacancy.

Proponents of the recall typically recruit
and endorse a replacement candidate and
campaign for his or her election. In the only
judicial recall election in Wisconsin, recall
proponents in 1977 did not endorse a replacement candidate for fear of dividing voters favoring the recall of Judge Archie Simonson of
Dane County.[23]

CAMPAIGN FINANCE

State corrupt practices acts regulate the financing of election and referenda campaigns.
Historically, these acts required the reporting
of campaign receipts and expenditures, and
limited the amount that may be contributed to
or spent in campaigns.

In 1976, the United States Supreme Court
in *Buckley* v. *Valeo* examined the Federal Election Campaign Act of 1971 and its 1974
amendments, and upheld the individual contribution limits, disclosure and reporting re-

quirements, and public financing provisions, but held "the limitations on expenditures, on independent expenditures by individuals and groups, and on expenditures by a candidate from his personal funds are constitutionally infirm."[24]

Two years later, the Court invalidated a Massachusetts statute restricting corporate contributions to referenda campaigns by ruling a corporation was protected by the First Amendment to the United States Constitution and could expend funds to publicize its views relative to a proposed state constitutional amendment authorizing the General Court to levy a graduated income tax.[25]

Statewide initiative, referendum, and recall campaigns are expensive because of the difficulties of obtaining the requisite number of certifiable signatures on petitions and the high cost of persuading the electorate to support or reject ballot propositions, or remove an officer. Proposition 15 on the 1982 California ballot would have placed controls on hand guns and resulted in approximately $10 million being spent by interest groups to secure its approval or defeat with the largest contribution, approximately $2.5 million, coming from the National Rifle Association.

The danger of "moneyed" interests employing the petition referendum and the initiative for their own benefit has been increased by the Court's decisions, yet evidence to date reveals that the side spending the most money in a campaign does not invariably win.

POPULISM REVIVED

Few question whether citizens are sovereign or the desirability of submitting proposed organic documents—state constitutions, constitutional amendments, local charters, and charter amendments—to the voters for a final determination. Strong objections, however, have been raised by many observers to the protest referendum, the initiative, and the recall on the ground that these devices undermine representative government.

The petition referendum is a form of citizens' veto designed to correct legislative sins of commission and should be available to voters as a safety valve to be employed to reverse unrepresentative legislative decisions. This type of referendum has not weakened representative government by discouraging many able individuals from seeking or continuing in legislative office, or by encouraging legislative bodies to shirk their responsibilities by employing the optional referendum (legislative placement of a proposition on the ballot).

One of the auxiliary advantages of the protest referendum, in conjunction with the initiative and the recall, is to encourage the electorate to revise state constitutions and local charters to make them short documents confined to fundamentals and readable by removing detailed restrictions since direct legislation and the recall provide the citizenry with mechanisms to ensure that legislators do not abuse the trust placed in them by the electorate.

Consideration should be given by states to a new type of petition referendum which, upon the filing of the requisite number of certified signatures, would suspend a law and require the legislative body to consider the repeal or amendment of the law within a stated number of days. Should the legislature fail to adopt the proposal contained in the petition within a specified number of days regardless of whether the legislature is in session on the day the petitions are certified, a referendum automatically would be held on the proposal. At present the filing of the requisite number of signatures results automatically in a referendum where voters are limited to a "yes" or "no" choice on the question of repealing the referred law. The proposed new type of petition referendum would encourage the legislative body to amend or repeal the law in question, thereby obviating the need for a referendum and its attendant expenses.

On balance, the indirect initiative strengthens the governance system. This type of initiative has the benefit of the legislative process, including public hearings and committee review, study, and recommendations. Should the legislative body fail to approve the proposition, voters have been advantaged in their decision-making capacity by the information on the proposition generated by the legislative process.

The indirect initiative can be an effective counterbalance to an unrepresentative legislative body and no more undermines representative government than the executive veto and the judicial veto. A major advantage of the initiative is the fact it makes the operation of interest groups more visible in comparison with their lobbying activities in a state or local legislative body. Furthermore, the availability of the initiative increases the citizen's stake in the government.

Support for the indirect initiative does not suggest that it should be employed frequently. It should be a reserve power or last resort weapon and the relative need for its use depends upon the degree of accountability, representativeness, and responsiveness of legislative bodies.

A model constitutional provision for the initiative should contain the following elements: (a) the attorney general and/or community affairs department should be directed to provide petition drafting services to sponsors of initiatives; (b) upon submission of a certified petition, a conference should be held at which the attorney general or community affairs department explains initiative wording problems, if any, to sponsors and suggests amendments if needed; (c) if a defeated proposition is resubmitted to the voters within two years, sponsors should be required to obtain additional signatures on petitions equal to 2 percent of the votes cast for governor in the last general election in the affected jurisdic-

tion; (d) the state constitution should authorize the employment of the initiative for purposes of placing the question of calling a constitutional convention on the ballot.

The question of adopting the recall has been the subject of controversy in many states and local jurisdictions, but not in most jurisdictions that have adopted it, when measured in terms of voluntary abandonment. Because citizen-initiated recall appears to be an application of modified direct democracy to representative democracy, philosophical arguments about it have abounded. State laws providing for the automatic vacating of a public office by an incumbent convicted of a felony have not generated controversy.

The recall possesses the potential for abuse unless the authorizing provision restricts its employment to cases involving malfeasance, misfeasance, or nonfeasance. If there are no restrictions upon the use of the recall, it may be employed by the losing candidate in the previous election in a second attempt to gain office, or the charges may be the result of a grudge or philosophical differences of opinion on issues. Experience reveals that the dangers of the unrestricted recall are small and are outweighed by its associated advantages.

The recall seldom has been used at the state level; only one governor—Lynn J. Frazier of North Dakota in 1981—has been recalled. Nevertheless, the recall can produce a major political change on the state level. Two Democratic state senators were recalled by Michigan voters in 1983 and replaced by Republicans, giving the Republicans control over the Senate.[26] The recall generally has been used on the local level to remove members of a city council who voted to fire a popular city manager.

To a certain extent, the infrequency of the use of the recall may be due to its restraining effect upon officers who recognize its existence is a threat to their continuance in office if they step out of line with majority opinion.

The recent and more frequent use of the direct initiative and the petition referendum should not obscure the fact that most representative governments have been responsive to the citizenry. Most citizens are interested chiefly in the delivery of quality public services at a reasonable cost. If legislative bodies ensure these two goals, use of direct legislation and recall should be uncommon.

No system of representation is perfect. Per consequens, a quadrivium of correctives—voting in regular elections, the direct initiative, the petition referendum, and the recall—should be available to the electorate, but preferably triggered only by gross misrepresentation.

NOTES

1. Nathaniel B. Shurtleff, ed. *Records of the Governor and Company of the Massachusetts Bay in New England* Vol. 1, (Boston: From the Press of William White, Printer to the Commonwealth, 1853), 293.

2. *The Acts and Resolves of the Province of the Massachusetts Bay* Vol. 2, (Boston: Wright and Potter, 1874), 30.

3. *Constitution of South Dakota*, Art. III, Section 1 (1898).

4. *Charter for the City and County of San Francisco*, Art. II, Chap. 1, Sections 20–22.

5. Frederick L. Bird and Frances M. Ryan, *The Recall of Public Officers: A Study of the Operation of the Recall in California* (New York: The Macmillan Company, 1930), 22.

6. *New Hampshire Revised Statutes*, Section 31.64 (1983 Supp.).

7. *Constitution of the Commonwealth of Massachusetts*, Articles of Amendment, Art. XLVIII.

8. Arkansas, Florida, Georgia, Hawaii, Massachusetts, Minnesota, Mississippi, Missouri, Nebraska, New Jersey, New Mexico, Ohio, Pennsylvania, South Dakota, Tennessee, West Virginia, and Wyoming.

9. *Constitution of Michigan*, Art. II, Section 8.

10. *Constitution of Washington*, Art. I, Section 33.

11. *Montana Laws of 1977*, Chap. 364, and *Revised Code of Montana*, Section 2-16-603 (1983).

12. *Greeley Colorado City Charter*, Section 4.3.

13. *Louisiana Acts of 1921*, extra session, No. 121, Section 9 and *Louisiana Revised Statutes*, Section 1300.13 (1956).

14. *Kansas Statutes Annotated*, Section 25-4302 (1981).

15. For an example of a statutory requirement, see *California Elections Code*, Sections 27007 and 27030.5 (1977 and 1984 Supp.).

16. *Alaska Laws of 1960*, Chap. 83, and *Alaska Statutes*, Section 15.45.480 (1982 Supp.).

17. *Kansas Laws of 1976*, Chap. 178, and *Kansas Statutes Annotated*, Section 25-4306 (1981).

18. For an example, see the *Constitution of Arizona*, Art. VIII, Section 2.

19. See *Revised Code of Washington*, Section 29.82.025 (1965 and 1984 Supp.).

20. For details, see *The Book of the States, 1980–81* (Lexington, Ky.: The Council of State Governments, 1980), 198.

21. For an example, see *Michigan Public Acts of 1978*, Public Act 533, Section 1, and *Michigan Compiled Laws Annotated*, Section 168.966 (1984 Supp.).

22. *Montana Laws of 1977*, Chap. 364, and *Revised Code of Montana*, Section 2-16-635 (1983).

23. "Winner in War Over Judge's Words," *The New York Times*, September 9, 1977, B1.

24. *Buckley* v. *Valeo*, 424 U.S. 1 at 143 (1976).

25. *First National Bank* v. *Bellotti*, 435 U.S. 765 (1978).

26. Candace Romig, "Two Michigan Legislators Recalled," *State Legislatures*, January 1984, 5.

CHAPTER 7
State Executives and Employees

Although most states elect several officials, attention is focussed upon the governor as chief executive. "A Day in the Life of a Governor" is followed by a discussion of why even the appointment of subordinates does not give control over administration programs. Operations are carried out by public employees who respond to criticism which they consider to be "bureaucrat bashing" by unionizing more highly than workers in the private sector. "The Rise of Government Unions and the Decline of the Work Ethic" is rebutted by an official of the largest union, the American Federation of State, County, and Municipal Employees (AFSCME), which contends that contracting out government's job to private business has serious shortcomings. In order to determine the scope of state and local governments, citizens need to decide which of these two opposing views raise the best arguments.

31

A Day in the Life of a Governor

THE NATIONAL GOVERNORS' ASSOCIATION

It is difficult to convey to a new Governor the importance of maintaining control over his time. One approach is to present a typical day of a Governor who has been in office for some time and is no longer concerned with transition problems. This section hypothetically portrays such a day—assuming that there is anything like a typical day (which there isn't)

From article of same title, in *State Government*, Summer 1979, pp. 110–116. This article was excerpted from The National Governors' Association, *Governing the American States: A Handbook for New Governors* (Washington, D.C.: 1978), pp. 10–20, and is reprinted by permission of The Council of State Governments.

of a typical Governor (which there isn't). It is presented here to point out the importance of managing time well, and of developing time-management ideas during the transition period.

8:00–9:00 A.M

Scheduled office time; no staff or calls allowed. The Governor instituted this practice after realizing that if he wanted to work alone for as much as an hour, he would have to demand it.

Reads newspaper stories on state government; dictates short congratulatory notes to juvenile delinquency director for fine press coverage on opening of new facility, and to editorial staff of major newspaper for editorial commending his support of the facility. Writes note to mental health director on press story about beating of retarded child in state facility.

Notes local controversy about highway location in southern part of state; makes mental note to discuss it with highway commissioner. Notes editorial and news comment that next legislative session is likely to be a rough one. Notes speculation that he is about to appoint Jones as new bank commissioner; tells press secretary to get speculation killed; he hasn't decided, but knows it won't be Jones.

Starts working on screened morning mail (a small part of mail actually received). Mayor of large city wants to be moved up on sewer project priority list; refers mayor's letter to the department. Official of smaller city complains that mass transportation money is unfairly going to larger cities; refers letter to department. National party chairman requests Governor's cooperation in upcoming congressional campaign financing; Governor writes a reminder to discuss with political advisor. Major contributor comments that branch banking law changes being considered by the staff would seriously threaten savings and loan institutions; Governor dictates letter in-

dicating he is aware of problems and is concerned.

Reviews telegrams from environmental groups requesting that he reverse his decision to support Corps of Engineers water supply project; other telegrams from local mayor and county leaders and builders ask him to reaffirm support of project. Decides to stay with earlier decision.

9:00 A.M

Receives delegation of legislators and mayor of suburban community seeking superhighway. Highway department briefing materials say that the road shouldn't be built at all; and if it is, it couldn't be started for 10 years, unless, of course, the Governor wants to propose new gasoline taxes to fund commitments to other areas. Governor tells delegation he is working on the problem and is sympathetic, but has other pressures for use of funds.

Asks friendly legislator to stay after the meeting, and finds out that the county chairman is wavering from support of his candidate for state senate and is unhappy with the way state party headquarters is run.

10:00 A.M

Kicks off National Cancer Week campaign with pictures and awards plus handshaking with county chairmen. One person catches him at end of meeting and asks that he solve problem of son who is in trouble with the Army. Governor pleads inability to handle problem, but offers to try. Calls federal relations aide aside to explain, and asks if aide can work something out to get friendly Congressman to check on the case.

10:30 A.M

Checks secretary for phone calls: has calls from two cabinet officers, one board chairman, his wife, two legislators, one local business leader, plus three aides who "must" see him.

Starts to return phone calls, but gets interrupted by press secretary who says major local issue is developing over announced layoff of 20 employees in state TB hospital; department says it's true; press secretary recommends saying Governor is looking into it and to tell the department to hold off. Governor tells press secretary to hold off comment until he has talked to department.

Now makes calls, postponing 11 A.M. meeting with transportation secretary and budget director on additional matching money for highway construction until 11:30 A.M., and 11:30 meeting with insurance commissioner until noon.

Mental health director advises that he is having some success with local mental health directors in meetings Governor had asked him to hold. Notes in passing (obviously real reason for call) that he is having some trouble with Governor's political advisor on staffing the department and is convinced that the professionalism of the department must remain inviolate.

Arts board chairman says he's getting lots of pressure from legislators for local interest arts projects and has decided to emphasize these projects almost solely in this year's fund allocation. Reports considerable sentiment in the business community that administration spending is getting out of hand and warns against proposing any tax increases.

Wife reminds him to do something about getting some state agency to support a statewide program to put art and music in state institutions for mentally retarded. Governor calls budget director and asks for prospects of doing it. Budget director believes the art board has no new statewide projects this year—concentrating on local concerns instead. Does Governor want it changed? Governor is not sure, and budget director offers a memo later in the week explaining the choices; Governor decides to wait for the memo.

Expecting the first of the legislators on the telephone, Governor gets his legislative aide instead—his secretary explaining that he had asked that Governor talk to him before the legislator. Legislative aide says legislator is extremely upset because Governor's budget bureau and perhaps higher education coordinating council are apparently not going to approve a community college for which locals have already raised money. Legislative aide feels it is absolutely essential that the project be approved before the fall election and asks the Governor to pry the issue out of whatever agency it is in.

Legislator says just what legislative aide said he would. Governor agrees to look into it and call him back.

The other legislator whose call Governor returns is concerned about a rumor that Governor is firing employees in TB hospital and planning to close it; says he understands problem but hopes that Governor will understand his, and that he'll have to issue a press release this afternoon criticizing lack of concern with TB patients and local community if Governor goes through with it. The local business leader is also concerned about the TB issue.

12:00 NOON

Secretary says transportation secretary, budget director, and transportation aide are waiting; also insurance commissioner. Meeting at 12:15 P.M. with major newspaper reporter pending, and more phone calls.

Governor has brief meeting on transportation funding. Budget director argues for passing up federal money for new highway construction on grounds of Governor's austerity program. Transportation secretary notes that funds are 80 percent federal and argues for a go-ahead. Governor says he'll read both memoranda and decide after checking with executive assistant.

Governor is scheduled to leave at 1 P.M. for a ribbon-cutting highway opening about an hour away. Asks secretary to see if he can scrub highway opening and to hold calls, and says he will see the reporter after press secretary has a minute to brief him. Press secretary says press is all over him on TB thing—what has the Governor decided? Governor asks secretary to get health director on phone, finds he is addressing public health association lunch right now—does the Governor want to interrupt? No, have him call just as soon as he is through speaking.

Reporter comes in to begin interview on whether governor is taking position in key party leadership fight over mayoral nomination in eastern part of the state; Governor sets ground rules as background and begins to expound on his preferences.

Secretary buzzes on intercom and reports that top aides (all of whom are now waiting to see him) advise OK to cancel highway opening, highway commissioner will handle but Governor should call mayor and apologize because there may be a big crowd which the mayor gathered. Governor tells her to call mayor on his behalf and explain situation, and that he will call the mayor himself later in the day.

Interview concluded, secretary brings in lunch that he was originally scheduled to have during trip to ribbon cutting.

1:15 P.M

Health director on the phone reminds Governor that there are no more TB patients to be cared for, that most of the people in TB sanitorium are alcoholics who can be readily cared for elsewhere, that firings are part of his budget plan, and that he has no funds to continue employees. Governor finds employees were offered jobs elsewhere, but many of them don't want to leave the community. Director says he can keep the facility open as long as the Governor provides the money. Governor asks press secretary to tell press of meeting on subject at 2 P.M.

Asks secretary to tell legislator to please hold off the press conference criticizing the TB closing for another day. She says she has had three calls from union leaders and a couple of legislative calls protesting the closing and that his political advisor wants to talk about them as well as other things. Governor sets up meeting for 2 P.M. with health director, budget director, press secretary and political advisor.

Secretary provides messages from other calls: . . . Three different people with candidates other than Jones called to express hope that the press story on Jones was not true. One wanted to talk to Governor before an apointment is made so he could tell him some confidential information about Jones . . . Jones called, said he didn't know he was being considered, but would be happy to talk about the job . . . Chairman of the commission on higher education said please make no commitment on the community college matter without talking to him. Budget director called with the same message . . . Federal relations aide called, wants a decision this afternoon on what to ask Senator Smith to do on strip-mine control amendments affecting state regulation. Senate votes tomorrow, and the Senator wants to go with Governor's position. Memo in in-box (which has been resting untouched on desk since 10 A.M.).

1:45 P.M

Governor tries to call federal relations aide while reading memorandum. Can't reach, he is on the way back from Washington. Governor asks secretary to find out whether he has talked to head of state environmental protection agency on subject . . . no one knows, he'll call in about an hour.

Governor tells secretary to tell insurance commissioner he is sorry to keep him waiting and for him to get lunch and check back about 3 P.M. Secretary says aides are still waiting, some of their business is pretty urgent, plus remember the 4 P.M. meeting on office space, and that he has an engagement this evening.

2:12 P.M

Meeting with health director and others (now including legislative personnel and legal advisors) on TB matter. Political and legislative advisors say they don't care how we got where we are, it is imperative that the state not be laying off employees right before election, and with key labor negotiations going on in other departments. Personnel advisor tends to agree, but notes that employees had some prior knowledge of likely layoffs. Budget director and health director are adamant on merits of closing the facility; health director says he will keep it open if budget is increased; budget director says no chance, the legislature cut the overall health budget last year. Legal advisor proposes compromise to keep the facility open until after election, funds to come from health budget, but administration would have to seek some supplemental appropriation to reimburse health budget. Health director is dubious, budget director opposed, personnel advisor says that where he comes from, if you are going to bite a bullet you do it all at once, not in stages. Meeting drags on. Obvious that these layoffs are just the beginning if Governor stays with health director's plan.

Meeting continues while Governor takes call from federal relations aide. Yes, he has talked to the environmental protection agency, and the position he recommends on strip mining is concurred in by them. Governor returns to TB meeting. Finds potential solution is to have mental health department take over part of facility instead of closing it. Unknown if mental health director will agree; health director is on phone to him now.

Governor leaves TB meeting with legal advisor to discuss status of suit by welfare rights organization to require higher welfare payments.

3:20 P.M

Returns to TB meeting, which now includes mental health director. Mental health director says he can't make a final decision now, needs to review the facility and prospects for transferring some patients and doctors from another of his facilities. Press secretary proposes to tell media the administration is looking into new possibility and layoffs are deferred. All agree, except budget director, who argues for closing, and political advisor, who urges a solution that will hold for a few months, not a few weeks. Governor accepts the solution anyhow. Instructs press secretary to inform media and legislative advisor to inform local legislators.

3:35 P.M

Secretary advises that insurance commissioner is back, other advisors are waiting, and Governor hasn't done anything about in-box. Plus more messages: . . . Neighboring Governor called and wants to discuss developing a common regional position on safety rules for zinc mining. Governor has secretary call federal relations aide to get in touch with neighboring Governor's staff to see what can be worked out . . . Press secretary calls with information that P.M. papers are breaking a story that a legislative leader of the Governor's party is suspected of selling real estate to the highway department, using inside information on new highway location . . . Highway commissioner is back from ribbon cutting and needs to talk . . . President of largest state university would like to chat briefly about prospects of a new law school . . . Speaker of the house wants to talk, important and personal . . . Secretary has arranged the scheduling meeting at 5 P.M., after the office space meeting.

Insurance commissioner is still waiting, has staff with him and two hours worth of visual aids. Governor calls the commissioner in alone—commissioner is prepared to talk about the new insurance consumer protection program he was asked to prepare; meeting was rescheduled twice already. Governor tells him he's sorry about the scheduling problem, asks him to leave the written material and promises to try to read it tonight and to make apologies to his staff.

Calls political advisor in. Asks about speaker's call; finds that speaker wants to be reassured that Governor would not back rival for speakership even if party wins handily in fall election. Political advisor says leave him hanging for awhile; call tomorrow and say that Governor doesn't control the membership but appreciates his support in the past, etc.

Political advisor discusses bank commissioner appointment and recommends someone other than Jones; Governor agrees and asks him to prepare press release. Political advisor stops at door to remind him that he had agreed to spend more time away from the office and with the people; says he must schedule more local events like the ribbon cutting today and then keep to the schedule; asks if mayor who arranged it has been called yet.

4:30 P.M

Governor calls the mayor and has a 15-minute conversation in which the mayor says pretty much what the political advisor did. Agrees to check a bridge situation within city limits and instructs secretary to check the point with the highway commissioner.

4:45 P.M

Governor begins the 4 P.M. office space meeting, knowing he still has the scheduling meeting and a couple of calls to go and that he should be receiving guests at the mansion at 6:30. The meeting requires his presence be-

cause the public works department, which allocates office space, is at loggerheads with the agencies. The agencies want more space—whether they have to lease it, get private companies to build it, or whatever—while public works wants to hold them off and build a new office building which would require the Governor's approval. The meeting is incredibly dull, with charts and graphs about office space, so at 5 P.M., the Governor leaves, indicating he has another meeting and leaving two or three agency heads, budget director and one aide with instructions to work out a recommendation for him that they can agree on.

5:00 P.M

Handles more messages. Has secretary get the facts on the law school from budget bureau and commissioner of higher education before calling president of university back tomorrow. Reminds secretary to call the speaker tomorrow. Calls the highway commissioner to find out what the mayor has already told him.

Has secretary tell aide who is waiting to talk about a project for cooperation between university students and law enforcement department to wait until tomorrow. Has consumer protection advisor do likewise.

Reviews brief remarks prepared for dinner session with group of business leaders. Remembers that one of the leaders is board chairman of the community college that all the fuss was about earlier in the day. Asks an aide to quickly collect the views of the higher education commissioner and the budget director and give him a briefing before he leaves the office.

5:30 P.M

Governor enters scheduling meeting. His secretary asks if he wants the aide left in the office space meeting or brought into the meeting; he answers "both." The scheduling meeting is no different from the last one, not likely to be different from the next.

The political advisor wants Governor to make fund-raising appearances at five geographically diverse places in the next week, appear at supermarkets with two legislative candidates, and attend two rallies for legislative candidates. In addition, advisor suggests strongly that Governor drop in at the Chinese-American society dinner next Saturday night and appear at a teacher's convention the following day.

Secretary says wife wants to hold Saturday all day at home and prefers to spend that evening with friends. Wife does not want to travel on Sunday, secretary says, reminding Governor that one of his children is making his debut as a high school football player on Friday. Governor's scheduler ticks off the remaining demands for time the following week:

One state trade association meeting (already accepted) and two more which request his presence and will schedule for a major address if he can make it;

One statewide labor meeting;

Three requests for local political functions, beyond the ones the political advisor knows the Governor had;

A request from the federal relations aide to visit the congressional delegation in Washington next week and deliver testimony for the National Governors' Association before a Senate subcommittee;

A request from two key agency directors to accompany them to Washington to resolve problems with federal agencies;

A request from the press aide for a news conference announcing the new bank commissioner, a backgrounder with a representative of a national magazine, and at least one additional general-purpose news conference during the week;

Six cabinet officers and three board or commission chairmen wanting to discuss one subject or another; and

Three county chairmen, four legislators, five major contributors, six local delegations seeking highways or other state construction, and the usual flow of private citizens wanting to see their Governor.

In addition, the schedulers report back on various events the Governor requests be scheduled, which have not been scheduled yet, including a visit to a mental hospital for inspection and employee relations, a meeting with educational advisors on potential for improving the state aid formula, a meeting with the planning director and several cabinet officers on land-use planning, and the remainder of the meetings on the consumer protection program similar to that with the insurance commissioner today.

Secretary reports Governor should take one complete day off just to concentrate on the paperwork in the in-box.

The scheduling meeting goes on to 6 P.M., at which time the Governor expresses preferences, delegates the exact schedule to the group, and receives a delegation from the office space meeting seeking to resolve a couple of questions. Indicating that he has to shower and change to be ready at the mansion by 6:30, Governor asks them either to write it up or talk to him in the morning (not remembering that tomorrow's schedule is worse than today's).

His secretary shouts out a couple of other phone calls; he says "tomorrow" and leaves office accompanied by aide trying to brief him on the community college situation, matching him pace for pace as he walks out. The community college situation is complicated indeed, so Governor decides not to decide yet and to finesse the question if it comes up in the evening.

After a quick shower and change accompanied by as much recitation of family affairs as time permits, Governor finds himself in the receiving line not quite promptly at 6:40, facing the ordeal of trying to remember 40 people whom he knows he should know. Cocktail conversation centers on bank regulation issues, exhortations to avoid tax increases, discussion of the business climate, costs of workers' compensation, and some general discussion of national politics. After dinner Governor talks briefly about some of his major programs and the need for good business climate in the state and retires to family quarters about 9:45 P.M.

In these moments of potential relaxation, Governor retrieves in-box correspondence from his brief case. First, the "information only" items consisting of magazine articles, FYI memos from staff, and the like; these he scans briefly, primarily to see if there is any action he need take. A memo from the welfare secretary which indicates negotiations may break down with hospitals over Medicaid reimbursement rates is sent to his political advisor with a question, "Can we handle this if negotiations fail?"

Now the "action" items. Some 20 letters to sign prepared by staff; 16 are OK, two require rewrite instructions to someone, and two more the Governor rewrites himself. Now it is 10:15 P.M., his definite cutoff time for relaxation and talking to his family, even though he has five or six complicated problems, including the community college issue, left hanging.

This example is obviously atypical for some, while typical for other Governors, only because it happens to cover a quiet time without a major crisis (prison riot, natural disaster), or having the legislature in session. It suggests the Governor's constant need to make choices in the use of his own time and more important, to avoid becoming a captive of the pressures on him. In a day such as the one described, it is hard to imagine the Governor contemplating, much less doing much about, his broad strategies for government leadership and party affairs.

When the moment of reflection does come, a Governor may find that his campaign did not result in his capturing the office, but in the office capturing him. He will see that many aspects of his predecessor's style that he wanted to change are things he is unable to change.

There is no obvious solution to these problems. There are ways to make it manageable only if the Governor designs his administration's priorities during transition—and avoids being totally "captured."

WHAT GOES ON AROUND THE GOVERNOR

While the governor goes through these frenetic paces, his staff attempts to stay one step behind—or at least only a few steps behind—anticipating his needs and following up commitments made on this typical day. Since a Governor is often judged by the quality and thoroughness of his staff's work, it is worth considering who did what around the Governor in connection with just a part of this "typical" day. Consider, for example, the 15 minutes at midday encompassing the highway-funding meeting and a few of the staff involved.

Three weeks previously, the Governor's scheduler had addressed some hard decisions. Should the Governor attend the highway ribbon cutting, or should he turn it down and send a representative? How many people would be annoyed or slighted? As the "typical" day approached, the scheduler had perhaps 20 or so similar decisions to make before making final the public portion of the Governor's day. And, even then, the schedule was changed.

Sitting with the Governor and the suburban legislators early in the day, the executive assistant to the Governor worried about his phone messages, large numbers of which mounted up in little pink piles on his desk. He usually kept two secretaries busy sorting correspondence, responding to requests, and placing calls. The suburban group's request for a new superhighway reminded him that the Governor was going to meet later in the morning with the budget director and transportation secretary on highway funding in general. The two men disagree and each will come well prepared with opposing arguments; he knows the Governor will ask him to help resolve the problem, but when will he have time to study it?

As the Governor's day unfolded, he reminded himself that his symbol of power—the office next door to the Governor's—was also a millstone around his neck. Much of his life, he realized, was taken up in "hand holding" and being a "sounding board." If only he could get caught up, he thought, he would be able to work on that new tax-reform initiative which the revenue department had failed to deliver in adequate form. But Senator Brown had called, and he had to get back to him before noon because the Governor might run into him at the ribbon cutting that afternoon. Perhaps this evening he could stop to think about the Governor's tax program.

"Why is the executive assistant allowing the transportation meeting to be delayed?" the budget director wondered at five minutes until noon as he waited to see the Governor. After all, the budget office's work on this issue had been going on—in fits and spurts—for six months. In fact, last night he and his unit chiefs were up until 3 A.M. completing the memorandum which would be devastating to the department of transportation's case for more highway construction. But if the Governor ran out of time this morning, the decision could be delayed again. The budget director had called the executive assistant to urge him to hurry the governor along, but his call was somewhere at the bottom of the pink pile in the inner office.

The Secretary of transportation didn't enjoy the budget director's dry personality, so he had passed the time waiting for the Gover-

nor's meeting by drifting across the hall to chat with the Governor's personal secretary. Besides the fact that he was a gregarious soul, he knew that staying on the good side of the Governor's secretary never hurt. Sometimes he absolutely had to talk to the Governor, and she would always put him through.

He was nervous about the Governor's reaction to his request for more highway money, in light of the Governor's austerity campaign. Just for instance, he had let the Governor's political advisor know that many of the campaign pledges made in the politically critical rural areas of the state could not be met without the road funds. And then, of course, there were 75 campaign workers from key areas of the state whom he had hired at the political advisor's request—they might have to be laid off if the new money was not found in the budget somewhere. He hoped that the advisor had mentioned these problems to the Governor. If it seemed that the decision was not going his way, he planned to ask for more study—a delaying tactic to ensure that the Governor would make the final decision only after being apprised of all the financial and political ramifications of the decision.

The planning director sat in his office working on the "Rural Development Plan" which the governor had promised during the campaign, and which was now six months and scores of public hearings in the making. He was worried because he feared that the Governor's meeting on road money was going to preempt consideration of the section on farm-to-market road repair, a centerpiece in the rural development program he was about to unveil. If the road funds were put into the budget, he might still have time to influence the pattern of expenditures. "If we don't rebuild the small bridges on our rural roads," he thought, "five years from now the farm economy will be in deep trouble." He knew that the budget director had been working on a memorandum to convince the Governor that the department of transportation's spending plan was premature, but the planner was unsure of the outcome. Until the issue was clearly resolved, he could not move forward on his development plans.

Others worked, watched, and waited on the outcome of the short meeting with the Governor.

The press secretary was concerned; the Washington office director wanted to be able to credit her office with getting the federal dollars; the environmental protection liaison was quietly lobbying against more highways.

In this "typical" day, these developments were only a small sample of the detailed staff work and intra-staff competition that are inevitable in the Governor's office.

32

The Gubernatorial Appointment Power: Too Much of a Good Thing?

DIANE KINCAID BLAIR

It is clear that gubernatorial appointment power is a significant tool in the governor's arsenal of weapons. Long touted as such by outside observers, governors also give it a high rating.[1]

Thad L. Beyle and Robert Dalton

An ample appoinitive power has been repeatedly identified by observers and governors alike as an essential component of an effective administration. It is therefore somewhat surprising that questions about the actual exercise of the appoinitive power seem to elicit so many rueful recollections from those very governors who simultaneously embrace the power's efficacy.[2] The adverse aspects of the appointment power are even more frequently and vehemently articulated by those aides who have assisted governors with the appoinitive process.[3]

What explains the aura of disappointment surrounding practitioners' discussions of the appointment power? Does it reflect mere distaste for this particular kind of decision-making? Or does it indicate more fundamental problems, which merit additional attention and concern?

GUBERNATORIAL VIEWS ON APPOINTMENT

To be sure, many of the appoinitive problems which governors recount have long been familiar to students of state politics and public administration. The potential pool of qualified appointees sometimes proves disappointingly

State Government, Vol.55, No.3 (Summer 1982), pp. 88–91.

thin,[4] while "many of the individuals who were looking for patronage were not individuals you'd like to patronize."[5] The ever-present possibility of scandal or embarrassment is evident in governors' warnings to get police checks on possible appointees,[6] to avoid appointing those with "weird hang-ups,"[7] to find appointees with the "ability to keep your head down and stay off the front page."[8]

Difficulties occasionally arise when square pegs are placed in round holes: "I think I made mistakes in some of my choices, not necessarily as it regards the man or woman, but as regards the position";[9] "Sometimes you make a bad decision about where a person fits."[10] Governors also refer to the problems created when appointees perform contrary to expectations, that "usually you can expect a change in that person, for the better or for the worse";[11] and, "The better the people you get, the more distance they place between themselves and you."[12]

Still another theme is the inevitable anger of those who were denied the appointments they sought: "[I] got into a lot of hot water because I refused to appoint some of the more prominent Democrats around the state";[13] "I now have twenty-three good friends who want on the Racing Commission. Soon I'll have twenty-two enemies and one ingrate."[14]

While governors have tried to make the appointment process easier with a variety of advisory mechanisms, the advisory apparatus itself can apparently lead to difficulties: "I had the county chairman of the Democratic executive committee in each of the counties as a member of this advisory commission. . . . My second term, I just abolished them . . . too frequently I would have to justify not taking the advisory committee's recommendation";[15] "Once they (a county delegation) actually come to you with a request, you've lost";[16] "I think screening committees are bad";[17] "One thing I will never do again is go to the blue-ribbon [search] committee."[18]

The detrimental side of the appointive process is strongly suggested by an Arkansas governor's expression of relief that, "We have it better here; at least the governor isn't involved in judgeships."[19] Even more explicit are the laments that "nothing can bedevil an administration more than weakness among appointees. Because if you pick wrong in one or two or three key cases, you find you're spending 90 percent of your time trying to deal with those weaknesses";[20] and, "If they're bad, you get more minuses for their being really bad than you get pluses out of their being good."[21]

AIDES' VIEWS ON APPOINTMENTS

The inimical aspects of the appointive process are expressed even more forcefully by the staff members. Their comments are liberally sprinkled with phrases like "geographic paranoia," "greedy legislators," and "those who see a new governor primarily as an instrument for getting rid of good people." They speak of constantly having had to "nag" the governor to fill openings, and of the whole process as a "necessary evil," "an incredible waste of time." Their suggested rules of procedure include few "Thou shall's" and many "Thou shall not's": do not consult too widely; do not delay, thereby letting pressures and expectations build; do not let applicants or their supporters see the governor personally; do not make appointments at the front end of a legislative session. The most frequently suggested guideline is simple, but unmistakably ominous: do not embarrass the governor. In fact, the observation of one aide encompasses the attitude of all: "We always began by looking for the most qualified person; we usually wound up going with the one least likely to embarrass the governor."[22]

While these candid comments identify some of the specific hazards inherent in the appointive process, they still do not wholly answer the questions raised at the outset. Why, given the universal agreement that "gubernatorial power of appointment is a most significant weapon in a governor's arsenal,"[23] do those who have employed these weapons sound so much like victims?

VOLUME OF GUBERNATORIAL APPOINTMENTS

One explanation, only hinted at above, may well be the sheer volume of appointments most governors must make. Wyner, in 1968, referred to "the average governor making approximately 400 statutory appointments, plus appointments to many more advisory boards and commissions."[24] Sabato, in 1978, noted that: "Each state government, even the smallest, includes scores of boards, agencies and commissions and requires the appointment of thousands of persons."[25] In a 1980 study of California, a state supposedly free of patronage, Bell and Price noted that the governor has about 170 appointments to make of heads and administrators of agencies; another 2,200 appointments of part-time members to over 300 state councils and commissions; about 160 judicial appointments in the average four-year term; and appointments to fill vacancies in otherwise elective positions, including those in local governments.[26] These staggering numbers are confirmed by contemporary governors themselves.[27]

Here, perhaps, lies at least a partial answer to the questions raised. While political scientists have traditionally measured the appointment power in terms of freedom to name the heads of major agencies,[28] such appointments are only the tip of the iceberg, both in visibility and in value. The advantages of having one's "own" budget director or health department director are so clearly advantageous in terms of policy imprint, administrative control, and political loyalty as to clearly outweigh whatever ill will may be raised in the appointment process. What, however, is to be gained from having one's own person on the Oil Museum Advisory Commission, or the State Capitol Cafeteria Commission or the Criminal Justice and Highway Safety Information Center Advisory Board? Indeed, since many statutes only permit gubernatorial appointment of one individual annually to a multimember board, even having one's own person on a University Board of Trustees, or State Highway Commission, may only provide a reliable informant, or an occasional transmitter of gubernatorial preferences. All too often, the only immediate consequence of many such appointments is the anger of the individual being replaced (since virtually everyone serving on such a commission develops a strong proprietary interest), and the resentment of those individuals who wanted to be named but were not.

THE APPOINTIVE PROCESS

Not only can political credit be squandered in the appointive process, but the drain on time and energy can be significant. While the key appointments are usually made early in the gubernatorial term, filling the thousands of lesser offices is an ongoing, unending operation, and although the position itself may seem petty to most observers, it may hold towering significance for those who desire it. The calls and correspondence to the governor's office on only one such appointment can be voluminous and frequently demand the governor's personal attention.

Whereas key appointments are characteristically made by the governor personally, with a minimum of consultation and checking,[29] the clearance mechanisms for minor appointments can consume inordinate quantities of staff time—a fact which may help to explain why appointment aides are even more critical than the governors themselves. Thousands of recommendations must be solicited and acknowledged. At the lowest levels of appointments (local vocational-technical school advisory committees, for example, or local water districts), nobody in the governor's office may be personally acquainted with any potential prospects; indeed, they may be unable to easily locate anyone who is.

Whether the prospect is a known quantity or not, even minor appointments usually require an elaborate clearance procedure with the appropriate legislators, campaign coordinators, relevant county party chairmen, affected professional or interest groups, and often members of the commission to which a new member is being named. All of those consulted must also be advised of the outcome. The process of checking out potential appointees frequently precipitates additional nominations, thereby generating additional clearance procedures and lengthening the list of those ultimately to be disappointed.

POLITICAL CONSEQUENCES OF APPOINTMENTS

If, as suggested above, the policy consequences of such appointments are frequently negligible, do the possible political benefits still result in a net plus to gubernatorial power? Again, these thousands of minor appointments are a decidedly double-edged sword. The governor may envision numerous possible political benefits to be reaped from a good appointment: the abiding gratitude of the appointee, which hopefully will translate into active political support and generous campaign contributions in the future; the indebtedness of an interest group; the favorable publicity that may ensue from the naming of some clearly meritorious individual; the applause for egalitarianism that may accompany the appointment of previously neglected minorities. A shrewd appointment may induce the legislative support of a recalcitrant senator or representative; may forestall the future candidacy of a potential opponent, or bind the wounds of a previous opponent; may demonstrate one's solidarity with party machinery, or one's sensitivity to a particular area or county, or one's flair for originality and independence.

Even this partial list of potential political benefits should be instructive: in extraordinarily fortuitous circumstances, a single appointment may accomplish several desirable purposes. Inevitably, however, some considerations—perhaps equally essential to the governor's political posture—must be not only ignored, but thwarted.

Indeed, even within one of these politically advantageous purposes lie a threatening host of possibly disadvantageous consequences: placating one legislator may arouse the jealousy of another; naming a woman may anger blacks; rewarding one county with an appointive plum may offend the geographic sensibilities of another area; indeed, satisfying one faction within a county may insure the undying hostility of another faction within that same county. If the governor bows to pressure from nurses (rather than doctors) for a seat on a health advisory board, there still remains the potentially explosive choice between registered nurses and practical nurses. Theoretically, there should ultimately be enough appointments to satisfy all; practically, it does not work that way. Interests and individuals wanting representation on the Board of Private Investigators and Private Security Guard Agencies cannot be placated with a seat on the Committee for Purchases of Workshop-Made Products.

CONFLICTING EXPECTATIONS SURROUNDING APPOINTMENTS

What confounds the appointing process even further is that whatever considerations finally prevail at the gubernatorial level, these inevitably differ from the purposes and expectations of those who are seeking gubernatorial appointments. Here, as well, an almost infinite panorama of possibilities exists.

Probably most prevalent is the coveted prestige that a gubernatorial appointment is seen to confer. For many appointment-seekers, this is the prime consideration (which helps to explain the dangerously wounded egos of those passed over). Other aspirants may have more specific axes to grind: the opportunity to influence, however slightly, decisions in behalf of one's ideals (protect the environment, promote school-book censorship), one's personal concerns (encourage awareness of spinal cord injuries, improve the status of women), one's professional ties (tighten up licensing requirements for realtors, weaken the standards for cosmetology inspections), one's economic interests (get more state funds deposited in savings and loan associations, encourage more state promotion of tourism), or one's locale (obtain a community college in the county, build a four-lane highway in the area). Others may be seeking a political stepping-stone, or at least a forum from which to speak and make useful contacts. Still others may desire various "perks" for themselves (per diem pay, travel expenses, good parking at football games, racing passes) and their friends (inside information on jobs and contracts). Gubernatorial aides report an astonishing number who confide that they just want a legitimate excuse to occasionally get away from home!

By now, the reasons for the rueful tone that permeates practitioners' discussions of the appointment power may be apparent. At the upper levels of administration, good appointments do produce, or at least have the strong potential for producing, highly beneficial results. At the lower levels, where the vast majority of appointments are made, the decision-making process is elaborate and exhausting, the policy consequences may be negligible, and the political consequences are frequently a net minus.

CONCLUSION

In his comprehensive treatment of contemporary governors, Sabato notes that patronage, the awarding of salaried state jobs to the party

faithful, has markedly diminished, and further concludes that:

> *The decline of patronage has been judged, somewhat surprisingly, as a boon for governors, since it has liberated them from a tedious, time-consuming, and frustrating chore that is outmoded in the modern political system. At the same time the governor has gained appointive powers where it really matters, at the top-level in policy making positions.[30]*

Perhaps it is time to do some equally vigorous pruning of the hundreds of non-salaried positions on advisory boards and councils and commissions to which governors must annually appoint thousands of individuals. How many of these entities are equally "outmoded in the modern political system"?

Many were originally established as buffers to protect agencies from the ravages of the spoils system. With the decline in patronage and growth of professionalism, their continued necessity is at least questionable. Others owe their origins to the once-felt necessity for patron boards, to build enthusiasm and credibility for a new state venture. If the service has acquired popularity and legitimacy, the patrons may no longer be necessary; if not, it may be time to abandon the quest. Many existing committees are enduring memorials to the classic response to a **bothersome interest** or problem: form a committee to study it. The resulting committee continues to require periodic appointments, but accomplishes little else. Some citizen boards were mandated by federal or state laws, now obsolete, or reflect a since-spent passion for citizen participation. In many other instances, while a totally legitimate function may exist, the necessity for gubernatorial involvement in the appointive process may be much less persuasive.

To summarize, while there is universal agreement on the necessity of ample gubernatorial power to appoint top-level administrators, there is some evidence that the power to make appointments to thousands of lower-level positions is so excessive as to be counter-productive. In that sense, perhaps governors possess too much of a good thing.

NOTES

1. Thad L. Beyle and Robert Dalton, "Appointment Power: Does It Belong to the Governor?" *State Government* 54, 1 (1981): 11.

2. Governors' comments drawn from interviews with 15 former governors published in Center for Policy Research, *Reflections on Being Governor* (Washington, D.C.: National Governors' Association, 1981), and from author's personal interviews with Arkansas Governors Dale Bumpers, David Pryor and Bill Clinton.

3. Aides' views and comments based on author's personal interviews with Appointment, Legislative and Executive Secretaries to Arkansas Governors Winthrop Rockefeller, Dale Bumpers, David Pryor and Bill Clinton.

4. Gov. James E. Holshouser Jr., *Reflections*, p. 138.

5. Gov. Robert F. Bennett, *Reflections*, p. 44.

6. Gov. Milton J. Shapp, *Reflections*, p. 210.

7. Gov. Blair Lee III, *Reflections*, p. 156.

8. Gov. Dan Walker, *Reflections*, p. 235.

9. Gov. James E. Holshouser Jr., *Reflections*, p. 138.

10. Gov. Jerry Apodoca, *Reflections*, p. 16.

11. Gov. David H. Pryor, *Reflections*, p. 166.

12. Gov. Dan Walker, *Reflections*, p. 234.

13. Gov. Milton J. Shapp, *Reflections*, p. 210.

14. Gov. David H. Pryor, personal interview, January 3, 1977.

15. Gov. Reubin O'D. Askew, *Reflections*, p. 28.

16. Gov. Bill Clinton, personal interview, June 19, 1981.

17. Gov. Jerry Apodoca, *Reflections*, p. 16.

18. Gov. Dan Walker, *Reflections*, p. 236.

19. Gov. Dale Bumpers, personal interview, December 30, 1976.

20. Gov. Michael S. Dukakis, *Reflections*, p. 67.

21. Gov. Dan Walker, *Reflections*, p. 234.

22. Aides to Governors Bumpers, Pryor, Clinton, personal interviews, 1976 to 1981.

23. Beyle and Dalton, "Appointment Power," p. 3.

24. Alan J. Wyner, "Gubernatorial Relations with Legislators and Administrators," *State Government* 41 (Summer, 1968): 200.

25. Larry Sabato, *Goodbye to Good-Time Charlie: The American Governor Transformed, 1950–1975* (Lexington, Mass: Lexington Books, 1978), p. 71. See also Center for Policy Research, *Governing the American States* (Washington, D.C.: National Governors' Association, 1978), pp. 71–72.

26. Charles Bell and Charles Price, *California Government Today: Politics of Reform* (Homewood, Ill.: Dorsey Press, 1980), pp. 218–22.

27. See *Reflections*, pp. 157, 210.

28. For example, see Joseph A. Schlesinger, "A Comparison of the Relative Positions of Governors," in Thad Beyle and Oliver Williams (eds.) *The American Governor in Behavioral Perspective* (New York: Harper & Row, 1972), p. 144. Also see Nelson C. Dometrius, "The Efficacy of a Governor's Formal Powers," *State Government* 52 (Summer 1979): 122–23. Similarly, interviews for *Reflections* asked the governors about criteria for "major personnel choices," or "key personnel in major administrative positions."

29. See for example Gov. Calvin L. Rampton, *Reflections*, pp. 179–80.

30. Sabato, pp. 71–74, 89. See also Lynn Muchmore and Thad Beyle, "The Governor as Party Leader," *State Government* 53 (Summer 1980): 123–24.

33

State Employee Bargaining: Policy and Organization

HELENE S. TANIMOTO AND GAIL F. INABA

At least 35 State governments engage in some type of labor negotiations with their employees, according to a survey conducted during the 1981–83 period by the Industrial Relations Center at the University of Hawaii at Manoa. A majority have formal negotiations; others have some type of "meet and confer" procedure.

States which engage in formal negotiations have bargaining units reflecting the history of organizing and negotiation activities in the respective States. The larger groups of organized State employees are in administrative/clerical, corrections, engineering/science, hospital, maintenance/trades, and public welfare occupations. Some professional employees—dentists, lawyers, doctors, teachers, engineers, and administrators—also are in bargaining units.

The American Federation of State, County, and Municipal Employees (AFSCME) is the major State employee union, representing 44 percent of the more than 943,000 covered employees in the survey. State employee associations represent about 75,000, or 18 percent of the employees, but the employee associations are affiliating with other unions, the most recent being the affiliation of the California State Employees' Association with the Service Employees International Union (AFL–CIO).

In the fall of 1981, a questionnaire was sent to the board responsible for collective bargaining procedures or the agency involved in personnel administration in each of the 50 State governments. By the fall of 1983, responses had been received from all States except New Mexico. The questionnaire was designed to identify States according to the extent of employee bargaining activity and to obtain basic data for a study of the characteristics of such activity. Questions were asked about State labor relations policy, organization of the administering agency, unit determination, and impasse resolution procedures. This summary discusses information related to policy and unit determination.

LABOR RELATIONS POLICY

Collective bargaining occurs in 27 State governments and, in most instances, is authorized by law. (See Table 1.) State employee collective bargaining is now authorized in Illinois by the Public Labor Relations Act (which became effective on July 1, 1984) and by the Education Labor Relations Act (effective January 1, 1984), and in Ohio with the enactment of a comprehensive statute (effective April 1, 1984). Informal consultations with no written agreements take place in four States—Utah, Indiana, Nevada, and Wyoming. In Utah, the State constitution[1] and attorney general opinion are the legal basis for such informal consultation. The other three States report no le-

U.S. Dept. of Labor, *Monthly Labor Review*, Vol.108, No.4 (April 1985), pp. 51–55.

gal basis for their policies. "Meet and confer" discussions with mutual understandings outlined in a memorandum of understanding occur in Alabama. Informal negotiations with written memorandum of understanding are authorized by State law and attorney general opinion in North Dakota. North Dakota also confers exclusive recognition status to unions for the purpose of informal negotiations. In Maryland and Missouri, informal "meet and confer" sessions are authorized by law. Such discussions are held between the Governor and the employee organizations in Maryland.

Five States—Arkansas, Mississippi, Oklahoma, South Carolina, and Texas—report that State employees had "no bargaining rights." There was no legal basis in Arkansas for this policy. Mississippi reported "there is no State legislation relative to collective bargaining in the public sector." Oklahoma and South Carolina replied that State employees were not among employees permitted to bargain, with South Carolina noting attorney general opinions and court rulings as the legal basis for not bargaining. Oklahoma did not provide the legal basis for the State policy. Texas reported that the "employer [is] not required to meet with employee groups, except to accept their grievances."

Arizona, Georgia, Idaho, Kentucky, and West Virginia reported simply that "bargaining does not occur." Georgia indicated only that "State employees are prohibited from striking—there are no unions or Board [Public Employee Relations Board]," without any reference to collective bargaining. Kentucky said that "employees have the right to collectively bargain, but [the] State isn't mandated to recognize. Bargaining does not occur." Citations to State law and an attorney general opinion were given as the legal basis for this policy.

Collective bargaining is prohibited in four States—by law in North Carolina and Colorado, by attorney general opinion in Tennessee, and by court ruling in Virginia.

Thus, while the policy and practices vary among States, some kind of negotiating activity—collective bargaining, meet and confer, consultation, or other mechanism—occurs in at least 35 States.

BARGAINING UNITS

More than 943,000 State employees are included in at least 470 bargaining units, according to responses from 27 States. (See Table 1.) Most (90 percent) of these employees are concentrated in 15 States. The State of New York employs some 161,000, or 17 percent; California has approximately 130,000, or 14 percent.

As a group, bargaining units carved along occupational lines (for example, nurses, teachers, guards) are found more frequently than units drawn along functional or departmental lines. Such occupational units are represented by unions or associations that limit membership according to a specific occupation or profession. For example, affiliates of the American Nurses Association represent 13 of the 15 units of nurses reported in this survey. However, there are certain groups of employees who, although organized in their own units, have chosen to be represented by broad-based unions, such as AFSCME.

States permitting collective bargaining generally have the appropriate bargaining units determined by Public Employee Relations Boards, other government agencies, or State officials. In Hawaii, Minnesota, and Wisconsin, bargaining units are set forth in the collective bargaining statutes; in Florida, they are established by rules promulgated by the Public Employees Relations Commission. In California, there are 46 potential units. The Public Employment Relations Board has carved 20 units for employees covered by the State Employer–Employee Relations Act; 17 units for the University of California system, and 9 units for the California State University system under the Higher Education Employer–Employee Relations Act. (At the time of the survey, only 9 higher education units

TABLE 1. STATE GOVERNMENT EMPLOYEES IN BARGAINING UNITS IN STATES IN WHICH COLLECTIVE BARGAINING IS AUTHORIZED, 1981–83

State	Number of Units	Employees Covered		Excluded Employees
		Number	Percent	
Total	470	943,042	100.0	
Alaska	11	11,541	1	Elected or appointed officials; teachers and noncertified employees of school districts covered by AS14.20.550 et seq. [Alaska teachers collective bargaining law].
California	29	130,497	14	Managerial and confidential employees.
Connecticut	27	41,452	4	Elected and appointed officials; board and commission members; managerial, part-time, and confidential employees; staff of Board of Labor Relations and Board of Mediation and Arbitration.
Delaware	30	4,768	1	Elected officials; appointees of Governor; public school teachers; prisoners.
Florida	10	68,210	7	Legislative employees; managerial and confidential employees; appointed and elected officials; agency heads; members of boards and commissions; militia; negotiating representatives; persons convicted of crime in State institutions; Federal and State fruit and vegetable inspectors; Public Employees Relations Commission employees.
Hawaii	12	31,629	3	Appointed and elected officials; members of boards and commissions; administrative officers, director or chief of a State agency or major division, and other top-level management and administrative personnel; individuals handling confidential matters.
Illinois	16	45,500	5	All State employees not under the jurisdiction of the Governor; supervisors; managers; confidential employees; temporary and emergency employees.
Iowa	7	14,830	2	Elected officials; appointees and members of boards or commissions, representatives of public employer; supervisory employees; school superintendents, assistant superintendents, principals, and assistant principals; confidential employees; students working part time; temporary employees; national guard; judges and other court employees; patients and inmates employed, sentenced, or committed to a State or local institution; Department of Justice and Commission for the Blind personnel.
Kansas	31	7,707	1	Supervisory and confidential employees.
Louisiana	20	9,800	1	None.
Maine	7	11,600	1	Certain appointees; department heads; temporary, seasonal, and on-call employees; employees with less than 6 months of service; militia; assistant attorneys general; elected officials; labor relations employees; confidential employees.
Massachusetts	45	61,280	6	Managerial and confidential employees.
Michigan	10	43,104	5	Supervisors, managers, and confidential employees.

State				Excluded employees
Minnesota	16	31,398	3	Managerial employees; physicians; unclassified employees appointed by the Governor, lieutenant governor, secretary of State, attorney general, treasurer, and auditor; all positions in the Bureau of Mediation Services and Public Employment Relations Board; hearing examiners in the Office of Administrative Hearings; confidential employees.
Montana	34	4,646	1	Elected officials; appointees of the Governor; supervisory employees; management officials; confidential employees; engineers.
Nebraska	15	7,359	1	National guard; militia.
New Hampshire	2	9,019	1	Unclassified and nonclassified employees; legislative service employees.
New Jersey	32	72,030	8	Confidential employees; managerial executives; elected officials; members of boards and commissions.
New York	9	161,300	17	Management; confidential employees.
Ohio	(1)	—	—	Supervisors; confidential and management-level employees.
Oregon	10	22,360	2	Supervisors; confidential employees.
Pennsylvania	25	88,398	9	Managerial and confidential employees.
Rhode Island	—	—	—	Governor and his designee; top-level supervisors.
South Dakota	3	2,550	(2)	Elected and appointed officials; administrators (except elementary and secondary school), administrative officers, directors, chief executive officers, chief deputies, first assistants, and others having authority to hire, transfer, suspend, layoff, recall, promote, discharge, assign, reward, or discipline other public employees or the responsibility to direct them, or to adjust their grievances or to recommend such action; students working 20 hours a week or less; temporary workers employed for 4 months or less; commissioned and enlisted personnel of the national guard; judges and employees of the unified court system; legislators and other employees of the legislature or any agency statutorily directed by the legislative branch.
Vermont	6	6,565	1	Employees exempt or excluded from State classified service; employees in the office of the lieutenant governor; legal assistants to the attorney general; department or agency head or deputy officer; head of an institution or a division director in the department of administration and similar positions in State colleges; managerial employees; private secretaries; Department of Personnel employees, budget and management analysts; revenue research analysts; director of budget and management operations; director of program formulation and evaluation; director of State information system.
Washington	51	24,061	3	Personnel exempt from civil service.
Wisconsin	12	27,916	3	University faculty and administrators; employees outside the classified service; limited term, sessional, and project employees; supervisory employees; management employees; confidential employees; Employment Relations Commission staff.

[1] Bargaining units were not defined in Ohio.
[2] Fewer than 1 percent

had exclusive representatives certified for representation purposes.) In Massachusetts, the Labor Relations Commission has established 10 statewide units of "nonprofessional" and professional employees, and 28 higher education units. Eight additional units (which cover State police, metropolitan district commission police, judiciary, and lottery commission employees) are set by statute.

The number of bargaining units ranges from two in New Hampshire to 51 in Washington; 13 States reported fewer than 15 units. The average number of units is 18. States tend to have relatively few units when employees are organized by occupation on a statewide basis, as is the case in Florida, Iowa, Maine, Michigan, New York, and Vermont (each of these States has 10 or fewer units). Other States (Minnesota with 16 statewide units and Hawaii and Wisconsin with 12 each) carve out additional units by separating subgroups of professional employees and establishing units for supervisory employees.

The case of Ohio is unusual. Prior to the 1983 passage of the collective bargaining law, the State had negotiated agreements with a number of employee organizations. However, the bargaining agent was recognized "based on a percentage of showing of interest determined by the appointing authority of each state agency evidenced by dues payment to an employee organization. Generally, employee organizations were granted the right to negotiate a contract when twenty (20) percent to thirty (30) percent of the total number of employees paid dues to an employee organization. . . . Therefore, recognition was granted based on this showing of interest and not through representation elections."

It was also explained that Ohio had "agreements which do not define the bargaining unit. In these instances, all dues-paying employees of an agency constitute the bargaining unit." Presently, the law authorizes the Ohio Public Employment Relations Board to determine the appropriate unit.

EXCLUDED EMPLOYEES

Information on type of employees excluded from bargaining was provided by the 27 States with collective bargaining activities. (See Table 1.) Only one State, Louisiana, extends bargaining to all employees, stating "no State employee groups are excluded from appropriate bargaining units." Managerial employees and confidential employees (generally those who have access to confidential information, or who participate in negotiating on behalf of the employer) are most often excluded (20 States), followed by elected and appointed officials (11) and supervisory employees (9).

Among the collective bargaining units in Alaska is a unit of confidential employees, who are defined as "classified employees of the Executive Branch who 'assist or act in a confidential capacity to a person who formulates, determines, and effectuates management policies in the area of collective bargaining.'" Ohio generally included supervisors in the bargaining units if they paid dues to an employee organization. However, some agreements in Ohio defined the bargaining unit to exclude supervisory, confidential, and management-level employees.

Practice varies in terms of coverage of supervisory employees under the bargaining laws. Supervisors are included in the same bargaining unit with nonsupervisory employees in Connecticut, Louisiana, and New York. Two broad supervisory units are set forth by law in Hawaii, but some units combine supervisory and nonsupervisory employees. In Delaware and Washington, most supervisors, if organized, are in units with other employees, although this practice may vary. Separate supervisory units are called for under the laws of Alaska, California, Florida, Maine, Minnesota, Nebraska, New Hampshire, New Jersey, Pennsylvania, and Vermont. In Alaska, however, the law grandfathers units that combined nonsupervisory and supervisory employees prior to the enactment of the

Public Employment Relations Act. In Florida, only the health care unit includes both supervisors and nonsupervisors, according to rules of the Public Employees Relations Commission. In New Jersey, the Public Employment Relations Commission is authorized to allow a bargaining unit made up of supervisory and nonsupervisory employees under special limited circumstances. Under the Pennsylvania law, supervisors are granted meet and discuss rights only. Supervisory employees in Michigan have only limited recognition rights.

BARGAINING ORGANIZATIONS

Unions enjoying exclusive representation rights in each of the States range in number from one (Louisiana) to 20 (Rhode Island). Washington has 51 bargaining units, but only eight unions are involved.

Affiliates of AFSCME are found in 24 States in the survey. In contrast, State employee associations, are recognized in 13[2] of the 26 States providing union representation information, and represent approximately 18 percent of the employees included in the survey. (In January 1984, the California State Employees' Association, with current membership of approximately 90,000, announced it would affiliate with the Service Employees International Union, thus reducing the percentage of employees in the survey represented by employee associations to 8 percent.)

A number of private sector unions hold exclusive representation rights among certain groups of State public employees. For example, the Communications Workers of America represents the largest number of employees, 42,313, in six units in New Jersey and one unit in California. The Service Employees International Union represents more than 34,000 employees in Illinois, Kansas, Michigan, New Jersey, Oregon, and Pennsylvania. Other private sector unions representing State employees include the International Federation of Professional and Technical Engineers (six

units with 9,000 employees in New Jersey and Washington), the Retail Clerks (four units with 3,380 employees in Montana, Nebraska, Pennsylvania, and Washington), and the Teamsters (11 units with 9,000 employees in Illinois, Massachusetts, Minnesota, Montana, New Jersey, Oregon, and Washington). At least 19 other private sector unions are represented in the survey.

In representing State government employees, the private sector unions follow jurisdictional lines in most cases (that is, the Painters, Electricians, and Machinist unions represent craft employees, and the Plant Guard Workers represent security employees). There are, however, variations. For example, the Teamsters union, which has primary interest in "transportation, warehousing, and the manufacture, procesing, sale, and distribution of food, milk, and dairy products,"[3] claims among its members a unit of university administrative employees in Minnesota. The Communications Workers of America, which began as a union of telephone employees,[4] represents State administrative, clerical, professional, and supervisory employees and psychiatric technicians. Until 1981, four of the six CWA units in New Jersey were jointly represented by the Civil Service Association and the State Employee Association.

By Occupation

Nearly 75,000 education employees in 21 States are represented by the American Federation of Teachers, National Education Association, American Association of University Professors, and other education employee organizations. These employees include both instructional and noninstructional professional personnel in institutions of higher education, community colleges, vocational-technical schools, schools for the blind and the deaf, and schools in correctional departments and hospitals. Affiliates of the American Federation of Teachers and the National Educa-

tion Association represent the largest numbers of employees, approximately 28,700 and
28,300, respectively, followed by the American Association of University Professors with
approximately 7,750. Three additional units

in Hawaii and Pennsylvania, totaling 7,770
faculty members, are represented jointly by
the American Association of University Pro-
fessors/National Education Association, and
American Association of University Profes-

**TABLE 2. PERCENT OF ORGANIZED FULL-TIME
EMPLOYEES IN STATE GOVERNMENT
AND IN PRIVATE NONAGRICULTURE INDUSTRIES,
SELECTED STATES, 1980**

State	State Government	Private Nonagriculture Industries
All States[1]	40.5	25.2
Alaska	67.9	33.7
California	48.1	27.0
Connecticut	78.5	23.0
Delaware	40.0	25.2
Florida	84.5	11.8
Hawaii	88.5	28.0
Illinois	44.5	30.4
Iowa	18.2	22.2
Kansas	17.3	15.4
Louisiana	15.7	16.4
Maine	69.4	24.1
Massachusetts	67.4	24.9
Michigan	54.0	37.3
Minnesota	54.3	26.2
Montana	53.7	29.2
Nebraska	17.9	18.1
New Hampshire	41.5	15.8
New Jersey	45.2	25.7
New York	82.6	38.8
Ohio	27.5	31.3
Oregon	48.3	26.1
Pennsylvania	60.3	34.6
Rhode Island	88.3	28.3
South Dakota	13.7	14.8
Vermont	65.5	18.0
Washington	36.2	34.4
Wisconsin	53.9	28.5

[1] Includes States other than those listed separately.
   NOTE. Only States with collective bargaining authorized for State employ-
ees were selected.
   SOURCE. Bureau of the Census and Bureau of Labor Statistics.

sors/American Federation of Teachers. Non-teacher organizations such as the California State Employees' Association, California Federation of the Union of American Physicians and Dentists, Statewide University Police Association, Nebraska Association of Public Employees, and AFSCME represent an additional 51 units consisting of 24,000 employees in education institutions; the majority (22,700) are noninstructional, nonprofessional employees.

Affiliates of the American Nurses Association represent 13 units comprising more than 12,700 nurses in Delaware, Florida, Illinois, Massachusetts, Minnesota, Montana, Oregon, Pennsylvania, and Washington. Two units, togther covering more than 2,400 registered nurses, are represented by the California State Employees' Association and the Hawaii Government Employees Association. In addition, a bargaining unit of 2,000 professional health care employees in Connecticut is represented by the N.E. Health Care Employees, District 1199, and a unit of 1,100 patient care employees in Wisconsin is represented by the United Professionals for Quality Health Care.

More than 20,700 State troopers and police were organized in 15 States. The Policemen's Benevolent Association is by far the largest, representing nearly 8,000 employees in Florida, New Jersey, and New York. The Fraternal Order of Police represents six units totaling 760 employees in Delaware, New Jersey, and Pennsylvania. Other police and state trooper organizations, representing more than 12,000 members, include the Alaska Public Safety Employees Association, California Association of Highway Patrolmen, Connecticut State Police Union, Iowa State Police Officers' Council, Kansas Troopers Association, Maine State Troopers Association, State Police Association of Massachusetts, Michigan State Police Troopers Association, Minnesota State Patrol Troopers Association, the State Troopers Fraternal Association of New Jersey, Inc., and the State Troopers Noncom-

missioned Officers Association of New Jersey, Inc. The Vermont State Employees Association represents a unit of State police officers in that State.

SOME OBSERVATIONS

The survey results presented here provide the basis for some general observations concerning characteristics of State government employee bargaining: the existence of a bargaining statute determines the bargaining unit coverage, but it may not be determinative of the extent of organization in terms of organized employees; and the extent of organization of the nonagriculture sector appears to influence the organization of State employees, although in States in which collective bargaining is authorized by law, the proportion of organized workers is larger in State government than in private nonagriculture industries. (See Table 2.)

The findings reveal State government bargaining characteristics which are not entirely like those that describe the private sector. This leads to questions which require further investigation. What factors other than the existence of a bargaining statute influence or promote organizations of State employees? Does the existence of a merit system affect the development of a State's labor relations policy and organization of employees? Are there differences in the bargaining outcomes developing out of State government bargaining? It may be that the perceived differences are only minor variations; but without further examination, it is not clear whether they reflect the environment unique to State government and the individual States.

NOTES

ACKNOWLEDGMENT: The authors thank Professor James L. Stern, University of Wisconsin–Madison for comments and suggestions.

1. According to the Utah respondent, the prohibition of collective bargaining by State Constitution is found in *Utah Code Annotated*, Secs. 34–34–1 to 34–34–17 (Utah's right-to-work law).
2. The States are Alaska, California, Connecticut, Illinois, Kansas, Maine, Michigan, Montana, Nebraska, New Hampshire, North Dakota, Vermont, and Washington.
3. See Jack Stieber, *Public Employee Unionism: Structure, Growth, Policy* (Washington, The Brookings Institution, 1973), p. 5.
4. See Jack Barbash, *Unions and Telephones* (New York, Harper & Row, 1952).

34

The Rise of Government Unions and the Decline of the Work Ethic

ALAN CRAWFORD

On November 8, 1982, a government watchdog group known as the Citizen's Budget Commission did what it does best. It issued a report. "Once again, the city of New York faces serious financial problems," the report observed, noting a projected $400 million deficit for the city in fiscal year 1983 and a $1.2 to $1.4 billion deficit in 1984.

This was about as new and exciting as George Steinbrenner firing another manager. What *was* new was the report's blunt talk about the major cause: the recently signed contracts that gave 180,000 non-uniformed workers and 35,000 uniformed employees wage hikes of 15 and 16 percent, respectively, over the next two years. The additional cost to the city for the hikes—which far exceeded projected inflation rates—was nearly $1.5 billion. "The sacrifices required to maintain the city's sound financial condition should be shared equitably," the report concluded. "The city should renegotiate the generous settlement[s]."

Renegotiate the contracts? (Tear down Yankee Stadium?). This not only was blunt talk, it was a call to arms. The proposal quickly became a target for organized labor and its traditional sympathizers. Victor Gotbaum, president of the city's largest union—District Council 37 of the American Federation of State, County, and Municipal Employees—immediately denounced the report and called for increased federal and state aid to ease the fiscal crisis. *The Village Voice* labeled the commission a "good government group whose board . . . would not know how to live on the salary of a teacher, cop, or city secretary" and called the raises "overdue and fair." *The New York Times* in an editorial rejected immediate renegotiation, saying that service cutbacks and lay-offs were the city's only choices. And Mayor Ed Koch—who had negotiated the contract for non-uniformed workers in the heat of his unsuccessful bid to win the Democratic gubernatorial primary—announced he'd rather raise taxes and cut ser-

---

The Washington Monthly, Vol.14, No.11 (January 1983), pp. 33–39. Reprinted with permission. Copyright by THE WASHINGTON MONTHLY CO., 1711 Connecticut Avenue, NW, Washington, DC 20009. (202) 462-0128.

vices first. Renegotiation would be a "last resort."

Though the commission's call for renegotiation likely will go unheeded, it's noteworthy nonetheless. Reformers in the city that made "fiscal crisis" a household word finally had to recognize that enough is enough—and that after two decades of uninterrupted growth in government payrolls, it was time to get serious. "Even in 1975, at the height of the city's fiscal crisis, the most we advocated was deferral of scheduled wage increases," explains James Hartman, executive director of the Citizen's Budget Commission. "I think this [call for renegotiation] is unprecedented—I don't think it's happened anywhere in the country."

And there's the rub. It's hard to deny that governments of all shapes and stripes are in worse shape this year than they have been for decades. The federal government's projected $200 billion deficit aside, 17 states have been forced to raise some new taxes in the last year and 28 have imposed a hiring freeze or laid off workers or done both. Michigan, wracked with a 16 percent unemployment rate in the wake of the automobile industry's decline, recently had to make up a projected $615 million deficit by temporarily raising taxes by more than $200 million and slashing its budget—which meant more than 1,600 workers got their pink slips.

Such cuts at first may sound like a long overdue chance to thin the ranks of government employees who spend their time counting paper clips. Would that it were so. Unfortunately, most of these cutbacks are not affecting these workers but the ones who provide government's most necessary services. In New York the likely lay-off victims are workers who clean streets, run subways, catch criminals, and put out fires.

It's not that such cutbacks are anything new. A decade ago most branch libraries in Washington, D.C., were open 72 hours a week; today the figure is 40. New York has slightly fewer policemen today than it did in 1954—and more than twice as many serious crimes. Because of a lack of maintenance crews and money, subway delays in New York City have climbed from 29,000 in 1977 to 63,000 in 1981. Indeed, long before the recession and the property tax revolt, cities and states were suffering a slow, almost imperceptible crumbling of services—which now threatens to become an avalanche.

One would think all this might trigger some new behavior on the part of government employees. Guess again. According to the Bureau of Labor Statistics, first-year wage hikes in state and local contracts involving 5,000 or more employees averaged 7.6 percent in the first half of this year. That compares to 7.4 percent for all of 1981, when inflation was far more a factor than it is today. Even more telling is the comparison with wage settlements in the private sector for the first six months of 1982, which averaged about 3 percent. The American Federation of Teachers, for example, reports settlements averaging 6 to 8 percent and boasts several double-digit contract gains. AFSCME reports 8 to 10 percent gains for its largest locals. When it comes to pay hikes for public employees, New York isn't the exception—it's the rule.

How strong are the unions? In the last two decades, the unionization of the nation's state, local, and federal workers has been one of the less noticed but important stories of the time. AFSCME, which had 220,000 members in 1964, now boasts over 1 million and is the largest single union within the AFL-CIO. The American Federation of Teachers and the National Education Association claim 2.2 million members. Today, one in every six American workers is employed by some level of government, and more than half belong to a union.

The real mandarins of the public employees, of course, are federal civil servants. More than 28,000 federal workers now make over $57,000 a year, many of them in jobs that have the responsibility of a middle-level administrative worker who might earn $25,000 to $35,000 in private business. High civil servant wages are a major reason Washington, D.C.'s per capita income of $13,539 is second only to Alaska's. This figure actually understates the District's relative affluence because fringe benefits are substantially higher for federal employees than private ones. Federal workers are covered by a generous pension system that has the taxpayers kick in $4 for every $1 the employees contribute. Because of automatic cost-of-living adjustments, these pensions often give retired workers far more than they earned while working. James Walker, who retired in 1967 as a $17,000-a-year economist and now gets $29,000 a year, recently told *The Washington Post* that it was "more than I deserve and a hell of a lot more than I need."

But compensation is only part of the reason federal employment is so cushy. Between civil service rules and the efforts of unions such as the American Federation of Government Employees, federal workers are virtually fire-proof; the discharge rate for government service is less than one-seventh of 1 percent. More important, federal employees are immune to any meaningful judgments about their competence. Throughout the '70s, for example, the proportion of federal employees who annually received "merit" pay increases was 99 percent.

Altogether, it's one sweet deal: generous pay and benefits, lifetime job security, meaningless performance evaluation, and, last but not least, protection from all the swings of fortune that affect workers in private industry. In 1982 one in five American households had an unemployed member sometime during the year. Leonard Reed, a writer and a retired civil servant, calculates that the total number of federal employees Reagan's budget cuts have sent packing is about 9,500, or about one in every 240 households.

MUNICIPAL IMMUNITY

State and local government workers haven't received nearly the critical attention that fed-eral employees have, but, as New York City's plight amply demonstrated, they deserve it. Indeed, in the last decade the extraordinary rise of government unions has led to exactly the same problems in local and state government that now plague the federal civil service: excessive pay and unproductive workers. And the rise of these problems coincides with the increasing power of government unions, which now represent over half the country's 13 million state and local workers.

These unions were formed for largely justifiable reasons. In the 1940s the women who dominated the teaching profession were grossly underpaid; some in Southern states received less than $1,000 a year. Black workers were victimized by both racism and low pay. (When Martin Luther King was assassinated in Memphis he was there to march on behalf of mistreated garbagemen.) Hospital workers also received short-shrift.

But things have changed dramatically since those days; most public workers now are no worse off than private workers in wages, decidedly better off when it comes to fringe benefits, and have advantages employees in most private jobs can only dream of: virtual lifetime job security, insulation against lay-offs, pay regardless of performance, and almost minimal pressure to increase productivity. So when CORE activist James Farmer called public employees the "niggers of the '70s" in an effort to rally support for them during a walkout in Atlanta, Mayor Maynard Jackson and the city's predominately black middle class knew better and the walkout was a resounding flop.

And with good reason, given what many government employees are now earning and what the public is getting in return. Teachers in Philadelphia, for example, make an average of almost $30,000 for a nine-month year; they also have one of the highest absentee rates in the nation, which further burdens taxpayers because schools must pay substitute teachers to replace them. Clerks who dispense subway tokens in New York start at $6.92 an hour and within two years make

$8.78; last year the New York Transit Authority received more than 20,000 applications for 400 new positions.

Then there are the fringe benefits. Los Angeles's Department of Finance estimates that by 1990 pension payments will be equal to 95 percent of its payroll costs; unlike the vast bulk of private pensions, the city's are indexed to inflation. The same is true in Washington, D.C.: If the city's recently retired fire chief lives to 77 he will have received more than $1 million in pension benefits.

New York City's pension costs also will increase dramatically—the result of pension plans that make the U.S. military's system look stingy by comparison. In that system, soldiers can retire at half pay after just 20 years. Sanitation workers, policemen, firemen, and bus drivers in New York get the same deal—except their pensions are based on their last year's earnings, *including overtime*. Reports by the New York Comptroller's Office in recent years have repeatedly documented dramatic increases of overtime in a worker's last year of work, which often resulted in pensions that were higher than his average earnings while working. One employee for the New York Transit Authority chalked up $51,000 his last year—more than double his normal salary.

To maintain the standard of living to which their members have grown accustomed, unions have employed a strategy over the years that is wholly logical from their point of view. In the face of budget restraint they've sacrificed the jobs of some members in order to keep salaries and benefits high for the rest. The laid-off workers tend to be the youngest and least powerful in the union, and any union leader who wishes to hang on to his post is not about to tell senior workers they should take a temporary pay cut to keep everyone working. When union leaders for Boston firemen recently agreed to some minor concessions, their angry members threw them out of office.

While union workers preserve their status, the public loses both ways: it pays substantially higher taxes for fewer services. Garbage doesn't get picked up as often; firemen take longer to reach a burning building; lines are longer when one applies for a building permit. But even more vexing is that government unions help ensure that, in the face of financial cutbacks, the most efficient way to deliver services won't be used. For to do so would be to violate a central tenet of public-employee unionism: workers should not be judged or rewarded for the quality of the work they do.

This attitude may be self-defeating, but it prevails in most cities. When Washington, D.C. public schools recently considered a plan to give "merit pay" increases only to teachers who had received ratings better than "satisfactory" after six years, the local teachers union hit the roof. Albert Shanker, president of the American Federation of Teachers, said such quality distinctions were impossible to make and would "demoralize" teachers who didn't get the bonuses. Instead of paying teachers according to their performance, teachers unions insist on paying them according to seniority and the possession of additional academic degrees. So if an incompetent teacher happens to have a Ph.D. in educational psychology, he'll receive substantially more than a colleague with the same experience who may be the finest teacher in the school but who lacks the same academic credentials. In the teachers-union world, of course, this does not "demoralize" the good teacher; it merely makes him want to go out and get a degree of his own, no matter how irrelevant it might be.

Promotion of bus mechanics in the District of Columbia's Metrobus system makes about as much sense. Supervisors must rely on the results of a written test and cannot take actual job performance into account. Police and firemen in Texas are promoted under the auspices of State Law 1269 M, which dictates promotions on the basis of seniority.

In the absence of performance standards, the result is predictable: government employees essentially have their jobs as long as they want them. The Philadelphia school system has fired just 24 of 13,000 employees for incompetence in the last six years—about four a year. Contract provisions there and in most school districts make firing a bad teacher so arduous that it often takes up to two years to claw one's way through the procedural hearings and evaluations.

Teachers aren't even the worst of the lot. Recently the New York transit authority installed a new computer system that helped discover more than 30 token-takers who owed the Authority more than $1,000. The agency dismissed the workers on the theory that they were either incompetent or crooked. The union protested and took the proceedings to arbitration, contending that since the rule against shortfalls had not been enforced for so long, employees first should have received a notice telling them such behavior was improper. An arbitrator bought the argument and reinstated the workers.

Performance evaluation isn't always fair or easy, and some workers are easier to evaluate than others. A bus mechanic can be judged by speed and number of mistakes; the efficiency of a government bureaucrat who spends the day writing memos is more difficult to assess. Indeed, too many memos may indicate that the worker has nothing productive to do.

What unions do is take the arguably difficult task of judging employees and then insist that it's not only difficult, but somehow undesirable. To the public employees union, there are just two kinds of workers: those who are doing their job, and those who aren't. All of the former should be paid and given automatic raises, if possible, through COLAs and other escalators regardless of whether they're making a minimal effort or going out of their way. The latter presumably should be fired— but only if the government is willing to negotiate the time-consuming process that unions insist must precede any dismissal. And, even in that case, the unions will defend the worker; he is, after all, a member of the union.

AFSCME NO MORE QUESTIONS

For years, conservatives have enjoyed skewering government unions but liberals have been conspicuously mute on the subject. So while public employees insist they be seen in the same light as the coal miners of the 1920s—oppressed workers struggling mightily against greedy bosses—Democratic politicians and most of the media have usually acquiesced in this fantasy.

There's a very good reason for this silent acceptance: those who shape public opinion are themselves part of the problem. Teachers and academicians, for example, enjoy the same isolation from performance evaluation through the tenure system. Among public school teachers, tenure commonly comes after just three years experience.

An even bigger culprit is the press, and a good example of the blinders it wears when it comes to government employees is provided by *The Washington Post*. Over the years it has seldom questioned the claims of federal workers seeking more civil service protection, higher pay, and ever-more-generous pensions. When federal workers demanded hefty raises on the pretense that there was a massive exodus of skilled federal workers from government, *Post* reporters accepted the pretense as fact. They didn't investigate the matter to discover that only a tiny percentage of federal employees fall into this category and that competition for most federal jobs is keen.

A similar blindness occurs with pensions. During the 1970s pensions for federal civil servants skyrocketed; in 1972 they cost $3.2 billion and in 1982 they cost $18.2 billion. Unless automatic cost-of-living adjustments are altered, pensions will go to $31 billion by 1990. Though the *Post* this summer called for federal pensioners to share in the government's budget cuts, the most courage it could muster was to call for a "thorough review" of the problem, repeating the canard that "the government needs adequate pension plans in order to recruit and retain high quality military and civilian personnel." This overlooks the fact that the government's difficulty in keeping people is often the result of workers taking advantage of the generous pension plan by retiring at 55, so they can find another job—thereby qualifying for social security as well.

Nearly 20 percent of the *Post's* readers work for the federal government, a figure that obviously doesn't include those who work for local governments in the Washington area. But an even stronger reason for the *Post's* kid-gloves approach is more personal: many reporters and editors believe they're entitled to exactly the same protections afforded civil servants.

Nothing better illustrates this than the Washington-Baltimore newspaper guild's proposal for a new *Post* contract. Among the guild's demands: a 28-hour work week with double-time pay for any work beyond that; five weeks of vacation a year; a 13-week paid vacation every five years; a nine-month sabbatical at half-pay for writing a book; promotions on the basis of seniority; bumping rights whereby laid-off employees can take the jobs of less senior workers with no loss of pay; and the right to arbitration in any firing proceedings. Reporters at the *Post* are entitled to a minimum of almost $30,000 a year after four years, but most get more.

The New York Times is no different—except that a reporter with two years' experience can expect a minimum salary of almost $40,000. And, like the *Post*, the *Times* historically has been noticeably sympathetic in its news coverage and editorials to government unions and their leaders.

The way the press has been co-opted on this issue was aptly illustrated in the person of the late Jerry Wurf, former president of AFSCME. Wurf began organizing poorly paid cafeteria workers in Manhattan during the 1940s. By the time he died in 1981 he was the head of one of the nation's most powerful unions.

If Wurf was unrelenting in his efforts to win higher wages and benefits for his members while protecting them against perfor-

mance standards, he endeared himself to many reporters with his liberal politics. He opposed the Vietnam War—often casting the only vote against it at AFL-CIO conventions. His politics were more liberal than most union leaders, and he was one of George Meany's most adamant foes.

But, perhaps most important, Wurf shared many of the prejudices of those who made their living covering him. He once referred to some fellow union members as "those goddamn bums in the building trades." And while he was colorful, profane, and quotable, he was also cultured. In a 1976 profile in *The New York Times Magazine*—whose headline, "How Jerry Wurf Walks on Water" left little doubt as to its sympathies—one of AFSCME's former executive secretaries, Paul Myer, was quoted approvingly as saying, "Jerry enjoys having the public think he's a coarse labor goon—but a lot of that is for effect . . . I learned a great deal about good wines and good foods from Jerry, and a lot about music and literature too. He's a guy who can be as comfortable with Elliot Richardson at the Court of St. James as he can be with a garbage collector in Memphis."

Wurf was more than just urbane, articulate, and liberal; he had a shrewd sense of the public's limits of tolerance. For example, he opposed the right to strike for firemen and policemen even though unionists like Meany taunted him for giving up this basic bargaining tool. But Wurf correctly appreciated that nothing will alienate public opinion faster than reports on the evening news of children and widows dying in their homes while firefighters stand idly by because they want more money.

The press' negligence also is reflected in the same people whom the public trusts to keep a close eye on government workers: the politicians. So many taxpayers are themselves public employees that politicians curry their favor rather than scrutinize their behavior. In many states teachers unions are the largest single source of money for legislative candidates; the recipients of this largesse obviously aren't on the front lines lobbying for stiffer competency standards for teachers and changes in the collective bargaining laws that would help link performance to pay. New York City's AFSCME leader, Victor Gotbaum, has boasted, "There's no question about it. We have the ability to elect our own boss." Elected officials are well aware of this; in 1975, Philadelphia Mayor Frank Rizzo gave a 12.8 percent pay raise to the city's civil servants two weeks before his crucial primary election. And Ed Koch's capitulation to the unions was directly tied to his hope of winning the New York governorship. But Koch unexpectedly lost—evidently forgetting that workers might be so grateful for his generosity that they wouldn't want him to leave for Albany.

UNIONS TO CITY: DROP DEAD

The result of this conspiracy of interests is that taxpayers end up getting far less than what they thought they'd bargained for. Rather than going to protect them from criminals or pick up their garbage, tax dollars are being used to keep unnecessary government employees on the payroll while services decline.

You knew it was coming . . . Yes, featherbedding by government unions is also a big problem. On the federal level, the most telling example was revealed in the wake of the 1981 strike by air traffic controllers. For some obscure reason, the controllers' union had insisted that staffing be on the basis of the 34th busiest day of the year—which meant that for much of the time controllers didn't have much to do. When this rule was abolished after the strike, 80 percent of the original traffic was handled by half the previous number of controllers.

The government could have saved money by hiring part-time air traffic controllers but the union contract prevented it. Simi-

lar prohibitions plague transit systems across the country that would prefer to hire part-time drivers for the morning and evening rush hours. Major systems like Chicago and New York still prohibit part-time bus drivers, and in some cities where they are allowed, union opposition has been fierce. Bus drivers in Los Angeles recently staged a five-day strike over the issue of additional part-time drivers. Though an arbitrator allowed the transit district to increase its part-time staff from 290 to 930, he stipulated that the number of full-time drivers could not drop below 4,090.

A variant of the "peak staffing" provisions in union contracts are "manning requirements." For example, because of contract provisions, New York City firetrucks can't leave the station without at least five firefighters, even though the city says fewer could do the job. Also in New York, a bitter battle was fought several years ago over the city's effort to replace three-man sanitation trucks with some manned by only two workers. The city finally won, and though it had to assuage the union with additional pay, it saved money. But even before the change, New York City was a paragon of efficiency compared to Rochester, New York, where union contracts specified five workers to a garbage crew. With so many garbagemen falling over one another, it became standard operating procedure to drop one man off to play Pac-man or nurse a beer for a few hours while the others collected garbage.

Then there's the phenomenon of two-man police cars. Over the years police forces have experienced a natural progression: from the officer walking the beat to the motorcycle cop to the policeman patrolling in a car. Many cities have gone one step further, putting two men in a patrol car, usually at the insistence of the police union. Yet an exhaustive study of the San Diego Police Department by the Police Foundation demonstrated there is virtually no difference in officer safety and effectiveness between a one-man and a two-man patrol car—though the latter costs nearly twice as much.

Has *any* city recognized the folly of capitulating to the public unions? A few. The best example comes from the Metropolitan Boston Transit Authority. Through the 1970s, the system was slowly crumbling. Service had been curtailed and necessary maintenance postponed while emergency infusions of cash were needed periodically to meet automatic cost-of-living allowances that were paid every quarter. Some subway operators made more than $50,000 a year. The MBTA contract further stipulated that all promotions were to be on the basis of seniority, with meaningful tests of ability prohibited; all overtime was awarded on the same basis. If the MBTA needed workers to stay overtime to fix a subway car, it was required to call the system's most senior employee first, even if he was 40 miles away. The authority, of course, also paid him for travel time.

In December 1980, these longstanding problems precipitated a major crisis as the system was forced to shut down. When the union refused to negotiate major changes, the MBTA took its case to the legislature, where none other than liberal Barney Frank championed its cause. The result was a series of sweeping changes that abolished archaic work rules and reduced costs substantially.

In the case of the MBTA, it was clear even to traditional union supporters that the situation had gotten out of hand. Unfortunately, few were willing to extend the same lesson to other government unions. Robert Kiley, MBTA's former president and a leading Massachusetts Democrat, explains, "Most liberals during the crisis got around asking the really tough questions by saying the transit workers were unique. The larger question—whether they were an extreme example of a more basic problem—was never really raised."

But that question needs to be raised—particularly as an increasing number of cities and states are whipsawed by declining revenues and increased need for city services. During New York's 1975 fiscal crisis, President Ford could tell the city to "drop dead," but Congress was still there to bail it out. With today's federal deficit, Congress not only would have to give Ford's same message to New York—it may be forced to give it to Detroit, Cleveland, Boston, San Francisco, and other beleaguered cities and states. As the Citizen's Budget Commission of New York City observed, while state and federal aid are desirable, they're also unlikely. New York, it concluded, would have to settle its problems by itself.

So will everyone else. Moreover, it should be clear that the necessary changes go beyond requiring that wage and benefit increases be tied to productivity gains in providing services. Even more important is smashing one of the underlying premises of government unions: that those who work for the public should somehow be protected from the same performance standards workers in private industry must meet each day. Setting up those standards may be difficult, but it is absolutely necessary.

The public can no longer afford—and never should have been asked to tolerate—featherbedded police and fire crews, automatic wage increases divorced from productivity gains, and work rules that make the deterioration of service inevitable while costs continue to climb. The question is when will labor's traditional supporters realize this—and begin to heed the call for sanity now coming out of New York.

35

Contracting Out: Public Employees' Group Contends the Practice Has Serious Shortcomings

LINDA LAMPKIN

The push to contract out public services—using private companies to perform the work of state and local governments—has increased dramatically in recent years. "Privatizing" has been promoted as the panacea for budget problems. However, evidence indicates that contracting out may not always be the answer for the tough fiscal problems faced by state and local governments today.

The American Federation of State, County and Municipal Employees (AFSCME) has studied the issue of contracting out for many years. The on-the-job experience of AFSCME's members has shown that contracting out has had serious shortcomings in a number of instances. Contractors providing government services may be more costly; contracting out may result in a reduction of the quality and efficiency in services and a lessening of public control; and there have been cases of crime and corruption associated with contracting out.

With competent public management, AFSCME contends, there would be no need to consider contracting out in many of the instances in which it is now used. Any state or local governmental agency should be able to effect the same kinds of economies and efficiencies that good private managers achieve, says the national group.

THE PENDULUM OF HISTORY

Historically, American government has provided many public services directly but there has always been some degree of contracting out, particularly on the federal level. In the early years of this century, cities and towns around the country turned to private companies to run local streetcar systems; to collect garbage; to provide fire protection; and to perform other basic public services, often because their communities lacked the needed public resources. But there were problems: some contractors were known to overcharge municipalities; some contractors made under-the-table payoffs; and some contractor-provided services were poor.

"Because of gross abuses," Ralph W. Widner, staff vice president of the Urban Land Institute, has noted, "the reform movement of the 1920s tried to professionalize the delivery of quality public services by making them part of the municipal government." Prodded by reformers, many municipalities decreased their dependence on contractors and delivered more services using the public work force.

Now, state and local governments are looking at returning to the use of private contractors. In 1982, Widner noted, "The pendu-

Reprinted from *American City & County*, Vol.99, No.2 (February 1984), pp. 49–50. © 1984 by Communication Channels Inc., Atlanta, GA, USA.

lum is swinging back the other way. It will continue to swing until there is another round of abuses and scandals and then (will) swing back the other way."

THE BUSINESS OF PUBLIC SERVICE

Contracting out is a high-stakes game, says AFSCME. On one side of the issue are the contractors, their trade associations, local chambers of commerce and many state and local public officials, as well as many powerful federal figures. These advocates of "privatization" claim that contracting out is a way for financially burdened state and local governments to trim budgets, to hold the line on taxes and to improve the delivery of services.

In seeking to involve the private sector more heavily in the delivery of basic public services at all levels of government, this group echoes a basic philosophy of the Reagan administration: that we have too much government, that government provides too many services, and that the private sector can provide whatever public services are needed more efficiently and more cheaply than public workers.

On the other side of the issue are public employees, public interest organizations, and many state and local government officials and community organizations who have experienced contracting out failures in their own jurisdictions. To these groups, contracting out, rather than always providing a panacea for state and local fiscal and service delivery problems, can increase governments' woes.

SQUEEZE PLAY ON GOVERNMENT

Although private firms regularly seek government contracts even in good economic times, a combination of factors in the 1970s and 1980s has accelerated private marketing activity. The recession, coupled with increased foreign competition in many markets, have caused many private firms to look increasingly to the public sector for new sources of revenue. At the same time, state and local governments are becoming increasingly cost-conscious. They have been hurt by inflation and their revenues have been cut due to the recession.

In addition, property tax-cutting initiatives, such as Proposition 13 in California and Proposition 2½ in Massachusetts, further reduced available revenues. By 1981, this combination of inflation, recession and taxing limitations had placed state and local governments in the difficult position of having to raise taxes or reduce services, or find other ways to reduce the costs of government.

With economic conditions deteriorating in recent years, and with city and state officials anxiously searching for ways to cut government operating costs, contracting out has sounded especially appealing. Private businesses, faced with depressed markets and often intense foreign competition, have viewed contracts in the public sector as a way to alleviate their own fiscal woes. Thus, contracting would appear to be a perfect match, offering state and local governments a way out of their financial problems while giving private firms a new market in the public sector.

Unfortunately, the partnership is too often unequal, says AFSCME. Private sector firms often make substantial profits; while state and local governments could realize short-term benefits through lowered personnel costs, they still maintain the responsibility for management, the quality of services may be diminished and costs may begin to escalate after an initial decrease.

ARGUMENTS AGAINST

Experience with contracting out at the state and local levels has demonstrated potential weaknesses, in some cases, in the practice of using private firms to deliver public services.

For example, rather than saving money for state and local governments, contracting out may result in higher costs—especially when all the true costs of contracting are actually considered. Private companies exist to make a profit and the necessity of a profit drives up the costs eventually, if not immediately. In addition, there are "hidden" government costs such as contract preparation, administration and monitoring of contractor performance, and use of public facilities and materials.

A key argument against contracting out is that it may result in poorer services for citizens, says AFSCME. Contractors are also looking for ways to reduce their costs and frequently this has led to charges that they have "cut corners" by hiring inexperienced, transient personnel at low wages, by ignoring contract requirements or by providing inadequate supervision.

The age-old problem of corruption in contracting out has not improved over time, according to AFSCME. As stated in a 1977 book, "Government for Sale," contracting may be associated with bribery, kickbacks and collusive bidding. Also, without proper controls, contracts could become tools of political patronage to reward supporters of successful candidates—just as in the days of the spoils system, when public jobs were doled out to winning candidates' backers.

INTERIM ARRANGEMENTS

Contractors also go in and out of business; sometimes they may be unable to complete a contract, leaving a jurisdiction high and dry. When a city finds it necessary to remove a contractor for poor performance, it is often forced to make expensive interim arrangements.

Cities and states may find that a contract, originally awarded at an attractive rate, be-

comes more expensive. This practice is called "buying in" or "low-balling." In order to obtain the contract and thus get a foot in the door, a firm could offer a very low price to perform a particular service. As contract performance continues, however, a city or state could find itself dependent on a particular contractor to such an extent that it cannot change contractors or cease the service. This might occur in long-term contracts for services, such as trash collection, which require expensive equipment that must be well-maintained. After contracting out such service, a municipality often sells equipment, leaving it little alternative except to use a contractor.

Another possible problem with contracting out is in the drafting of appropriate job specifications. State and local governments should know that it may be difficult to write a contract, which ensures that government gets what it wants for the agreed-upon price. They should also be aware that work performed by public employees may be covered under the agreement with the contractor.

MORE FLEXIBILITY

Public managers directing a public work force have a large degree of flexibility to respond to unforeseen circumstances. On the other hand, a contractor has the clear right to refuse to do anything that isn't in the contract. Even experienced contract writers may find it difficult to design a document for complex services that covers all unforeseen circumstances and emergencies. When a contract's performance specifications are too narrow or contain loopholes the result may be a decrease in the quality of services for the public.

True competition for contracts may be the exception rather than the rule in some state and local governmental jurisdictions. Contracts for trash collection, social services and architectural engineering and consulting services are often awarded under no-bid or negotiated-bid conditions. Where bidding occurs, there is the potential for collusion as recent paving and electrical contracting difficulties demonstrate.

Contracting out may result in less accountability by the government to its citizens, says AFSCME. When citizens complain about a contracted service, government officials could be left in the position with little more to do than to complain to the contractor, or enter either into costly contract renegotiations or termination proceedings. Any time when many citizens feel that government is too removed from the people it serves, AFSCME contends that contracting out pushes the level of accountability and responsiveness one more step away.

Responsible government requires improving the quality of public management and public service, not the selling off of government, says AFSCME. According to the federation, in every case of failure, in every case where the quality and efficiency of a public service has deteriorated and the cost increased, where control over public services has diminished, where corruption has occurred, the public endures the consequences and the public pays the bills.

CHAPTER 8

Financial Issues: More Than a Question of Money

Government's most important policy document is the budget, which allocates resources for each program. Whether each activity is financed primarily at the state or local government level, and what types of taxes are levied, varies by state, as described in the opening account by the ACIR. Which are used in your area? Do they meet the requisites of a quality tax system?

State financial systems are under increasing pressure and are turning to such alternatives as lotteries and user fees, whose merits are debated in two selections. Since state and local government revenues fluctuate with regional economic conditions, the level of services desired is balanced by the political obligation of levying taxes. The costs of turning government over to business enterprise or "privatization" are analyzed by Ted Kolderie, and Charles Goodsell responds with a defense of bureaucracy.

36

State Financial Systems

ADVISORY COMMISSION ON INTERGOVERNMENTAL RELATIONS

State financial systems exhibit much of the variety found in other aspects of state government. No two are exactly the same, although certain patterns of revenues, expenditures, and debt are evident. Any discussion of state finances must recognize this diversity as well as the states' interdependence with the local systems within their boundaries, the influence of federal fiscal actions, and the wide differences among states as to functional assignment patterns, wealth and policy preferences.

Confronted with the barrage of criticism directed at state financial systems, along with other aspects of state government, and faced with demands for increased services from their citizens, states transformed their financial systems in the past quarter century. They made major changes in expenditure patterns and altered their revenue raising structures. While this was underway, state taxing capacity and effort shifted among states, causing significant adjustments. In addition, debt burdens rose. . . .

STATE REVENUE SYSTEMS

Although federal financial assistance makes up about one-third of state expenditures, states raise most of the money in their general funds from their own taxes. Each state has its own individually designed tax system; however, sales and gross receipts taxes and indi-vidual income taxes are the workhorses of the state tax system.

Emphasis as to which specific tax produces the most revenue for the states has shifted over the years. Traditionally, property taxes were the major source. At the beginning of the present century, they made up more than half of state tax receipts, and as late as 1933 they constituted more than one-third. By the time of the Depression of the 1930s, however, property taxes had yielded first place to sales and gross receipts taxes, and in 1933 property tax levies brought in only 16.5% of state tax revenue. Since that time, their proportion has continued to shrink and they now produce only about 2%. Sales and gross receipts taxes remain the major source of state finances, although in recent years the spread of state income taxes made these newer levies major producers for the states. . . .

Requisites of a Quality Tax System

The general principles that mark a quality tax system have been prominent in public finance literature since Adam Smith discoursed on financial systems in his *Wealth of Nations*. Although different authorities emphasize different principles and may disagree as to their operationalization, there is consensus that a sound tax system should be fiscally adequate, elastic, diverse, economic in administration, simple and comprehensible, and equitable.

Advisory Commission on Intergovernmental Relations. *The Question of State Government Capability*, Report A–98, (Washington, D.C.: 1985), pp. 193, 204, 205, 207, 209. Footnotes have been omitted.

The ACIR has been concerned, also, with political accountability as well as with a balanced state-local system and the equilibrium between the growth of the public and private sectors.

Fiscal adequacy relates to whether or not the tax system brings in enough money to support the government. Meeting this requirement depends both on how much money the taxes yield and how much the government spends. State governments, with one exception—Vermont—are prohibited by their constitutions from operating with deficits, so obviously all meet this standard.

Elasticity is related to adequacy. Tax systems should be constructed in such a way that rates may be raised or lowered as economic conditions change. Motor fuels taxes, for example, sufficient to support the construction and maintenance of a highway system in an era of unlimited fuel supplies and large automobiles, may decline dramatically in an era of oil shortage when motorists drive less and in more fuel-efficient cars. This happened, as a matter of fact, in the recent fuel shortage, necessitating increases in gasoline tax rates in many states.

Diversity, too, is related to adequacy of income. A system with multiple taxes often can weather the exigencies of economic fluctuation better than one relying on one or a few taxes. Just as transportation facilities suffered when motor vehicle tax yields fell off, so do other governmental activities lose support if financed principally by sales taxes in a period of economic distress.

Economy of administration is concerned with ensuring that the tax collection process is not so expensive as to consume most of the funds produced, leaving little for support of policies the government wishes to pursue. Gasoline taxes, paid by retailers, for example, are costly to collect. Providing for the wholesalers to remit them involves fewer accounts and less administrative effort.

Although the principles, *simple and comprehensible*, would seem to speak for themselves, often they are not heard by designers of tax systems. Income taxes, in particular, are likely to violate these standards. Even where states have opted to make income tax form preparation easier by tying state taxes to the federal levy, the complications of the latter interfere with comprehensibility.

Equity involves fairness in the distribution of the tax burden across the population. It has two faces, both part of the principle that taxes should impose equal sacrifice. "Horizontal equity" is concerned with equal taxes for people in equal positions while "vertical equity" seeks a proper pattern of unequal taxes among people with unequal incomes. Whether vertical equity exists in a tax system hinges on whether the system is progressive or not. Under a progressive system, the tax burden rises with income. If, on the other hand, taxpayers with lower incomes experience greater burdens, the system is regressive. When taxpayers of all incomes have a similar tax burden, the tax is said to be proportional.

Political accountability, as perceived by the ACIR, means that tax-imposing bodies should answer to the people by making them aware of changes in the tax burden. When inflation drives incomes and expenditures into high brackets, it enables officials to benefit from increased revenues without the necessity for specific tax increases. The ACIR believes that tax rises should not occur automatically from changes in economic conditions, such as inflation, but only from overt discretionary actions by state-local officials.

State-local balance in revenue systems is achieved, in the ACIR view, when state revenues constitute 65% to 85% of total state-local taxes. This range was chosen because it should allow states to provide all of the nonfederal welfare funding and the majority of local education costs.

Public-private balance in revenue systems once was perceived by ACIR as one where the public sector grew at a higher rate than the economy. Since 1976, the perception has shifted to encompass public sector growth at about the same rate as the economy.

Tax diversity and equity have been the focus of most discussion of tax systems in recent years. Attention here will be directed principally at them along with the questions of political accountability and balance. It is impossible in a study of this breadth to assess other recommendations dealing with comprehensibility and simplicity of tax laws, elasticity and the economy of administration.

STATE PROGRESS IN ACHIEVING HIGHER QUALITY REVENUE SYSTEMS

Diversification in State Tax Systems

Revenue diversification can be provided by a balanced use of property, income and sales taxes. Since each of these has its own strengths and weaknesses, each can be used to provide balance in the tax structure. John Shannon points out that while this balanced use makes sense for most states, there are a fortunate few, namely the energy-rich and tourist-rich states, that are in a position to "export" a substantial portion of their taxes. In Texas, for example, it might be more advisable politically for the state to impose a severance tax on petroleum production than to levy an income tax on its own citizens. Much of the burden of the severance tax would then fall on those living and working outside its borders.

In general, states have diversified their tax systems with more states now relying on income as well as sales taxes as significant sources of funds. A total of 40 states now have broad-based individual income taxes, and three others—Connecticut, New Hampshire and Tennessee—have limited levies. Connecticut's tax applies only to capital gains and dividends, and New Hampshire and Tennessee tax only interest and dividends. Alaska, Florida, Nevada, South Dakota, Texas, Washington and Wyoming are the complete holdouts. In addition to the use of individual in-

come tax, all but five states impose corporate income taxes. Nevada, South Dakota, Texas, Washington and Wyoming are the only states that do not. As far as the general sales tax is concerned, all states except Alaska, Delaware, Montana, New Hampshire and Oregon now impose such taxes. . . .

The scarcity of available tax revenues stimulated increased reliance on user fees. Although their contribution to state income is relatively small, except for transportation funds, in recent years they have been imposed on more activities or increased in amount.

As a consequence of the diversification, states rely less heavily on the property tax. It brought in only 2% of the states' own-source tax funds in 1981. The property tax is still a major contributor to local government financing, however, and has undergone significant upgrading in its administration in recent years. State sales taxes, on the other hand, produced slightly more than half, 50.9%, of estimated tax revenues for 1981, and income (both personal and corporate) taxes provided 37.5%. . . .

Equity in State Tax Systems

Vertical equity—or a proper pattern of unequal taxes among unequal incomes—is the principal focus for securing fairness in state tax systems. Equity considerations require that the heaviest tax burden fall on those most able to pay and that subsistence income be exempt from taxation. Thus, state governments with regressive taxes, such as property and sales taxes, that bear most heavily on low-income residents increasingly provide some shields for these individuals. These can, and do, take the form of exemption of food and medicine from the sales tax, the granting of a tax credit or an income tax exemption in the state income tax, and some kind of "circuit breaker" to moderate the impact of the property tax. The latter, for example, might exempt property of individuals in low-income brackets from the property tax. . . .

The equity features states have adopted are . . . [as follows:] Of the 45 states with general sales taxes in 1981, 26 exempted food from coverage and two provided income tax credits. This compares with 16 out of 45 states with general sales taxes in 1970, an increase from 35.5% to 62.2%. In addition, 43 states do not impose the sales tax on prescription drugs. This is up from 25 states out of the 45 imposing the tax in 1970, an increase of 40%. To ease property tax burdens, 31 states have adopted state-financed circuit breakers. All homeowners and renters get the benefit of these arrangements in six states, while relief is limited to elderly homeowners and renters in 16. Practices in the remaining states vary among relief for elderly homeowners (6), all homeowners only (1), all renters only (1), and elderly renters (1). Circuit breakers are relatively recent innovations with Wisconsin adopting the first in 1964.

Increased state and local taxes together had a mixed effect on the fairness of the state-local systems. Personal income taxes were moderately progressive, amounting to 2.2% of the income of a family of four with an average income, 3.2% for a similar family with twice the average income, and 4.1% for a family with four times the average. . . . General sales and local property taxes, on the other hand, were regressive. The sales taxes consumed almost twice as large a percentage of the average family income as they did of incomes of the highest earners. Although the property tax gap between income levels was not as wide, that tax did bear heavier on the average family. It should be kept in mind that circuit breakers did not apply in most instances because they are directed at lower income families and the elderly. The latter are unlikely to be in households with two dependent children—an attribute of "average families."

Accountability

States are under pressure to exercise moderation in levying taxes both because profligate taxing burdens the citizenry and because it enables the public sector to expand to an unacceptable point. Public dissatisfaction has grown in recent years because inflation has pushed both incomes and property values into higher ranges, thus increasing the tax bite without overt actions on the part of taxing authorities. . . . Although, as a matter of political accountability, tax increases should be imposed specifically and not rise quietly as the result of inflationary factors, such is not always the case.

States have taken three principal types of action to deal with this specific problem and improve accountability. These are: (1) adoption of full disclosure laws, (2) reduction of property tax rates to offset large rises in assessments, and (3) indexation of the personal income tax.

"Full disclosure laws" mandate reduction of local tax rates on property to offset large assessment rises unless local taxing authorities advertise the need for a tax increase. Full disclosure requirements are in effect in ten states—Colorado, Florida, Hawaii, Kentucky, Maryland, Michigan, Montana, Tennessee, Texas and Virginia.

Provision for rolling back property tax rates to offset large rises in assessment have been adopted in ten states since 1971. They are: Arizona, Florida, Hawaii, Kentucky, Maryland, Montana, Rhode Island, Tennessee, Texas and Virginia.

Indexation adjusts provisions of the income tax law to account for inflation. It increases the fixed-dollar provisions of the tax code—such as standard deductions, personal exemptions, and income brackets—every year by the rate of inflation. Consequently, incomes that increase at the rate of inflation no longer are automatically subject to higher taxes and the original value of the exemptions and deductions is preserved. When indexation is not used in an inflationary period, taxes on lower incomes tend to rise more than those on higher incomes. A 1980 ACIR report pointed to the following advantages of indexation:

It removes the automatic, hidden tax increases that would otherwise result from the interaction of inflation and a progressive income tax.

It prevents arbitrary distortions of the legislated distribution of the tax burden and provides significant tax relief, particularly to those at the lower and upper ends of the income range.

It improves the ability of the voters to hold elected officials accountable for their taxing and spending decisions.

It helps slow the rate of growth in government and preserves the current balance of resources between the public and private sector.

It sustains the current intergovernmental fiscal balance and impedes the flow of resources and decisionmaking to higher levels of government.

No state indexed its personal income taxes prior to 1978 when Arizona, California and Colorado enacted indexing measures. They were joined later by Iowa, Minnesota and Wisconsin and subsequently by Montana, South Carolina, Oregon and Maine. The laws vary as to items indexed, timing of changes, limits imposed on the extent of rate modification and the price deflator employed.

Indexing is now in place in eight states—Arizona, Colorado, California, Wisconsin, Minnesota, Iowa, Oregon and South Carolina, although Colorado, California, Wisconsin, Minnesota, Iowa, temporarily suspended or postponed indexing provisions as a result of the recession.

States have adopted a variety of other measures to ensure moderation in taxation and spending. Although the idea of limiting taxes is not new, the adoption of the Jarvis-Gann-initiated Proposition 13 in California in 1978 stimulated a new round of enactments. More often than not, these apply to local government property taxation; nevertheless, state government fiscal powers are limited in 20 states. . . .

The limits slowed taxing and spending even in states that did not adopt them by demonstrating possible results if taxing and spending got out of hand.

Many students and practitioners of state government oppose the adoption of the levy limits, expenditure lids and assessment constraints, believing that it is better for the legislative authority to exercise the restraint rather than having restrictions imposed that impede flexibility. Nevertheless, a large segment of the public appears to favor the limits as a method of countering the influence of special interest groups that encourage government spending.

— **37** —

The Social and Economic Impact of State Lotteries

H. ROY KAPLAN

While the introduction of state lotteries is a recent development, beginning with the New Hampshire lottery in 1963, lotteries were popular at other times in our past.[1] Lotteries were firmly entrenched in England at the time of the colonization of the New World. The Virginia Company even used a series of lotteries to finance the development of its settlement in Jamestown. Lotteries were popular in the colonies and were patronized by many people, despite the high cost of tickets, which sometimes ran $30 or more. To hedge against the loss of such an investment, buyers could insure their tickets for a premium to make up the difference between the prize they might win and the cost of the ticket. Many of the Founding Fathers were avid lottery patrons. Despite his reputation for frugality, Benjamin Franklin was known to buy lottery tickets, and in a drawing in 1748, he wrote a friend, "I have not insured for anybody, so I shall neither lose nor gain that way."[2]

Later the practice of insuring developed into an alternative betting scheme whereby players could bet on the number of lots they thought might be taken from the wheel on a given day. If a person's guess was correct, he received the amount for which the lot was insured. Since drawings often lasted weeks or months, this was an interesting diversion that also heightened interest in the lottery.

There were two kinds of lotteries in the colonies: private drawings, which were run for personal profit, and legally sanctioned drawings, to provide capital for public projects. The most common private lotteries were raffles of merchandise, land, and even slaves. Many people utilized lotteries to pay debts, as did William Byrd III of Virginia. He divided his land, which was near the present city of Richmond, into 839 parcels and raffled them off. One of the winners was George Washington, who invested 50 pounds in the venture. At the age of 83, Thomas Jefferson tried to dispose of his land through a lottery to liquidate debts of $80,000. Ticket sales lagged, however, and his death on 4 July 1826 halted interest in it.

Lotteries were thought to be an easy method of raising revenue and were used by the colonies to help defray the costs of wars with the French and Indians and for public services. In 1777 the Continental Congress sponsored a lottery to raise funds for the Revolution, and four states—Massachusetts, Vermont, Rhode Island, and New York—also conducted them to aid the struggle for independence.

Countless lotteries were held by states and municipalities through the mid-1800s to finance public works projects, such as the construction of bridges, streets, courthouses, canals, hospitals, libraries, water systems, and wharves. A series of lotteries was held in the 1790s to finance the improvement and construction of Washington, D.C. Churches and colleges were not averse to relying on lotteries for raising needed revenue. From

The Annals of the American Academy of Political and Social Science, Vol.474 (July 1984), pp. 91–106. Copyright © 1984 The American Academy of Political and Social Science. Reprinted by permission of Sage Publications, Inc.

1790 to the Civil War, 47 colleges, including Harvard, Yale, Princeton, Dartmouth, Brown, Columbia, and Rutgers, approximately 300 lower schools, and some 200 church groups benefited from them.

Lotteries left an indelible stamp on the United States economy and business system through marketing, promotional, and organizational techniques that were developed by ticket brokers in the early 1800s. They were also the forerunner of private banking and stock brokerage chains, as they provided the means through which capital could be accumulated in small sums from many sources and later utilized for permanent investments.

The height of the lottery mania was reached in the mid-1800s. There were over 160 lottery shops in New York City in 1826, and in Philadelphia over 200 offices were selling chances for 420 different drawings, 394 of which violated Pennsylvania law. The competition for subscribers increased as private entrepreneurs entered the picture. Between 1790 and 1830, 21 states gave nearly 200 licenses for private and semiprivate lotteries. There was a lottery of some sort being held every day of the year by 1832. In 1826 the citizens of Rhode Island spent $1 million on lottery chances, while in New York the figure was nearly $1.5 million, and $750,000 in Massachusetts.[3]

Opponents of lotteries contended they were unfair methods for obtaining revenue because they induced working people to spend scarce resources in the hope of gaining sudden wealth. It was also believed that the commitment to work was diminished by the lure of easy money through wagering, reinforcing the supposed slothful nature of humans. The preamble of an act against lotteries in New York in 1747 stated that they were of "pernicious consequences" to the public because they encouraged "Numbers of Laboring People to Assemble together at Taverns where such Lotteries are usually Set on Foot and Drawn."[4]

The increase in lotteries also precipitated a corresponding increase in irregularities.

Misrepresentations, swindles, and riggings became widespread. Even in colonial days abuses occurred, such as awarding inferior goods as prizes or manipulating drawings so that valuable items remained undrawn. Some promoters even fled before drawings were held. As lotteries became bigger, so too did the magnitude of abuses. After a number of scandals involving the rigging of winners, organized opposition developed, which led to legislation banning lotteries by 1878 in all states except Louisiana, where they were barred 15 years later.

THE REEMERGENCE OF STATE LOTTERIES

Contemporary state lotteries were primarily developed for reasons similar to their eighteenth- and nineteenth-century predecessors: to raise revenue for financially pressed states. It is ironic that many of the 17 states[5] having lotteries today were among the original 13 colonies, and although a great deal of time has passed, categories of need have basically remained the same: health, education, and public welfare. The lingering recession of the 1970s and 1980s coupled with inflation and the shrinking tax base of cities created fiscal crises in many heavily industrial states, where lotteries have made the biggest comeback. As of May 1983, 27 other states and the U.S. Congress were also considering the legalization of lotteries.[6] Lotteries spread as adjacent states seek to capitalize on the mania and stop the flow of dollars across their borders.

The social climate is also ripe for the return of lotteries. The purchasing power of workers has been eroding, making it difficult for the middle and lower classes to maintain their life-styles. Added to the unemployed, they constitute a market for lotteries that dangle the tantalizing dream of instant wealth in front of them.

Another rationale for the reintroduction of lotteries has been the government's attempt to combat organized crime by depriving it of income. It was thought that lotteries could capitalize on the public's penchant for betting, especially in industrial states where illegal numbers games are ubiquitous, and put organized crime out of business.

Some people derive enjoyment from playing lotteries, and games have been developed to heighten the suspense and increase player participation. For the impatient, some tickets have an erasable mark so the purchaser can learn immediately whether she or he is an instant winner. Also, there are the daily numbers games, which afford bettors the chance to pick their own combinations of numbers. The recreational aspects of legalized gambling have not gone unnoticed, and although the lottery is one of the more unglamorous forms, there have been and will continue to be significant expenditures of energy devoted to increasing audience and player participation and enthusiasm.

REVENUE GENERATION

Since lotteries were introduced primarily to generate revenue for financially beleaguered states, the cogent question is whether they have achieved or can achieve this objective. Although they do raise revenue, they are not **able to generate sufficient funds to make significant contributions to state budgets.** The magnitude of this financial picture can be more fully comprehended when we consider that gross ticket sales for the active state lotteries in 1983 were approximately $5 billion, with the states receiving net revenues of $2 billion. The combined revenues for those states was $72.4 billion, which means lotteries contributed about 3 percent that year.[7]

Perhaps more than any other factor, the very nature of lotteries accounts for their relatively low yield. Lotteries are a voluntary form of fund-raising—a painless tax, and even though many people purchase tickets, most do not spend much money on them.

In New Jersey, which introduced the nation's first legal daily numbers game in 1975 and where 80 percent of the people eligible to buy tickets purchase them at one time or another, 1982 gross revenues hit nearly $518 million, or about $70 per capita. This was a 24 percent increase over the previous year. Much of the credit for the dramatic increase in sales goes to the introduction of legalized numbers games, which many other states have adopted.[8]

From its inception in 1970 to 1982, the New Jersey lottery contributed $380 million to higher education, $341 million to elementary and secondary education, and channeled an additional $425 million to institutions such as hospitals and correctional institutions.[9] This is an impressive amount of money, but taken over the 12-year history of the lottery, it amounts to less than $100 million per year; and, when compared to the total New Jersey expenditures on public education in 1981 alone of nearly $3.7 billion,[10] the lottery's contribution is relatively insignificant.

Less than half the revenue generated by a lottery finds its way into a state's treasury. In the past, administration, commissions to ticket agents, and advertising consumed 10 to 15 percent of the gross, but that share has been declining as sales have soared. Advertising is still one of the most expensive costs, accounting for approximately 30 percent of a state's operating budget. New Jersey spent $2.5 million on advertising in 1982, which accounted for one-third of its relatively low operating budget of approximately $7.5 million, or 1.4 cents of every dollar wagered. A network of agents is also required to sell tickets, as in New Jersey, where 4000 licensed agents provided this service and received over $37 million in 1982.

The largest drain on lottery revenues is mandated by law. Much of the revenue must be returned to players in the form of prizes. The amount varies from state to state but averages between 40 and 45 percent. Yet, even if all revenues were retained and no prizes awarded, the $5 billion raised by lotteries in 1983 would not solve the states' financial

TABLE 1. CHARACTERISTICS OF LOTTERIES IN THE UNITED STATES 1983

State	Year Enacted	Gross Revenue (Millions of Dollars)	Net Revenue (Millions of Dollars)	Type of Game	Top Prizes	Use of Funds
Arizona	1981	75	31.8	Continuous, instant	$1 million	Roads, transit, general fund
Colorado	1983	140 (January– 30 June, 1983)	42 (January– 30 June 1983	Continuous, instant	$1000 per week for life	Conservation, parks, capital construction
Connecticut	1972	188	80.5	Instant, weekly, numbers	Millions	General fund
Delaware	1975	30.1	11	Instant, daily, numbers	Millions	General fund
District of Columbia	1982	50.4 (25 August 1982– 25 June 1983)	13.1 (25 August 1982– 25 June 1983)	Instant, numbers (September 1983)	$1000 per week for life	General fund
Illinois	1974	495.4	214.1	Instant, daily, numbers, weekly	Millions	General fund
Maine	1974	13	3.7	Instant, daily, numbers	$25,000	General fund
Maryland	1973	462.8	198	Daily, weekly, numbers	Millions	General fund
Massachusetts	1972	312.1	104.6	Instant, daily, weekly, numbers	Millions	Local aid

State	Year			Games	Prize	Beneficiary
Michigan	1972	548.9	221.2	**Instant, daily, weekly, numbers**	Millions	Education
New Hampshire	1963	13.8	3.7	Instant, daily, weekly, numbers	$100,000	Education
New Jersey	1970	693.1	294.9	Daily, weekly, numbers, instant	Millions	Education, capital construction
New York	1967	645	275.2	Daily, instant, numbers	Millions	Education
Ohio	1974	397.8	145	Daily, numbers, weekly, instant	Millions	General fund (education as of 1 July 1983)
Pennsylvania	1972	885.4	355.4	Instant, daily, numbers	Millions	Senior citizens
Rhode Island	1974	43	14.7	Instant, daily, numbers, weekly	Millions	General fund
Vermont	1978	4.4	1.1	Instant, daily	$100,000	Debts, construction
Washington	1982	231.2 (15 November 1982 to 30 June 1983)	94.6 (15 November 1982 to 30 June 1983)	Instant	$1000 per week for life	General fund

SOURCES. Geoffrey Tomb, "Lotteries: 'Gimmicks' or Valid Fund Raisers?" *Miami Herald*, April 7, 1983; Larry Lang and Eric Nalder, "State Operated Lotteries," *Seattle Post-Intelligencer*, August 1, 1982; Bill Curry, "State Lotteries: Roses and Thorns," *State Legislatures*, March 1984, pp. 9–16; and information supplied by state lottery agencies.

problems. In this regard, the exceptions are New Jersey and Nevada. The combined income from legalized gambling activities in New Jersey accounted for 7 percent of its revenue in 1982, and the state of Nevada receives approximately 45 percent of its revenue that way, but these states are atypical because they permit casino gambling.

Lottery Contributions to State Budgets

Generally, lottery revenues account for only 2 to 3 percent of a state's budget, and economist Daniel Suits[11] predicted that even doubling such revenues would yield only 5 percent of a state's revenue. A National Science Foundation study[12] pointed out that states could generate the same amount of revenue derived from lotteries by increasing sales tax rates by half of a percent, and the error in predicting tax revenues for the coming year's budget has already exceeded lottery revenues in some states. Lotteries, then, by virtue of their voluntary nature and mandatory high prize returns, are unable to match the revenue generated by direct taxes.

While generating lottery revenues of $71 million in 1982, Connecticut considered a variety of new taxes in 1983, including a state income tax to make up for a shortfall of $265 million.

The Pennsylvania lottery grossed $885.4 million and netted $355.4 million in 1983, making it one of the most successful in the country. Nevertheless, the state increased its income tax rate from 2.2 percent to 2.45 percent, effective August 1983, to generate approximately $200 to $250 million in additional revenue. The state sales tax was also modified to encompass cigarettes and may thus generate an additional $60 million. Together, the sales and income taxes account for approximately $5 billion a year, nearly 15 times the net revenue generated by the state's lottery. In other words, raising the state income tax by one-quarter of a percent generates as much money as total net lottery revenues.

Lottery proponents counter that funds raised have found their way into needed programs and projects, and many states have earmarked lottery revenues for specified areas such as education. The more salient question is whether the funds would have been raised if the lotteries did not exist. In all probability, the odds are that programs deemed essential would have been funded if lotteries were not available.

In New Hampshire, lottery funds have contributed a sizable amount to education, but in 1981 New Hampshire ranked thirty-third among the states in the average funds spent per pupil in average daily attendance.[13] It is also reasonable to assume that the citizens of New Hampshire had, by 1963, recognized the necessity for increasing aid to education and would have embarked upon some other method if the lottery had not passed. Recently New Hampshire began a daily numbers game and doubled its gross revenues, but the proceeds provide only $4 million to the state's $342 million school budget. "I don't think a school district is going to succeed or fail because of the sweepstakes dollars," said Bruce Ryan, spokesman for the New Hampshire school system.[14]

There is no guarantee that earmarked categories will receive as much funding as they need. Recent financial crises in some states indicate that some special-interest categories for which lottery funds have been earmarked are still vulnerable and have been pared despite assistance from lotteries.

There are other drawbacks to the lottery solution to states' fiscal problems. The earmarking of funds can, under close scrutiny in some situations, be seen as nothing more than a neat bit of budgetary juggling. Some politicians look on earmarked lottery revenues—for example, in education, the most commonly earmarked category—as an exchange item in their budget. Moneys realized by a lottery are allocated for education, but total education funds may not be increased because a like amount may be withheld from other sources of funding. Students and institutions do not then receive, for example, a $50 million bonanza; they merely get what the legislature and governor felt they should have in the first place. The $50 million would probably have been raised from other sources, or programs would have been cut accordingly.

The Regressivity of Lotteries

According to George Rummel, deputy director of the Department of Revenue for the state of Illinois, lottery revenues literally staved off bankruptcy for his state on two occasions during 1975.[15] The $70 million that the lottery contributed to the general fund was only seven-tenths of 1 percent of the state's total revenues, but enough to fend off disaster. While such gestures seem heroic and timely, the legislatures of Illinois and other financially pressed states could be courting disaster by relying on lottery revenues. One of the greatest drawbacks of lotteries is the way they are used to substitute for dependable, equitable, and responsible methods of revenue generation. They perpetuate the muddle that many states are in. They impede tax reform and prevent the implementation of progressive taxes.

Furthermore, lotteries are quite regressive. A survey conducted for the national commission on gambling revealed that over 50 percent of the people in states having lotteries purchase tickets.[16] Purchase patterns vary, however: some people buy them sporadically, while others are steady patrons. Although the commission found that people with high income and education spent more, on the average, on lottery tickets than people with low income and education, poorer people spent proportionately more of their earnings, making lotteries more regressive than sales taxes.

Further evidence of their regressivity comes from research in Michigan. There, in fiscal year 1979-80, per capita sales of tickets were $75, but blacks spent more than whites, and a study reported by Suits[17] revealed that the proportion of family income spent on lot-

tery tickets declines almost 12 percent for every 10 percent increase in per capita income in that state. Suits calculated that the Michigan lottery is more than twice as regressive as that state's sales tax. He concludes that "the [Michigan] state lottery is one of the most regressive taxes known and imposes by far the heaviest relative burden on those least able to pay."[18]

Other proof of the regressive nature of lotteries comes from a 1977 report by the Connecticut State Commission on Special Revenue, which found that the state's daily numbers game primarily attracted the poor, the chronically unemployed, and the uneducated, while people with college degrees and incomes exceeding $25,000 largely ignored the state's various forms of legalized gambling.[19]

Using data for the states of Connecticut and Massachusetts, Brinner and Clotfelter[20] estimated that lotteries were equivalent to a state sales tax at a rate of 60 to 90 percent that fell disproportionately on lower income groups. Similarly, Spiro[21] analyzed questionnaires returned by 271 Pennsylvania lottery winners and found that the lottery was highly regressive for people in the $10,000-to-$15,000 income bracket. And Clotfelter,[22] using data from the Maryland lottery, calculated that the daily numbers game in that state was more regressive than the weekly game and only slightly less regressive than illegal numbers.

There is something cruelly perverse about states encouraging, even proselytizing, their poorest and least educated citizens to gamble often for the purpose of generating funds for education.

THE ILLEGAL SIDE OF LEGALIZED GAMBLING

Despite the impressive revenue figures that lottery officials proudly display, the fact remains that lotteries have not fulfilled another of their promises. They have not made significant inroads into illegal gambling. Numbers games flourish, especially among minorities. There are many reasons for the lack of success that lotteries have had in the war against organized crime. Smart bettors who are savvy about such things as payoffs and odds know that lotteries are bad bets. Although the odds in legal numbers games are comparable to their illegal counterparts for picking three numbers—often from 500 to 1 to 800 to 1—longer sequences of numbers push the odds much higher, often into the millions.

One of the arguments that proponents of legalized gambling, such as lotteries and off-track betting, use is the expectation that legalization will curtail illegal wagering in numbers and with bookies. This assumption, however, has not been substantiated. The national commission on gambling reported that there is more wagering in numbers and with bookies in states having lotteries and pari-mutuel betting than in states without them. Even when states modify their games—for example, by introducing daily numbers—in an attempt to compete more effectively, their illegal counterparts have been able to survive through some creative maneuvers of their own, such as lowering odds, increasing payoffs, extending credit, permitting smaller bets than do the legalized games, and offering the convenience of telephone services and house calls.

Since illegal games may be sold at places of business or even door-to-door, legal lotteries are at a competitive marketing disadvantage. But even more inhibiting is the fact that lottery winnings are taxed in the United States, often at several levels. For example, a big winner in New York City would receive a check minus 20 percent deducted for federal income tax and would then have to pay city and state income taxes, in addition to other federal tax obligations, depending on his or her tax bracket. Typically, winners of a million dollars or more—their numbers are approaching a thousand—will have to surrender one-third to one-half of their winnings to the Internal Revenue Service. This not only creates ill will, but has been frequently cited by players as false advertising, since the actual prize is half of the advertised sum. And not even death alleviates the big lottery winner's tax burden, since substantial state and federal inheritance taxes are deducted from the annual installments, often leaving a pittance for heirs.[23]

There may also be cultural norms favorable to the success of illegal games. Playing numbers is often institutionalized in urban neighborhoods among blacks and Hispanics, where the collection of a nickel, dime, or quarter is part of the routine of life.[24] These activities also provide otherwise unemployed persons with jobs and the opportunity to move up the organizational ladder in the local syndicate.

Illegal games are alluring to some people because they titillate noncomformists and thrill seekers who prefer the illegal route to sudden riches through the forbidden wager. But this can take on more ominous features, as when attempts are made to subvert legal games. One of the most notorious examples of this occurred in Pennsylvania on the night of 24 April 1980, when the master of ceremonies of the nightly televised lottery draw and the district manager of the lottery injected water into ping pong balls, save those numbered four and six, used to select the winning number. The winning number, 666, netted them and their accomplices $3.5 million, but officials, tipped by a suspicious bookmaker, investigated. Four of the conspirators later testified for the prosecution. The master of ceremonies received a 61-year sentence and the district manager 33 years. Ironically, lottery sales in Pennsylvania have continued to be brisk and may reach $1 billion annually by the mid-1980s.

Arizona's first lottery director was forced to resign after six months on the job because he was accused of favoritism in awarding lottery service contracts, and in the spring of 1983 the chairman of the New Jersey State

Lottery Commission stepped down after allegations were made of conflict of interest with vendors and the lottery's advertising agency.

Then there is the case of New York's ill-fated lottery, which folded in 1975 when it was divulged that less than half of the 42 draws produced winners because unsold tickets were eligible for prizes. The public was outraged and the entire administrative structure of the organization was replaced; yet this was a routine procedure in many states and in Canada at the time.

Actually, instances of fraud or collusion and other wrongdoing on the part of officials and agents among the lotteries have been relatively rare. This is laudable, since large sums of money are involved. But law enforcement agencies and lottery administrations must be vigilant to defend against attempts to subvert the games. Subversion takes many forms. For example, there have been attempts to sell counterfeit tickets, and individuals have tried to capture prizes by presenting forged replicas of winning tickets. A $5 million winner in the New York lottery recently told me about such a scheme that almost cheated him out of his prize.

GAMBLING AS RECREATION: A MORAL PARADOX

People have gambled from time immemorial, and a majority of our population not only believes many forms of gambling should be legalized, but participates in a wide variety of such activities. But not all laws or practices of government are popular, just as rules and regulations of parents may not meet with the enthusiastic support of their children. Certainly, state governments must devise methods for meeting their financial obligations, but one wonders how zealously they should promote gambling as a method for alleviating their economic problems.

Economist Frederick Stocker[25] observed that there is no other form of consumption that receives as much official state encouragement as legalized gambling. And while disclaimers such as New York's off-track betting slogan, Bet with Your Head, Not over It, may be aimed at infusing some rationality into the public's decision to wager, such attempts are few and rather faint. By legalizing more types of gambling and making it easier for people to engage in such activities, states may be creating a moral dilemma: a choice between their responsibility to provide for the general welfare of citizens on the one hand, and encouraging people to participate in activities that may be pathological on the other.

From Pennsylvania we hear that a young couple quit their jobs, sold their possessions, and invested their money in lottery tickets. For four months they purchased tickets in a losing attempt to beat the lottery. After spending $14,100 and losing $6,000 in wages to win $15,000 they decided to channel their energies into more constructive pursuits.[26] In Delaware a middle-aged housewife spent thousands in a vain effort to win the lottery; a similar story has emerged from Toronto, where a bank teller embezzled over $80,000, which she squandered on lottery tickets in an unsuccessful bid to capture a million-dollar prize.

While such accounts are rare, they are increasing and being encouraged by the relentless pitch of lotteries as the path to paradise. Gerry Fulcher, the head of the Delaware Council on Compulsive Gambling, recently reported the results of a study that alleged that the state was concentrating lottery ticket vending machines in poor areas of cities and was releasing hard-sell advertising on the dates welfare checks were being issued.[27]

Already some individual lottery prizes have surpassed $10 million, and a succession of new games and formats have been introduced to increase their excitement level and lure larger numbers of bettors. The national commission on gambling found that the public rated the excitement level of lotteries at the bottom of a list of gambling activities. To stim-

ulate interest, drawings are televised, and celebrities often participate. These shows frequently outdraw the competition and some
are broadcast nightly.[28]

Research for the national commission on
gambling indicates that availability of and
proximity to gambling activities leads to
greater participation. Nevada has the highest
proportion of bettors of any state, as well as
the greatest proportion of compulsive gamblers. While there might be some self-selec-
tive bias at work that attracts gamblers to Nevada, a similar phenomenon is now occurring
in and around Atlantic City, New Jersey.

Since the legalization of casinos in Atlantic City, the number of people seeking help
for compulsive gambling from local agencies
has dramatically increased. There has also
been a significant increase in the number of
people seeking treatment for compulsive
gambling at the Johns Hopkins Center for
Pathological Gambling, and some of these clients have also been abusing lotteries.[29]

It is widely believed among experts on
compulsive gambling that availability and
proximity to gambling are conducive to
abuse. This further complicates the state's position as a promoter of such activities. Lotteries generally do not possess the inherent
qualities of fast-paced action, risk, strategy,
and excitement that are characteristics of activities conducive to compulsive gambling.
The newer versions, however, are beginning
to incorporate some of these elements. There
are, for example, daily games that allow bettors to pick their own numbers, and instant
win cards in the form of baseball or other
games, such as slot machine combinations.

In their attempt to solve one kind of problem by introducing legalized gambling, legislatures may be creating a more insidious one.
It has been conservatively estimated that
there are more than 1 million compulsive
gamblers in the United States, and their numbers are increasing. Researchers at the Center
for Pathological Gambling at Johns Hopkins
University have estimated that the social and

economic costs of compulsive gambling run
over $34 billion annually.[30]

LOTTERIES AND SOCIAL CONTROL

Lotteries hold out the tantalizing promise of
instant riches to the public, and various promotions promise a lifetime of security and lei-
sure. In studies of million-dollar lottery winners in the United States and Canada[31] nearly
three-fourths quit their jobs—most within
two years after winning.[32] It is ironic that
states promote a no-work ethic on the one
hand while encouraging and even compelling
less fortunate people to work, on the other.

As lotteries and other forms of legalized
gambling become more widespread, a number of big winners may opt out of the labor
force, but more important, enormous numbers of citizens may be placing their aspira-
tions for better lives on the ephemeral possibility of winning. This illusory dream can also
be used as a method of social control—to placate people by diverting attention from their
misfortunes and meaningless lives. The social
control aspect of lotteries and legalized gambling assumes greater significance as they
proliferate. Even if politicians do not consciously utilize the diversionary potential of
gambling, an insidious volitional component
remains, raising the specter of a populace becoming a willing accomplice in its own undo-
ing. Our gullibility and propensity to be manipulated by such diversions is illustrated by
the behavior of lottery winners we studied,
who, despite their new-found wealth and
some negative experiences, almost universally continued purchasing tickets.

The social philosopher Herbert Marcuse
contended that advanced industrial societies
like the United States are characterized by
democratic unfreedom.[33] This seeming contradiction in terms becomes comprehensible
when applied to the social control quality of
legalized gambling, which allows people to

engage in previously forbidden activities for a price. States not only decriminalize gambling behavior, but they profit from it while gaining compliance to the existing social order from aspiring winners who docilely accept oppression, racism, exploitation, and injustice for the sake of that illusory win.

While this discussion may seem overly moralistic, and perhaps even outdated given the rapid social change that has characterized our attitudes toward legalized gambling in the last two decades, these issues deserve to be discussed. Gambling has been with us throughout history and no amount of legislation will eradicate it. But it has been our contention that the state has the responsibility to protect its citizens from the more negative impacts of gambling and their consequences and to pursue those courses of action that may permit gambling in a rational manner as well as providing resources for potential abusers. More important, it is the duty of the state to ameliorate social problems toward the end of promoting the public health and welfare and enhancing the quality of life of its citizens.

Certainly we cannot hold lottery officials and their agents responsible for the success of the games; it is their job. But just as certainly it is the job of our legislators to address forthrightly the critical issues confronting our society today. Lotteries and other forms of legalized gambling obfuscate these issues by impeding progress toward their amelioration. If they are used as escape mechanisms and painless methods of revenue generation, they will have a negative influence on society. They appear as red herrings in a sea populated by a plethora of political jellyfish without the back-bone to confront the unpopular but necessary issues of tax reform, fiscal responsibility, and long-range planning—the only ways sufficient funds can be generated to cope with the monumental problems of crime, energy, poverty, health, education, pollution, housing, and welfare.

As we have seen, lotteries are incapable of making significant contributions to states'

budgets. They are stopgap measures that lull the populace into a state of complacency while social and fiscal problems intensify. More people are joining welfare rolls, the ranks of the unemployed have swollen, health care has priced itself out of the free marketplace, housing is beyond the reach of most young couples, crime is rampant in cities and suburbs with people living in a state of siege, no energy policy exists by which we can rationally allocate our existing supplies of fossil fuels and develop clean and inexpensive substitutes, and education is severely affected because funds are being slashed by taxpayers to whom their leaders have not spoken candidly about the seriousness of the problems that confront them. Meanwhile, the public keeps buying tickets. Will lotteries and legalized gambling become the bread and circuses of a civilization tottering on the brink of social and economic disaster?

NOTES

1. The following history of lotteries in the United States is drawn from John Samuel Ezell, *Fortune's Merry Wheel: The Lottery in America* (Cambridge, MA: Harvard University Press, 1960).
2. Ibid., p. 95.
3. Ibid., pp. 99–100.
4. Ibid., p. 301.
5. New York, New Jersey, Massachusetts, Pennsylvania, Connecticut, Rhode Island, Maine, New Hampshire, Vermont, Ohio, Maryland, Delaware, Michigan, Illinois, Washington, Colorado, Arizona. The District of Columbia also has a lottery, as do Puerto Rico and the Virgin Islands.
6. Michael P. Davis, "The 'Lotterizing' of America," *Gaming Business Magazine* 4(5):6–10, 55 (May 1983).
7. U.S., Bureau of the Census, *Statistical Abstracts of the United States: 1984* (Washington, DC: Government Printing Office, 1984), p. 290. Data do not include Colorado, Washington, or the District of Columbia.
8. Daniel B. Suits, "Gambling as a Source of Revenue," in *Michigan's Fiscal and Economic Structure*, ed. Harvey E. Brazer and Deborah S. Laren

(Ann Arbor: University of Michigan Press, 1982), p. 832.

9. "Annual Report" (Trenton: New Jersey State Lottery, 1982).

10. U.S., Bureau of the Census, *Statistical Abstracts of the United States 1982–1983* (Washington, DC: Government Printing Office, 1983), p. 155.

11. Daniel B. Suits, "Gambling Taxes: Regressivity and Revenue Potential," *National Tax Journal*, 30(1):33 (Mar. 1977).

12. David Weinstein and Lillian Deitch, *The Impact of Legalized Gambling: The Socioeconomic Consequences of Lotteries and Off-Track Betting* (New York: Praeger, 1974), p. 74.

13. *Statistical Abstracts of the United States 1982–1983*, p. 155.

14. Eric Nalder and Larry Lange, "Lottery Mania Spreading West to Fill State Coffers," *Seattle Post-Intelligencer*, 2 Aug. 1982.

15. Address to the Third National Conference on Gambling, Las Vegas, NV, 19 Dec. 1976.

16. Commission on the Review of the National Policy toward Gambling, *Gambling in America* (Washington, DC: Government Printing Office, 1976).

17. Suits, "Gambling as a Source of Revenue," p. 833.

18. Ibid., pp. 833–34.

19. *New York Times*, 6 Jan. 1980.

20. Roger E. Brinner and Charles T. Clotfelter, "An Economic Appraisal of State Lotteries," *National Tax Journal* 28(4):402 (Dec. 1975).

21. Michael H. Spiro, "On the Tax Incidence of the Pennsylvania Lottery," *National Tax Journal*, 27(1):59 (Mar. 1974).

22. Charles T. Clotfelter, "On the Regressivity of State-Operated 'Numbers' Games," *National Tax Journal*, 32(4):546–47 (Mar. 1979).

23. H. Roy Kaplan, *Lottery Winners: How They Won and How Winning Changed Their Lives* (New York: Harper, & Row, 1978), pp. 134–53.

24. Ivan Light, "Numbers Gambling among Blacks: A Financial Institution," *American Sociological Review*, 42:892–904 (Dec. 1977).

25. Frederick D. Stocker, "State Sponsored Gambling as a Source of Public Revenue," *National Tax Journal*, 25(3):439–40 (Sept. 1972).

26. Kaplan, *Lottery Winners*, p. 12.

27. Personal communication with Gerry Fulcher; Ralph Batch, the director of the Delaware lottery, disputed these findings in a telephone interview.

28. See H. Roy Kaplan, "Sports, Gambling, and Television: The Emerging Alliance," *Arena Review*, 7(1):1–11 (Feb. 1983) for a discussion of the role of television in popularizing another form of gambling—sports betting.

29. Personal communication with Dr. Robert Politzer, director of the Johns Hopkins Center for Pathological Gambling.

30. Robert Politzer, James S. Morrow, and Sandra B. Leavey, "Report on the Societal Cost of Pathological Gambling and the Cost-Benefit/Effectiveness of Treatment" in *The Gambling Papers: Proceedings of the Fifth National Conference on Gambling and Risk Taking* (Reno: Bureau of Business and Economic Research, University of Nevada, 1982), vol. 3.

31. Kaplan, *Lottery Winners*, pp. 68–115; and H. Roy Kaplan, "Survey of Lottery Winners" (Final report to Loto Canada, 12 Feb. 1979).

32. The New Jersey income maintenance study and labor force projections further support these data, indicating a decreased commitment to work when economic alternatives to it are available. See Irwin Garfinkel, "Income Transfer Programs and Work Effort: A Review," in *How Income Supplements Can Affect Work Behavior* (Washington, DC: Government Printing Office, 1974).

33. Herbert Marcuse, *One Dimensional Man* (Boston: Beacon Press, 1964).

38

The User Fee Game

PHILIP ROSENBERG

User fees and charges pose unique concerns regarding the financing of service delivery. While there are a number of advantages for establishing a system of fees and charges, the public is clearly concerned with how much it will have to pay. In formulating user fee financing strategies, public officials must be prepared to deal with how service costs will be distributed among the various users, present and future.

Community investments support a diverse array of facilities, services and programs. Some facilities, such as recreational services, are used voluntarily, while other services benefit the general public, regardless of the needs or requirements of the individual. While certain facilities provide benefits in direct proportion to consumption, other services prove administratively difficult to measure on a usage basis.

In establishing pricing strategies, local officials should consider whether there needs to be a charge for those services that provide benefits to the entire population of the community or should the services be financed through general revenues.

Once a decision is made to establish a fee, what is the basis for the amount charged? Should the fee established recover a portion or the full cost of capital development? Should the fee cover only operating, maintenance and service delivery costs? Should everyone pay the same amount? Can the user and non-user be identified? Should persons of varying incomes pay the same amount? Should pricing include the marginal cost of capital development to meet the needs of particular users? Indeed, there are many questions to be answered, especially regarding the following pricing considerations:

Cost-oriented—Prices are generated to recover costs or revenues in excess of cost.

Competition-oriented—Prices are influenced in part by what the user would have to pay to obtain that service from an alternative available source.

Demand-oriented—Prices vary in relation to the number of persons who want the service in particular ways, during particular times, at particular locations.

Convenience-oriented—Prices vary to reflect the value of the convenience of the service or the manner in which the service is paid.

Society-oriented—Prices are adjusted to reflect societal objectives (lower prices for the poor, higher prices to discourage certain types of activities such as over-consumption of limited resources).

In selecting the appropriate strategy, the single major issue associated with fees and charges is related to the equity of pricing public goods and services. Although some officials may argue that fees are inherently equitable because the user pays for the goods and services consumed while the non-user does

Reprinted from *American City & County*, Vol.100, No.6 (June 1985) pp. 61–62. © 1985 by Communication Channels Inc., Atlanta, GA, USA.

not subsidize the capital cost provision, there are two dimensions to the establishment of a fee structure that is fair and equitable:

pricing to reflect the cost of serving the individual user; and

pricing to reflect the individual user's ability to pay.

Local government services are not provided to the public without cost. Yet, the equitable distribution of the cost is typically demanded by the public, since the portion of service costs not supported by fees represents a public subsidy.

If public officials could accurately apportion costs to the user, then everyone would pay their fair share. This would require the application of marginal pricing techniques wherein the user pays the precise portion of necessary costs. Marginal pricing is based on such variables as capital capacity and demand.

Strict adherence to marginal cost pricing could mean that full costs are not recovered. For example, one additional homeowner linked to a wastewater treatment facility that is operating under capacity adds very little to the operational and development costs of the facility. Because of these complexities, local officials either opt for a flat rate fee structure or a modified version of marginal pricing.

The degree of benefit an individual receives from a capital asset will also be variable, and the pricing strategy selected may reflect approximations of the benefits actually received. For example, capital improvements in a commercial development district may give a greater benefit for owners of developed land than owners of vacant land. In these cases, a certain degree of unfairness is inevitable and public officials must strive to select the pricing mechanism that offers the least net penalty.

HORIZONTAL EQUITY

One approach to establishing an equitable fee is to apply an identical charge across the en-

tire user population—horizontal equity. By creating a fee structure that promotes horizontal equity, local officials seek to collect a uniform amount that spreads program costs evenly among all users. In some cases, this approach is both rational and appropriate where those who make equal use of services pay equal amounts and where there is constant service demand throughout the year.

However, horizontal equity may not properly distribute the real cost to all users. A flat rate sewer charge means that those residents at some distance from the sewage treatment plant pay the same amount as those residents near the plant. The flat rate sewer charge may look fair (everyone receives service, everyone pays for it), but does not reflect the true capital cost per user since the community expends more dollars to provide the service as development spreads to new areas. Because infrastructure design must meet the potential demands of most peak load situations, a flat rate will not reflect the incremental or marginal capital cost associated with expanded capacity. Individuals using the facility in off-peak hours will, in essence, be subsidizing individuals who use the facility during peak load situations.

User fees have often been cited as a form of regressive taxation because lower income families and individuals pay a disproportionate share of their income for public goods and services. Instituting a fee to cover capital and operating costs may exclude the poor from benefitting from services that had previously been provided free of charge.

Additionally, some officials argue that fees are a more equitable pricing mechanism than the property tax. This argument suggests that low income persons, through the property tax or indirectly through rent, pay for services they may or may not use. In his book *Rebuilding America: Financing Public Works in the 1980s,* Roger J. Vaughn makes the case that low income households represent a disproportionate share of mass transit and public school users. Conversely, the poor use less than their population share of water, sanitation, library and museum services. Because fees offer the flexibility to select those public goods and services one wishes to consume, the poor will have an increased opportunity to pay for only those services they actually use.

In spite of these arguments, public officials have instituted differential pricing mechanisms that are designed to meet the needs of the low income, the elderly and the youth of their community. Vertical equity refers to the distribution of cost among users based on differing levels of income (ability-to-pay) or differing consumption levels. Senior citizen or youth fares for public transportation are not uncommon.

The decision to give preference to these groups in pricing may also be influenced by administrative simplicity. Pricing water on the basis of one's ability to pay may cause administrative nightmares. In these situations, it has been suggested that the poor be provided with some form of direct subsidy to pay for these services.

Local governments compete with each other to attract or retain business and industry. When establishing a fee structure, care must be taken to consider the fees imposed by neighboring jurisdictions and communities of similar size and service delivery. Do they charge a user fee? How much do they charge? What are the bases for the fee? If fees are too high and too numerous in comparison with comparable communities in the surrounding area, the community's competitive position can be adversely affected.

IDENTIFYING FEE SERVICES

Beyond the public policy and equity issues associated with the establishment of user fees, there are some questions that must be answered before a fee is determined. What services should be financed by fees? Who will pay? How much will they pay?

Generally, the use of fees to finance specific types of services will be influenced by the local government's legal capacity to levy a charge, the availability of alternative revenue sources, the social and political climate of the jurisdiction and the public's willingness to pay.

Service can be provided as a continuum with pure community-wide facilities (public schools, police protection) at one end and pure private-type facilities (public utilities) at the other end. Within the two extremes fall a number of services that have both public and private qualities. As the service provision moves across the continuum from public to private, the funding composition shifts from general revenue financing to fee-based financing. Those capital items falling in the middle may be financed, depending on public policy, by a combination of each revenue source.

Another important consideration is the ability to distinguish those who pay for service provision from the non-payer. There are a number of services for which it is relatively easy to identify and charge the consumer for service use.

Conversely, a betterment charge for the installation of street lighting may benefit not only residents of the street but those who travel through the area. If the non-payer cannot be excluded from the benefits of a fee-based service, there will be a number of negative results. First, those who pay for service will voice considerable protest to what they may consider to be an unfair charge. Second, no one will pay for the service if they can receive the benefits without cost. Third, those receiving service provision without cost may "overconsume."

DETERMINING PRICE

Ideally, no activity should have a singular basis for determining its price. The development of a fee structure has three essential elements:

Quantity—charge on the amount consumed;

Capacity—charge on the full cost of producing; and

Location—charge related to density and location.

A fee may be designed to incorporate components of each of these three elements. For example, water supply may incorporate zone (location), peakload (capacity) and the amount consumed (quantity).

Essential to establishing the fee is the availability of accurate cost information. The establishment of a rate that is built upon faulty cost information creates a multitude of problems.

The total cost of any activity is derived from two elements: direct costs and indirect costs. Direct costs can be readily attributable to the provision of a specific good or delivery of a particular service. Direct costs include labor and contracted services, materials and supplies. Indirect costs are not readily attributable to a service, yet the costs support service provision. Typically, indirect costs include data processing, finance, personnel, utility costs and other costs that cannot be related to a specific service or activity.

The fee selected will be influenced by a community's pricing objectives. If the principal aim of establishing a fee is to guarantee, where possible, full cost recovery, local officials need to examine the capability of the fee to generate revenue equal to the capital and operating cost of service. If the purpose of pricing is to control demand and lessen waste and over-consumption, the fee should reflect this concern. If there are significant capital, time or material cost differences, these factors likewise need to be considered in the pricing strategy.

Administrative capacity to establish, collect and monitor various types of fees should also influence the fee selection decision. The desire for administrative simplicity and the high costs associated with monitoring certain variable pricing structures may lead to the establishment of less precise pricing mechanisms. Where this is the case, a community may use such variables as land area, front footage or land value as proxies for more accurate indicators of individual use.

39

The Two Different Concepts of Privatization

TED KOLDERIE

Privatization is currently a hot topic, much in discussion and highly controversial.

Professional journals and business magazines have been filled with articles about it. Whole books have been written about the idea—some boosting it, such as E.S. Savas' *Privatizing the Public Sector* or Stuart Butler's *Privatizing Federal Spending;* some condemning it, such as *Passing the Bucks* by the American Federation of State, County and Municipal

---

Public Administration Review, Vol.46, No.4 (July–August 1986), pp. 285–291. Reprinted with permission from *Public Administration Review*. © 1986 by The American Society for Public Administration, 1120 G Street, NW, Suite 500, Washington, D.C. All rights reserved.

Employees. Centers are being formed to study or to promote the cause. Privatization now threatens to displace "partnerships" as the number one topic where people gather to talk about the contributions which business can make to the solution of problems which beset government.

Privatization is a live issue on the agendas of state, county, and city governments. It is becoming an issue in political campaigns. During the past year some particularly unusual and controversial proposals—especially, involving prisons—have brought privatization more to the attention of the media and of the general public. It is closely covered now, for example, by the *New York Times* and has become a favorite target for newspaper and magazine columnists, who tend to treat proposals for privatization as assertions that the market can replace government.

The discussion, the reporting, and the comment would be more helpful if there were some clarity about what the term *privatization* means. Much of the discussion is quite unclear—largely because two quite different ideas are being expressed by the use of the same word, and very different interests with very different implications for public policy are represented by those different ideas.

This article is an effort to sort out those two conflicting definitions of privatization.

WHAT ARE WE TALKING ABOUT PRIVATIZING?

Typically in a discussion about privatization it will be said that the Postal Service, or transit, or the fire service, or some other service should be "turned over to" the private sector. No useful discussion is possible in these terms. What does "turned over" mean? What precisely would be "turned over"?

Government performs two quite separate activities. It is essential to be clear which activity would be dropped under privatization. Is it the policy decision to *provide* a service? Or is

it the administrative action to *produce* a service? Is government to withdraw from its role as a buyer? Or from its role as a seller?

We cannot talk simply about a public sector and a private sector. Only a *four*-part concept of the sectors—combining providing and producing, government and non-government—will let us have a useful discussion about the roles of public and private and about the strategy of the privatization.

An example will help. Let's take the service called security. There are two pure cases and two mixed cases.

Case 1: Government does both—The legislature writes the law and provides the money; the Department of Corrections runs the prison. Neither function is private.

Case 2: Production is private—The City of Bloomington decides to provide security when the high school hockey teams play at the city arena, and it contracts with Pinkertons for the guards.

Case 3: Provision is private—Government sells to a market of private buyers. The North Stars hockey team wants security at Metropolitan Sports Center, and it contracts with the Bloomington city police.

Case 4: Both activities are private—A department store decides that it wants uniformed security and employs (or contracts privately for) its own guards. Government performs neither activity.

Case 1 is the pure-case public sector. The policy decision is governmental. A public bureau, at the same or at a different level, produces the service.

Case 2 is immediately recognizable as the—still controversial—system of contracting.

Case 3 is less familiar, although examples of government agencies selling to private buyers are in fact fairly common.

Case 4 is, again, well understood as the pure case of private agencies selling to private buyers.

The vocabulary *can* be confusing. Nothing is as troublesome as the ambiguous use of the word "providing." Some people talk in one breath about society providing medical care for the elderly and in the next describe doctors as the providers. Avoid such confusion: That way madness lies.

One distinct activity of government is to *provide* for its people. In other words: policy making, deciding, buying, requiring, regulating, franchising, financing, subsidizing.

A second and distinctly separate activity of government may be to *produce* the services it decides should be provided. In other words: operating, delivering, running, doing, selling, administering.

Each activity can be broken down into several parts; each of which might be privatized separately.

The *production* of a service is the less complicated of the two. It can be divided, for example, into the line service and into the support service; into the labor and into the equipment and facilities; into the work itself and into the management of the work. Any of these can, in turn, be divided into parts; the way a city might divide its refuse collection among several haulers or the management of its pension funds among several banks.

The *provision* of a service is more complicated. A service is publicly or socially provided (a) where the decision whether to have it (and the decisions about who shall have it and how much of it) is a political decision, (b) when government arranges for the recipients not to have to pay directly for the service themselves, and (c) when the government selects the producer that will serve them.

The service is privately provided (a) where individuals and nongovernmental organizations make their own decisions whether or not to have it, (b) where, if they choose to have it, they pay for it in full out of their own resources, whatever these may be, and (c) where they select the producer themselves.

Clearly there can be mixed cases. Government may make a service available but let citizens decide whether to use it; or the financing may be shared between public and private, with users paying a part and government paying a part of the cost; or some individuals may be asked to pay the cost in full **themselves while government pays the full cost for others; or government may pay the cost but allow the user to select the vendor, and so forth.**

Services provided publicly may be financed through taxes, as schools are. But government also uses nontax devices. One of these is regulation: Government provides us with clean restaurants by requiring their owners to clean them at their own expense. Franchising is another: Government provides to all parts of a city a uniform level of service by creating a monopoly that permits a utility to average its prices, overcharging some residents so as to subsidize others.

With this distinction clear, we can now look separately at what it means to privatize both provision and production.

PRIVATIZING PRODUCTION

Let's begin with the simpler activity of service production. Here privatization means simply that a governmental agency that had been producing a service is converted into, or is replaced by, a nongovernmental organization. This can occur either where the agency is selling to private buyers or where it is selling to government.

The British Example

In Britain privatization means transferring to private parties the ownership of a state industry that had been producing very largely for private buyers.

Over the years a number of private industries had been socialized by successive Labor governments, becoming British Steel, the Coal Board, British Gas, British Air, British Telecom, etc. These state industries served each other and the government, of course, but did business very largely with private firms and private households.

These are now being sold; sometimes to other firms, sometimes (through a stock issue) directly to individuals, sometimes to the workers. This "selling off the family silver" has been both popular (especially the sale of public housing units to their occupants, which has transformed tenants into owners) and profitable for the government.

As state industries, these enterprises had been under pressure to hold down their prices. Thus, year by year, deficits arose which the government had to cover. Year by year, the effort to limit the subsidy, as a way to force these industries to reduce their costs, had failed. So the Thatcher government decided to privatize these service producers. As private organizations, these industries will have to earn their revenues and will be forced to control costs and improve services in ways that, as public organizations, they were not.

The American Application

A few proposals for the sale of government enterprises have appeared here. Conrail is to be sold. President Reagan has proposed the sale of others, including power distribution facilities and selected petroleum reserves. But in this country (though called public utilities) the major energy, transportation, and communications systems (except for the Postal Service, TVA, and such distribution systems as Bonneville Power) have been in private ownership. The scope for the kind of privatization under way in the United Kingdom—transforming government-owned sellers of private services back into privately-owned sellers of private services—is limited in this country.

Here privatization has come to mean mainly the government turning more to private producers for services for which government remains responsible and which

government continues to finance. It has become simply a new name for contracting.

Contracting itself is not new in American government. It is traditional in public works at all levels, and it has been common in the rapid growth of human services since the 1960s. What is new is the proposal now to expand the practice and to apply it to service areas in which it had not previously been considered. There are proposals, for example, that a county board might privatize its hospital by turning over the management (or ownership) to, say, Hospital Corporation of America; or that a city might retain a private firm to finance and to operate, as well as to design and to build, a new waste-water-treatment plant; or that Tennessee might bring in the Corrections Corporation of America to run its state prisons.

These facilities and services would be turned over to private organizations in the sense that private organizations would run them (that is, become responsible for service production). But the responsibility for provision, the policy side, would remain governmental.

ISSUES IN PRIVATIZING PRODUCTION

The debate about this idea of privatizing production is now fully under way. While it has its ideological side, most of it is intensely practical. It is very much a clash between competing producers, both of which want the government's business.

The organizations of government employees, which would like to hold on to the business, say privatization will mean poorer service at higher cost. The American Federation of State, County and Municipal Employees has been running ads in the magazines read by city public-works directors, warning about the dangers of contracting, and has mailed copies of *Passing the Bucks* to 5,000 government officials.

Private firms that would like to get into the business say that privatization (contracting) offers better service at lower costs. In 1985 a number of firms created the Privatization Council, with offices at 30 Rockefeller Plaza, New York. The council sponsors conferences and publishes a journal, the *Privatization Review,* to promote this concept of privatization.

The problem is complex, falling roughly into six parts.

The Question of Competition

What actually happens as a result of a shift to contracting depends largely on whether the change is only the substitution of a monopoly private supplier for a monopoly public bureau or involves also the introduction of competition among producers.

If the change is simply from one monopoly supplier to another, then neither cost nor performance is likely to change very much. The government as buyer is still caught with a sole source arrangement. Some of the privatization in Britain has been of this sort. British Telecom has been sold to private owners, for example, but other communications companies have not been allowed to enter the market freely to compete with it. It is privatization without competition.

An argument can always be heard for this. Private and public organizations alike are quick to tell you how much better they could serve you if only they did not have to compete for your custom. But an effort at privatization should try to make the producers competitive. (Efforts are needed periodically to make even *private* industries competitive. The deregulation of railroads, aviation, over-the-road trucking, banking, health care, and telecommunications in the 1970s and 1980s was such an effort.)

The Question of "Creaming"

A common charge against privatization is that it will result in service going only to the easy and profitable customers, while the difficult and unprofitable customers are neglected.

This reflects a failure to distinguish between providing and producing. Creaming is a problem when producers sell to private buyers. It should not be a problem where government is the buyer. Government can get the service it wants to pay for. It will have to pay for what it wants. But if government wants rockets to the moon, it can get rockets to the moon. If it wants daily mail delivery to Lost Butte, Montana, it can get daily mail delivery to Lost Butte, Montana.

Government *will* have to be a smart buyer. Creaming, like corruption, *can* occur if the government is careless. Private contractors and public bureaus alike may tend to avoid the difficult work required in the poorer neighborhoods of a city. The government must be careful to specify the work it wants done, and it must inspect the work to make sure it gets what it wants.

The Question of Corruption

When a government buys from private producers, efforts must be made continually to detect and suppress anti-competitive behavior and the use of public office for private profit. The same is true when the producers are public.

We tend not to talk about corruption in the relationship between elected officials and their bureau. But this is also a noncompetitive arrangement, with the potential for problems (if, for example, wage increases are exchanged for contributions at campaign time). One good way to protect the public interest is to separate the governmental provider from its producers—public bureau or private contractor—through free-choice-of-vendor or voucher arrangements.

The Question of Cost

Where competition is introduced, costs are normally expected to fall. Thus, privatization of the producer side should be appealing not only to business firms eager for a chance to sell to the government but also to managers frustrated by a costly and unresponsive public bureau and to citizens eager to see service made more effective without an increase in their taxes. And probably competition does reduce costs per unit.

As the discussion goes along, however, concern is arising about a cost-*increasing* effect of contracting. This comes through strongly in the book, *Privatizing Federal Spending* by Stuart Butler, head of domestic policy studies at the Heritage Foundation in Washington. He argues that contracting expands "the spending coalition" that drives up the federal budget.

> *Moving the supply (producer) function out of government may replace a muted bureaucratic pressure for bigger programs with a well-financed, private-sector campaign. This significant drawback means that contracting should be viewed with caution as a means of privatization. Contracting can lead to more efficient government, but it does not guarantee smaller government.*

How you view contracting depends on what you are trying to do. If you think programs ought *not* to be expanded, you will probably want to resist its use. If you favor larger public programs, you may find it highly strategic to expand the use of this form of privatization.

A good example of this just now is in the field of corrections. One group wants to put more people behind bars and is advocating contracts with private firms to build and operate state prisons. Another thinks the industry of locking up people (especially kids) has already grown too large and wants to block contracting. The two groups disagree—except in their belief that contracting would mean more jails.

The Question of Control

Opponents of contracting argue that a government has better control when it *owns* its operations; that is, when the workers are permanent employees. Proponents argue that control is better when operations are handled by contract, because on contract—since an affirmative decision is required periodically to continue the relationship—the producer is always at risk.

The Question of Community

The term privatization—even if only of service production—suggests to some people that the public purpose of a program is somehow lost. Proposals are quickly drawn into an ideological debate—attacked as further eroding the sense of community in contemporary society and for intensifying the individualistic ethic of our time.

Here again the error lies in confusing production with provision. So far we have been talking only about a privatization of the *producer* role. The sense of community is not lost in this kind of privatization—unless the public character of a service depends on its being delivered by a specifically governmental producer. In some service areas and for some people, it may. This is clearly a reason for the resistance to contracting of prison services. Also, to most people, public education means a school run by government.

On the other hand, no strong feeling exists today that the public character of the program is lost if people needing medical care do not go to the county hospital or if people needing housing are not required to live in the project owned by the local housing authority.

When we're talking simply about nongovernmental *producers*, the social commitment to a program is generally maintained and, as we have seen, may even be enlarged. Hence, this kind of privatization does not put community seriously at risk.

The danger to community comes from

the other major concept of privatization, to which we now turn.

PRIVATIZING THE PROVISION OF SERVICE

It is quite possible, of course, to privatize the public role in the provision of benefits and services. Government would simply withdraw from (or reduce) its role as buyer, regulator, standard setter, or decision maker. People (or certain people for certain services thus privatized) would then be on their own to decide whether or not to have a service and to pay for it should they decide they want it.

Since the essence of government lies in this first function, of deciding what it will provide—what it will require and buy and make available; where and when and to whom and to what standard—*this* is the real (as Butler says, complete) privatization.

For those who care about government maintaining a strong policy role, health care is not privatized when the county board contracts the management of the public hospital to a private firm, when it sells the hospital to a private firm, or even when it closes the hospital and buys care from the other hospitals in the community. The responsibility to provide is truly privatized when the county board says it will no longer pay for the care of the medically indigent.

The Methods for Privatizing Provision

Government can withdraw from the provision of service in a variety of ways.

First, it can withdraw from the production of a service and not at the same time redesign that program into a purchase-of-service arrangement. This is load shedding, in the vocabulary of alternative service delivery. A city that simply stopped plowing snow out of alleys or stopped inspecting restaurants would be privatizing production and provision simultaneously.

Sometimes this occurs. Sometimes it does not. When government reduced its role in the production of housing (i.e., stopped building more housing projects), it redesigned public housing into a program in which it pays the rent for low-income families in privately owned houses and apartments.

Second, government can reduce or withdraw from its role as provider by introducing fees and charges for a service it continues to produce. In many cases the financing responsibility will still be shared between taxpayers and users. But the proportion paid by users will rise. It is a kind of creeping privatization.

Charges can be introduced at a flat rate for all, regardless of ability to pay. Or they can be introduced for some people and not for others, or set at a higher rate for some than for others. Discount transit fares for the elderly, sliding fee scales for day care, and checks to some people for winter heating bills (while other people pay full rate) come quickly to mind.

A similar privatization occurs as tax liability is extended to cover the cash payments received and the cash value of services received under benefit and entitlement programs. Above a certain income level, for example, social security payments are now taxable, and Colorado's Governor Richard Lamm has suggested this as a general policy where the pressure to offer services and benefits universally in the first instance cannot be resisted.

The Reasons for Privatizing Provision

Who would want to do anything so cold-hearted?

Actually, two very different interests, both deeply concerned about equity and about community, are coming together to reduce or limit the role of government as provider in America and in other western countries.

The first of the two efforts to limit the scope of government rises mainly from social and political concerns. In recent years some representatives of the poor and disadvantaged have increasingly resisted government housing, health care, and other social-welfare programs. For them effects are what count; not intentions. For the people they represent, programs have too often operated mainly to enlarge the income, status, and power of the industry of bureaucratic and professional service producers, whether governmental or private.

These advocates resist the idea that we find our community through politics and resist the extension of law and regulation that steadily deprives nongovernmental and nonprofessional institutions of the right to care for themselves and for each other in ways that private communities always have. Their efforts to maintain these rights for individuals, families, and voluntary organizations form an important part of the support for privatization.

The second and more conspicuous of the forces arises from the effort to restrain public expenditure—to relate needs and wants to what the city, state, or nation can realistically afford to pay.

The combination of client advocates, the media, and the political process has worked powerfully to turn needs into rights, rights into entitlements, entitlements into programs, and programs into budgets. At the same time, the combination of international and interstate economic competition, taxpayer resistance, and the need to stimulate entrepreneurship and investment has worked powerfully to constrain the resources that come into the economy and the amount available for public service provision.

In almost every country, public services have come under pressure. Something has had to give. One response has been to reduce services across the board, making no distinctions among users. Another is to shift from a universalist to a selective approach in social policy—that is, from a policy that makes services available to everyone at no charge regardless of ability to pay to a policy that asks those who can afford to pay to do so and reserves the limited public resources for those who genuinely cannot.

The latter approach, privatization, enhances equity better than an across-the-board reduction in service levels. It also eases the concern about what could happen to democratic institutions in a society in which more than half of the people have their incomes politically determined.

The people who want to limit what government provides are not necessarily coldhearted. They are skeptical about public officials' tendency to justify programs in terms of intentions. They worry about government's ability to drive out its competitors with the offer of free services. They seek to reduce the proportion of decisions made in a political process which they see as incapable, realistically, of resisting the pressure for irresponsible decisions to pay for services with other people's resources and to increase the proportion of decisions made in a process where private parties make responsible decisions about the use of their own resources.

The clear requirements for the success of a social policy of this sort, however, are almost certainly the provision of an adequate income to the poor—through transfers or through work—and the maintenance of community standards to those whose service is being paid for socially. It is hard to see that the effort at privatization is yet adequately sensitive to the practical and ethical importance of this idea of social equity.

A REASONABLE PROGRAM FOR PRIVATIZATION

Privatization can serve a useful purpose. It also carries some dangers. The effort should be to secure the former while avoiding the latter.

A reasonable program would involve some privatization of service production combined with some privatization of service provision.

Implementation of such a strategy would focus mainly on (a) maintaining the right and enlarging the responsibility of people to provide for their needs privately, where they can and where they wish; and, where government *is* responsible, (b) enlarging the opportunity for elected officials and for citizens to secure those services from private producers as well as from public agencies if they wish.

First, in the area of service *provision,* such a program would involve:

Being selective. *Targeting eligibility* to those in need.

Continuing to use *fees and charges with income offsets* for people of low income.

Taxing benefits, where benefits are granted universally in the first instance. (All of the above will privatize financial responsibility and thus help restrain expenditure.)

Fixing—*appropriating—the revenues* for programs and managing the eligibility as demand for the service changes. Commonly, today, programs fix the eligibility so that with a rise in demand it is the appropriation that becomes the variable.

Introducing voucher systems or other user-side subsidies that privatize and thereby depoliticize the vendor-selection decision where the service is governmentally paid and even where it is governmentally produced. This will guard against the problems that can arise in contracting, where elected or appointed officials select the vendor. It will also indicate more clearly the sort of service people really want.

Second, in the area of service *production,* such a program would involve:

A policy to *avoid sole sourcing,* whether the supplier is governmental or private. This will ensure competition. A public-bureau arrangement is essentially a long-term, noncompetitive, sole-source contract. (Note that it is possible to have competition without privatization. A government can contract with other governments, and free-choice-of-vendor arrangements can be introduced where the choice is simply among public agencies. Governor Rudy Perpich's proposal in 1985 for open enrollment among public school districts in Minnesota is an example of the latter.)

An effort to *disaggregate the elements of a service.* Breaking up a service into pieces will enlarge the opportunity to use different kinds of suppliers. This will allow changes to occur more gradually and thus lower both the political pain and the risk involved in service redesign.

Divestiture. A public policy body that serves also as the board of directors for the public agency producing its service is caught in a dual role which can at times become a conflict of interest. Separating the roles of provider and producer can make it easier to privatize production. This will be useful even in a general-purpose government organization, freeing the elected board to concentrate on policy and on ways to reduce the cost and to increase the quality of service. It is especially needed in single-purpose agencies such as transit commissions and public school districts.

Capitation. Paying the producer a lump sum, up front, and allowing that organization to keep whatever it does not need to spend introduces an incentive for producers to innovate. Teachers, for example, say that if given this incentive they would move quickly toward peer-teaching, independent study, parent involvement, the use of community resources, differentiated staffing, and new learning technology.

Co-production. In voucher arrangements clients can do much of the work themselves. They need not be required to spend the money on professional service. This will encourage strategies of prevention and self-help that can be, at the same time, less costly for payers and more supportive for users.

In Conclusion

Such a program ought to be possible.

For the moment, however, both the private leadership and the political leadership are mired in the old ways of thinking. Both are bogged down by traditional concepts of government that are insufficiently sensitive to needs for economy and responsiveness and by concepts of a private role that are insufficiently sensitive to the need for equity.

A new concept, combining equity in the provision of services with competition in their production, has yet to be articulated politically.

REFERENCES

Much of the literature on privatization is in articles and papers. A particularly extensive and useful bibliography can be found at the end of the generally negative view of privatization, in the article by Paul Starr, "The Meaning of Privatization," in: *Project on the Federal Social Role, Working Paper 6* (Washington: The National Conference on Social Welfare, 1985). The Local Government Center, a project of the Reason Foundation (1018 Garden Street, Santa Barbara, CA) keeps track of examples of efforts at privatization.

In many respects the fullest, most politically sophisticated, and therefore most important treatment of the subject is in: Stuart Butler, *Privatizing Federal Spending, A Strategy to Eliminate the Deficit* (Washington: The Heritage Foundation, 1985). Another effort to clarify the meaning of privatization, following the distinctions made by Vincent and Elinor Ostrom, is: E.S. Savas, *Privatizing the Public Sector* (Chatham, NJ: Chatham House, 1982).

Two particularly sensible comments by persons long in and around government and public administration are: Alan K. Campbell, *Testimony Before the Texas Commission on Economy and Efficiency* (Austin, TX: January 23, 1986), and Dick Netzer, "Privatization," in *Setting Municipal Priorities* (New York: Columbia University Press, 1985).

A summary of the varying approaches to privatization, in Britain and in other countries, appeared in *The Economist*, (December 21, 1985), p. 71.

40

Perspective on "Privatization": In Defense of Bureaucracy

CHARLES T. GOODSELL

"Privatization"—providing public sector services through private sector contracts—has been portrayed as a cure for the ills of government, a panacea that will reduce high taxes, lower the deficit, cut waste in government, and replenish inadequate public services.

State Government News, Vol.29, No.6 (July 1986), pp. 20–21.

But privatization or "contracting out" will not solve all our public-sector problems, no more than did earlier remedies, such as program budgeting and performance evaluation.

If this is not soon realized, the hype that surrounds the issue of privatization can only lead to disappointment. The states' approach to contracting out should not be that of the gullible enthusiast, but that of the responsible official who asks, "How can this idea be applied in our particular setting in the public interest?"

A JOB WELL DONE

A good reason for not rushing into the privatization of all public services is that government is not doing a bad job now. Our culture, traditionally suspicious of governmental power and economically reliant upon private capital, too often assumes anything done by the public sector is unsatisfactory. Countless voices—politicians seeking to discredit administrations in power, idealogues wishing to rail against government interference in business or suppression of minorities, and professors anxious to appear intellectually clever by denouncing all existing institutions—denigrate "bureaucracy" at every turn.

But government frequently performs a creditable job in a myriad of functions. Indeed, a substantial case can be made for public bureaucracy. More than 90 percent of Social Security checks arrive on time and in the proper amount. Approximately three-quarters of those receiving government services are personally satisfied with their treatment. The majority of government employees are honorable, effective, and hardworking men and women. Despite claims to the contrary, public services are not necessarily less efficiently performed by government than the private sector. For example, results are mixed and inconclusive on whether private or public refuse haulers are more productive.

For many of the nastier jobs government performs there are no comparative statistics. No contractor is interested in picking up the homeless from the streets, halting illegal immigration, or taking on the problem of drug abuse in the schools. Government always gets the thankless, impossible jobs of society, but this does not protect public servants from becoming scapegoats for public frustrations.

THE COMPETITIVE EDGE

Yet a case can be made for private sector contracting. Contracting out can temporarily increase output without making long-range commitments. It can bring fresh ideas and approaches into established programs. New talent can enliven old agencies. Even the possibility of contracting out can stimulate an agency's staff to improve. Then too, contracting out can save money if truly efficient contractors are hired, personnel and other costs are indeed lower, and the contract itself is properly negotiated, written, and enforced.

Privatization, then, is not a cure-all for sick or dying government, but rather a given medicine for a particular patient or illness. Public interest, *all* of the consequences for *all* citizens, should govern the decision to prescribe privatization. We must consider political accountability and social equity as well as economic efficiency and assess the impact on future generations as well as on today's taxpayers and voters.

THE DO'S AND DON'TS OF PRIVATIZATION

How can privatization be in the public interest? Consider some simple "do's and don'ts":

Make sure public authorities retain control from a political bargaining standpoint. For example, if one contractor performs all phases of a vital public function, it can become a monopoly, making bargaining difficult. Governments should instead divide important functions among multiple contractors.

Be wary of contractors with excessive political influence.

Do not permit contracting out to distort or erode the goals of public programs. Privately operated human service programs, for example, can emphasize delivery of benefits rather than outreach to the underprivileged. Refuse collection can be productive in terms of speedy completion of routes, but counterproductive in terms of noisy insensitivity to a quiet neighborhood.

Make certain the permanent workforce of government is not damaged by privatization. What is already "good" about government should not be derogated by attempting to make its services "better." The processes leading to contracting out can create serious morale problems. Workforces can be subjected to months or even years of critical evaluation, during which time government jobs are perceived as in grave jeopardy. A kind of "death row" syndrome results, adversely affecting both efficiency and morale. Another problem arises when reductions in force are necessary as a result of privatization. Rumor-generated attrition can result in the best workers securing new employment while the less competent stay behind.

Another danger is the diminishing of the challenges facing government administrators. Every time a program is contracted out, the private sector takes over program management. Public managers who are not satisfied with a monitoring role then have no reason to stay in government. Higher salaries offered by contractors could also lure good managers away. If carried too far, contracting out could indeed lead to a government of paper-shuffling "bureaucrats" rather than challenged line managers, a picture scarcely advocated by the proponents of privatization.

Finally, do not permit contracting out to reduce government to a less than vital force in soci-ety. No one advocates that all public functions be privatized. Nonetheless, too much privatization could, eventually, dismantle a state or local government. The combined pressures for privatization created by President Reagan's personal popularity, the skyrocketing deficit, Gramm-Rudman-Hollings budget requirements, the 1980s cutback mentality, and the political momentum of the privatization movement itself should not be underestimated.

It would be a colossal public-policy mistake to create the public-sector equivalent of what business magazines are currently calling the "hollow corporation." This is a company that consists of a financial-data processing headquarters and a diverse set of far-flung and semi-autonomous operations carried on by subsidiaries, contractors, and other independent units.

Excessive privatization in government could similarly create the "hollow state." This would be a government that: concerns itself more with monitoring the work of others than doing things itself; retains the responsibility for fulfillment of public needs but does not possess the direct authority to fulfill responsibilities; seeks minimal achievement of predetermined goals rather than new ways to serve its people; tries merely to save money rather than promote balanced achievement of all policy values; and ignores rather than preserves the symbolic bonds between citizens and policy that are fostered by the daily sights and sounds of the uniformed patrol officer, the rescue squad volunteer, the restaurant-inspecting sanitarian, and snowplow drivers in winter.

A brass tablet sunk into the surface of a sidewalk in my community reads, "Not Dedicated to Public Use." As we pick and choose what public services will be provided by private contractors, we should always insist that government and its contractors remain "Dedicated to Public Use."

CHAPTER 9

State and Local Judicial Systems

One of the long-standing controversies over the judiciary is whether judges should be elected or appointed. Both methods are widespread. Some states have adopted a merit system in which judges who initially were appointed because of their qualifications periodically "run against their own record." Voters are simply asked: "Shall Judge Blank be retained in office for another term?" Even in states with an elective judiciary, most judges initially ascend the bench by appointment. This is done by an informal agreement that judges planning to retire will resign before their term expires so that the governor can appoint someone else to fill the vacancy. Incumbent judges are rarely defeated for reelection, although California voters in 1986 refused to retain three justices of the California Supreme Court. Bar associations are likely to play a dominant role by recommending appointees or indicating their position on certain candidates.

We begin by examining the various approaches to judicial selection. Then Edmund Spaeth, a Pennsylvania appellate court judge, offers insights on the election process based on his personal experiences in campaigning for judicial office. The third article deals with the related—and at least equally difficult—problem of how to remove unqualified judges. It provides examples of incompetence and misconduct, and indicates the value of judicial investigative commissions established in many states. The remaining half of this chapter will consider four issues in the administration of justice: jury selection, plea bargaining, alternative means to settle disputes, and television coverage of trials.

41

Judicial Selection: Take Your Choice

JAMES J. ALFINI

Which method of judicial selection is most likely to produce a highly qualified, independent judiciary? . . . [T]he debate over the best method for selecting judges rages on unabated. One of the reasons why the debate has not been quelled is that, as one commentator has aptly stated, "the debate over judicial selection is being waged in a factual vacuum." Proponents and opponents of various judicial selection plans have tended to present their arguments in a highly emotional fashion, while disregarding or distorting facts that do not support their particular position.

At the present time, there are better than a dozen methods for selecting judges in use in the United States. However, many of these are simply variations of five basic methods.

The first of these basic selection methods is direct appointment by the chief executive. This, of course, is the selection method which is used in the federal system where the President appoints all of our federal judges subject to confirmation by the Senate. This method is also used in seven of the states, where appointments are made, of course, by the governor.

The second basic method is appointment by the legislature which at present is used in only three states.

The third method is popular election by *partisan* ballot which is used in 15 states.

The fourth method is popular election by *nonpartisan* ballot which is used in 17 states. (It

should be noted at this point that in the jurisdictions which employ popular election as the basic selection method, the chief executive normally has the power to appoint judges temporarily to judicial vacancies occurring between elections.)

The fifth, and now the most frequently used, method for selecting judges is the nonpartisan court plan, which has also been termed the Missouri Plan or the merit plan, and is presently in use in 22 states.

The reason these figures total more than 50 is that many states employ more than one selection method. For instance, in some states the trial court judges are elected while the appellate court judges are chosen by a merit plan.

Why so many methods for selecting judges? Traditionally, it has been assumed that judges selected for the wrong reasons may not possess the qualifications or motivations needed to perform all of the duties required of a judge. They are not selected by those who are responsible for their performance, nor are they responsible to higher authorities in ways in which other public officials are. Therefore, it has been assumed by many that there is a greater likelihood for corruption, laziness, intemperance, or incompetence among the judiciary than among officials of the other two branches of the government. Thus, at various points in our nation's history, new methods for selecting judges have been introduced in an attempt to mitigate these factors.

During the post-revolutionary period our state judges were generally *appointed* by the governor and confirmed by a council or the legislature or were chosen by the legislature itself. However, toward the middle of the nineteenth century, the influence of Jacksonian democracy led many of the existing states to abandon the appointive method for popular election of judges.

After the Civil War, the urban political machines began to dominate the judicial selection process and many of the modern bar associations were formed to counterbalance the influence of the political machines with the influence of the organized bar.

The bar leaders attempted to improve the judicial selection process by reforming the electoral process. They developed devices that were intended to aid the electorate, particularly in urban areas, in making informed, reasoned choices. In some cases they called for and got such reforms as having separate judicial nominating conventions, having direct primaries for judicial office, and having separate judicial elections. The principal reform promoted by the bar leaders was the popular election of judges on *nonpartisan* ballots. However, ex-President William Howard Taft, in an address before the American Bar Association in 1913, concluded that the nonpartisan election of judges had proved to be a failure.

In 1913, the American Judicature Society was founded to work for the improvement of the administration of justice. A major objective of the Society has been the development of a method of selection that would be most likely to assure a highly qualified, independent judiciary. The method ultimately proposed by the Society—the merit plan—contains three basic features.

First, the *nomination* of a list of qualified candidates, usually three, by a nonpartisan commission composed of lawyers and non-lawyers.

Second, the *appointment* of the judge by an elected official from the list compiled by the nominating commission.

Third, the *election*, after a short probationary period, of the judge in a yes-no retention election.

This plan was adopted by the House of Delegates of the American Bar Association in 1937 and three years later Missouri became the first state to adopt this plan for selection of its judges. Since that time, an additional 21 jurisdictions have adopted, in whole or in part, a selection plan similar to this model.

Over the years, proponents of each of the various plans have advanced arguments in support of their plan and arguments against the other plans. For the sake of convenience, the arguments for and against the four most frequently used methods of judicial selection—partisan election, nonpartisan election, the merit plan, and direct appointment by the executive—will be summarized.

The principal argument in favor of the partisan election system is that, in a democracy, the people have a right to select their public officials. But do the people actually select their judges through the partisan election process? It has been argued that in truly contested elections generally there is very little voter knowledge of the candidates on the ballot and, what is worse, the canons of judicial ethics prohibit a judge from doing anything which would commit "or appear to commit him in advance, with respect to any particular case or controversy." What this means in effect is that a judicial candidate cannot speak on any issue which could be properly assessed by the electorate.

It is further argued that few judicial elections are truly contested elections anyway. The traditional predominance of one political party over the other in many areas is so great that sometimes only one party nominates candidates for judgeships. . . . In other areas (particularly in New York City), the temporary political situation is often such that the political parties agree in advance that the slate to be offered the voters will be a "coalition" slate, whereby each party offers the voters the same slate of candidates. The result is that in most cases the party leaders rather than the voters exercise the real choice.

It [was] hoped that the nonpartisan election of judges, in conjunction with other electoral reform measures popular around the turn of the century, would return the choice to the electorate. However, it has been argued that the nonpartisan election of judges suffers from many of the same inadequacies attributed to the partisan election process.

A special citizen study committee in Wisconsin recently reported on their assessment of the nonpartisan election process presently in use in that state. The study committee found that, in practice, most Wisconsin judges are either appointed initially to fill interim vacancies rather than elected initially, or when they are actually elected they run unopposed. Even in contested elections, they found that voter participation was very low, that those who do vote have very little information on the candidates, and that those who do have information are likely to have acquired it from a political party. They found that most citizens have little basis for evaluating judicial candidates, that there are few issues in such contests, and that the lowest common denominator is voter appeal.

Perhaps their most telling observation was that the nonpartisan election system provides no opportunity to screen the qualifications for office of a particular candidate, and hence, there is nothing to insure election on the basis of ability and qualifications. They pointed out that at least where there are partisan judicial elections the screening of candidates for office is done by the political parties. Thus, at least the party leaders must accept some responsibility for slating unqualified candidates. They pointed out that in nonpartisan states such as Wisconsin, there is no one to accept responsibility for the poorly qualified, but "aesthetically pleasing" candidate.

Finally, without issues, without party identification, and frequently without bar evaluation, they argued that candidates for the bench in Wisconsin must rely on their own political or financial resources. This, of course, may tend to reduce the judges' independence and to create or appear to create obligations, financial or otherwise, to those who support him.

Next, we turn to the "merit plan" for selecting judges. It has been argued that the key to the success of this plan is the judicial nominating commission. At least theoretically, the nominating commission goes through a rigorous screening process for each of the judicial applicants. This process includes interviews of the candidates and contacts with references and other individuals who know something about the candidate's background and professional competence. The commission then meets as a body to discuss the qualifications of all the candidates and to narrow down the list of candidates to three individuals whom the commission considers to be the most highly qualified.

What is the merit to such a plan? Proponents of the plan claim that it takes the judge out of the political arena and thus gives him greater independence once he is placed on the bench. In addition, they claim that such a process has the greatest potential for placing the most highly qualified potential candidate on the bench by virtue of the rigorous screening process which the nominating commission goes through. The major argument against the plan is that it is undemocratic insofar as it takes, at least initially, the decision as to whether or not to place a particular person in public office out of the hands of the voters.

Opponents of the plan would probably find the plan to be more palatable if it could be assured that the judicial nominating commission would be representative of the community at large. However, they argue that since the judicial nominating commission is composed half of lawyers, who are placed on the commission by the bar, and half of non-lawyers, who are generally placed on the commission by the governor, the interests of the commission will not be representative of the broader interests of the community.

In addition, it is argued that political influences can be made to bear on commission deliberations. Since the governor appoints the non-lawyer members of the commission, there is nothing to prevent him from appointing people to the commission who are favorable to his interests and then attempting to influence the commission deliberations through these people to the extent that they nominate his previously hand-picked candidates.

Finally, opponents of the merit plan have argued that because of the composition of the commission, the commission will tend to nominate only the "bluebloods" of the legal profession. This particular assumption concerning the merit plan has been shown to be erroneous in an empirical study of the merit plan in Missouri. The political scientists conducting the study concluded that the merit selection system in Missouri is, "a highly pluralistic one that reflects diverse interests: upper- and lower-status lawyers; a range of social and economic institutions; sitting members of the judiciary; and the factions and gubernatorial followings of state politics."

The arguments for and against having judges appointed directly by the executive are somewhat similar to those relating to the merit plan. It is argued that it will increase the independence of the judiciary by taking them out of the political arena. It has also been argued that direct appointment is superior to the merit plan in that it places political responsibility squarely on the shoulders of the executive for the quality of judicial appointments; whereas the merit plan places such responsibility on a body without public accountability, the nominating commission. The detractors of direct appointment point to the fact that governors can and do use judicial appointments as a means of paying off political debts, with the qualifications of the appointee being of secondary importance.

Which of the selection methods, then, is the best? Both the recently promulgated American Bar Association *Standards Relating to Court Organization* and the standards of the *National Advisory Commission on Criminal Justice Standards and Goals* name the merit plan as the superior method of judicial selection.

Although the author intuitively agrees with these national standards, it must be pointed out, in all fairness, that there is no empirical evidence to support this position. No comprehensive study of judicial selection methods has compared the qualifications of judges selected under the various plans in an effort to demonstrate that the judges selected under any one plan are better than those selected under the other plans.

The principal reason that such a study has yet to be attempted is that it is widely assumed that we will never be able to reach a consensus as to what constitutes a good judge. This assumption is based on a belief that the business of judging is too complex to lend itself to measurement or evaluation. Thus, it is argued that if you are unable to evaluate a judge's performance, you will necessarily be unable to make meaningful comparisons of the performance of judges in an effort to determine which of the various selection methods chooses the best judges.

What is most perplexing about these arguments is that they use ignorance as an excuse. We will never be able to resolve the debate over judicial selection unless we are willing to address these underlying problems. We must be willing to conduct exhaustive studies of the judicial office and seek to develop a means of evaluating a judge's performance. Only then will we stand a chance of taking the sound and the fury out of the debate over judicial selection.

42

Reflections on a Judicial Campaign

EDMUND B. SPAETH, JR.

A great deal has been written about whether judges should be elected. Often, however, the argument is conducted in general terms, which makes the issues involved seem remote. I have campaigned for election to the Pennsylvania Superior Court (an intermediate appellate court of seven judges, each elected in a state-wide election), and have concluded that judges should not be elected.

I pretend to no certainty. Reasonable men will differ with my conclusions. . . . If we care about "the rule of law," the way in which we pick our judges is one of the most important decisions we must make.

ARGUMENTS AGAINST ELECTION

The Uninformed Electorate

In most elections, the electorate is informed. To begin with, the voters know whether the candidate is a Democrat or Republican, and while labels may not mean much, they mean something. In addition, most voters have a reasonably accurate idea of both the responsibilities of the office at stake and of how a particular candidate is likely to fulfill those responsibilities. In a judicial election, none of this is so.

A party label is, or should be, particularly meaningless when applied to a judicial candidate. If the election is for county trial judge, the voters will have a reasonably accurate idea

of the responsibilities of the office. This is not the case, I found, if the election is to fill an appellate court vacancy. Many people to whom I spoke did not know there *was* a Superior Court, and of those who did know, many thought it was a trial court.

In addition, judicial candidates attract little attention, and not many voters know who they are. I was invited to ride in the Labor Day parade in Elk County. The young man who was driving me around the state asked the police officer in charge of directing persons to the parade assembly area where he should take me, saying, "I have Judge Spaeth."

"Judge Spaeth?" said the officer. "Never heard of the man."

I freely admit that judges are likely to be impressed with their own importance and that this sort of experience is doubtless wholesome. But after you've won a contested primary election and have been campaigning all summer, it does make you wonder just what you've been doing.

It is unlikely that the electorate will ever be informed, either about the judicial candidate or about the court to which the would-be judge aspires. To be sure, if the candidate has been a judge for some time, he may be known to the newspapers in his community, and they will be able to speak up for or against him in their editorials. (This happened in my election, and I am sure it made a considerable difference.) Suppose, however, that the candidate has not been a judge, or has not been

Edmund B. Spaeth, Jr., "Reflections on a Judicial Campaign," *Judicature*, June–July 1976, pp. 10–20. Reprinted by permission of the publisher. Footnotes in original omitted.

one for very long. Then how does one decide whether to vote for him?

If a legislator concludes that too many persons are having trouble collecting on their automobile accident insurance, he may work for a new system of compensation, such as no-fault insurance. A candidate for legislative office may promise that, if elected, he will work for a given change (no-fault insurance) in a given situation (the settlement of claims arising from automobile accidents). This enables the voter to decide whether to support the candidate.

None of this applies to a candidate for judicial office. A judge does not deal in general situations; he works with specific cases, involving, say, whether a particular mother or a particular father should have custody of a particular child. Thus, all the judicial candidate can promise is that before deciding who is to have custody, he will look up the pertinent law and listen carefully to the evidence and arguments presented by both the mother and the father. One may forgive the voter who, after hearing such a promise, asks, "Isn't that what *any* judge is supposed to do?"

Nor can a judge promise much in the way of change. For example, I found many voters troubled by the decisions of the United States Supreme Court on the power of a state to make abortion criminal, and on the responsibility of the police to advise a suspect of his constitutional rights before asking him for a confession. I did my best to explain that what I thought of these decisions was quite irrelevant, for I was obliged to follow them. "Indeed," I would ask, "if a judge does not follow the law—and the Constitution as construed by the Supreme Court is the law—who will?"

Another example: I was sometimes asked whether I favored the death penalty, whether I thought it should be reinstated and broadened. The answer to this also involves the judge's obligation to follow the law, but it further involves some other constraints on his freedom to answer such questions, in contrast

to the freedom that other candidates enjoy. Thus, I would explain that the Pennsylvania legislature *had* reinstated the death penalty (though narrowing rather than broadening its application), and that I was obliged, whatever my personal convictions, to apply the law as enacted by the legislature. Then, however, I had to explain that whether the death penalty was constitutional was presently being decided by the Supreme Court, and that all courts would be bound by its decision. Finally, I observed that the Superior Court did not hear capital cases, so that the issue of the validity of the death penalty would not come before me. Once a questioner pressed on, asking, "Well, if it did come before you, how would you decide?" and I had to answer that I couldn't say—the question was very difficult, and any answer, without considering the evidence and hearing the arguments, would amount to prejudgment.

A final example: I was on several occasions asked whether I favored gun control. On each occasion I answered that the question was better addressed to a legislative candidate, adding that if the legislature enacted a gun control law, then it would be my responsibility to interpret and apply it.

I have no doubt of the propriety and necessity of such answers; if a judge does not give them, he demeans his office. Nevertheless, they are not complete. A judge does not simply look up and then follow the law, as a carpenter measures and then cuts a plank. Frequently the law is not clear; or it is in a state of flux; or factors beyond the law are pertinent to the case. In short, the way a judge looks at life will often be important. The voter senses this, and more often than not, when I was asked questions such as the ones I've mentioned, I felt that the questioner was not as interested in the specific issue as in trying to determine how I looked at life. However, political picnics seem to be for fun and hamburgers and for shaking as many hands as possible, not for philosophy. Almost never did I have the time, nor was it ever appropriate, to have more than a superficial discussion. As a result, I was left feeling as frustrated as my questioner.

I don't want to overstate. I remember being questioned by members of NOW (National Organization for Women) at a meeting in Pittsburgh. What started as a desultory and *pro forma* proceeding became an intense and searching discussion, which, I think, did give the members some basis for deciding whether they wanted to support me. We got well beyond noting the constraints on what a judicial candidate may properly say and into a consideration of how a judge's personal philosophy may affect his decisions. I was able to illustrate by discussing some specific cases in which a judge, while honoring precedent and legislative command, may nevertheless move the law along—open its windows to the sun, so to speak. Even so, the meeting ended in dissatisfaction, with my saying that I simply could not promise as much change as they would like, and that perhaps they should concern themselves more with the selection of legislative than judicial candidates. Still, we had had far more than a superficial discussion.

But this was an exceptional occasion. The questioning process was fairly summarized by a woman who asked, after listening to my carefully qualified answers, "But judge, if I don't know where you stand, how can I decide whether to vote for you?" I could only reply that I sympathized with her predicament; that when one votes for a judge, one is making a bet on character; and that I quite agreed that she did not know, and as a practical matter, would find it hard to learn, enough about me to decide whether my character was such that I would be a good judge.

The Judicial Campaign

Because the electorate is uninformed, a judicial candidate is tempted to make sensational statements, which he hopes will call the voters' attention to his candidacy and at the same time appeal to what he believes to be the majority view. I know one judge who campaigned throughout the state announcing that he was for the death penalty, another who promised that if elected he would "take the handcuffs off the police," another whose television advertisement showed him, in his robes, slamming shut a prison door. One can believe that the courts have sometimes erred in favor of the criminal and still recognize such campaigning as demeaning, both to the candidate and to the court to which he aspires.

It is a mistake to underestimate the damage such campaigning does. We are indeed wracked by crime. The courts do have important responsibilities with respect to crime. Not all of these responsibilities have been well discharged. Nevertheless, the courts do not define what activity is criminal; they do not catch criminals; they do not supervise them in prison or on probation or parole; and to whatever extent social conditions, such as poverty, prompt crime, the conditions are beyond the courts' control. To pretend that the problem of crime is simple, and that it will dissolve before a judge's decree, is to betray the ideals on which our nation rests. It deceives the people, it promises what cannot be performed, and, by raising hopes sure to be disappointed, it encourages persons to feel contempt for the courts and to take the law into their own hands.

Another unfortunate result of the electorate being uninformed is that the judicial candidate needs, or thinks he needs, money: if only he could print and distribute literature, and buy billboard space and radio and television time, his name would be recognized. It is, however, impossible for a judge to accept money to meet such campaign expenses without losing at least some of his impartiality.

In this respect there is an important difference between the legislative and executive branches and the judicial branch. A legislator or executive may to some extent represent special interests to whom he owes his election. To be sure, he should not put those interests ahead of the general welfare, but no one expects him to be impartial. A judge, however, who is not impartial is nothing. Worse, he is an oppression; only because of her blindfold is the goddess of justice given a sword.

Again, I do not mean to overstate. A judge is not, and should not be, a hermit. Especially if he is active in bar association affairs, he will have many lawyers among his friends, and it is to be expected that his friends will want to help him in his effort to be elected. But if the danger of money should not be overstated, neither should it be minimized.

In the first place, the contribution may not be small. It may be large, even very large, as when the lawyer not only makes a contribution himself but, because he is a senior partner in a large firm, is able to suggest that others contribute. Further, the judicial candidate cannot disentangle himself from the financial aspects of his campaign. I know, because I tried hard to do so. A citizens committee did all the solicitation, so that I was spared asking anyone to contribute; a secretary for the committee wrote the letters acknowledging the contributions; and the committee treasurer prepared and filed the reports required by Pennsylvania election law. As a result, in general I did not know who gave me money. Nevertheless, there were important exceptions. It happened that the Pennsylvania Bar Association supported my candidacy. Partly because of this, a small group of lawyers early in the campaign formed an informal sort of committee that met from time to time to raise money and otherwise support and guide the campaign. And, sometimes by accident, I learned of contributions by others.

Any contribution, whatever its size, may affect the professional relationship that should exist between the lawyer and the judge. No honorable lawyer wants his case decided on the basis of friendship. He knows that that way lies danger: in the next case, not

he but his opponent will win on friendship. The law is an all-or-nothing enterprise; treat all alike, whoever they may be, or surrender yourself to force and favoritism. The fact that candidates for judicial election must raise money works against the ideal of an impartial judiciary.

Not Merit but Chance

I was elected by a large margin. Afterwards, some of my friends said, "You see, the system works. The best man won." While courteous and flattering, such a remark is, I submit, mistaken. My election owed more to chance than to merit.

First, I happen to be a Democrat. In Pennsylvania, registered Democrats outnumber registered Republicans by half a million. Second, because a judicial candidate (especially a state-wide judicial candidate, like myself) is not well known, his election is likely to depend on the outcome of the numerous other elections being conducted at the same time—elections for county commissioners, sheriffs, district attorneys, mayors, and so on. Certain of these other elections happened to develop in a manner that helped me.

The leaders of the regular Democratic organization in Philadelphia, my home town, were steadfast in their support of me. (Indeed, their early support was critical to my nomination.) However, the Democratic incumbent for mayor and the organization were in a dispute, and since both the mayor and my opponent were "law and order" Italian-Americans, there was some talk that the mayor might support my opponent and undercut me. As it developed, this didn't happen. First, the regular organization's support of me never wavered. Second, the mayor, who had no particular differences with me (he had criticized some judges as being "soft on criminals," but I was not one), was determined to roll up a big vote for himself, and the best way to do that was to urge his supporters to get out a "straight" Democratic vote, which included me. Given this combination of effective regular organization support with factors personal to the mayor, the result was that I came out of Philadelphia with a 240,500 majority.

In Allegheny County, my opponent's own county, I ran a bad third in the primary. It happened, however, that after the primary, the Democratic party there resolved its differences, with the result that again I was the incidental beneficiary of a large straight Democratic vote. I also did well in populous counties next to Allegheny. This is steel country. During the fall, my opponent, while trying a case in which it was alleged that one of the large steel companies was polluting the atmosphere, made an off-the-cuff remark from the bench that infuriated the steel workers—they took him to mean that the pollution was their fault, not the company's.

I do not mean to pretend to a modesty I do not have. Although the situations I have mentioned arose largely as a matter of chance, I think—at least, I hope—I can take some credit for my good luck. In Philadelphia I had many friends, which at least to some extent was because they thought I had been a good judge. Even so, I remain persuaded that I was more lucky than good.

One other factor should be mentioned. I was told I proved to be a good campaigner. Suppose this was so. Does a person's ability as a campaigner really have much to do with his ability as a judge? To be effective, a campaigner must have some ability as a speaker, and must enjoy meeting many people he never saw before; but what do these abilities have to do with his ability to analyze a legal problem in an even-tempered way? Indeed, it may be that a good judge should not be a good campaigner; otherwise he may start dreaming of the senate or the governor's mansion, and write his opinions with his eyes not on his law books but on the vagaries of the Gallup polls.

It might seem that the element of chance in an election is of concern only to the candidates. And why worry about them? After all,

they chose to run, and knew, or should have known, what they were getting into. I suggest, however, that such an attitude would be mistaken. The difficulty is that in a judicial election, chance too often decides not simply which candidate wins but also who the candidates are. In other elections this is much less likely to be the case. In selecting a candidate to run for president, governor, senator, even congressman or mayor, the party leaders are under considerable pressure to pick someone who will appeal to voters throughout the election district, which is to say that external factors are taken into account. In selecting a candidate to run for judge, however, there is no such pressure, or very little. Since a judicial candidate brings little strength to the ticket but is likely to rise or fall with the fortunes of the other candidates, it is natural for a party leader to conclude that it does not much matter who the candidate is so long as he will not hurt the ticket. From this conclusion it is a short step to awarding the nomination as a political favor, with little reference to qualifications.

I know party leaders who are scrupulous in their concerns that a judicial candidate be qualified. Nevertheless, it cannot be denied that many people believe that often judges owe their nomination to favoritism or other factors unrelated to judicial ability. Justified or not, this belief is destructive of respect for the law.

ARGUMENTS FOR ELECTION

The Rewards of Campaigning

Once when I remarked during my campaign that running for election was good for a judge, a friend replied, "I don't see why. You certainly don't learn any law." He was right, you don't; but you do learn other things, of great value in applying the law.

In the course of campaigning—especially state-wide—a candidate visits many different communities. My campaign took me into almost every one of Pennsylvania's sixty-seven counties. Before I was done I had visited the northern woods, the southern farms and orchards, mill towns along the rivers, coal towns in the hills, fancy suburbs, cities great and small. I met a wonderful variety of people. It is impossible for a judge to come from such an experience without being uplifted.

A courtroom is an unhappy place. The parties are there because someone has been hurt, perhaps killed, in a crime or accident, or believes he has been cheated, or in some other way taken advantage of. Often a law suit brings out the worst in us, and is little more than an attempt to get more than our fair share or to hurt the other party. Of course there is drama in court, and sometimes humor, and bravery; but overall, sadness prevails, and this may skew a judge's attitudes.

Sadness does not prevail on the campaign trail. Again and again I was surprised, delighted, and touched by people's generosity and understanding. I am a shy man. It was not easy for me to walk into a room of several hundred people, none of whom I knew. Always, though, someone would come up to me and say something like, "You must be Judge Spaeth. Let me introduce you to my friends." And soon I would be talking to all sorts of pleasant people, learning all sorts of new things.

Many of these people were politicians. Politicians are in low repute these days, but I have come to have a high regard for them. I have already mentioned that a judicial candidate rarely brings any strength to a ticket. Certainly that was true of me; it was not only in Elk County that I was unknown. Nor was there any patronage that I could offer a local political leader. (I employ one secretary and my law clerks.) In short, there was little reason for a political leader to go out of his way to help me get elected; and in fact, some didn't.

But most of the politicians I met, great and small, could not have been more courteous or helpful. If I could not be at a dinner or picnic, often someone would speak on my behalf—without my having thought to ask him to. Some wrote special letters to their committee people, reminding them not to lose sight of me in their preoccupation with the local contests. Some wrote and even telephoned their opposite numbers in other counties. Some used their local party funds to buy me the radio and newspaper advertising I could not afford. There was no reason for these men and women to do so much, except that they deeply cared about the quality of the courts, and, generous to a fault, thought I was a good judge.

. . . I concede that some persons are in politics for unworthy reasons—greed, laziness, overweening ambition, whatever. Nevertheless, I am convinced from my experiences during the campaign that most people in politics are there because they want to improve their communities, and think that the way to do that is through their government.

Nor was I encouraged only by my experiences with people in politics. I had many conversations with everyday citizens, at picnics, county fairs, street corners and factory gates. I came from these convinced that people are far more thoughtful than many of their leaders, would-be leaders, and publicists realize. To be sure, I was favored with my fair share of prejudiced remarks. There are a certain number of people who believe that most of Pennsylvania's difficulties would disappear if only Philadelphia were sawed off and allowed to drift down the Delaware River and out to sea. There are others who have no idea that two-thirds of Pennsylvania is west of the Susquehanna River. Generally, however, I found people both idealistic and skeptical. Although worried about crime—which was usually a shorthand reference to the moral quality of our society—and concerned about an unjust and faltering economy, they were not dogmatic. Persuaded that there are some rather fundamental dislocations in our society, they remained wary of any easy statement of what those dislocations are, or of how they can be corrected.

Such experiences are important for a judge. If he is too overcome by the sadness in his courtroom, if he believes that most people are either knaves or fools, he cannot be a good judge. Imperfect as it is, the law is in essence an appeal to reason. To believe that such an appeal can succeed is to believe that man is more good than bad.

Finally, there is another way in which campaigning is good for a judge. Every occupation has its peculiar vice. The vice of judges is arrogance. So much is entrusted to a judge. He decides which witnesses to believe, what rules of law to apply. If he is not careful, he will come to think that because he has these great powers, he deserves them—that he really must be quite a fellow. I know of no experience more likely to dispel such an illusion than a political campaign. Partly this is true because the candidate is repeatedly cut down to size by incidents like my Elk County parade; partly it is because if he wins, he will reflect that he owes his victory more to chance than to merit. Mostly, however, it is because when he is done, he will have learned that he holds his office as trustee of his fellow citizens' dream of a just society.

Somewhere Judge Wyzanski remarked that when he had a particularly difficult decision to make, he would ask himself how one of the great judges—Holmes, for example, or Cardozo—would have decided. I myself have been sustained by this grand sentiment. Having campaigned, however, I have an additional source of inspiration. When a young woman who has never met you spends a cold day at a shopping center with her child, handing out leaflets simply because she heard you were a good judge, and when all sorts of people in all sorts of ways express their confidence in you, you want very much to do your best.

Opening Up the Judiciary

If government is to represent the people, it must be open to everyone, regardless of sex,

race, religion, or geography. We have been accustomed to this idea for some time as regards the legislative branch. Though our legislators are an imperfect mirror of our society, they are a very diverse group. As regards the executive branch, we have made progress. . . .

This quality of openness is equally important in the judicial branch. The distinctive feature of our society is not that it is democracy but that it is a democracy regulated by Constitutional guarantees, interpreted and enforced by the courts. It is therefore to the courts that the weak and the oppressed look for help. If that help is to be forthcoming, the courts cannot be the domain of any one class or group of people. That is why it was important to break the barrier against the appointment of a Jew to the United States Supreme Court, and of a black, and . . . of a woman.

While electing judges is not the only way to break such barriers, as the example of the Supreme Court shows, it is one way. Politics has long been an honorable resort of those excluded from a fair share of society's goods. Political leaders, moreover, like a "balanced ticket." When I was appointed a trial judge, it was as one of three. Of the two others, one judge was a Republican Catholic of Irish background, the other a Republican Catholic of Italian background. One of my friends explained: "Ned, you were appointed because you are [a] Democratic Anglo-Saxon Protestant who wears glasses."

SOME SUGGESTIONS FOR CHANGE

As I consider the foregoing advantages and disadvantages of electing judges, it seems to me that the advantages are the candidate's, the disadvantages the people's.

It is a common observation, sometimes made with some bitterness by judges themselves, that judges are often not respected. (Once, on a street corner in Donora, Pennsylvania, I introduced myself to an Ancient Mariner sort of man who, upon learning that I was a judge, fixed me with glittering eye and said, "You should be hung from that telephone pole.") This state of affairs is hardly surprising. The voter knows that too often in voting for a judicial candidate he is not making an informed choice. He also knows that too often the candidate was put on the ticket for political reasons, and not because of merit. He is therefore not surprised to find judicial performance that he regards as incompetent and irresponsible.

I was repeatedly asked during my campaign whether there was any "real issue" in the contest between my opponent and me. I always replied that there was, and that it was merit selection. I had been appointed to the Philadelphia trial bench by Governor William Scranton, a Republican, on the recommendation of a merit selection committee; and when Governor Shapp, a Democrat, appointed me to the Superior Court in December, 1973, it was again on the recommendation of a merit selection committee. Although I was a representative of the merit selection process, it was difficult for me to argue that this was a good process, for to do so might have suggested I thought I was above the electoral process, which I did not. I did say, however, that I believed the quality of the bench would improve if judicial appointments were made only upon the recommendation of a merit selection committee, and that if I were defeated, it would not be a personal defeat so much as a defeat for merit selection, and a consequent encouragement of increased partisanship in the selection of judges.

I have no way of knowing to what extent this argument affected the outcome of the election. I am convinced, however, that it had some effect, and that the effect was in my favor. I submit that the question has become not whether we should make changes in the present system of electing judges but what sort of changes we should make.

The system perhaps most often advocated by those critical of the partisan election of judges is the Missouri, or merit, plan. Stated generally, this plan operates as follows: A judge is appointed upon the recommendation of a merit selection committee. After serving for a year plus (the "plus" depending on the date of the next general election) he runs for "retention"; that is, the voters are asked to vote "yes" or "no" in response to the question, "Shall Judge ———— be retained in office?" If the vote is "no," another appointment is made, and the process starts over. If the vote is "yes," the judge serves a full term. The argument made in favor of this system is that it ensures merit selection while giving the electorate the last word.

There are a number of variations on the Missouri plan. At present in Pennsylvania, end-of-term vacancies are filled by partisan elections, but mid-term vacancies are filled through a merit process voluntarily established by Governor Shapp. I would like to see enacted into law a merit plan that would incorporate the following features:

First, the legislature should ensure that the merit selection committee will be both impartial and representative of the community. To accomplish this, some thought should be given to a fixed term for committee members; perhaps, too, their appointment should be subject to legislative confirmation.

Also, at least some of the committee members might be described by position. For example, the committee might be required to include one judge and two lawyers. . . . By similar specification, the legislature could ensure that the other committee members would come from throughout the state and from a representative variety of occupations (none political), and that each would be a person who, by the position he or she has achieved, has demonstrated both competence and the respect of a significant part of the community. Further, the legislature should provide the committee with a small full-time staff, and should insist upon rigorous procedures.

Second, the person nominated by the governor (upon recommendation of the merit selection committee) should not take office unless confirmed by the senate. The legislation should specify the confirmation procedure. There should be a hearing, open to the press and the general public, before an appropriate legislative committee. The nominee should be asked to appear before the legislative committee for questioning. To help this questioning to be effective, the merit selection committee should give the legislative committee such material as the nominee's answers to the merit selection committee's questionnaire.

Such a confirmation procedure would give reasonable assurance that all aspects of judicial appointment were appropriately recognized. The screening procedures of the merit selection committee should ensure that the nominee is a person of integrity and professional qualifications. The political leaders of both parties would be able to express their views. Also, the views of the legislators' constituents could be taken into account. There should also be arrangements for the nominee to be questioned by private citizens during the legislative committee hearing. Finally, I believe the press could be counted on to report the confirmation procedure and to comment editorially on the nominee's qualifications.

Third, the judicial term of office should be changed to provide that, if confirmed, the nominee would hold office with good behavior until reaching 65. The effect of this change would be to eliminate any election of judges, either partisan, for a judge's first term, or retention, for his second (or third) term.

I have already commented on the disadvantages of partisan election. I do not think much more of retention election. The electorate is likely to be even less well informed in a retention election than in a partisan election. As a result, the retention election is likely to be a desultory affair, and the candidate will almost surely be retained—at least that has been the usual experience in Pennsylvania. There is a qualification to this generalization, which points out a peculiar abuse to which a retention election may be subjected. A "no" campaign can be mounted by some special interest group angered by one of the judge's decisions, as for example in a controversial zoning case. Since the total vote is likely to be low, such a grudge vote may be decisive.

It may be suggested that the single, appointive, good-behavior term I propose would be too long. In fact, however, it would often work out to be not as long as many terms are now. In addition, if it were thought that no term should exceed twenty years, the legislature could so provide, though that might seem unfair to younger men and women. There is, moreover, an advantage to a single appointive term. The very fact that it may be long enhances its importance; recognition of this fact should encourage more careful selection and confirmation.

. . . Provision could be made for service as a senior judge if, upon retirement at 65, the judge were healthy and alert. The courts' work-loads are so heavy that there would be plenty for such senior judges to do.

The condition of good behavior is important. Pennsylvania is already one of the leaders in providing for the discipline of a judge upon complaint of a lawyer, litigant, or witness who has been mistreated by the judge. If a judge is to serve a substantial term, such disciplinary procedures should become a feature of judicial administration widely known by and readily accessible to not only lawyers but every citizen.

My family and I shall always be grateful for the experience of my campaign. As I have reflected on that experience, however, I am persuaded that our present way of selecting judges can be improved.

43

Now, the States Crack Down on Bad Judges

U.S. NEWS & WORLD REPORT

A broad attack on judicial misconduct and incompetence is developing in state capitals across the country at the very time when the power of courts to intervene in broad social questions is at an all-time high.

In state after state, special investigative units have been set up to dig into allegations against judges. The result: In the last four years alone, at least 52 judges, including some members of the highest state courts, have been either removed from the bench or censured.

Those found guilty of misconduct are very few in relation to the total number of judges. But the panels have unearthed instances of judges doing such things as:

Accepting bribes in return for light criminal sentences.

Offering to trade favors in court for sex with female defendants.

Treating lawyers, defendants or witnesses abusively and arbitrarily.

Failing to maintain a normal judicial workload because of senility.

Until a few years ago, most states had no practical means of policing misconduct and incompetence on the bench. State laws provided for removal of a judge only through impeachment by the legislature or petitioning for a recall election—procedures that are time-consuming and also frequently tainted by politics. Lesser sanctions, such as censure or reprimand, did not exist. Accordingly, incompetent or corrupt judges were rarely called to account. The seeds of the present crackdown go back to 1960, when California became the first state to streamline judicial disciplinary procedures.

It pioneered the idea of a permanent commission empowered to investigate charges against judges and recommend punishment, if warranted. The California Supreme Court then decides the question without resort to the legislature or the voting booth.

California's system is working well. In the century before the commission was set up, only four California judges were removed by the cumbersome methods of impeachment or recall. The new commission, in the last 18 years, has triggered the removal of four judges and the censure of six others.

Other states were slow to follow California's example. But in the last few years, as the power of courts grew and existing disciplinary commissions uncovered judicial wrongdoing, state after state rushed to adopt similar procedures. Today, there are special panels for investigating errant judges in 47 states and the District of Columbia. Maine, Mississippi and Washington are the only states that do not have such panels.

FROM LOWEST TO HIGHEST

The discipline commissions have found impropriety, incompetence or outright corruption at various levels of state judicial systems, from the lowest courts to the highest.

Associate Justice Donald B. Yarbrough of the Texas Supreme Court was sentenced in January to five years in prison for lying to a grand jury. Six months earlier, he had resigned from the bench under a hail of accusations. The state bar association had filed 80 charges of misconduct against him. . . .

Texas Judge Garth C. Bates was removed from the bench last summer on his indictment for accepting a bribe in return for not sentencing a defendant to prison. When picked up by the police, the judge was carrying $2,900 in $100 bills that matched part of a $59,000 cache given to a friend who arranged for the bribe. Bates is appealing his conviction on the bribery charge.

A few judges have been found using the power of their office to make sexual advances. Last fall, the U.S. Supreme Court turned down the appeal of a former Alabama judge sentenced to three years in prison for offering leniency to female defendants in return for sexual favors. One witness testified that Judge Thomas D. McDonald invited her into his office and told her that he would "maybe take care" of her grand-larceny charge if she met him at a Huntsville motel. . . .

A CODE FOR BEHAVIOR

Violations of law are the clearest reasons for disciplining a judge. But judges, unlike average citizens, also can be punished for arbitrary conduct that needlessly embarrasses parties in court or reflects poorly on the judicial system. The Code of Judicial Conduct of the American Bar Association, which has been adopted by many states, says "a judge should be patient, dignified and courteous to litigants, jurors, witnesses, lawyers and others with whom he deals in his official capacity."

Such standards of courtesy and fairness are difficult to enforce because they are so vague, trial lawyers say. An irascible judge might argue loudly with lawyers in front of the jury, but do so with respect and discretion. A loser in court may feel wronged by a judge merely because he ruled against him. Since judges suffer indigestion, headaches and hangovers like other people, their dispositions may vary drastically from day to day. Sometimes, however, a judge's conduct becomes so provocative that the disciplinary wheels start turning.

Municipal Court Judge William D. Spruance, for example, was removed by the California Supreme Court in 1975 for a variety of reasons, including improper "judicial temperament." According to the court, Spruance expressed his disbelief in the testimony of a defendant "by emitting a contemptuous sound commonly called a 'raspberry' " and "made a vulgar gesture in reprimanding a defendant for coming in late in a traffic matter."

HANDCUFFS OVER COFFEE

New York State Judge William M. Perry was removed from office in 1976 because he ordered three law officers to bring a coffee vendor before him, authorizing their use of handcuffs. According to testimony, the judge then shouted at the vendor about the quality of his coffee. In ordering his removal, the court said Perry worsened his offense by lying about the incident.

The Illinois Courts Commission ordered the removal of Circuit Judge William D. Vanderwater in 1976 for "willful misconduct in office and conduct that is prejudicial to the administration of justice and brings the judicial office into disrepute." The commission found that Judge Vanderwater personally arrested a man for trespassing in a building of which the judge was a part owner. According to testimony: At the police station, the judge summoned his partner to sign a complaint in blank form, then sentenced the man to eight months in jail after obtaining his signature on a guilty plea and waiver of the right to a jury trial.

In the 1976 suspension of Michigan Judge Willard L. Mikesell, it was found that, on one occasion, he reduced the bond for a defendant from $10,000 to $500 after forcing the defendant to get a haircut like Judge Mikesell's. The Michigan Supreme Court concluded that "the defendant was compelled to submit to some humiliating act or discipline of [Mikesell's] own devising without authority of law."

Detroit Recorders Court Judge James Del Rio was suspended from office last summer for five years by the Michigan Supreme Court after the state Judicial Tenure Commission accused him of numerous violations of judicial ethics. The court ruled that Del Rio threatened defendants who refused to plead guilty. It also found that he interceded in the Detroit courts on behalf of his friends. . . .

DIFFICULT CASES

Few judges are removed from the bench because of illness or senility. These cases are the most difficult for judicial-conduct commissions to handle because there is sympathy for the judge, who may not wish to admit to himself that he has gotten too old to handle his duties.

Last year, senility caused the only forced retirement of a state supreme-court judge in the nation's history. The California Commission on Judicial Performance recommended the retirement of 82-year-old Marshall McComb. Once considered to be an outstanding justice, McComb was accused by investigators of sleeping during court sessions, failing to pay attention during court conferences and

not doing his own work. McComb decided to fight the commission, but he lost his appeal, which was decided by a special panel of California judges.

All of these cases of judicial discipline are on the public record in states with active panels for the investigation of judicial misconduct. Typically, the panels have a small staff working under a commission of judges, lay people and lawyers. Anyone can file a complaint against a judge, but most are dismissed after a short investigation.

SORE LOSERS

Maurice S. Pipkin, executive director of the Texas State Judicial Qualifications Commission, says he receives "emotional letters" daily from people who lost their cases before various judges. The first step is to check the complaint with the letter writer's lawyer.

"Usually the lawyer is more dispassionate and says nothing was done wrong," Pipkin says. "If the lawyer says something was wrong, we'll go into it. We'll talk to the judge, examine the records and find out what happened."

To protect a judge's reputation, all states require that the panel's investigations be conducted in the strictest secrecy. The results are made public only if conduct warranting disciplinary action is uncovered. A public complaint is then filed with the state supreme court recommending censure, suspension, removal or, in the case of judges rendered incompetent by age, forced retirement. The court then decides whether to uphold the commission's recommendation and whether the punishment it suggests should be increased or reduced.

While much has been done, obstacles to the effective removal of state judges still remain.

For one thing, many lawyers are loath to get involved in disciplinary actions against judges. And investigations, once begun, can drag on for a long time before anything is settled. What's more, discipline-panel administrators in some states concede that judges tend to be unwilling to punish their fellow judges except in the clearest cases of misconduct.

Commission members make the point that while the number of judges disciplined may seem low to some people, it is significantly higher than it used to be. Moreover, some commission members insist that for every judge who is removed or publicly chastised, several others quietly resign or retire to avoid an investigation. On top of this, says one commission administrator, "there is a salutary effect on the conduct of judges just knowing that we exist."

Despite the difficulty of firing a judge, most lawyers rank the caliber of the bench high, especially at the federal level. A recent American Bar Association poll showed that only 3 percent of 602 lawyers surveyed found the quality of justice in federal courts wanting. When the Chicago Bar Association asked its members to recommend retention or rejec-

tion of 32 Illinois judges up for re-election, all but five were endorsed for another term.

INDEPENDENCE ISSUE

It is often suggested that if removal of judges is made too easy the independence of the courts will suffer. Many observers note that courts play an important role in protecting the rights of the minority against the popular will. They argue that to protect judges, and ultimately to protect rights guaranteed by the Constitution, removal should remain difficult.

Charles Morgan, a Washington, D.C., lawyer who spent years battling for civil rights in the South, holds that view. He argues that if removal had been easy, judges such as Frank M. Johnson, Jr., in Alabama and Elbert P. Tuttle on the U.S. Court of Appeals might have lost their seats for their defense of civil rights and civil liberties. "I'm willing to put up with some bad judges because easier removal also could apply to the great judges," Morgan says.

The next four articles discuss issues in the administration of justice. Trial lawyer Joseph Kelner gives other attorneys frank advice on jury selection (*voir dire* means "to see, to say"). Plea bargaining, where the accused pleads guilty in return for a lesser charge or lighter sentence, is extensively used in American courts. Why? It saves the state the time and expense of proving a case, encourages cooperation in investigations in return for leniency, and guarantees convictions. The judge does not have to accept a plea that has been bargained between the defendant's attorney and the prosecutor, and Judge Irving Kaufman tells why cases may be tried. The Sixth Amendment right to a speedy trial in criminal cases has caused backlogs in civil litigation, leading to alternative means of dispute resolution. Finally, each state must decide whether television coverage is to be allowed in its courts.

44

Jury Selection: The Prejudice Syndrome

JOSEPH KELNER

Prejudice is to prejudge. After decades of trials—and tribulations—I am convinced that the major factor determining the outcome of a jury trial is the prejudice that jurors bring with them to court.

No trial lawyer, no matter how experienced, is endowed with an omniscient X-ray vision enabling him or her to probe the brains and thought processes of prospective jurors.

Prejudice takes many virulent shapes and forms—racial, religious, ethnic, occupational, social, and professional. There are prejudices that infect women in their jealousies against other women. There are prejudices for or against physicians in malpractice cases. There are taxpayer prejudices against those who sue a municipality, and prejudices against divorced women. The variety of prejudices is infinite, running the gamut of all human hatreds and envies.

No ingenious techniques of oratory and persuasion are certain to eliminate prejudice from the all-powerful decisional processes of juries. However, counsel may devise techniques to neutralize, for the purpose of the case, the prejudices lurking in the psyches of the jurors.

A benign appraisal of human nature overlooks the fact that all human beings are subjected to numerous influences and pressures from cradle to grave. Such factors and sources as heredity, environment, parents, religion, education, and occupational influences and experiences inevitably color the thought processes of us all.

For example, on the average, nurses and ex-police officers are not happy choices by plaintiffs as jurors in personal injury cases. Though all nurses and police officers do not fit into the same mental mold, it may well be assumed that their daily contact with human pain and suffering would create in them some measure of reduced sensitivity to the pain and suffering of others. This premise concededly plays the assumed law of averages. The only alternative is to adopt the *laissez-faire* philosophy of accepting the first panel of jurors called. This we respectfully decline to do. Jury selection is a matter of personal judgment and use of the wits of the trial lawyer, whose judgment and instinct in the *voir dire* will be colored of necessity by his or her own experiences and knowledge of human nature and personal prejudices and biases.

Trial counsel, before trial, should make a careful survey of the factors involved in the case to determine the prototypes of jurors to be accepted or rejected. Counsel will consider the racial and national origin of both plaintiff and defendant, the nature of the accident, the types of jurors usually found on panels in this county, and the special circumstances to forecast and identify the nature and source of possible prejudice that may dictate the outcome of the case.

OBJECTIVE OF *VOIR DIRE*

The ultimate objective of *voir dire* is to ferret out the prejudice and bias that lurks in some area of the thinking of every juror. "Jury selection" is a misnomer. With the few peremptory challenges allotted, we do not "select" juries. We merely spend our few challenges to eliminate the jurors most likely to be prejudiced.

Female jurors may react subconsciously with aversion toward a younger or more attractive female litigant.

Jurors who in the past were sued as defendants in injury cases may classify all claimants as knaves.

Jurors who own commercial or apartment properties may regard each jury case as a lever for increasing their own insurance premiums. Many jurors have been brainwashed with insurance company leaflets, advertisements, and planted newspaper articles that, in recent years, have fostered the false concept that the juror's own automobile insurance premium rate is determined by the verdict rendered. Such jury tampering has been roundly condemned in many forums. It behooves each trial lawyer to ferret out such sentiments where possible.

It is axiomatic among trial lawyers that small homeowners are unfavorable jurors in actions against municipalities. The obvious deterrent is the juror's thought that his or her own taxes are affected adversely by a verdict for the plaintiff. On pretrial settlement discussions, some judges are disposed to recommend acceptance of a low offer to settle with the sage and true observation, "Remember, this is Blank County," (wherein dwell many small-minded homeowners and where verdicts against the city are reputedly as sparse as oases in the Sahara).

RACIAL PREJUDICE

Racial prejudice can be found in varying degrees in every state of the union. Discrimination exists in all walks of life, including social and religious groups, housing, athletics, politics, and education. While there is progress toward realization of the American dream of true equality, the trial lawyer on *voir dire* must face the facts of life as they now exist.

A black plaintiff is not necessarily assured of a fair trial merely because jurors born or raised in the South have been challenged from service by the plaintiff's counsel. The northern states have no dearth of bigots. The jury could be asked incisive and direct questions to elicit possible bias. Counsel should study the facial expressions and demeanor of the juror as well as the content of the juror's replies for a clue to possible bias lurking behind the mask of professed tolerance.

The juror should be told that every human being, by reason of environment or personal experiences, probably has some area of bias or prejudice, that it is a mark of courage and fairness to admit that he or she "may" have difficulty in being impartial in this case, that no one will quarrel with the juror's views, and that a fair trial can be had only if the juror will be outspoken and frank in this regard.

Some jurors, thus encouraged and coaxed, will readily admit to feelings of possible bias. Others, by their hesitant manner and averted eyes, permit counsel to reach the conclusion that bias exists.

An example: "Ladies and gentlemen, my client is Mrs. Julia Smith, who is a member of the black race. This is no time to debate bias and prejudice. I simply want to ask you, Mrs. Jones: Can Julia Smith get a fair trial with equal justice from you, the same as if she were a white person? Do you think she is entitled to equal justice? Would you have some discomfort or difficulty about that proposition?" Mrs. Jones' answers must be distrusted.

Such questions usually elicit responses such as, "There is no problem about that; she will get the same fair treatment as anyone else would." Or: "It will make no difference to me at all."

The content of such responses must be taken with a grain of salt. The prospective juror inevitably desires to serve on a case of importance and will suppress true feelings of prejudice. The manner in which the juror replies and the vibrations set up in the chemistry between counsel and the juror must determine counsel's instinct and decision to accept or reject the particular juror.

RELIGIOUS AND NATIONAL PREJUDICE

A juror who is a co-religionist with either party would seem normally to be a favorable bet for such party, but like all generalizations, this one is fallacious. I have had jury verdicts in which the only votes against the plaintiff came from co-religionists. They bent over backwards to the ultimate extreme! This is a field of inquiry that must be played by ear with the odds favoring acceptance of a co-religionist as a juror.

A more fertile source of prejudice may stem from nationality considerations. In years of discussion with active trial lawyers, I found that certain general notions have evolved with regard to certain national groups. The consensus is that:

An Irish juror must be assumed to be an unfavorable juror for an English plaintiff, and vice-versa.

A German juror who lived in Germany under Hitler would be assumed to be adverse to a Jewish plaintiff. The fallacy of this premise could be demonstrated only if information showing anti-Nazi sympathies of the juror were available to indicate that Nazi anti-Semitism never took root with this particular juror. Because such reliable information is not obtainable on *voir dire*, plaintiff's counsel must play the law of averages and should challenge the juror peremptorily.

Blacks, Mexicans, Puerto Ricans, or members of other economically depressed groups are considered pro-plaintiff in their sympathies. Local prejudice against them must be considered when they are the plaintiffs.

Jewish and Italian jurors often are considered sympathetic to plaintiffs by reason of their alleged emotional makeup or psychology as members of minority groups.

Conversely, German, Irish, Swedish, and Norwegian jurors are supposed to be conservative, less emotional, and hence pro-defendant in their sympathies.

Persons living in areas where racial or religious strife is known to have occurred should be examined carefully upon *voir dire*. For example, in New York City, where large numbers of Puerto Ricans have moved into certain areas of the city, a plaintiff of Puerto Rican heritage who reside[s in this area, may find jurors] may regard Puerto Ricans as invaders, or "foreigners." In Los Angeles a similar situation exists with regard to Mexicans.

A black juror is not likely to look kindly upon the cause of a plaintiff who is a police officer, for the tensions arising from allegations of police brutality are too well known to ignore.

All of these assumptions and generalities must give way to the reality of analysis of each individual juror, for all human beings differ from each other in personality and outlook and cannot be placed in a mold that stamps out identical philosophies, passions, and prejudices.

OCCUPATIONAL PREJUDICE

Examples of occupational prejudice may exist between members of different crafts in the same line of business. For example, there may be an intense disaffection between steelworkers and concrete workers in office building construction, or between sales clerks working for Macy's and those working for Gimbel's, or between hod carriers and bricklayers, or between taxi drivers and truck drivers, and so on *ad infinitum*. Utility company employees, such as telephone, gas, or electric workers, are regarded as pro-defendant in their sympathies, possibly because of "indoctrination" courses that they are alleged to receive from their employers to instill a pro-defendant psychology in them for future jury service. The allegation may or may not be true in given instances.

SOCIAL, ECONOMIC, AND REGIONAL PREJUDICES

Examples of prejudice include those prevailing among the various strata of social, economic, and regional groups, such as possible antipathy or envy of the poor juror as against a wealthy plaintiff, the Southerner against the Northerner, a business executive against a union organizer, or vice versa.

PROFESSIONAL PREJUDICES

Many persons are not enamored of physicians or lawyers. In medical malpractice cases it is vital for the plaintiff's counsel to query whether the juror is related to or has close friendships with physicians. If a doctor is a plaintiff in a negligence suit, it would be pertinent to know whether the juror has formed antipathies toward doctors, by reason of possible ill results of treatment or fancied high charges for medical treatment. Segments of the public label doctors as "pill pushers" and "quacks" as often as lawyers are designated "shysters" and "cheats." The lawyer or doctor who sues as plaintiff has a difficult row to hoe with such people on the jury.

FEMALE ENVY AND ANIMOSITY

The woman juror who is to decide the case of a young and attractive woman in some cases is apt to be a severe critic of the dress, speech, and deportment of the female plaintiff. The merits of the case may be only incidental. In one case in my experience, a beautiful 15-year-old girl who sustained injuries as a passenger in an automobile collision ran the gauntlet unsuccessfully and sustained the further injury of a defendant's verdict. A postmortem discussion with two middle-aged woman jurors disclosed that they had developed an unreasoning cold fury against the young but mature plaintiff. Her unforgivable offense was her beauty, a formidable factor that galvanized the two women jurors into persuading 10 compliant male jurors into a unanimous defendant's verdict. Their prejudice was the dominant ingredient of the verdict.

Counsel who brings a beautiful female to court as a plaintiff or witness must anticipate the subliminal effect on other women serving on juries.

PERSONAL INJURY EXPERIENCE

A juror who has sustained an injury similar to the one in suit likely will be an "authority" on the subject. His or her views of causation, permanency, and the dollar value of the injuries probably will be a powerful influence upon the jury. A juror who has accepted a relatively small award in workers' compensation for a back injury is not going to be disposed to giving a much higher award to a plaintiff for a similar injury.

In an actual case, my client was shot accidentally through the ankle by a police officer who had negligently handled a revolver. On *voir dire*, one of the jurors in the action against the city stated that he had been shot in the leg with three bullets while in army service. It was obvious, even without questions, that his injuries had been painful and had left permanent effects. Query: Should this juror be challenged peremptorily or permitted to serve?

I challenged him peremptorily on the premise that his gunshot wounds were as bad or worse than the injury of my client, that he would compare his veteran's pension with a reasonable award to be made to my client, and that the jury would look to him for leadership regarding the seriousness and extent of the injury and its monetary value.

During a recess at the trial, I met this challenged juror in the courthouse corridor. He stated sympathetically, "I'm sorry you challenged me, because I certainly would have been in favor of your client." I asked him how he would have evaluated my client's injury in awarding a verdict to him. He replied: "I might have given him as high as $15,000." The jury awarded many times as much money to the plaintiff.

PRIOR JURY EXPERIENCE

Jurors with prior jury experience may likely have been exposed to other cases of exaggerated injuries or poor liability. Accordingly, query:

Q. How many of you have sat as jurors in other injury cases?

Q. Did anything occur in these other cases that would make it difficult for you to be completely fair and impartial in this case?

Q. Do you think you can decide this case on its own facts regardless of the different situations you have seen in other cases?

Q. Do you think every case is different and that each case deserves a fair hearing on its own facts?

Regardless of the answers elicited, jurors who have served on more than two juries in injury cases should be excused. They have gone to the well too often.

THE JUROR WHO IS AGAINST "BIG VERDICTS"

Many jurors have read newspaper or magazine articles attacking high verdicts. The jury assembly rooms undoubtedly are the scene of much palaver upon this subject. The matter sometimes erupts unexpectedly during *voir dire* as follows:

Q. Is there anyone here who would be reluctant to render a substantial award of damages even if the evidence shows that a serious and permanent injury has been inflicted?

A. [By juror] I would have some trouble with that matter. [Here counsel must decide whether to challenge the juror in an attempt to bury the problem, or counsel may assume that the other jurors have similar thoughts they have no desire to express. If counsel decides to open up the subject and to meet it head on, query further:]

Q. Can you explain your thoughts?

A. Well, I have read a lot about high verdicts, and I do not agree with them.

Q. Do you mean you have read newspaper or magazine articles on this subject?

A. Yes.

Q. Have you discussed your thoughts with other jurors on this panel?

A. No.

Q. Would you agree that a small injury should get a small award and a large injury should get a larger award, commensurate with the seriousness of the injury?

A. I suppose so.

Q. Can you imagine any injury serious enough to deserve an award of $1 million or $5 million in spite of anything you may have read?

A. Yes.

Q. If you are selected as a juror, would you be able to promise on your oath as a juror to decide this case upon the evidence in this case alone and to disregard any outside influence of anything you have read or heard about so-called high verdicts?

A. Yes.

[Despite the above answers, this juror probably should be excused by wise counsel, for the brainwashing effect of propaganda may easily have influenced the juror's thinking beyond redemption. The questions are intended to induce the other jurors to be fair.]

VOIR DIRE BY COUNSEL
INVADING STRANGE TERRITORY

Frequently counsel will try cases in counties or states at considerable distance from home. The jurors in such situations will have a natural affinity to the defendant's counsel who is known to them as a local resident. Defense counsel may inject the local favoritism as follows in true hometown vernacular:

Q. Now, do any of you folks know this here lawyer from New York who's come upstate to try this case against us?

Or,

Q. Now this lawyer from Ohio is suing here in Indiana against Tom Jones, who lives right here in Kokomo, Indiana. Do any of you know this lawyer from Ohio?

Regarding such subtle ministrations, which are transparent devices to coax favoritism from the jury for their neighbor, counsel for the plaintiff may query as follows:

Q. Do you folks feel that you cannot grant a fair trial in Kokomo, Indiana, to my client, even though my client and I happen not to live in this county?

Q. Do you think the case should be decided on the evidence according to your oath as jurors, or do you feel that the main issue is where the lawyers or the parties hail from?

Q. Do you think that this court in Indiana can be the scene of a fair trial regardless of whether the lawyer is from another county or state?

Q. Do you think the main issue in this case will be who the lawyers are, or what the sworn evidence is upon which a just verdict should be rendered?

Q. My name is John Franklin. I do not happen to be fortunate enough to live in your beautiful area of this state; however, I ask you now, individually, whether it is possible for me to come into your county and get a fair and impartial trial for my client at your hands? [Question is to be put separately to all jurors, who will be reminded of their promise to be impartial on final argument.]

Q. Do you feel that a person who is injured through the fault of another should have a right to recover money damages if the evidence justifies it and if the law sanctions it?

Q. Do you feel that a person injured through the fault of another should merely absorb his or her injuries and do nothing about it even though the law, of course, is to the contrary and authorizes six [or 12] impartial persons on a jury to decide the honesty and the merits of the case?

Such questions usually elicit affirmative responses, but occasionally a juror will respond that many cases are exaggerated—a sure ticket to that juror's being peremptorily challenged.

MALPRACTICE CASES

Some individuals feel that doctors, the Good Samaritans of our society, can do no wrong. Some are related to doctors or are social friends of doctors. Such jurors should be eliminated because of their empathy and identification with the medical establishment. Lurking in their thought process is the likely feeling that the doctor, as a healer of the sick and the lame, should be forgiven "mistakes" and should not be penalized and disgraced by imposition of an adverse verdict.

Each juror should be asked:

Q. Do you understand that the license of this doctor to practice medicine is not going to be in jeopardy; that he is still practicing medicine and will continue to practice medicine regardless of the outcome of this case?

Q. Do you understand that this is not a criminal action in any sense of the word and that no one is going to jail as a result of your verdict?

Q. Do you understand that we are not contending that this doctor [or hospital] is a generally bad doctor [or hospital] or that this doctor [or hospital] is usually or always a bad doctor [or hospital]?

Q. Do you understand that we are merely claiming that *in this case* this doctor failed to conform to proper standards of care, deviating from normal, proper, accepted practice, inflicting serious injury upon Mrs. Smith; that the only consequence of this case will be a verdict for money damages if the evidence justifies it?

Q. Do you feel that doctors or hospitals should be placed upon a special pedestal of immunity that is not granted to the rest of us whether we are lawyers, plumbers, businessmen, teachers, or anyone else, that everyone is supposed to be equal before the law? [This is a reference to President Nixon, whose abrupt departure from the presidency and subsequent pardon has penetrated the psyche of all jurors everywhere.]

Equivocal responses such as "Well, yes but . . ." show empathy with the doctor.

AIRPLANE CASES
AND MOTORCYCLE CASES

In airplane crash cases, jurors on the panel should be asked to raise their hands if they never have flown in an airplane. Such individuals in this jet-age society may likely have the feeling that anyone who places his or life life at stake by flying in airplanes is foolhardy. Such reverse psychology would seem applicable in airplane crash cases, for the non-flier on the jury may apply the harsh doctrine of assumption of risk to bar a recovery to the airplane crash victim or the victim's survivors.

A similar type of prejudice applies to persons driving or riding on motorcycles or mopeds. To some jurors, anyone foolish enough to assume such risks has asked for and deserves the harsh fate of horrible injuries.

Jurors may be asked:

Q. Do you understand that Mr. Jones was a licensed motorcycle operator? We will prove he had much experience in operating motorcycles.

Q. Will you consider our evidence that Mr. Jones could not afford an automobile and used his motorcycle to go to and from work as a matter of economy?

Q. Do you believe that Mr. Jones is deserving of less consideration at your hands than a person who can afford to own and drive an automobile?

Q. Do you feel that a person who is operating a motorcycle is entitled to have the benefit of the same rules of the road as the driver of the automobile that struck him in the rear?

PRIOR LAWSUITS OR CLAIMS

It must be assumed that the defendant will have a record of all prior claims for workers' compensation or damages in negligence claims. The jury should be told about all such claims and queried as follows:

Q. Ladies and gentlemen, we expect to show that Mr. Jones, the plaintiff, was in excellent physical condition on the day of this accident. Four years earlier he had been injured while riding as a passenger in an automobile. In a lawsuit, he received some compensation for his injuries, which cleared up after five months and never bothered him again. The injuries were to the same part of his body in both accidents. Is that clear to you?

Q. Would the fact that Mr. Jones brought two separate lawsuits for injuries to his shoulder be considered improper by you?

Q. Would the coincidence of his having been injured twice in the shoulder in these accidents present any special problem to you, or could you decide the case fairly on the evidence?

Q. Would the fact that Mr. Jones, over the last 15 years, has had three lawsuits and three workers' compensation injuries lead you to be prejudiced against him, or would you be open-minded and decide this case strictly upon the evidence as to whether he was hurt in this accident, how seriously he was hurt, and whether it was the defendant's fault? Would you penalize him because he has been injured a number of times?

CONVICTION OF CRIMES

In preparation for trial, counsel must ascertain whether the plaintiff ever was convicted of a crime. If so, discretion may impel the decision to keep the plaintiff off the witness stand if independent testimony as to liability is available. If this is done, the defendant will be prevented from disclosing the plaintiff's criminal background because the conviction normally can be used by the defendant only to attack the plaintiff's credibility upon cross-examination.

Where the plaintiff's testimony is essential to prove a case, the jury should be conditioned via *voir dire* to accept this fact of life, as follows:

Q. May I inform you folks that when my client was younger, for various reasons that I cannot discuss in detail now, he got into trouble with the law. In 1959 he pleaded guilty to assault with a deadly weapon, a gun, and he was paroled for a period of three years; in 1962 he was convicted of armed robbery and was jailed for five years; in 1969 he was jailed for six months on a misdemeanor charge of simple assault to which he pleaded guilty. I expect to show that he has paid his debt to society for these wrongful, illegal acts and that he has worked hard and steadily for the past 11 years in his occupation of a brewer of beer without any further difficulties with the law. I now ask you:

Q. Do you feel that my client, who has paid his debt to society, has lost all rights to have a fair and impartial trial at your hands?

Q. Would these convictions so prejudice you that you would disbelieve anything and everything he may say in his sworn testimony?

Q. Would you be prejudiced against him because of his past record?

Q. Do you think it is possible that his case may be honest in spite of his background?

Q. Do you believe that American courts of justice should be closed to all persons who have ever been convicted of a crime?

Q. Can you decide this case on the evidence alone and not on the separate matter of these convictions, which had nothing to do with this automobile collision?

A CHECKLIST FOR *VOIR DIRE*

Make a short introductory statement to panel, briefly stating names of all attorneys and parties, nature of accident, date, place, and contentions regarding liability and injuries.

On *voir dire*, do I want to exclude persons of particular:

1. racial origin;
2. religious or national origin;
3. occupational groups;
4. social, economic, and regional groups;
5. professional groups or relatives of persons in certain professions or occupations;
6. women jurors;
7. aged jurors;
8. kingpin or leader types?

On *voir dire*, check jurors on possible relationships to casualty insurance companies as officer, stockholder, director, or employee in the past or at present (if local procedural rules so permit).

Check on whether:

1. any jurors ever were sued, or members of their families ever were sued, in injury claims at any time;
2. any jurors have any feelings regarding rendering substantial verdicts in injury cases;
3. any jurors have read or heard brainwashing publicity, propaganda, or discussion on personal injury litigation (this depends on whether this is a particular problem in certain areas; it must be recognized that there is authority, deemed by this author to be unsound, that questions cannot be asked on *voir dire* as to

exposure to literature dealing with insurance premiums and amounts of awards);

4. any jurors have had prior jury service in injury cases; if so, whether they have carried over any general sentiments against claimants in such cases (ideally, first-time jurors are preferable).

Gain jury acceptance of problems by broaching them on *voir dire*. For example:

1. darting-child situations (show perfection of care by child not required);
2. pedestrian knockdown (discuss right-of-way of pedestrian);
3. malpractice situations (knock out immunity of doctor);

4. prior lawsuits or claims by plaintiff (make full disclosure to jury);
5. prior pathology or prior injuries of plaintiff (make full disclosure);
6. conviction of crimes by plaintiff (make full disclosure);
7. trick questions or prejudicial material by defendant, e.g., injection of sympathy for defendant (counteract);
8. elimination of impatient jurors;
9. obtain a ruling before *voir dire* to quash prejudicial material;
10. avoid levity during *voir dire*. If deponent indulges in it, terminate it by remark, "This is a serious matter. My client has serious and permanent injuries. It is no time to indulge in jokes."

45

The Injustices of Plea-Bargaining

IRVING R. KAUFMAN

Prison revolt is the product of felt injustice rather than physical hardship. It is now widely recognized that prison inmates' grievances are fueled by unexplained—and sometimes inexplicable disparities in their sentences. But I believe that the pervasive practice of plea-bargaining is a yet more profound cause of the disrespect prisoners feel for the criminal justice system.

A criminal trial is a rarity. With very few exceptions, virtually all criminal convictions are entered by a guilty plea. No criminal defendant or prosecutor should, in a properly functioning judicial system, be bludgeoned by cost or delay into bargaining for a plea. To the degree that a judicial system falls short of this ideal, it will certainly breed cynicism and distrust.

When one reflects on the charges leveled at our criminal-justice system, the conclusion is inescapable that the criminal trial provides the only assurance of just, consistent and sure law enforcement. Of even greater importance, however, is the impressive ritual of the legal proceeding itself.

The trial embodies our highest ideals of fairness. Its preoccupation with the presumption of innocence and its requirement of proof to a moral certainty express society's fundamental regard that justice be done to the accused. And the pronouncement of judgment based on the unanimous verdict of a jury of one's peers is as solemn an act, as fraught with grandeur, as society can devise to impress upon the lawbreaker the enormity of his conduct. The process of trial may often be crucial in justifying punishment to the accused and demonstrating to society the fairness, and firmness, of its legal system.

We cannot ignore the perversions of justice that may be engendered by bargained pleas. There are lawyers who never try a case. Their fees are based on the assumption that the client will plead guilty, and they are conscious of the financial imperative of inducing the client to do so. The defense attorney often paints the possibility of a favorable outcome at trial in the darkest hues.

In difficult cases, he may even recruit friends and family members to implore the defendant to enter a guilty plea. In many instances, the lawyer's advice may be wise. But a guilty plea brought about by a system that encourages such pressures always risks undermining faith in our criminal-justice system.

The pressure to induce a guilty plea undermines respect for law in a more direct way. A criminal defendant begins with a corrupt view of the world. The secrecy of plea-bargaining reinforces these unfortunate convictions. Indeed, a lawyer whose time is exclusively devoted to plea-bargaining is always tempted to permit the impression that the bargain was won through favoritism and personal ties. A process that ought to be a lesson in honesty and fair play merely confirms the cynicism of those subject to it.

The response is made that elimination of plea-bargaining would further delay a "justice" that is already far from swift. We are warned that increased delay would weaken deterrence and prolong the agony of defendants languishing in jails awaiting trial. It is true that mandating a trial of almost all criminal cases in our financially starved courts would increase the difficulties for an already overworked and overwhelmed criminal-justice system.

But we must candidly face up to the ugly price we are paying by relying almost exclusively on bargained guilty pleas. A system of penal law cannot aspire to be effective unless those subject to it, and the general community, consider it just. Plainly, treatment that the accused believes to be contrived is not rehabilitative. And it is equally apparent that, at least in a democratic society, punishment that is viewed as oppressive cannot deter.

Justice is a moral imperative. It cannot be sacrificed to expediency without undermining society's very foundations. Encouraging plea-bargains as a means of expediting the criminal process is a mere palliative, and ultimately self-defeating.

The "economies" resulting from plea-bargaining can be exaggerated all too easily. Years before prosecutors and defense counsel became addicted to the negotiated plea, defendants often pleaded guilty in open court, freely and willingly. Many defendants are eager to confess their guilt before the judge and assuage a troubled conscience. In the small number of jurisdictions that have eliminated plea-bargaining, prosecutors have abjured "overcharging," and the courts have not been inundated by a cascade of criminal trials. And let us not overlook that plea-bargaining itself is often time-consuming and productive of delay.

Some problems of delay will result from abolishing plea-bargaining. The appropriate response to this marginal increase in undue delay is more efficient use of the courts. A wise investment of resources in the trial phase of the judicial process will, of course, be required. And we must recognize that the courts cannot continue to bear the full brunt of society's ills. If they are to perform their more important tasks well, it is urgent that they be relieved of less critical matters.

To assure everyone accused of crime his day in court will greatly tax our ingenuity and commitment to justice. But the stakes are high, and the regeneration of our respect for law well worth the sacrifice.

— **46** —

Private Judging: A New Variation of Alternative Dispute Resolution

ERIC D. GREEN

Recently, some California litigants in complex commercial cases and in such other nasty disputes as divorce cases with large amounts of property at stake have voluntarily availed themselves of a binding variation of court-ordered arbitration—the use of a private judge or "referee" pursuant to the California general reference statute.[1] Dubbed by the popular press as "rent-a-judge," the procedure resembles private arbitration, but differs in certain important ways.

By agreement of the parties, the court refers the case to a privately selected and paid neutral "referee." In the broadest applications of this process (as in California), the referee has all the powers of a judge except the contempt power, and the referee's decision is entered as binding by the trial court. Thus, private judging closely resembles private arbitration in that the third party's decision is binding. But unlike arbitration, once the referee's decision is entered as a judgment, it may be appealed for errors of law or on the ground that the judgment is against the weight of evidence.

Like private arbitration, the minitrial, and some court-ordered arbitration programs, private judging permits litigants to have their cases heard privately and quickly by a third party of their own choosing. Also like the minitrial, private judging has established such an impressive track record where it has been applied that it has attracted the attention of lawyers, judges, and business people nationwide. Yet this attention has resulted in mixed reviews. Private judging has been hailed as a flexible and efficient alternative to adjudication[2] and condemned as "rich man's

© 1985 Association of Trial Lawyers of America. Reprinted with permission from *Trial*, Vol.21, No.10 (October 1985), pp. 36–43. This article is based on a paper presented to the 1985 Chief Justice Earl Warren Conference on Advocacy, sponsored by the Roscoe Pound-American Trial Lawyers Foundation.

justice" that undermines the public dispute resolution system and threatens constitutional values.[3]

HOW PRIVATE JUDGING WORKS

The essence of the California reference procedure is the provision that allows the court "upon the agreement of the parties" to appoint anyone it deems qualified as "referee" to "try any or all of the issues in an action . . . whether of fact or of law, and to report a finding and judgment thereon" or "to ascertain a fact necessary to enable the court to determine an action."[4] The parties may stipulate to the choice of a single referee or of up to three.[5]

In certain specified cases, if the parties do not agree on a referee, on the application of either party, or on its own motion, the court may appoint a special referee or referees "against whom there is no legal objection" to determine an account or report on a single fact.[6] A legal objection may be based on the bias or interest[7] of the referee or, in environmental cases, "on the ground that he is not technically qualified with respect to the particular subject matter of the proceedings."[8] Yet, generally, and especially in private-judging cases that have attracted the most interest from corporate counsel seeking a way out of crowded public courtrooms, the referee has been appointed under the general reference provisions and has been selected by mutual agreement of the parties.

A case may be referred to a referee at any time—even before the filing of the complaint—by the filing of a petition and proposed order. In most cases, the referee is appointed after the answer and any counterclaims have been filed. Since the referee has all the power of a judge to hear and decide motions and discovery matters, however, early appointment of a referee can greatly reduce the cost of pretrial conflict.

The procedure at the trial may range from traditional court proceedings to the more informal procedures of arbitration. Witnesses are sworn, but the evidence taken need not be reported or even recorded if the parties desire.[9] The referee is obliged to follow both substantive law and evidentiary rules, but the parties may agree, subject to some limitations, to modify or disregard most formal rules of procedure, evidence, and pleading. The parties and referee may also agree on the date of the "trial" and on the disputed issues to be tried.

The referee must submit a written report to the appointing court within 20 days of the close of testimony. Generally, this report consists of findings of fact and conclusions of law, which must be stated separately.[10] Yet, apparently, if the parties and referee agree, detailed findings and conclusions may be dispensed with and only brief findings and conclusions reported—e.g., liability in a certain amount or nonliability. If the similar judge pro tem process[11] is used instead of the general reference statute, findings may be waived totally.

The most important aspect of the California process is that "the finding of the referee . . . upon the whole issue *must* stand as the finding of the court, and . . . judgment may be entered thereon in the same manner as if the action had been tried by the court."[12] Several California Supreme Court cases[13] and the Code Commissioners' Note to this section state that the finding of a general referee is "conclusive" and that mandamus lies to compel the court to enter judgment on the report of a referee. Unlike arbitration, however, appeal rights are preserved just as they would be with any other judgment.[14]

Despite the fact that a private judge's decision becomes the judgment of a court, it has no precedential value. Since it is not a decision of a higher court, it has no binding effect on a trial court. And since it is the decision of another trial judge, it has no stare decisis effect either. If a reference-based judgment were appealed and affirmed by a higher court, however, then the decision of the higher court would be a binding precedent regardless of whether the initial decision was by a private, regular, or administrative judge. In this respect, private judging is no different from arbitration.

Costs, including the referee's fee, are chargeable to the parties, who may stipulate whatever sharing arrangement they desire.

Although California's procedure has attracted the lion's share of national attention, nearly every state has some general reference statute or rule-based system. These programs span a broad spectrum.[15]

Some limit the subject matter of cases that may be referred. Some treat the referee's decision as merely advisory, which is essentially indistinguishable from nonbinding arbitration or a minitrial. Some limit use of the procedure to "exceptional" cases.[16] Some permit trial court review of the referee's conclusions of law but not of the referee's findings of fact. Others, like California, give the referee's decision the full weight of a judicial judgment.[17]

When compared with adjudication or most court-ordered arbitration programs, private judging is distinguished by several attractions. First and foremost, litigants choose the third party who will decide their dispute rather than trusting the luck of the draw in the assignment of a trial judge. This can be crucial in a complex commercial case, in a dispute involving difficult technical questions, or in a case simply involving a large amount of money or a vital aspect of a company's business. Parties are likely to attach greater credibility to a decision handed down by someone they had some role in choosing.

As private judging is more widely employed, the hypothesis that reference judgments are more accepted and, hence, less often appealed by the parties can be put to the test by comparing the rates of appeals of referee and traditional trial judgments. One would expect fewer appeals from referees'

judgments because they represent a self-selected category of cases in which disputants have sought a quick resolution and have presumably chosen a judge less error prone.

CONVENIENCE AND FLEXIBILITY

Parties trapped in traditional court litigation have virtually no control over the timing of the trial or the scheduling of hearing dates. In such large jurisdictions as Los Angeles Superior Court and Suffolk County (Massachusetts) Superior Court, the time between the filing of a complaint and the start of a trial commonly runs from four to five years or more. Since "justice delayed is justice denied," finding ingenious ways to advance one's case on the calendar has now become a valuable litigation tactic. Yet counsel can often do nothing to break out of this legal logjam but wait and hope that witnesses do not die or forget testimony and that parties do not lose interest and give up. Nothing, that is, except get the court to appoint a referee, hire a retired judge, and go to trial whenever the parties are ready.

With private judging, the parties can schedule their trial at a convenient place, date, and time and be certain of the arrangements. One attorney who has participated in several reference procedures claims private judging saves "80 percent of the delays, 80 percent of the legal fees, and 80 percent of the aggravation" encountered in the courts.

Another major advantage over adjudication enjoyed by private judging is its flexible rules and procedures. Parties wanting the formality and procedures of a trial—black-robed judge, paneled courtroom, reporter, and all the "tosh"[18]—can have them under the reference provisions. But as with private alternate dispute resolution, most procedural and evidentiary rules can be relaxed if the parties want. By waiving general rules, the parties can design rules of evidence and procedures that meet their needs. Revising the rules is, of course, not revolutionary but the essence of arbitration. And in traditional adjudication, it is not unusual for the parties and the court to agree to dispense with some of the trappings of due process. On the other hand, the obligations of the referee to apply substantive law and the availability of an appeal for errors of law sharply distinguish the reference procedure from arbitration.

CONFIDENTIALITY

Once the matter is referred to the referee, nothing more need be reported or made public except the referee's findings of fact and conclusions of law. Apparently even this to a large extent may be waived by the parties. If an appeal is taken after a reference of this sort, the parties will have to stipulate to a record on appeal. According to those experienced with the procedure, in practice this has not been a problem.[19]

In contrast, a regular trial is a completely public event. Anyone is free to attend, including the parties' competitors. Exhibits and testimony are available to anyone who wants access. Even a protective order may not effectively preserve the confidentiality of discovery materials. In cases involving trade secrets or closely guarded business methods that are not quite trade secrets but understandably regarded as private, or in cases where the parties may be concerned about bad publicity, confidentiality may be a sufficient reason for parties to "go private." This is often the motivation for using the reference procedure in contested divorces or in cases involving celebrities.

Another advantage of the reference procedure over traditional litigation is the speed with which a decision is rendered after the trial. Unfortunately, a delay of many months between the close of a court-tried case and a decision is not unusual. Under the California

reference procedure, a decision is expected within 20 days.

The assurance of a final binding and appealable decision is a major advantage of the reference procedure over court-ordered arbitration, the minitrial, and other nonbinding processes. The quid pro quo for this, however, is that the decision is imposed by a third party rather than designed by the parties themselves. This has some important byproducts. For example, since the referee's decision is handed down by a judicial figure and incorporated into a judgment, it is much more likely to resemble the winner-take-all, money-based nature of most common law judgments rather than the more flexible, creative, and mutually compensatory character of voluntary settlements.

Private judging also provides more flexible relief than does court adjudication because of its opportunities for mediation, negotiation, and voluntary settlement before judgment. A reference proceeding conducted by an experienced former judge or attorney sensitive to the procedure's mediational possibilities provides the next best settlement forum to a minitrial. But the main point is that the result of an adjudication before a referee is much more likely to resemble that of a traditional adjudication than that of an arbitration, negotiation, mediation, or minitrial. Of course, this—and the right of appeal—may be just what the parties want.

Experience with the binding reference procedure has so far been largely confined to California and is relatively recent. The procedure has been on the books in that state for more than a century, but was used in alternative dispute resolution for the first time in 1976. Since then it has been used in Los Angeles alone in more than 300 cases, most of which were large, time-consuming matters.[20]

A typical example of the reference procedure was a breach of contract, defective product case involving a major auto manufacturer, the designer, and the manufacturer of a component part. Five suits and countersuits were filed when the product allegedly failed and the automaker canceled the contracts. Unable to obtain a trial in the public courts, the parties had a referee appointed. After 15 days of trial, scheduled at the convenience of the parties and witnesses, a judgment was handed down. Reportedly, even the losing party praised the process.[21]

DEFUSING THE CRITICISM

With all of the advantages over traditional adjudication, what points can be made against expanded use of the reference procedure? Paradoxically, most criticism seems to be based precisely on the assumption that adjudication by referee is better than adjudication by the court.

Critics claim that since litigants must pay the referee themselves while the court system is almost completely supported by taxes, the availability of private judging creates two kinds of justice—"rich man's justice" and "poor man's justice."

Such criticism is understandable but invalid. First, use by some litigants of the reference process does not deprive other litigants of anything they now have. The quality of justice available in the courts is not adversely affected by the diversion of some cases to referees. On the contrary, removing complex business disputes from the courts can only have a positive impact on court calendars and increase everyone else's access to justice. Indeed, some believe that commercial disputes between private litigants, which are the staple of the reference process, ought not to be allowed in court at all. These cases, the critics claim, unfairly consume the scarce resources of the court system at the expense of criminal defendants and individual claimants awaiting trial. Under this view, the public dispute resolution system should be reserved for disputes in which the public has a more substantial interest—criminal cases, civil rights cases, and individual grievances that require the leverage of the state for resolution. Although extreme, this view somewhat reflects the present system. Speedy trial provisions for criminal cases and priority treatment for cases involving public law issues seek to ensure greater access to the courts for these disputes at the expense of commercial litigants. But the point is pushed too far to claim that the public has *no* interest in the efficient and fair resolution of private commercial disputes or that such disputants have no right of access to the public system when necessary.

Guaranteeing a right of access differs, however, from saying that commercial disputants *must* adjudicate their disputes in court despite their belief that they have found a better way in a better forum. After all, the resolution of commercial litigation by negotiation between the principals alone or by their agreement to seek a decision from a referee is somewhat a continuation of the business dealings that first led to the dispute. Viewed in this light, why should those wishing to employ the services of a referee and willing to pay what amounts to a user's fee for the service be denied that option? Even taxpayers benefit when private parties decide on the reference process—the state saves the cost of the judge and all other court personnel. Thus to the extent that using referees works a reallocation of resources, the reallocation is in economists' terms, "Pareto-superior"; in everyday language, no one is worse off and at least one person is better off.

In addition, the underlying assumptions of the "rich man's justice" criticism are questionable. Experience indicates and studies of civil litigation corroborate that, in many cases, only the wealthy can afford the justice now dispensed by the public system and the private bar. Although disputants must pay a private judge while they would otherwise receive the services of a judge at no cost, they will usually save so much in reduced delay, inconvenience, disruption, and unnecessary formality that the reference procedure will more than pay for itself. Unfortunately, too often it is today's public justice system that dispenses "rich man's justice," which is what reference disputants seek to avoid.

A more valid concern is that if private judging becomes commonplace for business, it could result in a withdrawal from the public system of powerful, private interests, which could drain off resources necessary for the reform and improvement of the courts. Yet, this is unlikely. No matter how attractive private judging and other alternate dispute resolution become, even the most powerful and resourceful components of society will resort to the public system. The existence of all alternative dispute resolution depends on a strong, open court system and a strong trial bar. Even the most powerful companies and individuals cannot prevent themselves from being summoned into court by a complainant and kept there. Reference takes two to tango. In many cases, one party will not want to dance.

Another criticism of private judging deserving serious consideration relates to its confidentiality. Secret trials offend our notion of open government and public courts and may offend the public's "first amendment right to know" about the conduct of government. The parties in private reference disputes would deny that the public interest is protected and the first amendment served by revealing the details of their business disputes and how they are resolved. To them, the disputes are merely the continuation of private transactions that went awry. They would contend that straightening out a transaction need not be any more public than its making.

The weakness of this reasoning is that at least one of the parties to the dispute has invoked the assistance of a public agency (the court) and both have then agreed to employ officially sanctioned dispute resolution. The parties' claim to privacy is more convincing where they have resolved their dispute through negotiation, mediation, or a mini-trial, without the aid of the court. But under private judging, the parties obtain a judgment enforceable with all the power of the state

normally available to victorious litigants. If the parties want the imprimatur and power of a judgment, the critics of privacy would say, the trade-off is openness. Considering the possible antitrust implications of a referee-ordered judgment, this argument has some force. It does not account for the fact, however, that parties to a lawsuit can generally settle a case themselves privately and ask the court to enter a judgment incorporating the terms of the settlement. If there is no right of access to settlement negotiations in this situation, why need there be in the reference?

Another criticism of reference is that private judges may favor frequent users of the system, i.e., large institutions:

> *Payments to free market referees raise particular concerns insofar as referees may be influenced to decide cases in favor of the party more likely to bring cases to them in the future. To a certain extent, this problem would be solved by the consent requirement, since no one would consent to a reference if he knew the referee would favor his opponent. As a safeguard, however, consent would only be effective in protecting the integrity of reference proceedings if all parties had perfect knowledge about all referee decisions. Those parties with the greatest experience with reference, however, would have superior knowledge. Similar parties in other contexts have been called "repeat players," but under the market conditions that prevail in reference, they might better be termed steady customers. Steady customers represent an important asset to any seller and a referee would find it in his self-interest to favor these parties where possible. Of course, any favoritism could not be overt, for then the opponents of the steady customers would refuse to consent. But over time, referees could safely give steady customers the benefit of the doubt more often than not. Steady customers would suspect that their status was giving them a small edge, and this would bring them back into reference for future fights. But their opponents, the one-time customers, would not be aware of the subtle systemic bias working against them. They*

could not therefore make a fully informed choice when they consented to the reference. The risk of a due process violation would be especially great if the delay in the state courts had compelled a party with less than full information to agree to reference.[22]

Any process that employs neutral third parties who have their own economic interest in being hired confronts this problem. The same danger exists with arbitration. In the labor context, the problem is diminished because both sides are repeat players, the disputants and arbitrators are all members of a close-knit community, and the range of issues with which arbitrators deal is narrow enough so that the arbitrators' track records are readily known to both sides. But in commercial arbitration, none of these conditions is present. The only safeguards are such administrative oversight of arbitration institutions as the AAA, word-of-mouth, and the individual integrity of the third party. These safeguards are far from perfect, however, which is why parties should exercise great care in the selection of a neutral for any binding process.

NOTES

1. CAL. CIV. PROC. CODE §§ 638–645 (West 1976).
2. See G. GOLDBERG, E. GREEN & E.F. SANDER, DISPUTE RESOLUTION 285–93 (1985); Green, *Avoiding the Legal Logjam—Private Justice California Style,* in CORPORATE DISPUTE MANAGEMENT 65 (1982), from which most of this section is taken; Hufstedler, *The Future of Civil Litigation,* 1980 UTAH L. REV. 753. See generally DISPUTE RESOLUTION 280–281, 285–293, 306.
3. See Note, *The California Rent-a-Judge Experiment: Constitutional and Policy Consideration of Pay as You Go Courts,* 94 HARV. L. REV. 1592 (1981); R. Bird, State of the Judiciary Address, in San Diego, Cal. (Oct. 11, 1981).
4. CAL. CIV. PROC. CODE § 638 (West 1976).
5. *Id.* at § 640.
6. *Id.* at §§ 639, 640.
7. *Id.* at § 641.
8. *Id.* at § 641.2.
9. *Id.* at § 643. See Chapman v. Gipson, 229 P.2d 834 (Cal. Ct. App. 1951).
10. CAL. CIV. PROC. CODE § 643.
11. See CAL. CONST. art VI, § 21; Rule 244(a) CAL. R. CT.
12. See CAL. CIV. PROC. CODE § 644 (emphasis added).
13. *See, e.g.,* Ellsworth v. Ellsworth, 269 P.2d 3 (Cal. 1954); Lewis v. Grunberg, 270 P. 181 (Cal. 1928).
14. CAL. CIV. PROC. CODE § 645.
15. For an excellent summary of state reference processes, see Note, *supra* note 3, at 1594–1597; Green, *supra note* 2, at 76–79.
16. This form of reference is, in essence, incorporated into Rule 53, FED. R. CIV. P. (Special Masters), unless the referee happens to be a United States magistrate, in which case the "exceptional" requirement is dispensed with. See 28 U.S.C. § 636(c)(1) Federal Magistrate Act of 1979, Pub. L. No. 96-82, 93 Stat. 643; Rules 72–76, FED. R. CIV. P.; De Costa v. Columbia Broadcasting Sys., 520 F.2d 499, 507 (1st Cir. 1975), *cert. denied,* 96 S. Ct. 856 (1976); Note, *Article III Constraints and the Expanding Civil Jurisdiction of Federal Magistrates: A Dissenting View,* 88 YALE L.J. 1023 (1979).
17. Examples of provisions that would permit parties to obtain "private judging" of a dispute similar to the California model include:

    N.Y. CIV. PRAC. LAW §§ 4301–4321 (McKinney 1974). (N.Y. CIV. PRAC. LAW § 4317 provides: "The parties may stipulate that any issue shall be determined by a referee. Upon the filing of the stipulation with the clerk, the clerk shall forthwith enter an order referring the issue for trial to the referee named therein. Where the stipulation does not name a referee, the court shall designate a referee.")

    WASH. REV. CODE ANN. §§ 4.48.010–4.48.100 (1974). (WASH. REV. CODE ANN. § 4.48.030 is identical to OR. REV. STAT. § 17.730.)

    NEB. REV. STAT. § § 25-1129 to 25-1137 (1975). (NEB. REV. STAT. § 25-1132 provides: "In all cases of reference, the parties, except when an infant may be a party, may agree upon suitable person or persons, not exceeding three, and the reference shall be ordered accordingly; and if the par-

ties do not agree, the court shall appoint one or more referees, not exceeding three, who shall be free from exception.").

R.I. GEN. LAWS § 9-15-1 to 9-15-21 (1971). (R.I. GEN. LAWS § 9-15-1 provides: "Any court may permit the parties in any civil action pending therein to enter into a rule of court to refer such action to the decision of one or more referees, to be agreed on by the parties, and also to refer in the same rule any other actions, causes of action or suits, that may exist between them either jointly or severally, generally or specially.")

Examples of schemes that, although not as close to California as the first five, would permit parties to obtain private judging of their dispute by a decision-maker of their choice include:

KAN. CIV. PRO. CODE ANN. § 60-253 (Vernon 1983) (reference procedure; omits provision requiring parties to stipulate to the identify of the referee);

OHIO CT.R. 53 (following Fed. R. Civ. P. 53 re masters but without the federal limitation to "exceptional cases"; referee must be an attorney "admitted to practice in this state");

N.H. REV. STAT. ANN. §§ 519:9-519: 16 (1974) (reference procedure; manner of selecting referee not specified in statute, but may be provided for by rule of court);

WIS. STAT. ANN. § 805.06 (West 1983) (follows Fed. R. Civ. P. 53, but accompanying interpretive commentary indicates that "except in divorce and annulment, all or any of the issues may be referred");

CONN. GEN. STAT. §§ 52-425 to 52-434 (1960) (allows for both a reference "committee" and a procedure for a judge pro tem);

FLA. R. CIV. PROC. 1.490 (essentially a judge pro tem procedure);

S.D. COMP. LAWS ANN. § 15-6-53; S.D. COMP. LAWS ANN. §§ 15-13-1 to 15-13-4 (while S.D. Compiled Laws Ann. § 15-6-53 limits the use of a referee to "exceptional cases," S.D. Comp. Laws Ann. § 15-13-1 et seq. provides for a reference procedure similar to that used in California).

18. This is Lon Fuller's term for the ritualistic elements of courts. Fuller, *The Forms and Limits of Adjudication*, 92 HARV. L. REV. 353, 357 (1978).
19. *See* Note, *supra* note 3, at 1598 n.25.
20. Christenson, *Private Justice: California's General Reference Procedures*, 1982 ABA FOUND. RES. J. 79, 102.
21. Green, *supra* note 2, at 75. *See also* Knight, *Private Dispute Resolution—A Going Concern in California*, in CORPORATE DISPUTE MANAGEMENT 113 (1982).
22. Note, *supra* note 3, at 1608.

47

Television in Our Courts: The Proven Advantages, the Unproven Dangers

NORMAN DAVIS

For two full years—one under an experimental rule, the other under a permanent order—television and still cameras have been given access to all state courts in Florida on a daily basis, almost unfettered. The separate cases or trials covered for broadcast number in the hundreds; the number of days on which cameras have televised trials in Florida courtrooms can be counted in the thousands.

Almost three dozen states now permit photographic coverage or are actively considering it.[1] Florida has far and away the most experience because its rule for access has been the most relaxed for the longest period of time. Not a shred of material evidence has emerged to show that camera access has been incompatible with the right to due process and a fair trial. To the contrary, because a camera has an inherent capability that pencil and paper do not, television conveys the *reality* of the courtroom far more accurately than any other reportorial tool, and conveying that reality advances the ends of justice.[2]

Those who are most anxious about television's impact on the judicial process tend to be those with little or no exposure to the actual coverage. One hears amazing tales and conjecture from critics in various forums around the country who project a list of horribles if television coverage takes hold. In places like Florida, where pictures from the courtroom are commonplace on a day-in day-out basis, the real world bears no resemblance whatever to the doomsday forecasts.

Some social observers predict the worst outcome simply because television is involved. In a recent issue of *Judicature*, George Gerbner, the dean of the Annenberg School of Communications at the University of Pennsylvania, roundly condemned television's pursuit of news photographic coverage in courtrooms and accused television of trying to remake our system of justice "in its own image."[3] The ugly process and harmful outcomes Dean Gerbner describes is one which those of us in Florida and elsewhere who have pursued access for cameras do not want, do not expect, and do not see reflected in the now-common broadcasts of courtroom trials.

CRITICS, BUT NO EVIDENCE

Where is the evidence that television in its journalism role has actually affected other institutions in a negative way? TV cameras long have been trained on legislatures, school boards, county commissions, zoning boards, the U.S. House of Representatives, and myriad other public institutions—even the Christmas mass in St. Peter's—without "remaking" the institutions. Television in the courtroom need not be any different.[4]

Judicature, Vol.64, No.2 (August 1980), pp. 85–92. Reprinted by permission of the publisher.

Legislatures, like the courts, deal with issues affecting lives, liberty, and property. Allen Morris, the highly regarded clerk of the Florida House of Representatives and a historian and student of the legislature for half a century, has this observation about TV coverage:

> [Television] has subtly altered the legislative process for the better. Many of our legislators had their doubts about the wisdom of gavel-to-gavel televising because they feared television would encourage grandstanding. This did not happen. Instead, television coverage had a favorable impact on the lawmaking process.
>
> No one mumbles bills through. You seldom see legislators reading newspapers and never see them eating lunch at their desks during debate anymore. . . . Nowadays, under the eye of the television cameras, those sponsoring bills are far more careful to give the House and the viewing public an adequate explanation of what the pending measure does. In other words, debate has become far more structured.[5]

Television as a medium and an industry deserves all of the intense scrutiny it receives, but not all of the criticism is valid or fair. Those who equate television coverage of courts with a greedy search for entertainment, ratings and profits grossly distort television journalism. The *New York Times* and the *Wall Street Journal* also base their advertising charges on the size and make-up of audiences they deliver and they constantly reach for larger audiences. But it doesn't follow that their news coverage is necessarily predicated on such considerations.

Many of the issues raised by opponents of camera access, like the one questioning the motives of television journalists, smack of a double standard—tests never applied to other media. The Florida Supreme Court, in its final order amending the code of judicial conduct, noted that newspapers and magazines also deal in entertainment, and asked

> Is a 'men's entertainment' magazine more calculated to educate and less to entertain than the local television station? At best the answer to that question is a value judgment, but no one would seriously suggest that a reporter for such a magazine should be precluded from covering and reporting a trial because it is not intended to educate or inform the public—that it intends to exploit the courts commercially.[6]

SPECTACLE . . . OR WITNESS?

From his premise that television's goal is entertainment (and ratings), Dean Gerbner concludes that televised trials represent a modern-day equivalent of "show trials and public confessions" of the Middle Ages, which, he says, "were a part of the entertainment mainstream, now joined by much of what we call news, compelling attention, exposing deviation, spreading fear and cultivating conformity."

What Dean Gerbner watches I do not know, but the thousands of samples of televised courtroom coverage—*thousands*—which Florida and other states have provided make both his premise and his conclusions just plain wrong. Nothing appearing on television sets in Florida almost nightly matches, singly or collectively, the frightening prospects he imagines.

Opponents of televised trials often decry the "spectacle" of the "trial conducted in an arena," but so do the advocates. A trial unfolding before 100,000 people in a stadium or a colosseum is a phenomenon far, far different from one conducted in a decorous courtroom under careful rules with 100,000 people looking on from their living rooms. The first is spectacle; the second is witness.

Justice Clark, writing for the majority in *Estes* in a different era and in a completely different factual setting, worried that

> from the moment the trial judge announces that a case will be televised it becomes a cause célèbre . . . The approaching trial immediately assumes an important status in the public press and the

accused is highly publicized along with the offense with which he is charged. . . . And we must remember that realistically it is only the notorious trial which will be broadcast . . .[7]

Notorious trials there certainly are, but courtroom television didn't invent them and television doesn't cause them. There were no cameras present during the trials of Patty Hearst, Sacco and Vanzetti, John Peter Zenger, the Chicago Seven, the Scottsboro Boys, Murph the Surf, or Joan Little. Even so, all those trials were notorious.

On the other hand, a single unobtrusive TV camera *was* present at several Florida trials which achieved great notoriety: those of Ronny Zamora, Theodore Bundy, Johnny Jones, and the four police officers accused of killing black motorcyclist Arthur McDuffie. But *all* of those cases generated high public interest—contrary to Justice Clark's prediction—long *before* the trial and long *before* TV coverage of each one was contemplated. And it isn't hard to see why.[8]

Zamora's murder defense was based on an exotic concept of television-induced insanity. Bundy allegedly had traveled across the United States on a killing spree. Jones, head of one of the largest school districts in the country and one of our ranking black educators, was charged with using school system funds for his vacation home. The black community was upset for months before the trial of the police who beat McDuffie because many blacks believed there was a double standard in the administration of justice in Dade County.

These cases, like those farther removed in history, were "notorious" in their own right. The lone camera which looked on inside the trial chamber neither fomented the notoriety nor aggravated that which already existed. Each case received exhaustive coverage from newspapers and other media before and during the trial. Even without an in-court camera, each case would have received similar coverage by television stations (including squads of cameras around the courthouse) because of the inherent public interest in the issues involved.[9]

SEEING THE PROCESS AS IT IS

Dean Gerbner has rightly detailed the distortions of lawyers, judges, and the courts which commonly have been woven through entertainment programs on television, but then he proceeds with nothing more than supposition to assert that in TV coverage of the real thing "trials will be picked and edited to fit that dramatic ritual."

His assertion collides with reality. In the *real* world of televised courtrooms, viewers have seen nothing whatever that remotely resembles Perry Mason. Instead, they see a slow process which is mostly low-key, rules which are complex, arguments which focus on technical procedure, and attorneys and judges who pause and stumble and fluff their lines just like the rest of us. The courtroom doesn't look like a Hollywood set and the participants don't look and act like a Hollywood cast. No responsible journalist wants it otherwise.

Indeed, during two years of intensive media coverage, Florida has not seen any salivating mobs in the streets yelling for more "public confessions." Almost unanimously, the telephone and mail feedback to television stations has reflected one degree or another of wonderment at seeing the process as it actually is—hardly surprising since the televised coverage can be infinitely more informative and revealing than news reports filtered through the minds of even the best reporters. For the vast majority of citizens, indeed, it has been the very first look inside the chambers of justice.

As long as cameras don't create a circus environment—and no one advocates that—it is socially useful for citizens to see, with the unique realism which only the camera can provide, justice at work. The *Mayberry* decision in 1971 noted that while public trial "is essentially a right of the accused . . . there is, however, a correlative right to preserve the public's right to be informed about criminal prosecutions in the best interests of all its citizens."[10]

In another federal decision a few years earlier, the court observed that

> The public notice of a judicial proceeding tends to improve the quality of testimony, first, by producing in a witness' mind a disinclination to falsify, and second, by securing the presence of other nonparties who may be able to furnish testimony to contradict falsifiers.
>   . . . Other reasons . . . for proceeding publicly rather than privately in the law are (1) the participants, judge, jury and counsel, are moved to stricter conscientiousness in the performance of their duties; (2) persons not parties to the action may be affected by pending litigation and have a right to know what is going on; and (3) public attendance has an educative effect which can increase respect for law and provide confidence in judicial remedies.[11]

Television can enhance these ends more completely and more directly than any other single element. Weigh in your own mind, the next time you see artists' sketches of a court proceeding on a news broadcast, the relative accuracy and fairness they are able to communicate as measured against a camera.

A RIGHT TO OBSERVE

And note, too, that the importance of witness by the general public has just been underscored by the U.S. Supreme Court in the landmark case of *Richmond Newspapers, Inc. v. Virginia.* Writing for the majority, Chief Justice Burger observed that

> . . . when the ancient 'town meeting' form of trial became too cumbersome, twelve members of the community were delegated to act as its surro-

gates, but the community did not surrender its right to observe the conduct of trials. The people retained a 'right of visitation' which enabled them to satisfy themselves that justice was in fact being done.
> People in an open society do not demand infallibility from their institutions, but it is difficult for them to accept what they are prohibited from observing. When a criminal trial is conducted in the open, there is at least an opportunity both for understanding the system in general and its workings in a particular case.[12]

Justice Brennan, joined by Justice Marshall, wrote in a concurring opinion that

> . . . the trial is more than a demonstrably just method of adjudicating disputes and protecting rights. It plays a pivotal role in the entire judicial process, and, by extension, in our form of government. Under our system, judges are not mere umpires, but, in their own sphere, lawmakers—a coordinate branch of government. While individual cases turn upon the controversies between parties, or involve particular prosecutions, court rulings impose official and practical consequences upon members of society at large. Thus . . . it is a genuine government proceeding.[13]

While the *Richmond Newspapers* decision didn't address the issue of cameras in courtrooms, a footnote included in the majority opinion authored by the chief justice is interesting:

> That the right to attend may be exercised by people less frequently today when information as to trials generally reaches them by way of print and electronic media in no way alters the basic right. Instead of relying on personal observation or reports from neighbors as in the past, most people receive information concerning trials through the media whose representatives 'are entitled to the same rights [to attend trials] as the general public.' Estes v. Texas, 381 U.S. at 540.[14]

Opponents of camera coverage—usually those who have seen little of it—are tempted to warn that only "snippets" of a given day's proceedings will emerge on the evening news. Those of the snippet school overlook the fact that virtually *all* news reports in every medium consist of brief digests of events. Even large daily newspapers devote limited column-inches to a report of a full day of activity in court. When, in fact, has a newspaper or magazine *ever* provided the complete start-to-finish coverage television has given to three important trials in Florida?

It is crucial to remember that TV reporters will be in the courtroom even if the camera is not, and without pictures they will continue to report their impressions of what happens—detractors would say in "snippet" fashion. Television news directors in Florida indicate that the availability of photographic and sound material has resulted in the main in longer and more comprehensive reports than previously.

LITTLE EFFECT
ON PARTICIPANTS

Perceptions from outside the courtroom are one thing; what about perceptions from the inside? Does the presence of the camera, even under rigid guidelines, cause witnesses, jurors, lawyers, or judges to behave in such a way that justice is perverted? The development of measured, objective evidence may be impossible to obtain, because what ultimately is required is somehow to determine psychological impacts on the participants in a trial with the camera present, and then to measure impacts on the same participants in the same trial circumstances without the camera. But even then the result wouldn't be instructive, since the participants could be equally impacted by a host of other factors in the courtroom: the robed judge, the uniformed bailiff, an imposing battery of attorneys, from one to half a dozen sketch artists busily drawing, the court reporter's stenotype machine, and many others.

Twenty-five years ago, a leading newspaper editor compared a camera to a live gallery:

It can be argued that the camera is a lot less disconcerting in some ways than a courtroom spectator. No camera ever let out an involuntary exclamation of horror, dismay or amusement on the utterance of a witness. No camera ever grimaced or coughed during testimony. No gallery of cameras ever burst into applause and had to be rapped to order by the court. No camera ever wept or laughed.[15]

The anxiety level concerning potential impacts on witnesses and jurors which existed in Florida before the introduction of cameras seemingly has diminished with experience. Circuit Judge Arthur Franza, summarizing the results of a survey which he conducted among his colleagues throughout the state, noted that in certain respects "some Judges have strong opinions," but concluded "From the whole, I think Courts do not object to the use of cameras in the courtroom now that they have had some experience."[16] Even some defense lawyers who were among the most apprehensive now discreetly admit that the presence of the single camera has not been harmful.

At the conclusion of the year of experimentation it had ordered, the Florida Supreme Court saw none of the adverse effects which opponents had predicted—grandstanding lawyers, posturing judges, intimidated witnesses, distracted or fearful jurors. The court concluded that "the assertions are but assumptions unsupported by any evidence. No respondent has been able to point to any instance during the pilot program period where these fears were substantiated."[17]

Such evidence as exists would appear to refute the assumptions. A survey of about two-thirds of the participants shows that the assumed effects of TV on their behavior varied in degree from little to none. More importantly, participants saw no significant difference in the presence or degree of these influences when they compared the electronic and print media.[18]

WHAT PARTICIPANTS SAID ABOUT TELEVISING FLORIDA'S TRIALS

At the conclusion of Florida's experimental year of camera access two years ago, the Florida Supreme Court commissioned a survey of participants in trials which electronic media had covered. The Office of the State Courts Administrator distributed questionnaires to witnesses, jurors, attorneys, and court personnel. Roughly two-thirds of those in each category responded—a total of 1,349 individuals. It is the most extensive measurement ever attempted, and the Florida Supreme Court expressly relied on the results in its deliberations.

The survey was incomplete in many respects. The Court itself cautioned that "the survey results are nonscientific and reflect only the respondents' attitudes and perceptions. . . ." The inquiry focused attention on camera and microphone almost exclusively; only four of the 55 questions examined "newspaper coverage." No other potentially enhancing, distracting, or inhibiting factors in the courtroom were mentioned. Television coverage during the survey period was something of a novelty, and for the trial participants the questions emphasized that novelty.

(To call attention to the unfairness of singling out cameras, Miami television station WPLG filed with the state supreme court the results of a hasty and admittedly imperfect telephone survey it had conducted among 262 respondents selected randomly by a computer in Dade and Broward counties. The station asked one question: "During court trials, newspaper reporters frequently are on hand, along with artists sketching witnesses for TV news programs. Do you believe the presence of newspaper reporters and sketch artists affects the testimony of witnesses in a negative way?" About 30 per cent said yes.)

Nonetheless, the officially sanctioned survey has been cited far and wide by advocates and opponents alike who pick and choose among the disputed results for support.

Court personnel and attorneys generally were less favorable toward cameras than witnesses and jurors were. Even so, a third of the court staffers and attorneys said that television and photographic coverage had made them feel "more favorable towards the Florida courts."

Some of the results appeared contradictory or offsetting. Forty percent of the attorneys thought the camera made other attorneys "nervous," but fully a third said other attorneys also were "more attentive." About one-fourth of court personnel responding saw judges made nervous by the coverage, but one-third among them said the judges were more attentive.

Jurors were asked whether the presence of photographic equipment affected their "ability to judge the truthfulness of the witness:" 3.8 per cent said they were somewhat hindered; 4.8 per cent said they were helped. Among witnesses, slightly more than half reported that the equipment made them self-conscious; in another response more than a third said they felt more responsible for their actions because the camera was there.

Jurors and witnesses were asked whether, during the trial, they had wanted "to see or hear yourself in the media." About a fourth of the jurors and a third of the witnesses expressed some interest. Whether they also would have liked to read about themselves in the newspaper wasn't asked, nor do the results relate in any way this interest in media coverage to the respondents' ability to perform their sworn duties in court.

When directly compared with newspapers, television fared no better and no worse with the respondents. Witnesses, for example, were asked if they were "concerned that someone may try to harm you in some way because of your appearance as a . . . witness . . . being on television?" About 29 per cent said yes. But an almost equal number—28 per cent—feared harm from "being in the newspapers."

When jurors were asked if they had been "concerned that people would know you were serving on a particular jury and try to influence your decision as a result of the **newspaper coverage of the trial?" 14 per cent** responded positively. When "television coverage" was the issue, 18 per cent were affirmative.

The pitfalls and inadequacies of such research are obvious, but camera access scored impressively well even within the disputed circumstances of the Florida survey. "Overall," one question asked, "would you favor or oppose allowing television, photographic, or radio coverage in the courtroom?" Responding favorably or with no opinion were 73 percent of the jurors, 64 per cent of the witnesses, 58 per cent of the court personnel, and 58 per cent of the attorneys.

No evidence has emerged during the full year of experience following the Florida court's final order which would support suppositions of harm.

There is no shortage of academics and others who want to conduct formalized research on whether the supposed impacts are real. Advocates as well as opponents of cameras need to be receptive to hard evidence whatever the outcome, but the researchers have a heavy responsibility not to tilt the studies against television by focusing on it to the exclusion of other factors and conditions.

OTHER PROBLEMS . . .
AND SOLUTIONS

In Florida, the petitioners for access have conceded all along that the appearance of certain witnesses and defendants may not be appropriate for photographic coverage. Examples are rape victims, children in custody cases, undercover law enforcement agents, crucial witnesses in terrorism cases, and so on.

Apparently mindful that even in such categories protection could be sought on superficial grounds, the Florida Supreme Court prescribed in careful words a fact-finding standard:

> The presiding judge may exclude electronic media coverage of a particular participant only upon a finding that such coverage will have a substantial effect upon the particular individual which would be qualitatively different from the effect on members of the public in general and such effect will be qualitatively different from coverage by other types of media.[19]

Thus far, judges and media officials in Florida have tended to be comfortable with the language. The key to the successful application of such a standard is a proper hearing to discover facts against which it can be measured.

One entirely unexpected bonus from having a TV camera inside the courtroom at major trials is that it encourages almost all other media representatives to operate elsewhere. High public interest usually brings dozens of reporters to a courtroom, but Miami media people, with the cooperation of the chief judges, have pioneered the "media room" remote from the courtroom itself where pooling television crews can set up their bulky equipment. Print journalists prefer to monitor the trial from the room since they can talk and move there without restriction. The trial itself thus is spared the throngs of note-taking journalists.

Another welcome by-product hailed by many judges has been the virtual disappearance of the photographic herd which stalked the steps and the hallways of the courthouse waiting to pounce on lawyers and witnesses moving into and out of the trial room. When the camera can focus on the trial itself, the undignified shouting and shoving matches **outside are no longer necessary.**

Florida's unparalleled application of the concept of truly open government to its courts was launched in 1975 by a petition from the two Post-Newsweek television stations in Miami and Jacksonville.[20] In their report to the state supreme court at the end of the one-year-experiment, the stations told the court that they:

> sought only that access provided to others—the right to be present at public proceedings and to report proceedings without disruption. Properly controlled, that access can be allowed under the decisions of all courts which have addressed the subject. When that access is allowed, principles of open government will be advanced, the values of the First and Sixth Amendments vindicated and a great tradition of the common law maintained for modern times.[21]

In terms of media coverage of the courts, we have seen the future in Florida—and it works.

NOTES

1. "Television in the Courtroom—Recent Developments," National Center for State Courts, May 1, 1980.
2. The U.S. Supreme Court has agreed to hear a case in which a defendant objected to the Florida rule, Chandler v. Florida, 48 U.S.L.W., W. 3645 (April 8, 1980); probable jurisdiction noted, 48 U.S.L., W. 3677 (April 22, 1980). But the defendant makes only *constitutional* arguments in his brief, insisting the camera is unconstitutional *per se*. He points to no "specific mischief" to the rights of his client because of the presence of the camera.
3. Television has had its most profound impact, perhaps, on political campaigns. Candidates and parties have altered strategies to accommodate television because it best meets their need for intimate contact with as many people as possible.
4. Gerbner, *Trial by television: are we at the point of no return?*, 63 JUDICATURE 416 (April 1980).
5. Remarks by Allen Morris, Clerk, Florida House of Representatives, at Annual Meeting of the American Society of Legislative Clerks and Sec-

retaries, New Orleans, Louisiana, November 29, 1977.
6. Petition of Post-Newsweek Stations, Florida, Inc., 370 So. 2d 764.
7. Estes v. Texas, 381 U.S. at 545.
8. I find it preposterous that a few critics think that Miami riots were in any way the result of camera television coverage of the McDuffie trial. *See, e.g.,* Weingarten, *Riot puts TV court coverage on trial*, NATIONAL LAW JOURNAL, June 2, 1980, page 10. But as I said in a letter in response, there were deep feelings and resentments for at least a year prior to the McDuffie trial covering a range of perceived injustices in Dade County. Television covered the essence of the courtroom proceedings comprehensively and fairly. None of what was shown was inflammatory merely because television showed it. Davis, *Television's Coverage of the McDuffie Trial* (letter), NATIONAL LAW JOURNAL, June 23, 1980, page 15.
9. Nor was Justice Clark correct in his prediction that "only the notorious trial will be broadcast." For every Bundy or Zamora case seen on television in Florida, scores of lesser known proceedings have also been covered.
10. U.S. ex rel. Mayberry v. Yeager, 321 F. Supp. 199, 204 (D.N.J. 1971).
11. U.S. v. American Radiator & Standard Sanitary Corp., 274 F. Supp. at 794.
12. Richmond Newspapers, Inc. v. Virginia, 48 U.S. L.W. 5008, 5012 (June 24, 1980).
13. Richmond Newspapers, Inc. v. Virginia, Brennan, J., concurring, 48 U.S. L. W. 5008, 5019 (June 24, 1980).
14. Richmond Newspapers, Inc. v. Virginia, 48 U.S. L. W. 5008, 5014 n. 12 (June 24, 1980).
15. Wiggins, *The Public's Right to Public Trial*, 19 F.R.D. 25 (1955).
16. Letter to Chairman, Conference of Circuit Judges (Fla.), May 9, 1978.
17. Petition for Modification of Code of Judicial Conduct, *Petition of Post-Newsweek Stations, Florida, Inc.*, 270 So. 2d 764 (Fla. 1979).
18. 370 So.2d 764 (Fla. 1979).
19. *Id. See also* Hoyt, *Prohibiting courtroom cameras: it's up to the judge in Florida and Wisconsin*, 63 JUDICATURE 290 (1979).
20. Petition, *supra* n. 17.
21. Report of Post-Newsweek Stations, Florida, Inc., *Petition of Post-Newsweek Stations*, 270 So.2d 764 (Fla. 1979).

CHAPTER 10

City Councils
and City Executives

Life on the city council, in fact, twenty-four hours a day, is described by Robert Morlan. While mayoral candidates are increasingly using mass-media campaigning, Stephen K. Bailey found life as mayor of Middletown, Connecticut quite different from his college lectures on management theory. Two selections assess the council-manager form of government, and the relationship between managers and council members. All the contributors, in describing the "structured interaction" down at city hall, emphasize the human interactive process rather than a structural description of the form of government.

48

Life on the City Council:
Realities of Legislative Politics

ROBERT L. MORLAN

Probably the single most important factor conditioning the distinctiveness of local legislative politics is sheer proximity to the elector-ate. The local legislator, especially in the smaller and middle-size communities, must indeed operate in what Burke termed "the

From *Politics in California* by Robert L. Morlan and Leroy C. Hardy. Reprinted by permission of Anne M. Morlan, executrix of the Morlan estate.

strictest union with his constituents"—right in the middle of them, in fact, twenty-four hours a day. Although he may be in a formal legislative session only once every couple of weeks, there are endless other meetings: with fellow officials, interest groups, and private citizens. He can scarcely walk down Main Street or shop in a supermarket without being engaged in conversation by someone concerned with local government actions of one sort or another. His constituents are omnipresent; they can pick up the telephone and talk with their representative at almost any moment, and it is no problem at all to appear at his front door.

At least in this sense, if not in others, the job is often a tougher one than that facing state and national legislators. Whatever their efforts to remain in close touch with the voters, they are a bit more remote. . . . Even the "status gap" is larger. It is also true that it is vastly easier for groups interested in a specific policy to attend the meetings of a local governing body, and to exert the kind of pressure that only physical presence can apply. The new councilman or board member soon learns that few if any visitors will attend who do not have an axe to grind. In the few moments before a meeting is formally opened members survey the audience, recognizing certain groups and the cause they represent, jestingly speculating with one another about those they do not recognize. "What do *they* want?" is the standard question. From the standpoint of proximity there is little difference between cities and counties of about the same size, but in each case the differences between units of large and small populations are much more noticeable. Members of special district boards are far less close to their constituents, not because of geography but as a result of the general low level of public interest in their activities, with school districts once again an occasional exception. All do remain fairly readily accessible, however.

One of the characteristics most striking to the uninitiated observer of local legislative bodies is the rather remarkable degree of informality in their proceedings. Rules of parliamentary order are not uncommonly honored in the breach. Votes may be inaudible except in the rare circumstance of a sharp division. Citizens participate from the audience in debate, though, of course, only when recognized to do so, and both the council and members of the audience frequently address one another by first names. Unhappily, from the board member's perspective, while groups of citizens will from time to time appear to support a favorite project, few persons attend with sufficient continuity to gain a broad understanding, and when really tough decisions have to be made those who are sympathetic to the position of the board are prone to shy away from combat and leave the board to face its critics completely devoid of the inestimable help of visible public backing.

The larger the city or county, the more formality there is likely to be in legislative operations, but relative ease of citizen access and participation is still a hallmark. . . . The formal machinery is familiar enough, but it is vitally important to ask the question, "What about the politics that breathes life into institutions?"—or, more down to earth, "How are things actually done, in practice?" Though we shall for convenience use a middle-size city for illustrative purposes, most of the observations are equally applicable to any city or to the county and district boards. Both of the latter generally possess somewhat less discretionary authority, being subject to more detailed state regulation, and the bulk of the districts are concerned with a single function rather than a multitude. But politics is simply one aspect of human behavior, the relationship among human beings in the official sphere, and our focus now is on one special facet of that behavior.

Despite all possible divergences of opinion, and even on the occasions when there is mutual dislike, the council and mayor sitting together as a legislative body possess a special type of unity. They are bound together as those who have survived the election battles and represent the people's choice; by possession of a body of common knowledge about city problems far more thorough than that of the best-informed private citizen; by common pressures from the outside; by a common sense of responsibility; by a common awareness that they no longer possess the luxury of criticism without responsibility but that they must ultimately vote—and be accountable for that vote. Not only is there this degree of common bond against the "outsider," but they are also the inheritors of a long tradition of a society basically desirous of working out disputes by peaceful means and aware of the necessity for toleration of opposing ideas.

The casual or occasional visitor to the city council meeting is often distressed at what he thinks he sees: major pieces of legislation passed by unanimous vote with little or no discussion, while an hour is spent hashing over the implications of an apparently minor request for a zoning reclassification. What he does not realize is that in the latter case he is seeing the whole play, while in the former he is witnessing only the final curtain. That major ordinance, now passed with scarcely a ripple, has no doubt been the subject of discussion and negotiation, perhaps heated controversy, for many months.

It originated, in all probability, in a recommendation from the city manager, from one of the executive departments, or from an interest group, in any of which situations it had undergone extensive study. More and more it is true that local legislative bodies have available to them a considerable amount of expert advice, but the view of the specialist is not the only one to be taken into account. Because the council saw possible merit in the proposal, it was put in proper legal language by the city attorney and then introduced by a member at a regular meeting, but from that time on the skein is tangled. Once it was publicized by introduction, individuals and interest groups who saw serious objections to all or part of the bill began to talk to the council-

men. As the weeks went by, the councilmen compared notes with one another, frequently in random conversations in the city hall, over coffee on Main Street, at social affairs. They discussed various aspects in late-at-night bull sessions in the manager's office as they sweated out details of next year's budget. Tentative changes were tried out on opposing interest groups from time to time, in an effort to find a way to accomplish the central purpose while eliminating as many objections as possible. After several amendments and modifications, when the council had at last negotiated into a reasonable compromise the differences among its individual members, the new version was presented and discussed at length in informal meetings with each of the major pressure groups concerned. Finally a public hearing was advertised and held during a regular meeting, the suggestions from all such discussions being incorporated where feasible. The vote on final passage, witnessed by our observer, was thus merely a ratification of the treaties already concluded.

One of the true essentials of this process is that of carrying the public along. It, of course, cannot be fully informed of all details and nuances, nor does it wish to be, but it must not be taken by surprise. Throughout all the long steps, time must be devoted to effective public relations even when the information is seemingly being ignored. Above all, the press must be catered to: invited to every informal meeting of the council and with the pressure groups, fed special interest features, kept informed in advance of possible future developments not yet ready for publicity. While the latter is risky, the risks of failing to inform the press are usually greater. A successful legislative effort must ordinarily be matched by at least an equal amount of effort at paving the way through development of public understanding. In addition to the usual media of information, it is common in certain situations, such as capital improvements, for the council to use the technique of appointing a "citizens advisory commission" of well-

known persons. Their activities gain additional publicity, and they themselves normally become effective missionaries.

Not every ordinance, of course, goes
through every element of the process we have
been recounting. A great many acts of any
legislative body are noncontroversial, but for
most major and controversial ones this is a
fairly accurate picture. It is extremely time
consuming, frequently frustrating, yet clearly
the essence of a mature democracy. A local
governing body is continuous; it does not
meet in time-limited sessions as do most state
legislatures, and its work may be spread over
long periods. The product may also be subsequently amended with relative ease. Given
the process described above, it is hardly surprising that the great majority of votes in local
legislatures are unanimous. Until the whole
council is reasonably satisfied, the issue may
simply not be brought to a vote. Naturally,
there will be times when this cannot be
achieved, but even on the split votes there is
seldom much debate on final passage. The
minority knows it has already lost and contents itself with a statement, however vehe-
ment, for the public record.

What we have been examining is a council where such splits as occur come on the
basis of disagreement on specific issues or
policy. There are also some few councils and
boards on which there exist "prevailing
splits," although the two types of splits are
not mutually exclusive. The causes of consistently similar split voting on a council, almost
regardless of the issues at hand, may include
such factors as serious divisions within the
community, personality clashes, differences
in age, length of residence, length of service
on the council—and, despite . . . nonpartisan elections, party affiliation. Where genuinely permanent splits are present the processes of legislative politics are not necessarily
very different; there are simply some official
outsiders when the compromises are reached.

And what of the pressures to which the
legislators are exposed during the long devel-

opment of legislation? A great deal of the
ceaseless barrage is, in fact, but a part of the
thoroughly legitimate effort of every group to
be sure that the councilmen are fully informed
of its viewpoint, and subsequently of the bargaining necessary to achieve a final resolution. But there are other facets. Where possible each side will seek to have councilmen
approached by persons who were active in
their campaigns or who were contributors to
it. Others will call who are fellow members of
the same clubs, unions, trade associations,
and churches. When the stakes are high there
will be organized telephoning, presuming to
represent the voice of the people, until a
councilman is sorely tempted to rip the phone
from its moorings. In such a case there will
also be threats, some direct and some anonymous, mostly promising defeat at the next
election if the vote is not right. Unfortunately,
there may even be cranks with veiled or blatant threats of violence. But the pressure felt
the most by any conscientious legislator is not
direct pressure at all in any usual sense of the
term; it is the "widows and orphans" pressure—his desire to avoid governmental or
private actions that may in some way disadvantage elements of the community population who can least afford it and are least able
to protect their own interests.

Decisions of local councils are influenced
by a number of things that may sometimes
seem irrelevant to the immediate issue at
hand: the danger of establishing precedents
that will later return to haunt them, or the
interpretation of their legal powers and limitations by the city or county attorney, upon
whose advice they are quite dependent.
There is also the omnipresent question of
whether funds will be available to support a
particular project, no matter how worthy it
may be. . . .

Citizens are often irked at what they consider the excessive cautiousness of politicians
when first presented with a new policy proposal, however minor. Such caution is likely
to have been born of sad experience, how-

ever, inasmuch as it is virtually a political ax-
iom that even the most innocent-appearing
proposition has the capacity to become incredibly complicated and controversial. It is
an unwary councilman who commits himself
to an idea at first blush; the inclination of the
experienced member is to ask time to study it
and investigate the implications, for he has
found that although he sees no objection on
the face of it, almost certainly outraged
groups will materialize from somewhere
pointing out all manner of unforeseen and potentially horrible results. To the bright-eyed
proponent the idea of anyone's opposing so
worthy a project is utterly inconceivable. So
why the procrastination? He suspects devious
political machinations.

Much of this discussion has suggested
the rather vast gulf in certain respects that lies
between the public official and the citizen, between the insider and the outsider in politics.
There is a gulf in level and scope of information, in the sense of personal responsibility, in
freedom of criticism, in the pressures under
which one must work, in awareness of complexities. The mercurial nature of public reactions is a constant headache; any councilman
knows that a dog-control ordinance will stir
an emotional public response far beyond that
generated by a multimillion-dollar project to
rehabilitate the entire downtown business
district. It is not enough for the legislator to
make the soundest decisions in the world, unless he is also able to persuade the public of
the wisdom of his actions.

In spite of his greater base of information
and awareness of ramifications (perhaps in
large part because of them), he is more
acutely aware of his own fallibility. He well
knows that the tough decisions are never between right and wrong, good and bad, although this is a common public view. There
are always those aggravating mixtures of
good and bad, but sooner or later he must
vote. There are sleepless nights as against his
will the mind reviews uncertainties again and
again—how to be sure? Out of the welter of
conflicting interests, knowing that he is hearing loudly from the few and nothing from the
many, how can he be certain even of what
"the public" wants, let alone determine
clearly the direction of that tantalizing goal,
the public interest? He will recognize in time
that he cannot, perfectly. He can only use his
judgment as fairly and honestly as possible,
listen with an open mind, seek to be able to
live with his own conscience—and submit
that stewardship periodically to the will of the
voters, a submission that . . . he is not likely
to leave purely to chance outcome.

49

Mayoral Candidates Enter the Big Time Using Costly TV Ads and Consultants

JERRY HAGSTROM AND ROBERT GUSKIND

LOS ANGELES—It's a bare five months since the 1984 presidential elections and the residents of the nation's second-largest city are already being subjected to another barrage of political commercials.

Viewers of the morning television news shows often tune in to find Mayor Tom Bradley reminding his constituents of how many skyscrapers have sprouted in downtown Los Angeles since he took office in 1973. On another channel, commercials for his main opponent, city council member John Ferraro, suggest that Bradley would use another mayoral term only as a stepping stone to run for governor of California in 1986. When they get home from work, Angelenos find their mailboxes stuffed with candidate literature appealing to every demographic breakdown from ethnic background to age.

Los Angeles is undergoing another campaign more quickly than most cities because it holds a nonpartisan mayoral election on April 9. A runoff will be held on June 4 if no candidate receives 50 per cent of the vote.

By November, 1,200 cities from New York (population 7.8 million) to Hickory Flat, Miss. (population 458), will hold mayoral elections. Increasingly, the campaigns are professional affairs with all the trappings usually associated with congressional and gubernatorial races.

Most mayoral candidates in cities with populations of at least 100,000 are using professional polling, radio and TV advertisements and direct-mail consultants to build their images. And there is evidence that modern political techniques are seeping into mayoral and even city council races in smaller cities. Even if local candidates wanted to return to the old style of campaigning, relying on personal appearances and volunteer help, it would not work, say campaign experts.

As candidates have become more dependent on TV and radio ads and direct-mail appeals, campaign costs have skyrocketed. Because most of the campaign money is raised from firms and individuals that do business with the cities, questions of conflict of interest and political favoritism are arising. Ethical questions have been raised, particularly about campaign contributions from real estate interests, as growth—both too much and too little of it—has become a controversial campaign issue in many communities.

In the largest cities and especially in media-conscious Los Angeles, polling, mailed campaign literature and radio and TV commercials are nothing new in mayoral races. Bradley, for example, used polling, direct-mail appeals and TV and radio spots when he ran for the first time, unsuccessfully, in 1969. But over the past decade, politicians in smaller cities have begun to hire consultants, according to Geoffrey D. Garin, president of Peter D. Hart Research Associates Inc., the Washington, D.C.-based polling firm that has

National Journal, Vol.17, No.14 (April 6, 1985), pp. 737–742. Copyright 1985 by National Journal Inc. All Rights Reserved. Reprinted by permission.

worked in dozens of national campaigns. "Even though the candidates live in small towns, they are used to seeing all the commercials for a Senate or gubernatorial race. It's raised expectations—if not of voters, at least of the politicians—of what a campaign should be."

In some cases, mayoral candidates use sophisticated campaign techniques as preparation for future national or statewide campaigns, said Daniel B. Payne, a Boston-based media consultant. The most ambitious small-town politicians, Payne said, "believe if they are ever going to become big-time political figures, they've got to start to understand this stuff."

The newer campaign techniques are particularly popular among mayoral candidates in the fast-growing South and West, where powerful party organizations are lacking because the municipal elections frequently are nonpartisan. "In a smaller, stable community, over time you could build a reputation by being active in your union or your church or ethnic or fraternal organization, by raising a good family, paying your bills and taking care of your yard," said Daniel K. Whitehurst, mayor of Fresno, Calif., from 1977–85 and currently a fellow at Harvard University's Institute of Politics. "In a California city that had 30,000 people 30 years ago and today has a quarter million, you don't have a reputation. What you have, maybe, is an image. And if you don't have one, you go out and buy one."

The same is true in Texas, according to Louis Hulme, president of Louis Hulme Associates, a Fort Worth (Texas) political consulting firm. "Growth destroys complacency on your part," said Hulme, "because you can't depend on the old established groups to reach the new people, and you've got to reach them with information and issues that are pertinent to them. You still have the same enemy you had before: apathy. You've got to get enough people interested in the race, and it makes it more expensive."

REGIONAL DIFFERENCES

Arlington, Texas, which elects a mayor on April 6, is a good example of how growth can affect mayoral politics. Once a sleepy suburb between Dallas and Fort Worth, Arlington's population has mushroomed from 45,000 people in 1960 to 160,000 in 1980. Since 1980, the Arlington Chamber of Commerce estimates, the city has added nearly 30,000 residents.

Rapid growth in Arlington has put the established political order of conservative Democratic businessmen in a precarious position. Tom J. Vandergriff held the nonpartisan post of mayor for 26 years before winning election to Congress as a Democrat for one term in 1982. His protege and successor, Harold E. Patterson, a well-known local banker, is now being challenged by city council member Gary Bruner, an oil company public relations executive and relative newcomer to the city. Both candidates have hired professional campaign managers, direct-mail specialists and phone bank operators to conduct their campaigns. Patterson, once expected to hold the mayor's post as long as Vandergriff did, is believed to be facing a stiff challenge.

"Growth in Arlington means there are an awful lot of people the name Patterson doesn't mean a damned thing to," said Hulme. "The name Vandergriff doesn't even carry much weight anymore. Just a few years ago everybody thought these people were unbeatable."

The heavy use of direct mail to persuade voters is typical of mayoral races in suburbs outside large cities. TV advertising is an efficient expenditure of money for mayoral candidates in central cities and occasionally in the very largest suburbs, but because ad rates are based on the size of the entire viewing public, candidates from smaller jurisdictions served by a station can rarely afford TV spots.

Direct mail also allows the campaign to target voters. "If you're running a mayoral campaign, you don't want to mail to 900,000 households because only 30 per cent turn out," said Dan Siwulec, vice president of Below, Tobe & Associates Inc., a Culver City (Calif.) direct-mail firm that has worked for candidates in 38 states. "So you pick a target group—people who are going to vote and vote for you."

Slowly, but surely, the modern campaign techniques are also seeping into mayoral campaigns in the Northeast and Midwest. In 1979, when the Cleveland business community was determined to wrest control of the mayor's office from populist Democratic incumbent Dennis J. Kucinich, his Republican challenger, George V. Voinovich, hired Detroit-based Market Opinion Research Inc. to conduct polls and a Cleveland public relations firm to create commercials in the officially nonpartisan election. Kucinich, who produced his own campaign commercials and had his campaign staff conduct polls, called the campaign "a marked shift from grass roots to electronic roots."

In office, Voinovich has continued to commission public opinion polls. One poll showed that Cleveland residents were upset about cuts in fire protection, and the mayor's office launched a public relations campaign to convince the public that the fire department was being run more efficiently.

Voinovich and his staff point out, however, that they still maintain a large grassroots effort in each area of the city. "We run different mini-campaigns in each of the city's wards and ethnic areas," said James Conrad, Voinovich's campaign manager. "On the Westside you run a different grass-roots effort than on the Eastside, which is black. A homogeneous campaign won't be at all successful."

Kucinich maintains that he is not bitter about having lost to a candidate who ran a more professional campaign, but still notes somewhat sadly "that politics is becoming detached and somewhat esoteric and maybe less important to most people than the World Series." The choice between grass-roots campaigns and media politics, he said, is like "the difference between participatory democracy and selling cornflakes. I like cornflakes. The problem is that I like participatory democracy even more."

The negative reactions of older politicians to the hiring of consultants and the heavy use of media are motivated more by dismay over the death throes of machine politics than by dislike of media politics, said I. Robert Goodman, a Brooklandville (Md.)-based media consultant. "City pols are completely peeved that their 'walking around money' is now going on the tube. The old-time bosses have lost their power because politicians can now go directly to the public at large in 30 seconds. So television has invaded their profession."

Opposition, Goodman contends, is centered in cities where large portions of campaign budgets now go toward purchasing TV airtime. "Twenty years ago the ad man would get 10 per cent of the budget," he said. "Now, he gets 80 per cent. It really hurts the boys who used to pick up their $100, stash $90, give away $10 and then pray they delivered their precincts."

Some popular mayors have managed to avoid the new techniques. St. Paul (Minn.) Mayor George Latimer, a Democrat who has been in office since 1976, scoffs at the technology his counterparts are using. "We just haven't been very scientific," he said. "I've got an old world charm approach to elections."

Latimer said he has never produced a TV commercial, has commissioned only one poll and limits his direct-mail appeals to "a sample ballot that includes us with the rest of the Democrats and goes to targeted Democratic-Farmer-Labor households."

Latimer also said that his five elections have cost a total of $223,000. "I could probably raise a large amount of money and have a big media campaign, but I think it would offend an awful lot of St. Paulites," he said. But he concedes that his low-key approach "is refreshing as long as you win with it. It won't be so refreshing when I get clobbered."

CAMPAIGN COSTS

The use of media and direct mail have caused most campaign budgets to skyrocket, especially in growing cities that are just entering the political big leagues. The most expensive items are mailed campaign literature and TV advertising. The cost of TV spots is increasing 15 per cent a year, according to Goodman.

Fresno's advertising rates are relatively low compared with major metropolitan areas, but, even in Fresno, half the campaign budget goes for media costs, former mayor Whitehurst said. His campaign budget escalated from $30,000 in 1977 to $70,000 in 1981, and if he had run for reelection in 1985, he expected spending to reach $200,000. Dale Doig, who won a five-candidate race on March 5 to succeed Whitehurst, spent $300,000.

In the nation's 30 largest cities, campaign budgets can easily hit the $500,000–$1 million mark. Voinovich spent just under $1 million in 1979 to defeat Kucinich, who had only $145,000 in his coffers. This year, Voinovich said, he will spend $500,000–$750,000, depending on the strength of his opposition.

St. Louis Mayor Vincent C. Schoemehl Jr. spent $685,000 to win the 1985 Democratic primary with 70 per cent of the vote. In Los Angeles, Bradley spent $1 million on his 1969 race, and, this year, he expects to spend $1.6 million, with the increase reflecting higher TV and radio costs. Ferraro plans to spend $1 million–$2 million to oppose Bradley, a campaign spokeswoman said.

The people the candidates turn to for contributions are the same ones who have financed municipal races for generations: personal friends and business associates, real estate developers and investors, political parties and labor unions. In recent years, political action committees (PACs) have also begun contributing to mayoral campaigns.

Candidates often go to great lengths to tell reporters and the public about their $10 and $25 "home parties" and barbecue fundraisers, but most of the money in big mayoral campaigns comes from big contributors. A March 11 Los Angeles Times analysis of campaign contributions received by Bradley and Ferraro from November 1982–December 1984 found that fewer than 0.5 per cent of the contributions were under $100. The study also found that 42 per cent of the contributors either did business with the city or required city approval for their own or their clients' projects. The study further revealed that 25 per cent of the contributors were in the real estate business, 14 per cent were in the financial industry and 13 per cent were PACs. A third of the contributors had family incomes above $200,000 a year.

Throughout the country, developers and real estate investors have the biggest stakes in the decisions of city governments and contribute the most money to local campaigns. In the Sunbelt and in fast-growing suburbs, developers are the dominant contributors to mayoral campaigns, but they also participate in campaigns in older, central cities where massive commercial development has taken place in recent years.

Most of the money for mayoral races is raised locally because the issues in those campaigns are of little interest to outsiders. There are a few exceptions, however. Black mayoral candidates, for example, have begun traveling to other cities to raise money from black professionals. New York city council president Carol Bellamy hopes to raise money for her race this year against New York Mayor Edward I. Koch through a national direct-mail solicitation targeted to those who want to support women candidates, said her political consultant, Bill Zimmerman, president of Zimmerman, Galanty & Finman in Santa Monica, Calif.

Businesses and firms dealing with cities treasure their established relationships, giving incumbents a tremendous advantage in the early stages of both fund raising and campaigning. But this advantage can easily be lost if the challenger shows the incumbent to be weak or catches on with the public.

Because campaign contributions are not limited in most mayoral races, Garin said, "you can do a lot more with a sugar daddy" than you can in Senate and House races. "All you need is one rich friend, and it changes the dynamics a great deal."

Bradley followed that route when, as a black challenger to incumbent Mayor Sam Yorty in 1969, he found it almost impossible to raise money in the Los Angeles business community. "In order to get the campaign off the ground, it was necessary to borrow a large sum of money," Bradley said. "One of my backers, [financier] Max Palevsky, put up $300,000. At that time, there were no [other] businessmen in the city willing to back a challenger. One exception stands out in my mind—Philip Hawley, now chief executive officer of Carter Hawley Hale stores."

Once a mayoral candidate appears likely to win, the business contributors usually jump on board. During Houston Mayor Kathryn J. Whitmire's first campaign in 1981, "we raised about as much money between the primary and the runoff election as we did before the primary," said Clintine Cashion, Whitmire's campaign manager and now director of the city's office of intergovernmental affairs.

The specter of big budgets has raised questions in some places about just what the big contributors are getting from city hall and has spurred proposals to reform municipal campaign finance, including one on the ballot in Los Angeles in June.

In addition to the business community, the other major power in municipal elections is organized labor. The officially nonpartisan status of many municipal elections and the weakening of local political parties in recent years have increased the value of union support. Unions make financial contributions but their most important asset for a candidate is an experienced campaign apparatus. Albert Shanker, president of the American Federation of Teachers, AFL-CIO, said: "We're about the biggest political machine in town.

And our endorsement means hundreds of volunteers, loads of telephones, literature distributions, palm cards on Election Day and substantial financial contributions."

The American Federation of State, County and Municipal Employees, AFL-CIO (AFSCME), whose membership usually has a direct stake in mayoral races, budgets $500,000 per year for local races, funnels contributions from its national office to local unions and often contributes in-kind polling and media consulting services to candidates. In the past, AFSCME has hired the Peter D. Hart firm and William R. Hamilton & Staff Inc. to work on behalf of mayoral candidates. Endorsement decisions are left entirely to the locals, "because they're the ones that have to live with the candidates," said Jerry Clark, AFSCME's political director.

Incumbents usually have a better chance of getting union endorsement and support. "If you have an incumbent who has done a pretty good job in terms of our issues, then you always re-endorse him, no matter how nice and shiny the new guy that comes along is," said Shanker.

Candidates and union officials agree that the unions' campaigning abilities are more important today than their endorsements, which may turn off nonunion voters. Even if candidates don't openly covet local union endorsements, most of the unions have too much power in big cities to be ignored.

At the very least, mayoral candidates seek neutrality from unions that might otherwise oppose them. "This is a union town," said a Seattle official. "You don't want the aerospace mechanics and Boeing's union with 70,000 members against you."

Unions representing public and private workers usually try to act together in mayoral races, but sometimes their agendas conflict. In the 1982 Washington, D.C., mayoral election, construction unions supported incumbent Marion S. Barry in the decisive Democratic primary, largely because of the number of union jobs provided by construction of the city's convention center, while service workers and hotel and restaurant unions supported Barry's opponent, the late Patricia Roberts Harris, because Barry had supported changes they disliked in city workers' compensation laws.

IMAGES

No matter how many modern campaign techniques are adapted to local races, running for mayor still has its unique qualities.

One reason is that 70 per cent of the nation's cities hold officially nonpartisan elections. The first election attracts many candidates, including representatives of fringe elements—one woman in Los Angeles is running on the "song and dance" ticket. A runoff is then held between the top two vote-getters. In some older cities with overwhelming Democratic voter registration, the nonpartisan election is really a contest among Democrats.

Partisan elections are far more common in the mid-Atlantic states, where 89 per cent of the cities permit party designations for mayoral candidates, and in New England where 41 per cent of the races are partisan. In the South, the Mountain states and especially the Pacific states—where cities were incorporated during the local political reform era of the early 20th century—nonpartisan elections are the rule.

In many cities today, says pollster Garin, "the two political parties essentially are anti-growth and pro-growth even though [those labels] don't appear on the ballot anywhere." The role of growth issues, he added, depends on the phase of "a city's life cycle." In high-growth areas such as Virginia Beach, Va., where Garin has conducted polls in recent elections, the major issue is controlling and directing growth, and the residents want someone who will stand up to the developers. "In a lot of places, the developers become the bogeyman," he said. "And in a lot of respects, the developers do it to themselves.

They are terribly heavy-handed about their involvement in local politics."

Where economic and population growth haven't reached explosive levels, Garin said, campaigns focus on which candidate will attract more new development to the city.

"In thinking about media," said consultant Payne, "you always have to be talking about accomplishments and talking in a very hardheaded way about future economic gains." For example, Payne created a series of commercials showing Detroit Mayor Coleman A. Young making his pitch from construction sites.

Polling questions in mayoral races, which are an indicator of what the experts believe concerns the public, tend to focus on job performance and future expectations for the city. As a consultant put it: "A lot more time [is spent in the polls] asking about the nitty-gritty of sewers and stop lights and trash collection. The fascinating thing is people have a lot more to say about their garbage collection than they do about strategic arms limitation."

In the nation's biggest cities, with the most diverse populations, the personalities and race of the candidates often supersede job performance issues. Both news media and polling specialists say that the longer a mayor is in office, the more he is sold, and criticized, on the basis of his personality. New York's Mayor Koch and former Boston Mayor Kevin H. White are prime examples of this phenomenon.

The toughest campaigns for media specialists are those in which a black candidate is running seriously for the first time. In 1983, when former Philadelphia Mayor Frank L. Rizzo tried to regain the top office in his increasingly black city, he was plagued with the racist baggage of his previous campaigns. Rizzo's first consultant tried to clean up his image, but when tracking polls showed the candidate wasn't improving, Rizzo fired him and hired consultant Goodman, who described the first commercials as making Rizzo "look like he'd been embalmed by the fireplace."

Goodman designed spots that reminded Philadelphians of Rizzo's toughness and criticized his black opponent, W. Wilson Goode, for his performance as city manager. But neither campaign succeeded in reselling Rizzo.

The same year, consultant Zimmerman faced the opposite job of selling a black mayoral candidate, Harold Washington, in the racially charged political atmosphere of Chicago. Zimmerman first tried TV commercials that avoided race and stressed Washington's capabilities, but finally Zimmerman felt compelled by the Republican opposition's ads to take on the race issue directly.

Zimmerman desperately needed to reach the undecided white voter. The logical technique would have been to design a direct-mail piece aimed specifically at those voters, but Zimmerman decided the situation called for an emotional appeal that could be better displayed on TV.

The night before the election, Zimmerman bought simultaneous air-time on all three network stations and aired a commercial saying that Chicagoans should be "as ashamed" of the booing of Washington and former Vice President Walter F. Mondale at a Chicago church as Americans are of the assassinations of President Kennedy and Martin Luther King Jr.

Zimmerman admitted in an interview that the connection between the incidents "would not have held up" to multiple viewings, but the next day the results showed. Turnout was 81 per cent among whites, 79 per cent among blacks, and Washington won by 3 percentage points.

Political Volunteerism Turns Professional

Political volunteers are still alive and well in most mayoral campaigns. But grass-roots volunteer efforts are not quite the Mom and Pop operations they used to be.

Just ask Phoenix political consultant Richard DeGraw. His firm, Roots Development Inc., helped Phoenix Mayor Terry Goddard recruit and organize his volunteer work force in 1983. During the past two years, DeGraw has worked on more than 80 campaigns in the Rocky Mountain states, including school board races, state legislative contests, gubernatorial elections, Senate races, initiative and referendum drives and the presidential campaigns of Edward M. Kennedy in 1980 and Walter F. Mondale in 1984. He has run grass-roots efforts for three Phoenix mayoral candidates and 12 city council candidates in Phoenix and Tucson.

There is a growing demand for his services, DeGraw said, because volunteer coordination in most campaigns is "haphazardly done" and most staffs have neither the time nor the manpower or technology to manage big volunteer staffs. "We're the only company in the West that takes the traditional shit work of a campaign and organizes it," DeGraw said. "We get our hands dirty." DeGraw supervises volunteer recruitment and scheduling and provides food and transportation for volunteers if necessary. On occasion, he will hire paid workers. The extra care and supervision is critical, he said, because in most campaigns, "volunteers slip through the cracks and never come back."

Volunteer operations are particularly difficult to manage in the Sunbelt, according to DeGraw. "It's different here than in the East," he said, "because Maricopa County, for instance, [which includes Phoenix] is the size of the state of Maryland. To do get-out-the-vote work in Maricopa County you have to position teams 100 miles apart in select neighborhoods."

Fort Worth (Texas) political consultant

Louis Hulme, who manages municipal campaigns, said the job of political persuasion in Sunbelt cities—many of which are run by professional city managers and civil servants and thus have no patronage jobs—requires bigger campaign budgets for hired help. "The days of old when your volunteers figured that there were going to be plums passed out after election day are gone," he said. "Volunteer work is great in theory, but we've found that if you get 25 volunteers who promise to stuff envelopes, you'll be lucky if 5 show up."

The market for professional volunteer services is more limited in older cities, where party and precinct organizations provide campaign help. Volunteer recruitment for this year's mayoral race began last year in St. Louis, where Democratic ward captains still distribute food baskets and patronage jobs. Mayor Vincent C. Schoemehl Jr.'s reelection campaign has built a volunteer base in each of the city's 28 wards, said campaign manager Nancy Rice. The three million pieces of literature that the organization distributed were either mailed or taken door-to-door by volunteers. On Election Day, 1,500 of Schoemehl's volunteers hit the streets to knock on doors and, if needed, take voters to the polls.

Cleveland's Republican Mayor George V. Voinovich said volunteer workers are "essential." His reelection team "will organize every ward in the city and have a chairman, vice chairman and people working in their own areas," said Voinovich. He already has a good head start. When his direct-mail consultants sent out 230,000 reelection announcements, they included "volunteer cards" for the fall race. The campaign has already accumulated 1,500 names.

Even in Sunbelt cities, most volunteer operations are still managed by the campaign staff. In 1981, Houston Mayor Kathryn J. Whitmire's staff assembled 12,000 volunteers who manned the campaign's phone bank, direct-mail, door-to-door and get-out-the-vote operations.

After taking office, Whitmire set up a full-time volunteer office which keeps computerized lists of 25,000 unpaid workers from her 1981 and 1983 campaigns who are available to make phone calls, distribute literature, host fund-raising parties in their homes and even program computers. Whitmire has precinct coordinators and volunteers in 400 of the city's 500 precincts.

Whitmire's office, which keeps in touch with volunteers year-round through a newsletter and social gatherings, may have discovered the secret to making free labor work. The problem with most campaigns is that "they don't spend any time on their volunteers," said DeGraw. "They treat people like drones."

DeGraw recruits campaign workers from lists of Democratic volunteers, contributors and his own computerized files from past campaigns. He promises campaign staffs "a cadre of volunteers loyal to my firm and to me." To cultivate workers, he arranges parties, buys them tickets to rock concerts and arranges other functions for them in the off-season.

In Goddard's get-out-the-vote effort, DeGraw recruited and scheduled 4,000 volunteers for a final two-day blitz tied to the campaign's heaviest use of paid media. The volunteers also worked for two "ideologically similar" city council candidates at the same time. On Election Day, working out of eight locations around Phoenix and using "highly targeted walking lists" of likely Democratic voters, the volunteers fanned out around the city.

Meanwhile, DeGraw, sitting in the campaign headquarters, followed the pattern of voter turnout precinct by precinct on his computer. Checking turnout at two-hour intervals, he calculated where turnout in Democratic precincts was below target levels for winning. "I [knew] at 9 A.M., 11 A.M., 1 P.M. and 4 P.M. what precincts [were not] performing," he said. "And I have time to shift volunteers around and go in and turn things around."

Cities Ponder Donation Limits

The campaign finance reform movement inspired by the Watergate scandal of the early 1970s has largely eluded municipal elections. Candidates for President and Congress must follow federal disclosure and contribution limit guidelines, and most gubernatorial candidates must comply with some type of state regulation, but candidates for municipal offices are bound by minimal, if any, controls.

But that has begun to change. On June 4, Los Angeles voters will consider a proposed city charter amendment to impose contribution limits of $1,000 to citywide candidates and $500 to city council candidates. Mayor Tom Bradley and some of the city's leading fund raisers are backing the proposal.

Tucson, Ariz., is considering a new city charter that includes restrictions on campaign finances. And the increase in contributions from political action committees (PACs) to city council candidates in Pasadena, Calif., has prompted the city council to consider campaign contribution legislation.

The municipal campaign reform movement pleases Daniel K. Whitehurst, former mayor of Fresno, Calif., and now a fellow at Harvard University's Institute of Politics. During his administration, Fresno imposed a $375 limit on contributions to municipal candidates from individuals, PACs or corporations.

"Being a candidate and an officeholder today is out of whack," Whitehurst said. "After you are elected, you continue to raise money, and it has an impact on the way you can do your job. You can't help but consider the fund-raising implications of decisions you make. And it got worse and worse each year during the time I was in office."

Even a few of the consultants whose bread and butter depends on these big contributions have begun to question whether selling access to city hall is a good idea.

"I don't know if this is corrupt or not," said Boston-based media consultant Daniel B. Payne, who has worked for former Boston Mayor Kevin H. White, Detroit's Coleman A. Young and New Orleans's Ernest N. (Dutch) Morial, among others. "People aren't contributing money because they think someone will make a good spokesman for the city. They want him because they want to be able to go downtown and get some help if they need it. They want to know someone will answer the phone if they need a zoning variance, or that they'll be able to get their brother-in-law a job in the summer picking up paper. It's gut-level politics. Everybody is looking for a way to get the administration's ear."

The Tucson charter proposal was inspired by Seattle, which, in 1979, established the nation's only local public finance campaign system. That system, which was revised in 1983, provides for matching public funds for all contributions up to $50. It also limits contributions from individuals, corporations and PACs to $350 in a single year. Beginning in 1987, campaign spending will be limited to $250,000 for mayoral candidates and $75,000 for other citywide races.

The Seattle law has "worked like a charm," said Alan W. Miller, head of the Seattle office of election administration. "The law significantly reduced the average size of contributions, increased the number of individual contributors and reduced the number of contributions of $100 or more. That's exactly what it was supposed to do."

A study of financing of city council races from 1975–83 by the Seattle elections office substantiated Miller's view. In 1977, the study found that the average number of contributors to a city campaign was 778. In 1979, the year the law took effect, the figure rose to 1,063 and, in 1981, to 1,114. By 1983, during a period when the ordinance was allowed to lapse, the number of contributors dropped back to 698.

Under many state incorporation laws, cities do not have the power to set their own campaign finance guidelines. Seventeen states do not require municipal candidates to file any financial disclosure reports, although some localities in those states have imposed their own guidelines. Only 12 states limit contributions to local candidates, with caps ranging from $300 in Montana to $3,000 in Kentucky.

— 50 —

A Structured Interaction Pattern for Harpsichord and Kazoo

STEPHEN K. BAILEY

"And so, gentlemen, I would conclude that proper delegation, a reasonable span of control, an executive budget, a well-organized personnel system, a clear division between line and staff, and a properly structured interaction pattern for decision-making are the **necessary ingredients of good administration.** Next hour we shall discuss headquarters-field relationships."

The well-trained bell rings. I gather up my notes, drop them on my cluttered desk, grab my hat, trot down the stone steps in front of Fisk Hall, and slide into the front seat of a waiting police cruiser.

"Good morning, Mayor. City Hall?"

"Hi, Al. Yes, City Hall."

The cruiser burps and purrs and turns down College Street.

"Say, Mayor."

"Yes, Al?"

"We gonna get a raise this year?"

"Gee, Al, I dunno. Depends. . . ."

"On what, Mayor?"

"Well, Al, it depends on the chief—and on the Police Commission. And, of course, I don't know what the Board of Finance will say—or the Merit Rating Board—or the Council. And, of course, if you fellows get a raise, what will the firemen and the boys in Public Works say. And the School Board. To say nothing of the party."

"Election year, huh, Mayor?"

"Yuh."

"Guess things are tough all over, huh, Mayor?"

"You can say that again, Al."

"Yuh."

"I'll do what I can for the boys, Al. But you know that I'm only the mayor. And in Centerville, here, we have no scalar system and damn little posdcorb."

"How's that, Mayor?"

Public Administration Review, Summer 1954, pp. 202–204. Reprinted with permission from the *Public Administration Review*, © 1954 by the American Society for Public Administration, 1120 G Street, NW, Suite 500, Washington, D.C. All rights reserved.

"Skip it, Al. Thanks for the ride."

"O.K., Mayor."

As the elevator creeps toward the fourth floor, I turn to the elevator operator.

"Anyone waiting, Fred?"

"I think the comptroller wants to see you, Mayor. He's down in Bill Blake's office."

"O.K., Fred. Thanks."

I find Harry as directed.

"Oh, Mayor. Bill and I want to talk to you about the sewer bond."

"Sewer thing, Harry. Shoot." (I always pun when I know I'm in trouble.)

"Mayor, do you want these on short terms or 20-year reinvested?"

(With serious tone) "Well, Harry, there is of course a great deal to be said on both sides. Incidentally, how's the market?" (This last question I'd overheard Harry asking a banker on the phone the previous week, and it sounded dandy.)

"It's good, Mayor. It's good."

"Well, in that case, Harry, why not?"

"Why not *what*, Mayor?"

"Er—ah—why not follow the market?"

"You mean 20-year bonds, Mayor?"

"If that's what you and Bill think best, Harry, go right ahead."

"O.K., Mayor, we ought to get them for one-ninety or two."

"Yeah, Mayor," Bill breaks in. "It was up to two-forty last August."

Me, horrified, "You mean it's gone *down?*"

(Bill and Harry together) "But that's *good,* Mayor."

(Me, laughingly) "Oh, is it—I mean—well, ain't I the old card, boys?"

(Harry and Bill, shaking their heads good naturedly) "You sure are, Mayor."

Ellen has been avoiding my glances for about a week. She's a good secretary, but her morale is obviously not high. (What *was* it Elton Mayo said to do in cases like this?)

(Jovially) "Good morning, Ellen!"

(Matter of factly) "Good morning, Mayor."

(Ebulliently) "Quite a day, Ellen, huh?"

(Glumly) "I guess some people might think so, Mayor."

It is quite obvious that something has to be done about Ellen's attitude.

"Ellen."

"Yes, Mayor."

"Is something wrong?"

"Nope."

"Ellen. Look at me. There *is* something wrong, isn't there?"

(Avoiding my penetrating eyes) "Is there?"

"Yes, Ellen, there is. For a week now you've been treating me like a discontinuous continuum."

"A what, Mayor?"

"A—oh, never mind. Now what is it, Ellen?"

(Pause. Then with a burst) "You know as well as I do what the trouble is, Mayor. You gave that—that—that *woman* on the third floor a raise. She's now in *my* classification, and she—she—she—OH!"

"But, Ellen, she . . ."

"She doesn't deserve a clerk-typist rating, that's what. It's all politics, and I could just die."

"But, Ellen, the Merit Rating Board upon recommendation of the Ernst and Ernst study changed that one. She's been working for the city for twenty-eight years. You've only been here six."

"I do six times the work *she* does, that's what."

"But, Ellen, everyone knows that. Everyone knows you're the best, most hardworking, most efficient girl in the building. You know I'd be lost without you. And you realize of course that the whole city would grind to a halt if you were not at the helm."

"There's no sense talking about it, Mayor. I've been hurt and you know it."

(Lamely) "I'm sorry, Ellen."

The telephone buzzer buzzes.

"Yes, Ellen."

"Mr. Dugan on two, Mayor."

I push the button.

"Hello, Jack? How the heck are you? . . . You're what Jack? . . . But, Jack, I never said that. I must have been misquoted. . . . The *Bridgeport Herald* said what? . . . Jack, that's ridiculous. Why would I call one of my own councilmen, and one of my own party, a 'pinhead'? . . . No, I did *not* say that. I simply told the reporter you had one of the sharpest heads on the Council. . . . Jack . . . Jack . . . Hello? Hello?"

"Mayor."

"Yes, Joe."

"You asked me the other day about, what did you call it, central purchasing or something? Would you spell that out again please?"

"Sure, Joe. It's just this. I figure you in Public Works buy tires, and the Second District Highway buys tires, and Police buys tires, and the Fire Department buys tires. Instead of each one of you going down to a local filling station and buying retail, why don't you pool your orders and buy wholesale?"

"And go *outside* the city, Mayor?"

"Well, not necessarily. Can't you buy wholesale inside the city?"

"Not if you got to bid. The big distributors in Hartford and New Haven would cream the locals."

"They would?"

"Sure. And what'll the local filling stations say if you start buying out of town?"

"Why, they'll say—they'll say that I'm saving the taxpayers' money. That's what they'll say."

"Oh, Mayor—you slay me! You slay me, Mayor."

"Charter Revision Committee will come to order. Minutes of the previous meeting? What is the pleasure of the committee?"

"I move they be approved and placed on file."

"Without objection, so ordered. Well, gentlemen, this evening the first item on the agenda is what to do about the councilmanic

committee system. It's my own feeling that councilmanic committees should not have administrative control over departments. We must not fuzz up responsibility."

"Well, Mayor, who *should* the department heads be responsible to?"

"Well, I should say—and I don't want you to feel that I want power for *myself* here—this is a matter of administrative principle—I should say they should be responsible to the chief executive."

(Vehemently) "We don't want any dictators in Centerville."

"No, no. You don't understand. For instance, who runs a big industry?"

"A board of directors."

"Well, yes, in one sense. But you have a general manager *under* the board of directors. Now the Common Council is like the . . ."

"Who's going to control the Mayor?"

"The people."

"Yeah, like stockholders control G.E."

"No, it's not quite the same. You see, in industry, management is not in a goldfish bowl. In government, I suffer, the city suffers, from lateral pressures on the hierarchy."

"Pepto-bismol will fix that up in a jiffy, Mayor."

(6:30 A.M. My wife, sleepily) "Hello? You want to speak to the Mayor? Well, it's awfully early in the morning . . . All right, just a minute. (Poking me) Hey! Psst! It's for you, Highness."

(Early morning bass) "This is the Mayor speaking."

"Mayor?"

"Yes. Who is this?"

"This is a taaaaxpayer."

"What can I do for you?"

"Mayor. I seen that big pitchur in the paper last night about redoin' the whole East Side—tearin' down all those tenements and puttin' up a new civic center. That your idea?"

(A little proudly) "Why, yes."

"Mayor."

"Yes."

"Why the hell don't you stop tryin' to build Radio City and come down here and collect my garbage. It *stinks!*" (Click!)

"And I give you a man who needs no introduction to the Civitans—a man who, though young in years, has certainly done a great deal for—well, that is, has certainly caused much comment during his tour of duty at City Hall. Your Mayor and mine. . . ." (Polite applause)

"Mr. Chairman, distinguished guests, members of Rotary—I mean Civitans—I'm not very good at telling stories, and you have probably all heard this one about the politician and the kangaroo. Well, it seems there was a politician and he went to the zoo one day and he went over to the kangaroo cage. Well, sir, that old kangaroo backed away and said, 'Here's *one* pocket you don't get your hands into,' and the politician said. . . ."

"Mayor."

"Yes, Ellen."

"You look tired."

"A little weary, Ellen. What have I got on tonight?"

"Tonight isn't bad. Sports banquet and Park Board. But tomorrow there's Zoning Board of Appeals at 9:00; Red Cross proclamation over WCNX at 10:00; lunch at Rotary; Planning and Development at 2:00; party caucus at 5:30; dinner with the Parking Authority; and a long session with the Board of Finance on the Town School budget in the evening."

"At least I have no classes tomorrow, Ellen."

"Day *after* tomorrow, Mayor."

"Gentlemen. As I was saying last time, a pyramidal structure with proper staff-line relationships, emphasis upon a proper organizational theory, with a functional decision-making interaction pattern—these make up what might be called the administrative way of life."

51

Assessment of the Council-Manager Form of Government Today

KARL F. JOHNSON AND C.J. HEIN

The Council-Manager Form of Government has been for so long the standard against which other forms of local government are measured that, when an occasional flurry of challenges arises, supporters of council-manager government become concerned. While there is a record of continued growth and solid achievement, in recent years the academic literature has contained considerable criticism of city managers and the form of

Reprinted from *Public Management*, Vol.67, No.7 (July 1985), pp. 4–6, by special permission, © 1985, The International City Management Association, Washington, D.C.

government. What is perhaps the most successful governmental reform in the United States finds itself challenged by a new group of reformers who regard it as failing in some important respects.

The arguments have been that city managers are (1) not fiscally responsible (i.e., city manager cities spend more than other cities); (2) not responsive to the city council; and (3) not responsive to citizen needs. The proposed alternative is to abolish the professional manager position and replace it with a mayor-council cum neighborhoods system of government, sometimes in effect replacing the manager with the "professional amateur government official," a full-time mayor often with full-time councilmembers, all paid full-time salaries and supplied with full-time paid staff. Other reformers prefer a more formal role for neighborhoods (with full-time staffs) in the governmental system.

C-M RESEARCH

In some recent research (Johnson and Hein, 1984), we used ICMA recognition of cities as one variable in a regression analysis of city revenues, expenditures, and selected other factors. Some of our findings reflect favorably on the performance of city manager cities and run counter to the criticisms noted.

As part of the reform movement, local government management has been expected to adhere to the principles of good business practice, efficiency, and neutrality (Banfield and Wilson, 1963; Stillman, 1977). In contrast, Morgan and Pelissero (1980) compared a few council-manager cities with a "matched" group of control cities over an 11-year period and found that the council-manager cities spent more money, on the average; thereby refuting the reason for reforming a city with a city manager. Even setting aside Morgan and Pelissero's small sample size, Hofferbert (1981) made the cogent point that the finding

may reflect only some short-term fluctuations and, therefore, merely fall into the "cumulative-marginality fallacy." Our findings, in contrast to those of Morgan and Pelissero, suggest that manager cities currently tend to operate as originally suggested by reform advocates; ICMA-recognized ones tend to raise less revenue and spend less than do nonrecognized cities. On the other hand, this relationship might lead some to the conclusion that the council-manager form of government is too fiscally conservative.

Some authors push further and argue that the council-manager form is not very open to the needs of deprived groups in the community, as may be evidenced by a manager's alleged lack of interest in citizen participation. For example, Almy (1977) points out that city managers tended not to involve citizen participation in the decisions related to revenue-sharing funds. Further, Huntley and MacDonald (1975) found that one of the activities city managers preferred least was to speak on controversial issues to civic groups, church groups, and so on. The decision to avoid citizen participation in policymaking about revenue sharing may thus have been concerned with avoiding controversy. Walking a fine line between politics and professional expertise is one aspect of the manager's job. While being discreet about the use of power, the manager has more latitude in fiscal decision making when there is polarization among citizen groups (Huntley and MacDonald, 1975).

Critics charge that the council-manager form of government stifles the give and take of interest positions in the community, forcing the council to take a back seat and even threatening democracy (Wood, 1959; Lineberry and Fowler, 1967). The analysis in our study showed significant participation by the ICMA city management variable in implementing revenue and spending. But the findings can represent a manager and council working together within a normal interplay of interest groups in the community, along with instances of greater influence by the managers and their staffs.

Local government officials have expressed concerns about fiscal problems (McGowan and Stevens, 1982), and tighter budget control was one solution increasingly followed by city managers (Stillman, 1982). But this does not mean that managers are moving to usurp the council's or mayor's roles in the political arena. The manager's participation in the more political aspects of city affairs was one of those activities least favored by city managers (Stillman, 1982). If anything, managers found that a good deal of their time and activity was spent resisting attempts by the mayor and council to intrude in administrative affairs (Huntley and MacDonald, 1975; Stillman, 1982).

Where conflict and transition are occurring, the city manager may be expected to be drawn further into the policy affairs of city government, while such elected officials as the mayor may continue to receive the benefits "of public exposure with little political risk" (Sanders, 1982). Thus, as resources become more scarce, the threat to a professional city manager and this form of government becomes more acute; scapegoats are needed to handle the frustration of having no resources to deliver to the citizens who provide electoral support.

The major effect shown in our study between the ICMA management variable and revenue and expenditure patterns was at the link with conventional revenue sources like property taxes (Johnson and Hein, 1984). Substantial concern with state and federal revenues is shown by city management (McGowan and Stevens, 1982). What we feel might be taking place is that city managers are having to offset declining funds, due to program cuts at the federal and state levels, with traditional city revenues and revenue-sharing funds, if possible.

Critics attack city managers from both sides. Sometimes the complaint is that city managers have thwarted democracy by being too conservative, because the empirical findings indicate a lower response to certain ethnic or implied community demands (Lineberry and Fowler, 1967). Or perhaps managers have been too liberal by increasing revenues and expenditures, as indicated by Morgan and Pelissero (1980). But there is some evidence in the literature that they are balanced in their approach to social issues.

Managers have initiated significant changes in social policy within their administrations. Over 80 percent of those cities with populations greater than 25,000 that have adopted affirmative action plans for minorities and women have done so at the initiation of their ICMA-recognized city management (Huntley and MacDonald, 1975). At the same time, these managements were cautious about participating in employment programs that legally committed them to provide employment opportunities and quotas (Huntley and MacDonald, 1975).

Thus, the commitment is to move, at least symbolically, partially toward social equity and concern. Yet the manager must be cautious about the administration's fiscal response to the community consensus. The future roles of the manager have been seen as a balance between "back to the fundamentals" pure management and the "forward to the new horizons" broker/negotiator, change agent, facilitator of new innovations (Stillman, 1982). The successful blend of these roles in relation to the future consequences of the fiscal picture for local governments warrants careful study.

Another major concern of the critics of the council-manager form of government, especially among political scientists who are worried about the deterioration of the political party system in the United States, is that the city management form contributes to the weakening of local party organizations, thus making it possible for national political organizations and one-issue groups to gain disproportionate control over our political parties. Other institutional changes such as the increasing influence of electronic media in elections also contribute to the deterioration of local party organizations.

There may not be a Democratic or Republican way to pave a street, as supporters of the council-manager form often say, but if strong, active local Republican and Democratic party organizations are a needed counterweight to such things as media dominance of our political system, we may need to consider ways to encourage local party organizations to help frame the issues and debate the policies of our city governments. The issue, of course, is nonpartisanship or partisanship of the electorate and the governing body, not the continuing nonpartisanship of the city manager. It may be more difficult to be nonpartisan in a partisan environment, but if that is an important element in our democracy, city managers may have to try to work in a more partisan governing system.

Increased partisanship, however, does not seem to fit in very well with another solution offered by the critics of the council-manager system, namely, to give an increased role in policy and spending decisions to neighborhood organizations. None of these proposals envision Republicans and Democrats competing for control of the neighborhood council. The neighborhood is viewed as a small, nonpartisan element representing the views of the residents, presumably arrived at by democratic give and take. Perhaps a potential alliance exists between supporters of nonpartisan neighborhoods and nonpartisan city managers. In any case, critics of the council-manager system sometimes present conflicting demands, such as nonpartisan neighborhoods vs. strong local party organizations.

CURRENT TRENDS

Probably the growth rate of the council-manager form of government has been gradually slowing down, and naturally there is concern about whether it has reached its peak. Some people also may be concerned about whether we can expect more cities to abandon the form and move to some other form such as the strong mayor plan.

Sanders (1982) reported that from 1970 to mid-1981, some 3.5 percent of cities with the council-manager form had discontinued it. In the same period, about 10 percent of cities with the mayor-council form of government shifted to the council-manager form. We would expect that, in the period of tight finances since 1981, the change rate will have slowed down, because campaigns to change the form of government may have been viewed as an unnecessary expense.

One imponderable for the future is whether the "lean and mean" budget posture adopted by some city managers these past few years is viewed positively or negatively by citizens and their elected representatives. Mayors and councilmembers seemed to like having the city manager propose spending cuts. Citizens whose programs were cut were often not pleased. To the extent that managers have an internal drive to cut expenditures, it may come into conflict with citizen desires for additional services. Very few cities are now providing an optimum level of services. To the extent that this is blamed on (credited to?) the city manager, there may be further citizen discontent with the form of government.

Our view is that, over the long haul, the professionalism of the council-manager form of government will find support from citizens. Most people want fair, effective, and efficient government. When the information needed to make reasoned comparisons is made available, the sense of balance conveyed by the council-manager form of government will prevail.

REFERENCES

Almy, T.A., 1977, "City managers, public avoidance, and revenue sharing," *Public Administration Review* 37 (January/February): 19–17.

Banfield, E.C. and J.Q. Wilson, 1963, *City Politics*, New York, N.Y.: Vintage Books.

Hofferbert, R.I., 1981, "Communication on 'Morgan and Pelissero,'" *American Political Science Review* 75 (September): 722–725.

Huntley, R.J. and R.J. MacDonald, 1975, "Urban managers: Organizational preferences, managerial styles, and social policy roles," *Municipal Year Book* 1975 (Washington, D.C.: ICMA): 149–159.

Johnson, K.F. and C.J. Hein, 1984, "Reform, suburban cities and public opinion policy in relation to municipal revenues and expenditures: A first look," Prepared for the Western Social Science Association meetings, San Diego, Calif.: April 1984.

Lineberry, R.L. and E.P. Fowler, 1967, "Reformism and public policies in American cities," *American Political Science Review* 61 (September): 701–716.

McGowan, R.P. and J.M. Stevens, 1982, "Survey of local government officials: Analysis of current issues and future trends," *Urban Interest* 4 (Spring): 49–56.

Morgan, D.R. and J.P. Pelissero, 1980, "Urban policy: Does political structure matter?" *American Political Science Review* 74 (December): 999–1006.

Sanders, H.T. 1982, "The government of American cities: Continuity and change in structure," *Municipal Year Book* 1982 (Washington, D.C.: ICMA): 178–186.

Stillman, R.J. II, 1977, "City manager—professional helping hand or political hired hand," *Public Administration Review* 37 (November/December): 659–670.

————, 1982, "Local public management in transition: A report on the current state of the **profession,**" *Municipal Year Book* 1982 (Washington, D.C.: ICMA): 161–173.

Wood, R.C., 1959, *Suburbia*, Boston, Mass.: Houghton-Mifflin.

52

Managers and Councilmembers: Comparing Their Political Attitudes

JAMES E. NEAL

As one of the few who have made the transition from manager to councilmember, I am happy to report that the journey from manager to legislator is not as fraught with peril as you might believe. In fact, it can be an enlightening process, once you get over having to answer the obvious inquiry of "Why did you want to run for city council?" for the hundredth time. A former city manager who has the opportunity to serve on a city council has a unique opportunity to learn the differences and similarities between the roles of the manager and the councilmember and to gain a better understanding of each role. The answer to the question is, "I ran for the city council because I had just retired and had the time and wanted to continue my involvement in my profession, which I had always enjoyed. I

Reprinted from *Public Management*, Vol.68, No.1 (January 1986), pp. 13–14, by special permission, © 1986, The International City Management Association, Washington, D.C.

felt I had a wealth of knowledge I could contribute to my community, and it was something I had always wanted to do."

To begin with, and what is very important, is that a councilmember's livelihood or career does not depend on the job of city councilmember, whereas, if the city manager loses the job, his or her likelihood and career are in jeopardy. Councilmembers have the security of knowing that, once elected, their job (which is, in fact, a second job) is relatively secure for at least four years, barring a recall effort. A manager, on the other hand, may keep the job by virtue of only one vote on the council—hardly what one would call security.

That councilmembers and managers need to have a better understanding and appreciation of each other's roles is obvious, yet one finds many serious problems in council/manager relations, as evidenced by the short tenure of managers over the years.

From its inception, the council/manager form of government has produced relationships between elected officials and appointed executive officers that have ranged, like marriages, from those that apparently were made in heaven to those that seemingly were forged in hell. Those instances where the council and the manager understood and respected each other's strengths, shortcomings, and area of expertise have resulted in strong, well-run cities. Conversely, no one benefits when council and manager are pitted against one another, either personally or professionally.

FRAUGHT WITH DISASTER

It was once thought that the proper relations between council and manager were that the manager stayed out of policy and politics and simply ran the administrative arm of the city government, while the council strictly handled policy and gave direction to the manager. Then came the council/manager team idea, where both the manager and the council were involved in developing policy and the manager was tolerant when councilmembers occasionally got involved in administrative matters. The council/manager team approach, however (although there have been numerous articles about it during recent years supporting and applauding it), appears to be changing. Some of this change is due to Proposition #13, wherein with such tremendous shortage of funds, councils became involved in administrative research and decision making. Also, councils, perhaps because of exposure to the team concept and numerous and varied training sessions sponsored by the League of California Cities and several California universities, have become better educated and more sophisticated in the field of public administration.

Now, after being on the council for three years and doing a lot of talking to my colleagues on different councils throughout the state, I find that many councilmembers today feel that they can become involved in just about anything that interests them, including administrative matters. Thus, the lines of authority are becoming blurred once again.

In view of this trend, it is not surprising that a manager turned councilmember might be even more tempted than other councilmembers to act like a second manager. After all, the former manager has been professionally involved in administrative responsibilities for years. It, therefore, seems logical that the former manager would be interested in those aspects of city government, especially when colleagues on the council seek advice on administrative matters. The manager turned councilmember must continually be aware that there is a responsibility to the city manager not to usurp the city manager's authority as the appointed executive officer. If a balance can be struck between these two, the manager turned councilmember will be an asset to both the council and the manager. If not, the situation is fraught with disaster for both.

THE POLITICAL PULSE

Having gone through the election process, I can see now why councilmembers are more knowledgeable about political matters than the manager. For most councilmembers, some of this information comes early in their political careers as they walk precincts and talk to residents of the community—something managers normally do not do. As a result, councilmembers become known to hundreds of citizens who tell them what they like and don't like about the city. People and groups who are relatively quiet all year suddenly become active as they express their support for a particular candidate.

Perhaps the most active and influential of these groups is a councilmember's election committee or political action committee. This committee consists of those close supporters who helped the councilmember get elected, who came to all of the political meetings, who helped raise funds, who met at the councilmember's house night after night, and who provided close support during the exciting election times. The influence of this group often continues long after the election is over and provides the councilmember with a political network of information and opinion. Thus, a councilmember has his fingers pretty much on the political pulse of the community and becomes actually a center of political activity, an accomplishment the city manager may never achieve. The wise manager, therefore, will pick the brain of every councilmember about his political expertise. This information is very valuable and will give the manager insight into the political activities of the community. It often explains what puzzles so many managers about why councilmembers sometimes vote the way they do.

LARGER EGOS

As a group, city managers tend to maintain a low profile. A councilmember, on the other hand, has greater visibility by virtue of being an elected official. In fact, visibility is probably the single most important element in being elected. (So far, I have been unable to make this change—I still maintain a low profile in the city. I do expect, though, if I run again, that I will have to make a change in order to get reelected.)

A councilmember does not like to be upstaged by a bright and interesting city manager. If any egos are larger than the managers, they are the egos of the councilmembers. If quotes are made in the newspaper, most councilmembers like to make these quotes and get their names in the paper, on the radio or television. The city manager who has done an excellent job in completing a councilmember's favorite project sometimes wonders why the councilmember isn't pleased when the story comes out in the newspaper—quoting the city manager.

THE FAVORED PROJECT

Since being elected to the council, I have gained a better appreciation of something that the manager involved in the pressure cooker atmosphere of the day-to-day job may choose to ignore. A councilmember may devote an extraordinary amount of time and energy to a few projects or issues that the councilmember needs to have completed. The manager, on the other hand, is concerned about the orderly progress and development of a whole host of issues and feels responsible for accomplishing them. The manager must realize that a lot more time is going to have to be spent on a councilmember's favorite projects than on other goals. The councilmembers should appreciate the fact that their goals are not the only matters with which the city manager must deal and be tolerant if the project does not come to fruition as soon as they would like.

As city manager, one of my priorities was to see that the councilmembers received information on a variety of issues in a timely and expeditious manner. Now that I am on the council, I am even more convinced of the importance of information provided to the council by the manager. A councilmember's nightmare is to be asked a question by a resident, or worse—a representative of the media, about an important occurrence or problem and not be aware of the matter at all or have insufficient information to be able to respond. Agenda communications are extremely important, also. Councilmembers like to be kept informed on an almost daily basis of what is going on at city hall. The councilmember appreciates the phone call, and it often brings thoughts to mind that are of interest to both parties. When I was a manager, I arranged to know whenever councilmembers were visiting city hall and made sure I talked to them before they left.

POLITICS AND POWER

Let's face it—both the members of the city council and the manager are politicians. The manager, in order to be effective, has to be an astute politician despite denials from managers that they are involved in politics. The politics I have in mind here are not partisan politics but the politics of influencing people and politicians to get things done by majority consensus—in short, the power of persuasion and sometimes manipulation and control.

The manager is a very powerful person as the administrative head of an organization that affects the lives of many people in his community. The organization gets things done and controls and spends millions of dollars of taxpayers' funds. The council is more powerful as a unit but not necessarily as individuals. To get their way, they have to arrive at a consensus among themselves, which is sometimes extremely difficult, and then work through the political process. If a single councilmember decides he is opposed to the city manager for whatever reason, however, he can eventually force the manager to resign. A councilmember can be the manager's greatest ally or biggest obstacle to getting a particular program approved by the council.

Councilmembers mostly seek a different kind of power than the manager. Councilmembers, in addition to getting their projects and goals of the city accomplished, also sometimes seek individual control of the council. In fact, more of some councilmembers' time appears to be spent in getting control than in getting projects accomplished.

In closing, I would like to say that very few managers I have talked to have indicated any desire to be a councilmember. I have found it to be an exciting and exhilarating experience, however, even though at times it is frustrating. In fact, I have enjoyed it so much I am seriously thinking of running for a second term.

CHAPTER 11

How Many Governments Does It Take?

America is unique in the number of its local governments: there are more than 80,000 nationwide. While a few New England states have abolished counties and transferred their functions, the number of separately incorporated municipalities, and special districts, newly formed in order to provide services, continues to increase. Americans like to have their "own" community, with the ability to determine service levels and to control land use and tax rates. But in many urban areas this proliferation of local governmental entities has fragmented financial resources and divided responsibility for comprehensive solutions. A long-time observer of local communities, Joseph Zimmerman asks *can* government functions be "rationally reassigned?"

Four selections review counties, town meetings, and special-district governments. The population of counties into which most states are divided range from a few thousand people to several million, and typically provide basic services (the sheriff, courts, secondary roads, and schools) outside incorporated cities. Most must deal with both rural and urban problems, as Richard Black points out in "Full Partnership for Counties." In contrast, the direct citizen participation in a New England town meeting is only possible in small communities, but it is a valued heritage of American democracy. The demand for more local services is likely to result in the formation of a special district, whose service area may cross other jurisdictions. Special districts are convenient to form, are legally able to set their own tax rates and user fees, or to borrow money. Are special districts therefore a new "dark continent" of unknown governments? The most numerous type of special districts provide education—and much more, as Professor Gerald Pomper found in "Practicing Political Science on a Local School Board."

53

Can Governmental Functions Be "Rationally Reassigned"?

JOSEPH F. ZIMMERMAN

The governance system in New York State is complex, and its complexity in metropolitan areas is increasing as the state and the national governments become more deeply involved in attempts to solve areawide problems. Currently, there are 1,607 units of general purpose local government in the state—57 counties (excluding New York City which contains five counties), 62 cities, 931 towns and 557 villages. In addition, there are 743 school districts, other special districts (such as fire and water) that are units of government, and "special districts" within towns and counties that are not units of government. Further complicating the governance system are 42 state-controlled public authorities operating on a statewide or regional basis—18 for transportation, six for commerce and development, three for port development, 13 for finance and housing, and two for marketing.

Reformers since the 1890s have been proposing structural changes in the New York local government system to establish clear lines of authority and responsibility, and ensure that services are provided in the most cost effective and efficient manner. Influenced over the years by the scientific management movement that originated in private industry and demonstrated economies of scale in the production of goods and services, and by the Populist and Progressive movements, reformers until the 1960s placed heavy emphasis on the need for a reduction in the number of local governments, functional consolidation, and creation of the position of a strong mayor or city manager in whom responsibility for administration would be centralized.

The existence of numerous local governments fragmented the governance system and was held to be responsible for conflicts of authority, duplication of services, needs-fiscal resources mismatches, inadequate service levels, a long ballot, lack of areawide programming and other problems. While the arguments on the surface appeared to be persuasive, voters generally rejected reform proposals. In the early 1960s, a number of reformers and interest groups began to turn their attention to the higher levels of government for metropolitan solutions.

Two new groups of reformers advocating political decentralization emerged in the 1960s. The first group urges the breaking up of large cities into neighborhood governments or conversion of the cities into two-tier governmental systems. The second group developed the public choice theory which innately supports the existing fractionated system. These theorists favor a large number of small units of local government on the grounds that they maximize citizen participation, governmental responsiveness, and choice of residential location on the basis of services offered and taxes levied. The theory, of course is predicated largely on the existence of a broad

National Civic Review, Vol.73, No.3 (March 1984), pp. 125–131.

grant of discretionary authority by the state to its general purpose political subdivisions.

The views of neighborhood government advocates and public choice theorists are supported in part by empirical studies. The United States Advisory Commission on Intergovernmental Relations (ACIR) concluded that the size of a city in the population range of 25,000 to 250,000 has no significant relationship to economies or diseconomies of scale, but the law of diminishing returns applies as size exceeds 250,000, resulting in significant diseconomies of scale. The largest diseconomies were found to be associated with the police function ("Size Can Make a Difference—A Closer Look," *ACIR Information Bulletin,* September 16, 1970).

APPROACHES TO "SORTING OUT"

All of the municipal reformers placed heavy emphasis on structural changes to achieve a "rational" assignment of functional responsibilities. Interest in structural changes continues, even though relatively few have been initiated in recent decades as reliance generally has been on other approaches.

Structural Changes

There are three broad categories of proposals for structural changes—annexation, a one-tier system and a two-tier system.

Annexation. Central cities historically were authorized to annex contiguous territory as it became urbanized, and the suggestion has been advanced that the failure of boundary extensions to keep pace with urbanization has been a root cause of the metropolitan problem (see the REVIEW, June 1977, page 278). Most recent annexations have been small, except in certain areas in the southwest, and there is no evidence that the procedure holds the potential for the creation of a unitary government in most areas.

The New York general municipal law contains provisions authorizing cities, towns and villages to annex adjoining territory, but the enabling sections are encumbered by restrictions which make it difficult to actually use.

A One-tier System. Consolidation may be either complete or partial. In a complete consolidation, a new government is formed by the amalgamation of the county and municipal governments. Partial consolidation may involve the merger of most county functions with the central city to form a new consolidated government with the county continuing to exist for the performance of the few functions required by the state constitution. A second form of partial consolidation involves the merger of several but not all municipalities with the county.

The New York town law since 1973 has authorized the consolidation of two or more towns, but the enabling statute has not been used. The state legislature has plenary power to dissolve units of local government (it last exercised the power in 1898). Dissolution of units obviously would reduce overlapping jurisdictions.

A Two-tier System. Two varieties of a two-layer system—the county and the special district—have been used in the United States. Since responsibility for certain functions is consolidated in the upper tier, each variety may be viewed as a type of semi-consolidation. A new unit of government is formed on the upper-tier level when a decision is made to establish a special district, whereas the modernized county model provides for strengthening of the powers of an existing unit to enable it to serve as the areawide government.

Every metropolitan reorganization approved by the voters since 1947 has involved the county, and it is evident that there is less political opposition to the modernization of a county government than there is to a proposal for the creation of a new, multi-functional, upper-tier unit.

A county government with sufficient

powers and resources to serve as an effective upper-tier government can be established by either the incremental assignment of additional powers or the adoption of a charter making the change. Los Angeles County is the outstanding example of the incremental approach, and Dade County, Florida, is the only example of the second method. New York State voters have the constitutional authority to modify an existing county charter or adopt one granting authority to solve areawide problems.

Functional transfers from the municipal to the county level have occurred in New York and a number of other states. The New York constitution requires separate approval by voters of cities as a unit and of towns as a second unit within a county before a function can be transferred to the county (*Town of Lockport* v. *Citizens for Community Action at the Local Level,* 423 U.S. 808 (1977)). The transfer of a village function to the county is more difficult since a triple concurrent majority is required.

Although most functional transfers occur voluntarily, state legislatures have authority to mandate them. The Florida legislature in 1970 transferred property tax administration to the county level, and the New York legislature in 1972 shifted most welfare functions to the county level.

Three Florida counties adopted charters partially preempting responsibility for functions. The 1957 Dade County charter authorizes the board of county commissioners to *"set reasonable minimum standards for all governmental units in the County for the performance of any service or functions."* If a municipality fails to comply with the standards, the county *"may take over and perform, regulate, or grant franchises to operate any such service."* The county has not exercised this power.

The Volusia County charter, approved by the voters in 1970, grants the county the power of preemption with respect to the protection of the environment. The power has been exercised once, to regulate the location,

construction, repair and abandonment of wells, and the installation and repair of pumps and pumping equipment.

The Broward County charter, adopted in 1974, authorizes the county planning council to prepare a land use plan, and to approve or reject any such plan submitted by any governmental unit within the county. If a local plan is found to be in substantial conformity, it is certified and becomes effective. If a plan is rejected or a unit fails to submit one for certification, the county land use plan becomes effective.

The failure of comprehensive areawide reorganization plans to win voter approval has promoted the organization of numerous special districts. It is important to distinguish special districts that are units of government from service and tax districts labeled "special districts" that are under the control of town boards and county governing bodies in New York State.

A district has a number of advantages in being able to solve a specific areawide problem. The principal advantage is the relative ease of formation, since a proposal to create a district typically does not generate the strenuous political opposition that develops when a proposal is advanced for the creation of a multi-purpose district or modernization of the county government. The single function assigned to a district may not be perceived as a threat by municipal officials who either have not been responsible for the function or had problems with it. And, of course, the district may be established to perform a wholesaling function, e.g., water supply, with the municipalities performing the retailing function, i.e., distribution. A district often is able to take advantage of economies of scale and specialization by concentrating on the provision of one service in a relatively large geographical area; it does not have to consider competing interests.

In New York State, a constitutional amendment and referendum are not required to create such districts, which often rely on user charges for revenue and, consequently, are not restricted by constitutional and statutory tax limits. The absence of the power to tax makes the proposal for a district more acceptable to some taxpayers. And revenue bonds, exempt from debt limits, can be issued without referendum.

Reformers tend to object to unifunctional special districts for two major reasons. First, a new district further fragments the political system, thereby making the government of the area more complex. Second, it may be more difficult to achieve a comprehensive approach to areawide development, as the activities of an autonomous special district may affect adversely other governmental programs, e.g., bridge and tunnel authorities in metropolitan areas have injured public transportation by facilitating the movement of automobiles.

Forty-two special districts in New York are controlled by the state. Special districts can be controlled by local governments if local elected officials are designated by the enabling statute to serve as the ex officio directors or are authorized to appoint the directors. The enabling statute also can authorize the voters to elect the directors of a public authority. The Connecticut legislature converted the metropolitan district commission in the Hartford area from a state-controlled to a voter-controlled special district.

Non-Structural Changes

Writing in 1965, political economist Charles E. Lindblom of Yale University maintained that political problems could be resolved through mutual adjustments made by the actors. Supporters of the cooperative approach to areawide problems in effect had been saying the same thing. They are convinced that such problems can be solved by local governments acting on the basis of comity, and support their position by pointing out that the fragmented local government system has averted collapse by adaptive responses to the pressures of urbanization.

Councils of Governments. Ecumenicists, convinced that regional planning commissions and councils of governments (COGs) can develop areawide plans that will be implemented by the cooperative action of local governments, received encouragement from the federal government which in the period 1966–1982 required that all applications for numerous federal grants-in-aid be channeled for review through a commission or COG.

The advantages of COGs are several, including their relative ease of organization, provision of a forum for the discussion of areawide problems, and service as a coordinating mechanism for local governments. Unfortunately, COGs suffer all the disadvantages of the United Nations, including the inability to rise above narrow self-interest. No COG has solved a major problem, and many have become inactive. COGs have concentrated on the solution of relatively minor problems and undoubtedly will continue to do so.

Service Agreements. Intergovernmental service agreements, formal and informal, have been used for well over a century by local governments. These agreements enable a political subdivision to obtain a service or a product which the government itself cannot produce or could produce only at an excessively high cost. The provider of the service also benefits if the agreement permits economies of scale.

One of the broadest grants of power to local governments to cooperate with other governments is found in the New York State constitution: *"Local governments shall have the power to agree, as authorized by act of the legislature, with the Federal government, a State or one or more other governments within or without the State to provide cooperatively, jointly, or by contract any facilities, services, activity, or undertaking which each participating local government has the power to provide separately."* The grant contains a limitation, however, that local governments may enter into service agreements only if each has the power to provide the services separately.

According to a 1972 survey, 44 of 84 (52 percent) responding New York State municipalities had entered into formal and informal service agreements. Sixty-two percent of the municipalities reported that they provided services to another municipality. The respondents also reported they most often entered into agreements with municipalities (50 percent) followed by counties (38 percent), special districts other than school districts (25 percent), school districts (25 percent), and the state (22 percent). All respondents checked "to take advantage of economies of scale" as the reason for entering into such agreements.

Functional Transfers. The voluntary transfer of functional responsibility by one local government to another is a non-coercive approach to resolving an areawide problem. As pointed out in an earlier section, most functional transfers are locally initiated but the state legislatures can mandate them.

In a 1975 national study conducted by the author, 1,039 of the 3,319 responding municipalities (31 percent) had transferred responsibility for one or more functions or components of functions during the previous 10 years to another municipality, the county, the state, special districts and councils of governments. Fifty-eight percent of the reporting municipalities checked to "achieve economies of scale" as a reason for shifting the responsibility. In addition, respondents checked the following reasons: eliminate duplication (44 percent), lack of facilities and equipment (41 percent), fiscal restraints (29 percent), lack of personnel (26 percent), inadequate services (22 percent), jurisdictional or geographic limitations (21 percent), and federal aid requirements/incentives (20 percent).

Property Tax Base Sharing. In 1971, the Minnesota legislature initiated an innovative program to reduce the "fiscal mismatch" in the seven-county Twin Cities metropolitan area by mandating the partial sharing by local governments of the growth in the commer-

cial-industrial property tax base. The program is an attempt to reduce gross fiscal disparities among municipalities by requiring that the revenue produced by 40 percent of the new nonresidential construction be deposited in the municipal equity account in the state treasury and distributed to municipalities according to a need and population formula (see *National Civic Review*, Vol.73, No.2 (February 1984), page 89).

CONCLUSIONS

Darwinism does not pervade the New York State local government system, as very few of the "weaker" units fail to survive, and political realities suggest that a comprehensive structural reorganization of the system is improbable in the foreseeable future. In consequence, the state legislature wisely is examining functional assignments to determine whether a realignment of responsibilities is needed.

Power sharing is essential in today's complex society, and many governmental decisions will continue to be made through the process of negotiation by the principal participants, including quasi-public and private ones. We anticipate that critical problems generally will be alleviated or solved by intergovernmental cooperation and tinkering. Service agreements, often arranged on a trade-off basis, will be entered into more frequently by local governments, and responsibility for a troublesome function on occasion will be transferred upward to the county or the state, or to a newly established unifunctional regional special district. The state legislature and associations of local governments also should work for the removal of constitutional provisions hindering the development of an effective regional governance system.

To reduce the "needs-fiscal resources mismatch," serious consideration could be given by the state legislature to the adoption of a partial property tax base sharing program, or the establishment of regional services financing districts with authority to raise sufficient funds to allow existing local governments cooperatively to solve areawide problems. In addition, the desirability of state assumption of responsibility for the performance or the complete financing of expensive functions, such as public welfare, should be explored.

54

Full Partnership for Counties

RICHARD L. BLACK

Even if county government had not previously existed in the American governmental system, the second half of the 20th Century would have produced such a form. This is the belief of a substantial number of practitioners and students of government grappling with **urban and rural problems and the need for an effective governmental mechanism below the state and above the municipal level.**

Fragmented urban service delivery systems, the impact of special interest government, declining rural areas, the voracious consumption of land and water resources, the undisciplined spawning of hundreds of special districts, the bitter feud between some states and their local subdivisions—these are but a few of the unaddressed problems which involve counties directly and in some cases, preeminently. Any success in solving these problems challenging our social, economic, and governmental systems, rests in no small way on how well and how soon counties assume their proper role as full partners in the

area of public policy and decision making in our governmental system.

Ninety-eight percent of all citizens in the United States are served by one of the nation's 3,101 county governments, whether they live in a central city, suburb, or a rural area. And 74 million Americans, or about one-third of the total population of this country, live in one of the 500 counties and 37 states where the appointed county administrator form of government exists. The appointed administrator form of county government in most states is modeled after the council-manager form used so extensively in municipal governments.

Under this form, the county administrator is appointed by and responsible to the county governing body, usually a county council. While there are variations of this form from state to state, the usual practice finds the appointed administrator responsible for managing the day-to-day operations and affairs of the county government. The appointed administrator form is the fastest

Reprinted from *Public Management*, Vol.63, No.12 (December 1981), pp. 2–4, by special permission, © 1981, The International City Management Association, Washington, D.C.

growing plan of county government in the United States today.

FUNCTIONAL SHIFTS

The county has emerged over the past three decades as the principal service delivery arm of government for many citizens for an impressive array of municipal-type services, and for most services and programs involving health, education, and welfare programs. The process and influence of urbanization, particularly since World War II, have fashioned significant change in the governmental structure in this country and the resultant relationship among the governmental units of all levels. One of the most striking changes involves the new and enhanced status of counties and their elected and appointed officials. This evolving change has occurred in part through the shift of traditional service delivery responsibilities from city to county governments. Functional areas typically shifted include planning, solid waste collection and disposal, public health, public safety, including regulatory code administration, sewage collection and treatment, and public finance, including assessment and taxation.

County governments are the service delivery units to which municipal services are most likely to be shifted and many municipal officials are supportive of the position that county governments should play a greater role in providing municipal-type services. It is noteworthy that municipal officials supporting this view are most likely to be found in states where counties have already taken on the new urban role and provide a relatively wide range of municipal-type services.

The 20th Century will produce dramatic change for counties in their long-time identification as the lowly dark continent of American government to a more appropriate role as the most important sub-state unit in the American governmental system. With the ever-increasing responsibilities and enhanced role of county governments has generally come the modernization of county government structure, organization, and operations. This has been achieved in most instances through home rule legislation and the subsequent adoption of modern forms which require more sophisticated management and administrative leadership and expertise.

PROFESSIONAL ADMINISTRATION

The incidence of an appointed professional administrator is directly related to county population—the larger the county, the more likely it is to have an appointed administrator. The jurisdictions with populations above 100,000 account for 80.5 percent of all people living in counties with an appointed administrator. Professional, nonpolitical leadership in counties which have modernized has been provided in many instances by careerists in public administration. Typical county administrators have spent most of their professional career in local government. Their training, experience, and mobility are essentially the same as that possessed by their city counterparts. Basic differences between county and city administrators are generally more apparent than real. In balance, professional county and city administrators are expected to fill a role with formal authority which revolves around such management activities as planning, organizing, staffing, coordinating, directing, reporting, budgeting, facilitating, and educating.

Today's county administrators, particularly in urban settings, must be professional. They place great emphasis on graduate level education in public administration to deal with the 3 Ms of general management—manpower, money, and materiel. These administrators are people-oriented and view their major responsibility as achieving the mission and goals of the organization through leading and motivating the work force.

The county administrator's position of public trust requires an understanding of and sensitivity to the broad and marbleized array of community problems which have been produced in great measure by urban expansion and rural decline. The county administrator is expected to give direction through anticipation and accurate assessment of public issues of the day, and to assist in the definition and clarification of complex community goals amidst a welter of special interests.

Administrators must continually identify and concentrate on community goals which are seemingly unidentifiable. Professional appointed county administrators must fill many roles—all equally well. They use techniques, methodology, and strategies to anticipate and identify issues, gather and analyze data, propose solutions, and communicate and explain all of this to (1) the governing body they serve; (2) the internal managers and supervisors of the organization; and (3) the work force. The administrators' leadership role, even though "issues oriented," must consistently represent private, not public, leadership. They propose and the elected council disposes. It is essential that the administrators recognize this and other nuances and subleties of their role and relationship with the governing body.

THE URBAN-RURAL MIX

Any comparison of the respective roles of county and city administrators should begin with a recognition of some of the basic similarities of and differences between typical county and city jurisdictions. Most counties in this country are larger, more expansive, and less symmetrical than the average city and thus present unique operational problems and constraints. The population of the county compared with that of the city is generally larger, spread out, more homogeneous, and conservative. And the social, economic, and political characteristics of the county, including the influence of whatever urbanism exists within its boundaries, introduce new dimensions to the problem solving and service delivery responsibilities of the county administrator.

For example, the dual nature of most counties, with their mix of urban and rural areas, means that counties must simultaneously deal with the perennial problems of urban expansion and rural decline and the growing city/farm dichotomy. County government policies, strategies, and procedures' are usually designed to factor and accommodate the impact on the rural as well as urban residents. The ambivalence required of county administrators is under constant pressure as they attempt to deal effectively with the incorporated (urban) as well as the unincorporated (rural) areas of the county.

The traditional role of the county as an agency or arm of the state government influences and has a profound effect on the county's policy making and service delivery systems. Today, those systems must recognize the unique transportation needs of many citizens which grow out of the county's expansive geography, and those factors produced by its peculiar social and economic mix. The traditional operational and political drag identified with county governments resulting from state mandates and close political and operational ties with the state must also be recognized as influential factors in the county policy making and service delivery systems. Always a factor affecting those systems is the duplication of service and competition produced by municipal and special service district operations within or contiguous to the county jurisdiction.

Newly implemented municipal-type functions and policies such as land use control and regulatory code enforcement in previously uncontrolled and unregulated areas of any county require well-timed, skillful, and ingenious administrative strategies designed to achieve acceptance by and produce desired results for a public usually suspicious and

TABLE 1. COUNTY GOVERNMENTS BY 1980 POPULATION AND REGION

Classification	No. of Local Governments	Counties No.	Counties Population
Total	26,210	3,042	203,722,908
Population group			
1,000,000 +	26	20	39,594,339
500,000–999,999	66	48	32,665,066
250,000–499,999	125	88	30,273,223
100,000–249,999	336	218	33,321,229
50,000– 99,999	660	375	26,276,426
25,000– 49,999	1,244	609	21,449,829
10,000– 24,999	2,618	958	15,863,945
5,000– 9,999	2,478	449	3,436,779
2,500– 4,999	3,022	176	677,227
Under 2,500	15,635	101	164,845
Geographic division			
New England	1,650	52	7,638,534
Mid-Atlantic	4,827	144	28,028,934
East North Central	4,327	436	40,904,505
West North Central	5,190	617	16,730,981
South Atlantic	2,883	546	32,752,424
East South Central	1,831	362	13,980,906
West South Central	2,927	468	22,819,488
Mountain	1,361	274	10,794,027
Pacific	1,214	143	30,073,109

hostile to any type of public control of private property. Such factors and conditions describe in part many county governments as they exist today, and cast the mold and institutional environment into which those who provide professional leadership and management for those counties must fit.

ADMINISTRATIVE LEADERSHIP

While there are no universal conditions, forms, systems, or management styles found among counties, few if any fundamental differences exist between professional county and city administrators in their responsibility for and execution of management and administrative functions.

Today, the county administrator possesses or should possess management expertise and be capable of leading and directing a strong, cohesive management team. This is the key to the excellence of administration modern counties require and must achieve considering their new role and responsibilities to the public. A professional administrator brings to the governmental scene an experience—a set of values reflected in both performance and leadership. These values and professional experience condition the individual's professional style—the way an administrator sees and responds to the surrounding institutional, political, and organizational environment.

A major contribution of professional county administrators is realized through the merger of their principal talent (the "how to") with the council's responsibility (the "what to"). Through that merger the political leadership of the county governing body is supported by providing it with the full benefit of all possible options and proposals in its decision-making role. Such an approach allows for the full benefit of professional expertise in strategy development and policy making by the legislative body, but avoids the triumph of technique over purpose.

THE POLICY PROCESS

In today's complex, marbleized, changing, and sometimes confused governmental system, the emerging leadership role of county government is strengthened by the implementation of policies and strategies finally approved by county council after having been researched and put into workable form by a professional staff led by and including the county administrator. If this process is to be effective, an atmosphere of mutual trust, open discussion, and teamwork is essential in the council-administrator policymaking relationship. This can best be achieved through the professional administrator serving as the catalyst and coordinator of the county government's technical and professional resources.

In balance, whatever the professional style and characteristics of the county administrator, and however he or she interprets and fills that role, public or political leadership is the prerogative and responsibility of the elected governing body. Such leadership is aimed at deliberating and controlling public policy while leadership of the appointed county administrator must consistently be private and organizational. When either the county council or county administrator fails to understand or interpret their respective roles or the subtleties of the plan correctly, it can easily fall into disarray.

--- **55** ---

Town Meetings: Folksy Democracy

GEORGE B. MERRY

Thomas Jefferson never lived in New England, but the early American patriot from Virginia was impressed with its town meetings. He termed them "the wisest invention ever devised by the wit of man for the perfect exercise of self-government and for its preservation."

Despite population growth and the increased complexities of modern life, once-tiny Yankee villages are tenaciously clinging to the 3½-century tradition of folksy democracy in action.

These yearly do-it-yourself government sessions, now in full swing in Massachusetts, are wrestling with a myriad of challenges ranging from solid-waste disposal to pay raises for inflation-squeezed employees.

Some town meetings, as in the past, are able to take care of everything in a matter of a few hours at a single session.

Many, however, are finding it increasingly difficult to do so. Four to six sessions, on consecutive nights or spread over several weeks, are not uncommon, especially in some larger towns where allowing everyone "their 2 cents worth" in debate slows proceedings.

A few dozen Massachusetts towns, many of them in the Greater Boston area, in recent decades have abandoned open participation at the meetings. A more workable arrangement, they have found, is to elect town-meeting members to make the decisions. Other interested townspeople may observe from the sidelines.

Even in towns where everybody can have a piece of the action, the town-meeting function has changed somewhat, with more authority vested in boards of selectmen and various other elected town bodies.

But there is little sentiment in most communities for shifting to some other form of government, even though poor attendance at town meetings is a frequent problem. Nowadays needed quorums are sometimes hard to come by, resulting in postponements.

In smaller towns, police and others are sometimes dispatched to round up enough people so a meeting can begin. The old fishing village of Marblehead, Mass., for instance, plans to send town criers through the streets to rally residents for its May 5 gathering.

Although it may result in less debate and shorter sessions, low attendance also makes it easier for special interests, such as town employees, to get their measures approved.

While town warrants, the formal agendas for the meetings, vary widely both in length and content from one community to another, the biggest and most widely debated item is the municipal budget.

Unlike last year, when cost-pruning was prevalent at these annual sessions, the current round of meetings is producing generally bigger budgets. Appropriation increases offered from the floor are more readily accepted.

Marjorie Battin, president of the Massachusetts Municipal Association and former chairman of the Lexington Board of Selectmen, notes that in her town meeting this year backers of spending increases have generally had little difficulty winning the two-thirds vote support needed to override the now year-old, state-imposed municipal budget cap.

This included a $510,000 appropriation for a new curbside trash-collection program made necessary by the state-ordered closing of the Lexington dump.

In neighboring Bedford, the big issue at the recent town meeting was the taking by eminent domain of a tract of land for new town wells. The town's wells had had to be shut down because of contamination, forcing the purchase of water from another municipality.

Other town-meeting issues sparking citizen discussion, if not oratory, include proposals for regionalized services between several adjoining communities, local school closings, zoning changes, and new snowplows and graders for highway departments.

The Bay State's smallest town, Mount Washington, for example, has on its May 6 agenda a measure to increase the responsibilities of the roads supervisor, the only full-time employee. He would do double-duty as chief of police as well.

This rural hamlet, nestled in the southwestern corner of Massachusetts, a stone's throw from both Connecticut and New York, now has only one part-time policeman to serve its 78 residents.

About half of Mount Washington's 59 voters are expected to attend the annual session in the century-old white clapboard Town

Hall. A year ago local citizens went on a spending spree, nearly doubling the budget and boosting the property tax rate from a modest $18 to $33.75.

"We don't have much in the way of services, and most of what we spend is for roads which we must have since our people have to go out of town to work and shop," explains

Alan Copland, chairman of the Mount Washington Board of Selectmen.

Mr. Copland, a lifelong town resident and publisher of the Berkshire Courier in Great Barrington some 12 miles away, hopes for funds for a part-time secretary to serve the town offices now manned entirely by volunteers.

56

Special District Government: A New "Dark Continent"?

NATIONAL CIVIC REVIEW

Adoption of new spending and taxing limitations on municipalities has had the unanticipated consequence of contributing to the creation of more units of local government. The result has been a decrease in accountability. The proliferation of special purpose districts during the last five years has occurred because general purpose local government did not or could not perform services which citizens demand. Paradoxically, one of the reasons has been the new limitations forced on local government by citizens.

The census bureau has just reported the latest enumeration of local governmental units—3,041 counties, 19,083 municipalities, 16,748 townships; 15,032 independent school districts. Only the number of special districts has increased significantly since the last count in 1977; it is up 11 percent to 28,733. Even more striking is the increase in spending, $9 billion in 1977, almost $25 billion in 1980 and

still growing. A large percentage of special district revenue is from user fees not included in the tax levy. A systematic review of the situation is needed.

John C. Bollens of the University of California at Los Angeles warns that special districts represent a "new dark continent" of American government. "They are a strange breed," he says. "Some of them serve very useful purposes. But many of them are not accountable. Even when their officials are elected, the candidates usually have no opposition. They are shadow governments."

There are circumstances in which special districts are appropriate mechanisms for providing services jointly for several municipal jurisdictions and thus constitute a more effective approach to service delivery. Sometimes, where limited services are needed in a growing area, a special district is a useful interim arrangement prior to the establishment of a

Editorial Comment, *National Civic Review*, Vol.71, No.8 (September 1982), pp. 397–398.

full-service municipal government. In other circumstances, residents of an area may want to provide an added service and create a special district for that purpose. But the rapid recent growth in the number of special districts also reflects efforts to circumvent tax, debt and spending limits in municipalities. Unquestionably, this further fragments and complicates local government, and whenever a particular service comes under special district jurisdiction it is removed from the process whereby general purpose governing bodies evaluate service needs and assign priorities.

At a time when citizens are unusually tax conscious and have succeeded in placing tax and expenditure caps on general government, they still demand services. They complain about taxes imposed by cities and counties but are willing to pay service charges or special levies to districts providing basic services—fire protection, parks, health care, libraries, water and sewage disposal. When special districts are subordinate to general government, and thus reflect differentiated service levels within a single jurisdiction, elected city council members or county commissions can still be held accountable, but the special districts reported by the census are actually separate governments, and how they are to be held accountable is another story.

We are alarmed by the low voter turnout in all elections, but despite the calls for keeping government close to the people the lowest turnout is in the election of low-visibility trustees or commissioners of special districts. These fragments of the total governmental picture are often the most unaccountable. Few citizens know who is in charge. Complaints about deficiencies in special district service are likely to be lodged with city hall. When the response is that it has no responsibility for that special district service, the citizens accuse city hall of buck passing. Public confidence is further eroded. Ardent advocates are pleased to remove their pet services from the budgetary process of general government and maintain it in isolation—take the service "out of politics" they say. Actually, doing this is nothing new and it has been reinforced by intensified special interest politics and encouraged when by doing so tax and expenditure limits can be circumvented. When city and county officials have promoted this they have become participants in the fragmentation process.

In the multi-level American governmental system, the role of the citizen is always an exacting one. Holding elected officials accountable for particular services is confusing at best. When local government has the overlay of special districts, confusion is compounded. Once established, these units can become an almost anonymous part of the political system with self-perpetuating bodies. For whatever reason these units exist they should be in the "sunshine." If they perform well and responsibly this should be known, but if not they should be subject to public scrutiny and those that do not should be modified or abolished. Unfortunately, too often the record of performance is unclear, in some cases deliberately so. It is also most important to monitor the creation of new special units, to be sure they are needed as an alternative to general government. If they are simply a subterfuge to get around legal limits, something is amiss. In such cases the limits may well be a disservice to accountable government. Rather than circumventing limits, an honest appraisal of them is in order.

57

Practicing Political Science on a Local School Board

GERALD M. POMPER

If politics is the art of the possible, political scientists have much to learn through the practice of government. Accepting this premise, many political scientists, following the example of Charles Merriam, have taken on political and governmental jobs. In this informal article, I want to report on my own experience.

My involvement is minor—one member of a nine-person school board, in a small community of 14,000 people and 1,600 students, with an annual budget of $8 million. The scope is relatively small, but I still find the lessons I have learned widely applicable. I have been particularly gratified to find that political science *is* relevant. The small matters that constitute the work of a small political entity have been illuminated by the generalizations of the discipline. In turn, these experiences have deepened my knowledge of political science—and provided good illustrative material for my courses.

I will briefly deal with four subjects: elections, interest groups, bureaucratic politics, and the political community. Inevitably, this is a personal report, but still, I hope, one that will be of more than parochial interest.

GETTING ELECTED

School boards are voluntary and unpaid bodies. There are few "self-starters" and political parties usually refrain from involvement. "Recruitment," in this case, is not only a category of analysis, but a reality. Probably like most candidates, I was asked to run, and had to be persuaded.

Once committed to the race, however, the campaign becomes as personally absorbing and important as a contest for offices with far greater power and personal rewards. It almost seemed as if I were running for president—but in an alternate universe in which every political variable had been compressed to microscopic size. Fundraising and spending limits were important, even though the legal limit on expenditures was only $1,000. We considered gender balance, and concluded that I had an advantage over my female opponent when five of the other eight positions on the Board were already filled by women. Discussions of means to attract the "black vote," the "Catholic vote," etc. were as earnest as any in the Democratic National Committee. The difference was that we were talking about how to win support from 50 blacks, or 500 Catholics, not millions.

These small numbers underlined the truth of the old adage, "All politics is local." One of my unofficial "campaign managers" persuasively argued that every campaign is an effort to establish a personal tie between the candidate and each voter. Presidential candidates must do this artificially, by bogus personal letters and media messages. In a

The American Political Science Association, *PS* (Spring 1984), pp. 220–225.

school board campaign, where 800 ballots would probably win, I could realistically hope to reach every voter. On the strategic level, this fact meant targeting specific individuals. Tactically, it led to an hour of telephoning every night for a month, holding 20 informal coffees for groups of as few as three people and no more than 15, and shaking hands for hours at the local supermarket, our functional equivalent of the traditional general store.

Personal contact is more important than I had believed. Early in the campaign, I went to a meeting of parents favoring an all-day kindergarten, one of the most visible school issues. By attending and declaring my support, I hoped to win the support of this group of voters—and to counter the appeal of my opponent, who had been one of the prime advocates of the program. The next day, however, I learned that I had lost rather than won votes, despite my being scored "right" on the issues. My mistake was in leaving the meeting at its formal end. What the parents had wanted was not only my programmatic support, but personal contact, the opportunity to "schmooz," and "press the flesh." After that, I never left a meeting until the hostess began yawning.

In these meetings, I deepened my understanding of the impact of issues on voting behavior. Educational issues are quite specific, proximate, and personal. Parents are often the true experts when it comes to the needs of their children, and parents of schoolchildren (and resident teachers) are the essential constituency in a school election. As a result, public opinion is highly informed, and a candidate must be both knowledgeable and ready to learn. At the same time, the voters I met seemed to me to be realistic in their expectations. They knew that no elected official could solve even the small problems of one school district and were willing to allow discretion and to follow leadership. In short, I found no "democratic distemper" but a healthy dialogue.

Most generally, I came to value elections in a personal way that reinforced my academic appreciation. We have long known about the "arrogance of power," and academicians often have inflated egos. But in the voting booth, all women and men are equal—and you, as a candidate, eagerly want their approval. I spent four hours one evening listening to three people tell me about the decline of morality in contemporary society (i.e., beer bottles on the high school football field) and the extravagance of government (i.e., the cost of lettuce for home economics classes). Yet, despite the fact that I held a Ph.D. and have taught for 25 years, I listened respectfully to them. Once elected, I was eager to support policies to bar drinking from school grounds and to reduce food purchasing bills. On large as well as trivial matters the dependence of elected officials on their constituents makes them responsive to their democratic masters. Mill, I found, was right: "Rulers and ruling classes are under a necessity of considering the interests of those who have the suffrage; but of those who are excluded, it is in their option whether they will do so or not."

INTEREST GROUP POLITICS

Once sworn into office, I found myself in still another universe, a pluralistic world apparently designed by David Truman. Decisions often depended on the resolution of conflicts between self-interested groups. Intensity and proximity made some groups more influential than their numbers warranted, but considerations of the general public interest did have an impact.

One example is provided by our biennial negotiations for a teacher contract. Despite the decline in the national rate of inflation and despite a comparatively high salary schedule, the premise of our negotiations was that a settlement would require at least an annual seven percent increase in teacher salaries. The teachers were the only organized interest group involved. Moreover, many of their members were local voters, and their cooperation was obviously central to any improvement in the schools. Parents, the only other obvious interest group, typified Walter Lippmann's "phantom public"—wanting a resolution of the conflict and unwilling to deal with specific issues in dispute. The "general interest" may have been that of the taxpayers, who were already typically paying $3,000 annually in property taxes for the schools, but it was not represented specifically. Speaking for this interest, the Board was able to win some concessions that would effect future economies—but at a price.

A second case involved the sale of a school building closed as the result of declining enrollment. Two alternatives were possible—selling to a developer who would convert the building to condominium apartments or tearing it down and selling subdivided lots for single-family homes. The first option would produce the most revenue for the schools, but the loudest demands came from a handful of persons near the school, who favored single-family homes on many grounds, including the resultant increase in the value of their own property. A majority of the Board was prepared to listen to this limited public, until—following Schattschneider—the "scope of conflict" was changed. A federal mandate to equalize girls' athletic facilities suddenly required the Board to find a large new source of revenue. Forced to concentrate on the schools' own needs, the Board decided to sell to the highest bidder.

BUREAUCRATIC POLITICS

Most of a school board's time is spent with professional administrators. Working full-time, versed in the educational lore and jargon, regulated and protected by state laws their colleagues often have drafted, the staff

has immense advantages in any conflict with a volunteer and amateur Board. Not surprisingly, scholarly studies have found that these boards exercise relatively little real authority over the professionals. School governance sometimes is undiluted symbolic politics, a la Edelman, as boards go through impotent rituals of power. All appointments are formally made by roll-call votes, even when they involve tenured personnel who could be removed only for the most flagrant moral abuses. Similarly, each new course and each financial transaction requires a roll-call, even though the members must necessarily follow staff recommendations in almost all details.

The effective place for citizen control is the budget. As representatives of the taxpayers, who in many states vote directly on the school budget, Board members attempt to hold down spending to limit tax rates. School bureaucrats have their established routines to counter these economy drives, many of them resembling the techniques used by the Pentagon to resist cuts in defense spending. "We can't fall behind the Russians" is a slogan that can be employed to buy either multi-warhead missiles or the newest science texts. "Most of the increase is due to inflation" can explain expensive tanks or new $45 basketballs. As we know from Wildavsky, bureaucrats build budgets incrementally, assuming that past expenditures are unquestionable, and that only new spending for the coming fiscal year requires discussion.

The best technique to use in this situation is to make the professional educators directly aware of the tradeoffs inherent in any social policy, including a school budget. This cannot be done by asking abstractly, "Which programs are of lower priority?" The answer will inevitably be that everything is indispensable, whether it is sewing in the fourth grade, calculus for a handful of advanced students, or separate whirlpools for girl and boy athletes. Instead, there must first be a total limit placed on spending, forcing prioritizing among programs and, not incidentally, providing a defense against the many particular interests that will want a "small" increase for their pet programs. Seeing the process at work, I am now far more sympathetic to such proposals as mandatory ceilings on taxes. Imposing real, even seemingly arbitrary, limits prods administrators to think creatively and to question past assumptions. When there is no new money for math courses, an additional secretary becomes less indispensable. In the end, school administrators will usually make the choices that are best for the children—but they can use some encouragement.

This strategy is particularly necessary in education policy, for school spending is likely to rise annually, whatever the level of inflation or the school enrollment. Spending groups are identifiable and organized. The basic object of this spending, our children, are the embodiment of our dearest hopes. The natural generosity we feel toward their education inherently cannot be tested against any measures of cost-effectiveness. Still more is this the case when the nation has become alarmed over "a rising tide of mediocrity" (or at least a "rising tide of reports") in the schools.

Budgets have the advantage for the citizen Board member of being tangible and precise. More difficult to control are the curriculum and administrative matters that come before the Board. On such matters, professors are likely to be misled by analogies to higher education. They believe that universities are, or at least ought to be, governed and collegial, while public schools are administered and hierarchical. Other Board members' experience may be even less relevant. In their efforts to improve the schools, most representatives follow two very different strategies—suggesting "grand ideas" ("back to basics") or dealing with very specific grievances ("Why do the buses come late on Third Avenue?"). These interventions can be very valuable, but they typically miss the middle range of activity,

such as program development and implementation that comprises most of the actual management of any bureaucracy, including schools.

This pattern leaves school administrators free to shape most policy, unless a school board member is unusually pointed and persistent. (But, as Neustadt asked of presidents, how often does a Board member ask three times about the same issue?) Even then, it is hard to "command" such desired outcomes as "creative thinking" (and Neustadt reminds us how rarely direct command is used). If challenged, administrators use some common bureaucratic defenses. Delay, as I have just suggested, is one. A second is to argue that law or practice will not allow innovation, e.g., "the state (union/commissioner/insurance company) won't permit it." Lacking expertise and time for research, the Board member must usually accept the answer. Another defensive technique is over-compliance. A new policy is followed to a logical absurdity, so that the Board member learns to mind his own business. A request for information is dutifully answered by reams of paper, the mass of detail burying the Board member's original thought. In dealing with academicians, like myself, a particular variant is to cite the research literature in education. As you might guess, the reference is not necessarily enlightening.

Political science suggests some ways to deal with these problems. Here are a few recommendations. Create competing interests within the bureaucracy. Thus, if dissatisfied with the results of English instruction, establish a new "writing across the curriculum" program. Provide incentives, such as competitive awards for new teaching techniques. Rotate administrators, so that undesirably entrenched patterns are necessarily disrupted. Define issues so that the Board sets the terms of the agenda, rather than the school hierarchy. For example, reduce the time devoted to woodworking by emphasizing additional language instruction, rather than debating the merits of ripsaws. Perhaps most important, remember that organizations are not simply goal-oriented groups, but are natural systems in which individual needs and interpersonal relationships must be nurtured.

THE POLITICAL COMMUNITY

Much of this essay suggests that school board membership is frustrating and that the idealistic goal of educating our children faces great obstacles in voter resistance, interest group parochialism, and administrative routines. All of that is true.

Nevertheless, it is a rewarding experience, and I suspect the rewards are even greater in positions of greater responsibility. It is a learning experience, and professors can and should always learn. It is a real experience, more so than most of what we do in the classroom or research center. In our academic work, we may talk about the relative desirability of spending public money for an MX missile or a food stamps program, but we are only talking theoretically. It is quantitatively much less important, but qualitatively more meaningful, actually to find means to reduce the cost of health insurance by $50,000, so that you can begin to teach computer literacy to 1,600 students who are your friends' children and your neighbors. It is also an enlarging experience. The office-holder necessarily becomes conscious of acting, however inexpertly and bounded, on behalf of larger interests, and this feeling may be most satisfying when acting for a powerless group, such as children.

The benefits of political involvement go beyond these personal satisfactions, toward the discovery of public life in a deeper sense. As de Tocqueville warned us early, the greatest defect in American life is likely to be the lack of community, the absence of personal ties which gain meaning in common enterprises. That defect is even more apparent today, when we have necessarily delegated much of the work of government to distant sites, when we live in transient communities, when material and emotional demands force a concentration on our personal well-being.

Political life counteracts this absence of community. In holding even a minor public office, your relationships to others in the community change. Conversations are more likely to be on the general issues with which you deal. Neighbors talk not only about the weather or the grocery prices, but about the desirability of revising the science curriculum. The relationship is not less friendly or less egalitarian (there is no "power" involved), but it is more *public*, more concerned with your common lives.

That talk educates both the public official and his or her constituents. After my election, I fulfilled a campaign pledge to go back monthly to some of the homes where I had campaigned and to discuss school developments. It is a sad commentary on the trust voters have in politicians that my hosts were surprised that I bothered to return, and one assumed, incorrectly, that I was running for a new term. Otherwise, these were heartening evenings. We discussed not theories of education, but classroom instruction in the fourth grade. While I tried to explain our new program budget, I also was taught the realities of raising children in single-parent families. Amid the fun and the coffee cake, all of us learned. Madison was right in thinking that the election of representatives would "refine and enlarge the public views," but he neglected to mention the same effect of community activity upon the representatives themselves.

My experience has convinced me that there is still great potential for a public life, at least in small localities. Residents have a vast reservoir of knowledge about their towns; on one occasion, I found that there was cumulative local experience of over 200 years among ten householders on a single street. Schools—and other issues—do matter to the voters, whether they view them as past or present students, parents or grandparents, or taxpayers. And there is a desire, inexpert but warm, to "do good," for children and for the community.

Democratic political theorists have based their philosophies on such optimistic premises. In current political dialogue, however, they are often forgotten, as both academicians and electoral candidates stress self-interest and group competition. As political scientists, we might do better to teach these other lessons, not only in our schools, but to our national leaders.

CHAPTER 12

Participation in State and Local Politics

Relatively few people are active citizens in the governments closest to them. This concluding chapter examines a variety of reasons why this is so. Two selections offer a framework for analysis of urban black politics, and that demographics indicate increasing political clout for Hispanics. Turning from this "macro" approach, we then take the "micro" approach, that of human motivations. A "bureaucrat" finds government "a profoundly human affair," and LeRoy Harlow details the corruption and "violations of the public trust" which disillusion citizens. Finally, the choices: why participate in party politics, or else be a lonely independent as "The Reformer" concludes *Capitol, Courthouse, and City Hall*.

58

Citizen Participation:
Walking the Municipal Tightrope

THOMAS W. FLETCHER

What has happened to urban government in America?

The harsh fact is that through many years, the American poor and, to a lesser degree, Americans in general have become more and more lost in the sea of government. Quite clearly American citizens have lost much of their ability to influence government. Simple arithmetic can tell us part of this story. Thirty years ago a city councilman might represent 15,000 voters; today he may represent 100,000, 250,000, or more.

Then, too, in our thrust away from politically run cities we have reformed out of existence the precinct captain. Despite his sometime reputation and behavior, this was a man who could connect an individual's small needs and problems with government's larger concerns. He got street lights fixed, found jobs, cut red tape, and in general gave people a feeling that they could still touch and use government. In large part, that is no longer true, instead of reforming this liaison system, we destroyed it.

The result is that powerful individuals and organized groups can still touch government, but too often John Q. Citizen cannot. In the suburbs, the slum, and even the university, many citizens feel they have no voice, no say, no influence on the thousands of government decisions affecting them each year. And they do not.

At the same time, government has failed to discover the uncontrolled, uncoordinated monster that it has become. As cities have grown, sprawling across vast new areas or packing citizens more and more tightly into inner cores, they have let themselves become an almost unmanageable, unresponsive, and incomprehensible maze. Administrative charts paint a neat but oversimplified picture of government from a central administrator's point of view. The fact is a government organization must be measured not only by how much coordination it has at the top but also by how much teamwork and delivery it has at the bottom of the organization pyramid—in the city's subcommunities where the people and the problems actually live...

How businesslike is it for a city to measure its workload by the evident demand, the citizens who walk up to counters and ask for city services, when many thousands more, uninformed and unbelieving, spend lifetimes with needs that could be satisfied?

Why hasn't government approached its problem of service delivery as business and the medical profession have in recent years? Identify the areas of need. Don't simply count the cases, the customers, the complainants, but actually survey, as business does, and identify the needy and the needs in city areas and proceed to meet both needs in those city communities where the problems are.

Reprinted from *Public Management*, July 1969, by special permission © 1969, The International City Management Association, Washington, D.C.

This is what business has done with its clusters of stores, with its supermarkets. This is what the medical profession has done with its clinics. They have moved to the market . . . as must city government.

And city government must make certain that its market areas, its subcommunities, its regions of varying economic, social, and service needs receive services tailored to the region. . . .

Two problems, among many others, are pressing here. One is the need at the local level to pull together, by reorganization or by cooperation, the many service delivery agencies, public and nonpublic, which exist side by side, overlap, and all too often do not plan and work together. There are myriad examples: jealously independent school systems, semi-independent health and welfare agencies, completely independent nonpublic organizations, whose caseworkers often cover the same communities, deal with the same problems—sharing neither information nor energies.

The second is the need for state and federal governments to require local general government coordination of the programs they fund in municipalities, the programs that often spring up on city landscapes without the knowledge of concerned city planners. The federal government, for example, must decide that the projects it funds must be linked with plans being pressed by city government to improve living for its citizens. . . .

However, the key word in this new thrust is "responsiveness." This is the basic issue. Many of the problems we confront today in city organization and in city service delivery would not exist if people had asked themselves the question, "Are these new programs and the way they are being administered responsive to actual individual-people needs and community needs?"

To assure that level of responsibility on the part of government, there must be informed, influential community, subcity organizations capable of raising issues, of promoting ideas, of influencing government direction. Because government must be responsive, it also has the responsibility of encouraging, assisting, staffing, and heading such community organizations.

In this connection, I certainly agree with [the] statement that, "Commitment to neighborhood involvement does not imply abdication of municipal responsibility for the city's well-being."

But we must make certain that the voice of the people is heard and that government, the servant of the people, responds.

This is no easy task. The division between government and people has deepened and widened. Suspicion, mistrust, urgent needs, and militancy put fantastic pressures on the effort to achieve some kind of effective partnership.

Community organizations will grow, thrive, and hopefully develop that degree of influence which will spell governmental responsiveness, but those same organizations will splinter if they bureaucratize themselves, if they become so laden with structure and operational concerns that they become "too busy" to represent their constituencies.

We in government must recognize the tightrope we must walk to achieve maximum community influence—and continuing progress in our cities.

59

A Framework for the Analysis of Urban Black Politics

JOHN R. HOWARD

Richard Hatcher, Mayor of Gary, Indiana, identified the holding of political office as the only important power resource blacks collectively possess in American society:

Blacks still do not control the real power centers in this country. We do not have large accumulations of personal wealth. We do not run any of the nation's largest two hundred corporations. We do not have influence within the military-industrial networks. . . . We do not have much say with the councils of organized labor.

Our major gains so far have been limited to local government. Here we do indeed control terrain that was formerly beyond our grasp.[1]

In examining the policy consequences of significant black municipal office-holding we are also examining the viability of the American politico-economic system. If the formal political system proves to be an ineffective instrument for meliorating black ills, then existing racial tensions will become more intense. As the resentment and aggression of the urban black underclass grows, the fear and hostility of whites, perceiving threats to their physical safety and to the established social order, will mount.

The capacity of the system in its present form to survive such tensions is doubtful. A drift toward authoritarian solutions, guaranteeing safety to whites by keeping a heavy hand on the black underclass, would not be unlikely, but would diminish the sum of liberty available to each person in the society. The stakes, then, in urban black politics are fairly high, and the policy and program outcomes of black leadership at the municipal level are still in doubt.

. . . [A]t least two questions become central in the analysis of urban black politics:

1. Around what set of concerns, issues, and problems does it revolve; or, in other words, public policy with regard to what? This question breaks down in two further parts: (a) how recalcitrant are the municipal problems confronting black officeholders? and (b) are those problems substantially those of blacks or do they also plague other important sectors of the electorate? . . .

2. It is also essential in the analysis of urban black office-holding to understand the context within which policy is formulated and implemented. This entails examining the structural and economic parameters within which decision-making occurs. Since the urban black officeholder is, after all, black, it also entails examining the impact of considerations of race and racism on their political behavior. Again, the major question breaks

---

John R. Howard, "A Framework for the Analysis of Urban Black Politics," *The Annals of the American Academy of Political and Social Science,* September 1978, pp. 2–14. Edited and reprinted by permission of the author. Some footnotes in original omitted.

down into more specific questions. It becomes important in understanding the context within which urban black leaders pursue their objectives to know: (a) the extent to which white attitudes do or do not accommodate such leadership; (b) the extent to which important sectors of the white population, attitudes aside, may have an instrumental stake in discriminatory practices—some of the financial rewards which may accrue from perpetuating a segregated housing market, for example. Additionally, a grasp of the parameters within which urban black leaders function entails examining the impact of federal and state policies on municipalities.

The balance of this essay is given over to examining both the magnitude of the problems confronting black officeholders at the municipal level and the politico-social context within which black leadership seeks to confront those problems. . . .

BLACK NEEDS AND URBAN POLICY

Although black mayors have been elected in over 130 cities, the bulk of the attention in terms of black municipal office-holding has been given to the major urban centers with substantial black populations: Detroit, Newark, Gary, Atlanta, Washington, D.C., Oakland, California, and New Orleans; and to a host of smaller, substantially black communities like Compton, California and East St. Louis, Illinois.

Several cities with black populations of 10 percent or less have had black chief executives, including Boulder, Colorado, College Park, Maryland, Grand Rapids, Michigan, and Chapel Hill, North Carolina. The prototypic situation, however, is found in a Gary or a Newark, rather than in these smaller, substantially white, more affluent cities. And it is

undoubtedly the case that the fate of urban black politics will be determined in the Newarks rather than in the Boulder, Colorados.[2]

The more typical cities with black leadership have similar, although not identical, profiles. They are cities which are older, blacker, and poorer than most in the United States. The primary policy concerns of urban black leadership relate directly or indirectly to the problems generated by the poverty of a substantial portion of their black constituents. These problems are multifaceted and interconnected. For example, the amount of a city's nontaxable church property or of its nontaxed cultural facilities has an impact on the revenues available to finance the social services received by the poor.

Although the problem of urban poverty is well-known in its general dimensions (most informed citizens know that there are a lot of poor people in Newark), it may be instructive to review them in detail. Such a review will provide a clearer grasp of the problems confronting urban black leadership. Indeed, demographic data indicate that, for certain dimensions of well-being or standard of living, the black population of the United States is more like the population of certain Third World countries than it is like this country's white population.

From the standpoint of black officeholders, the problems fall into a number of policy areas: employment, housing, health, transportation, public safety, and education are, perhaps, the most important. The powers of black officeholders in terms of these areas are a function of the structure of city government, the statutory relations between city and state, and the extent of the fiscal and programmatic obligations assumed by the federal government. Nevertheless, blacks at the local level are looked to for leadership and may indeed contribute to the formulation of policy, even for issues where the major responsibilities are fixed at other levels of government.

Perhaps the clearest way of conveying the full dimensions of the problems faced by black chief executives in some of our major cities is to review the key areas of employment and unemployment.

Employment, Unemployment, and Income Among Urban Blacks

Central to the problems of the ghetto, and therefore a major source of the problems confronting black chief executives, is the high rate of urban black unemployment. The high rate of unemployment has a ripple effect, generating a host of other problems. The lack of effective demand, that is, demand which can be backed up with dollars, hurts ghetto business, black and white. It affects choice in the housing market, questions of discrimination in housing aside, and determines the quality of the health care received. Also, as many observers have pointed out, it decreases local revenues while increasing the need for publicly supported services.

As many scholars have noted, Bureau of Labor Statistics data tend to understate the actual extent of joblessness in the nation by excluding workers who have become discouraged and ceased seeking employment and those with part-time jobs who want full-time jobs. The National Urban League Research Department, drawing on a formula developed by the Joint Economic Committee of Congress, developed a Hidden Employment Index that allows for adding both groups to those officially listed as unemployed. The use of this formula indicated an actual unemployment rate among blacks in urban low income areas of 25.8 percent, this figure rising in 1975 in some areas to over 30 percent. . . .

. . . Employment and other data to be cited indicate that while the white population demographically is similar to the populations of countries in Western Europe (with the exception of Portugal), the nonwhite population of the United States in certain demographic respects looks like the populations found in parts of the Caribbean or in certain Central and South American countries. Indeed, the

"two nations" alluded to as a possibility in the Kerner Commission's report on the urban riots of the 1960s, in some respects already exists. The urban ghetto is, in black novelist James Baldwin's words "Another Country."

Unemployment has been a longstanding problem in the black community. Only three times between 1949 and 1974 did the official black unemployment rate fall below 6 percent, 1954 being the last year in which this occurred; while for whites during the same period only twice did it rise above 6 percent.

In a very real sense, then, the Depression of the 1930s never ended for blacks. Given that indices of hidden unemployment suggest that the official unemployment figures are low, black unemployment rates may for decades actually have approached those of whites during the 1930s. The problems inherited by urban black leadership, therefore, are historically very long-standing and have never officially been wholly recognized. Put somewhat differently, urban blacks have for decades experienced a chronic recession, but in the 1970s, as blacks assumed power at the municipal level, the chronic recession became a depression.

Contrary to popular belief, federal and state income transfer policies in the form of unemployment benefits do not provide significant economic relief for the ghetto. Only about half of the 8 million persons officially listed as unemployed in 1975 received unemployment compensation and ". . . only about 37 percent of the 1.5 million blacks [officially] without jobs received benefits."

Where does an unemployed black go who is either ineligible for unemployment compensation or who has used up his or her eligibility? Presumably—if they do not turn to stealing—on to welfare. A mass of data indicates, however, that most poor families do not participate in income transfers through public assistance programs. In 1974, 40 percent of the black families below the officially determined poverty line did not receive any form of public assistance. And, according to a

report of the National Governor's Conference, in 1974 only 62 percent of the poor were
eligible for cash grants through either Aid to
Families with Dependent Children (AFDC),
aimed primarily at single-parent families, or
Supplemental Security Income (SSI) for the
aged, the blind, and the disabled, but, of
course, not all of those eligible actually received assistance. Insofar as adequate relief is
not provided by the state or federal governments, cities are left either to draw on their
own revenues or face the consequences of
large numbers of impoverished and discon-
tented people within their boundaries.

In contrast to the 1930s, when rising unemployment was accompanied by a fall in
price levels, in the 1970s price levels and unemployment rates rose together. . . . It is the
case, of course, that prices also rose in cities
with white leadership. The difference between black- and white-led cities is that black
leadership is more likely to be looked to by
struggling black constituents for relief.

The problem of urban black poverty is
not solely a problem of the unemployed. Indeed, most of the poor are wage earners, but
they do not make enough to rise above the
poverty line by any of several definitions of
poverty. . . . Thus, central among the problems confronting urban black leadership is
poverty. . . .

The economic weakness of the ghetto is
reflected in the meager dimensions of black
business. Black-owned business constitutes
neither an important locus of black employment nor a significant source of public revenue. . . . Most are small, family-owned enterprises, at best yielding a living to a few
family members.

There is a reciprocal relationship between
the impoverished state of black business in
the ghetto and the high rate of unemployment. Indeed, the high rate of unemployment
has a ripple effect, the lack of effective black
demand limiting the economic viability of
most black-owned business. Insofar as such
businesses depend largely or totally on black

clientele, they are leaning on an economically
weak market. The limited business that this
condition generates prevents black businesses
from expanding to become important ghetto
employers.

Other Aspects of the Problem of Poverty

The massive problems of poverty in the
ghetto produce a host of interrelated problems; for example, the small size of most black
businesses means that most blacks have to
seek employment outside their community.

At that point problems of transportation
become important, and the negative impact of
federal and state policies promoting the use of
automobile over public transportation becomes clear. . . . Thus, not surprisingly,
more black poverty area residents use public
transportation to get to work than make use
of an automobile. Additionally, black central
city residents are more likely than white central city residents to use public transportation
to get to work, whether their jobs are inside or
outside the central city.

Poverty is also associated with ill health,
and ill health affects rate of participation in the
labor force, and rate of participation in the
labor force is associated for any group with
the group's rate of poverty. Put somewhat
differently, the poor are more likely to be ill
than the nonpoor and are, partially because of
this, less likely to be in the labor force. Not
being in the labor force denies them an adequate income and therefore increases the
probability that health status will be a factor
keeping them idle. . . .

The poverty of the ghetto is also associated with high rates of crime and of fatal violence, the latter stemming both from police
action to control what in the nineteenth century were termed "the dangerous classes"
and from intragroup violence among ghetto
residents. In terms of such intragroup fatal
violence, homicide is nationally the second
leading cause of death among young black

males. Indeed, in 1974 the absolute number of males who fell victim to homicide was greater for the roughly 12 percent nonwhite minority than for the 88 percent white majority (8,755 to 7,992). For young white males, accidents of one type or another and, curiously, suicide are the leading causes of death.

Urban black leadership, then, confronts problems of enormous magnitude. Questions of housing, transportation, public safety, health and hospital care are all related, however, to the problem of poverty.

Let us turn now to a discussion of the second essential element in a framework for the analysis of urban black politics.

THE CONTEXT WITHIN WHICH BLACK LEADERSHIP IS EXERCISED

All politicians operate within certain externally imposed constraints. . . . The nature of the constraints differs from one historical period and one type of political system to another, but the limits are always there.

There are a variety of constraints confronting urban black leadership in terms of the development and implementation of meliorative policy with regard to the ghetto problems. Among these constraints are (a) the political (and moral) inaccessibility of certain policy approaches theoretically available to white leadership; (b) the fiscal strain, of varying degrees of severity, depending on the particular city; (c) the apportioning of power among city offices as this is reflected in the structure of city government; (d) the dependence on state and federal policy initiatives; and (e) racism as it is manifested in institutional and affective forms. Of these, the latter is both the most powerful and the most elusive.

Regressive Policy and Urban Black Leadership

The problems of many cities with black leadership derive, at least in part, from the fact that their populations are comprised of substantial numbers of poor people. Clearly one approach to solving the problems represented by the poor is to advocate the expulsion of the poor from the city.

Experienced analysts of the urban scene have advanced this policy with regard to the problems of New York City and, by inference, to those of other cities with substantial minority and low-income populations. Thus, in 1977 Roger Starr, New York's Housing and Development Administrator, encouraged the "planned shrinkage" of low-income and minority communities as an alternative to city-wide cuts in service. In other words, services to the nonpoor were to be maintained by inducing the poor to leave the city.

Later that year, in a series of recommendations to incoming New York City Mayor Edward Koch, . . . a Columbia University Business School professor urged cutting municipal services to the poor to encourage them to leave the city. His plan entailed, among other steps, closing municipal hospitals, closing day care centers, and raising tuition at the city colleges in order to shut out poor students. Managing "negative growth" would . . . maintain the quality of life in the city for the nonpoor. Lowering the quality of life for the poor would result from these policies, thereby presumably forcing the poorest segments of the population to seek refuge elsewhere.

Richard P. Nathan, Senior Fellow at the Brookings Institution, alluded to some of the benefits some observers see these policies as yielding:

> . . . the bravest among municipal leaders have suggested that certain metropolitan areas . . . should consciously adopt a policy abandoning the most hopelessly blighted areas. There are also observers who see the build up of low priced vacant land in the inner city as a hidden asset. They see rising fuel prices (which discourage large communities), an available labor force, access to rail and sea transportation and urban services as ultimately bringing a resurgence for the nation's troubled inner cities.[3]

But presumably this would be a resurgence involving repopulation of the inner city with mostly white suburbanites and young professionals who prefer urban to suburban life.

Clearly, for political reasons, urban black leadership might find it more difficult than white to entertain such proposals for coping with the municipal problems presented by poverty. Politically, the black community, poor and nonpoor, provides the black politician with his primary base of support. The black politician, then, is constrained to seek melioration for the ghetto rather than the physical removal of the poor from the city.

Fiscal Strain

Cities vary in their capacity to support services at levels which are commensurate with the health and safety for their citizens. In general, cities with black leadership show somewhat greater problems in the area than cities without black leadership. Most, though not all black cities, show fiscal strain. . . .

Herrington Bryce, formerly Director of Research at the Joint Center for Political Studies, . . . measured municipal fiscal capacity in terms of per capita income as an indicant "of the amount of money a mayor can potentially raise by taxes or fees to conduct the affairs of government." Comparing cities with black mayors with cities of similar size, and cities in the same state with white mayors, he concluded that ". . . among cities which might have to supply a given set of goods and services at a roughly similar per unit cost, those with black mayors are less able to raise the necessary funds through taxation unless they enact exorbitant tax rates."

In terms of the context, then, within which urban black leadership confronts municipal problems, certain policy options theoretically open to white leadership are closed to black leadership, and it must seek to meet a wider range of publicly supported needs from a narrower fiscal base than that available to white leadership in cities of comparable size or cities in the same state.

Let us now look at the structural framework within which leadership is exercised.

The Structure of Government and Urban Black Leadership

There are wide variations in the forms of government in municipalities with black leadership. At the risk of oversimplification, however, they may be categorized in terms of the amount of power they yield to the chief executive.

Commission and council-manager forms of city government yield less power to mayors while mayor-council forms of government (sometimes with a chief administrative officer appointed by the mayor) yield more power. . . . A number of black-led cities have the council-manager form of government, including Compton, Insker, Pontiac, and Cincinnati. In Pontiac and Cincinnati, however, the mayor is elected by the council, which, in principle, should make for more harmonious relations between the mayor and the city manager. . . .

In the larger black-led cities, Detroit, Atlanta, Newark, Gary, and in some of the more demographically typical smaller cities like East Orange and New Brunswick in New Jersey, the mayor-council form of government yields greater mayoral power in terms of the budget, vetoes over council ordinances and resolutions, and appointments.

The structure of city government is thus an important variable in terms of the capacity of black leadership to formulate and implement programs responsive to constituent problems.

Federal and State Initiatives

Clearly federal and state policies are crucial to the fate of cities, both in terms of the budgetary and fiscal obligations they impose and in terms of the monetary relief they provide. Model Cities (1966), the Housing and Urban Development Act (1968), and the Housing and Community Development Act of 1974 have been of enormous importance. The Housing and Community Development Act, with its goals of "expansion and improvement of the quantity and quality of community services, principally for people of low and moderate income (and) reduction of the isolation of economic groups within communities and geographic areas through spacial deconcentration of housing opportunities for low-income people," sought to address the danger identified by former secretary of Housing and Urban Development, Robert Weaver, that ". . . if current trends continue, the central city could function as a reservation for the poor. . . ."

Institutional and Affective Racism

Clearly the dynamics of urban black politics in the United States cannot be understood without reference to the racism which has been an indelible part of American history. Although there have been episodes of xenophobia and nativism in American history, and despite the fact that Orientals, Jews, Mexicans, and other ethnic or religious groups have from time to time been or continue to be the objects of contumely, the experience of blacks in the United States has been unique.

This uniqueness means that black phenomena have to be studied in their own terms. The models and theories with regard to assimilation mobility, group self-identity and the like, which might be used analytically with other groups, are not wholly appropriate or applicable for blacks. The central fact in the history of blacks in the United States has been the tenacious and pervasive character of white racism. Therefore, in the discussion of the context within which urban black leadership is exercised it is essential to examine the pressures against meliorative change which emanate from white racism.

Institutional Racism

The essence of the concept of institutional racism is that on issues of real substance, issues involving the distribution of opportunities and resources, large numbers of whites with or without personal hostility may have a stake in institutional arrangements which work to the detriment of blacks. Put somewhat differently: "The rules of the game" in terms of access . . . may not in given cases be racist in content, but may have racially biased consequences. This has particularly important consequences in terms of cities. As Herrington Bryce stated, "In the view of some observers, blacks have inherited the city after other ethnic groups have become well entrenched in the police force, the sanitation department, and education and welfare bureaucracies."

The locus of conflict in terms of black access to employment in these bureaucracies has been civil service and other testing procedures which are not necessarily job related and which systematically disqualify a disproportionately large number of black and other minority job applicants. The white stake in the municipal status quo is often materially substantial. As the sociologist Frances Fox Piven pointed out, "Whites and blacks are pitted against each other in a struggle for the occupational and political benefits attached to public employment. Whites now have the bulk of these benefits and blacks want a greater share of them."

A number of cases filed by blacks and other minorities have attacked testing and screening procedures for public employment, seemingly neutral in character but with racially differential outcomes in terms of the identification of prospective new hires. And whites have fought to retain control of public sector unions representing firemen, policemen, teachers, and sanitation men, having gone to court to resist measures which would have increased the number of blacks in their ranks.

Institutional racism extends beyond the public service unions to the practices of a variety of urban institutions and organizations. Thus, the United States League of Savings Associations urged its members, in response to charges of refusing to lend for mortgage or home improvement in largely or entirely black neighborhoods, to "make clear that in weighing the social merit of any loan application against your fiduciary responsibility you must put the interests of your savers first." This practice, of course, creates a self-fulfilling prophecy, the channeling of money from urban neighborhoods to potentially more lucrative fields, resulting in accelerating deterioration of those neighborhoods.

Insofar as black-led cities tend to have a higher proportion black population than non-black-led cities of comparable size, their problems of institutional racism are more severe. The existence of an array of institutional practices, seemingly benign or neutral in character but racially-biased in practice, form part of the context in which leadership is exercised.

Affective Racism

In the two decades following World War II, the major approach in the social sciences to the study of race was psychological. Economics gave relatively little attention to the economics of discrimination while political science failed to develop an extensive literature on the enfranchisement or disenfranchisement of blacks. . . .

In the late 1960s, this approach gave way to analyses of the political economy of discrimination. In other words, research shifted away from attempting to discover why individual whites are anti-black to looking at those aspects of the political and economic systems which sustained or even reinforced black and minority subordination.

Irrespective of this shift in the attention of scholars, there was a fundamental truth in the earlier psychological approach to the study of race problems in the United States. There are whites who hate blacks not because of the high black crime rate, or the number of blacks on welfare, or the alleged black influence on property values; rather, they hate blacks because blacks exist. Put somewhat differently, there are whites who have a deep-seated, tenacious antipathy toward blacks,

the verbalized particulars of the anti-black stereotype being essentially rationalizations for that antipathy.

Perhaps the clearest way of discerning the impact of white attitudes toward black life is to review some of the data on white attitudes concerning specific measures and policies affecting blacks. Thus, a Harris poll involving a nationwide sample of adult whites, conducted for the National Urban League and reported in 1975, indicated, more than a decade and a half after *Brown* v. *Board of Education,* that 38 percent of white ethnics (Irish, Italians, and Poles) disapproved of the Supreme Court decision banning mandatory segregation in public schools, while 48 percent of white Protestants disapproved. Indeed, 10 percent of white ethnics and 30 percent of white Protestants favored racially segregated schools. White support for specific legislation shoring up black rights is also less than solid. A 1970 Harris poll indicated that 43 percent of whites did not support voting rights legislation while 34 percent were against public accommodations laws, and 38 percent opposed fair employment practices legislation.

This is not to say that all those whites opposed to judicial and legislative reform in the area of race are ineluctable racists; given individuals may have varying philosophical objections to these laws. Individuals may even favor racial reforms but object to these public actions on tactical grounds. Clearly, however, there are a considerable number of whites who are opposed to racial reform because they are anti-black. Irrespective of polls showing modification of white attitudes, the electoral facts of the matter with regard to urban black leadership are that black candidates running in cities with a substantial black population have rarely received major white support.

The tangible consequences of racism may be that the yardstick used to measure the performance of black leadership may be different than that used to measure the performance of white leadership. The leeway given black leadership for error and experimentation may be considerably less than that afforded white leadership. Whereas white leadership may be assumed to be competent and honest until it demonstrates lack of these qualities, black leadership is more likely to be viewed as incompetent and dishonest until it proves otherwise. Race and racism are inevitably part of the situation within which urban black leadership performs.

. . . I have attempted to present a framework for the analysis of urban black politics. Essential to an understanding of the dynamics of urban black politics is a grasp of the demographic character of the major cities in which blacks govern. These cities present a profile which differentiates them from most American cities of similar size. The dimensions of the problems confronting most black leadership in cities of 25,000 or more are greater than those confronting white leadership in cities of comparable size. These prob-

lems are of long historical derivation, but the pressures on black leadership to deal with them effectively over a short period of time are fairly great. . . .

NOTES

1. Richard G. Hatcher, "Minority Objection," *New York Affairs*, Vol.3, No.3 (Spring 1976), p. 69.
2. Throughout this discussion Los Angeles is not given attention, as its status as a large city with a substantially white population but a black chief executive is atypical. In certain respects the problems Bradley faces overlap with those of a Gibson or a Hatcher, but the differences are so great as to make Los Angeles an exception to most of the generalizations that would hold true of other black governed cities.
3. Richard P. Nathan, "Is There a National Urban Crisis?" *New York Affairs*, Vol.3, No.4 (Summer–Fall 1976), p. 10.

— **60** —

Political Clout of Hispanics Grows as Their Numbers Swell

JOHN DILLIN

Miami, Denver, San Antonio, and a number of other major cities are sending the United States a message: Hispanic political power is on the rise.

Miami was the latest. The election last week of Miami's first Cuban-American mayor, Xavier Suarez, sent a wave of pride

through the Magic City's Spanish-speaking neighborhoods. It was an event comparable to the election of the first Irish-American mayor of Boston in 1885, or the first black mayor of Los Angeles in 1973.

It was also one more signal that Hispanics are finally beginning to flex their muscles.

Reprinted by permission from *The Christian Science Monitor*, Vol.77, No.251, November 20, 1985, pp. 1, 5, 6. © 1985 The Christian Science Publishing Society. All rights reserved.

As millions of immigrants pour into the U.S. from Mexico, Cuba, and other Latin nations, Hispanic votes are beginning to change the face of American politics.

That change is almost certain to accelerate. Because of a high birthrate, and because of both legal and illegal immigration, Hispanics are the fastest-growing population segment.

The U.S. has not yet felt the full impact of Hispanics' power. Politically, they are like a 100-watt bulb that is producing about 40 watts of light. Although they now total 7.5 percent of the US population, Hispanics made up only 3 percent of the voters in last year's presidential and congressional elections, according to ABC News exit surveys.

In fact, the record of Hispanic voting is even lower than the traditionally poor record of blacks.

Despite their low turnout, political experts say that Hispanics' voting power bears close watching. Not only are their numbers increasing, but Hispanic population growth is concentrated in some of the most crucial electoral states.

Hispanics have gravitated in the greatest numbers to California, Texas, Florida, Illinois, and New York. Those five states alone have 58 percent of the electoral votes (157) needed to elect a president.

The Hispanic population that is of voting age in California, for example, surged 117 percent from 1970 to 1980. And, according to a private research group, rapid increases in California's Hispanic and Asian populations could lead to the white population's losing its majority status within 25 years. The Hispanic voting-age population of California climbed to 2,775,170 in 1980 and has continued moving upward at a rapid rate since that last official census. In Florida, growth was 130 percent, in Texas, 82 percent.

What does this mean politically?

First, it should be wonderful news for Democrats. Both Mexican-Americans and Puerto Ricans (concentrated in New York State) usually vote Democratic.

In the 1982 elections for Congress, for example, 82 percent of Hispanic voters supported Democratic candidates; only 16 percent, Republican, according to NBC/Associated Press exit surveys.

Presidential voting is usually the same. In 1980, Hispanics supported Democrat Jimmy Carter over Republican Ronald Reagan by 70 to 25, according to the Southwest Voter Education Project.

The exception to this rule is the Cuban-American. Cubans, strongly anticommunist because of their experience with Fidel Castro, support a tough defense policy. Most, therefore, register Republican.

If Hispanic immigration continues at a high rate, it could conceivably derail Republican plans to become the majority party in the U.S. House of Representatives in the early 1990s. The GOP is counting on dozens of new congressmen from the Sunbelt—precisely where Hispanic power will be concentrated.

Republican leaders, who read the census data as well as anyone, have made Hispanics a vital target group. President Reagan went all out to court Hispanics in 1984—apparently with positive results. ABC exit polls found Reagan received 44 percent of the Hispanic vote, 19 percentage points more than in 1980.

Hispanic voting power is already having a notable effect on some sensitive political issues, such as abortion, school prayer, immigration reform, aid to religious schools, and even foreign policy.

Hispanics are generally, regarded as liberal on economic issues, conservative on social issues. But a study by the National Council of La Raza indicates such generalizations are not always true.

A survey by the Southwest Voter Education Project found that in East Los Angeles and San Antonio 75 percent of all Mexican-Americans favor the Equal Rights Amendment; 64 percent favor abortion under some, or all, circumstances.

Even so, some generalizations seem to hold true. A majority of Hispanics in the

Southwest Voter poll said they wanted more federal funds for social programs.

The vast majority of Hispanics are Roman Catholic, a factor that could also influence national and state policy. A Republican strategist working for President Reagan in 1984 said one key reason the White House backs tuition tax credits for parochial school costs is the need to court middle-class Catholic voters, including Hispanics. Similar considerations played a role in Mr. Reagan's decision to send an ambassador to the Vatican.

Just last week, Education Secretary William J. Bennett showed that the GOP plans to continue this courtship of Catholic voters when he unveiled his new plan to provide federal money, through vouchers, to 5 million low-income children to attend school, many of them parochial.

Earlier efforts to sluice government money into religious schools have been ruled unconstitutional by the courts. But pressure could increase as the number of Catholic voters grows. Nearly 3 of every 10 voters in the 1984 election were Catholic, according to ABC News surveys.

If there is one issue that most concerns Hispanics, it is the high level of unemployment. While generally lower than black unemployment, Hispanic joblessness is usually above the level for whites.

Hispanics blame a number of factors: lack of job skills and confidence, discrimination. But the most important, they believe, is poor education. Which means better schools may be the most important key to winning this new Hispanic vote.

61

Government: "A Profoundly Human Affair"

BILL JAMIESON, JR.

I have worked in or around government since I graduated from the University of Arizona in 1965. First, there was a 4-year hitch in the Navy; then, after a short stay in my family's business, I worked for 3 years in community programs that were funded by the government. I also spent 1 year at the federal level and 11 years in state government.

This has been an always fascinating, and sometimes frustrating, odyssey. It has given me the opportunity to observe "up close and personal" how government works, and how it does not work. I have watched—and participated in—the delicate and constantly shifting balance of power between people, and between the branches and levels of government.

From all of this, I have come to understand that the operation of government is a profoundly human affair. Contrary to what seems to be the popular opinion, government is not a faceless abstraction. Rather, it is a living organism that thinks and acts through

Reprinted from *Public Management*, Vol.67, No.5 (May 1985), pp. 19–20, by special permission, © 1985, The International City Management Association, Washington, D.C.

thousands of people: people who are mayors, governors, and councilmembers; doctors, nurses, maintenance workers, accountants, educators, lawyers, and typists. They are all people—real people with real dreams; real people with real abilities; real people with real faults; real people who, just like their private sector colleagues, want to feel a sense of pride in their work.

When an elected official or the press or the public refers to the generic "lazy bureaucrat," or talks about "cutting the fat" from the "bloated bureaucracy," a message is delivered to these people about how other people value them and their profession. How many of us would be able to work enthusiastically and cooperatively today to accomplish the goals of somebody who yesterday labeled us a "fat, lazy bureaucrat"?

Elected officials, the public, and the press make great sport of blasting the bureaucrat and blaming him or her for most of society's woes. But who are the bureaucrats? Well, he and she are just like their colleagues in the private sector. They are professionals who, like their colleagues, want to have pride in their work; they are mothers and fathers who want their children to be proud of what they do; are members of local service clubs and active participants in their communities.

People who work in the government are not much different from those who work in private bureaucracies: There are some who are extraordinary, who exceed all expectations. There are a few who don't meet expectations. The majority are people who do a good job.

It is very difficult for them to function professionally when their leader is quoted in the newspaper as saying that they are a drain on the people they have dedicated their career to serving. Their boss—elected or appointed—has campaigned for or agreed to take a position that makes him or her a leader: a leader of bureaucrats. That makes the leader part of the bureaucratic team.

This team is charged with seeking effi-

ciency. Everybody is for efficiency, which can be defined in this case as improved services and lower costs. Everyone is for it. The public is for it, appointed leaders are for it, and bureaucrats are for it. Yet, campaigning for efficiency and running an efficient government are two different things. The elected or appointed leaders can't collect all of the trash by themselves; they can't pave all of the roads by themselves; they can't run the airport by themselves; they can't police the streets by themselves; they can't deliver quality education by themselves.

They need the very bureaucrats they often refer to in derogatory terms to do it for them. Bureaucrats are, unfortunately, blamed for all of the inefficiencies in government, most of which are not of their making. For instance, to make government truly efficient, you would have to make several very controversial changes. You would have to repeal the open meeting law, make it easier to hire and fire people by weakening the civil service, remove some of the procedural restrictions on purchasing, increase the power of the executive at the expense of the legislative and judicial branches of government. These and other restrictions are put on government, not by the bureaucrats, but by the elected leaders. They are part of legislation or ordinances, and bureaucrats are required to live by them.

I am not advocating that all of these changes be made, but simply using them as examples to illustrate that perhaps efficiency is not what we really want. We have a system of government—at all levels of government—that provides an elaborate set of checks and balances. Checks and balances are designed to ensure that the public is protected from the abuse of power, that public funds are protected from improper use, and, I would sometimes argue, that the wheels of government grind slowly enough for the press and public to watch every single little action.

This brings up another heavy constraint placed on the bureaucrat. Public employees are required to work under a kind of scrutiny that the private sector seldom knows. An error by a mid-level accountant in government is likely to be debated in a public meeting; an honest mistake in judgment by a mid-level manager is likely to end up as front page news; a personnel action by a government manager is likely to be second-guessed publicly for weeks.

What do public employees want from you? Public employees—those referred to as bureaucrats—want the same things out of their profession that people in the private sector want from theirs: to make a good living for their family, to have pride in their work, to believe in what they do, and to have some job satisfaction and some fun. People don't come into public service with the goal of getting rich. People come into public service with the goal of serving. Public employees want to have good leaders. It is when the leadership fails—when they look to the leaders and do not get respect, but get ridicule, that they turn to organization. It is then they look outside their management to reorganizing.

When I was appointed the director of Arizona's Department of Administration, I took on responsibility for the state's personnel system and, thus, the task of working with the state employees association (AFSCME). Since I didn't have any experience in working with labor organizations, I talked to everyone I could about them. I talked to leaders of organized labor; I talked to management leaders from companies that were organized and from companies that were nonunion. Perhaps the best and wisest counsel of all came from a lawyer who had the reputation of being a union buster. He told me, simply, that any company that is organized deserves to be. Any company that has an antagonistic labor organization has likely failed in its leadership responsibilities. He told me to concentrate not on beating a union, but on being pro-employee.

I ask each of you: Do employees who work for you—the people who work in your cities and towns—believe (CAN they believe by listening to what you say; CAN they believe by watching your actions) that you respect their work? That you respect them professionally? If they can believe that, my guess is that you have an efficient and effective government. If they don't believe that, if the rhetoric is anti-employee and anti-public administration as a profession, my guess is that you have labor problems.

It is really tough for people to feel good about what they do when their leaders are saying that it isn't worth anything. It is equally tough for them to serve the public with enthusiasm. You can argue that public employees are paid to do their job and that they darn well better do it well and with a smile on their face or they will have to go out in the real world and make a payroll.

Whether or not this is a fair assessment, it isn't a realistic one. It is also one that, in my opinion, is a cop-out for those of us who consider ourselves leaders. Our job is not merely to represent our constituents to government—but also to represent government to our constituents. It is to lead and to set an atmosphere of management for employees who work in government so that they will deliver. More often than not, in my experience, the failure to deliver is a failure of leadership, not a failure of the bureaucracy.

The people who live in your community and the people who work for you in government are the same people. They want to have pride in their work, and pride in their government, and I believe that they have earned it—and I believe that you can help them get it.

62

Violations of the Public Trust

LEROY F. HARLOW

Our nation was formed in the late 1700s largely in revolt against abuse of governmental power by monarchs, parliaments, and lesser officials. It was founded on the noble ideal of government of the people, by the people, and for the people. Yet our history is replete with examples of the misuse of governmental power entrusted to officials and employees at all levels—from the highest national offices to the lowest village clerkships.

From about 1820 on, the nineteenth century was marked by the spoils and patronage systems at all levels of government. The mid-1800s were a time of buying and selling state legislatures, of the rise of big-city bossism. At the federal level, following the assassination of President Garfield by a disappointed office seeker, the spoils system was slowed somewhat by the 1887 adoption of competitive (civil-service) examination for appointive offices. The opening of the twentieth century saw the beginning of a reform movement that later included the era of "muckraking" journalism (ironically so named in derogation by reform President Theodore Roosevelt), reduction of the power of the state legislatures, and the invention and spread of the council-manager plan of local government.

Currently . . . we seem to have reverted to practices of earlier eras. Men and women who have been elected, appointed, or employed to preserve and enhance the public interest are found using their positions as places of leverage and power to achieve ends contrary to the public good and for personal benefit of themselves, other venal government officials and employees, and corrupt private citizens. Whether violations of public trust are accelerating (as some believe), are decreasing (as others claim), or are "same as always" (as noted by cynical veteran observers), we know that lack of integrity and the extent of corruption among government officials and employees have seriously eroded the confidence of the American public in their public-service personnel.

For readers unacquainted with the venality and corruption to which local governments are subject, the following litany of wrongdoing may be of interest. Because some taxpayer-readers may be helping, unknowingly, to pay the added costs of such misgovernment, and some employees and officials may be insensitive to or naive about this part of the real world of local government, both groups may benefit from being able to recognize similar activities in their communities or in the governments where they have responsibility. Most of these examples come from my direct personal exposure and my file of ethics materials. Keep in mind (1) that each of the activities listed may take different forms, (2) that all may be immoral or unethical, but not necessarily illegal in every public jurisdiction, and (3) that the classifications presented here sometimes overlap.

Election Irregularities. Local misgovernment starts with the elective process. A corrupt ad-

LeRoy F. Harlow, *Servants of All*. (Provo, Utah: Brigham Young University Press, 1981), pp. 308–313.

ministration may hand-pick election officials to be sure the vote is delivered, whatever the means. The means may include fraudulent voter lists that include names of fictitious persons, of persons deceased, and of persons no longer residing within the governmental jurisdiction. Floaters may vote more than once at the same polling place or at more than one polling place. People who protest about apparent irregularities may be intimidated by threats or be physically assaulted. Ballots and voting machines may be tampered with. Voters may be paid to vote "right"—so many dollars each—or they may be promised government jobs in return for their campaign efforts and votes.

Kickbacks. Often local-government corruption is a two-way street, a kind of mutual-aid arrangement. ("You support me for office; if elected, I'll give you a government job. Then you'll kick back to me part of your salary either directly, as a straight political contribution, or to a flower fund [ostensibly to pay for cards, flowers, etc., when a fellow employee is ill or has a death in the family]. Your contribution will help pay the costs of the next campaign. This way we'll both have good jobs and a steady income.") (For female employees the kickback may be not in money but in intimate favors.)

Bribery. Once in office, elected and appointed officials and employees may be offered or solicit bribes of various kinds in return for some official but wrongful acts. The inducement may be money, gifts, trips, or other valuable considerations. The purpose of a bribe may be to buy a favorable vote or decision on a rezoning, an award of a contract or franchise, the purchase of goods or services, the granting of a license, or the certifying of an inspection that was not made.

Of course the government people don't openly solicit bribes. They only signal in various ways that they might be willing to consider a bribe. This may include: frustrating and costly delays in getting the official approvals you are required to have, for no apparent reason (and especially when others get prompt approvals); suggestions that you engage a designated party to help process your application or request; offers to "work something out" or overlook a technical violation; awards of purchases and contracts on a noncompetitive negotiated basis; a shortage of reputable bidders; and frequent rejections of low bidders for not meeting "responsible-bidder" qualifications.

Pilferage and Theft. Corruption does not always directly involve parties outside the government. Stealing is an example. Pilfering small sums from a petty-cash fund and taking small objects can be the forerunners of more significant thefts. City offices may use an excess amount of stationery about the time the school year starts. Workmen may supply themselves and friends with materials and small tools from a city shop. Parking-meter collectors have been known to skim the meter receipts, and treasurers to cover up the "uncollectibles" they have pocketed by keeping a second set of books. City employees have built private buildings, using city materials and equipment, while working on city time. Others have had their personal autos serviced, repaired, and filled with tax-exempt gasoline at the city garage. I know of one popular city-works superintendent who spent time in the state penitentiary after selling a piece of the city's earth-moving equipment and pocketing the payment.

Fraud. This kind of intentional deception takes many forms. Some of the more common might include falsifying applications for public funds, appraisal and inventory records, reports of inspections made, and certificates of work performed or goods delivered; forging signatures; misusing government credit cards; not showing at work, but having fellow employees punch their time cards; writing bogus work orders and invoices; altering receipt copies; bootlegging government revenue-producing goods; overlooking defalcations and falsifying audit reports; selling employment examination tests and altered examination results.

These kinds of fraudulent activities have

long been practiced. A more recent innovation is the fraudulent use of computers by inputting false data, manipulating correct data, and producing false information. Possible indicators of fraudulent activities might be increasing numbers of citizens' complaints, unexplained changes in revenue collections, sensitivity to routine questioning, financial personnel putting in excessive overtime, and **evidence of double sets of books.**

Fixing. In corrupt situations, some people may make a living as fixers. They may claim to have, or actually have, connections and influence that enable them to get favorable action that is beyond the reach of the ordinary citizen. If they are part of the local political machine, they may assist confused, anxious, or frustrated citizens without charge but for the purpose of building up IOUs to be collected by the machine in the form of loyal support of the machine between elections and at the polls. Or for a fee they will get a traffic ticket "taken care of" (canceled), a license approved, a request or application expedited, or a court-imposed penalty reduced. To get results, they may have to act illegally; at the very least they will conspire with local-government officials or employees with whom they split their fee.

Favoritism. Because of the many contacts local-government people have with citizens, there are numerous opportunities to be partial in the kind, amount, and quality of service rendered. Office holders and employees may give their friends and political associates preferential treatment. There may be favoritism without a formal agreement of *quid pro quo* (one thing in return for another). However, since few people are totally altruistic, the private citizen who makes a contribution to a public official usually expects something in return, either immediately or some time in the future; similarly, the official who uses his office and governmental power to show more consideration or indulgence to one citizen than another is likely to expect something in return. Thus, favoritism and bribery overlap.

Protection. Prostitution, gambling, pornography, drug and liquor pushing, and other vices cannot survive in a community without public patronage and tacit or outright official cooperation. Because officials run some risk of job loss or worse when they provide protection for these illegal activities, they demand at least equivalent payment. The *quid pro quo* is payment by the vice operators for partial or **total protection against police harassment,** raids, prosecution, and heavy fines. Of course, this means that to be effective the arrangements must involve the police, the city's legal counsel, and the courts.

Payoffs. Bribery, theft, fraud, fixing, favoritism, protection, and other activities inimicable to efficient and impartial local government involve an exchange between local-government personnel and one or more other parties. Because the arrangements usually are illegal, the parties cannot resolve in open court any differences they may have. They must rely on their own codes of conduct. This gives local officials, who have the powers and facilities of government at their command, a clear advantage. A second party who fails to pay off as agreed could suffer severe and lasting penalties. Probably the default rate of payoffs to public officials by individuals engaged in illegal activities is small.

Embezzlement. Local officials and employees often have large sums of money and materials, and costly equipment and facilities entrusted to their care and security. For various reasons, they may take personal possession of these items for their own use. They may blame their embezzlement on unsatisfactory salary, fringe benefits, and working conditions; on family problems; or on financial difficulties. Or they may simply be crooks who found an easy place to ply their criminal trade. Some early-warning signals of possible embezzlement are officials and employees living beyond their means, gambling, and drinking more than usual. Another hint may be cash-handling personnel who do not issue official receipts, saying, "Your check will be your receipt."

Payroll Padding. Compared with the sophisticated schemes sometimes devised to cover up embezzlement and fraud, payroll padding is rather straightforward. It is a matter of adding fictitious or extra names to payrolls, and getting control of paychecks. Its success is often traced to loose payroll, personnel, and accounting procedures and records, and to carelessly placing too much trust in the people who prepare the payrolls and distribute the checks. Again, living beyond one's means and gambling are possible evidence of this kind of unethical and illegal behavior.

Harassment. Because of the many contacts that local governments have with citizens, hardly any organization in the community is in a better position to torment the citizens. Harassment may be an indication that an officer or employee is open to a bribe. Sudden enforcement of little-known and relatively unimportant regulations, with no prior warning, may indicate that inspectors, refuse collectors, police officers, and others are under pressure from higher up to increase their contributions to the political organization, and are using this means to meet their quotas.

Threats. Citizens who fail to cooperate with dishonest and unfair office holders and employees may receive verbal or anonymous written threats of injury or worse to their families and themselves. The aim is to intimidate the citizen into a state of civic paralysis, or to coerce him into complying with the officials' wishes.

Extortion. Businessmen and other private citizens who conclude that they cannot afford to defy the crooks in office, whether for economic reasons or for the physical safety of themselves and their families, and yield to the financial and other demands of these governmental leeches, only encourage bolder and expanded extortion.

Reprisals. Citizens who defy the dishonest and illegal acts of local officials and their bosses, and thus keep the latter from achieving their goals, may find themselves subjected to more than one kind of reprisal. For instance, they may get no response to their requests for service, or get careless service—garbage strewn on their property and containers unnecessarily damaged. They may be prosecuted and fined for minor violations. Or they may have their property assessment doubled or tripled, and their taxes increased accordingly.

Criminal Syndicates. Perhaps the ultimate in violation of the public trust is what has come to be known as "burglars in blue"—policemen who have organized crime rings within their own departments. Several cities have been plagued by these unconscionable situations. In Denver, for example, residents who responded to the police-department invitation to let the department know when they would be out of town so that the department would be able to provide additional surveillance, returned home to find their homes completely cleaned out. Later it was discovered that the department's own officers, from top to bottom, had organized themselves into burglary teams and, using large vans, had systematically entered the homes and carted off household goods and family belongings that they sold through illegal outlets ("fences").

So much for examples of wrongdoing by persons holding positions of public trust in local government.

When you read or hear of public officials and employees being apprehended while engaged in questionable activities and being charged with a crime, you may not recognize the nature of the wrongdoing by the terms used. Instead of being charged with "bribery," "fraud," "payroll padding," "extortion," and so on, the suspects may be charged with "nonfeasance," "misfeasance," or "malfeasance." These terms come from the root *feasance*, which a dictionary might define as "the doing of an act as an obligation or duty." Hence, "nonfeasance" is failure to perform an obligatory duty, "misfeasance" is the improper or wrongful performance of an act which is normally proper and lawful, and "malfeasance" is the commission of a wrongful or illegal act by a public official. Whether called by what they are, or by some obscure legal term, the above examples are not the only misdeeds ever committed by people occupying local-government offices. But they may be enough to suggest the nature of violations of the public trust and why they, along with the shortage of good people to run for or accept public office, the lack of effective management tools, and the number of self-serving people in the public service, are impediments to better local government.

63

Why Participate in Party Politics?

CITIZENSHIP CLEARING HOUSE

The future of free representative democracy is seriously endangered when a high proportion of men and women of character and intelligence flinch at the thought of participation in partisan politics. Some say in defense of nonparticipation that they do not wish to risk misrepresentation of their character and motives. Others say that they find the rough and tumble of partisan politics extremely distasteful. Still others are held back by considerations of the possible effects of political participation on their business or home life. These are mere pinpricks compared to what the citizen-soldier is called upon to endure in war for the preservation of democracy. A free and healthy system of representative government is unattainable without well-organized political parties led by honest and intelligent men and women devoted to the common good.

No generally applicable device other than political parties has yet been developed for coalescing a multitude of individual opinions to the point where democratic government becomes possible. It is true that special interest groups sometimes provide an effective means of influencing elections and the conduct of legislative bodies. But to the extent that such groups are successful it means the triumph of special interests over the general public interest. Parties represent, albeit sometimes imperfectly, the general interest. When special interest groups grow strong parties grow weak. In seeking the greatest good for the greatest number, therefore, it is essential that the strength of the parties be maintained, but the political parties cannot be more honest, more intelligent, or more patriotic than their leaders.

Many persons, including some college teachers of politics, believe that the independent citizen is more influential than the party man on the theory that the parties must woo his support to win. The independent, however, sacrifices the chance to share in the nomination of candidates and in the determination of party principles and programs. His choice at the election is too often between two evils. The machinery through which the individual voter can work most effectively for the improvement of politics is that of his political party.

Better Minds for Better Politics, pamphlet published by the Citizenship Clearing House, New York, pp. 4–8.

No machinery, however, can be expected to operate successfully, if its management is abandoned by honest, intelligent, and patriotic citizens and abused by those to whom it goes by default. . . .

In a free representative democracy a high premium must be placed on training young men and women for intelligent and effective participation in politics. Preservation of our democratic processes depends not only on knowledge and interest but also on developing a willingness among the able, well-trained, and interested students to participate in the drama and dynamics of American politics. . . . Whatever success the colleges and universities have in preparing their students for positions of prominence and leadership in the professions, they will stand to lose much if not all of their greatness as seats of learning if they fail to supply the nation with intelligent, active, and devoted participants in party politics.

64

The Reformer

RICHARD S. CHILDS

A reformer is one who sets forth cheerfully toward defeat. It is his peculiar function to embrace the hopeless cause when it can win no other friends and when its obvious futility repels that thick-necked, practical, timorous type of citizen to whom the outward appearance of success is so dear. His persistence against stone walls invites derision from those who have never been touched by his religion and do not know what fun it is. He never seems victorious, for if he were visibly winning, he would forthwith cease to be dubbed "reformer."

Yet in time, the Reformer's little movement becomes respectable and his little minority proves that it can grow and presently the Statesman joins it and takes all the credit, cheerfully handed to him by the Reformer as bribe for his support.

And then comes the Politician, rushing grandly to the succor of the victor!

And all the Crowd!

The original Reformer is lost in the shuffle then, but he doesn't care. For as the great bandwagon which he started goes thundering past with trumpets, the Crowd in the intoxication of triumph leans over the side to jeer at him—a forlorn and lonely crank mustering a pitiful little odd-lot of followers along the roadside and setting them marching, while over their heads he lifts the curious banner of his next crusade!

Richard S. Childs, "The Reformer," *National Municipal Review*, July 1927, reverse of title page. Reprinted by permission of the publisher.